Mnemonics	ARM ISA	Description
QADD	v5E	signed saturated 32-bit add
QDADD	v5E	signed saturated double and 32-bit add
QDSUB	v5E	signed saturated double and 32-bit subtract
QSUB	v5E	signed saturated 32-bit subtract
RSB	v1	reverse subtract of two 32-bit values
RSC	v1	reverse subtract with carry of two 32-bit integers
SBC	v1	subtract with carry of two 32-bit values
SMLAxy	v5E	signed multiply accumulate instructions $((16 \times 16) + 32 = 32\text{-bit})$
SMLAL	v3M	signed multiply accumulate long $((32 \times 32) + 64 = 64\text{-bit})$
SMLALxy	v5E	signed multiply accumulate long $((16 \times 16) + 64 = 64\text{-bit})$
SMLAWy	v5E	signed multiply accumulate instruction $(((32 \times 16) \gg 16) + 32 = 32\text{-bit})$
SMULL	v3M	signed multiply long $(32 \times 32 = 64\text{-bit})$
SMULxy	v5E	signed multiply instructions $(16 \times 16 = 32\text{-bit})$
SMULWy	v5E	signed multiply instruction $((32 \times 16) \gg 16 = 32\text{-bit})$
STC STC2	v2 v5	store to memory single or multiple 32-bit values from coprocessor
STM	v1	store multiple 32-bit registers to memory
STR	v1 v4 v5E	store register to a virtual address in memory
SUB	v1	subtract two 32-bit values
SWI	v1	software interrupt
SWP	v2a	swap a word/byte in memory with a register, without interruption
TEQ	v1	test for equality of two 32-bit values
TST	v1	test for bits in a 32-bit value
UMLAL	v3M	unsigned multiply accumulate long $((32 \times 32) + 64 = 64\text{-bit})$
UMULL	v3M	unsigned multiply long $(32 \times 32 = 64\text{-bit})$

ARM SYSTEM DEVELOPER'S GUIDE

DESIGNING AND OPTIMIZING SYSTEM SOFTWARE

ABOUT THE AUTHORS

Andrew N. Sloss

Andrew Sloss received a B.Sc. in Computer Science from the University of Herefordshire (UK) in 1992 and was certified as a Chartered Engineer by the British Computer Society (C.Eng, FBCS). He has worked in the computer industry for over 16 years and has been involved with the ARM processor since 1987. He has gained extensive experience developing a wide range of applications running on the ARM processor. He designed the first editing systems for both Chinese and Egyptian Hieroglyphics executing on the ARM2 and ARM3 processors for Emerald Publishing (UK). Andrew Sloss has worked at ARM Inc. for over six years. He is currently a Technical Sales Engineer advising and supporting companies developing new products. He works within the U.S. Sales Organization and is based in Los Gatos, California.

Dominic Symes

Dominic Symes is currently a software engineer at ARM Ltd. in Cambridge, England, where he has worked on ARM-based embedded software since 1995. He received his B.A. and D.Phil. in Mathematics from Oxford University. He first programmed the ARM in 1989 and is particularly interested in algorithms and optimization techniques. Before joining ARM, he wrote commercial and public domain ARM software.

Chris Wright

Chris Wright began his embedded systems career in the early 80s at Lockheed Advanced Marine Systems. While at Advanced Marine Systems he wrote small software control systems for use on the Intel 8051 family of microcontrollers. He has spent much of his career working at the Lockheed Palo Alto Research Laboratory and in a software development group at Dow Jones Telerate. Most recently, Chris Wright spent several years in the Customer Support group at ARM Inc., training and supporting partner companies developing new ARM-based products. Chris Wright is currently the Director of Customer Support at Ultimodule Inc. in Sunnyvale, California.

John Rayfield

John Rayfield, an independent consultant, was formerly Vice President of Marketing, U.S., at ARM. In this role he was responsible for setting ARM's strategic marketing direction in the U.S., and identifying opportunities for new technologies to serve key market segments. John joined ARM in 1996 and held various roles within the company, including Director of Technical Marketing and R&D, which were focused around new product/technology development. Before joining ARM, John held several engineering and management roles in the field of digital signal processing, software, hardware, ASIC and system design. John holds an M.Sc. in Signal Processing from the University of Surrey (UK) and a B.Sc.Hons. in Electronic Engineering from Brunel University (UK).

ARM System Developer's Guide

Designing and Optimizing System Software

Andrew N. Sloss

Dominic Symes

Chris Wright

With a contribution by John Rayfield

AMSTERDAM · BOSTON · HEIDELBERG · LONDON
NEW YORK · OXFORD · PARIS · SAN DIEGO
SAN FRANCISCO · SINGAPORE · SYDNEY · TOKYO

Morgan Kaufmann is an imprint of Elsevier

Senior Editor	Denise E.M. Penrose
Publishing Services Manager	Simon Crump
Project Manager	Sarah M. Hajduk
Developmental Editor	Belinda Breyer
Editorial Assistant	Summer Block
Cover Design	Dick Hannus
Cover Image	Red Wing No.6 by Charles Biederman
	Collection Walker Art Center, Minneapolis
	Gift of the artist through the Ford Foundation Purchase Program, 1964
Technical Illustration	Dartmouth Publishing
Composition	Cepha Imaging, Ltd.
Copyeditor	Ken Dellapenta
Proofreader	Jan Cocker
Indexer	Ferreira Indexing
Interior printer	The Maple-Vail Book Manufacturing Group
Cover printer	Phoenix Color

Morgan Kaufmann Publishers is an imprint of Elsevier.
500 Sansome Street, Suite 400, San Francisco, CA 94111

Library of Congress Cataloging-in-Publication Data
Sloss, Andrew N.
  ARM system developer's guide: designing and optimizing system software/Andrew N.
Sloss, Dominic Symes, Chris Wright.
     p. cm.
  Includes bibliographical references and index.
  ISBN-13: 978-1-55860-874-0 ISBN-10: 1-55860-874-5 (alk. paper)
   1. Computer software–Development. 2. RISC microprocessors. 3. Computer
architecture. I. Symes, Dominic. II. Wright, Chris, 1953- III. Title.

  QA76.76.D47S565 2004
  005.1–dc22

                                                    2004040366

ISBN-13: 978-1-55860-874-0
ISBN-10: 1-55860-874-5

For information on all Morgan Kaufmann publications,
visit our Web site at *www.mkp.com*.

Printed in the United States of America
08 07   5 4

CONTENTS

PREFACE

Increasingly, embedded systems developers and system-on-chip designers select specific microprocessor cores and a family of tools, libraries, and off-the-shelf components to quickly develop new microprocessor-based products. A major player in this industry is ARM. Over the last 10 years, the ARM architecture has become the most pervasive 32-bit architecture in the world, with more than 2 billion ARM-based processors shipped at the time of this writing. ARM processors are embedded in products ranging from cell/mobile phones to automotive braking systems. A worldwide community of ARM partners and third-party vendors has developed among semiconductor and product design companies, including hardware engineers, system designers, and software developers. To date, no book has directly addressed their need to develop the system and software for an ARM-based embedded design. This text fills that gap.

Our goal has been to describe the operation of the ARM core from a product developer's perspective with a clear emphasis on software. Because we have written this book specifically for engineers who are experienced with embedded systems development but who may be unfamiliar with the ARM architecture, we have assumed no previous ARM experience.

To help our readers become productive as quickly as possible, we have included a suite of ARM software examples that can be integrated into commercial products or used as templates for the quick creation of productive software. The examples are numbered so that readers can easily locate the source code on the publisher's Web site. The examples are also valuable to people with ARM design experience who want to make the most efficient use of an ARM-based embedded system.

ORGANIZATION OF THE BOOK

The book begins by briefly noting the ARM processor design philosophy and discussing how and why it differs from the traditional RISC philosophy. The first chapter also introduces a simple embedded system based on the ARM processor.

Chapter 2 digs more deeply into the hardware, focusing on the ARM processor core and presenting an overview of the ARM cores currently in the marketplace.

The ARM and Thumb instruction sets are the focus of Chapters 3 and 4, respectively, and form the fundamental basis for the rest of the book. Explanations of key instructions include complete examples, so these chapters also serve as a tutorial on the instruction sets.

Chapters 5 and 6 demonstrate how to write efficient code with scores of example that we have developed while working with ARM customers. Chapter 5 teaches proven techniques and rules for writing C code that will compile efficiently on the ARM architecture, and it helps determine which code should be optimized. Chapter 6 details best practices for writing and optimizing ARM assembly code—critical for improving performance by reducing system power consumption and clock speed.

Because primitives are basic operations used in a wide range of algorithms, it's worthwhile to learn how they can be optimized. Chapter 7 discusses how to optimize primitives for specific ARM processors. It presents optimized reference implementations of common primitives as well as of more complicated mathematical operations for those who wish to take a quick reference approach. We have also included the theory behind each implementation for those who wish to dig deeper.

Audio and video embedded systems applications are increasingly in demand. They require digital signal processing (DSP) capability that until recently would have been provided by a separate DSP processor. Now, however, the ARM architecture offers higher memory bandwidths and faster multiply accumulate operations, permitting a single ARM core design to support these applications. Chapter 8 examines how to maximize the performance of the ARM for digital processing applications and how to implement DSP algorithms.

At the heart of an embedded system lie the exception handlers. Efficient handlers can dramatically improve system performance. Chapter 9 covers the theory and practice of handling exceptions and interrupts on the ARM processor through a set of detailed examples.

Firmware, an important part of any embedded system, is described in Chapter 10 by means of a simple firmware package we designed, called Sandstone. The chapter also reviews popular industry firmware packages that are available for the ARM.

Chapter 11 demonstrates the implementation of embedded operating systems through an example operating system we designed, called Simple Little Operating System.

Chapters 12, 13, and 14 focus on memory issues. Chapter 12 examines the various cache technologies that surround the ARM cores, demonstrating routines for controlling the cache on specific cache-enabled ARM processors. Chapter 13 discusses the memory protection unit, and Chapter 14 discusses the memory management unit.

Finally, in Chapter 15, we consider the future of the ARM architecture, highlighting new directions in the instruction set and new technologies that ARM is implementing in the next few years.

The appendices provide detailed references on the instruction sets, cycle timing, and specific ARM products.

EXAMPLES ON THE WEB

As we noted earlier, we have created an extensive set of tested practical examples to reinforce concepts and methods. These are available on the publisher's Web site at *www.mkp.com/companions/1558608745*.

ACKNOWLEDGMENTS

First, of course, are our wives—Shau Chin Symes and Yulian Yang—and families who have been very supportive and have put up with us spending a large proportion of our home time on this project.

This book has taken many years to complete, and many people have contributed with encouragement and technical advice. We would like to personally thank all the people involved. Writing a technical book involves a lot of painstaking attention to detail, so a big thank you to all the reviewers who spent time and effort reading and providing feedback—a difficult activity that requires a special skill. Reviewers who worked with the publisher during the developmental process were Jim Turley (Silicon-Insider), Peter Maloy (CodeSprite), Chris Larsen, Peter Harrod (ARM, Ltd.), Gary Thomas (MLB Associates), Wayne Wolf (Princeton University), Scott Runner (Qualcomm, Inc.), Niall Murphy (PanelSoft), and Dominic Sweetman (Algorithmics, Ltd.).

A special thanks to Wilco Dijkstra, Edward Nevill, and David Seal for allowing us to include selected examples within the book. Thanks also to Rod Crawford, Andrew Cummins, Dave Flynn, Jamie Smith, William Rees, and Anne Rooney for helping throughout with advice. Thanks to the ARM Strategic Support Group—Howard Ho, John Archibald, Miguel Echavarria, Robert Allen, and Ian Field—for reading and providing quick local feedback.

We would like to thank John Rayfield for initiating this project and contributing Chapter 15. We would also like to thank David Brash for reviewing the manuscript and allowing us to include ARMv6 material in this book.

Lastly, we wish to thank Morgan Kaufmann Publishers, especially Denise Penrose and Belinda Breyer for their patience and advice throughout the project.

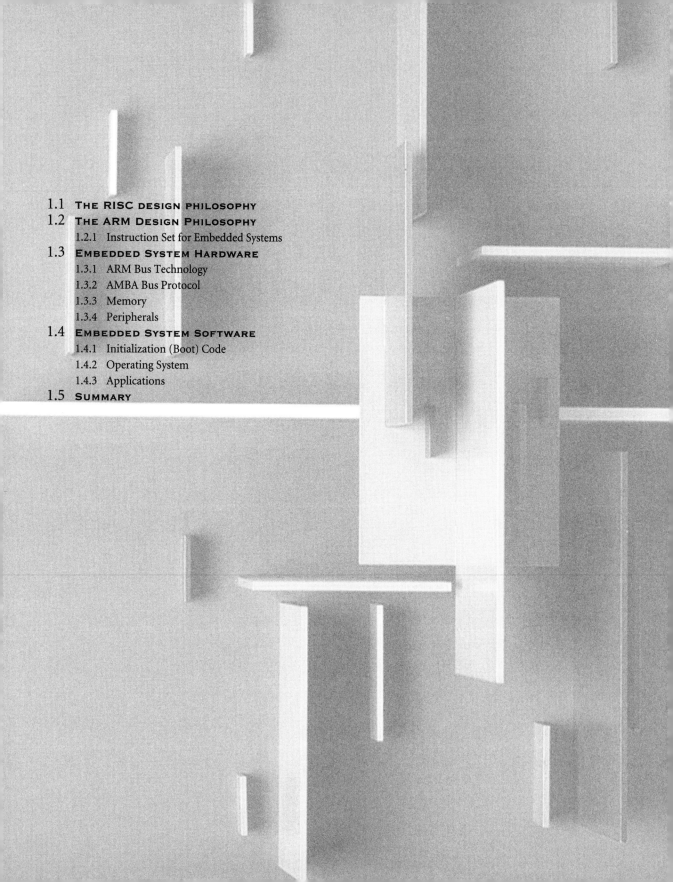

CHAPTER 1

ARM EMBEDDED SYSTEMS

The ARM processor core is a key component of many successful 32-bit embedded systems. You probably own one yourself and may not even realize it! ARM cores are widely used in mobile phones, handheld organizers, and a multitude of other everyday portable consumer devices.

ARM's designers have come a long way from the first ARM1 prototype in 1985. Over one billion ARM processors had been shipped worldwide by the end of 2001. The ARM company bases their success on a simple and powerful original design, which continues to improve today through constant technical innovation. In fact, the ARM core is not a single core, but a whole family of designs sharing similar design principles and a common instruction set.

For example, one of ARM's most successful cores is the ARM7TDMI. It provides up to 120 Dhrystone MIPS[1] and is known for its high code density and low power consumption, making it ideal for mobile embedded devices.

In this first chapter we discuss how the RISC (reduced instruction set computer) design philosophy was adapted by ARM to create a flexible embedded processor. We then introduce an example embedded device and discuss the typical hardware and software technologies that surround an ARM processor.

---

1. Dhrystone MIPS version 2.1 is a small benchmarking program.

1.1 THE RISC DESIGN PHILOSOPHY

The ARM core uses a RISC architecture. RISC is a design philosophy aimed at delivering simple but powerful instructions that execute within a single cycle at a high clock speed. The RISC philosophy concentrates on reducing the complexity of instructions performed by the hardware because it is easier to provide greater flexibility and intelligence in software rather than hardware. As a result, a RISC design places greater demands on the compiler. In contrast, the traditional complex instruction set computer (CISC) relies more on the hardware for instruction functionality, and consequently the CISC instructions are more complicated. Figure 1.1 illustrates these major differences.

The RISC philosophy is implemented with four major design rules:

1. *Instructions*—RISC processors have a reduced number of instruction classes. These classes provide simple operations that can each execute in a single cycle. The compiler or programmer synthesizes complicated operations (for example, a divide operation) by combining several simple instructions. Each instruction is a fixed length to allow the pipeline to fetch future instructions before decoding the current instruction. In contrast, in CISC processors the instructions are often of variable size and take many cycles to execute.

2. *Pipelines*—The processing of instructions is broken down into smaller units that can be executed in parallel by pipelines. Ideally the pipeline advances by one step on each cycle for maximum throughput. Instructions can be decoded in one pipeline stage. There is no need for an instruction to be executed by a miniprogram called microcode as on CISC processors.

3. *Registers*—RISC machines have a large general-purpose register set. Any register can contain either data or an address. Registers act as the fast local memory store for all data

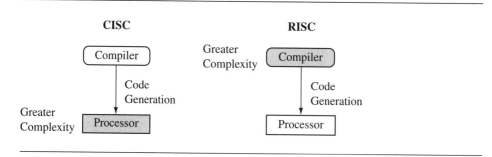

Figure 1.1   CISC vs. RISC. CISC emphasizes hardware complexity. RISC emphasizes compiler complexity.

processing operations. In contrast, CISC processors have dedicated registers for specific purposes.

4. *Load-store architecture*—The processor operates on data held in registers. Separate load and store instructions transfer data between the register bank and external memory. Memory accesses are costly, so separating memory accesses from data processing provides an advantage because you can use data items held in the register bank multiple times without needing multiple memory accesses. In contrast, with a CISC design the data processing operations can act on memory directly.

These design rules allow a RISC processor to be simpler, and thus the core can operate at higher clock frequencies. In contrast, traditional CISC processors are more complex and operate at lower clock frequencies. Over the course of two decades, however, the distinction between RISC and CISC has blurred as CISC processors have implemented more RISC concepts.

1.2 THE ARM DESIGN PHILOSOPHY

There are a number of physical features that have driven the ARM processor design. First, portable embedded systems require some form of battery power. The ARM processor has been specifically designed to be small to reduce power consumption and extend battery operation—essential for applications such as mobile phones and personal digital assistants (PDAs).

High code density is another major requirement since embedded systems have limited memory due to cost and/or physical size restrictions. High code density is useful for applications that have limited on-board memory, such as mobile phones and mass storage devices.

In addition, embedded systems are price sensitive and use slow and low-cost memory devices. For high-volume applications like digital cameras, every cent has to be accounted for in the design. The ability to use low-cost memory devices produces substantial savings.

Another important requirement is to reduce the area of the die taken up by the embedded processor. For a single-chip solution, the smaller the area used by the embedded processor, the more available space for specialized peripherals. This in turn reduces the cost of the design and manufacturing since fewer discrete chips are required for the end product.

ARM has incorporated hardware debug technology within the processor so that software engineers can view what is happening while the processor is executing code. With greater visibility, software engineers can resolve issues faster, which has a direct effect on the time to market and reduces overall development costs.

The ARM core is not a pure RISC architecture because of the constraints of its primary application—the embedded system. In some sense, the strength of the ARM core is that it does not take the RISC concept too far. In today's systems the key is not raw processor speed but total effective system performance and power consumption.

1.2.1 INSTRUCTION SET FOR EMBEDDED SYSTEMS

The ARM instruction set differs from the pure RISC definition in several ways that make the ARM instruction set suitable for embedded applications:

- *Variable cycle execution for certain instructions*—Not every ARM instruction executes in a single cycle. For example, load-store-multiple instructions vary in the number of execution cycles depending upon the number of registers being transferred. The transfer can occur on sequential memory addresses, which increases performance since sequential memory accesses are often faster than random accesses. Code density is also improved since multiple register transfers are common operations at the start and end of functions.

- *Inline barrel shifter leading to more complex instructions*—The inline barrel shifter is a hardware component that preprocesses one of the input registers before it is used by an instruction. This expands the capability of many instructions to improve core performance and code density. We explain this feature in more detail in Chapters 2, 3, and 4.

- *Thumb 16-bit instruction set*—ARM enhanced the processor core by adding a second 16-bit instruction set called Thumb that permits the ARM core to execute either 16- or 32-bit instructions. The 16-bit instructions improve code density by about 30% over 32-bit fixed-length instructions.

- *Conditional execution*—An instruction is only executed when a specific condition has been satisfied. This feature improves performance and code density by reducing branch instructions.

- *Enhanced instructions*—The enhanced digital signal processor (DSP) instructions were added to the standard ARM instruction set to support fast 16×16-bit multiplier operations and saturation. These instructions allow a faster-performing ARM processor in some cases to replace the traditional combinations of a processor plus a DSP.

These additional features have made the ARM processor one of the most commonly used 32-bit embedded processor cores. Many of the top semiconductor companies around the world produce products based around the ARM processor.

1.3 EMBEDDED SYSTEM HARDWARE

Embedded systems can control many different devices, from small sensors found on a production line, to the real-time control systems used on a NASA space probe. All these devices use a combination of software and hardware components. Each component is chosen for efficiency and, if applicable, is designed for future extension and expansion.

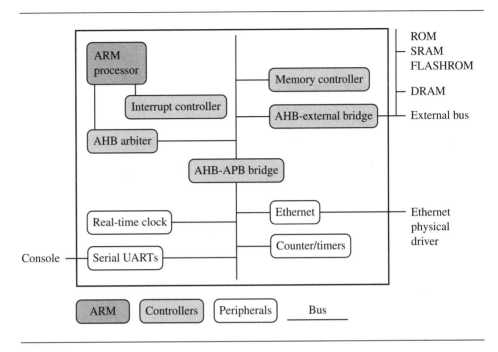

Figure 1.2   An example of an ARM-based embedded device, a microcontroller.

Figure 1.2 shows a typical embedded device based on an ARM core. Each box represents a feature or function. The lines connecting the boxes are the buses carrying data. We can separate the device into four main hardware components:

- The *ARM processor* controls the embedded device. Different versions of the ARM processor are available to suit the desired operating characteristics. An ARM processor comprises a core (the execution engine that processes instructions and manipulates data) plus the surrounding components that interface it with a bus. These components can include memory management and caches.

- *Controllers* coordinate important functional blocks of the system. Two commonly found controllers are interrupt and memory controllers.

- The *peripherals* provide all the input-output capability external to the chip and are responsible for the uniqueness of the embedded device.

- A *bus* is used to communicate between different parts of the device.

1.3.1 ARM BUS TECHNOLOGY

Embedded systems use different bus technologies than those designed for x86 PCs. The most common PC bus technology, the Peripheral Component Interconnect (PCI) bus, connects such devices as video cards and hard disk controllers to the x86 processor bus. This type of technology is external or off-chip (i.e., the bus is designed to connect mechanically and electrically to devices external to the chip) and is built into the motherboard of a PC.

In contrast, embedded devices use an on-chip bus that is internal to the chip and that allows different peripheral devices to be interconnected with an ARM core.

There are two different classes of devices attached to the bus. The ARM processor core is a *bus master*—a logical device capable of initiating a data transfer with another device across the same bus. Peripherals tend to be *bus slaves*—logical devices capable only of responding to a transfer request from a bus master device.

A bus has two architecture levels. The first is a physical level that covers the electrical characteristics and bus width (16, 32, or 64 bits). The second level deals with *protocol*—the logical rules that govern the communication between the processor and a peripheral.

ARM is primarily a design company. It seldom implements the electrical characteristics of the bus, but it routinely specifies the bus protocol.

1.3.2 AMBA BUS PROTOCOL

The Advanced Microcontroller Bus Architecture (AMBA) was introduced in 1996 and has been widely adopted as the on-chip bus architecture used for ARM processors. The first AMBA buses introduced were the ARM System Bus (ASB) and the ARM Peripheral Bus (APB). Later ARM introduced another bus design, called the ARM High Performance Bus (AHB). Using AMBA, peripheral designers can reuse the same design on multiple projects. Because there are a large number of peripherals developed with an AMBA interface, hardware designers have a wide choice of tested and proven peripherals for use in a device. A peripheral can simply be bolted onto the on-chip bus without having to redesign an interface for each different processor architecture. This plug-and-play interface for hardware developers improves availability and time to market.

AHB provides higher data throughput than ASB because it is based on a centralized multiplexed bus scheme rather than the ASB bidirectional bus design. This change allows the AHB bus to run at higher clock speeds and to be the first ARM bus to support widths of 64 and 128 bits. ARM has introduced two variations on the AHB bus: Multi-layer AHB and AHB-Lite. In contrast to the original AHB, which allows a single bus master to be active on the bus at any time, the Multi-layer AHB bus allows multiple active bus masters. AHB-Lite is a subset of the AHB bus and it is limited to a single bus master. This bus was developed for designs that do not require the full features of the standard AHB bus.

AHB and Multi-layer AHB support the same protocol for master and slave but have different interconnects. The new interconnects in Multi-layer AHB are good for systems with multiple processors. They permit operations to occur in parallel and allow for higher throughput rates.

The example device shown in Figure 1.2 has three buses: an AHB bus for the high-performance peripherals, an APB bus for the slower peripherals, and a third bus for external peripherals, proprietary to this device. This external bus requires a specialized bridge to connect with the AHB bus.

1.3.3 MEMORY

An embedded system has to have some form of memory to store and execute code. You have to compare price, performance, and power consumption when deciding upon specific memory characteristics, such as hierarchy, width, and type. If memory has to run twice as fast to maintain a desired bandwidth, then the memory power requirement may be higher.

1.3.3.1 Hierarchy

All computer systems have memory arranged in some form of hierarchy. Figure 1.2 shows a device that supports external off-chip memory. Internal to the processor there is an option of a cache (not shown in Figure 1.2) to improve memory performance.

Figure 1.3 shows the memory trade-offs: the fastest memory cache is physically located nearer the ARM processor core and the slowest secondary memory is set further away. Generally the closer memory is to the processor core, the more it costs and the smaller its capacity.

The cache is placed between main memory and the core. It is used to speed up data transfer between the processor and main memory. A cache provides an overall increase in performance but with a loss of predictable execution time. Although the cache increases the

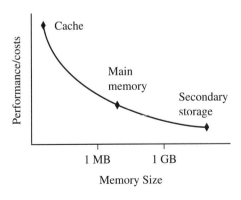

Figure 1.3   Storage trade-offs.

general performance of the system, it does not help real-time system response. Note that many small embedded systems do not require the performance benefits of a cache.

The main memory is large—around 256 KB to 256 MB (or even greater), depending on the application—and is generally stored in separate chips. Load and store instructions access the main memory unless the values have been stored in the cache for fast access. Secondary storage is the largest and slowest form of memory. Hard disk drives and CD-ROM drives are examples of secondary storage. These days secondary storage may vary from 600 MB to 60 GB.

1.3.3.2   Width

The memory width is the number of bits the memory returns on each access—typically 8, 16, 32, or 64 bits. The memory width has a direct effect on the overall performance and cost ratio.

If you have an uncached system using 32-bit ARM instructions and 16-bit-wide memory chips, then the processor will have to make two memory fetches per instruction. Each fetch requires two 16-bit loads. This obviously has the effect of reducing system performance, but the benefit is that 16-bit memory is less expensive.

In contrast, if the core executes 16-bit Thumb instructions, it will achieve better performance with a 16-bit memory. The higher performance is a result of the core making only a single fetch to memory to load an instruction. Hence, using Thumb instructions with 16-bit-wide memory devices provides both improved performance and reduced cost.

Table 1.1 summarizes theoretical cycle times on an ARM processor using different memory width devices.

1.3.3.3   Types

There are many different types of memory. In this section we describe some of the more popular memory devices found in ARM-based embedded systems.

Read-only memory (ROM) is the least flexible of all memory types because it contains an image that is permanently set at production time and cannot be reprogrammed. ROMs are used in high-volume devices that require no updates or corrections. Many devices also use a ROM to hold boot code.

Table 1.1   Fetching instructions from memory.

Instruction size	8-bit memory	16-bit memory	32-bit memory
ARM 32-bit	4 cycles	2 cycles	1 cycle
Thumb 16-bit	2 cycles	1 cycle	1 cycle

Flash ROM can be written to as well as read, but it is slow to write so you shouldn't use it for holding dynamic data. Its main use is for holding the device firmware or storing long-term data that needs to be preserved after power is off. The erasing and writing of flash ROM are completely software controlled with no additional hardware circuity required, which reduces the manufacturing costs. Flash ROM has become the most popular of the read-only memory types and is currently being used as an alternative for mass or secondary storage.

Dynamic random access memory (DRAM) is the most commonly used RAM for devices. It has the lowest cost per megabyte compared with other types of RAM. DRAM is *dynamic*—it needs to have its storage cells refreshed and given a new electronic charge every few milliseconds, so you need to set up a DRAM controller before using the memory.

Static random access memory (SRAM) is faster than the more traditional DRAM, but requires more silicon area. SRAM is *static*—the RAM does not require refreshing. The access time for SRAM is considerably shorter than the equivalent DRAM because SRAM does not require a pause between data accesses. Because of its higher cost, it is used mostly for smaller high-speed tasks, such as fast memory and caches.

Synchronous dynamic random access memory (SDRAM) is one of many subcategories of DRAM. It can run at much higher clock speeds than conventional memory. SDRAM synchronizes itself with the processor bus because it is clocked. Internally the data is fetched from memory cells, pipelined, and finally brought out on the bus in a burst. The old-style DRAM is asynchronous, so does not burst as efficiently as SDRAM.

1.3.4 PERIPHERALS

Embedded systems that interact with the outside world need some form of peripheral device. A peripheral device performs input and output functions for the chip by connecting to other devices or sensors that are off-chip. Each peripheral device usually performs a single function and may reside on-chip. Peripherals range from a simple serial communication device to a more complex 802.11 wireless device.

All ARM peripherals are *memory mapped*—the programming interface is a set of memory-addressed registers. The address of these registers is an offset from a specific peripheral base address.

Controllers are specialized peripherals that implement higher levels of functionality within an embedded system. Two important types of controllers are memory controllers and interrupt controllers.

1.3.4.1 Memory Controllers

Memory controllers connect different types of memory to the processor bus. On power-up a memory controller is configured in hardware to allow certain memory devices to be active. These memory devices allow the initialization code to be executed. Some memory devices must be set up by software; for example, when using DRAM, you first have to set up the memory timings and refresh rate before it can be accessed.

1.3.4.2 Interrupt Controllers

When a peripheral or device requires attention, it raises an interrupt to the processor. An interrupt controller provides a programmable governing policy that allows software to determine which peripheral or device can interrupt the processor at any specific time by setting the appropriate bits in the interrupt controller registers.

There are two types of interrupt controller available for the ARM processor: the standard interrupt controller and the vector interrupt controller (VIC).

The standard interrupt controller sends an interrupt signal to the processor core when an external device requests servicing. It can be programmed to ignore or mask an individual device or set of devices. The interrupt handler determines which device requires servicing by reading a device bitmap register in the interrupt controller.

The VIC is more powerful than the standard interrupt controller because it prioritizes interrupts and simplifies the determination of which device caused the interrupt. After associating a priority and a handler address with each interrupt, the VIC only asserts an interrupt signal to the core if the priority of a new interrupt is higher than the currently executing interrupt handler. Depending on its type, the VIC will either call the standard interrupt exception handler, which can load the address of the handler for the device from the VIC, or cause the core to jump to the handler for the device directly.

1.4 EMBEDDED SYSTEM SOFTWARE

An embedded system needs software to drive it. Figure 1.4 shows four typical software components required to control an embedded device. Each software component in the stack uses a higher level of abstraction to separate the code from the hardware device.

The initialization code is the first code executed on the board and is specific to a particular target or group of targets. It sets up the minimum parts of the board before handing control over to the operating system.

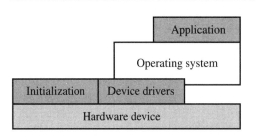

Figure 1.4   Software abstraction layers executing on hardware.

The operating system provides an infrastructure to control applications and manage hardware system resources. Many embedded systems do not require a full operating system but merely a simple task scheduler that is either event or poll driven.

The device drivers are the third component shown in Figure 1.4. They provide a consistent software interface to the peripherals on the hardware device.

Finally, an application performs one of the tasks required for a device. For example, a mobile phone might have a diary application. There may be multiple applications running on the same device, controlled by the operating system.

The software components can run from ROM or RAM. ROM code that is fixed on the device (for example, the initialization code) is called *firmware*.

1.4.1 INITIALIZATION (BOOT) CODE

Initialization code (or boot code) takes the processor from the reset state to a state where the operating system can run. It usually configures the memory controller and processor caches and initializes some devices. In a simple system the operating system might be replaced by a simple scheduler or debug monitor.

The initialization code handles a number of administrative tasks prior to handing control over to an operating system image. We can group these different tasks into three phases: initial hardware configuration, diagnostics, and booting.

Initial hardware configuration involves setting up the target platform so it can boot an image. Although the target platform itself comes up in a standard configuration, this configuration normally requires modification to satisfy the requirements of the booted image. For example, the memory system normally requires reorganization of the memory map, as shown in Example 1.1.

Diagnostics are often embedded in the initialization code. Diagnostic code tests the system by exercising the hardware target to check if the target is in working order. It also tracks down standard system-related issues. This type of testing is important for manufacturing since it occurs after the software product is complete. The primary purpose of diagnostic code is fault identification and isolation.

Booting involves loading an image and handing control over to that image. The boot process itself can be complicated if the system must boot different operating systems or different versions of the same operating system.

Booting an image is the final phase, but first you must load the image. Loading an image involves anything from copying an entire program including code and data into RAM, to just copying a data area containing volatile variables into RAM. Once booted, the system hands over control by modifying the program counter to point into the start of the image.

Sometimes, to reduce the image size, an image is compressed. The image is then decompressed either when it is loaded or when control is handed over to it.

EXAMPLE
1.1

Initializing or organizing memory is an important part of the initialization code because many operating systems expect a known memory layout before they can start.

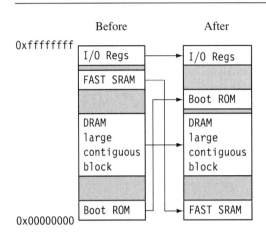

Figure 1.5   Memory remapping.

Figure 1.5 shows memory before and after reorganization. It is common for ARM-based embedded systems to provide for memory remapping because it allows the system to start the initialization code from ROM at power-up. The initialization code then redefines or remaps the memory map to place RAM at address 0x00000000—an important step because then the exception vector table can be in RAM and thus can be reprogrammed. We will discuss the vector table in more detail in Section 2.4.

1.4.2 OPERATING SYSTEM

The initialization process prepares the hardware for an operating system to take control. An operating system organizes the system resources: the peripherals, memory, and processing time. With an operating system controlling these resources, they can be efficiently used by different applications running within the operating system environment.

ARM processors support over 50 operating systems. We can divide operating systems into two main categories: real-time operating systems (RTOSs) and platform operating systems.

RTOSs provide guaranteed response times to events. Different operating systems have different amounts of control over the system response time. A hard real-time application requires a guaranteed response to work at all. In contrast, a soft real-time application requires a good response time, but the performance degrades more gracefully if the response time overruns. Systems running an RTOS generally do not have secondary storage.

Platform operating systems require a memory management unit to manage large, non-real-time applications and tend to have secondary storage. The Linux operating system is a typical example of a platform operating system.

These two categories of operating system are not mutually exclusive: there are operating systems that use an ARM core with a memory management unit and have real-time characteristics. ARM has developed a set of processor cores that specifically target each category.

1.4.3 APPLICATIONS

The operating system schedules applications—code dedicated to handling a particular task. An application implements a processing task; the operating system controls the environment. An embedded system can have one active application or several applications running simultaneously.

ARM processors are found in numerous market segments, including networking, automotive, mobile and consumer devices, mass storage, and imaging. Within each segment ARM processors can be found in multiple applications.

For example, the ARM processor is found in networking applications like home gateways, DSL modems for high-speed Internet communication, and 802.11 wireless communication. The mobile device segment is the largest application area for ARM processors because of mobile phones. ARM processors are also found in mass storage devices such as hard drives and imaging products such as inkjet printers—applications that are cost sensitive and high volume.

In contrast, ARM processors are not found in applications that require leading-edge high performance. Because these applications tend to be low volume and high cost, ARM has decided not to focus designs on these types of applications.

1.5 SUMMARY

Pure RISC is aimed at high performance, but ARM uses a modified RISC design philosophy that also targets good code density and low power consumption. An embedded system consists of a processor core surrounded by caches, memory, and peripherals. The system is controlled by operating system software that manages application tasks.

The key points in a RISC design philosophy are to improve performance by reducing the complexity of instructions, to speed up instruction processing by using a pipeline, to provide a large register set to store data near the core, and to use a load-store architecture.

The ARM design philosophy also incorporates some non-RISC ideas:

- It allows variable cycle execution on certain instructions to save power, area, and code size.
- It adds a barrel shifter to expand the capability of certain instructions.
- It uses the Thumb 16-bit instruction set to improve code density.

- It improves code density and performance by conditionally executing instructions.
- It includes enhanced instructions to perform digital signal processing type functions.

An embedded system includes the following hardware components: ARM *processors* are found embedded in chips. Programmers access *peripherals* through memory-mapped registers. There is a special type of peripheral called a *controller*, which embedded systems use to configure higher-level functions such as memory and interrupts. The AMBA on-chip *bus* is used to connect the processor and peripherals together.

An embedded system also includes the following software components: *Initialization code* configures the hardware to a known state. Once configured, *operating systems* can be loaded and executed. Operating systems provide a common programming environment for the use of hardware resources and infrastructure. *Device drivers* provide a standard interface to peripherals. An *application* performs the task-specific duties of an embedded system.

ARM Processor Fundamentals

Chapter 1 covered embedded systems with an ARM processor. In this chapter we will focus on the actual processor itself. First, we will provide an overview of the processor core and describe how data moves between its different parts. We will describe the programmer's model from a software developer's view of the ARM processor, which will show you the functions of the processor core and how different parts interact. We will also take a look at the core extensions that form an ARM processor. Core extensions speed up and organize main memory as well as extend the instruction set. We will then cover the revisions to the ARM core architecture by describing the ARM core naming conventions used to identify them and the chronological changes to the ARM instruction set architecture. The final section introduces the architecture implementations by subdividing them into specific ARM processor core families.

A programmer can think of an ARM core as functional units connected by data buses, as shown in Figure 2.1, where, the arrows represent the flow of data, the lines represent the buses, and the boxes represent either an operation unit or a storage area. The figure shows not only the flow of data but also the abstract components that make up an ARM core.

Data enters the processor core through the *Data* bus. The data may be an instruction to execute or a data item. Figure 2.1 shows a Von Neumann implementation of the ARM—data items and instructions share the same bus. In contrast, Harvard implementations of the ARM use two different buses.

The instruction decoder translates instructions before they are executed. Each instruction executed belongs to a particular instruction set.

The ARM processor, like all RISC processors, uses a *load-store architecture*. This means it has two instruction types for transferring data in and out of the processor: load instructions copy data from memory to registers in the core, and conversely the store

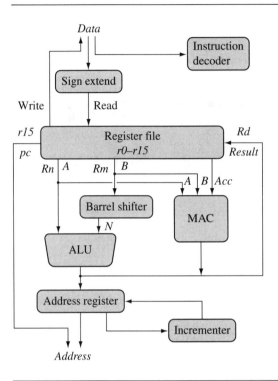

Figure 2.1   ARM core dataflow model.

instructions copy data from registers to memory. There are no data processing instructions that directly manipulate data in memory. Thus, data processing is carried out solely in registers.

Data items are placed in the *register file*—a storage bank made up of 32-bit registers. Since the ARM core is a 32-bit processor, most instructions treat the registers as holding signed or unsigned 32-bit values. The sign extend hardware converts signed 8-bit and 16-bit numbers to 32-bit values as they are read from memory and placed in a register.

ARM instructions typically have two source registers, *Rn* and *Rm*, and a single result or destination register, *Rd*. Source operands are read from the register file using the internal buses *A* and *B*, respectively.

The ALU (arithmetic logic unit) or MAC (multiply-accumulate unit) takes the register values *Rn* and *Rm* from the *A* and *B* buses and computes a result. Data processing instructions write the result in *Rd* directly to the register file. Load and store instructions use the ALU to generate an address to be held in the address register and broadcast on the *Address* bus.

One important feature of the ARM is that register *Rm* alternatively can be preprocessed in the barrel shifter before it enters the ALU. Together the barrel shifter and ALU can calculate a wide range of expressions and addresses.

After passing through the functional units, the result in *Rd* is written back to the register file using the *Result* bus. For load and store instructions the incrementer updates the address register before the core reads or writes the next register value from or to the next sequential memory location. The processor continues executing instructions until an exception or interrupt changes the normal execution flow.

Now that you have an overview of the processor core we'll take a more detailed look at some of the key components of the processor: the registers, the current program status register (*cpsr*), and the pipeline.

2.1 REGISTERS

General-purpose registers hold either data or an address. They are identified with the letter *r* prefixed to the register number. For example, register 4 is given the label *r4*. Figure 2.2 shows the active registers available in *user* mode—a protected mode normally

Figure 2.2 Registers available in *user* mode.

used when executing applications. The processor can operate in seven different modes, which we will introduce shortly. All the registers shown are 32 bits in size.

There are up to 18 active registers: 16 data registers and 2 processor status registers. The data registers are visible to the programmer as *r0* to *r15*.

The ARM processor has three registers assigned to a particular task or special function: *r13*, *r14*, and *r15*. They are frequently given different labels to differentiate them from the other registers.

In Figure 2.2, the shaded registers identify the assigned special-purpose registers:

- Register *r13* is traditionally used as the stack pointer (*sp*) and stores the head of the stack in the current processor mode.

- Register *r14* is called the link register (*lr*) and is where the core puts the return address whenever it calls a subroutine.

- Register *r15* is the program counter (*pc*) and contains the address of the next instruction to be fetched by the processor.

Depending upon the context, registers *r13* and *r14* can also be used as general-purpose registers, which can be particularly useful since these registers are banked during a processor mode change. However, it is dangerous to use *r13* as a general register when the processor is running any form of operating system because operating systems often assume that *r13* always points to a valid stack frame.

In ARM state the registers *r0* to *r13* are *orthogonal*—any instruction that you can apply to *r0* you can equally well apply to any of the other registers. However, there are instructions that treat *r14* and *r15* in a special way.

In addition to the 16 data registers, there are two program status registers: *cpsr* and *spsr* (the current and saved program status registers, respectively).

The register file contains all the registers available to a programmer. Which registers are visible to the programmer depend upon the current mode of the processor.

2.2 CURRENT PROGRAM STATUS REGISTER

The ARM core uses the *cpsr* to monitor and control internal operations. The *cpsr* is a dedicated 32-bit register and resides in the register file. Figure 2.3 shows the basic layout of a generic program status register. Note that the shaded parts are reserved for future expansion.

The *cpsr* is divided into four fields, each 8 bits wide: flags, status, extension, and control. In current designs the extension and status fields are reserved for future use. The control field contains the processor mode, state, and interrupt mask bits. The flags field contains the condition flags.

Some ARM processor cores have extra bits allocated. For example, the *J* bit, which can be found in the flags field, is only available on Jazelle-enabled processors, which execute

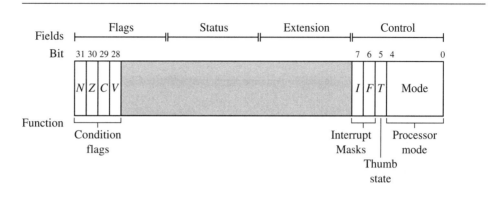

Figure 2.3   A generic program status register (*psr*).

8-bit instructions. We will discuss Jazelle more in Section 2.2.3. It is highly probable that future designs will assign extra bits for the monitoring and control of new features.

For a full description of the *cpsr*, refer to Appendix B.

2.2.1 PROCESSOR MODES

The processor mode determines which registers are active and the access rights to the *cpsr* register itself. Each processor mode is either privileged or nonprivileged: A privileged mode allows full read-write access to the *cpsr*. Conversely, a nonprivileged mode only allows read access to the control field in the *cpsr* but still allows read-write access to the condition flags.

There are seven processor modes in total: six privileged modes (*abort, fast interrupt request, interrupt request, supervisor, system,* and *undefined*) and one nonprivileged mode (*user*).

The processor enters *abort* mode when there is a failed attempt to access memory. *Fast interrupt request* and *interrupt request* modes correspond to the two interrupt levels available on the ARM processor. *Supervisor* mode is the mode that the processor is in after reset and is generally the mode that an operating system kernel operates in. *System* mode is a special version of *user* mode that allows full read-write access to the *cpsr*. *Undefined* mode is used when the processor encounters an instruction that is undefined or not supported by the implementation. *User* mode is used for programs and applications.

2.2.2 BANKED REGISTERS

Figure 2.4 shows all 37 registers in the register file. Of those, 20 registers are hidden from a program at different times. These registers are called *banked registers* and are identified by the shading in the diagram. They are available only when the processor is in a particular

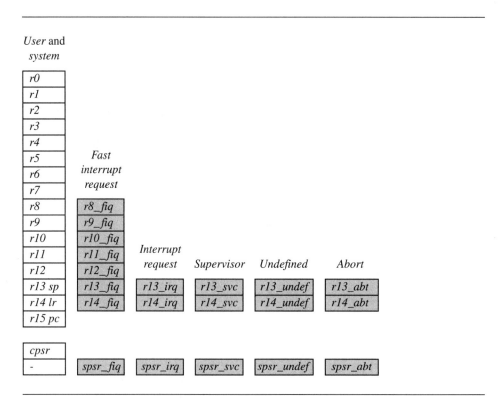

Figure 2.4   Complete ARM register set.

mode; for example, *abort* mode has banked registers *r13_abt, r14_abt* and *spsr_abt.* Banked registers of a particular mode are denoted by an underline character post-fixed to the mode mnemonic or *_mode.*

Every processor mode except *user* mode can change mode by writing directly to the mode bits of the *cpsr.* All processor modes except *system* mode have a set of associated banked registers that are a subset of the main 16 registers. A banked register maps one-to-one onto a *user* mode register. If you change processor mode, a banked register from the new mode will replace an existing register.

For example, when the processor is in the *interrupt request* mode, the instructions you execute still access registers named *r13* and *r14.* However, these registers are the banked registers *r13_irq* and *r14_irq.* The *user* mode registers *r13_usr* and *r14_usr* are not affected by the instruction referencing these registers. A program still has normal access to the other registers *r0* to *r12.*

The processor mode can be changed by a program that writes directly to the *cpsr* (the processor core has to be in privileged mode) or by hardware when the core responds to

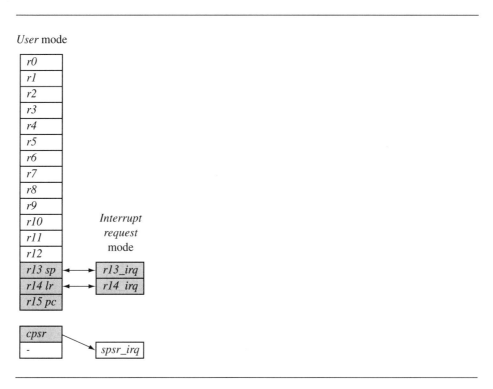

User mode

Figure 2.5   Changing mode on an exception.

an exception or interrupt. The following exceptions and interrupts cause a mode change: *reset, interrupt request, fast interrupt request, software interrupt, data abort, prefetch abort,* and *undefined instruction.* Exceptions and interrupts suspend the normal execution of sequential instructions and jump to a specific location.

Figure 2.5 illustrates what happens when an interrupt forces a mode change. The figure shows the core changing from *user* mode to *interrupt request* mode, which happens when an *interrupt request* occurs due to an external device raising an interrupt to the processor core. This change causes *user* registers *r13* and *r14* to be banked. The *user* registers are replaced with registers *r13_irq* and *r14_irq*, respectively. Note *r14_irq* contains the return address and *r13_irq* contains the stack pointer for *interrupt request* mode.

Figure 2.5 also shows a new register appearing in *interrupt request* mode: the saved program status register *(spsr)*, which stores the previous mode's *cpsr*. You can see in the diagram the *cpsr* being copied into *spsr_irq*. To return back to *user* mode, a special return instruction is used that instructs the core to restore the original *cpsr* from the *spsr_irq* and bank in the *user* registers *r13* and *r14*. Note that the *spsr* can only be modified and read in a privileged mode. There is no *spsr* available in *user* mode.

Table 2.1   Processor mode.

Mode	Abbreviation	Privileged	Mode[4:0]
Abort	abt	yes	10111
Fast interrupt request	fiq	yes	10001
Interrupt request	irq	yes	10010
Supervisor	svc	yes	10011
System	sys	yes	11111
Undefined	und	yes	11011
User	usr	no	10000

Another important feature to note is that the *cpsr* is not copied into the *spsr* when a mode change is forced due to a program writing directly to the *cpsr*. The saving of the *cpsr* only occurs when an exception or interrupt is raised.

Figure 2.3 shows that the current active processor mode occupies the five least significant bits of the *cpsr*. When power is applied to the core, it starts in *supervisor* mode, which is privileged. Starting in a privileged mode is useful since initialization code can use full access to the *cpsr* to set up the stacks for each of the other modes.

Table 2.1 lists the various modes and the associated binary patterns. The last column of the table gives the bit patterns that represent each of the processor modes in the *cpsr*.

2.2.3   STATE AND INSTRUCTION SETS

The state of the core determines which instruction set is being executed. There are three instruction sets: ARM, Thumb, and Jazelle. The ARM instruction set is only active when the processor is in ARM state. Similarly the Thumb instruction set is only active when the processor is in Thumb state. Once in Thumb state the processor is executing purely Thumb 16-bit instructions. You cannot intermingle sequential ARM, Thumb, and Jazelle instructions.

The Jazelle *J* and Thumb *T* bits in the *cpsr* reflect the state of the processor. When both *J* and *T* bits are 0, the processor is in ARM state and executes ARM instructions. This is the case when power is applied to the processor. When the T bit is 1, then the processor is in Thumb state. To change states the core executes a specialized branch instruction. Table 2.2 compares the ARM and Thumb instruction set features.

The ARM designers introduced a third instruction set called *Jazelle*. *Jazelle* executes 8-bit instructions and is a hybrid mix of software and hardware designed to speed up the execution of Java bytecodes.

To execute Java bytecodes, you require the Jazelle technology plus a specially modified version of the Java virtual machine. It is important to note that the hardware portion of Jazelle only supports a subset of the Java bytecodes; the rest are emulated in software.

Table 2.2   ARM and Thumb instruction set features.

	ARM (*cpsr* $T = 0$)	Thumb (*cpsr* $T = 1$)
Instruction size	32-bit	16-bit
Core instructions	58	30
Conditional execution[a]	most	only branch instructions
Data processing instructions	access to barrel shifter and ALU	separate barrel shifter and ALU instructions
Program status register	read-write in privileged mode	no direct access
Register usage	15 general-purpose registers +*pc*	8 general-purpose registers +7 high registers +*pc*

[a] See Section 2.2.6.

Table 2.3   Jazelle instruction set features.

	Jazelle (*cpsr* $T = 0, J = 1$)
Instruction size	8-bit
Core instructions	Over 60% of the Java bytecodes are implemented in hardware; the rest of the codes are implemented in software.

The Jazelle instruction set is a closed instruction set and is not openly available. Table 2.3 gives the Jazelle instruction set features.

2.2.4   INTERRUPT MASKS

Interrupt masks are used to stop specific interrupt requests from interrupting the processor. There are two interrupt request levels available on the ARM processor core—*interrupt request* (IRQ) and *fast interrupt request* (FIQ).

The *cpsr* has two interrupt mask bits, 7 and 6 (or *I* and *F*), which control the masking of IRQ and FIQ, respectively. The *I* bit masks IRQ when set to binary 1, and similarly the *F* bit masks FIQ when set to binary 1.

2.2.5   CONDITION FLAGS

Condition flags are updated by comparisons and the result of ALU operations that specify the S instruction suffix. For example, if a SUBS subtract instruction results in a register value of zero, then the *Z* flag in the *cpsr* is set. This particular subtract instruction specifically updates the *cpsr*.

Table 2.4   Condition flags.

Flag	Flag name	Set when
Q	Saturation	the result causes an overflow and/or saturation
V	oVerflow	the result causes a signed overflow
C	Carry	the result causes an unsigned carry
Z	Zero	the result is zero, frequently used to indicate equality
N	Negative	bit 31 of the result is a binary 1

With processor cores that include the DSP extensions, the Q bit indicates if an overflow or saturation has occurred in an enhanced DSP instruction. The flag is "sticky" in the sense that the hardware only sets this flag. To clear the flag you need to write to the *cpsr* directly.

In Jazelle-enabled processors, the J bit reflects the state of the core; if it is set, the core is in Jazelle state. The J bit is not generally usable and is only available on some processor cores. To take advantage of Jazelle, extra software has to be licensed from both ARM Limited and Sun Microsystems.

Most ARM instructions can be executed conditionally on the value of the condition flags. Table 2.4 lists the condition flags and a short description on what causes them to be set. These flags are located in the most significant bits in the *cpsr*. These bits are used for conditional execution.

Figure 2.6 shows a typical value for the *cpsr* with both DSP extensions and Jazelle. In this book we use a notation that presents the *cpsr* data in a more human readable form. When a bit is a binary 1 we use a capital letter; when a bit is a binary 0, we use a lowercase letter. For the condition flags a capital letter shows that the flag has been set. For interrupts a capital letter shows that an interrupt is disabled.

In the *cpsr* example shown in Figure 2.6, the C flag is the only condition flag set. The rest *nzvq* flags are all clear. The processor is in ARM state because neither the Jazelle *j* or Thumb *t* bits are set. The IRQ interrupts are enabled, and FIQ interrupts are disabled. Finally, you

Figure 2.6   Example: *cpsr* = *nzCvqjiFt_SVC*.

Table 2.5   Condition mnemonics.

Mnemonic	Name	Condition flags
EQ	equal	Z
NE	not equal	z
CS HS	carry set/unsigned higher or same	C
CC LO	carry clear/unsigned lower	c
MI	minus/negative	N
PL	plus/positive or zero	n
VS	overflow	V
VC	no overflow	v
HI	unsigned higher	zC
LS	unsigned lower or same	Z or c
GE	signed greater than or equal	NV or nv
LT	signed less than	Nv or nV
GT	signed greater than	NzV or nzv
LE	signed less than or equal	Z or Nv or nV
AL	always (unconditional)	ignored

can see from the figure the processor is in *supervisor* (*SVC*) mode since the mode[4:0] is equal to binary 10011.

2.2.6 CONDITIONAL EXECUTION

Conditional execution controls whether or not the core will execute an instruction. Most instructions have a condition attribute that determines if the core will execute it based on the setting of the condition flags. Prior to execution, the processor compares the condition attribute with the condition flags in the *cpsr*. If they match, then the instruction is executed; otherwise the instruction is ignored.

The condition attribute is postfixed to the instruction mnemonic, which is encoded into the instruction. Table 2.5 lists the conditional execution code mnemonics. When a condition mnemonic is not present, the default behavior is to set it to always (**AL**) execute.

2.3 PIPELINE

A pipeline is the mechanism a RISC processor uses to execute instructions. Using a pipeline speeds up execution by fetching the next instruction while other instructions are being decoded and executed. One way to view the pipeline is to think of it as an automobile assembly line, with each stage carrying out a particular task to manufacture the vehicle.

Figure 2.7   ARM7 Three-stage pipeline.

Figure 2.7 shows a three-stage pipeline:

■ *Fetch* loads an instruction from memory.

■ *Decode* identifies the instruction to be executed.

■ *Execute* processes the instruction and writes the result back to a register.

Figure 2.8 illustrates the pipeline using a simple example. It shows a sequence of three instructions being fetched, decoded, and executed by the processor. Each instruction takes a single cycle to complete after the pipeline is filled.

The three instructions are placed into the pipeline sequentially. In the first cycle the core fetches the ADD instruction from memory. In the second cycle the core fetches the SUB instruction and decodes the ADD instruction. In the third cycle, both the SUB and ADD instructions are moved along the pipeline. The ADD instruction is executed, the SUB instruction is decoded, and the CMP instruction is fetched. This procedure is called *filling the pipeline*. The pipeline allows the core to execute an instruction every cycle.

As the pipeline length increases, the amount of work done at each stage is reduced, which allows the processor to attain a higher operating frequency. This in turn increases the performance. The system *latency* also increases because it takes more cycles to fill the pipeline before the core can execute an instruction. The increased pipeline length also means there can be data dependency between certain stages. You can write code to reduce this dependency by using *instruction scheduling* (for more information on instruction scheduling take a look at Chapter 6).

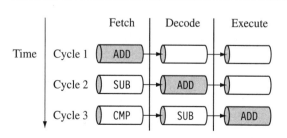

Figure 2.8   Pipelined instruction sequence.

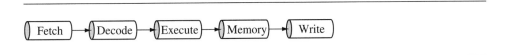

Figure 2.9   ARM9 five-stage pipeline.

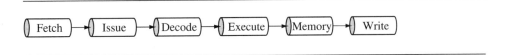

Figure 2.10   ARM10 six-stage pipeline.

The pipeline design for each ARM family differs. For example, The ARM9 core increases the pipeline length to five stages, as shown in Figure 2.9. The ARM9 adds a memory and writeback stage, which allows the ARM9 to process on average 1.1 Dhrystone MIPS per MHz—an increase in instruction throughput by around 13% compared with an ARM7. The maximum core frequency attainable using an ARM9 is also higher.

The ARM10 increases the pipeline length still further by adding a sixth stage, as shown in Figure 2.10. The ARM10 can process on average 1.3 Dhrystone MIPS per MHz, about 34% more throughput than an ARM7 processor core, but again at a higher latency cost.

Even though the ARM9 and ARM10 pipelines are different, they still use the same *pipeline executing characteristics* as an ARM7. Code written for the ARM7 will execute on an ARM9 or ARM10.

2.3.1   PIPELINE EXECUTING CHARACTERISTICS

The ARM pipeline has not processed an instruction until it passes completely through the execute stage. For example, an ARM7 pipeline (with three stages) has executed an instruction only when the fourth instruction is fetched.

Figure 2.11 shows an instruction sequence on an ARM7 pipeline. The MSR instruction is used to enable IRQ interrupts, which only occurs once the MSR instruction completes the execute stage of the pipeline. It clears the *I* bit in the *cpsr* to enable the IRQ interrupts. Once the ADD instruction enters the execute stage of the pipeline, IRQ interrupts are enabled.

Figure 2.12 illustrates the use of the pipeline and the program counter *pc*. In the execute stage, the *pc* always points to the address of the instruction plus 8 bytes. In other words, the *pc* always points to the address of the instruction being executed plus two instructions ahead. This is important when the *pc* is used for calculating a relative offset and is an

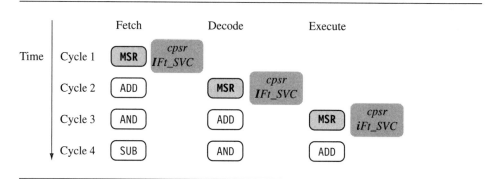

Figure 2.11   ARM instruction sequence.

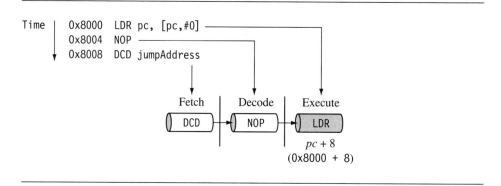

Figure 2.12   Example: *pc* = address + 8.

architectural characteristic across all the pipelines. Note when the processor is in Thumb state the *pc* is the instruction address plus 4.

There are three other characteristics of the pipeline worth mentioning. First, the execution of a branch instruction or branching by the direct modification of the *pc* causes the ARM core to flush its pipeline.

Second, ARM10 uses branch prediction, which reduces the effect of a pipeline flush by predicting possible branches and loading the new branch address prior to the execution of the instruction.

Third, an instruction in the execute stage will complete even though an interrupt has been raised. Other instructions in the pipeline will be abandoned, and the processor will start filling the pipeline from the appropriate entry in the vector table.

2.4 EXCEPTIONS, INTERRUPTS, AND THE VECTOR TABLE

When an exception or interrupt occurs, the processor sets the *pc* to a specific memory address. The address is within a special address range called the *vector table*. The entries in the vector table are instructions that branch to specific routines designed to handle a particular exception or interrupt.

The memory map address 0x00000000 is reserved for the vector table, a set of 32-bit words. On some processors the vector table can be optionally located at a higher address in memory (starting at the offset 0xffff0000). Operating systems such as Linux and Microsoft's embedded products can take advantage of this feature.

When an exception or interrupt occurs, the processor suspends normal execution and starts loading instructions from the exception vector table (see Table 2.6). Each vector table entry contains a form of branch instruction pointing to the start of a specific routine:

- *Reset vector* is the location of the first instruction executed by the processor when power is applied. This instruction branches to the initialization code.

- *Undefined instruction vector* is used when the processor cannot decode an instruction.

- *Software interrupt vector* is called when you execute a SWI instruction. The SWI instruction is frequently used as the mechanism to invoke an operating system routine.

- *Prefetch abort vector* occurs when the processor attempts to fetch an instruction from an address without the correct access permissions. The actual abort occurs in the decode stage.

- *Data abort vector* is similar to a prefetch abort but is raised when an instruction attempts to access data memory without the correct access permissions.

- *Interrupt request vector* is used by external hardware to interrupt the normal execution flow of the processor. It can only be raised if IRQs are not masked in the *cpsr*.

Table 2.6   The vector table.

Exception/interrupt	Shorthand	Address	High address
Reset	RESET	0x00000000	0xffff0000
Undefined instruction	UNDEF	0x00000004	0xffff0004
Software interrupt	SWI	0x00000008	0xffff0008
Prefetch abort	PABT	0x0000000c	0xffff000c
Data abort	DABT	0x00000010	0xffff0010
Reserved	—	0x00000014	0xffff0014
Interrupt request	IRQ	0x00000018	0xffff0018
Fast interrupt request	FIQ	0x0000001c	0xffff001c

■   *Fast interrupt request vector* is similar to the interrupt request but is reserved for hardware requiring faster response times. It can only be raised if FIQs are not masked in the *cpsr*.

2.5   CORE EXTENSIONS

The hardware extensions covered in this section are standard components placed next to the ARM core. They improve performance, manage resources, and provide extra functionality and are designed to provide flexibility in handling particular applications. Each ARM family has different extensions available.

There are three hardware extensions ARM wraps around the core: cache and tightly coupled memory, memory management, and the coprocessor interface.

2.5.1   CACHE AND TIGHTLY COUPLED MEMORY

The cache is a block of fast memory placed between main memory and the core. It allows for more efficient fetches from some memory types. With a cache the processor core can run for the majority of the time without having to wait for data from slow external memory. Most ARM-based embedded systems use a single-level cache internal to the processor. Of course, many small embedded systems do not require the performance gains that a cache brings.

ARM has two forms of cache. The first is found attached to the Von Neumann–style cores. It combines both data and instruction into a single unified cache, as shown in Figure 2.13. For simplicity, we have called the glue logic that connects the memory system to the AMBA bus *logic and control*.

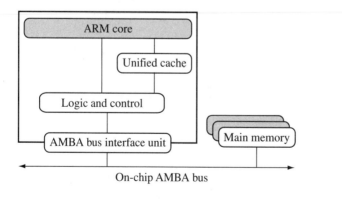

Figure 2.13   A simplified Von Neumann architecture with cache.

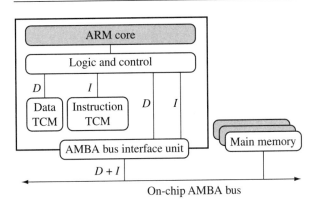

Figure 2.14   A simplified Harvard architecture with TCMs.

By contrast, the second form, attached to the Harvard-style cores, has separate caches for data and instruction.

A cache provides an overall increase in performance but at the expense of predictable execution. But for real-time systems it is paramount that code execution is *deterministic*— the time taken for loading and storing instructions or data must be predictable. This is achieved using a form of memory called *tightly coupled memory* (TCM). TCM is fast SRAM located close to the core and guarantees the clock cycles required to fetch instructions or data—critical for real-time algorithms requiring deterministic behavior. TCMs appear as memory in the address map and can be accessed as fast memory. An example of a processor with TCMs is shown in Figure 2.14.

By combining both technologies, ARM processors can have both improved performance and predictable real-time response. Figure 2.15 shows an example core with a combination of caches and TCMs.

2.5.2   MEMORY MANAGEMENT

Embedded systems often use multiple memory devices. It is usually necessary to have a method to help organize these devices and protect the system from applications trying to make inappropriate accesses to hardware. This is achieved with the assistance of memory management hardware.

ARM cores have three different types of memory management hardware—no extensions providing no protection, a memory protection unit (MPU) providing limited protection, and a memory management unit (MMU) providing full protection:

- *Nonprotected memory* is fixed and provides very little flexibility. It is normally used for small, simple embedded systems that require no protection from rogue applications.

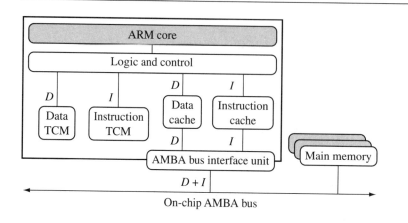

Figure 2.15   A simplified Harvard architecture with caches and TCMs.

- *MPUs* employ a simple system that uses a limited number of memory regions. These regions are controlled with a set of special coprocessor registers, and each region is defined with specific access permissions. This type of memory management is used for systems that require memory protection but don't have a complex memory map. The MPU is explained in Chapter 13.

- *MMUs* are the most comprehensive memory management hardware available on the ARM. The MMU uses a set of translation tables to provide fine-grained control over memory. These tables are stored in main memory and provide a virtual-to-physical address map as well as access permissions. MMUs are designed for more sophisticated platform operating systems that support multitasking. The MMU is explained in Chapter 14.

2.5.3   COPROCESSORS

Coprocessors can be attached to the ARM processor. A coprocessor extends the processing features of a core by extending the instruction set or by providing configuration registers. More than one coprocessor can be added to the ARM core via the coprocessor interface.

The coprocessor can be accessed through a group of dedicated ARM instructions that provide a load-store type interface. Consider, for example, coprocessor 15: The ARM processor uses coprocessor 15 registers to control the cache, TCMs, and memory management.

The coprocessor can also extend the instruction set by providing a specialized group of new instructions. For example, there are a set of specialized instructions that can be added to the standard ARM instruction set to process vector floating-point (VFP) operations.

These new instructions are processed in the decode stage of the ARM pipeline. If the decode stage sees a coprocessor instruction, then it offers it to the relevant coprocessor. But if the coprocessor is not present or doesn't recognize the instruction, then the ARM takes an undefined instruction exception, which allows you to emulate the behavior of the coprocessor in software.

2.6 ARCHITECTURE REVISIONS

Every ARM processor implementation executes a specific *instruction set architecture* (ISA), although an ISA revision may have more than one processor implementation.

The ISA has evolved to keep up with the demands of the embedded market. This evolution has been carefully managed by ARM, so that code written to execute on an earlier architecture revision will also execute on a later revision of the architecture.

Before we go on to explain the evolution of the architecture, we must introduce the ARM processor nomenclature. The nomenclature identifies individual processors and provides basic information about the feature set.

2.6.1 NOMENCLATURE

ARM uses the nomenclature shown in Figure 2.16 to describe the processor implementations. The letters and numbers after the word "ARM" indicate the features a processor

---

ARM{x}{y}{z}{T}{D}{M}{I}{E}{J}{F}{-S}

x—family
y—memory management/protection unit
z—cache
T—Thumb 16-bit decoder
D—JTAG debug
M—fast multiplier
I—EmbeddedICE macrocell
E—enhanced instructions (assumes TDMI)
J—Jazelle
F—vector floating-point unit
S—synthesizible version

Figure 2.16   ARM nomenclature.

may have. In the future the number and letter combinations may change as more features are added. Note the nomenclature does not include the architecture revision information. There are a few additional points to make about the ARM nomenclature:

- All ARM cores after the ARM7TDMI include the *TDMI* features even though they may not include those letters after the "ARM" label.

- The processor *family* is a group of processor implementations that share the same hardware characteristics. For example, the ARM7TDMI, ARM740T, and ARM720T all share the same family characteristics and belong to the ARM7 family.

- *JTAG* is described by IEEE 1149.1 Standard Test Access Port and boundary scan architecture. It is a serial protocol used by ARM to send and receive debug information between the processor core and test equipment.

- *EmbeddedICE macrocell* is the debug hardware built into the processor that allows breakpoints and watchpoints to be set.

- *Synthesizable* means that the processor core is supplied as source code that can be compiled into a form easily used by EDA tools.

2.6.2 ARCHITECTURE EVOLUTION

The architecture has continued to evolve since the first ARM processor implementation was introduced in 1985. Table 2.7 shows the significant architecture enhancements from the original architecture version 1 to the current version 6 architecture. One of the most significant changes to the ISA was the introduction of the Thumb instruction set in ARMv4T (the ARM7TDMI processor).

Table 2.8 summarizes the various parts of the program status register and the availability of certain features on particular instruction architectures. "All" refers to the ARMv4 architecture and above.

2.7 ARM PROCESSOR FAMILIES

ARM has designed a number of processors that are grouped into different families according to the core they use. The families are based on the ARM7, ARM9, ARM10, and ARM11 cores. The postfix numbers 7, 9, 10, and 11 indicate different core designs. The ascending number equates to an increase in performance and sophistication. ARM8 was developed but was soon superseded.

Table 2.9 shows a rough comparison of attributes between the ARM7, ARM9, ARM10, and ARM11 cores. The numbers quoted can vary greatly and are directly dependent upon the type and geometry of the manufacturing process, which has a direct effect on the frequency (MHz) and power consumption (watts).

Table 2.7   Revision history.

Revision	Example core implementation	ISA enhancement
ARMv1	ARM1	First ARM processor
		26-bit addressing
ARMv2	ARM2	32-bit multiplier
		32-bit coprocessor support
ARMv2a	ARM3	On-chip cache
		Atomic swap instruction
		Coprocessor 15 for cache management
ARMv3	ARM6 and ARM7DI	32-bit addressing
		Separate *cpsr* and *spsr*
		New modes—*undefined instruction* and *abort*
		MMU support—virtual memory
ARMv3M	ARM7M	Signed and unsigned long multiply instructions
ARMv4	StrongARM	Load-store instructions for signed and unsigned halfwords/bytes
		New mode—*system*
		Reserve SWI space for architecturally defined operations
		26-bit addressing mode no longer supported
ARMv4T	ARM7TDMI and ARM9T	Thumb
ARMv5TE	ARM9E and ARM10E	Superset of the ARMv4T
		Extra instructions added for changing state between ARM and Thumb
		Enhanced multiply instructions
		Extra DSP-type instructions
		Faster multiply accumulate
ARMv5TEJ	ARM7EJ and ARM926EJ	Java acceleration
ARMv6	ARM11	Improved multiprocessor instructions
		Unaligned and mixed endian data handling
		New multimedia instructions

Within each ARM family, there are a number of variations of memory management, cache, and TCM processor extensions. ARM continues to expand both the number of families available and the different variations within each family.

You can find other processors that execute the ARM ISA such as StrongARM and XScale. These processors are unique to a particular semiconductor company, in this case Intel.

Table 2.10 summarizes the different features of the various processors. The next subsections describe the ARM families in more detail, starting with the ARM7 family.

Table 2.8   Description of the *cpsr*.

Parts	Bits	Architectures	Description
Mode	4:0	all	processor mode
T	5	ARMv4T	Thumb state
I & F	7:6	all	interrupt masks
J	24	ARMv5TEJ	Jazelle state
Q	27	ARMv5TE	condition flag
V	28	all	condition flag
C	29	all	condition flag
Z	30	all	condition flag
N	31	all	condition flag

Table 2.9   ARM family attribute comparison.

	ARM7	ARM9	ARM10	ARM11
Pipeline depth	three-stage	five-stage	six-stage	eight-stage
Typical MHz	80	150	260	335
mW/MHz[a]	0.06 mW/MHz	0.19 mW/MHz (+ cache)	0.5 mW/MHz (+ cache)	0.4 mW/MHz (+ cache)
MIPS[b]/MHz	0.97	1.1	1.3	1.2
Architecture	Von Neumann	Harvard	Harvard	Harvard
Multiplier	8 × 32	8 × 32	16 × 32	16 × 32

[a] Watts/MHz on the same 0.13 micron process.
[b] MIPS are Dhrystone VAX MIPS.

2.7.1   ARM7 FAMILY

The ARM7 core has a Von Neumann–style architecture, where both data and instructions use the same bus. The core has a three-stage pipeline and executes the architecture ARMv4T instruction set.

The ARM7TDMI was the first of a new range of processors introduced in 1995 by ARM. It is currently a very popular core and is used in many 32-bit embedded processors. It provides a very good performance-to-power ratio. The ARM7TDMI processor core has been licensed by many of the top semiconductor companies around the world and is the first core to include the Thumb instruction set, a fast multiply instruction, and the EmbeddedICE debug technology.

Table 2.10   ARM processor variants.

CPU core	MMU/MPU	Cache	Jazelle	Thumb	ISA	E[a]
ARM7TDMI	none	none	no	yes	v4T	no
ARM7EJ-S	none	none	yes	yes	v5TEJ	yes
ARM720T	MMU	unified—8K cache	no	yes	v4T	no
ARM920T	MMU	separate—16K /16K $D + I$ cache	no	yes	v4T	no
ARM922T	MMU	separate—8K/8K $D + I$ cache	no	yes	v4T	no
ARM926EJ-S	MMU	separate—cache and TCMs configurable	yes	yes	v5TEJ	yes
ARM940T	MPU	separate—4K/4K $D + I$ cache	no	yes	v4T	no
ARM946E-S	MPU	separate—cache and TCMs configurable	no	yes	v5TE	yes
ARM966E-S	none	separate—TCMs configurable	no	yes	v5TE	yes
ARM1020E	MMU	separate—32K/32K $D + I$ cache	no	yes	v5TE	yes
ARM1022E	MMU	separate—16K/16K $D + I$ cache	no	yes	v5TE	yes
ARM1026EJ-S	MMU and MPU	separate—cache and TCMs configurable	yes	yes	v5TE	yes
ARM1136J-S	MMU	separate—cache and TCMs configurable	yes	yes	v6	yes
ARM1136JF-S	MMU	separate—cache and TCMs configurable	yes	yes	v6	yes

[a] E extension provides enhanced multiply instructions and saturation.

One significant variation in the ARM7 family is the ARM7TDMI-S. The ARM7TDMI-S has the same operating characteristics as a standard ARM7TDMI but is also synthesizable.

ARM720T is the most flexible member of the ARM7 family because it includes an MMU. The presence of the MMU means the ARM720T is capable of handling the Linux and Microsoft embedded platform operating systems. The processor also includes a unified 8K cache. The vector table can be relocated to a higher address by setting a coprocessor 15 register.

Another variation is the ARM7EJ-S processor, also synthesizable. ARM7EJ-S is quite different since it includes a five-stage pipeline and executes ARMv5TEJ instructions. This version of the ARM7 is the only one that provides both Java acceleration and the enhanced instructions but without any memory protection.

2.7.2   ARM9 FAMILY

The ARM9 family was announced in 1997. Because of its five-stage pipeline, the ARM9 processor can run at higher clock frequencies than the ARM7 family. The extra stages improve the overall performance of the processor. The memory system has been redesigned to follow the Harvard architecture, which separates the data D and instruction I buses.

The first processor in the ARM9 family was the ARM920T, which includes a separate $D + I$ cache and an MMU. This processor can be used by operating systems requiring virtual memory support. ARM922T is a variation on the ARM920T but with half the $D + I$ cache size.

The ARM940T includes a smaller $D + I$ cache and an MPU. The ARM940T is designed for applications that do not require a platform operating system. Both ARM920T and ARM940T execute the architecture v4T instructions.

The next processors in the ARM9 family were based on the ARM9E-S core. This core is a synthesizable version of the ARM9 core with the E extensions. There are two variations: the ARM946E-S and the ARM966E-S. Both execute architecture v5TE instructions. They also support the optional *embedded trace macrocell* (ETM), which allows a developer to trace instruction and data execution in real time on the processor. This is important when debugging applications with time-critical segments.

The ARM946E-S includes TCM, cache, and an MPU. The sizes of the TCM and caches are configurable. This processor is designed for use in embedded control applications that require deterministic real-time response. In contrast, the ARM966E does not have the MPU and cache extensions but does have configurable TCMs.

The latest core in the ARM9 product line is the ARM926EJ-S synthesizable processor core, announced in 2000. It is designed for use in small portable Java-enabled devices such as 3G phones and personal digital assistants (PDAs). The ARM926EJ-S is the first ARM processor core to include the Jazelle technology, which accelerates Java bytecode execution. It features an MMU, configurable TCMs, and $D + I$ caches with zero or nonzero wait state memories.

2.7.3   ARM10 FAMILY

The ARM10, announced in 1999, was designed for performance. It extends the ARM9 pipeline to six stages. It also supports an optional vector floating-point (VFP) unit, which adds a seventh stage to the ARM10 pipeline. The VFP significantly increases floating-point performance and is compliant with the IEEE 754.1985 floating-point standard.

The ARM1020E is the first processor to use an ARM10E core. Like the ARM9E, it includes the enhanced E instructions. It has separate 32K $D + I$ caches, optional vector floating-point unit, and an MMU. The ARM1020E also has a dual 64-bit bus interface for increased performance.

ARM1026EJ-S is very similar to the ARM926EJ-S but with both MPU and MMU. This processor has the performance of the ARM10 with the flexibility of an ARM926EJ-S.

2.7.4 ARM11 FAMILY

The ARM1136J-S, announced in 2003, was designed for high performance and power-efficient applications. ARM1136J-S was the first processor implementation to execute architecture ARMv6 instructions. It incorporates an eight-stage pipeline with separate load-store and arithmetic pipelines. Included in the ARMv6 instructions are single instruction multiple data (SIMD) extensions for media processing, specifically designed to increase video processing performance.

The ARM1136JF-S is an ARM1136J-S with the addition of the vector floating-point unit for fast floating-point operations.

2.7.5 SPECIALIZED PROCESSORS

StrongARM was originally co-developed by Digital Semiconductor and is now exclusively licensed by Intel Corporation. It is has been popular for PDAs and applications that require performance with low power consumption. It is a Harvard architecture with separate $D + I$ caches. StrongARM was the first high-performance ARM processor to include a five-stage pipeline, but it does not support the Thumb instruction set.

Intel's XScale is a follow-on product to the StrongARM and offers dramatic increases in performance. At the time of writing, XScale was quoted as being able to run up to 1 GHz. XScale executes architecture v5TE instructions. It is a Harvard architecture and is similar to the StrongARM, as it also includes an MMU.

SC100 is at the other end of the performance spectrum. It is designed specifically for low-power security applications. The SC100 is the first SecurCore and is based on an ARM7TDMI core with an MPU. This core is small and has low voltage and current requirements, which makes it attractive for smart card applications.

2.8 SUMMARY

In this chapter we focused on the hardware fundamentals of the actual ARM processor. The ARM processor can be abstracted into eight components—ALU, barrel shifter, MAC, register file, instruction decoder, address register, incrementer, and sign extend.

ARM has three instruction sets—ARM, Thumb, and Jazelle. The register file contains 37 registers, but only 17 or 18 registers are accessible at any point in time; the rest are banked according to processor mode. The current processor mode is stored in the *cpsr*. It holds the current status of the processor core as well interrupt masks, condition flags, and state. The state determines which instruction set is being executed.

An ARM processor comprises a core plus the surrounding components that interface it with a bus. The core extensions include the following:

- *Caches* are used to improve the overall system performance.
- *TCMs* are used to improve deterministic real-time response.

- *Memory management* is used to organize memory and protect system resources.

- *Coprocessors* are used to extend the instruction set and functionality. Coprocessor 15 controls the cache, TCMs, and memory management.

An ARM processor is an implementation of a specific instruction set architecture (ISA). The ISA has been continuously improved from the first ARM processor design. Processors are grouped into implementation families (ARM7, ARM9, ARM10, and ARM11) with similar characteristics.

INTRODUCTION TO THE ARM INSTRUCTION SET

This introduction to the ARM instruction set is a fundamental chapter since the information presented here is used throughout the rest of the book. Consequently, it is placed here before we start going into any depth on optimization and efficient algorithms. This chapter introduces the most common and useful ARM instructions and builds on the ARM processor fundamentals covered in the last chapter. Chapter 4 introduces the Thumb instruction set, and Appendix A gives a complete description of all ARM instructions.

Different ARM architecture revisions support different instructions. However, new revisions usually add instructions and remain backwardly compatible. Code you write for architecture ARMv4T should execute on an ARMv5TE processor. Table 3.1 provides a complete list of ARM instructions available in the ARMv5E instruction set architecture (ISA). This ISA includes all the core ARM instructions as well as some of the newer features in the ARM instruction set. The "ARM ISA" column lists the ISA revision in which the instruction was introduced. Some instructions have extended functionality in later architectures; for example, the CDP instruction has an ARMv5 variant called CDP2. Similarly, instructions such as LDR have ARMv5 additions but do not require a new or extended mnemonic.

We illustrate the processor operations using examples with pre- and post-conditions, describing registers and memory before and after the instruction or instructions are

Table 3.1   ARM instruction set.

Mnemonics	ARM ISA	Description
ADC	v1	add two 32-bit values and carry
ADD	v1	add two 32-bit values
AND	v1	logical bitwise AND of two 32-bit values
B	v1	branch relative $+/-$ 32 MB
BIC	v1	logical bit clear (AND NOT) of two 32-bit values
BKPT	v5	breakpoint instructions
BL	v1	relative branch with link
BLX	v5	branch with link and exchange
BX	v4T	branch with exchange
CDP CDP2	v2 v5	coprocessor data processing operation
CLZ	v5	count leading zeros
CMN	v1	compare negative two 32-bit values
CMP	v1	compare two 32-bit values
EOR	v1	logical exclusive OR of two 32-bit values
LDC LDC2	v2 v5	load to coprocessor single or multiple 32-bit values
LDM	v1	load multiple 32-bit words from memory to ARM registers
LDR	v1 v4 v5E	load a single value from a virtual address in memory
MCR MCR2 MCRR	v2 v5 v5E	move to coprocessor from an ARM register or registers
MLA	v2	multiply and accumulate 32-bit values
MOV	v1	move a 32-bit value into a register
MRC MRC2 MRRC	v2 v5 v5E	move to ARM register or registers from a coprocessor
MRS	v3	move to ARM register from a status register (*cpsr* or *spsr*)
MSR	v3	move to a status register (*cpsr* or *spsr*) from an ARM register
MUL	v2	multiply two 32-bit values
MVN	v1	move the logical NOT of 32-bit value into a register
ORR	v1	logical bitwise OR of two 32-bit values
PLD	v5E	preload hint instruction
QADD	v5E	signed saturated 32-bit add
QDADD	v5E	signed saturated double and 32-bit add
QDSUB	v5E	signed saturated double and 32-bit subtract
QSUB	v5E	signed saturated 32-bit subtract
RSB	v1	reverse subtract of two 32-bit values
RSC	v1	reverse subtract with carry of two 32-bit integers
SBC	v1	subtract with carry of two 32-bit values
SMLA*xy*	v5E	signed multiply accumulate instructions $((16 \times 16) + 32 = 32\text{-bit})$
SMLAL	v3M	signed multiply accumulate long $((32 \times 32) + 64 = 64\text{-bit})$
SMLAL*xy*	v5E	signed multiply accumulate long $((16 \times 16) + 64 = 64\text{-bit})$
SMLAW*y*	v5E	signed multiply accumulate instruction $(((32 \times 16) \gg 16) + 32 = 32\text{-bit})$
SMULL	v3M	signed multiply long $(32 \times 32 = 64\text{-bit})$

continued

Table 3.1   ARM instruction set. (*Continued*)

Mnemonics	ARM ISA	Description
SMUL*xy*	v5E	signed multiply instructions ($16 \times 16 = 32$-bit)
SMULW*y*	v5E	signed multiply instruction ((32×16) $\gg$ $16 = 32$-bit)
STC STC2	v2 v5	store to memory single or multiple 32-bit values from coprocessor
STM	v1	store multiple 32-bit registers to memory
STR	v1 v4 v5E	store register to a virtual address in memory
SUB	v1	subtract two 32-bit values
SWI	v1	software interrupt
SWP	v2a	swap a word/byte in memory with a register, without interruption
TEQ	v1	test for equality of two 32-bit values
TST	v1	test for bits in a 32-bit value
UMLAL	v3M	unsigned multiply accumulate long ((32×32) $+ 64 = 64$-bit)
UMULL	v3M	unsigned multiply long ($32 \times 32 = 64$-bit)

executed. We will represent hexadecimal numbers with the prefix 0x and binary numbers with the prefix 0b. The examples follow this format:

```
PRE    <pre-conditions>
       <instruction/s>
POST   <post-conditions>
```

In the pre- and post-conditions, memory is denoted as

```
mem<data_size>[address]
```

This refers to *data_size* bits of memory starting at the given byte *address*. For example, *mem32*[1024] is the 32-bit value starting at address 1 KB.

ARM instructions process data held in registers and only access memory with load and store instructions. ARM instructions commonly take two or three operands. For instance the ADD instruction below adds the two values stored in registers *r1* and *r2* (the source registers). It writes the result to register *r3* (the destination register).

Instruction Syntax	Destination register (*Rd*)	Source register 1 (*Rn*)	Source register 2 (*Rm*)
ADD r3, r1, r2	*r3*	*r1*	*r2*

In the following sections we examine the function and syntax of the ARM instructions by instruction class—data processing instructions, branch instructions, load-store instructions, software interrupt instruction, and program status register instructions.

3.1   DATA PROCESSING INSTRUCTIONS

The data processing instructions manipulate data within registers. They are move instructions, arithmetic instructions, logical instructions, comparison instructions, and multiply instructions. Most data processing instructions can process one of their operands using the barrel shifter.

If you use the S suffix on a data processing instruction, then it updates the flags in the cpsr. Move and logical operations update the carry flag C, negative flag N, and zero flag Z. The carry flag is set from the result of the barrel shift as the last bit shifted out. The N flag is set to bit 31 of the result. The Z flag is set if the result is zero.

3.1.1   MOVE INSTRUCTIONS

Move is the simplest ARM instruction. It copies N into a destination register Rd, where N is a register or immediate value. This instruction is useful for setting initial values and transferring data between registers.

Syntax: `<instruction>{<cond>}{S} Rd, N`

MOV	Move a 32-bit value into a register	$Rd = N$
MVN	move the NOT of the 32-bit value into a register	$Rd = \sim N$

Table 3.3, to be presented in Section 3.1.2, gives a full description of the values allowed for the second operand N for all data processing instructions. Usually it is a register Rm or a constant preceded by #.

EXAMPLE
3.1

This example shows a simple move instruction. The MOV instruction takes the contents of register $r5$ and copies them into register $r7$, in this case, taking the value 5, and overwriting the value 8 in register $r7$.

```
PRE    r5 = 5
       r7 = 8
       MOV    r7, r5    ; let r7 = r5
POST   r5 = 5
       r7 = 5
```

3.1.2 BARREL SHIFTER

In Example 3.1 we showed a MOV instruction where N is a simple register. But N can be more than just a register or immediate value; it can also be a register Rm that has been preprocessed by the barrel shifter prior to being used by a data processing instruction.

Data processing instructions are processed within the arithmetic logic unit (ALU). A unique and powerful feature of the ARM processor is the ability to shift the 32-bit binary pattern in one of the source registers left or right by a specific number of positions before it enters the ALU. This shift increases the power and flexibility of many data processing operations.

There are data processing instructions that do not use the barrel shift, for example, the MUL (multiply), CLZ (count leading zeros), and QADD (signed saturated 32-bit add) instructions.

Pre-processing or shift occurs within the cycle time of the instruction. This is particularly useful for loading constants into a register and achieving fast multiplies or division by a power of 2.

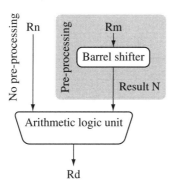

Figure 3.1   Barrel shifter and ALU.

To illustrate the barrel shifter we will take the example in Figure 3.1 and add a shift operation to the move instruction example. Register Rn enters the ALU without any pre-processing of registers. Figure 3.1 shows the data flow between the ALU and the barrel shifter.

EXAMPLE   We apply a logical shift left (LSL) to register Rm before moving it to the destination register.
3.2   This is the same as applying the standard C language shift operator $\ll$ to the register. The MOV instruction copies the shift operator result N into register Rd. N represents the result of the LSL operation described in Table 3.2.

```
PRE    r5 = 5
       r7 = 8
```

```
        MOV     r7, r5, LSL #2   ; let r7 = r5*4 = (r5<<2)
POST    r5 = 5
        r7 = 20
```

The example multiplies register *r5* by four and then places the result into register *r7*.

The five different shift operations that you can use within the barrel shifter are summarized in Table 3.2.

Figure 3.2 illustrates a logical shift left by one. For example, the contents of bit 0 are shifted to bit 1. Bit 0 is cleared. The *C* flag is updated with the last bit shifted out of the register. This is bit $(32 - y)$ of the original value, where *y* is the shift amount. When *y* is greater than one, then a shift by *y* positions is the same as a shift by one position executed *y* times.

Table 3.2   Barrel shifter operations.

Mnemonic	Description	Shift	Result	Shift amount y
LSL	logical shift left	$x\,\text{LSL}\,y$	$x \ll y$	#0–31 or *Rs*
LSR	logical shift right	$x\,\text{LSR}\,y$	$(\text{unsigned})x \gg y$	#1–32 or *Rs*
ASR	arithmetic right shift	$x\,\text{ASR}\,y$	$(\text{signed})x \gg y$	#1–32 or *Rs*
ROR	rotate right	$x\,\text{ROR}\,y$	$((\text{unsigned})x \gg y) \mid (x \ll (32 - y))$	#1–31 or *Rs*
RRX	rotate right extended	$x\,\text{RRX}$	$(c\ \text{flag} \ll 31) \mid ((\text{unsigned})x \gg 1)$	none

Note: *x* represents the register being shifted and *y* represents the shift amount.

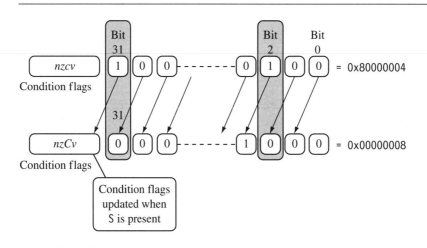

Figure 3.2   Logical shift left by one.

Table 3.3   Barrel shift operation syntax for data processing instructions.

N shift operations	Syntax
Immediate	`#immediate`
Register	`Rm`
Logical shift left by immediate	`Rm, LSL #shift_imm`
Logical shift left by register	`Rm, LSL Rs`
Logical shift right by immediate	`Rm, LSR #shift_imm`
Logical shift right with register	`Rm, LSR Rs`
Arithmetic shift right by immediate	`Rm, ASR #shift_imm`
Arithmetic shift right by register	`Rm, ASR Rs`
Rotate right by immediate	`Rm, ROR #shift_imm`
Rotate right by register	`Rm, ROR Rs`
Rotate right with extend	`Rm, RRX`

EXAMPLE   This example of a `MOVS` instruction shifts register $r1$ left by one bit. This multiplies register
3.3 $r1$ by a value 2^1. As you can see, the C flag is updated in the *cpsr* because the S suffix is
           present in the instruction mnemonic.

```
PRE     cpsr = nzcvqiFt_USER
        r0 = 0x00000000
        r1 = 0x80000004

        MOVS    r0, r1, LSL #1

POST    cpsr = nzCvqiFt_USER
        r0 = 0x00000008
        r1 = 0x80000004
```

Table 3.3 lists the syntax for the different barrel shift operations available on data processing instructions. The second operand N can be an immediate constant preceded by #, a register value Rm, or the value of Rm processed by a shift.

3.1.3   ARITHMETIC INSTRUCTIONS

The arithmetic instructions implement addition and subtraction of 32-bit signed and unsigned values.

Syntax: `<instruction>{<cond>}{S} Rd, Rn, N`

ADC	add two 32-bit values and carry	$Rd = Rn + N +$ `carry`
ADD	add two 32-bit values	$Rd = Rn + N$
RSB	reverse subtract of two 32-bit values	$Rd = N - Rn$
RSC	reverse subtract with carry of two 32-bit values	$Rd = N - Rn -$ `!(carry flag)`
SBC	subtract with carry of two 32-bit values	$Rd = Rn - N -$ `!(carry flag)`
SUB	subtract two 32-bit values	$Rd = Rn - N$

N is the result of the shifter operation. The syntax of shifter operation is shown in Table 3.3.

EXAMPLE
3.4
This simple subtract instruction subtracts a value stored in register *r2* from a value stored in register *r1*. The result is stored in register *r0*.

PRE   r0 = 0x00000000
       r1 = 0x00000002
       r2 = 0x00000001

       SUB r0, r1, r2

POST   r0 = 0x00000001

EXAMPLE
3.5
This reverse subtract instruction (RSB) subtracts *r1* from the constant value #0, writing the result to *r0*. You can use this instruction to negate numbers.

PRE   r0 = 0x00000000
       r1 = 0x00000077

       RSB r0, r1, #0   ; Rd = 0x0 - r1

POST   r0 = -r1 = 0xffffff89

EXAMPLE
3.6
The SUBS instruction is useful for decrementing loop counters. In this example we subtract the immediate value one from the value one stored in register *r1*. The result value zero is written to register *r1*. The *cpsr* is updated with the *ZC* flags being set.

PRE   cpsr = nzcvqiFt_USER
       r1 = 0x00000001

       SUBS r1, r1, #1

POST   cpsr = nZCvqiFt_USER
        r1 = 0x00000000

3.1.4 USING THE BARREL SHIFTER WITH ARITHMETIC INSTRUCTIONS

The wide range of second operand shifts available on arithmetic and logical instructions is a very powerful feature of the ARM instruction set. Example 3.7 illustrates the use of the inline barrel shifter with an arithmetic instruction. The instruction multiplies the value stored in register *r1* by three.

EXAMPLE 3.7   Register *r1* is first shifted one location to the left to give the value of twice *r1*. The ADD instruction then adds the result of the barrel shift operation to register *r1*. The final result transferred into register *r0* is equal to three times the value stored in register *r1*.

PRE   r0 = 0x00000000
        r1 = 0x00000005

        ADD   r0, r1, r1, LSL #1

POST   r0 = **0x0000000f**
        r1 = 0x00000005

3.1.5 LOGICAL INSTRUCTIONS

Logical instructions perform bitwise logical operations on the two source registers.

Syntax: <instruction>{<cond>}{S} Rd, Rn, N

AND	logical bitwise AND of two 32-bit values	$Rd = Rn \& N$
ORR	logical bitwise OR of two 32-bit values	$Rd = Rn \mid N$
EOR	logical exclusive OR of two 32-bit values	$Rd = Rn \,^\wedge N$
BIC	logical bit clear (AND NOT)	$Rd = Rn \& \sim N$

EXAMPLE 3.8   This example shows a logical OR operation between registers *r1* and *r2*. *r0* holds the result.

PRE   r0 = 0x00000000
        r1 = 0x02040608
        r2 = 0x10305070

```
            ORR   r0, r1, r2
```

POST   r0 = **0x12345678**

EXAMPLE   This example shows a more complicated logical instruction called BIC, which carries out
 3.9   a logical bit clear.

PRE   r1 = 0b1111
            r2 = 0b0101

```
            BIC   r0, r1, r2
```

POST   r0 = **0b1010**

This is equivalent to

            Rd = Rn **AND NOT**(N)

In this example, register *r2* contains a binary pattern where every binary 1 in *r2* clears
a corresponding bit location in register *r1*. This instruction is particularly useful when
clearing status bits and is frequently used to change interrupt masks in the *cpsr*.

The logical instructions update the *cpsr* flags only if the S suffix is present. These
instructions can use barrel-shifted second operands in the same way as the arithmetic
instructions.

3.1.6 COMPARISON INSTRUCTIONS

The comparison instructions are used to compare or test a register with a 32-bit value.
They update the *cpsr* flag bits according to the result, but do not affect other registers.
After the bits have been set, the information can then be used to change program flow by
using conditional execution. For more information on conditional execution take a look
at Section 3.8. You do not need to apply the S suffix for comparison instructions to update
the flags.

Syntax: <instruction>{<cond>} Rn, N

CMN	compare negated	flags set as a result of $Rn + N$
CMP	compare	flags set as a result of $Rn - N$
TEQ	test for equality of two 32-bit values	flags set as a result of $Rn \wedge N$
TST	test bits of a 32-bit value	flags set as a result of $Rn \& N$

N is the result of the shifter operation. The syntax of shifter operation is shown in Table 3.3.

EXAMPLE
3.10

This example shows a CMP comparison instruction. You can see that both registers, *r0* and *r9*, are equal before executing the instruction. The value of the *z* flag prior to execution is 0 and is represented by a lowercase *z*. After execution the *z* flag changes to 1 or an uppercase *Z*. This change indicates *equality*.

```
PRE    cpsr = nzcvqiFt_USER
       r0 = 4
       r9 = 4

       CMP   r0, r9

POST   cpsr = nZcvqiFt_USER
```

The CMP is effectively a subtract instruction with the result discarded; similarly the TST instruction is a logical AND operation, and TEQ is a logical exclusive OR operation. For each, the results are discarded but the condition bits are updated in the *cpsr*. It is important to understand that comparison instructions only modify the condition flags of the *cpsr* and do not affect the registers being compared.

3.1.7 MULTIPLY INSTRUCTIONS

The multiply instructions multiply the contents of a pair of registers and, depending upon the instruction, accumulate the results in with another register. The long multiplies accumulate onto a pair of registers representing a 64-bit value. The final result is placed in a destination register or a pair of registers.

```
Syntax: MLA{<cond>}{S} Rd, Rm, Rs, Rn
        MUL{<cond>}{S} Rd, Rm, Rs
```

MLA	multiply and accumulate	$Rd = (Rm^*Rs) + Rn$
MUL	multiply	$Rd = Rm^*Rs$

```
Syntax: <instruction>{<cond>}{S} RdLo, RdHi, Rm, Rs
```

SMLAL	signed multiply accumulate long	$[RdHi, RdLo] = [RdHi, RdLo] + (Rm^*Rs)$
SMULL	signed multiply long	$[RdHi, RdLo] = Rm^*Rs$
UMLAL	unsigned multiply accumulate long	$[RdHi, RdLo] = [RdHi, RdLo] + (Rm^*Rs)$
UMULL	unsigned multiply long	$[RdHi, RdLo] = Rm^*Rs$

The number of cycles taken to execute a multiply instruction depends on the processor implementation. For some implementations the cycle timing also depends on the value in *Rs*. For more details on cycle timings, see Appendix D.

EXAMPLE
3.11

This example shows a simple multiply instruction that multiplies registers *r1* and *r2* together and places the result into register *r0*. In this example, register *r1* is equal to the value 2, and *r2* is equal to 2. The result, 4, is then placed into register *r0*.

```
PRE     r0 = 0x00000000
        r1 = 0x00000002
        r2 = 0x00000002

        MUL   r0, r1, r2   ; r0 = r1*r2

POST    r0 = 0x00000004
        r1 = 0x00000002
        r2 = 0x00000002
```

The long multiply instructions (SMLAL, SMULL, UMLAL, and UMULL) produce a 64-bit result. The result is too large to fit a single 32-bit register so the result is placed in two registers labeled *RdLo* and *RdHi*. *RdLo* holds the lower 32 bits of the 64-bit result, and *RdHi* holds the higher 32 bits of the 64-bit result. Example 3.12 shows an example of a long unsigned multiply instruction.

EXAMPLE
3.12

The instruction multiplies registers *r2* and *r3* and places the result into register *r0* and *r1*. Register *r0* contains the lower 32 bits, and register *r1* contains the higher 32 bits of the 64-bit result.

```
PRE     r0 = 0x00000000
        r1 = 0x00000000
        r2 = 0xf0000002
        r3 = 0x00000002

        UMULL   r0, r1, r2, r3   ; [r1,r0] = r2*r3

POST    r0 = 0xe0000004 ; = RdLo
        r1 = 0x00000001 ; = RdHi
```

3.2 BRANCH INSTRUCTIONS

A branch instruction changes the flow of execution or is used to call a routine. This type of instruction allows programs to have subroutines, *if-then-else* structures, and loops.

The change of execution flow forces the program counter *pc* to point to a new address. The ARMv5E instruction set includes four different branch instructions.

Syntax: B{<cond>} label
        BL{<cond>} label
        BX{<cond>} Rm
        BLX{<cond>} label | Rm

B	branch	$pc = label$
BL	branch with link	$pc = label$ lr = address of the next instruction after the BL
BX	branch exchange	$pc = Rm$ & 0xfffffffe, $T = Rm$ & 1
BLX	branch exchange with link	$pc = label$, $T = 1$ $pc = Rm$ & 0xfffffffe, $T = Rm$ & 1 lr = address of the next instruction after the BLX

The address *label* is stored in the instruction as a signed *pc*-relative offset and must be within approximately 32 MB of the branch instruction. *T* refers to the Thumb bit in the *cpsr*. When instructions set *T*, the ARM switches to Thumb state.

EXAMPLE
3.13
This example shows a forward and backward branch. Because these loops are address specific, we do not include the pre- and post-conditions. The forward branch skips three instructions. The backward branch creates an infinite loop.

```
        B       forward
        ADD     r1, r2, #4
        ADD     r0, r6, #2
        ADD     r3, r7, #4
forward
        SUB     r1, r2, #4
```

```
backward
        ADD     r1, r2, #4
        SUB     r1, r2, #4
        ADD     r4, r6, r7
        B       backward
```

Branches are used to change execution flow. Most assemblers hide the details of a branch instruction encoding by using labels. In this example, *forward* and *backward* are the labels. The branch labels are placed at the beginning of the line and are used to mark an address that can be used later by the assembler to calculate the branch offset.

EXAMPLE 3.14   The branch with link, or BL, instruction is similar to the B instruction but overwrites the link register *lr* with a return address. It performs a subroutine call. This example shows a simple fragment of code that branches to a subroutine using the BL instruction. To return from a subroutine, you copy the link register to the *pc*.

```
        BL      subroutine  ; branch to subroutine
        CMP     r1, #5      ; compare r1 with 5
        MOVEQ   r1, #0      ; if (r1==5) then r1 = 0
        :
subroutine
        <subroutine code>
        MOV     pc, lr      ; return by moving pc = lr
```

The branch exchange (BX) and branch exchange with link (BLX) are the third type of branch instruction. The BX instruction uses an absolute address stored in register *Rm*. It is primarily used to branch to and from Thumb code, as shown in Chapter 4. The *T* bit in the *cpsr* is updated by the least significant bit of the branch register. Similarly the BLX instruction updates the *T* bit of the *cpsr* with the least significant bit and additionally sets the link register with the return address.

3.3   LOAD-STORE INSTRUCTIONS

Load-store instructions transfer data between memory and processor registers. There are three types of load-store instructions: single-register transfer, multiple-register transfer, and swap.

3.3.1   SINGLE-REGISTER TRANSFER

These instructions are used for moving a single data item in and out of a register. The datatypes supported are signed and unsigned words (32-bit), halfwords (16-bit), and bytes. Here are the various load-store single-register transfer instructions.

Syntax: <LDR|STR>{<cond>}{B} Rd,addressing[1]
        LDR{<cond>}{SB|H|SH} Rd, addressing[2]
        STR{<cond>}H Rd, addressing[2]

LDR	load word into a register	$Rd \leftarrow mem32[address]$
STR	save byte or word from a register	$Rd \rightarrow mem32[address]$
LDRB	load byte into a register	$Rd \leftarrow mem8[address]$
STRB	save byte from a register	$Rd \rightarrow mem8[address]$

LDRH	load halfword into a register	$Rd <- mem16[address]$
STRH	save halfword into a register	$Rd -> mem16[address]$
LDRSB	load signed byte into a register	$Rd <- SignExtend$ $(mem8[address])$
LDRSH	load signed halfword into a register	$Rd <- SignExtend$ $(mem16[address])$

Tables 3.5 and 3.7, to be presented is Section 3.3.2, describe the *addressing*[1] and *addressing*[2] syntax.

EXAMPLE
3.15

LDR and STR instructions can load and store data on a boundary alignment that is the same as the datatype size being loaded or stored. For example, LDR can only load 32-bit words on a memory address that is a multiple of four bytes—0, 4, 8, and so on. This example shows a load from a memory address contained in register *r1*, followed by a store back to the same address in memory.

```
;
; load register r0 with the contents of
; the memory address pointed to by register
; r1.
;
        LDR     r0, [r1]          ; = LDR r0, [r1, #0]
;
; store the contents of register r0 to
; the memory address pointed to by
; register r1.
;
        STR     r0, [r1]          ; = STR r0, [r1, #0]
```

The first instruction loads a word from the address stored in register *r1* and places it into register *r0*. The second instruction goes the other way by storing the contents of register *r0* to the address contained in register *r1*. The offset from register *r1* is zero. Register *r1* is called the *base address register*.

3.3.2 SINGLE-REGISTER LOAD-STORE ADDRESSING MODES

The ARM instruction set provides different modes for addressing memory. These modes incorporate one of the indexing methods: preindex with writeback, preindex, and postindex (see Table 3.4).

Table 3.4   Index methods.

Index method	Data	Base address register	Example
Preindex with writeback	*mem[base + offset]*	*base + offset*	LDR r0,[r1,#4]!
Preindex	*mem[base + offset]*	*not updated*	LDR r0,[r1,#4]
Postindex	*mem[base]*	*base + offset*	LDR r0,[r1],#4

Note: ! indicates that the instruction writes the calculated address back to the base address register.

EXAMPLE
3.16

Preindex with writeback calculates an address from a base register plus address offset and then updates that address base register with the new address. In contrast, the preindex offset is the same as the preindex with writeback but does not update the address base register. Postindex only updates the address base register after the address is used. The preindex mode is useful for accessing an element in a data structure. The postindex and preindex with writeback modes are useful for traversing an array.

```
PRE     r0 = 0x00000000
        r1 = 0x00090000
        mem32[0x00009000] = 0x01010101
        mem32[0x00009004] = 0x02020202

        LDR    r0, [r1, #4]!
```

Preindexing with writeback:

```
POST(1)  r0 = 0x02020202
         r1 = 0x00009004

         LDR    r0, [r1, #4]
```

Preindexing:

```
POST(2)  r0 = 0x02020202
         r1 = 0x00009000

         LDR    r0, [r1], #4
```

Postindexing:

```
POST(3)  r0 = 0x01010101
         r1 = 0x00009004
```

Table 3.5   Single-register load-store addressing, word or unsigned byte.

Addressing[1] mode and index method	Addressing[1] syntax
Preindex with immediate offset	`[Rn, #+/-offset_12]`
Preindex with register offset	`[Rn, +/-Rm]`
Preindex with scaled register offset	`[Rn, +/-Rm, shift #shift_imm]`
Preindex writeback with immediate offset	`[Rn, #+/-offset_12]!`
Preindex writeback with register offset	`[Rn, +/-Rm]!`
Preindex writeback with scaled register offset	`[Rn, +/-Rm, shift #shift_imm]!`
Immediate postindexed	`[Rn], #+/-offset_12`
Register postindex	`[Rn], +/-Rm`
Scaled register postindex	`[Rn], +/-Rm, shift #shift_imm`

This example shows how each indexing method effects the address held in register *r1*, as well as the data loaded into register *r0*. Each instruction shows the result of the index method with the same pre-condition.

The addressing modes available with a particular load or store instruction depend on the instruction class. Table 3.5 shows the addressing modes available for load and store of a 32-bit word or an unsigned byte.

A signed offset or register is denoted by "+/−", identifying that it is either a positive or negative offset from the base address register *Rn*. The base address register is a pointer to a byte in memory, and the offset specifies a number of bytes.

Immediate means the address is calculated using the base address register and a 12-bit offset encoded in the instruction. *Register* means the address is calculated using the base address register and a specific register's contents. *Scaled* means the address is calculated using the base address register and a barrel shift operation.

Table 3.6 provides an example of the different variations of the LDR instruction. Table 3.7 shows the addressing modes available on load and store instructions using 16-bit halfword or signed byte data.

These operations cannot use the barrel shifter. There are no STRSB or STRSH instructions since STRH stores both a signed and unsigned halfword; similarly STRB stores signed and unsigned bytes. Table 3.8 shows the variations for STRH instructions.

3.3.3 MULTIPLE-REGISTER TRANSFER

Load-store multiple instructions can transfer multiple registers between memory and the processor in a single instruction. The transfer occurs from a base address register *Rn* pointing into memory. Multiple-register transfer instructions are more efficient from single-register transfers for moving blocks of data around memory and saving and restoring context and stacks.

Table 3.6 Examples of LDR instructions using different addressing modes.

	Instruction	$r0 =$	$r1 + =$
Preindex with writeback	LDR r0,[r1,#0x4]!	mem32[r1 + 0x4]	0x4
	LDR r0,[r1,r2]!	mem32[r1+r2]	r2
	LDR r0,[r1,r2,LSR#0x4]!	mem32[r1 + (r2 LSR 0x4)]	(r2 LSR 0x4)
Preindex	LDR r0,[r1,#0x4]	mem32[r1 + 0x4]	*not updated*
	LDR r0,[r1,r2]	mem32[r1 + r2]	*not updated*
	LDR r0,[r1,-r2,LSR #0x4]	mem32[r1-(r2 LSR 0x4)]	*not updated*
Postindex	LDR r0,[r1],#0x4	mem32[r1]	0x4
	LDR r0,[r1],r2	mem32[r1]	r2
	LDR r0,[r1],r2,LSR #0x4	mem32[r1]	(r2 LSR 0x4)

Table 3.7 Single-register load-store addressing, halfword, signed halfword, signed byte, and doubleword.

Addressing^2 mode and index method	Addressing^2 syntax
Preindex immediate offset	[Rn, #+/-offset_8]
Preindex register offset	[Rn, +/-Rm]
Preindex writeback immediate offset	[Rn, #+/-offset_8]!
Preindex writeback register offset	[Rn, +/-Rm]!
Immediate postindexed	[Rn], #+/-offset_8
Register postindexed	[Rn], +/-Rm

Table 3.8 Variations of STRH instructions.

	Instruction	Result	$r1 + =$
Preindex with writeback	STRH r0,[r1,#0x4]!	mem16[r1+0x4]=r0	0x4
	STRH r0,[r1,r2]!	mem16[r1+r2]=r0	r2
Preindex	STRH r0,[r1,#0x4]	mem16[r1+0x4]=r0	*not updated*
	STRH r0,[r1,r2]	mem16[r1+r2]=r0	*not updated*
Postindex	STRH r0,[r1],#0x4	mem16[r1]=r0	0x4
	STRH r0,[r1],r2	mem16[r1]=r0	r2

Load-store multiple instructions can increase interrupt latency. ARM implementations do not usually interrupt instructions while they are executing. For example, on an ARM7 a load multiple instruction takes $2 + Nt$ cycles, where N is the number of registers to load and t is the number of cycles required for each sequential access to memory. If an interrupt has been raised, then it has no effect until the load-store multiple instruction is complete.

Compilers, such as armcc, provide a switch to control the maximum number of registers being transferred on a load-store, which limits the maximum interrupt latency.

Syntax: `<LDM|STM>{<cond>}<addressing mode> Rn{!},<registers>{^}`

LDM	load multiple registers	$\{Rd\}^{*N}$ <- mem32[start address + 4*N] optional Rn updated
STM	save multiple registers	$\{Rd\}^{*N}$ -> mem32[start address + 4*N] optional Rn updated

Table 3.9 shows the different addressing modes for the load-store multiple instructions. Here N is the number of registers in the list of registers.

Any subset of the current bank of registers can be transferred to memory or fetched from memory. The base register Rn determines the source or destination address for a load-store multiple instruction. This register can be optionally updated following the transfer. This occurs when register Rn is followed by the ! character, similiar to the single-register load-store using preindex with writeback.

Table 3.9 Addressing mode for load-store multiple instructions.

Addressing mode	Description	Start address	End address	Rn!
IA	increment after	Rn	$Rn + 4^*N - 4$	$Rn + 4^*N$
IB	increment before	$Rn + 4$	$Rn + 4^*N$	$Rn + 4^*N$
DA	decrement after	$Rn - 4^*N + 4$	Rn	$Rn - 4^*N$
DB	decrement before	$Rn - 4^*N$	$Rn - 4$	$Rn - 4^*N$

EXAMPLE
3.17

In this example, register $r0$ is the base register Rn and is followed by !, indicating that the register is updated after the instruction is executed. You will notice within the load multiple instruction that the registers are not individually listed. Instead the "-" character is used to identify a range of registers. In this case the range is from register $r1$ to $r3$ inclusive.

Each register can also be listed, using a comma to separate each register within "{" and "}" brackets.

```
PRE    mem32[0x80018] = 0x03
       mem32[0x80014] = 0x02
```

```
mem32[0x80010] = 0x01
r0 = 0x00080010
r1 = 0x00000000
r2 = 0x00000000
r3 = 0x00000000

LDMIA    r0!, {r1-r3}
```

POST   r0 = 0x0008001c
          r1 = 0x00000001
          r2 = 0x00000002
          r3 = 0x00000003

Figure 3.3 shows a graphical representation.

The base register *r0* points to memory address 0x80010 in the PRE condition. Memory addresses 0x80010, 0x80014, and 0x80018 contain the values 1, 2, and 3 respectively. After the load multiple instruction executes registers *r1*, *r2*, and *r3* contain these values as shown in Figure 3.4. The base register *r0* now points to memory address 0x8001c after the last loaded word.

Now replace the LDMIA instruction with a load multiple and increment before LDMIB instruction and use the same PRE conditions. The first word pointed to by register *r0* is ignored and register *r1* is loaded from the next memory location as shown in Figure 3.5.

After execution, register *r0* now points to the last loaded memory location. This is in contrast with the LDMIA example, which pointed to the next memory location.

The decrement versions DA and DB of the load-store multiple instructions decrement the start address and then store to ascending memory locations. This is equivalent to descending memory but accessing the register list in reverse order. With the increment and decrement load multiples, you can access arrays forwards or backwards. They also allow for stack push and pull operations, illustrated later in this section.

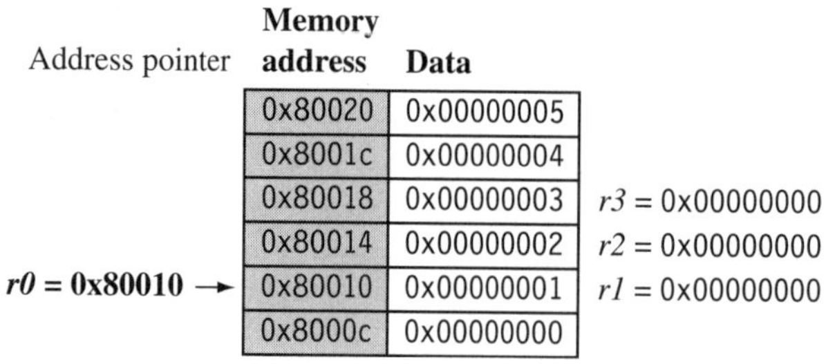

Address pointer	**Memory address**	**Data**	
	0x80020	0x00000005	
	0x8001c	0x00000004	
	0x80018	0x00000003	*r3* = 0x00000000
	0x80014	0x00000002	*r2* = 0x00000000
r0 = **0x80010** →	0x80010	0x00000001	*r1* = 0x00000000
	0x8000c	0x00000000	

Figure 3.3   Pre-condition for LDMIA instruction.

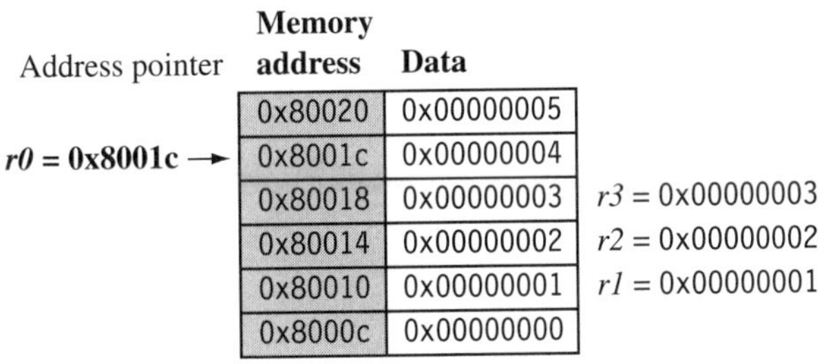

Figure 3.4   Post-condition for LDMIA instruction.

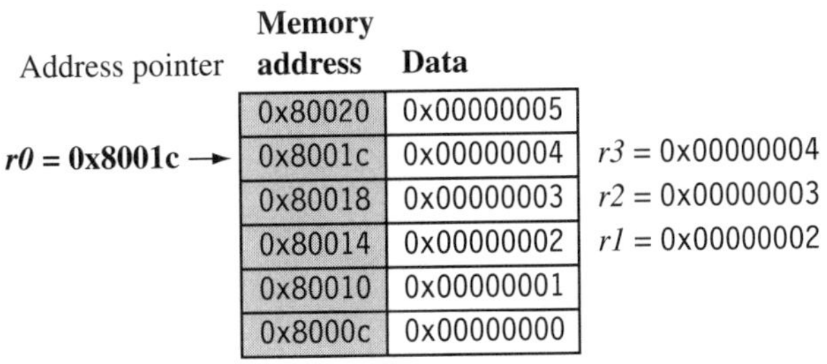

Figure 3.5   Post-condition for LDMIB instruction.

Table 3.10   Load-store multiple pairs when base update used.

Store multiple	Load multiple
STMIA	LDMDB
STMIB	LDMDA
STMDA	LDMIB
STMDB	LDMIA

Table 3.10 shows a list of load-store multiple instruction pairs. If you use a store with base update, then the paired load instruction of the same number of registers will reload the data and restore the base address pointer. This is useful when you need to temporarily save a group of registers and restore them later.

EXAMPLE 3.18   This example shows an STM *increment before* instruction followed by an LDM *decrement after* instruction.

```
PRE      r0 = 0x00009000
         r1 = 0x00000009
         r2 = 0x00000008
         r3 = 0x00000007

         STMIB    r0!, {r1-r3}

         MOV      r1, #1
         MOV      r2, #2
         MOV      r3, #3

PRE(2)   r0 = 0x0000900c
         r1 = 0x00000001
         r2 = 0x00000002
         r3 = 0x00000003

         LDMDA r0!, {r1-r3}

POST     r0 = 0x00009000
         r1 = 0x00000009
         r2 = 0x00000008
         r3 = 0x00000007
```

The STMIB instruction stores the values 7, 8, 9 to memory. We then corrupt register *r1* to *r3*. The LDMDA reloads the original values and restores the base pointer *r0*.

EXAMPLE 3.19   We illustrate the use of the load-store multiple instructions with a *block memory copy* example. This example is a simple routine that copies blocks of 32 bytes from a source address location to a destination address location.

The example has two load-store multiple instructions, which use the same *increment after* addressing mode.

```
; r9 points to start of source data
; r10 points to start of destination data
; r11 points to end of the source

loop
        ; load 32 bytes from source and update r9 pointer
        LDMIA    r9!, {r0-r7}
```

```
; store 32 bytes to destination and update r10 pointer
STMIA   r10!, {r0-r7} ; and store them

; have we reached the end
CMP     r9, r11
BNE     loop
```

This routine relies on registers *r9*, *r10*, and *r11* being set up before the code is executed. Registers *r9* and *r11* determine the data to be copied, and register *r10* points to the destination in memory for the data. LDMIA loads the data pointed to by register *r9* into registers *r0* to *r7*. It also updates *r9* to point to the next block of data to be copied. STMIA copies the contents of registers *r0* to *r7* to the destination memory address pointed to by register *r10*. It also updates *r10* to point to the next destination location. CMP and BNE compare pointers *r9* and *r11* to check whether the end of the block copy has been reached. If the block copy is complete, then the routine finishes; otherwise the loop repeats with the updated values of register *r9* and *r10*.

The BNE is the branch instruction B with a condition mnemonic NE (not equal). If the previous compare instruction sets the condition flags to *not equal*, the branch instruction is executed.

Figure 3.6 shows the memory map of the block memory copy and how the routine moves through memory. Theoretically this loop can transfer 32 bytes (8 words) in two instructions, for a maximum possible throughput of 46 MB/second being transferred at 33 MHz. These numbers assume a perfect memory system with fast memory.

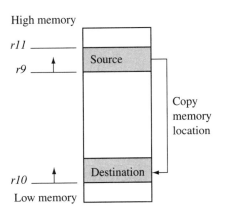

Figure 3.6   Block memory copy in the memory map.

3.3.3.1 Stack Operations

The ARM architecture uses the load-store multiple instructions to carry out stack operations. The *pop* operation (removing data from a stack) uses a load multiple instruction; similarly, the *push* operation (placing data onto the stack) uses a store multiple instruction.

When using a stack you have to decide whether the stack will grow up or down in memory. A stack is either *ascending* (A) or *descending* (D). Ascending stacks grow towards higher memory addresses; in contrast, descending stacks grow towards lower memory addresses.

When you use a *full stack* (F), the stack pointer *sp* points to an address that is the last used or full location (i.e., *sp* points to the last item on the stack). In contrast, if you use an *empty stack* (E) the *sp* points to an address that is the first unused or empty location (i.e., it points after the last item on the stack).

There are a number of load-store multiple addressing mode aliases available to support stack operations (see Table 3.11). Next to the *pop* column is the actual load multiple instruction equivalent. For example, a full ascending stack would have the notation FA appended to the load multiple instruction—LDMFA. This would be translated into an LDMDA instruction.

ARM has specified an ARM-Thumb Procedure Call Standard (ATPCS) that defines how routines are called and how registers are allocated. In the ATPCS, stacks are defined as being full descending stacks. Thus, the LDMFD and STMFD instructions provide the pop and push functions, respectively.

EXAMPLE
3.20

The STMFD instruction pushes registers onto the stack, updating the *sp*. Figure 3.7 shows a push onto a full descending stack. You can see that when the stack grows the stack pointer points to the last full entry in the stack.

```
PRE    r1 = 0x00000002
       r4 = 0x00000003
       sp = 0x00080014

       STMFD   sp!, {r1,r4}
```

Table 3.11   Addressing methods for stack operations.

Addressing mode	Description	Pop	= LDM	Push	= STM
FA	full ascending	LDMFA	LDMDA	STMFA	STMIB
FD	full descending	LDMFD	LDMIA	STMFD	STMDB
EA	empty ascending	LDMEA	LDMDB	STMEA	STMIA
ED	empty descending	LDMED	LDMIB	STMED	STMDA

PRE	Address	Data		POST	Address	Data
	0x80018	0x00000001			0x80018	0x00000001
sp →	0x80014	0x00000002			0x80014	0x00000002
	0x80010	*Empty*			0x80010	0x00000003
	0x8000c	*Empty*		sp →	0x8000c	0x00000002

Figure 3.7   STMFD instruction—full stack push operation.

POST   r1 = 0x00000002
r4 = 0x00000003
sp = 0x0008000c

EXAMPLE
3.21

In contrast, Figure 3.8 shows a push operation on an empty stack using the STMED instruction. The STMED instruction pushes the registers onto the stack but updates register *sp* to point to the next empty location.

PRE   r1 = 0x00000002
r4 = 0x00000003
sp = 0x00080010

STMED   sp!, {r1,r4}

POST   r1 = 0x00000002
r4 = 0x00000003
sp = 0x00080008

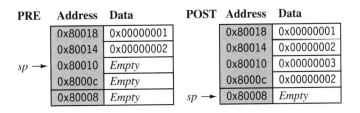

PRE	Address	Data		POST	Address	Data
	0x80018	0x00000001			0x80018	0x00000001
	0x80014	0x00000002			0x80014	0x00000002
sp →	0x80010	*Empty*			0x80010	0x00000003
	0x8000c	*Empty*			0x8000c	0x00000002
	0x80008	*Empty*		sp →	0x80008	*Empty*

Figure 3.8   STMED instruction—empty stack push operation.

When handling a checked stack there are three attributes that need to be preserved: the *stack base*, the *stack pointer*, and the *stack limit*. The stack base is the starting address of the stack in memory. The stack pointer initially points to the stack base; as data is pushed onto the stack, the stack pointer descends memory and continuously points to the top of stack. If the stack pointer passes the stack limit, then a *stack overflow error* has occurred. Here is a small piece of code that checks for stack overflow errors for a descending stack:

```
; check for stack overflow

SUB sp, sp, #size
CMP sp, r10
BLLO _stack_overflow ; condition
```

ATPCS defines register *r10* as the stack limit or *sl*. This is optional since it is only used when stack checking is enabled. The BLLO instruction is a branch with link instruction plus the condition mnemonic LO. If *sp* is less than register *r10* after the new items are pushed onto the stack, then stack overflow error has occurred. If the stack pointer goes back past the stack base, then a *stack underflow error* has occurred.

3.3.4 SWAP INSTRUCTION

The swap instruction is a special case of a load-store instruction. It swaps the contents of memory with the contents of a register. This instruction is an *atomic operation*—it reads and writes a location in the same bus operation, preventing any other instruction from reading or writing to that location until it completes.

Syntax: SWP{B}{<cond>} Rd,Rm,[Rn]

SWP	swap a word between memory and a register	$tmp = mem32[Rn]$ $mem32[Rn] = Rm$ $Rd = tmp$
SWPB	swap a byte between memory and a register	$tmp = mem8[Rn]$ $mem8[Rn] = Rm$ $Rd = tmp$

Swap cannot be interrupted by any other instruction or any other bus access. We say the system "holds the bus" until the transaction is complete.

EXAMPLE 3.22   The swap instruction loads a word from memory into register *r0* and overwrites the memory with register *r1*.

```
PRE     mem32[0x9000] = 0x12345678
        r0 = 0x00000000
        r1 = 0x11112222
        r2 = 0x00009000

        SWP    r0, r1, [r2]
```

POST   mem32[0x9000] = **0x11112222**
        r0 = 0x12345678
        r1 = 0x11112222
        r2 = 0x00009000

This instruction is particularly useful when implementing semaphores and mutual exclusion in an operating system. You can see from the syntax that this instruction can also have a byte size qualifier B, so this instruction allows for both a word and a byte swap.

EXAMPLE
3.23

This example shows a simple data guard that can be used to protect data from being written by another task. The SWP instruction "holds the bus" until the transaction is complete.

```
spin
        MOV    r1, =semaphore
        MOV    r2, #1
        SWP    r3, r2, [r1] ; hold the bus until complete
        CMP    r3, #1
        BEQ    spin
```

The address pointed to by the semaphore either contains the value 0 or 1. When the semaphore equals 1, then the service in question is being used by another process. The routine will continue to loop around until the service is released by the other process—in other words, when the semaphore address location contains the value 0.

3.4 SOFTWARE INTERRUPT INSTRUCTION

A software interrupt instruction (SWI) causes a software interrupt exception, which provides a mechanism for applications to call operating system routines.

Syntax: SWI{<cond>} SWI_number

SWI	software interrupt	lr_svc = address of instruction following the SWI
		$spsr\_svc$ = $cpsr$
		pc = vectors + 0x8
		$cpsr$ mode = SVC
		$cpsr$ I = 1 (mask IRQ interrupts)

When the processor executes an SWI instruction, it sets the program counter *pc* to the offset 0x8 in the vector table. The instruction also forces the processor mode to *SVC*, which allows an operating system routine to be called in a privileged mode.

Each SWI instruction has an associated SWI number, which is used to represent a particular function call or feature.

EXAMPLE 3.24
Here we have a simple example of an SWI call with SWI number 0x123456, used by ARM toolkits as a debugging SWI. Typically the SWI instruction is executed in user mode.

```
PRE     cpsr = nzcVqift_USER
        pc = 0x00008000
        lr = 0x003fffff; lr = r14
        r0 = 0x12

        0x00008000   SWI      0x123456

POST    cpsr = nzcVqIft_SVC
        spsr = nzcVqift_USER
        pc = 0x00000008
        lr = 0x00008004
        r0 = 0x12
```

Since SWI instructions are used to call operating system routines, you need some form of parameter passing. This is achieved using registers. In this example, register *r0* is used to pass the parameter 0x12. The return values are also passed back via registers.

Code called the *SWI handler* is required to process the SWI call. The handler obtains the SWI number using the address of the executed instruction, which is calculated from the link register *lr*.

The SWI number is determined by

```
SWI_Number = <SWI instruction> AND NOT(0xff000000)
```

Here the *SWI instruction* is the actual 32-bit SWI instruction executed by the processor.

EXAMPLE 3.25
This example shows the start of an SWI handler implementation. The code fragment determines what SWI number is being called and places that number into register *r10*. You can see from this example that the load instruction first copies the complete SWI instruction into register *r10*. The BIC instruction masks off the top bits of the instruction, leaving the SWI number. We assume the SWI has been called from ARM state.

```
SWI_handler
        ;
        ; Store registers r0-r12 and the link register
```

```
;
STMFD    sp!, {r0-r12, lr}

; Read the SWI instruction
LDR      r10, [lr, #-4]

; Mask off top 8 bits
BIC      r10, r10, #0xff000000

; r10 - contains the SWI number
BL       service_routine

; return from SWI handler
LDMFD    sp!, {r0-r12, pc}^
```

The number in register *r10* is then used by the SWI handler to call the appropriate SWI service routine.

3.5 PROGRAM STATUS REGISTER INSTRUCTIONS

The ARM instruction set provides two instructions to directly control a program status register (*psr*). The MRS instruction transfers the contents of either the *cpsr* or *spsr* into a register; in the reverse direction, the MSR instruction transfers the contents of a register into the *cpsr* or *spsr*. Together these instructions are used to read and write the *cpsr* and *spsr*.

In the syntax you can see a label called *fields*. This can be any combination of control (*c*), extension (*x*), status (*s*), and flags (*f*). These fields relate to particular byte regions in a *psr*, as shown in Figure 3.9.

```
Syntax: MRS{<cond>} Rd,<cpsr|spsr>
        MSR{<cond>} <cpsr|spsr>_<fields>,Rm
        MSR{<cond>} <cpsr|spsr>_<fields>,#immediate
```

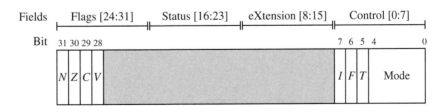

Figure 3.9   *psr* byte fields.

MRS	copy program status register to a general-purpose register	$Rd = psr$
MSR	move a general-purpose register to a program status register	$psr[field] = Rm$
MSR	move an immediate value to a program status register	$psr[field] = immediate$

The *c* field controls the interrupt masks, Thumb state, and processor mode. Example 3.26 shows how to enable IRQ interrupts by clearing the *I* mask. This operation involves using both the MRS and MSR instructions to read from and then write to the *cpsr*.

EXAMPLE
3.26
The MSR first copies the *cpsr* into register *r1*. The BIC instruction clears bit 7 of *r1*. Register *r1* is then copied back into the *cpsr*, which enables IRQ interrupts. You can see from this example that this code preserves all the other settings in the *cpsr* and only modifies the *I* bit in the control field.

```
PRE    cpsr = nzcvqIFt_SVC

       MRS    r1, cpsr
       BIC    r1, r1, #0x80 ; 0b01000000
       MSR    cpsr_c, r1

POST   cpsr = nzcvqiFt_SVC
```

This example is in *SVC* mode. In *user* mode you can read all *cpsr* bits, but you can only update the condition flag field *f*.

3.5.1   COPROCESSOR INSTRUCTIONS

Coprocessor instructions are used to extend the instruction set. A coprocessor can either provide additional computation capability or be used to control the memory subsystem including caches and memory management. The coprocessor instructions include data processing, register transfer, and memory transfer instructions. We will provide only a short overview since these instructions are coprocessor specific. Note that these instructions are only used by cores with a coprocessor.

```
Syntax: CDP{<cond>} cp, opcode1, Cd, Cn {, opcode2}
        <MRC|MCR>{<cond>} cp, opcode1, Rd, Cn, Cm {, opcode2}
        <LDC|STC>{<cond>} cp, Cd, addressing
```

CDP	coprocessor data processing—perform an operation in a coprocessor
MRC MCR	coprocessor register transfer—move data from/to coprocessor registers
LDC STC	coprocessor memory transfer—load and store blocks of memory to/from a coprocessor

In the syntax of the coprocessor instructions, the *cp* field represents the coprocessor number between *p0* and *p15*. The *opcode* fields describe the operation to take place on the coprocessor. The *Cn*, *Cm*, and *Cd* fields describe registers within the coprocessor. The coprocessor operations and registers depend on the specific coprocessor you are using. Coprocessor 15 (CP15) is reserved for system control purposes, such as memory management, write buffer control, cache control, and identification registers.

EXAMPLE
3.27

This example shows a CP15 register being copied into a general-purpose register.

```
; transferring the contents of CP15 register c0 to register r10
        MRC p15, 0, r10, c0, c0, 0
```

Here CP15 *register-0* contains the processor identification number. This register is copied into the general-purpose register *r10*.

3.5.2 COPROCESSOR 15 INSTRUCTION SYNTAX

CP15 configures the processor core and has a set of dedicated registers to store configuration information, as shown in Example 3.27. A value written into a register sets a configuration attribute—for example, switching on the cache.

CP15 is called the *system control coprocessor*. Both MRC and MCR instructions are used to read and write to CP15, where register *Rd* is the core destination register, *Cn* is the primary register, *Cm* is the secondary register, and *opcode2* is a secondary register modifier. You may occasionally hear secondary registers called "extended registers."

As an example, here is the instruction to move the contents of CP15 control register *c1* into register *r1* of the processor core:

```
        MRC p15, 0, r1, c1, c0, 0
```

We use a shorthand notation for CP15 reference that makes referring to configuration registers easier to follow. The reference notation uses the following format:

CP15:cX:cY:Z

The first term, *CP15*, defines it as coprocessor 15. The second term, after the separating colon, is the primary register. The primary register *X* can have a value between 0 and 15. The third term is the secondary or extended register. The secondary register *Y* can have a value between 0 and 15. The last term, *opcode2*, is an instruction modifier and can have a value between 0 and 7. Some operations may also use a nonzero value *w* of *opcode1*. We write these as *CP15:w:cX:cY:Z*.

3.6 Loading Constants

You might have noticed that there is no ARM instruction to move a 32-bit constant into a register. Since ARM instructions are 32 bits in size, they obviously cannot specify a general 32-bit constant.

To aid programming there are two pseudoinstructions to move a 32-bit value into a register.

Syntax: LDR Rd, =constant
        ADR Rd, label

| LDR | load constant pseudoinstruction | *Rd* = 32-bit constant |
| ADR | load address pseudoinstruction | *Rd* = 32-bit relative address |

The first pseudoinstruction writes a 32-bit constant to a register using whatever instructions are available. It defaults to a memory read if the constant cannot be encoded using other instructions.

The second pseudoinstruction writes a relative address into a register, which will be encoded using a *pc*-relative expression.

EXAMPLE 3.28   This example shows an LDR instruction loading a 32-bit constant 0xff00ffff into register *r0*.

```
        LDR     r0, [pc, #constant_number-8-{PC}]
        :
constant_number
        DCD     0xff00ffff
```

This example involves a memory access to load the constant, which can be expensive for time-critical routines.

Example 3.29 shows an alternative method to load the same constant into register *r0* by using an MVN instruction.

Table 3.12   LDR pseudoinstruction conversion.

Pseudoinstruction	Actual instruction
`LDR r0, =0xff`	`MOV r0, #0xff`
`LDR r0, =0x55555555`	`LDR r0, [pc, #offset_12]`

EXAMPLE
3.29

Loading the constant `0xff00ffff` using an `MVN`.

PRE   none...

       `MVN     r0, #0x00ff0000`

POST   r0 = **0xff00ffff**

As you can see, there are alternatives to accessing memory, but they depend upon the constant you are trying to load. Compilers and assemblers use clever techniques to avoid loading a constant from memory. These tools have algorithms to find the optimal number of instructions required to generate a constant in a register and make extensive use of the barrel shifter. If the tools cannot generate the constant by these methods, then it is loaded from memory. The LDR pseudoinstruction either inserts an MOV or MVN instruction to generate a value (if possible) or generates an LDR instruction with a *pc*-relative address to read the constant from a *literal pool*—a data area embedded within the code.

Table 3.12 shows two pseudocode conversions. The first conversion produces a simple MOV instruction; the second conversion produces a *pc*-relative load. We recommended that you use this pseudoinstruction to load a constant. To see how the assembler has handled a particular load constant, you can pass the output through a disassembler, which will list the instruction chosen by the tool to load the constant.

Another useful pseudoinstruction is the ADR instruction, or *address relative*. This instruction places the address of the given *label* into register *Rd*, using a *pc*-relative add or subtract.

3.7 ARMv5E Extensions

The ARMv5E extensions provide many new instructions (see Table 3.13). One of the most important additions is the signed multiply accumulate instructions that operate on 16-bit data. These operations are single cycle on many ARMv5E implementations.

ARMv5E provides greater flexibility and efficiency when manipulating 16-bit values, which is important for applications such as 16-bit digital audio processing.

Table 3.13   New instructions provided by the ARMv5E extensions.

Instruction	Description
CLZ {<cond>} Rd, Rm	count leading zeros
QADD {<cond>} Rd, Rm, Rn	signed saturated 32-bit add
QDADD{<cond>} Rd, Rm, Rn	signed saturated double 32-bit add
QDSUB{<cond>} Rd, Rm, Rn	signed saturated double 32-bit subtract
QSUB{<cond>} Rd, Rm, Rn	signed saturated 32-bit subtract
SMLAxy{<cond>} Rd, Rm, Rs, Rn	signed multiply accumulate 32-bit (1)
SMLALxy{<cond>} RdLo, RdHi, Rm, Rs	signed multiply accumulate 64-bit
SMLAWy{<cond>} Rd, Rm, Rs, Rn	signed multiply accumulate 32-bit (2)
SMULxy{<cond>} Rd, Rm, Rs	signed multiply (1)
SMULWy{<cond>} Rd, Rm, Rs	signed multiply (2)

3.7.1   COUNT LEADING ZEROS INSTRUCTION

The count leading zeros instruction counts the number of zeros between the most significant bit and the first bit set to 1. Example 3.30 shows an example of a CLZ instruction.

EXAMPLE   You can see from this example that the first bit set to 1 has 27 zeros preceding it. CLZ is
3.30   useful in routines that have to normalize numbers.

PRE   r1 = 0b00000000000000000000000000010000

CLZ r0, r1

POST   r0 = **27**

3.7.2   SATURATED ARITHMETIC

Normal ARM arithmetic instructions wrap around when you overflow an integer value. For example, 0x7fffffff + 1 = -0x80000000. Thus, when you design an algorithm, you have to be careful not to exceed the maximum representable value in a 32-bit integer.

EXAMPLE   This example shows what happens when the maximum value is exceeded.
3.31

PRE   cpsr = nzcvqiFt_SVC
r0 = 0x00000000
r1 = 0x70000000 (positive)
r2 = 0x7fffffff (positive)

```
                ADDS    r0, r1, r2
```

POST   cpsr = **NzcVqiFt_SVC**
             r0 = **0xefffffff (negative)**

In the example, registers *r1* and *r2* contain positive numbers. Register *r2* is equal to
0x7fffffff, which is the maximum positive value you can store in 32 bits. In a perfect world adding these numbers together would result in a large positive number. Instead
the value becomes negative and the overflow flag, *V*, is set.

In contrast, using the ARMv5E instructions you can *saturate* the result—once the highest
number is exceeded the results remain at the maximum value of 0x7fffffff. This avoids
the requirement for any additional code to check for possible overflows. Table 3.14 lists all
the ARMv5E saturation instructions.

Table 3.14   Saturation instructions.

Instruction	Saturated calculation
QADD	$Rd = Rn + Rm$
QDADD	$Rd = Rn + (Rm*2)$
QSUB	$Rd = Rn - Rm$
QDSUB	$Rd = Rn - (Rm*2)$

EXAMPLE   This example shows the same data being passed into the QADD instruction.
3.32

PRE   cpsr = nzcvqiFt_SVC
           r0 = 0x00000000
           r1 = 0x70000000 (positive)
           r2 = 0x7fffffff (positive)

           QADD   r0, r1, r2

POST   cpsr = nzcv**Q**iFt_SVC
            r0 = **0x7fffffff**

You will notice that the saturated number is returned in register *r0*. Also the Q bit (bit 27
of the *cpsr*) has been set, indicating saturation has occurred. The Q flag is sticky and will
remain set until explicitly cleared.

3.7.3 ARMv5E MULTIPLY INSTRUCTIONS

Table 3.15 shows a complete list of the ARMv5E multiply instructions. In the table,
x and y select which 16 bits of a 32-bit register are used for the first and second

Table 3.15   Signed multiply and multiply accumulate instructions.

Instruction	Signed Multiply [Accumulate]	Signed result	Q flag updated	Calculation
SMLAxy	(16-bit *16-bit)+ 32-bit	32-bit	yes	$Rd = (Rm.x * Rs.y) + Rn$
SMLALxy	(16-bit *16-bit)+ 64-bit	64-bit	—	$[RdHi, RdLo] + = Rm.x * Rs.y$
SMLAWy	((32-bit *16-bit) $\gg$ 16)+ 32-bit	32-bit	yes	$Rd = ((Rm * Rs.y) \gg 16) + Rn$
SMULxy	(16-bit *16-bit)	32-bit	—	$Rd = Rm.x * Rs.y$
SMULWy	((32-bit *16-bit) $\gg$ 16)	32-bit	—	$Rd = (Rm * Rs.y) \gg 16$

operands, respectively. These fields are set to a letter T for the top 16-bits, or the letter B for the bottom 16 bits. For multiply accumulate operations with a 32-bit result, the Q flag indicates if the accumulate overflowed a signed 32-bit value.

EXAMPLE 3.33   This example shows how you use these operations. The example uses a signed multiply accumulate instruction, SMLATB.

```
PRE    r1 = 0x20000001
       r2 = 0x20000001
       r3 = 0x00000004

       SMLATB r4, r1, r2, r3

POST   r4 = 0x00002004
```

The instruction multiplies the top 16 bits of register *r1* by the bottom 16 bits of register *r2*. It adds the result to register *r3* and writes it to destination register *r4*.

3.8   CONDITIONAL EXECUTION

Most ARM instructions are *conditionally executed*—you can specify that the instruction only executes if the condition code flags pass a given condition or test. By using conditional execution instructions you can increase performance and code density.

The condition field is a two-letter mnemonic appended to the instruction mnemonic. The default mnemonic is AL, or *always execute*.

Conditional execution reduces the number of branches, which also reduces the number of pipeline flushes and thus improves the performance of the executed code. Conditional execution depends upon two components: the condition field and condition flags. The condition field is located in the instruction, and the condition flags are located in the *cpsr*.

EXAMPLE
3.34

This example shows an ADD instruction with the EQ condition appended. This instruction will only be executed when the zero flag in the *cpsr* is set to 1.

```
; r0 = r1 + r2 if zero flag is set
ADDEQ r0, r1, r2
```

Only comparison instructions and data processing instructions with the S suffix appended to the mnemonic update the condition flags in the *cpsr*.

EXAMPLE
3.35

To help illustrate the advantage of conditional execution, we will take the simple C code fragment shown in this example and compare the assembler output using nonconditional and conditional instructions.

```
while (a!=b)
{
  if (a>b) a -= b; else b -= a;
}
```

Let register *r1* represent *a* and register *r2* represent *b*. The following code fragment shows the same algorithm written in ARM assembler. This example only uses conditional execution on the branch instructions:

```
        ; Greatest Common Divisor Algorithm
gcd
        CMP     r1, r2
        BEQ     complete
        BLT     lessthan
        SUB     r1, r1, r2
        B       gcd

lessthan
        SUB     r2, r2, r1
        B       gcd

complete
...
```

Now compare the same code with full conditional execution. As you can see, this dramatically reduces the number of instructions:

```
gcd
        CMP     r1, r2
```

```
SUBGT   r1, r1, r2
SUBLT   r2, r2, r1
BNE     gcd
```

3.9 SUMMARY

In this chapter we covered the ARM instruction set. All ARM instructions are 32 bits in length. The arithmetic, logical, comparisons, and move instructions can all use the inline barrel shifter, which pre-processes the second register *Rm* before it enters into the ALU.

The ARM instruction set has three types of load-store instructions: single-register load-store, multiple-register load-store, and swap. The multiple load-store instructions provide the push-pop operations on the stack. The ARM-Thumb Procedure Call Standard (ATPCS) defines the stack as being a full descending stack.

The software interrupt instruction causes a software interrupt that forces the processor into *SVC* mode; this instruction invokes privileged operating system routines. The program status register instructions write and read to the *cpsr* and *spsr*. There are also special pseudoinstructions that optimize the loading of 32-bit constants.

The ARMv5E extensions include count leading zeros, saturation, and improved multiply instructions. The count leading zeros instruction counts the number of binary zeros before the first binary one. Saturation handles arithmetic calculations that overflow a 32-bit integer value. The improved multiply instructions provide better flexibility in multiplying 16-bit values.

Most ARM instructions can be conditionally executed, which can dramatically reduce the number of instructions required to perform a specific algorithm.

C H A P T E R 4

INTRODUCTION TO THE THUMB INSTRUCTION SET

This chapter introduces the Thumb instruction set. Thumb encodes a subset of the 32-bit ARM instructions into a 16-bit instruction set space. Since Thumb has higher performance than ARM on a processor with a 16-bit data bus, but lower performance than ARM on a 32-bit data bus, use Thumb for memory-constrained systems.

Thumb has higher *code density*—the space taken up in memory by an executable program—than ARM. For memory-constrained embedded systems, for example, mobile phones and PDAs, code density is very important. Cost pressures also limit memory size, width, and speed.

On average, a Thumb implementation of the same code takes up around 30% less memory than the equivalent ARM implementation. As an example, Figure 4.1 shows the same divide code routine implemented in ARM and Thumb assembly code. Even though the Thumb implementation uses more instructions, the overall memory footprint is reduced. Code density was the main driving force for the Thumb instruction set. Because it was also designed as a compiler target, rather than for hand-written assembly code, we recommend that you write Thumb-targeted code in a high-level language like C or C++.

Each Thumb instruction is related to a 32-bit ARM instruction. Figure 4.2 shows a simple Thumb ADD instruction being decoded into an equivalent ARM ADD instruction.

Table 4.1 provides a complete list of Thumb instructions available in the THUMBv2 architecture used in the ARMv5TE architecture. Only the branch relative instruction can be conditionally executed. The limited space available in 16 bits causes the barrel shift operations ASR, LSL, LSR, and ROR to be separate instructions in the Thumb ISA.

```
ARM code                            Thumb code
ARMDivide                           ThumbDivide
; IN:  r0(value),r1(divisor)        ; IN:  r0(value),r1(divisor)
; OUT: r2(MODulus),r3(DIVide)       ; OUT: r2(MODulus),r3(DIVide)

        MOV   r3,#0                         MOV   r3,#0
loop                                loop
        SUBS  r0,r0,r1                      ADD   r3,#1
        ADDGE r3,r3,#1                      SUB   r0,r1
        BGE   loop                          BGE   loop
        ADD   r2,r0,r1                      SUB   r3,#1
                                            ADD   r2,r0,r1

  5 × 4 = 20  bytes                   6 × 2 = 12  bytes
```

Figure 4.1   Code density.

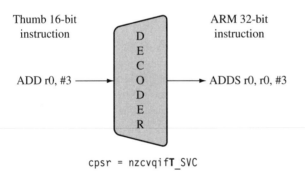

Thumb 16-bit
instruction

ARM 32-bit
instruction

ADD r0, #3 ──────▶ DECODER ──────▶ ADDS r0, r0, #3

cpsr = nzcvqifT_SVC

Figure 4.2   Thumb instruction decoding.

We only describe a subset of these instructions in this chapter since most code is compiled from a high-level language. See Appendix A for a complete list of Thumb instructions.

This chapter covers Thumb register usage, ARM-Thumb interworking, branch instructions, data processing instructions, load-store instructions, stack operations, and software interrupts.

Table 4.1 Thumb instruction set.

Mnemonics	THUMB ISA	Description
ADC	v1	add two 32-bit values and carry
ADD	v1	add two 32-bit values
AND	v1	logical bitwise AND of two 32-bit values
ASR	v1	arithmetic shift right
B	v1	branch relative
BIC	v1	logical bit clear (AND NOT) of two 32-bit values
BKPT	v2	breakpoint instructions
BL	v1	relative branch with link
BLX	v2	branch with link and exchange
BX	v1	branch with exchange
CMN	v1	compare negative two 32-bit values
CMP	v1	compare two 32-bit integers
EOR	v1	logical exclusive OR of two 32-bit values
LDM	v1	load multiple 32-bit words from memory to ARM registers
LDR	v1	load a single value from a virtual address in memory
LSL	v1	logical shift left
LSR	v1	logical shift right
MOV	v1	move a 32-bit value into a register
MUL	v1	multiply two 32-bit values
MVN	v1	move the logical NOT of 32-bit value into a register
NEG	v1	negate a 32-bit value
ORR	v1	logical bitwise OR of two 32-bit values
POP	v1	pops multiple registers from the stack
PUSH	v1	pushes multiple registers to the stack
ROR	v1	rotate right a 32-bit value
SBC	v1	subtract with carry a 32-bit value
STM	v1	store multiple 32-bit registers to memory
STR	v1	store register to a virtual address in memory
SUB	v1	subtract two 32-bit values
SWI	v1	software interrupt
TST	v1	test bits of a 32-bit value

4.1 THUMB REGISTER USAGE

In Thumb state, you do not have direct access to all registers. Only the low registers *r0* to *r7* are fully accessible, as shown in Table 4.2. The higher registers *r8* to *r12* are only accessible with MOV, ADD, or CMP instructions. CMP and all the data processing instructions that operate on low registers update the condition flags in the *cpsr*.

Table 4.2   Summary of Thumb register usage.

Registers	Access
r0–r7	fully accessible
r8–r12	only accessible by MOV, ADD, and CMP
r13 sp	limited accessibility
r14 lr	limited accessibility
r15 pc	limited accessibility
cpsr	only indirect access
spsr	no access

You may have noticed from the Thumb instruction set list and from the Thumb register usage table that there is no direct access to the *cpsr* or *spsr*. In other words, there are no MSR- and MRS-equivalent Thumb instructions.

To alter the *cpsr* or *spsr*, you must switch into ARM state to use MSR and MRS. Similarly, there are no coprocessor instructions in Thumb state. You need to be in ARM state to access the coprocessor for configuring cache and memory management.

4.2 ARM-THUMB INTERWORKING

ARM-Thumb interworking is the name given to the method of linking ARM and Thumb code together for both assembly and C/C++. It handles the transition between the two states. Extra code, called a *veneer*, is sometimes needed to carry out the transition. ATPCS defines the ARM and Thumb procedure call standards.

To call a Thumb routine from an ARM routine, the core has to change state. This state change is shown in the *T* bit of the *cpsr*. The BX and BLX branch instructions cause a switch between ARM and Thumb state while branching to a routine. The BX *lr* instruction returns from a routine, also with a state switch if necessary.

The BLX instruction was introduced in ARMv5T. On ARMv4T cores the linker uses a veneer to switch state on a subroutine call. Instead of calling the routine directly, the linker calls the veneer, which switches to Thumb state using the BX instruction.

There are two versions of the BX or BLX instructions: an ARM instruction and a Thumb equivalent. The ARM BX instruction enters Thumb state only if bit 0 of the address in *Rn* is set to binary 1; otherwise it enters ARM state. The Thumb BX instruction does the same.

```
Syntax: BX    Rm
        BLX   Rm | label
```

BX	Thumb version branch exchange	$pc = Rn$ & 0xfffffffe $T = Rn[0]$
BLX	Thumb version of the branch exchange with link	$lr = $ (instruction address after the BLX) $+ 1$ $pc = label, \ T = 0$ $pc = Rm$ & 0xfffffffe, $T = Rm[0]$

Unlike the ARM version, the Thumb BX instruction cannot be conditionally executed.

EXAMPLE   This example shows a small code fragment that uses both the ARM and Thumb versions of
4.1   the BX instruction. You can see that the branch address into Thumb has the lowest bit set.
This sets the *T* bit in the *cpsr* to Thumb state.

The return address is not automatically preserved by the BX instruction. Rather the code
sets the return address explicitly using a MOV instruction prior to the branch:

```
; ARM code
        CODE32                  ; word aligned
        LDR     r0, =thumbCode+1 ; +1 to enter Thumb state
        MOV     lr, pc          ; set the return address
        BX      r0              ; branch to Thumb code & mode
        ; continue here
; Thumb code
        CODE16                  ; halfword aligned
thumbCode
        ADD   r1, #1
        BX    lr                ; return to ARM code & state
```

A branch exchange instruction can also be used as an absolute branch providing bit 0
isn't used to force a state change:

```
; address(thumbCode) = 0x00010000

; cpsr = nzcvqIFt_SVC
; r0 = 0x00000000

0x00009000        LDR r0, =thumbCode+1

; cpsr = nzcvqIFt_SVC
; r0 = 0x00010001

0x00009008        BX    r0
```

```
; cpsr = nzcvqIFT_SVC
; r0 = 0x00010001
; pc = 0x00010000
```

You can see that the least significant bit of register *r0* is used to set the *T* bit of the *cpsr*. The *cpsr* changes from *IFt*, prior to the execution of the BX, to *IFT*, after execution. The *pc* is then set to point to the start address of the Thumb routine.

EXAMPLE   Replacing the BX instruction with BLX simplifies the calling of a Thumb routine since it sets
  4.2   the return address in the link register *lr*:

```
        CODE32
        LDR    r0, =thumbRoutine+1    ; enter Thumb state
        BLX    r0                     ; jump to Thumb code
        ; continue here

        CODE16
thumbRoutine
        ADD    r1, #1
        BX     r14                    ; return to ARM code and state
```

4.3 OTHER BRANCH INSTRUCTIONS

There are two variations of the standard branch instruction, or B. The first is similar to the ARM version and is conditionally executed; the branch range is limited to a signed 8-bit immediate, or −256 to +254 bytes. The second version removes the conditional part of the instruction and expands the effective branch range to a signed 11-bit immediate, or −2048 to +2046 bytes.

The conditional branch instruction is the only conditionally executed instruction in Thumb state.

```
Syntax: B<cond> label
        B label
        BL label
```

B	branch	$pc = label$
BL	branch with link	$pc = label$ $lr = $ (instruction address after the BL) + 1

The BL instruction is not conditionally executed and has an approximate range of +/−4 MB. This range is possible because BL (and BLX) instructions are translated into a pair of 16-bit

Thumb instructions. The first instruction in the pair holds the high part of the branch offset, and the second the low part. These instructions must be used as a pair.

The code here shows the various instructions used to return from a BL subroutine call:

```
MOV      pc, lr
```

```
BX       lr
```

```
POP      {pc}
```

To return, we set the *pc* to the value in *lr*. The stack instruction called POP will be discussed in more detail in Section 4.7.

4.4 DATA PROCESSING INSTRUCTIONS

The data processing instructions manipulate data within registers. They include move instructions, arithmetic instructions, shifts, logical instructions, comparison instructions, and multiply instructions. The Thumb data processing instructions are a subset of the ARM data processing instructions.

Syntax:
```
<ADC|ADD|AND|BIC|EOR|MOV|MUL|MVN|NEG|ORR|SBC|SUB>  Rd, Rm
<ADD|ASR|LSL|LSR|ROR|SUB> Rd, Rn #immediate
<ADD|MOV|SUB> Rd,#immediate
<ADD|SUB> Rd,Rn,Rm
 ADD Rd,pc,#immediate
 ADD Rd,sp,#immediate
<ADD|SUB> sp, #immediate
<ASR|LSL|LSR|ROR> Rd,Rs
<CMN|CMP|TST> Rn,Rm
 CMP Rn,#immediate
 MOV Rd,Rn
```

ADC	add two 32-bit values and carry	$Rd = Rd + Rm + C$ flag
ADD	add two 32-bit values	$Rd = Rn + immediate$ $Rd = Rd + immediate$ $Rd = Rd + Rm$ $Rd = Rd + Rm$ $Rd = (pc \mathbin{\&} \text{0xfffffffc}) + (immediate \ll 2)$ $Rd = sp + (immediate \ll 2)$ $sp = sp + (immediate \ll 2)$

AND	logical bitwise AND of two 32-bit values	$Rd = Rd \ \& \ Rm$
ASR	arithmetic shift right	$Rd = Rm \gg immediate,$ $C \ \text{flag} = Rm[immediate - 1]$ $Rd = Rd \gg Rs, \ C \ \text{flag} = Rd[Rs - 1]$
BIC	logical bit clear (AND NOT) of two 32-bit values	$Rd = Rd \ \text{AND NOT}(Rm)$
CMN	compare negative two 32-bit values	$Rn + Rm \qquad \textit{sets flags}$
CMP	compare two 32-bit integers	$Rn - immediate \quad \textit{sets flags}$ $Rn - Rm \qquad \textit{sets flags}$
EOR	logical exclusive OR of two 32-bit values	$Rd = Rd \ \text{EOR} \ Rm$
LSL	logical shift left	$Rd = Rm \ll immediate,$ $C \ \text{flag} = Rm[32 - immediate]$ $Rd = Rd \ll Rs, \ C \ \text{flag} = Rd[32 - Rs]$
LSR	logical shift right	$Rd = Rm \gg immediate,$ $C \ \text{flag} = Rd[immediate - 1]$ $Rd = Rd \gg Rs, \ C \ \text{flag} = Rd[Rs - 1]$
MOV	move a 32-bit value into a register	$Rd = immediate$ $Rd = Rn$ $Rd = Rm$
MUL	multiply two 32-bit values	$Rd = (Rm * Rd)[31{:}0]$
MVN	move the logical NOT of a 32-bit value into a register	$Rd = \text{NOT}(Rm)$
NEG	negate a 32-bit value	$Rd = 0 - Rm$
ORR	logical bitwise OR of two 32-bit values	$Rd = Rd \ \text{OR} \ Rm$
ROR	rotate right a 32-bit value	$Rd = Rd \ \text{RIGHT\_ROTATE} \ Rs,$ $C \ \text{flag} = Rd[Rs - 1]$
SBC	subtract with carry a 32-bit value	$Rd = Rd - Rm - \text{NOT}(C \ \text{flag})$
SUB	subtract two 32-bit values	$Rd = Rn - immediate$ $Rd = Rd - immediate$ $Rd = Rn - Rm$ $sp = sp - (immediate \ll 2)$
TST	test bits of a 32-bit value	$Rn \ \text{AND} \ Rm \qquad \textit{sets flags}$

These instructions follow the same style as the equivalent ARM instructions. Most Thumb data processing instructions operate on low registers and update the *cpsr*. The exceptions are

```
MOV    Rd,Rn
ADD    Rd,Rm
CMP    Rn,Rm
ADD    sp, #immediate
SUB    sp, #immediate
ADD    Rd,sp,#immediate
ADD    Rd,pc,#immediate
```

which can operate on the higher registers *r8–r14* and the *pc*. These instructions, except for CMP, do not update the condition flags in the *cpsr* when using the higher registers. The CMP instruction, however, always updates the *cpsr*.

EXAMPLE
4.3

This example shows a simple Thumb ADD instruction. It takes two low registers *r1* and *r2* and adds them together. The result is then placed into register *r0*, overwriting the original contents. The *cpsr* is also updated.

```
PRE    cpsr = nzcvIFT_SVC
       r1 = 0x80000000
       r2 = 0x10000000

       ADD    r0, r1, r2

POST   r0 = 0x90000000
       cpsr = NzcvIFT_SVC
```

EXAMPLE
4.4

Thumb deviates from the ARM style in that the barrel shift operations (ASR, LSL, LSR, and ROR) are separate instructions. This example shows the logical left shift (LSL) instruction to multiply register *r2* by 2.

```
PRE    r2 = 0x00000002
       r4 = 0x00000001

       LSL    r2, r4

POST   r2 = 0x00000004
       r4 = 0x00000001
```

See Appendix A for a complete list of Thumb data processing instructions.

4.5 SINGLE-REGISTER LOAD-STORE INSTRUCTIONS

The Thumb instruction set supports load and storing registers, or LDR and STR. These instructions use two preindexed addressing modes: offset by register and offset by immediate.

```
Syntax: <LDR|STR>{<B|H>} Rd, [Rn,#immediate]
        LDR{<H|SB|SH>} Rd,[Rn,Rm]
        STR{<B|H>} Rd,[Rn,Rm]
        LDR Rd,[pc,#immediate]
        <LDR|STR> Rd,[sp,#immediate]
```

LDR	load word into a register	Rd <- $mem32[address]$
STR	save word from a register	Rd -> $mem32[address]$
LDRB	load byte into a register	Rd <- $mem8[address]$
STRB	save byte from a register	Rd -> $mem8[address]$
LDRH	load halfword into a register	Rd <- $mem16[address]$
STRH	save halfword into a register	Rd -> $mem16[address]$
LDRSB	load signed byte into a register	Rd <- $SignExtend(mem8[address])$
LDRSH	load signed halfword into a register	Rd <- $SignExtend(mem16[address])$

You can see the different addressing modes in Table 4.3. The offset by register uses a base register *Rn* plus the register offset *Rm*. The second uses the same base register *Rn* plus a 5-bit immediate or a value dependent on the data size. The 5-bit offset encoded in the instruction is multiplied by one for byte accesses, two for 16-bit accesses, and four for 32-bit accesses.

Table 4.3   Addressing modes.

Type	Syntax
Load/store register	[Rn, Rm]
Base register + offset	[Rn, #immediate]
Relative	[pc|sp, #immediate]

EXAMPLE 4.5   This example shows two Thumb instructions that use a preindex addressing mode. Both use the same pre-condition.

```
PRE     mem32[0x90000] = 0x00000001
        mem32[0x90004] = 0x00000002
        mem32[0x90008] = 0x00000003
        r0 = 0x00000000
        r1 = 0x00090000
        r4 = 0x00000004


        LDR  r0, [r1, r4]    ; register

POST    r0 = 0x00000002
        r1 = 0x00090000
        r4 = 0x00000004


        LDR   r0, [r1, #0x4]   ; immediate

POST    r0 = 0x00000002
```

Both instructions carry out the same operation. The only difference is the second LDR uses a fixed offset, whereas the first one depends on the value in register *r4*.

4.6 MULTIPLE-REGISTER LOAD-STORE INSTRUCTIONS

The Thumb versions of the load-store multiple instructions are reduced forms of the ARM load-store multiple instructions. They only support the increment after (IA) addressing mode.

```
Syntax : <LDM|STM>IA Rn!, {low Register list}
```

LDMIA	load multiple registers	$\{Rd\}^{*N}$ <- mem32[Rn + 4*N], Rn = Rn + 4*N
STMIA	save multiple registers	$\{Rd\}^{*N}$ -> mem32[Rn + 4*N], Rn = Rn + 4*N

Here *N* is the number of registers in the list of registers. You can see that these instructions always update the base register *Rn* after execution. The base register and list of registers are limited to the low registers *r0* to *r7*.

EXAMPLE 4.6   This example saves registers *r1* to *r3* to memory addresses 0x9000 to 0x900c. It also updates base register *r4*. Note that the update character ! is not an option, unlike with the ARM instruction set.

```
PRE     r1 = 0x00000001
        r2 = 0x00000002
```

```
            r3 = 0x00000003
            r4 = 0x9000

            STMIA    r4!,{r1,r2,r3}
```

POST   mem32[0x9000] = **0x00000001**
        mem32[0x9004] = **0x00000002**
        mem32[0x9008] = **0x00000003**
        r4 = **0x900c**

4.7 STACK INSTRUCTIONS

The Thumb stack operations are different from the equivalent ARM instructions because they use the more traditional POP and PUSH concept.

```
Syntax: POP {low_register_list{, pc}}
        PUSH {low_register_list{, lr}}
```

POP	pop registers from the stacks	${Rd}^{*N}$ <- mem32[sp + 4*N], sp = sp + 4*N
PUSH	push registers on to the stack	${Rd}^{*N}$ -> mem32[sp + 4*N], sp = sp − 4*N

The interesting point to note is that there is no stack pointer in the instruction. This is because the stack pointer is fixed as register *r13* in Thumb operations and *sp* is automatically updated. The list of registers is limited to the low registers *r0* to *r7*.

The PUSH register list also can include the link register *lr*; similarly the POP register list can include the *pc*. This provides support for subroutine entry and exit, as shown in Example 4.7.

The stack instructions only support full descending stack operations.

EXAMPLE 4.7   In this example we use the POP and PUSH instructions. The subroutine ThumbRoutine is called using a branch with link (BL) instruction.

```
            ; Call subroutine
            BL      ThumbRoutine
            ; continue

ThumbRoutine
            PUSH    {r1, lr}      ; enter subroutine
            MOV     r0, #2
            POP     {r1, pc}      ; return from subroutine
```

The link register *lr* is pushed onto the stack with register *r1*. Upon return, register *r1* is popped off the stack, as well as the return address being loaded into the *pc*. This returns from the subroutine.

4.8 SOFTWARE INTERRUPT INSTRUCTION

Similar to the ARM equivalent, the Thumb software interrupt (SWI) instruction causes a software interrupt exception. If any interrupt or exception flag is raised in Thumb state, the processor automatically reverts back to ARM state to handle the exception.

Syntax: SWI immediate

SWI	software interrupt	lr_svc = address of instruction following the SWI
		$spsr\_svc = cpsr$
		pc = vectors + 0x8
		$cpsr$ mode $= SVC$
		$cpsr\ I = 1$ (mask IRQ interrupts)
		$cpsr\ T = 0$ (ARM state)

The Thumb SWI instruction has the same effect and nearly the same syntax as the ARM equivalent. It differs in that the SWI number is limited to the range 0 to 255 and it is not conditionally executed.

EXAMPLE
4.8

This example shows the execution of a Thumb SWI instruction. Note that the processor goes from Thumb state to ARM state after execution.

```
PRE     cpsr = nzcVqifT_USER
        pc = 0x00008000
        lr = 0x003fffff        ; lr = r14
        r0 = 0x12


    0x00008000    SWI    0x45


POST    cpsr = nzcVqIft_SVC
        spsr = nzcVqifT_USER
        pc = 0x00000008
        lr = 0x00008002
        r0 = 0x12
```

4.9 SUMMARY

In this chapter we covered the Thumb instruction set. All Thumb instructions are 16 bits in length. Thumb provides approximately 30% better code density over ARM code. Most code written for Thumb is in a high-level language such as C and C++.

ATPCS defines how ARM and Thumb code call each other, called *ARM-Thumb interworking*. Interworking uses the branch exchange (BX) instruction and branch exchange with link (BLX) instruction to change state and jump to a specific routine.

In Thumb, only the branch instructions are conditionally executed. The barrel shift operations (ASR, LSL, LSR, and ROR) are separate instructions.

The multiple-register load-store instructions only support the increment after (IA) addressing mode. The Thumb instruction set includes POP and PUSH instructions as stack operations. These instructions only support a full descending stack.

There are no Thumb instructions to access the coprocessors, *cpsr*, and *spsr*.

CHAPTER 5

EFFICIENT C PROGRAMMING

The aim of this chapter is to help you write C code in a style that will compile efficiently on the ARM architecture. We will look at many small examples to show how the compiler translates C source to ARM assembler. Once you have a feel for this translation process, you can distinguish fast C code from slow C code. The techniques apply equally to C++, but we will stick to plain C for these examples.

We start with an overview of C compilers and optimization, which will give an idea of the problems the C compiler faces when optimizing your code. By understanding these problems you can write source code that will compile more efficiently in terms of increased speed and reduced code size. The following sections are grouped by topic.

Sections 5.2 and 5.3 look at how to optimize a basic C loop. These sections use a data packet checksum as a simple example to illustrate the ideas. Sections 5.4 and 5.5 look at optimizing a whole C function body, including how the compiler allocates registers within a function and how to reduce the overhead of a function call.

Sections 5.6 through 5.9 look at memory issues, including handling pointers and how to pack data and access memory efficiently. Sections 5.10 through 5.12 look at basic operations that are usually not supported directly by ARM instructions. You can add your own basic operations using inline functions and assembler.

The final section summarizes problems you may face when porting C code from another architecture to the ARM architecture.

5.1   OVERVIEW OF C COMPILERS AND OPTIMIZATION

This chapter assumes that you are familiar with the C language and have some knowledge of assembly programming. The latter is not essential, but is useful for following the compiler output examples. See Chapter 3 or Appendix A for details of ARM assembly syntax.

Optimizing code takes time and reduces source code readability. Usually, it's only worth optimizing functions that are frequently executed and important for performance. We recommend you use a performance profiling tool, found in most ARM simulators, to find these frequently executed functions. Document nonobvious optimizations with source code comments to aid maintainability.

C compilers have to translate your C function literally into assembler so that it works for all possible inputs. In practice, many of the input combinations are not possible or won't occur. Let's start by looking at an example of the problems the compiler faces. The memclr function clears N bytes of memory at address data.

```
void memclr(char *data, int N)
{
  for (; N>0; N--)
  {
    *data=0;
    data++;
  }
}
```

No matter how advanced the compiler, it does not know whether N can be 0 on input or not. Therefore the compiler needs to test for this case explicitly before the first iteration of the loop.

The compiler doesn't know whether the data array pointer is four-byte aligned or not. If it is four-byte aligned, then the compiler can clear four bytes at a time using an int store rather than a char store. Nor does it know whether N is a multiple of four or not. If N is a multiple of four, then the compiler can repeat the loop body four times or store four bytes at a time using an int store.

The compiler must be conservative and assume all possible values for N and all possible alignments for *data*. Section 5.3 discusses these specific points in detail.

To write efficient C code, you must be aware of areas where the C compiler has to be conservative, the limits of the processor architecture the C compiler is mapping to, and the limits of a specific C compiler.

Most of this chapter covers the first two points above and should be applicable to any ARM C compiler. The third point will be very dependent on the compiler vendor and compiler revision. You will need to look at the compiler's documentation or experiment with the compiler yourself.

To keep our examples concrete, we have tested them using the following specific C compilers:

- *armcc* from ARM Developer Suite version 1.1 (ADS1.1). You can license this compiler, or a later version, directly from ARM.

- *arm-elf-gcc* version 2.95.2. This is the ARM target for the GNU C compiler, *gcc*, and is freely available.

We have used *armcc* from ADS1.1 to generate the example assembler output in this book. The following short script shows you how to invoke *armcc* on a C file `test.c`. You can use this to reproduce our examples.

```
armcc -Otime -c -o test.o test.c
fromelf -text/c test.o > test.txt
```

By default *armcc* has full optimizations turned on (the `-O2` command line switch). The `-Otime` switch optimizes for execution efficiency rather than space and mainly affects the layout of `for` and `while` loops. If you are using the *gcc* compiler, then the following short script generates a similar assembler output listing:

```
arm-elf-gcc -O2 -fomit-frame-pointer -c -o test.o test.c
arm-elf-objdump -d test.o > test.txt
```

Full optimizations are turned off by default for the GNU compiler. The `-fomit-frame-pointer` switch prevents the GNU compiler from maintaining a frame pointer register. Frame pointers assist the debug view by pointing to the local variables stored on the stack frame. However, they are inefficient to maintain and shouldn't be used in code critical to performance.

5.2 BASIC C DATA TYPES

Let's start by looking at how ARM compilers handle the basic C data types. We will see that some of these types are more efficient to use for local variables than others. There are also differences between the addressing modes available when loading and storing data of each type.

ARM processors have 32-bit registers and 32-bit data processing operations. The ARM architecture is a RISC load/store architecture. In other words you must load values from memory into registers before acting on them. There are no arithmetic or logical instructions that manipulate values in memory directly.

Early versions of the ARM architecture (ARMv1 to ARMv3) provided hardware support for loading and storing unsigned 8-bit and unsigned or signed 32-bit values.

Table 5.1   Load and store instructions by ARM architecture.

Architecture	Instruction	Action
Pre-ARMv4	LDRB	load an unsigned 8-bit value
	STRB	store a signed or unsigned 8-bit value
	LDR	load a signed or unsigned 32-bit value
	STR	store a signed or unsigned 32-bit value
ARMv4	LDRSB	load a signed 8-bit value
	LDRH	load an unsigned 16-bit value
	LDRSH	load a signed 16-bit value
	STRH	store a signed or unsigned 16-bit value
ARMv5	LDRD	load a signed or unsigned 64-bit value
	STRD	store a signed or unsigned 64-bit value

These architectures were used on processors prior to the ARM7TDMI. Table 5.1 shows the load/store instruction classes available by ARM architecture.

In Table 5.1 loads that act on 8- or 16-bit values extend the value to 32 bits before writing to an ARM register. Unsigned values are zero-extended, and signed values sign-extended. This means that the cast of a loaded value to an int type does not cost extra instructions. Similarly, a store of an 8- or 16-bit value selects the lowest 8 or 16 bits of the register. The cast of an int to smaller type does not cost extra instructions on a store.

The ARMv4 architecture and above support signed 8-bit and 16-bit loads and stores directly, through new instructions. Since these instructions are a later addition, they do not support as many addressing modes as the pre-ARMv4 instructions. (See Section 3.3 for details of the different addressing modes.) We will see the effect of this in the example checksum_v3 in Section 5.2.1.

Finally, ARMv5 adds instruction support for 64-bit load and stores. This is available in ARM9E and later cores.

Prior to ARMv4, ARM processors were not good at handling signed 8-bit or any 16-bit values. Therefore ARM C compilers define char to be an unsigned 8-bit value, rather than a signed 8-bit value as is typical in many other compilers.

Compilers *armcc* and *gcc* use the datatype mappings in Table 5.2 for an ARM target. The exceptional case for type char is worth noting as it can cause problems when you are porting code from another processor architecture. A common example is using a char type variable i as a loop counter, with loop continuation condition i ≥ 0. As i is unsigned for the ARM compilers, the loop will never terminate. Fortunately *armcc* produces a warning in this situation: *unsigned comparison with 0*. Compilers also provide an override switch to make char signed. For example, the command line option -fsigned-char will make char signed on *gcc*. The command line option -zc will have the same effect with *armcc*.

For the rest of this book we assume that you are using an ARMv4 processor or above. This includes ARM7TDMI and all later processors.

Table 5.2   C compiler datatype mappings.

C Data Type	Implementation
char	unsigned 8-bit byte
short	signed 16-bit halfword
int	signed 32-bit word
long	signed 32-bit word
long long	signed 64-bit double word

5.2.1 LOCAL VARIABLE TYPES

ARMv4-based processors can efficiently load and store 8-, 16-, and 32-bit data. However, most ARM data processing operations are 32-bit only. For this reason, you should use a 32-bit datatype, int or long, for local variables wherever possible. Avoid using char and short as local variable types, even if you are manipulating an 8- or 16-bit value. The one exception is when you want wrap-around to occur. If you require modulo arithmetic of the form $255 + 1 = 0$, then use the char type.

To see the effect of local variable types, let's consider a simple example. We'll look in detail at a checksum function that sums the values in a data packet. Most communication protocols (such as TCP/IP) have a checksum or cyclic redundancy check (CRC) routine to check for errors in a data packet.

The following code checksums a data packet containing 64 words. It shows why you should avoid using char for local variables.

```
int checksum_v1(int *data)
{
  char i;
  int sum = 0;

  for (i = 0; i < 64; i++)
  {
    sum += data[i];
  }
  return sum;
}
```

At first sight it looks as though declaring i as a char is efficient. You may be thinking that a char uses less register space or less space on the ARM stack than an int. On the ARM, both these assumptions are wrong. All ARM registers are 32-bit and all stack entries are at least 32-bit. Furthermore, to implement the i++ exactly, the compiler must account for the case when $i = 255$. Any attempt to increment 255 should produce the answer 0.

Consider the compiler output for this function. We've added labels and comments to make the assembly clear.

```
checksum_v1
        MOV     r2,r0               ; r2 = data
        MOV     r0,#0               ; sum = 0
        MOV     r1,#0               ; i = 0
checksum_v1_loop
        LDR     r3,[r2,r1,LSL #2]   ; r3 = data[i]
        ADD     r1,r1,#1            ; r1 = i+1
        AND     r1,r1,#0xff         ; i = (char)r1
        CMP     r1,#0x40            ; compare i, 64
        ADD     r0,r3,r0            ; sum += r3
        BCC     checksum_v1_loop    ; if (i<64) loop
        MOV     pc,r14              ; return sum
```

Now compare this to the compiler output where instead we declare i as an unsigned int.

```
checksum_v2
        MOV     r2,r0               ; r2 = data
        MOV     r0,#0               ; sum = 0
        MOV     r1,#0               ; i = 0
checksum_v2_loop
        LDR     r3,[r2,r1,LSL #2]   ; r3 = data[i]
        ADD     r1,r1,#1            ; r1++
        CMP     r1,#0x40            ; compare i, 64
        ADD     r0,r3,r0            ; sum += r3
        BCC     checksum_v2_loop    ; if (i<64) goto loop
        MOV     pc,r14              ; return sum
```

In the first case, the compiler inserts an extra AND instruction to reduce i to the range 0 to 255 before the comparison with 64. This instruction disappears in the second case.

Next, suppose the data packet contains 16-bit values and we need a 16-bit checksum. It is tempting to write the following C code:

```
short checksum_v3(short *data)
{
  unsigned int i;
  short sum=0;

  for (i = 0; i < 64; i++)
  {
    sum = (short)(sum + data[i]);
```

```
    }
    return sum;
}
```

You may wonder why the for loop body doesn't contain the code

```
sum += data[i];
```

With *armcc* this code will produce a warning if you enable implicit narrowing cast warnings using the compiler switch -W + n. The expression sum + data[i] is an integer and so can only be assigned to a short using an (implicit or explicit) narrowing cast. As you can see in the following assembly output, the compiler must insert extra instructions to implement the narrowing cast:

```
checksum_v3
        MOV     r2,r0               ; r2 = data
        MOV     r0,#0               ; sum = 0
        MOV     r1,#0               ; i = 0
checksum_v3_loop
        ADD     r3,r2,r1,LSL #1     ; r3 = &data[i]
        LDRH    r3,[r3,#0]          ; r3 = data[i]
        ADD     r1,r1,#1            ; i++
        CMP     r1,#0x40            ; compare i, 64
        ADD     r0,r3,r0            ; r0 = sum + r3
        MOV     r0,r0,LSL #16
        MOV     r0,r0,ASR #16       ; sum = (short)r0
        BCC     checksum_v3_loop    ; if (i<64) goto loop
        MOV     pc,r14              ; return sum
```

The loop is now three instructions longer than the loop for example checksum_v2 earlier! There are two reasons for the extra instructions:

- The LDRH instruction does not allow for a shifted address offset as the LDR instruction did in checksum_v2. Therefore the first ADD in the loop calculates the address of item i in the array. The LDRH loads from an address with no offset. LDRH has fewer addressing modes than LDR as it was a later addition to the ARM instruction set. (See Table 5.1.)
- The cast reducing total + array[i] to a short requires two MOV instructions. The compiler shifts left by 16 and then right by 16 to implement a 16-bit sign extend. The shift right is a sign-extending shift so it replicates the sign bit to fill the upper 16 bits.

We can avoid the second problem by using an int type variable to hold the partial sum. We only reduce the sum to a short type at the function exit.

However, the first problem is a new issue. We can solve it by accessing the array by incrementing the pointer *data* rather than using an index as in data[i]. This is efficient regardless of array type size or element size. All ARM load and store instructions have a postincrement addressing mode.

EXAMPLE
5.1
The checksum_v4 code fixes all the problems we have discussed in this section. It uses int type local variables to avoid unnecessary casts. It increments the pointer data instead of using an index offset data[i].

```
short checksum_v4(short *data)
{
  unsigned int i;
  int sum=0;

  for (i=0; i<64; i++)
  {
    sum += *(data++);
  }
  return (short)sum;
}
```

The *(data++) operation translates to a single ARM instruction that loads the data and increments the data pointer. Of course you could write sum += *data; data++; or even *data++ instead if you prefer. The compiler produces the following output. Three instructions have been removed from the inside loop, saving three cycles per loop compared to checksum_v3.

```
checksum_v4
        MOV     r2,#0               ; sum = 0
        MOV     r1,#0               ; i = 0
checksum_v4_loop
        LDRSH   r3,[r0],#2          ; r3 = *(data++)
        ADD     r1,r1,#1            ; i++
        CMP     r1,#0x40            ; compare i, 64
        ADD     r2,r3,r2            ; sum += r3
        BCC     checksum_v4_loop    ; if (sum<64) goto loop
        MOV     r0,r2,LSL #16
        MOV     r0,r0,ASR #16       ; r0 = (short)sum
        MOV     pc,r14              ; return r0
```

The compiler is still performing one cast to a 16-bit range, on the function return. You could remove this also by returning an int result as discussed in Section 5.2.2.

5.2.2 FUNCTION ARGUMENT TYPES

We saw in Section 5.2.1 that converting local variables from types char or short to type int increases performance and reduces code size. The same holds for function arguments. Consider the following simple function, which adds two 16-bit values, halving the second, and returns a 16-bit sum:

```
short add_v1(short a, short b)
{
  return a + (b >> 1);
}
```

This function is a little artificial, but it is a useful test case to illustrate the problems faced by the compiler. The input values a, b, and the return value will be passed in 32-bit ARM registers. Should the compiler assume that these 32-bit values are in the range of a short type, that is, −32,768 to +32,767? Or should the compiler force values to be in this range by sign-extending the lowest 16 bits to fill the 32-bit register? The compiler must make compatible decisions for the function caller and callee. Either the caller or callee must perform the cast to a short type.

We say that function arguments are passed *wide* if they are not reduced to the range of the type and *narrow* if they are. You can tell which decision the compiler has made by looking at the assembly output for add_v1. If the compiler passes arguments wide, then the callee must reduce function arguments to the correct range. If the compiler passes arguments narrow, then the caller must reduce the range. If the compiler returns values wide, then the caller must reduce the return value to the correct range. If the compiler returns values narrow, then the callee must reduce the range before returning the value.

For *armcc* in ADS, function arguments are passed narrow and values returned narrow. In other words, the caller casts argument values and the callee casts return values. The compiler uses the ANSI prototype of the function to determine the datatypes of the function arguments.

The *armcc* output for add_v1 shows that the compiler casts the return value to a short type, but does not cast the input values. It assumes that the caller has already ensured that the 32-bit values r0 and r1 are in the range of the short type. This shows narrow passing of arguments and return value.

```
add_v1
        ADD     r0,r0,r1,ASR #1      ; r0 = (int)a + ((int)b >> 1)
        MOV     r0,r0,LSL #16
        MOV     r0,r0,ASR #16        ; r0 = (short)r0
        MOV     pc,r14               ; return r0
```

The *gcc* compiler we used is more cautious and makes no assumptions about the range of argument value. This version of the compiler reduces the input arguments to the range of a short in both the caller and the callee. It also casts the return value to a short type. Here is the compiled code for add_v1:

```
add_v1_gcc
        MOV     r0, r0, LSL #16
        MOV     r1, r1, LSL #16
        MOV     r1, r1, ASR #17      ; r1 = (int)b >> 1
        ADD     r1, r1, r0, ASR #16  ; r1 += (int)a
        MOV     r1, r1, LSL #16
        MOV     r0, r1, ASR #16      ; r0 = (short)r1
        MOV     pc, lr               ; return r0
```

Whatever the merits of different narrow and wide calling protocols, you can see that char or short type function arguments and return values introduce extra casts. These increase code size and decrease performance. It is more efficient to use the int type for function arguments and return values, even if you are only passing an 8-bit value.

5.2.3   Signed versus Unsigned Types

The previous sections demonstrate the advantages of using int rather than a char or short type for local variables and function arguments. This section compares the efficiencies of signed int and unsigned int.

If your code uses addition, subtraction, and multiplication, then there is no performance difference between signed and unsigned operations. However, there is a difference when it comes to division. Consider the following short example that averages two integers:

```
int average_v1(int a, int b)
{
  return (a+b)/2;
}
```

This compiles to

```
average_v1
        ADD     r0,r0,r1             ; r0 = a + b
        ADD     r0,r0,r0,LSR #31     ; if (r0<0) r0++
        MOV     r0,r0,ASR #1         ; r0 = r0 >> 1
        MOV     pc,r14               ; return r0
```

Notice that the compiler adds one to the sum before shifting by right if the sum is negative. In other words it replaces $x/2$ by the statement:

$$(x<0) \ ? \ ((x+1) >> 1): \ (x >> 1)$$

It must do this because x is signed. In C on an ARM target, a divide by two is not a right shift if x is negative. For example, $-3 \gg 1 = -2$ but $-3/2 = -1$. Division rounds towards zero, but arithmetic right shift rounds towards $-\infty$.

It is more efficient to use unsigned types for divisions. The compiler converts unsigned power of two divisions directly to right shifts. For general divisions, the divide routine in the C library is faster for unsigned types. See Section 5.10 for discussion on avoiding divisions completely.

SUMMARY   **The Efficient Use of C Types**

- For local variables held in registers, don't use a `char` or `short` type unless 8-bit or 16-bit modular arithmetic is necessary. Use the `signed` or `unsigned int` types instead. Unsigned types are faster when you use divisions.

- For array entries and global variables held in main memory, use the type with the smallest size possible to hold the required data. This saves memory footprint. The ARMv4 architecture is efficient at loading and storing all data widths provided you traverse arrays by incrementing the array pointer. Avoid using offsets from the base of the array with `short` type arrays, as `LDRH` does not support this.

- Use explicit casts when reading array entries or global variables into local variables, or writing local variables out to array entries. The casts make it clear that for fast operation you are taking a narrow width type stored in memory and expanding it to a wider type in the registers. Switch on *implicit narrowing cast* warnings in the compiler to detect implicit casts.

- Avoid implicit or explicit narrowing casts in expressions because they usually cost extra cycles. Casts on loads or stores are usually free because the load or store instruction performs the cast for you.

- Avoid `char` and `short` types for function arguments or return values. Instead use the `int` type even if the range of the parameter is smaller. This prevents the compiler performing unnecessary casts.

5.3 C LOOPING STRUCTURES

This section looks at the most efficient ways to code `for` and `while` loops on the ARM. We start by looking at loops with a fixed number of iterations and then move on to loops with a variable number of iterations. Finally we look at loop unrolling.

5.3.1 LOOPS WITH A FIXED NUMBER OF ITERATIONS

What is the most efficient way to write a `for` loop on the ARM? Let's return to our checksum example and look at the looping structure.

Here is the last version of the 64-word packet checksum routine we studied in Section 5.2. This shows how the compiler treats a loop with incrementing count i++.

```
int checksum_v5(int *data)
{
  unsigned int i;
  int sum=0;

  for (i=0; i<64; i++)
  {
    sum += *(data++);
  }
  return sum;
}
```

This compiles to

```
checksum_v5
          MOV     r2,r0           ; r2 = data
          MOV     r0,#0           ; sum = 0
          MOV     r1,#0           ; i = 0
checksum_v5_loop
          LDR     r3,[r2],#4      ; r3 = *(data++)
          ADD     r1,r1,#1        ; i++
          CMP     r1,#0x40        ; compare i, 64
          ADD     r0,r3,r0        ; sum += r3
          BCC     checksum_v5_loop ; if (i<64) goto loop
          MOV     pc,r14          ; return sum
```

It takes three instructions to implement the for loop structure:

- An ADD to increment i
- A compare to check if i is less than 64
- A conditional branch to continue the loop if i < 64

This is not efficient. On the ARM, a loop should only use two instructions:

- A subtract to decrement the loop counter, which also sets the condition code flags on the result
- A conditional branch instruction

The key point is that the loop counter should count down to zero rather than counting up to some arbitrary limit. Then the comparison with zero is free since the result is stored in the condition flags. Since we are no longer using i as an array index, there is no problem in counting down rather than up.

EXAMPLE
5.2

This example shows the improvement if we switch to a decrementing loop rather than an incrementing loop.

```
int checksum_v6(int *data)
{
  unsigned int i;
  int sum=0;

  for (i=64; i!=0; i--)
  {
    sum += *(data++);
  }
  return sum;
}
```

This compiles to

```
checksum_v6
        MOV     r2,r0               ; r2 = data
        MOV     r0,#0               ; sum = 0
        MOV     r1,#0x40            ; i = 64
checksum_v6_loop
        LDR     r3,[r2],#4          ; r3 = *(data++)
        SUBS    r1,r1,#1            ; i-- and set flags
        ADD     r0,r3,r0            ; sum += r3
        BNE     checksum_v6_loop    ; if (i!=0) goto loop
        MOV     pc,r14              ; return sum
```

The SUBS and BNE instructions implement the loop. Our checksum example now has the minimum number of four instructions per loop. This is much better than six for checksum_v1 and eight for checksum_v3.

For an unsigned loop counter i we can use either of the loop continuation conditions i!=0 or i>0. As i can't be negative, they are the same condition. For a signed loop counter, it is tempting to use the condition i>0 to continue the loop. You might expect the compiler to generate the following two instructions to implement the loop:

```
SUBS  r1,r1,#1   ; compare i with 1, i=i-1
BGT   loop       ; if (i+1>1) goto loop
```

In fact, the compiler will generate

```
SUB    r1,r1,#1      ; i--
CMP    r1,#0         ; compare i with 0
BGT    loop          ; if (i>0) goto loop
```

The compiler is not being inefficient. It must be careful about the case when i = -0x80000000 because the two sections of code generate different answers in this case. For the first piece of code the SUBS instruction compares i with 1 and then decrements i. Since -0x80000000 < 1, the loop terminates. For the second piece of code, we decrement i and then compare with 0. Modulo arithmetic means that i now has the value +0x7fffffff, which is greater than zero. Thus the loop continues for many iterations.

Of course, in practice, i rarely takes the value -0x80000000. The compiler can't usually determine this, especially if the loop starts with a variable number of iterations (see Section 5.3.2).

Therefore you should use the termination condition i!=0 for signed or unsigned loop counters. It saves one instruction over the condition i>0 for signed i.

5.3.2 LOOPS USING A VARIABLE NUMBER OF ITERATIONS

Now suppose we want our checksum routine to handle packets of arbitrary size. We pass in a variable N giving the number of words in the data packet. Using the lessons from the last section we count down until N = 0 and don't require an extra loop counter i.

The checksum_v7 example shows how the compiler handles a for loop with a variable number of iterations N.

```
int checksum_v7(int *data, unsigned int N)
{
  int sum=0;

  for (; N!=0; N--)
  {
    sum += *(data++);
  }
  return sum;
}
```

This compiles to

```
checksum_v7
        MOV    r2,#0              ; sum = 0
        CMP    r1,#0              ; compare N, 0
        BEQ    checksum_v7_end    ; if (N==0) goto end
```

```
checksum_v7_loop
        LDR     r3,[r0],#4          ; r3 = *(data++)
        SUBS    r1,r1,#1            ; N-- and set flags
        ADD     r2,r3,r2           ; sum += r3
        BNE     checksum_v7_loop   ; if (N!=0) goto loop
checksum_v7_end
        MOV     r0,r2              ; r0 = sum
        MOV     pc,r14             ; return r0
```

Notice that the compiler checks that N is nonzero on entry to the function. Often this check is unnecessary since you know that the array won't be empty. In this case a do-while loop gives better performance and code density than a for loop.

EXAMPLE
5.3

This example shows how to use a do-while loop to remove the test for N being zero that occurs in a for loop.

```
int checksum_v8(int *data, unsigned int N)
{
  int sum=0;

  do
  {
    sum += *(data++);
  } while (--N!=0);
  return sum;
}
```

The compiler output is now

```
checksum_v8
        MOV     r2,#0              ; sum = 0
checksum_v8_loop
        LDR     r3,[r0],#4         ; r3 = *(data++)
        SUBS    r1,r1,#1           ; N-- and set flags
        ADD     r2,r3,r2          ; sum += r3
        BNE     checksum_v8_loop  ; if (N!=0) goto loop
        MOV     r0,r2             ; r0 = sum
        MOV     pc,r14            ; return r0
```

Compare this with the output for checksum_v7 to see the two-cycle saving.

5.3.3 LOOP UNROLLING

We saw in Section 5.3.1 that each loop iteration costs two instructions in addition to the body of the loop: a subtract to decrement the loop count and a conditional branch.

We call these instructions the *loop overhead.* On ARM7 or ARM9 processors the subtract takes one cycle and the branch three cycles, giving an overhead of four cycles per loop.

You can save some of these cycles by *unrolling* a loop—repeating the loop body several times, and reducing the number of loop iterations by the same proportion. For example, let's unroll our packet checksum example four times.

EXAMPLE
5.4

The following code unrolls our packet checksum loop by four times. We assume that the number of words in the packet N is a multiple of four.

```c
int checksum_v9(int *data, unsigned int N)
{
  int sum=0;

  do
  {
    sum += *(data++);
    sum += *(data++);
    sum += *(data++);
    sum += *(data++);
    N -= 4;
  } while ( N!=0);
  return sum;
}
```

This compiles to

```
checksum_v9
        MOV    r2,#0        ; sum = 0
checksum_v9_loop
        LDR    r3,[r0],#4    ; r3 = *(data++)
        SUBS   r1,r1,#4      ; N -= 4 & set flags
        ADD    r2,r3,r2      ; sum += r3
        LDR    r3,[r0],#4    ; r3 = *(data++)
        ADD    r2,r3,r2      ; sum += r3
        LDR    r3,[r0],#4    ; r3 = *(data++)
        ADD    r2,r3,r2      ; sum += r3
        LDR    r3,[r0],#4    ; r3 = *(data++)
        ADD    r2,r3,r2      ; sum += r3
        BNE    checksum_v9_loop ; if (N!=0) goto loop
        MOV    r0,r2         ; r0 = sum
        MOV    pc,r14        ; return r0
```

We have reduced the loop overhead from 4N cycles to (4N)/4 = N cycles. On the ARM7TDMI, this accelerates the loop from 8 cycles per accumulate to 20/4 = 5 cycles per accumulate, nearly doubling the speed! For the ARM9TDMI, which has a faster load instruction, the benefit is even higher.

There are two questions you need to ask when unrolling a loop:

- How many times should I unroll the loop?
- What if the number of loop iterations is not a multiple of the unroll amount? For example, what if N is not a multiple of four in checksum_v9?

To start with the first question, only unroll loops that are important for the overall performance of the application. Otherwise unrolling will increase the code size with little performance benefit. Unrolling may even reduce performance by evicting more important code from the cache.

Suppose the loop is important, for example, 30% of the entire application. Suppose you unroll the loop until it is 0.5 KB in code size (128 instructions). Then the loop overhead is at most 4 cycles compared to a loop body of around 128 cycles. The loop overhead cost is 3/128, roughly 3%. Recalling that the loop is 30% of the entire application, overall the loop overhead is only 1%. Unrolling the code further gains little extra performance, but has a significant impact on the cache contents. It is usually not worth unrolling further when the gain is less than 1%.

For the second question, try to arrange it so that array sizes are multiples of your unroll amount. If this isn't possible, then you must add extra code to take care of the leftover cases. This increases the code size a little but keeps the performance high.

EXAMPLE 5.5   This example handles the checksum of any size of data packet using a loop that has been unrolled four times.

```
int checksum_v10(int *data, unsigned int N)
{
  unsigned int i;
  int sum=0;

  for (i=N/4; i!=0; i--)
  {
    sum += *(data++);
    sum += *(data++);
    sum += *(data++);
    sum += *(data++);
  }
  for (i=N&3; i!=0; i--)
  {
```

```
    sum += *(data++);
  }
  return sum;
}
```

The second for loop handles the remaining cases when N is not a multiple of four. Note that both N/4 and N&3 can be zero, so we can't use do-while loops.

Writing Loops Efficiently

- Use loops that count down to zero. Then the compiler does not need to allocate a register to hold the termination value, and the comparison with zero is free.

- Use unsigned loop counters by default and the continuation condition i!=0 rather than i>0. This will ensure that the loop overhead is only two instructions.

- Use do-while loops rather than for loops when you know the loop will iterate at least once. This saves the compiler checking to see if the loop count is zero.

- Unroll important loops to reduce the loop overhead. Do not overunroll. If the loop overhead is small as a proportion of the total, then unrolling will increase code size and hurt the performance of the cache.

- Try to arrange that the number of elements in arrays are multiples of four or eight. You can then unroll loops easily by two, four, or eight times without worrying about the leftover array elements.

5.4 REGISTER ALLOCATION

The compiler attempts to allocate a processor register to each local variable you use in a C function. It will try to use the same register for different local variables if the use of the variables do not overlap. When there are more local variables than available registers, the compiler stores the excess variables on the processor stack. These variables are called *spilled* or *swapped out* variables since they are written out to memory (in a similar way virtual memory is swapped out to disk). Spilled variables are slow to access compared to variables allocated to registers.

To implement a function efficiently, you need to

- minimize the number of spilled variables
- ensure that the most important and frequently accessed variables are stored in registers

First let's look at the number of processor registers the ARM C compilers have available for allocating variables. Table 5.3 shows the standard register names and usage when following the ARM-Thumb procedure call standard (ATPCS), which is used in code generated by C compilers.

Table 5.3   C compiler register usage.

Register number	Alternate register names	ATPCS register usage
r0	a1	Argument registers. These hold the first four function
r1	a2	arguments on a function call and the return value on a
r2	a3	function return. A function may corrupt these registers and
r3	a4	use them as general scratch registers within the function.
r4	v1	General variable registers. The function must preserve the callee
r5	v2	values of these registers.
r6	v3	
r7	v4	
r8	v5	
r9	v6 sb	General variable register. The function must preserve the callee value of this register except when compiling for *read-write position independence* (RWPI). Then *r9* holds the *static base* address. This is the address of the read-write data.
r10	v7 sl	General variable register. The function must preserve the callee value of this register except when compiling with stack limit checking. Then *r10* holds the stack limit address.
r11	v8 fp	General variable register. The function must preserve the callee value of this register except when compiling using a frame pointer. Only old versions of *armcc* use a frame pointer.
r12	ip	A general scratch register that the function can corrupt. It is useful as a scratch register for function veneers or other intraprocedure call requirements.
r13	sp	The stack pointer, pointing to the full descending stack.
r14	lr	The link register. On a function call this holds the return address.
r15	pc	The program counter.

Provided the compiler is not using software stack checking or a frame pointer, then the C compiler can use registers *r0* to *r12* and *r14* to hold variables. It must save the callee values of *r4* to *r11* and *r14* on the stack if using these registers.

In theory, the C compiler can assign 14 variables to registers without spillage. In practice, some compilers use a fixed register such as *r12* for intermediate scratch working and do not assign variables to this register. Also, complex expressions require intermediate working registers to evaluate. Therefore, to ensure good assignment to registers, you should try to limit the internal loop of functions to using at most 12 local variables.

If the compiler does need to swap out variables, then it chooses which variables to swap out based on frequency of use. A variable used inside a loop counts multiple times. You can guide the compiler as to which variables are important by ensuring these variables are used within the innermost loop.

The register keyword in C hints that a compiler should allocate the given variable to a register. However, different compilers treat this keyword in different ways, and different architectures have a different number of available registers (for example, Thumb and ARM). Therefore we recommend that you avoid using register and rely on the compiler's normal register allocation routine.

SUMMARY   **Efficient Register Allocation**

- Try to limit the number of local variables in the internal loop of functions to 12. The compiler should be able to allocate these to ARM registers.

- You can guide the compiler as to which variables are important by ensuring these variables are used within the innermost loop.

5.5 FUNCTION CALLS

The ARM Procedure Call Standard (APCS) defines how to pass function arguments and return values in ARM registers. The more recent ARM-Thumb Procedure Call Standard (ATPCS) covers ARM and Thumb interworking as well.

The first four integer arguments are passed in the first four ARM registers: *r0, r1, r2,* and *r3*. Subsequent integer arguments are placed on the full descending stack, ascending in memory as in Figure 5.1. Function return integer values are passed in *r0*.

This description covers only integer or pointer arguments. Two-word arguments such as long long or double are passed in a pair of consecutive argument registers and returned in *r0, r1*. The compiler may pass structures in registers or by reference according to command line compiler options.

The first point to note about the procedure call standard is the *four-register rule*. Functions with four or fewer arguments are far more efficient to call than functions with five or more arguments. For functions with four or fewer arguments, the compiler can pass all the arguments in registers. For functions with more arguments, both the caller and callee must access the stack for some arguments. Note that for C++ the first argument to an object method is the *this* pointer. This argument is implicit and additional to the explicit arguments.

If your C function needs more than four arguments, or your C++ method more than three explicit arguments, then it is almost always more efficient to use structures. Group related arguments into structures, and pass a structure pointer rather than multiple arguments. Which arguments are related will depend on the structure of your software.

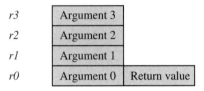

sp + 16	Argument 8
sp + 12	Argument 7
sp + 8	Argument 6
sp + 4	Argument 5
sp	Argument 4

r3	Argument 3
r2	Argument 2
r1	Argument 1
r0	Argument 0 / Return value

Figure 5.1   ATPCS argument passing.

The next example illustrates the benefits of using a structure pointer. First we show a typical routine to insert N bytes from array data into a queue. We implement the queue using a cyclic buffer with start address Q_start (inclusive) and end address Q_end (exclusive).

```
char *queue_bytes_v1(
  char *Q_start,        /* Queue buffer start address */
  char *Q_end,          /* Queue buffer end address */
  char *Q_ptr,          /* Current queue pointer position */
  char *data,           /* Data to insert into the queue */
  unsigned int N)       /* Number of bytes to insert */
{
  do
  {
    *(Q_ptr++) = *(data++);

    if (Q_ptr == Q_end)
    {
      Q_ptr = Q_start;
    }
  } while (--N);
  return Q_ptr;
}
```

This compiles to

```
queue_bytes_v1
        STR     r14,[r13,#-4]!   ; save lr on the stack
        LDR     r12,[r13,#4]     ; r12 = N
queue_v1_loop
        LDRB    r14,[r3],#1      ; r14 = *(data++)
        STRB    r14,[r2],#1      ; *(Q_ptr++) = r14
        CMP     r2,r1            ; if (Q_ptr == Q_end)
        MOVEQ   r2,r0            ;     {Q_ptr = Q_start;}
        SUBS    r12,r12,#1       ; --N and set flags
        BNE     queue_v1_loop    ; if (N!=0) goto loop
        MOV     r0,r2            ; r0 = Q_ptr
        LDR     pc,[r13],#4      ; return r0
```

Compare this with a more structured approach using three function arguments.

EXAMPLE
5.6
The following code creates a Queue structure and passes this to the function to reduce the number of function arguments.

```
typedef struct {
  char *Q_start;         /* Queue buffer start address */
  char *Q_end;           /* Queue buffer end address */
  char *Q_ptr;           /* Current queue pointer position */
} Queue;

void queue_bytes_v2(Queue *queue, char *data, unsigned int N)
{
  char *Q_ptr = queue->Q_ptr;
  char *Q_end = queue->Q_end;

  do
  {
    *(Q_ptr++) = *(data++);

    if (Q_ptr == Q_end)
    {
      Q_ptr = queue->Q_start;
    }
  } while (--N);
  queue->Q_ptr = Q_ptr;
}
```

This compiles to

```
queue_bytes_v2
        STR     r14,[r13,#-4]!   ; save lr on the stack
        LDR     r3,[r0,#8]       ; r3 = queue->Q_ptr
        LDR     r14,[r0,#4]      ; r14 = queue->Q_end
queue_v2_loop
        LDRB    r12,[r1],#1      ; r12 = *(data++)
        STRB    r12,[r3],#1      ; *(Q_ptr++) = r12
        CMP     r3,r14           ; if (Q_ptr == Q_end)
        LDREQ   r3,[r0,#0]       ;    Q_ptr = queue->Q_start
        SUBS    r2,r2,#1         ; --N and set flags
        BNE     queue_v2_loop    ; if (N!=0) goto loop
        STR     r3,[r0,#8]       ; queue->Q_ptr = r3
        LDR     pc,[r13],#4      ; return
```

The queue_bytes_v2 is one instruction longer than queue_bytes_v1, but it is in fact more efficient overall. The second version has only three function arguments rather than five. Each call to the function requires only three register setups. This compares with four register setups, a stack push, and a stack pull for the first version. There is a net saving of two instructions in function call overhead. There are likely further savings in the callee function, as it only needs to assign a single register to the Queue structure pointer, rather than three registers in the nonstructured case.

There are other ways of reducing function call overhead if your function is very small and corrupts few registers (uses few local variables). Put the C function in the same C file as the functions that will call it. The C compiler then knows the code generated for the callee function and can make optimizations in the caller function:

■ The caller function need not preserve registers that it can see the callee doesn't corrupt. Therefore the caller function need not save all the ATPCS corruptible registers.

■ If the callee function is very small, then the compiler can inline the code in the caller function. This removes the function call overhead completely.

EXAMPLE
5.7
The function uint_to_hex converts a 32-bit unsigned integer into an array of eight hexadecimal digits. It uses a helper function nybble_to_hex, which converts a digit d in the range 0 to 15 to a hexadecimal digit.

```
unsigned int nybble_to_hex(unsigned int d)
{
  if (d<10)
  {
    return d + '0';
```

```
  }
  return d - 10 + 'A';
}

void uint_to_hex(char *out, unsigned int in)
{
  unsigned int i;

  for (i=8; i!=0; i--)
  {
    in = (in<<4) | (in>>28); /* rotate in left by 4 bits */
    *(out++) = (char)nybble_to_hex(in & 15);
  }
}
```

When we compile this, we see that uint_to_hex doesn't call nybble_to_hex at all!
In the following compiled code, the compiler has inlined the uint_to_hex code. This is
more efficient than generating a function call.

```
uint_to_hex
        MOV     r3,#8              ; i = 8
uint_to_hex_loop
        MOV     r1,r1,ROR #28      ; in = (in<<4)|(in>>28)
        AND     r2,r1,#0xf         ; r2 = in & 15
        CMP     r2,#0xa            ; if (r2>=10)
        ADDCS   r2,r2,#0x37        ;   r2 +='A'-10
        ADDCC   r2,r2,#0x30        ; else r2 +='0'
        STRB    r2,[r0],#1         ; *(out++) = r2
        SUBS    r3,r3,#1           ; i-- and set flags
        BNE     uint_to_hex_loop   ; if (i!=0) goto loop
        MOV     pc,r14             ; return
```

The compiler will only inline small functions. You can ask the compiler to inline
a function using the __inline keyword, although this keyword is only a hint and the
compiler may ignore it (see Section 5.12 for more on inline functions). Inlining large
functions can lead to big increases in code size without much performance improvement.

SUMMARY   **Calling Functions Efficiently**

■   Try to restrict functions to four arguments. This will make them more efficient to
     call. Use structures to group related arguments and pass structure pointers instead of
     multiple arguments.

- Define small functions in the same source file and before the functions that call them. The compiler can then optimize the function call or inline the small function.

- Critical functions can be inlined using the __inline keyword.

5.6 POINTER ALIASING

Two pointers are said to *alias* when they point to the same address. If you write to one pointer, it will affect the value you read from the other pointer. In a function, the compiler often doesn't know which pointers can alias and which pointers can't. The compiler must be very pessimistic and assume that any write to a pointer may affect the value read from any other pointer, which can significantly reduce code efficiency.

Let's start with a very simple example. The following function increments two timer values by a step amount:

```
void timers_v1(int *timer1, int *timer2, int *step)
{
  *timer1 += *step;
  *timer2 += *step;
}
```

This compiles to

```
timers_v1
        LDR     r3,[r0,#0]        ; r3 = *timer1
        LDR     r12,[r2,#0]       ; r12 = *step
        ADD     r3,r3,r12         ; r3 += r12
        STR     r3,[r0,#0]        ; *timer1 = r3
        LDR     r0,[r1,#0]        ; r0 = *timer2
        LDR     r2,[r2,#0]        ; r2 = *step
        ADD     r0,r0,r2          ; r0 += r2
        STR     r0,[r1,#0]        ; *timer2 = t0
        MOV     pc,r14            ; return
```

Note that the compiler loads from step twice. Usually a compiler optimization called *common subexpression elimination* would kick in so that *step was only evaluated once, and the value reused for the second occurrence. However, the compiler can't use this optimization here. The pointers timer1 and step might alias one another. In other words, the compiler cannot be sure that the write to timer1 doesn't affect the read from step.

In this case the second value of *step is different from the first and has the value *timer1. This forces the compiler to insert an extra load instruction.

The same problem occurs if you use structure accesses rather than direct pointer access. The following code also compiles inefficiently:

```
typedef struct {int step;} State;
typedef struct {int timer1, timer2;} Timers;

void timers_v2(State *state, Timers *timers)
{
  timers->timer1 += state->step;
  timers->timer2 += state->step;
}
```

The compiler evaluates state->step twice in case state->step and timers->timer1 are at the same memory address. The fix is easy: Create a new local variable to hold the value of state->step so the compiler only performs a single load.

EXAMPLE
5.8

In the code for timers_v3 we use a local variable step to hold the value of state->step. Now the compiler does not need to worry that state may alias with timers.

```
void timers_v3(State *state, Timers *timers)
{
    int step = state->step;

    timers->timer1 += step;
    timers->timer2 += step;
}
```

You must also be careful of other, less obvious situations where aliasing may occur. When you call another function, this function may alter the state of memory and so change the values of any expressions involving memory reads. The compiler will evaluate the expressions again. For example suppose you read state->step, call a function and then read state->step again. The compiler must assume that the function could change the value of state->step in memory. Therefore it will perform two reads, rather than reusing the first value it read for state->step.

Another pitfall is to take the address of a local variable. Once you do this, the variable is referenced by a pointer and so aliasing can occur with other pointers. The compiler is likely to keep reading the variable from the stack in case aliasing occurs. Consider the following example, which reads and then checksums a data packet:

```
int checksum_next_packet(void)
{
  int *data;
  int N, sum=0;
```

```
  data = get_next_packet(&N);

  do
  {
    sum += *(data++);
  } while (--N);

  return sum;
}
```

Here get_next_packet is a function returning the address and size of the next data packet. The previous code compiles to

```
checksum_next_packet
        STMFD   r13!,{r4,r14}       ; save r4, lr on the stack
        SUB     r13,r13,#8          ; create two stacked variables
        ADD     r0,r13,#4           ; r0 = &N, N stacked
        MOV     r4,#0               ; sum = 0
        BL      get_next_packet     ; r0 = data
checksum_loop
        LDR     r1,[r0],#4          ; r1 = *(data++)
        ADD     r4,r1,r4            ; sum += r1
        LDR     r1,[r13,#4]         ; r1 = N (read from stack)
        SUBS    r1,r1,#1            ; r1-- & set flags
        STR     r1,[r13,#4]         ; N = r1 (write to stack)
        BNE     checksum_loop       ; if (N!=0) goto loop
        MOV     r0,r4               ; r0 = sum
        ADD     r13,r13,#8          ; delete stacked variables
        LDMFD   r13!,{r4,pc}        ; return r0
```

Note how the compiler reads and writes N from the stack for every N--. Once you take the address of N and pass it to get_next_packet, the compiler needs to worry about aliasing because the pointers data and &N may alias. To avoid this, don't take the address of local variables. If you must do this, then copy the value into another local variable before use.

You may wonder why the compiler makes room for two stacked variables when it only uses one. This is to keep the stack eight-byte aligned, which is required for LDRD instructions available in ARMv5TE. The example above doesn't actually use an LDRD, but the compiler does not know whether get_next_packet will use this instruction.

Avoiding Pointer Aliasing

- Do not rely on the compiler to eliminate common subexpressions involving memory accesses. Instead create new local variables to hold the expression. This ensures the expression is evaluated only once.

- Avoid taking the address of local variables. The variable may be inefficient to access from then on.

5.7   STRUCTURE ARRANGEMENT

The way you lay out a frequently used structure can have a significant impact on its performance and code density. There are two issues concerning structures on the ARM: alignment of the structure entries and the overall size of the structure.

For architectures up to and including ARMv5TE, load and store instructions are only guaranteed to load and store values with address aligned to the size of the access width. Table 5.4 summarizes these restrictions.

For this reason, ARM compilers will automatically align the start address of a structure to a multiple of the largest access width used within the structure (usually four or eight bytes) and align entries within structures to their access width by inserting padding.

For example, consider the structure

```
struct {
  char a;
  int b;
  char c;
  short d;
}
```

For a little-endian memory system the compiler will lay this out adding padding to ensure that the next object is aligned to the size of that object:

Address	+3	+2	+1	+0
+0	pad	pad	pad	a
+4	b[31,24]	b[23,16]	b[15,8]	b[7,0]
+8	d[15,8]	d[7,0]	pad	c

Table 5.4   Load and store alignment restrictions for ARMv5TE.

Transfer size	Instruction	Byte address
1 byte	LDRB, LDRSB, STRB	any byte address alignment
2 bytes	LDRH, LDRSH, STRH	multiple of 2 bytes
4 bytes	LDR, STR	multiple of 4 bytes
8 bytes	LDRD, STRD	multiple of 8 bytes

To improve the memory usage, you should reorder the elements

```
struct {
  char a;
  char c;
  short d;
  int b;
}
```

This reduces the structure size from 12 bytes to 8 bytes, with the following new layout:

Address	+3	+2	+1	+0
+0	d[15,8]	d[7,0]	c	a
+4	b[31,24]	b[23,16]	b[15,8]	b[7,0]

Therefore, it is a good idea to group structure elements of the same size, so that the structure layout doesn't contain unnecessary padding. The *armcc* compiler does include a keyword __packed that removes all padding. For example, the structure

```
__packed struct {
  char a;
  int b;
  char c;
  short d;
}
```

will be laid out in memory as

Address	+3	+2	+1	+0
+0	b[23,16]	b[15,8]	b[7,0]	a
+4	d[15,8]	d[7,0]	c	b[31,24]

However, packed structures are slow and inefficient to access. The compiler emulates unaligned load and store operations by using several aligned accesses with data operations to merge the results. Only use the __packed keyword where space is far more important than speed and you can't reduce padding by rearragement. Also use it for porting code that assumes a certain structure layout in memory.

The exact layout of a structure in memory may depend on the compiler vendor and compiler version you use. In API (Application Programmer Interface) definitions it is often a good idea to insert any padding that you cannot get rid of into the structure manually. This way the structure layout is not ambiguous. It is easier to link code between compiler versions and compiler vendors if you stick to unambiguous structures.

Another point of ambiguity is enum. Different compilers use different sizes for an enumerated type, depending on the range of the enumeration. For example, consider the type

```
typedef enum {
  FALSE,
  TRUE
} Bool;
```

The *armcc* in ADS1.1 will treat Bool as a one-byte type as it only uses the values 0 and 1. Bool will only take up 8 bits of space in a structure. However, *gcc* will treat Bool as a word and take up 32 bits of space in a structure. To avoid ambiguity it is best to avoid using enum types in structures used in the API to your code.

Another consideration is the size of the structure and the offsets of elements within the structure. This problem is most acute when you are compiling for the Thumb instruction set. Thumb instructions are only 16 bits wide and so only allow for small element offsets from a structure base pointer. Table 5.5 shows the load and store base register offsets available in Thumb.

Therefore the compiler can only access an 8-bit structure element with a single instruction if it appears within the first 32 bytes of the structure. Similarly, single instructions can only access 16-bit values in the first 64 bytes and 32-bit values in the first 128 bytes. Once you exceed these limits, structure accesses become inefficient.

The following rules generate a structure with the elements packed for maximum efficiency:

- Place all 8-bit elements at the start of the structure.
- Place all 16-bit elements next, then 32-bit, then 64-bit.
- Place all arrays and larger elements at the end of the structure.
- If the structure is too big for a single instruction to access all the elements, then group the elements into substructures. The compiler can maintain pointers to the individual substructures.

Table 5.5   Thumb load and store offsets.

Instructions	Offset available from the base register
LDRB, LDRSB, STRB	0 to 31 bytes
LDRH, LDRSH, STRH	0 to 31 halfwords (0 to 62 bytes)
LDR, STR	0 to 31 words (0 to 124 bytes)

SUMMARY **Efficient Structure Arrangement**

- Lay structures out in order of increasing element size. Start the structure with the smallest elements and finish with the largest.

- Avoid very large structures. Instead use a hierarchy of smaller structures.

- For portability, manually add padding (that would appear implicitly) into API structures so that the layout of the structure does not depend on the compiler.

- Beware of using enum types in API structures. The size of an enum type is compiler dependent.

5.8 BIT-FIELDS

Bit-fields are probably the least standardized part of the ANSI C specification. The compiler can choose how bits are allocated within the bit-field container. For this reason alone, avoid using bit-fields inside a union or in an API structure definition. Different compilers can assign the same bit-field different bit positions in the container.

It is also a good idea to avoid bit-fields for efficiency. Bit-fields are structure elements and usually accessed using structure pointers; consequently, they suffer from the pointer aliasing problems described in Section 5.6. Every bit-field access is really a memory access. Possible pointer aliasing often forces the compiler to reload the bit-field several times.

The following example, dostages_v1, illustrates this problem. It also shows that compilers do not tend to optimize bit-field testing very well.

```
void dostageA(void);
void dostageB(void);
void dostageC(void);

typedef struct {
  unsigned int stageA : 1;
  unsigned int stageB : 1;
  unsigned int stageC : 1;
} Stages_v1;

void dostages_v1(Stages_v1 *stages)
{
  if (stages->stageA)
  {
    dostageA();
  }
```

```
         if (stages->stageB)
         {
            dostageB();
         }
         if (stages->stageC)
         {
            dostageC();
         }
      }
```

Here, we use three bit-field flags to enable three possible stages of processing. The example compiles to

```
dostages_v1
         STMFD    r13!,{r4,r14}      ; stack r4, lr
         MOV      r4,r0              ; move stages to r4
         LDR      r0,[r0,#0]         ; r0 = stages bitfield
         TST      r0,#1              ; if (stages->stageA)
         BLNE     dostageA           ;     {dostageA();}
         LDR      r0,[r4,#0]         ; r0 = stages bitfield
         MOV      r0,r0,LSL #30      ; shift bit 1 to bit 31
         CMP      r0,#0              ; if (bit31)
         BLLT     dostageB           ;     {dostageB();}
         LDR      r0,[r4,#0]         ; r0 = stages bitfield
         MOV      r0,r0,LSL #29      ; shift bit 2 to bit 31
         CMP      r0,#0              ; if (!bit31)
         LDMLTFD  r13!,{r4,r14}      ;     return
         BLT      dostageC           ; dostageC();
         LDMFD    r13!,{r4,pc}       ; return
```

Note that the compiler accesses the memory location containing the bit-field three times. Because the bit-field is stored in memory, the dostage functions could change the value. Also, the compiler uses two instructions to test bit 1 and bit 2 of the bit-field, rather than a single instruction.

You can generate far more efficient code by using an integer rather than a bit-field. Use enum or #define masks to divide the integer type into different fields.

EXAMPLE
5.9
The following code implements the dostages function using logical operations rather than bit-fields:

```
typedef unsigned long Stages_v2;

#define STAGEA (1ul << 0)
```

```
#define STAGEB (1ul << 1)
#define STAGEC (1ul << 2)

void dostages_v2(Stages_v2 *stages_v2)
{
  Stages_v2 stages = *stages_v2;

  if (stages & STAGEA)
  {
    dostageA();
  }
  if (stages & STAGEB)
  {
    dostageB();
  }
  if (stages & STAGEC)
  {
    dostageC();
  }
}
```

Now that a single unsigned long type contains all the bit-fields, we can keep a copy of their values in a single local variable stages, which removes the memory aliasing problem discussed in Section 5.6. In other words, the compiler must assume that the dostage*X* (where *X* is A, B, or C) functions could change the value of *stages_v2.

The compiler generates the following code giving a saving of 33% over the previous version using ANSI bit-fields:

```
dostages_v2
        STMFD     r13!,{r4,r14}    ; stack r4, lr
        LDR       r4,[r0,#0]       ; stages = *stages_v2
        TST       r4,#1            ; if (stage & STAGEA)
        BLNE      dostageA         ;     {dostageA();}
        TST       r4,#2            ; if (stage & STAGEB)
        BLNE      dostageB         ;     {dostageB();}
        TST       r4,#4            ; if (!(stage & STAGEC))
        LDMNEFD   r13!,{r4,r14}    ; return;
        BNE       dostageC         ; dostageC();
        LDMFD     r13!,{r4,pc}     ; return
```

You can also use the masks to set and clear the bit-fields, just as easily as for testing them. The following code shows how to set, clear, or toggle bits using the STAGE masks:

```
stages |= STAGEA;              /* enable stage A */
```

```
stages &= ~STAGEB;        /* disable stage B */
stages ^= STAGEC;         /* toggle stage C */
```

These bit set, clear, and toggle operations take only one ARM instruction each, using ORR, BIC, and EOR instructions, respectively. Another advantage is that you can now manipulate several bit-fields at the same time, using one instruction. For example:

```
stages |= (STAGEA | STAGEB);       /* enable stages A and B */
stages &= ~(STAGEA | STAGEC);      /* disable stages A and C */
```

SUMMARY   **Bit-fields**

- Avoid using bit-fields. Instead use #define or enum to define mask values.

- Test, toggle, and set bit-fields using integer logical AND, OR, and exclusive OR operations with the mask values. These operations compile efficiently, and you can test, toggle, or set multiple fields at the same time.

5.9 UNALIGNED DATA AND ENDIANNESS

Unaligned data and endianness are two issues that can complicate memory accesses and portability. Is the array pointer aligned? Is the ARM configured for a big-endian or little-endian memory system?

The ARM load and store instructions assume that the address is a multiple of the type you are loading or storing. If you load or store to an address that is not aligned to its type, then the behavior depends on the particular implementation. The core may generate a data abort or load a rotated value. For well-written, portable code you should avoid unaligned accesses.

C compilers assume that a pointer is aligned unless you say otherwise. If a pointer isn't aligned, then the program may give unexpected results. This is sometimes an issue when you are porting code to the ARM from processors that do allow unaligned accesses. For *armcc*, the __packed directive tells the compiler that a data item can be positioned at any byte alignment. This is useful for porting code, but using __packed will impact performance.

To illustrate this, look at the following simple routine, readint. It returns the integer at the address pointed to by data. We've used __packed to tell the compiler that the integer may possibly not be aligned.

```
int readint(__packed int *data)
{
  return *data;
}
```

This compiles to

```
readint
        BIC     r3,r0,#3            ; r3 = data & 0xFFFFFFFC
        AND     r0,r0,#3            ; r0 = data & 0x00000003
        MOV     r0,r0,LSL #3        ; r0 = bit offset of data word
        LDMIA   r3,{r3,r12}         ; r3, r12 = 8 bytes read from r3
        MOV     r3,r3,LSR r0        ; These three instructions
        RSB     r0,r0,#0x20         ; shift the 64 bit value r12.r3
        ORR     r0,r3,r12,LSL r0    ; right by r0 bits
        MOV     pc,r14              ; return r0
```

Notice how large and complex the code is. The compiler emulates the unaligned access using two aligned accesses and data processing operations, which is very costly and shows why you should avoid _packed. Instead use the type char * to point to data that can appear at any alignment. We will look at more efficient ways to read 32-bit words from a char * later.

You are likely to meet alignment problems when reading data packets or files used to transfer information between computers. Network packets and compressed image files are good examples. Two- or four-byte integers may appear at arbitrary offsets in these files. Data has been squeezed as much as possible, to the detriment of alignment.

Endianness (or byte order) is also a big issue when reading data packets or compressed files. The ARM core can be configured to work in *little-endian* (least significant byte at lowest address) or *big-endian* (most significant byte at lowest address) modes. Little-endian mode is usually the default.

The endianness of an ARM is usually set at power-up and remains fixed thereafter. Tables 5.6 and 5.7 illustrate how the ARM's 8-bit, 16-bit, and 32-bit load and store instructions work for different endian configurations. We assume that byte address A is aligned to

Table 5.6 Little-endian configuration.

Instruction	Width (bits)	b31..b24	b23..b16	b15..b8	b7..b0
LDRB	8	0	0	0	B(A)
LDRSB	8	S(A)	S(A)	S(A)	B(A)
STRB	8	X	X	X	B(A)
LDRH	16	0	0	B(A+1)	B(A)
LDRSH	16	S(A+1)	S(A+1)	B(A+1)	B(A)
STRH	16	X	X	B(A+1)	B(A)
LDR/STR	32	B(A+3)	B(A+2)	B(A+1)	B(A)

Table 5.7   Big-endian configuration.

Instruction	Width (bits)	b31..b24	b23..b16	b15..b8	b7..b0
LDRB	8	0	0	0	B(A)
LDRSD	8	S(A)	S(A)	S(A)	B(A)
STRB	8	X	X	X	B(A)
LDRH	16	0	0	B(A)	B(A+1)
LDRSH	16	S(A)	S(A)	B(A)	B(A+1)
STRH	16	X	X	B(A)	B(A+1)
LDR/STR	32	B(A)	B(A+1)	B(A+2)	B(A+3)

Notes:
> B(A): The byte at address A.
> S(A): 0xFF if bit 7 of B(A) is set, otherwise 0x00.
>   X: These bits are ignored on a write.

the size of the memory transfer. The tables show how the byte addresses in memory map into the 32-bit register that the instruction loads or stores.

What is the best way to deal with endian and alignment problems? If speed is not critical, then use functions like readint_little and readint_big in Example 5.10, which read a four-byte integer from a possibly unaligned address in memory. The address alignment is not known at compile time, only at run time. If you've loaded a file containing big-endian data such as a JPEG image, then use readint_big. For a bytestream containing little-endian data, use readint_little. Both routines will work correctly regardless of the memory endianness ARM is configured for.

EXAMPLE 5.10   These functions read a 32-bit integer from a bytestream pointed to by data. The bytestream contains little- or big-endian data, respectively. These functions are independent of the ARM memory system byte order since they only use byte accesses.

```
int readint_little(char *data)
{
  int a0,a1,a2,a3;

  a0 = *(data++);
  a1 = *(data++);
  a2 = *(data++);
  a3 = *(data++);
  return a0 | (a1<<8) | (a2<<16) | (a3<<24);
}


int readint_big(char *data)
```

```
{
  int a0,a1,a2,a3;

  a0 = *(data++);
  a1 = *(data++);
  a2 = *(data++);
  a3 = *(data++);
  return (((((a0 << 8) | a1) << 8) | a2) << 8) | a3;
}
```

If speed is critical, then the fastest approach is to write several variants of the critical routine. For each possible alignment and ARM endianness configuration, you call a separate routine optimized for that situation.

EXAMPLE   The read_samples routine takes an array of N 16-bit sound samples at address in. The
5.11   sound samples are little-endian (for example from a.wav file) and can be at any byte
            alignment. The routine copies the samples to an aligned array of short type values pointed
            to by out. The samples will be stored according to the configured ARM memory endianness.
            The routine handles all cases in an efficient manner, regardless of input alignment and
            of ARM endianness configuration.

```
void read_samples(short *out, char *in, unsigned int N)
{
  unsigned short *data; /* aligned input pointer */
  unsigned int sample, next;

  switch ((unsigned int)in & 1)
  {
    case 0: /* the input pointer is aligned */
      data = (unsigned short *)in;
      do
      {
        sample = *(data++);
#ifdef __BIG_ENDIAN
        sample = (sample >> 8) | (sample << 8);
#endif
        *(out++) = (short)sample;
      } while (--N);
      break;

    case 1: /* the input pointer is not aligned */
      data = (unsigned short *)(in-1);
      sample = *(data++);
```

```
#ifdef __BIG_ENDIAN
        sample = sample & 0xFF; /* get first byte of sample */
#else
        sample = sample>>8;     /* get first byte of sample */
#endif
        do
        {
        next = *(data++);
        /* complete one sample and start the next */
#ifdef __BIG_ENDIAN
        *out++ = (short)((next & 0xFF00) | sample);
        sample = next & 0xFF;
#else
        *out++ = (short)((next<<8) | sample);
        sample = next>>8;
#endif
        } while (--N);
        break;
    }
}
```

The routine works by having different code for each endianness and alignment. Endianness is dealt with at compile time using the __BIG_ENDIAN compiler flag. Alignment must be dealt with at run time using the switch statement.

You can make the routine even more efficient by using 32-bit reads and writes rather than 16-bit reads and writes, which leads to four elements in the switch statement, one for each possible address alignment modulo four.

SUMMARY **Endianness and Alignment**

- Avoid using unaligned data if you can.

- Use the type char * for data that can be at any byte alignment. Access the data by reading bytes and combining with logical operations. Then the code won't depend on alignment or ARM endianness configuration.

- For fast access to unaligned structures, write different variants according to pointer alignment and processor endianness.

5.10 DIVISION

The ARM does not have a divide instruction in hardware. Instead the compiler implements divisions by calling software routines in the C library. There are many different types of division routine that you can tailor to a specific range of numerator and denominator values. We look at assembly division routines in detail in Chapter 7. The standard integer division routine provided in the C library can take between 20 and 100 cycles, depending on implementation, early termination, and the ranges of the input operands.

Division and modulus (/ and %) are such slow operations that you should avoid them as much as possible. However, division by a constant and repeated division by the same denominator can be handled efficiently. This section describes how to replace certain divisions by multiplications and how to minimize the number of division calls.

Circular buffers are one area where programmers often use division, but you can avoid these divisions completely. Suppose you have a circular buffer of size buffer_size bytes and a position indicated by a buffer offset. To advance the offset by increment bytes you could write

```
offset = (offset + increment) % buffer_size;
```

Instead it is far more efficient to write

```
offset += increment;
if (offset>=buffer_size)
{
    offset -= buffer_size;
}
```

The first version may take 50 cycles; the second will take 3 cycles because it does not involve a division. We've assumed that increment < buffer_size; you can always arrange this in practice.

If you can't avoid a division, then try to arrange that the numerator and denominator are unsigned integers. Signed division routines are slower since they take the absolute values of the numerator and denominator and then call the unsigned division routine. They fix the sign of the result afterwards.

Many C library division routines return the quotient and remainder from the division. In other words a free remainder operation is available to you with each division operation and vice versa. For example, to find the (x, y) position of a location at offset bytes into a screen buffer, it is tempting to write

```
typedef struct {
  int x;
  int y;
} point;

point getxy_v1(unsigned int offset, unsigned int bytes_per_line)
{
  point p;
```

```
      p.y = offset / bytes_per_line;
      p.x = offset - p.y * bytes_per_line;
      return p;
  }
```

It appears that we have saved a division by using a subtract and multiply to calculate p.x, but in fact, it is often more efficient to write the function with the modulus or remainder operation.

EXAMPLE   In getxy_v2, the quotient and remainder operation only require a single call to a division
5.12   routine:

```
point getxy_v2(unsigned int offset, unsigned int bytes_per_line)
{
  point p;

  p.x = offset % bytes_per_line;
  p.y = offset / bytes_per_line;
  return p;
}
```

There is only one division call here, as you can see in the following compiler output. In fact, this version is four instructions shorter than getxy_v1. Note that this may not be the case for all compilers and C libraries.

```
getxy_v2
        STMFD    r13!,{r4, r14}   ; stack r4, lr
        MOV      r4,r0            ; move p to r4
        MOV      r0,r2            ; r0 = bytes_per_line
        BL       __rt_udiv        ; (r0,r1) = (r1/r0, r1%r0)
        STR      r0,[r4,#4]       ; p.y = offset / bytes_per_line
        STR      r1,[r4,#0]       ; p.x = offset % bytes_per_line
        LDMFD    r13!,{r4,pc}     ; return
```

5.10.1 REPEATED UNSIGNED DIVISION WITH REMAINDER

Often the same denominator occurs several times in code. In the previous example, bytes_per_line will probably be fixed throughout the program. If we project from three to two cartesian coordinates, then we use the denominator twice:

$$(x, y, z) \rightarrow (x/z, y/z)$$

In these situations it is more efficient to *cache* the value of $1/z$ in some way and use a multiplication by $1/z$ instead of a division. We will show how to do this in the next subsection. We also want to stick to integer arithmetic and avoid floating point (see Section 5.11).

The next description is rather mathematical and covers the theory behind this conversion of repeated divisions into multiplications. If you are not interested in the theory, then don't worry. You can jump directly to Example 5.13, which follows.

5.10.2 CONVERTING DIVIDES INTO MULTIPLIES

We'll use the following notation to distinguish exact mathematical divides from integer divides:

- n/d = the integer part of n divided by d, rounding towards zero (as in C)

- n%d = the remainder of n divided by d which is $n - d(n/d)$

- $\dfrac{n}{d} = nd^{-1}$ = the true mathematical divide of n by d

The obvious way to estimate d^{-1}, while sticking to integer arithmetic, is to calculate $2^{32}/d$. Then we can estimate n/d

$$\left(n(2^{32}/d)\right)/2^{32} \tag{5.1}$$

We need to perform the multiplication by n to 64-bit accuracy. There are a couple of problems with this approach:

- To calculate $2^{32}/d$, the compiler needs to use 64-bit long long type arithmetic because 2^{32} does not fit into an unsigned int type. We must specify the division as $(1\text{ull} \ll 32)/d$. This 64-bit division is much slower than the 32-bit division we wanted to perform originally!

- If d happens to be 1, then $2^{32}/d$ will not fit into an unsigned int type.

It turns out that a slightly cruder estimate works well and fixes both these problems. Instead of $2^{32}/d$, we look at $(2^{32} - 1)/d$. Let

```
s = 0xFFFFFFFFul / d;   /* s = (2^32-1)/d */
```

We can calculate s using a single unsigned int type division. We know that

$$2^{32} - 1 = sd + t \text{ for some } 0 \le t < d \tag{5.2}$$

Therefore

$$s = \frac{2^{32}}{d} - e_1, \quad \text{where } 0 < e_1 = \frac{1 + t}{d} \le 1 \tag{5.3}$$

Next, calculate an estimate q to n/d:

```
q = (unsigned int)( ((unsigned long long)n * s) >> 32);
```

Mathematically, the shift right by 32 introduces an error e_2:

$$q = ns2^{-32} - e_2 \text{ for some } 0 \le e_2 < 1 \tag{5.4}$$

Substituting the value of s:

$$q = \frac{n}{d} - ne_1 2^{-32} - e_2 \tag{5.5}$$

So, q is an underestimate to n/d. Now

$$0 \le ne_1 2^{-32} + e_2 < e_1 + e_2 < 2 \tag{5.6}$$

Therefore

$$n/d - 2 < q \le n/d \tag{5.7}$$

So $q = n/d$ or $q = (n/d) - 1$. We can find out which quite easily, by calculating the remainder $r = n - qd$, which must be in the range $0 \le r < 2d$. The following code corrects the result:

```
r = n-q * d;     /* the remainder in the range 0 <= r < 2 * d */
if (r >= d)      /* if correction is required */
{
   r -= d;       /* correct the remainder to the range 0 <= r < d */
   q++;          /* correct the quotient */
}
/* now q = n / d and r = n % d */
```

EXAMPLE The following routine, scale, shows how to convert divisions to multiplications in practice.
5.13 It divides an array of N elements by denominator d. We first calculate the value of s as above. Then we replace each divide by d with a multiplication by s. The 64-bit multiply is cheap because the ARM has an instruction UMULL, which multiplies two 32-bit values, giving a 64-bit result.

```
void scale(
   unsigned int *dest,          /* destination for the scale data */
   unsigned int *src,           /* source unscaled data */
   unsigned int d,              /* denominator to divide by */
   unsigned int N)              /* data length */
{
   unsigned int s = 0xFFFFFFFFu / d;
```

```
do
{
  unsigned int n, q, r;

  n = *(src++);
  q = (unsigned int)(((unsigned long long)n * s) >> 32);
  r = n - q * d;
  if (r >= d)
  {
    q++;
  }
  *(dest++) = q;
} while (--N);
}
```

Here we have assumed that the numerator and denominator are 32-bit unsigned integers. Of course, the algorithm works equally well for 16-bit unsigned integers using a 32-bit multiply, or for 64-bit integers using a 128-bit multiply. You should choose the narrowest width for your data. If your data is 16-bit, then set $s = (2^{16} - 1)/d$ and estimate q using a standard integer C multiply.

5.10.3 UNSIGNED DIVISION BY A CONSTANT

To divide by a constant c, you could use the algorithm of Example 5.13, precalculating $s = (2^{32} - 1)/c$. However, there is an even more efficient method. The ADS1.2 compiler uses this method to synthesize divisions by a constant.

The idea is to use an approximation to d^{-1} that is sufficiently accurate so that multiplying by the approximation gives the exact value of n/d. We use the following mathematical results:[1]

$$\text{If } 2^{N+k} \le ds \le 2^{N+k} + 2^k, \text{ then } n/d = (ns) \gg (N + k) \text{ for } 0 \le n < 2^N. \quad (5.8)$$

$$\text{If } 2^{N+k} - 2^k \le ds < 2^{N+k}, \text{ then } n/d = (ns + s) \gg (N + k) \text{ for } 0 \le n < 2^N. \quad (5.9)$$

---

1. For the first result see a paper by Torbjorn Granlund and Peter L. Montgomery, "Division by Invariant Integers Using Multiplication," in *proceedings of the SIG-PLAN PLDI'94 Conference,* June 1994.

Since $n = (n/d)d + r$ for $0 \le r \le d - 1$, the results follow from the equations

$$ns - (n/d)2^{N+k} = ns - \frac{n-r}{d}2^{N+k} = n\frac{ds - 2^{N+k}}{d} + \frac{r2^{N+k}}{d} \qquad (5.10)$$

$$(n+1)s - (n/d)2^{N+k} = (n+1)\frac{ds}{d} - \frac{2^{N+k}}{d} + \frac{(r+1)2^{N+k}}{d} \qquad (5.11)$$

For both equations the right-hand side is in the range $0 \le x < 2^{N+k}$. For a 32-bit unsigned integer n, we take $N = 32$, choose k such that $2^k < d \le 2^{k+1}$, and set $s = (2^{N+k} + 2^k)/d$. If $ds \ge 2^{N+k}$, then $n/d = (ns) \gg (N + k)$; otherwise, $n/d = (ns + s) \gg (N + k)$. As an extra optimization, if d is a power of two, we can replace the division with a shift.

EXAMPLE
5.14 The `udiv_by_const` function tests the algorithm described above. In practice d will be a fixed constant rather than a variable. You can precalculate s and k in advance and only include the calculations relevant for your particular value of d.

```c
unsigned int udiv_by_const(unsigned int n, unsigned int d)
{
  unsigned int s,k,q;

  /* We assume d!=0 */

  /* first find k such that (1<<k) <= d < (1<<(k+1)) */
  for (k=0; d/2>=(1u<<k); k++);

  if (d==1u<<k)
  {
    /* we can implement the divide with a shift */
    return n>>k;
  }

  /* d is in the range (1<<k) < d < (1<<(k+1)) */
  s = (unsigned int)(((1ull<<(32+k))+(1ull<<k))/d);

  if ((unsigned long long)s*d >= (1ull<<(32+k)))
  {
      /* n/d = (n*s) >> (32+k) */
      q = (unsigned int)(((unsigned long long)n*s) >> 32);
      return q>>k;
  }

  /* n/d = (n*s+s) >> (32+k) */
```

```
q = (unsigned int)(((unsigned long long)n*s + s) >> 32);
return q >> k;
}
```

If you know that $0 \le n < 2^{31}$, as for a positive signed integer, then you don't need to bother with the different cases. You can increase k by one without having to worry about s overflowing. Take $N = 31$, choose k such that $2^{k-1} < d \le 2^k$, and set $s = (s^{N+k}+2^k-1)/d$. Then $n/d = (ns) \gg (N + k)$.

5.10.4 SIGNED DIVISION BY A CONSTANT

We can use ideas and algorithms similar to those in Section 5.10.3 to handle signed constants as well. If $d < 0$, then we can divide by $|d|$ and correct the sign later, so for now we assume that $d > 0$. The first mathematical result of Section 5.10.3 extends to signed n. If $d > 0$ and $2^{N+k} < ds \le 2^{N+k} + 2^k$, then

$$n/d = (ns) \gg (N + k) \text{ for all } 0 \le n < 2^N \qquad (5.12)$$

$$n/d = ((ns) \gg (N + k)) + 1 \text{ for all } -2^N \le n < 0 \qquad (5.13)$$

For 32-bit signed n, we take $N = 31$ and choose $k \le 31$ such that $2^{k-1} < d \le 2^k$. This ensures that we can find a 32-bit unsigned $s = (2^{N+k} + 2^k)/d$ satisfying the preceding relations. We need to take special care multiplying the 32-bit signed n with the 32-bit unsigned s. We achieve this using a signed long long type multiply with a correction if the top bit of s is set.

EXAMPLE
5.15
The following routine, sdiv_by_const, shows how to divide by a signed constant d. In practice you will precalculate k and s at compile time. Only the operations involving n for your particular value of d need be executed at run time.

```
int sdiv_by_const(int n, int d)
{
  int s,k,q;
  unsigned int D;

  /* set D to be the absolute value of d, we assume d!=0 */
  if (d>0)
  {
    D=(unsigned int)d;    /* 1 <= D <= 0x7FFFFFFF */
  }
  else
```

```
{
  D=(unsigned int) - d; /* 1 <= D <= 0x80000000 */
}

/* first find k such that (1<<k) <- D < (1<<(k+1)) */
for (k=0; D/2>=(1u<<k); k++);

if (D==1u<<k)
{
    /* we can implement the divide with a shift */
    q = n>>31;         /* 0 if n>0, -1 if n<0 */
    q = n + ((unsigned)q>>(32-k)); /* insert rounding */
    q = q>>k;          /* divide */
    if (d < 0)
    {
      q = -q;            /* correct sign */
    }
    return q;
}

/* Next find s in the range 0<=s<=0xFFFFFFFF */
/* Note that k here is one smaller than the k in the equation */
s = (int)(((1ull<<(31+(k+1)))+(1ull<<(k+1)))/D);

if (s>=0)
{
  q = (int)(((signed long long)n*s)>>32);
}
else
{
  /* (unsigned)s = (signed)s + (1<<32) */
  q = n + (int)(((signed long long)n*s)>>32);
}
q = q>>k;

/* if n<0 then the formula requires us to add one */
q += (unsigned)n>>31;

/* if d was negative we must correct the sign */
if (d<0)
{
  q = -q;
}
```

```
    return q;
}
```

Section 7.3 shows how to implement divides efficiently in assembler.

SUMMARY   **Division**

- ■ Avoid divisions as much as possible. Do not use them for circular buffer handling.

- ■ If you can't avoid a division, then try to take advantage of the fact that divide routines often generate the quotient n/d and modulus n%d together.

- ■ To repeatedly divide by the same denominator d, calculate $s = (2^k - 1)/d$ in advance. You can replace the divide of a k-bit unsigned integer by d with a $2k$-bit multiply by s.

- ■ To divide unsigned $n < 2^N$ by an unsigned constant d, you can find a 32-bit unsigned s and shift k such that n/d is either $(ns) \gg (N + k)$ or $(ns + s) \gg (N + k)$. The choice depends only on d. There is a similar result for signed divisions.

5.11 FLOATING POINT

The majority of ARM processor implementations do not provide hardware floating-point support, which saves on power and area when using ARM in a price-sensitive, embedded application. With the exceptions of the Floating Point Accelerator (FPA) used on the ARM7500FE and the Vector Floating Point accelerator (VFP) hardware, the C compiler must provide support for floating point in software.

In practice, this means that the C compiler converts every floating-point operation into a subroutine call. The C library contains subroutines to simulate floating-point behavior using integer arithmetic. This code is written in highly optimized assembly. Even so, floating-point algorithms will execute far more slowly than corresponding integer algorithms.

If you need fast execution and fractional values, you should use *fixed-point* or *block-floating* algorithms. Fractional values are most often used when processing digital signals such as audio and video. This is a large and important area of programming, so we have dedicated a whole chapter, Chapter 8, to the area of digital signal processing on the ARM. For best performance you need to code the algorithms in assembly (see the examples of Chapter 8).

5.12 INLINE FUNCTIONS AND INLINE ASSEMBLY

Section 5.5 looked at how to call functions efficiently. You can remove the function call overhead completely by inlining functions. Additionally many compilers allow you to include inline assembly in your C source code. Using inline functions that contain assembly you can get the compiler to support ARM instructions and optimizations that aren't usually available. For the examples of this section we will use the inline assembler in *armcc*.

Don't confuse the inline assembler with the main assembler *armasm* or *gas*. The inline assembler is part of the C compiler. The C compiler still performs register allocation, function entry, and exit. The compiler also attempts to optimize the inline assembly you write, or deoptimize it for debug mode. Although the compiler output will be functionally equivalent to your inline assembly, it may not be identical.

The main benefit of inline functions and inline assembly is to make accessible in C operations that are not usually available as part of the C language. It is better to use inline functions rather than #define macros because the latter doesn't check the types of the function arguments and return value.

Let's consider as an example the saturating multiply double accumulate primitive used by many speech processing algorithms. This operation calculates $a + 2xy$ for 16-bit signed operands x and y and 32-bit accumulator a. Additionally, all operations saturate to the nearest possible value if they exceed a 32-bit range. We say x and y are Q15 fixed-point integers because they represent the values $x2^{-15}$ and $y2^{-15}$, respectively. Similarly, a is a Q31 fixed-point integer because it represents the value $a2^{-31}$.

We can define this new operation using an inline function qmac:

```
__inline int qmac(int a, int x, int y)
{
  int i;

  i = x*y; /* this multiplication cannot saturate */
  if (i>=0)
  {
    /* x*y is positive */
    i = 2*i;
    if (i<0)
    {
      /* the doubling saturated */
      i = 0x7FFFFFFF;
    }
    if (a + i < a)
    {
      /* the addition saturated */
      return 0x7FFFFFFF;
    }
    return a + i;
  }
  /* x*y is negative so the doubling can't saturate */
```

```
    if (a + 2*i > a)
    {
        /* the accumulate saturated */
        return - 0x80000000;
    }
    return a + 2*i;
}
```

We can now use this new operation to calculate a saturating correlation. In other words, we calculate $a = 2x_0y_0 + \cdots 2x_{N-1}y_{N-1}$ with saturation.

```
int sat_correlate(short *x, short *y, unsigned int N)
{
  int a=0;

  do
  {
    a = qmac(a, *(x++), *(y++));
  } while (--N);
  return a;
}
```

The compiler replaces each qmac function call with inline code. In other words it inserts the code for qmac instead of calling qmac. Our C implementation of qmac isn't very efficient, requiring several if statements. We can write it much more efficiently using assembly. The inline assembler in the C compiler allows us to use assembly in our inline C function.

EXAMPLE 5.16   This example shows an efficient implementation of qmac using inline assembly. The example supports both *armcc* and *gcc* inline assembly formats, which are quite different. In the *gcc* format the "cc" informs the compiler that the instruction reads or writes the condition code flags. See the *armcc* or *gcc* manuals for further information.

```
__inline int qmac(int a, int x, int y)
{
  int i;
  const int mask = 0x80000000;

  i = x*y;
#ifdef __ARMCC_VERSION        /* check for the armcc compiler */
  __asm
  {
    ADDS i, i, i                /* double */
    EORVS i, mask, i, ASR 31 /* saturate the double */
```

```
        ADDS a, a, i                /* accumulate */
        EORVS a, mask, a, ASR 31 /* saturate the accumulate */
    }
#endif
#ifdef __GNUC__ /* check for the gcc compiler */
    asm("ADDS %0,%1,%2          ":"=r" (i):"r" (i)    ,"r" (i):"cc");
    asm("EORVS %0,%1,%2,ASR#31":"=r" (i):"r" (mask),"r" (i):"cc");
    asm("ADDS %0,%1,%2          ":"=r" (a):"r" (a)    ,"r" (i):"cc");
    asm("EORVS %0,%1,%2,ASR#31":"=r" (a):"r" (mask),"r" (a):"cc");
#endif

    return a;
}
```

This inlined code reduces the main loop of sat_correlate from 19 instructions to
9 instructions.

EXAMPLE   Now suppose that we are using an ARM9E processor with the ARMv5E extensions. We can
5.17   rewrite qmac again so that the compiler uses the new ARMv5E instructions:

```
__inline int qmac(int a, int x, int y)
{
    int i;

    __asm
    {
        SMULBB i, x, y /* multiply */
        QDADD a, a, i /* double + saturate + accumulate + saturate */
    }
    return a;
}
```

This time the main loop compiles to just six instructions:

```
sat_correlate_v3
            STR      r14,[r13,#-4]!    ; stack lr
            MOV      r12,#0            ; a = 0
sat_v3_loop
            LDRSH    r3,[r0],#2        ; r3 = *(x++)
            LDRSH    r14,[r1],#2       ; r14 = *(y++)
            SUBS     r2,r2,#1          ; N-- and set flags
```

```
SMULBB    r3,r3,r14    ; r3 = r3 * r14
QDADD     r12,r12,r3   ; a = sat(a+sat(2*r3))
BNE       sat_v3_loop  ; if (N!=0) goto loop
MOV       r0,r12       ; r0 = a
LDR       pc,[r13],#4  ; return r0
```

Other instructions that are not usually available from C include coprocessor instructions. Example 5.18 shows how to access these.

EXAMPLE   This example writes to coprocessor 15 to flush the instruction cache. You can use similar
5.18   code to access other coprocessor numbers.

```
void flush_Icache(void)
{
#ifdef __ARMCC_VERSION /* armcc */
  __asm {MCR p15, 0, 0, c7, c5, 0}
#endif
#ifdef __GNUC__ /* gcc */
  asm ( "MCR p15, 0, r0, c7, c5, 0" );
#endif
}
```

SUMMARY   **Inline Functions and Assembly**

- Use inline functions to declare new operations or primitives not supported by the C compiler.
- Use inline assembly to access ARM instructions not supported by the C compiler. Examples are coprocessor instructions or ARMv5E extensions.

5.13 PORTABILITY ISSUES

Here is a summary of the issues you may encounter when porting C code to the ARM.

- *The char type.* On the ARM, char is unsigned rather than signed as for many other processors. A common problem concerns loops that use a char loop counter i and the continuation condition $i \geq 0$, they become infinite loops. In this situation, *armcc* produces a warning of unsigned comparison with zero. You should either use a compiler option to make char signed or change loop counters to type int.

- *The int type.* Some older architectures use a 16-bit int, which may cause problems when moving to ARM's 32-bit int type although this is rare nowadays. Note that expressions are promoted to an int type before evaluation. Therefore if i = -0x1000, the expression i == 0xF000 is true on a 16-bit machine but false on a 32- bit machine.

- *Unaligned data pointers.* Some processors support the loading of short and int typed values from unaligned addresses. A C program may manipulate pointers directly so that they become unaligned, for example, by casting a char * to an int *. ARM architectures up to ARMv5TE do not support unaligned pointers. To detect them, run the program on an ARM with an alignment checking trap. For example, you can configure the ARM720T to data abort on an unaligned access.

- *Endian assumptions.* C code may make assumptions about the endianness of a memory system, for example, by casting a char * to an int *. If you configure the ARM for the same endianness the code is expecting, then there is no issue. Otherwise, you must remove endian-dependent code sequences and replace them by endian-independent ones. See Section 5.9 for more details.

- *Function prototyping.* The *armcc* compiler passes arguments narrow, that is, reduced to the range of the argument type. If functions are not prototyped correctly, then the function may return the wrong answer. Other compilers that pass arguments wide may give the correct answer even if the function prototype is incorrect. Always use ANSI prototypes.

- *Use of bit-fields.* The layout of bits within a bit-field is implementation and endian dependent. If C code assumes that bits are laid out in a certain order, then the code is not portable.

- *Use of enumerations.* Although enum is portable, different compilers allocate different numbers of bytes to an enum. The *gcc* compiler will always allocate four bytes to an enum type. The *armcc* compiler will only allocate one byte if the enum takes only eight-bit values. Therefore you can't cross-link code and libraries between different compilers if you use enums in an API structure.

- *Inline assembly.* Using inline assembly in C code reduces portability between architectures. You should separate any inline assembly into small inlined functions that can easily be replaced. It is also useful to supply reference, plain C implementations of these functions that can be used on other architectures, where this is possible.

- *The volatile keyword.* Use the volatile keyword on the type definitions of ARM memory-mapped peripheral locations. This keyword prevents the compiler from optimizing away the memory access. It also ensures that the compiler generates a data access of the correct type. For example, if you define a memory location as a volatile short type, then the compiler will access it using 16-bit load and store instructions LDRSH and STRH.

5.14 SUMMARY

By writing C routines in a certain style, you can help the C compiler to generate faster ARM code. Performance-critical applications often contain a few routines that dominate the performance profile; concentrate on rewriting these routines using the guidelines of this chapter.

Here are the key performance points we covered:

- Use the `signed` and `unsigned int` types for local variables, function arguments, and return values. This avoids casts and uses the ARM's native 32-bit data processing instructions efficiently.

- The most efficient form of loop is a `do-while` loop that counts down to zero.

- Unroll important loops to reduce the loop overhead.

- Do not rely on the compiler to optimize away repeated memory accesses. Pointer aliasing often prevents this.

- Try to limit functions to four arguments. Functions are faster to call if their arguments are held in registers.

- Lay structures out in increasing order of element size, especially when compiling for Thumb.

- Don't use bit-fields. Use masks and logical operations instead.

- Avoid divisions. Use multiplications by reciprocals instead.

- Avoid unaligned data. Use the `char *` pointer type if the data could be unaligned.

- Use the inline assembler in the C compiler to access instructions or optimizations that the C compiler does not support.

WRITING AND OPTIMIZING ARM ASSEMBLY CODE

Embedded software projects often contain a few key subroutines that dominate system performance. By optimizing these routines you can reduce the system power consumption and reduce the clock speed needed for real-time operation. Optimization can turn an infeasible system into a feasible one, or an uncompetitive system into a competitive one.

If you write your C code carefully using the rules given in Chapter 5, you will have a relatively efficient implementation. For maximum performance, you can optimize critical routines using hand-written assembly. Writing assembly by hand gives you direct control of three optimization tools that you cannot explicitly use by writing C source:

- *Instruction scheduling:* Reordering the instructions in a code sequence to avoid processor stalls. Since ARM implementations are pipelined, the timing of an instruction can be affected by neighboring instructions. We will look at this in Section 6.3.

- *Register allocation:* Deciding how variables should be allocated to ARM registers or stack locations for maximum performance. Our goal is to minimize the number of memory accesses. See Section 6.4.

- *Conditional execution:* Accessing the full range of ARM condition codes and conditional instructions. See Section 6.5.

It takes additional effort to optimize assembly routines so don't bother to optimize noncritical ones. When you take the time to optimize a routine, it has the side benefit of giving you a better understanding of the algorithm, its bottlenecks, and dataflow.

Section 6.1 starts with an introduction to assembly programming on the ARM. It shows you how to replace a C function by an assembly function that you can then optimize for performance.

We describe common optimization techniques, specific to writing ARM assembly. Thumb assembly is not covered specifically since ARM assembly will always give better performance when a 32-bit bus is available. Thumb is most useful for reducing the compiled size of C code that is not critical to performance and for efficient execution on a 16-bit data bus. Many of the principles covered here apply equally well to Thumb and ARM.

The best optimization of a routine can vary according to the ARM core used in your target hardware, especially for signal processing (covered in detail in Chapter 8). However, you can often code a routine that is reasonably efficient for all ARM implementations. To be consistent this chapter uses ARM9TDMI optimizations and cycle counts in the examples. However, the examples will run efficiently on all ARM cores from ARM7TDMI to ARM10E.

6.1   WRITING ASSEMBLY CODE

This section gives examples showing how to write basic assembly code. We assume you are familiar with the ARM instructions covered in Chapter 3; a complete instruction reference is available in Appendix A. We also assume that you are familiar with the ARM and Thumb procedure call standard covered in Section 5.4.

As with the rest of the book, this chapter uses the ARM macro assembler *armasm* for examples (see Section A.4 in Appendix A for *armasm* syntax and reference). You can also use the GNU assembler *gas* (see Section A.5 for details of the GNU assembler syntax).

EXAMPLE
6.1

This example shows how to convert a C function to an assembly function—usually the first stage of assembly optimization. Consider the simple C program main.c following that prints the squares of the integers from 0 to 9:

```
#include <stdio.h>

int square(int i);

int main(void)
{
  int i;

  for (i=0; i<10; i++)
  {
    printf("Square of %d is %d\n", i, square(i));
  }
}

int square(int i)
```

```
{
  return i*i;
}
```

Let's see how to replace `square` by an assembly function that performs the same action. Remove the C definition of `square`, but not the declaration (the second line) to produce a new C file `main1.c`. Next add an *armasm* assembler file `square.s` with the following contents:

```
        AREA    |.text|, CODE, READONLY

        EXPORT  square

        ; int square(int i)
square
        MUL    r1, r0, r0   ; r1 = r0 * r0
        MOV    r0, r1       ; r0 = r1
        MOV    pc, lr       ; return r0
        END
```

The AREA directive names the area or code section that the code lives in. If you use nonalphanumeric characters in a symbol or area name, then enclose the name in vertical bars. Many nonalphanumeric characters have special meanings otherwise. In the previous code we define a read-only code area called .text.

The EXPORT directive makes the symbol `square` available for external linking. At line six we define the symbol `square` as a code label. Note that *armasm* treats nonindented text as a label definition.

When `square` is called, the parameter passing is defined by the ATPCS (see Section 5.4). The input argument is passed in register *r0*, and the return value is returned in register *r0*. The multiply instruction has a restriction that the destination register must not be the same as the first argument register. Therefore we place the multiply result into *r1* and move this to *r0*.

The END directive marks the end of the assembly file. Comments follow a semicolon.

The following script illustrates how to build this example using command line tools.

```
armcc -c main1.c
armasm square.s
armlink -o main1.axf main1.o square.o
```

Example 6.1 only works if you are compiling your C as ARM code. If you compile your C as Thumb code, then the assembly routine must return using a BX instruction.

EXAMPLE **6.2**   When calling ARM code from C compiled as Thumb, the only change required to the assembly in Example 6.1 is to change the return instruction to a BX. BX will return to ARM or Thumb state according to bit 0 of *lr*. Therefore this routine can be called from ARM or Thumb. Use BX `lr` instead of MOV `pc,lr` whenever your processor supports BX (ARMv4T and above). Create a new assembly file `square2.s` as follows:

```
        AREA     |.text|, CODE, READONLY

        EXPORT   square

        ; int square(int i)
square
        MUL    r1, r0, r0   ; r1 = r0 * r0
        MOV    r0, r1       ; r0 = r1
        BX     lr           ; return r0

        END
```

With this example we build the C file using the Thumb C compiler *tcc*. We assemble the assembly file with the interworking flag enabled so that the linker will allow the Thumb C code to call the ARM assembly code. You can use the following commands to build this example:

```
tcc -c main1.c
armasm -apcs /interwork square2.s
armlink -o main2.axf main1.o square2.o
```

EXAMPLE
6.3
This example shows how to call a subroutine from an assembly routine. We will take Example 6.1 and convert the whole program (including `main`) into assembly. We will call the C library routine `printf` as a subroutine. Create a new assembly file `main3.s` with the following contents:

```
        AREA     |.text|, CODE, READONLY

        EXPORT   main

        IMPORT   |Lib$$Request$$armlib|, WEAK
        IMPORT   __main    ; C library entry
        IMPORT   printf    ; prints to stdout
i       RN 4

        ; int main(void)
main
        STMFD  sp!, {i, lr}
        MOV    i, #0
```

```
loop
        ADR     r0, print_string
        MOV     r1, i
        MUL     r2, i, i
        BL      printf
        ADD     i, i, #1
        CMP     i, #10
        BLT     loop
        LDMFD   sp!, {i, pc}


print_string
        DCB     "Square of %d is %d\n", 0


        END
```

We have used a new directive, IMPORT, to declare symbols that are defined in other files. The imported symbol Lib$$Request$$armlib makes a request that the linker links with the standard ARM C library. The WEAK specifier prevents the linker from giving an error if the symbol is not found at link time. If the symbol is not found, it will take the value zero. The second imported symbol __main is the start of the C library initialization code. You only need to import these symbols if you are defining your own main; a main defined in C code will import these automatically for you. Importing printf allows us to call that C library function.

The RN directive allows us to use names for registers. In this case we define *i* as an alternate name for register *r4*. Using register names makes the code more readable. It is also easier to change the allocation of variables to registers at a later date.

Recall that ATPCS states that a function must preserve registers *r4* to *r11* and *sp*. We corrupt *i*(*r4*), and calling printf will corrupt *lr*. Therefore we stack these two registers at the start of the function using an STMFD instruction. The LDMFD instruction pulls these registers from the stack and returns by writing the return address to *pc*.

The DCB directive defines byte data described as a string or a comma-separated list of bytes.

To build this example you can use the following command line script:

```
armasm main3.s
armlink -o main3.axf main3.o
```

Note that Example 6.3 also assumes that the code is called from ARM code. If the code can be called from Thumb code as in Example 6.2 then we must be capable of returning to Thumb code. For architectures before ARMv5 we must use a BX to return. Change the last instruction to the two instructions:

```
        LDMFD   sp!, {i, lr}
        BX      lr
```

Finally, let's look at an example where we pass more than four parameters. Recall that ATPCS places the first four arguments in registers *r0* to *r3*. Subsequent arguments are placed on the stack.

EXAMPLE
6.4

This example defines a function sumof that can sum any number of integers. The arguments are the number of integers to sum followed by a list of the integers. The sumof function is written in assembly and can accept any number of arguments. Put the C part of the example in a file main4.c:

```c
#include <stdio.h>

/* N is the number of values to sum in list ... */
int sumof(int N, ...);

int main(void)
{
    printf("Empty sum=%d\n", sumof(0));
    printf("1=%d\n", sumof(1,1));
    printf("1+2=%d\n", sumof(2,1,2));
    printf("1+2+3=%d\n", sumof(3,1,2,3));
    printf("1+2+3+4=%d\n", sumof(4,1,2,3,4));
    printf("1+2+3+4+5=%d\n", sumof(5,1,2,3,4,5));
    printf("1+2+3+4+5+6=%d\n", sumof(6,1,2,3,4,5,6));
}
```

Next define the sumof function in an assembly file sumof.s:

```
        AREA    |.text|, CODE, READONLY

        EXPORT  sumof

N       RN 0    ; number of elements to sum
sum     RN 1    ; current sum

        ; int sumof(int N, ...)
sumof
        SUBS    N, N, #1        ; do we have one element
        MOVLT   sum, #0         ; no elements to sum!
        SUBS    N, N, #1        ; do we have two elements
        ADDGE   sum, sum, r2
        SUBS    N, N, #1        ; do we have three elements
        ADDGE   sum, sum, r3
        MOV     r2, sp          ; top of stack
loop
        SUBS    N, N, #1        ; do we have another element
        LDMGEFD r2!, {r3}       ; load from the stack
```

```
        ADDGE   sum, sum, r3
        BGE     loop
        MOV     r0, sum
        MOV     pc, lr          ; return r0

        END
```

The code keeps count of the number of remaining values to sum, N. The first three values are in registers *r1, r2, r3*. The remaining values are on the stack. You can build this example using the commands

```
armcc -c main4.c
armasm sumof.s
armlink -o main4.axf main4.o sumof.o
```

6.2 PROFILING AND CYCLE COUNTING

The first stage of any optimization process is to identify the critical routines and measure their current performance. A *profiler* is a tool that measures the proportion of time or processing cycles spent in each subroutine. You use a profiler to identify the most critical routines. A *cycle counter* measures the number of cycles taken by a specific routine. You can measure your success by using a cycle counter to benchmark a given subroutine before and after an optimization.

The ARM simulator used by the ADS1.1 debugger is called the ARMulator and provides profiling and cycle counting features. The ARMulator profiler works by sampling the program counter *pc* at regular intervals. The profiler identifies the function the *pc* points to and updates a hit counter for each function it encounters. Another approach is to use the trace output of a simulator as a source for analysis.

Be sure that you know how the profiler you are using works and the limits of its accuracy. A *pc*-sampled profiler can produce meaningless results if it records too few samples. You can even implement your own *pc*-sampled profiler in a hardware system using timer interrupts to collect the *pc* data points. Note that the timing interrupts will slow down the system you are trying to measure!

ARM implementations do not normally contain cycle-counting hardware, so to easily measure cycle counts you should use an ARM debugger with ARM simulator. You can configure the ARMulator to simulate a range of different ARM cores and obtain cycle count benchmarks for a number of platforms.

6.3 INSTRUCTION SCHEDULING

The time taken to execute instructions depends on the implementation pipeline. For this chapter, we assume ARM9TDMI pipeline timings. You can find these in Section D.3 of

Appendix D. The following rules summarize the cycle timings for common instruction classes on the ARM9TDMI.

Instructions that are conditional on the value of the ARM condition codes in the *cpsr* take one cycle if the condition is not met. If the condition is met, then the following rules apply:

- ALU operations such as addition, subtraction, and logical operations take one cycle. This includes a shift by an immediate value. If you use a register-specified shift, then add one cycle. If the instruction writes to the *pc*, then add two cycles.

- Load instructions that load *N* 32-bit words of memory such as LDR and LDM take *N* cycles to issue, but the result of the last word loaded is not available on the following cycle. The updated load address is available on the next cycle. This assumes zero-wait-state memory for an uncached system, or a cache hit for a cached system. An LDM of a single value is exceptional, taking two cycles. If the instruction loads *pc*, then add two cycles.

- Load instructions that load 16-bit or 8-bit data such as LDRB, LDRSB, LDRH, and LDRSH take one cycle to issue. The load result is not available on the following two cycles. The updated load address is available on the next cycle. This assumes zero-wait-state memory for an uncached system, or a cache hit for a cached system.

- Branch instructions take three cycles.

- Store instructions that store *N* values take *N* cycles. This assumes zero-wait-state memory for an uncached system, or a cache hit or a write buffer with *N* free entries for a cached system. An STM of a single value is exceptional, taking two cycles.

- Multiply instructions take a varying number of cycles depending on the value of the second operand in the product (see Table D.6 in Section D.3).

To understand how to schedule code efficiently on the ARM, we need to understand the ARM pipeline and dependencies. The ARM9TDMI processor performs five operations in parallel:

- *Fetch:* Fetch from memory the instruction at address *pc*. The instruction is loaded into the core and then processes down the core pipeline.

- *Decode:* Decode the instruction that was fetched in the previous cycle. The processor also reads the input operands from the register bank if they are not available via one of the forwarding paths.

- *ALU:* Executes the instruction that was decoded in the previous cycle. Note this instruction was originally fetched from address $pc - 8$ (ARM state) or $pc - 4$ (Thumb state). Normally this involves calculating the answer for a data processing operation, or the address for a load, store, or branch operation. Some instructions may spend several cycles in this stage. For example, multiply and register-controlled shift operations take several ALU cycles.

Instruction address	pc	$pc-4$	$pc-8$	$pc-12$	$pc-16$
Action	Fetch	Decode	ALU	LS1	LS2

Figure 6.1   ARM9TDMI pipeline executing in ARM state.

- *LS1:* Load or store the data specified by a load or store instruction. If the instruction is not a load or store, then this stage has no effect.

- *LS2:* Extract and zero- or sign-extend the data loaded by a byte or halfword load instruction. If the instruction is not a load of an 8-bit byte or 16-bit halfword item, then this stage has no effect.

Figure 6.1 shows a simplified functional view of the five-stage ARM9TDMI pipeline. Note that multiply and register shift operations are not shown in the figure.

After an instruction has completed the five stages of the pipeline, the core writes the result to the register file. Note that pc points to the address of the instruction being fetched. The ALU is executing the instruction that was originally fetched from address $pc - 8$ in parallel with fetching the instruction at address pc.

How does the pipeline affect the timing of instructions? Consider the following examples. These examples show how the cycle timings change because an earlier instruction must complete a stage before the current instruction can progress down the pipeline. To work out how many cycles a block of code will take, use the tables in Appendix D that summarize the cycle timings and interlock cycles for a range of ARM cores.

If an instruction requires the result of a previous instruction that is not available, then the processor stalls. This is called a pipeline *hazard* or pipeline *interlock*.

EXAMPLE
6.5

This example shows the case where there is no interlock.

```
ADD    r0, r0, r1
ADD    r0, r0, r2
```

This instruction pair takes two cycles. The ALU calculates $r0 + r1$ in one cycle. Therefore this result is available for the ALU to calculate $r0 + r2$ in the second cycle.

EXAMPLE
6.6

This example shows a one-cycle interlock caused by load use.

```
LDR    r1, [r2, #4]
ADD    r0, r0, r1
```

This instruction pair takes three cycles. The ALU calculates the address $r2 + 4$ in the first cycle while decoding the ADD instruction in parallel. However, the ADD cannot proceed on

Pipeline	Fetch	Decode	ALU	LS1	LS2
Cycle 1	...	ADD	LDR	...	
Cycle 2		...	*ADD*	LDR	...
Cycle 3		...	ADD	—	LDR

Figure 6.2   One-cycle interlock caused by load use.

the second cycle because the load instruction has not yet loaded the value of *r1*. Therefore the pipeline stalls for one cycle while the load instruction completes the LS1 stage. Now that *r1* is ready, the processor executes the ADD in the ALU on the third cycle.

Figure 6.2 illustrates how this interlock affects the pipeline. The processor stalls the ADD instruction for one cycle in the ALU stage of the pipeline while the load instruction completes the LS1 stage. We've denoted this stall by an italic ADD. Since the LDR instruction proceeds down the pipeline, but the ADD instruction is stalled, a gap opens up between them. This gap is sometimes called a pipeline *bubble*. We've marked the bubble with a dash.

EXAMPLE
6.7

This example shows a one-cycle interlock caused by delayed load use.

```
LDRB    r1, [r2, #1]
ADD     r0, r0, r2
EOR     r0, r0, r1
```

This instruction triplet takes four cycles. Although the ADD proceeds on the cycle following the load byte, the EOR instruction cannot start on the third cycle. The *r1* value is not ready until the load instruction completes the LS2 stage of the pipeline. The processor stalls the EOR instruction for one cycle.

Note that the ADD instruction does not affect the timing at all. The sequence takes four cycles whether it is there or not! Figure 6.3 shows how this sequence progresses through the processor pipeline. The ADD doesn't cause any stalls since the ADD does not use *r1*, the result of the load.

Pipeline	Fetch	Decode	ALU	LS1	LS2
Cycle 1	EOR	ADD	LDRB	...	
Cycle 2	...	EOR	ADD	LDRB	...
Cycle 3		...	*EOR*	ADD	LDRB
Cycle 4		...	EOR	—	ADD

Figure 6.3   One-cycle interlock caused by delayed load use.

Pipeline	Fetch	Decode	ALU	LS1	LS2
Cycle 1	AND	B	MOV	...	
Cycle 2	EOR	AND	B	MOV	...
Cycle 3	SUB	—	—	B	MOV
Cycle 4	...	SUB	—	—	B
Cycle 5		...	SUB	—	—

Figure 6.4   Pipeline flush caused by a branch.

EXAMPLE This example shows why a branch instruction takes three cycles. The processor must flush
6.8 the pipeline when jumping to a new address.

```
        MOV    r1, #1
        B      case1
        AND    r0, r0, r1
        EOR    r2, r2, r3
        ...
case1
        SUB    r0, r0, r1
```

The three executed instructions take a total of five cycles. The MOV instruction executes on the first cycle. On the second cycle, the branch instruction calculates the destination address. This causes the core to flush the pipeline and refill it using this new *pc* value. The refill takes two cycles. Finally, the SUB instruction executes normally. Figure 6.4 illustrates the pipeline state on each cycle. The pipeline drops the two instructions following the branch when the branch takes place.

6.3.1 SCHEDULING OF LOAD INSTRUCTIONS

Load instructions occur frequently in compiled code, accounting for approximately one-third of all instructions. Careful scheduling of load instructions so that pipeline stalls don't occur can improve performance. The compiler attempts to schedule the code as best it can, but the aliasing problems of C that we looked at in Section 5.6 limits the available optimizations. The compiler cannot move a load instruction before a store instruction unless it is certain that the two pointers used do not point to the same address.

Let's consider an example of a memory-intensive task. The following function, str_tolower, copies a zero-terminated string of characters from in to out. It converts the string to lowercase in the process.

```
void str_tolower(char *out, char *in)
{
  unsigned int c;

  do
  {
    c = *(in++);
    if (c>='A' && c<='Z')
    {
      c = c + ('a' -'A');
    }
    *(out++) = (char)c;
  } while (c);
}
```

The ADS1.1 compiler generates the following compiled output. Notice that the compiler optimizes the condition (c>='A' && c<='Z') to the check that 0<=c-'A'<='Z'-'A'. The compiler can perform this check using a single unsigned comparison.

```
str_tolower
        LDRB    r2,[r1],#1    ; c = *(in++)
        SUB     r3,r2,#0x41   ; r3 = c -'A'
        CMP     r3,#0x19      ; if (c <='Z'-'A')
        ADDLS   r2,r2,#0x20   ;    c +='a'-'A'
        STRB    r2,[r0],#1    ; *(out++) = (char)c
        CMP     r2,#0         ; if (c!=0)
        BNE     str_tolower   ;    goto str_tolower
        MOV     pc,r14        ; return
```

Unfortunately, the SUB instruction uses the value of c directly after the LDRB instruction that loads c. Consequently, the ARM9TDMI pipeline will stall for two cycles. The compiler can't do any better since everything following the load of c depends on its value. However, there are two ways you can alter the structure of the algorithm to avoid the cycles by using assembly. We call these methods load scheduling by *preloading* and *unrolling*.

6.3.1.1 Load Scheduling by Preloading

In this method of load scheduling, we load the data required for the loop at the end of the previous loop, rather than at the beginning of the current loop. To get performance improvement with little increase in code size, we don't unroll the loop.

EXAMPLE
6.9

This assembly applies the preload method to the str_tolower function.

```
out     RN 0    ; pointer to output string
in      RN 1    ; pointer to input string
```

```
c          RN 2    ; character loaded
t          RN 3    ; scratch register
           ; void str_tolower_preload(char *out, char *in)
str_tolower_preload
           LDRB    c, [in], #1      ; c = *(in++)
loop
           SUB     t, c, #'A'       ; t = c-'A'
           CMP     t, #'Z'-'A'      ; if (t <= 'Z'-'A')
           ADDLS   c, c, #'a'-'A'   ;   c += 'a'-'A';
           STRB    c, [out], #1     ; *(out++) = (char)c;
           TEQ     c, #0            ; test if c==0
           LDRNEB  c, [in], #1      ; if (c!=0) { c=*in++;
           BNE     loop             ;             goto loop; }
           MOV     pc, lr           ; return
```

The scheduled version is one instruction longer than the C version, but we save two cycles for each inner loop iteration. This reduces the loop from 11 cycles per character to 9 cycles per character on an ARM9TDMI, giving a 1.22 times speed improvement.

The ARM architecture is particularly well suited to this type of preloading because instructions can be executed conditionally. Since loop i is loading the data for loop $i + 1$ there is always a problem with the first and last loops. For the first loop, we can preload data by inserting extra load instructions before the loop starts. For the last loop it is essential that the loop does not read any data, or it will read beyond the end of the array. This could cause a data abort! With ARM, we can easily solve this problem by making the load instruction conditional. In Example 6.9, the preload of the next character only takes place if the loop will iterate once more. No byte load occurs on the last loop.

6.3.1.2   Load Scheduling by Unrolling

This method of load scheduling works by unrolling and then interleaving the body of the loop. For example, we can perform loop iterations $i, i + 1, i + 2$ interleaved. When the result of an operation from loop i is not ready, we can perform an operation from loop $i + 1$ that avoids waiting for the loop i result.

EXAMPLE 6.10   The assembly applies load scheduling by unrolling to the str_tolower function.

```
out    RN 0    ; pointer to output string
in     RN 1    ; pointer to input string
ca0    RN 2    ; character 0
t      RN 3    ; scratch register
```

```
ca1      RN 12   ; character 1
ca2      RN 14   ; character 2
         ; void str_tolower_unrolled(char *out, char *in)
str_tolower_unrolled
         STMFD   sp!, {lr}          ; function entry
loop_next3
         LDRB    ca0, [in], #1      ; ca0 = *in++;
         LDRB    ca1, [in], #1      ; ca1 = *in++;
         LDRB    ca2, [in], #1      ; ca2 = *in++;
         SUB     t, ca0, #'A'       ; convert ca0 to lower case
         CMP     t, #'Z'-'A'
         ADDLS   ca0, ca0, #'a'-'A'
         SUB     t, ca1, #'A'       ; convert ca1 to lower case
         CMP     t, #'Z'-'A'
         ADDLS   ca1, ca1, #'a'-'A'
         SUB     t, ca2, #'A'       ; convert ca2 to lower case
         CMP     t, #'Z'-'A'
         ADDLS   ca2, ca2, #'a'-'A'
         STRB    ca0, [out], #1     ; *out++ = ca0;
         TEQ     ca0, #0            ; if (ca0!=0)
         STRNEB  ca1, [out], #1     ;    *out++ = ca1;
         TEQNE   ca1, #0            ; if (ca0!=0 && ca1!=0)
         STRNEB  ca2, [out], #1     ;    *out++ = ca2;
         TEQNE   ca2, #0            ; if (ca0!=0 && ca1!=0 && ca2!=0)
         BNE     loop_next3         ;    goto loop_next3;
         LDMFD   sp!, {pc}          ; return;
```

This loop is the most efficient implementation we've looked at so far. The implementation requires seven cycles per character on ARM9TDMI. This gives a 1.57 times speed increase over the original str_tolower. Again it is the conditional nature of the ARM instructions that makes this possible. We use conditional instructions to avoid storing characters that are past the end of the string.

However, the improvement in Example 6.10 does have some costs. The routine is more than double the code size of the original implementation. We have assumed that you can read up to two characters beyond the end of the input string, which may not be true if the string is right at the end of available RAM, where reading off the end will cause a data abort. Also, performance can be slower for very short strings because (1) stacking *lr* causes additional function call overhead and (2) the routine may process up to two characters pointlessly, before discovering that they lie beyond the end of the string.

You should use this form of scheduling by unrolling for time-critical parts of an application where you know the data size is large. If you also know the size of the data at compile time, you can remove the problem of reading beyond the end of the array.

SUMMARY   **Instruction Scheduling**

- ARM cores have a pipeline architecture. The pipeline may delay the results of certain instructions for several cycles. If you use these results as source operands in a following instruction, the processor will insert stall cycles until the value is ready.

- Load and multiply instructions have delayed results in many implementations. See Appendix D for the cycle timings and delay for your specific ARM processor core.

- You have two software methods available to remove interlocks following load instructions: You can preload so that loop i loads the data for loop $i + 1$, or you can unroll the loop and interleave the code for loops i and $i + 1$.

6.4 REGISTER ALLOCATION

You can use 14 of the 16 visible ARM registers to hold general-purpose data. The other two registers are the stack pointer *r13* and the program counter *r15*. For a function to be ATPCS compliant it must preserve the callee values of registers *r4* to *r11*. ATPCS also specifies that the stack should be eight-byte aligned; therefore you must preserve this alignment if calling subroutines. Use the following template for optimized assembly routines requiring many registers:

```
routine_name
        STMFD   sp!,        {r4-r12, lr}      ; stack saved registers
          ; body of routine
          ; the fourteen registers r0-r12 and lr are available
        LDMFD   sp!,        {r4-r12, pc}      ; restore registers and return
```

Our only purpose in stacking *r12* is to keep the stack eight-byte aligned. You need not stack *r12* if your routine doesn't call other ATPCS routines. For ARMv5 and above you can use the preceding template even when being called from Thumb code. If your routine may be called from Thumb code on an ARMv4T processor, then modify the template as follows:

```
routine_name
        STMFD   sp!,        {r4-r12, lr}      ; stack saved registers
          ; body of routine
          ; registers r0-r12 and lr available
        LDMFD   sp!,        {r4-r12, lr}      ; restore registers
        BX          lr                        ; return, with mode switch
```

In this section we look at how best to allocate variables to register numbers for register-intensive tasks, how to use more than 14 local variables, and how to make the best use of the 14 available registers.

6.4.1 ALLOCATING VARIABLES TO REGISTER NUMBERS

When you write an assembly routine, it is best to start by using names for the variables, rather than explicit register numbers. This allows you to change the allocation of variables to register numbers easily. You can even use different register names for the same physical register number when their use doesn't overlap. Register names increase the clarity and readability of optimized code.

For the most part ARM operations are orthogonal with respect to register number. In other words, specific register numbers do not have specific roles. If you swap all occurrences of two registers *Ra* and *Rb* in a routine, the function of the routine does not change. However, there are several cases where the physical number of the register is important:

- *Argument registers.* The ATPCS convention defines that the first four arguments to a function are placed in registers *r0* to *r3*. Further arguments are placed on the stack. The return value must be placed in *r0*.

- *Registers used in a load or store multiple.* Load and store multiple instructions LDM and STM operate on a list of registers in order of ascending register number. If *r0* and *r1* appear in the register list, then the processor will always load or store *r0* using a lower address than *r1* and so on.

- *Load and store double word.* The LDRD and STRD instructions introduced in ARMv5E operate on a pair of registers with sequential register numbers, *Rd* and *Rd* + 1. Furthermore, *Rd* must be an even register number.

For an example of how to allocate registers when writing assembly, suppose we want to shift an array of *N* bits upwards in memory by *k* bits. For simplicity assume that *N* is large and a multiple of 256. Also assume that $0 \leq k < 32$ and that the input and output pointers are word aligned. This type of operation is common in dealing with the arithmetic of multiple precision numbers where we want to multiply by 2^k. It is also useful to block copy from one bit or byte alignment to a different bit or byte alignment. For example, the C library function memcpy can use the routine to copy an array of bytes using only word accesses.

The C routine shift_bits implements the simple *k* bit shift of *N* bits of data. It returns the *k* bits remaining following the shift.

```
unsigned int shift_bits(unsigned int *out, unsigned int *in,
                        unsigned int N, unsigned int k)
{
  unsigned int carry=0, x;

  do
  {
    x = *in++;
    *out++ = (x << k) | carry;
```

```
    carry = x >> (32-k);
    N -= 32;
  } while (N);

  return carry;
}
```

The obvious way to improve efficiency is to unroll the loop to process eight words of 256 bits at a time so that we can use load and store multiple operations to load and store eight words at a time for maximum efficiency. Before thinking about register numbers, we write the following assembly code:

```
shift_bits
        STMFD    sp!, {r4-r11, lr}          ; save registers
        RSB      kr, k, #32                 ; kr = 32-k;
        MOV      carry, #0
loop
        LDMIA    in!, {x_0-x_7}             ; load 8 words
        ORR      y_0, carry, x_0, LSL k     ; shift the 8 words
        MOV      carry, x_0, LSR kr
        ORR      y_1, carry, x_1, LSL k
        MOV      carry, x_1, LSR kr
        ORR      y_2, carry, x_2, LSL k
        MOV      carry, x_2, LSR kr
        ORR      y_3, carry, x_3, LSL k
        MOV      carry, x_3, LSR kr
        ORR      y_4, carry, x_4, LSL k
        MOV      carry, x_4, LSR kr
        ORR      y_5, carry, x_5, LSL k
        MOV      carry, x_5, LSR kr
        ORR      y_6, carry, x_6, LSL k
        MOV      carry, x_6, LSR kr
        ORR      y_7, carry, x_7, LSL k
        MOV      carry, x_7, LSR kr
        STMIA    out!, {y_0-y_7}            ; store 8 words
        SUBS     N, N, #256                 ; N -= (8 words * 32 bits)
        BNE      loop                       ; if (N!=0) goto loop;
        MOV      r0, carry                  ; return carry;
        LDMFD    sp!, {r4-r11, pc}
```

Now to the register allocation. So that the input arguments do not have to move registers, we can immediately assign

```
out    RN 0
in     RN 1
```

```
N       RN 2
k       RN 3
```

For the load multiple to work correctly, we must assign x_0 through x_7 to sequentially increasing register numbers, and similarly for y_0 through y_7. Notice that we finish with x_0 before starting with y_1. In general, we can assign x_n to the same register as y_{n+1}. Therefore, assign

```
x_0     RN 5
x_1     RN 6
x_2     RN 7
x_3     RN 8
x_4     RN 9
x_5     RN 10
x_6     RN 11
x_7     RN 12
y_0     RN 4
y_1     RN x_0
y_2     RN x_1
y_3     RN x_2
y_4     RN x_3
y_5     RN x_4
y_6     RN x_5
y_7     RN x_6
```

We are nearly finished, but there is a problem. There are two remaining variables *carry* and *kr*, but only one remaining free register *lr*. There are several possible ways we can proceed when we run out of registers:

- Reduce the number of registers we require by performing fewer operations in each loop. In this case we could load four words in each load multiple rather than eight.

- Use the stack to store the least-used values to free up more registers. In this case we could store the loop counter N on the stack. (See Section 6.4.2 for more details on swapping registers to the stack.)

- Alter the code implementation to free up more registers. This is the solution we consider in the following text. (For more examples, see Section 6.4.3.)

We often iterate the process of implementation followed by register allocation several times until the algorithm fits into the 14 available registers. In this case we notice that the carry value need not stay in the same register at all! We can start off with the carry value in y_0 and then move it to y_1 when x_0 is no longer required, and so on. We complete the routine by allocating *kr* to *lr* and recoding so that carry is not required.

EXAMPLE
6.11

This assembly shows our final `shift_bits` routine. It uses all 14 available ARM registers.

```
kr   RN lr

shift_bits
              STMFD   sp!, {r4-r11, lr}      ; save registers
              RSB     kr, k, #32             ; kr = 32-k;
              MOV     y_0, #0                ; initial carry
loop
              LDMIA   in!, {x_0-x_7}         ; load 8 words
              ORR     y_0, y_0, x_0, LSL k   ; shift the 8 words
              MOV     y_1, x_0, LSR kr       ; recall x_0 = y_1
              ORR     y_1, y_1, x_1, LSL k
              MOV     y_2, x_1, LSR kr
              ORR     y_2, y_2, x_2, LSL k
              MOV     y_3, x_2, LSR kr
              ORR     y_3, y_3, x_3, LSL k
              MOV     y_4, x_3, LSR kr
              ORR     y_4, y_4, x_4, LSL k
              MOV     y_5, x_4, LSR kr
              ORR     y_5, y_5, x_5, LSL k
              MOV     y_6, x_5, LSR kr
              ORR     y_6, y_6, x_6, LSL k
              MOV     y_7, x_6, LSR kr
              ORR     y_7, y_7, x_7, LSL k
              STMIA   out!, {y_0-y_7}        ; store 8 words
              MOV     y_0, x_7, LSR kr
              SUBS    N, N, #256             ; N -= (8 words * 32 bits)
              BNE     loop                   ; if (N!=0) goto loop;
              MOV     r0, y_0                ; return carry;
              LDMFD   sp!, {r4-r11, pc}
```

6.4.2 USING MORE THAN 14 LOCAL VARIABLES

If you need more than 14 local 32-bit variables in a routine, then you must store some variables on the stack. The standard procedure is to work outwards from the innermost loop of the algorithm, since the innermost loop has the greatest performance impact.

EXAMPLE
6.12

This example shows three nested loops, each loop requiring state information inherited from the loop surrounding it. (See Section 6.6 for further ideas and examples of looping constructs.)

```
nested_loops
        STMFD   sp!, {r4-r11, lr}
        ; set up loop 1
loop1
        STMFD   sp!, {loop1 registers}
        ; set up loop 2
loop2
        STMFD   sp!, {loop2 registers}
        ; set up loop 3
loop3
        ; body of loop 3
        B{cond} loop3
        LDMFD   sp!, {loop2 registers}
        ; body of loop 2
        B{cond} loop2
        LDMFD   sp!, {loop1 registers}
        ; body of loop 1
        B{cond} loop1
        LDMFD   sp!, {r4-r11, pc}
```

You may find that there are insufficient registers for the innermost loop even using the construction in Example 6.12. Then you need to swap inner loop variables out to the stack. Since assembly code is very hard to maintain and debug if you use numbers as stack address offsets, the assembler provides an automated procedure for allocating variables to the stack.

EXAMPLE 6.13 This example shows how you can use the ARM assembler directives MAP (alias ^) and FIELD (alias #) to define and allocate space for variables and arrays on the processor stack. The directives perform a similar function to the struct operator in C.

```
            MAP     0       ; map symbols to offsets starting at offset 0
a           FIELD   4       ; a is 4 byte integer (at offset 0)
b           FIELD   2       ; b is 2 byte integer (at offset 4)
c           FIELD   2       ; c is 2 byte integer (at offset 6)
d           FIELD   64      ; d is an array of 64 characters (at offset 8)
length      FIELD   0       ; length records the current offset reached

example
            STMFD   sp!, {r4-r11, lr}  ; save callee registers
            SUB     sp, sp, #length    ; create stack frame
            ; ...
            STR     r0, [sp, #a]       ; a = r0;
            LDRSH   r1, [sp, #b]       ; r1 = b;
```

```
ADD     r2, sp, #d          ; r2 = &d[0]
; ...
ADD     sp, sp, #length     ; restore the stack pointer
LDMFD   sp!, {r4-r11, pc}   ; return
```

6.4.3 MAKING THE MOST OF AVAILABLE REGISTERS

On a load-store architecture such as the ARM, it is more efficient to access values held in registers than values held in memory. There are several tricks you can use to fit several sub-32-bit length variables into a single 32-bit register and thus can reduce code size and increase performance. This section presents three examples showing how you can pack multiple variables into a single ARM register.

EXAMPLE
6.14

Suppose we want to step through an array by a programmable increment. A common example is to step through a sound sample at various rates to produce different pitched notes. We can express this in C code as

```
sample = table[index];
index += increment;
```

Commonly index and increment are small enough to be held as 16-bit values. We can pack these two variables into a single 32-bit variable indinc:

$$indinc = (index \ll 16) + increment = \begin{array}{|c|c|}\hline \text{Bit } 31 \quad\quad 16 & 15 \quad\quad\quad\quad 0 \\\hline index & increment \\\hline\end{array}$$

The C code translates into assembly code using a single register to hold indinc:

```
LDRB    sample, [table, indinc, LSR#16]  ; table[index]
ADD     indinc, indinc, indinc, LSL#16   ; index+=increment
```

Note that if index and increment are 16-bit values, then putting index in the top 16 bits of indinc correctly implements 16-bit-wrap-around. In other words, index = (short)(index + increment). This can be useful if you are using a buffer where you want to wrap from the end back to the beginning (often known as a *circular buffer*).

EXAMPLE
6.15

When you shift by a register amount, the ARM uses bits 0 to 7 as the shift amount. The ARM ignores bits 8 to 31 of the register. Therefore you can use bits 8 to 31 to hold a second variable distinct from the shift amount.

This example shows how to combine a register-specified shift `shift` and loop counter `count` to shift an array of 40 entries right by `shift` bits. We define a new variable `cntshf` that combines `count` and `shift`:

```
                            Bit  31                    8 7            0
cntshf = (count<<8) + shift =  [        count          |    shift    ]
```

```
out     RN 0  ; address of the output array
in      RN 1  ; address of the input array
cntshf  RN 2  ; count and shift right amount
x       RN 3  ; scratch variable
        ; void shift_right(int *out, int *in, unsigned shift);
shift_right
        ADD   cntshf, cntshf, #39<<8  ; count = 39
shift_loop
        LDR   x, [in], #4
        SUBS  cntshf, cntshf, #1<<8   ; decrement count
        MOV   x, x, ASR cntshf        ; shift by shift
        STR   x, [out], #4
        BGE   shift_loop              ; continue if count>=0
        MOV   pc, lr
```

EXAMPLE If you are dealing with arrays of 8-bit or 16-bit values, it is sometimes possible to manipulate
6.16   multiple values at a time by packing several values into a single 32-bit register. This is called *single issue multiple data* (SIMD) processing.

ARM architecture versions up to ARMv5 do not support SIMD operations explicitly. However, there are still areas where you can achieve SIMD type compactness. Section 6.6 shows how you can store multiple loop values in a single register. Here we look at a graphics example of how to process multiple 8-bit pixels in an image using normal ADD and MUL instructions to achieve some SIMD operations.

Suppose we want to merge two images X and Y to produce a new image Z. Let x_n, y_n, and z_n denote the nth 8-bit pixel in these images, respectively. Let $0 \leq a \leq 256$ be a scaling factor. To merge the images, we set

$$z_n = (ax_n + (256 - a)y_n)/256 \qquad (6.1)$$

In other words image Z is image X scaled in intensity by $a/256$ added to image Y scaled by $1 - (a/256)$. Note that

$$z_n = w_n/256, \quad \text{where } w_n = a(x_n - y_n) + 256y_n \qquad (6.2)$$

Therefore each pixel requires a subtract, a multiply, a shifted add, and a right shift. To process multiple pixels at a time, we load four pixels at once using a

word load. We use a bracketed notation to denote several values packed into the
same word:

$$[x3, x2, x1, x0] = x_3 2^{24} + x_2 2^{16} + x_1 2^8 + x_0 =$$

Bit	24	16	8	0
	x_3	x_2	x_1	x_0

We then unpack the 8-bit data and promote it to 16-bit data using an AND with a mask
register. We use the notation

$$[x2, x0] = x_2 2^{16} + x_0 =$$

Bit	31	16	15	0
	x_2		x_0	

Note that even for signed values $[a, b] + [c, d] = [a + b, c + d]$ if we interpret $[a, b]$ using
the mathematical equation $a2^{16} + b$. Therefore we can perform SIMD operations on these
values using normal arithmetic instructions.

The following code shows how you can process four pixels at a time using only two
multiplies. The code assumes a 176×144 sized quarter CIF image.

```
IMAGE_WIDTH        EQU 176      ; QCIF width
IMAGE_HEIGHT       EQU 144      ; QCIF height

pz      RN 0    ; pointer to destination image (word aligned)
px      RN 1    ; pointer to first source image (word aligned)
py      RN 2    ; pointer to second source image (word aligned)
a       RN 3    ; 8-bit scaling factor (0-256)

xx      RN 4    ; holds four x pixels [x3, x2, x1, x0]
yy      RN 5    ; holds four y pixels [y3, y2, y1, y0]
x       RN 6    ; holds two expanded x pixels [x2, x0]
y       RN 7    ; holds two expanded y pixels [y2, y0]
z       RN 8    ; holds four z pixels [z3, z2, z1, z0]
count   RN 12   ; number of pixels remaining
mask    RN 14   ; constant mask with value 0x00ff00ff

        ; void merge_images(char *pz, char *px, char *py, int a)
merge_images
        STMFD   sp!, {r4-r8, lr}
        MOV     count, #IMAGE_WIDTH*IMAGE_HEIGHT
        LDR     mask, =0x00FF00FF    ; [    0, 0xFF,    0, 0xFF ]
  merge_loop
        LDR     xx, [px], #4         ; [   x3,   x2,   x1,   x0 ]
        LDR     yy, [py], #4         ; [   y3,   y2,   y1,   y0 ]
        AND     x, mask, xx          ; [    0,   x2,    0,   x0 ]
        AND     y, mask, yy          ; [    0,   y2,    0,   y0 ]
        SUB     x, x, y              ; [  (x2-y2),     (x0-y0)  ]
```

```
MUL    x, a, x               ; [  a*(x2-y2),    a*(x0-y0)  ]
ADD    x, x, y, LSL#8        ; [        w2,          w0  ]
AND    z, mask, x, LSR#8     ; [  0,    z2,    0,    z0  ]
AND    x, mask, xx, LSR#8    ; [  0,    x3,    0,    x1  ]
AND    y, mask, yy, LSR#8    ; [  0,    y3,    0,    y1  ]
SUB    x, x, y               ; [   (x3-y3),     (x1-y1)  ]
MUL    x, a, x               ; [  a*(x3-y3),   a*(x1-y1)  ]
ADD    x, x, y, LSL#8        ; [        w3,          w1  ]
AND    x, mask, x, LSR#8     ; [  0,    z3,    0,    z1  ]
ORR    z, z, x, LSL#8        ; [  z3,   z2,    z1,   z0  ]
STR    z, [pz], #4           ; store four z pixels
SUBS   count, count, #4
BGT    merge_loop
LDMFD  sp!, {r4-r8, pc}
```

The code works since

$$0 \leq w_n \leq 255a + 255(256 - a) = 256 \times 255 = 0xFF00 \qquad (6.3)$$

Therefore it is easy to separate the value $[w_2, w_0]$ into w_2 and w_0 by taking the most significant and least significant 16-bit portions, respectively. We have succeeded in processing four 8-bit pixels using 32-bit load, stores, and data operations to perform operations in parallel.

SUMMARY **Register Allocation**

- ARM has 14 available registers for general-purpose use: *r0* to *r12* and *r14*. The stack pointer *r13* and program counter *r15* cannot be used for general-purpose data. Operating system interrupts often assume that the *user* mode *r13* points to a valid stack, so don't be tempted to reuse *r13*.

- If you need more than 14 local variables, swap the variables out to the stack, working outwards from the innermost loop.

- Use register names rather than physical register numbers when writing assembly routines. This makes it easier to reallocate registers and to maintain the code.

- To ease register pressure you can sometimes store multiple values in the same register. For example, you can store a loop counter and a shift in one register. You can also store multiple pixels in one register.

6.5 CONDITIONAL EXECUTION

The processor core can conditionally execute most ARM instructions. This conditional execution is based on one of 15 condition codes. If you don't specify a condition, the assembler defaults to the execute always condition (AL). The other 14 conditions split into seven pairs of complements. The conditions depend on the four condition code flags N, Z, C, V stored in the *cpsr* register. See Table A.2 in Appendix A for the list of possible ARM conditions. Also see Sections 2.2.6 and 3.8 for an introduction to conditional execution.

By default, ARM instructions do not update the N, Z, C, V flags in the ARM *cpsr*. For most instructions, to update these flags you append an S suffix to the instruction mnemonic. Exceptions to this are comparison instructions that do not write to a destination register. Their sole purpose is to update the flags and so they don't require the S suffix.

By combining conditional execution and conditional setting of the flags, you can implement simple if statements without any need for branches. This improves efficiency since branches can take many cycles and also reduces code size.

EXAMPLE
6.17

The following C code converts an unsigned integer $0 \leq i \leq 15$ to a hexadecimal character c:

```
if (i<10)
{
  c = i + '0';
}
else
{
  c = i + 'A'-10;
}
```

We can write this in assembly using conditional execution rather than conditional branches:

```
CMP     i, #10
ADDLO   c, i, #'0'
ADDHS   c, i, #'A'-10
```

The sequence works since the first ADD does not change the condition codes. The second ADD is still conditional on the result of the compare. Section 6.3.1 shows a similar use of conditional execution to convert to lowercase.

Conditional execution is even more powerful for cascading conditions.

EXAMPLE
6.18

The following C code identifies if c is a vowel:

```
if (c=='a' || c=='e' || c=='i' || c=='o' || c=='u')
{
    vowel++;
}
```

In assembly you can write this using conditional comparisons:

```
TEQ     c, #'a'
TEQNE   c, #'e'
TEQNE   c, #'i'
TEQNE   c, #'o'
TEQNE   c, #'u'
ADDEQ   vowel, vowel, #1
```

As soon as one of the TEQ comparisons detects a match, the *Z* flag is set in the *cpsr*. The following TEQNE instructions have no effect as they are conditional on *Z* = 0.

The next instruction to have effect is the ADDEQ that increments vowel. You can use this method whenever all the comparisons in the if statement are of the same type.

EXAMPLE 6.19

Consider the following code that detects if c is a letter:

```
if ((c>='A' && c<='Z') || (c>='a' && c<='z'))
{
    letter++;
}
```

To implement this efficiently, we can use an addition or subtraction to move each range to the form $0 \le c \le limit$. Then we use unsigned comparisons to detect this range and conditional comparisons to chain together ranges. The following assembly implements this efficiently:

```
SUB     temp, c, #'A'
CMP     temp, #'Z'-'A'
SUBHI   temp, c, #'a'
CMPHI   temp, #'z'-'a'
ADDLS   letter, letter, #1
```

For more complicated decisions involving switches, see Section 6.8.

Note that the logical operations AND and OR are related by the standard logical relations as shown in Table 6.1. You can invert logical expressions involving OR to get an expression involving AND, which can often be useful in simplifying or rearranging logical expressions.

SUMMARY   **Conditional Execution**

■   You can implement most if statements with conditional execution. This is more efficient than using a conditional branch.

Table 6.1   Inverted logical relations

Inverted expression	Equivalent
!(a && b)	(!a) || (!b)
!(a || b)	(!a) && (!b)

- You can implement `if` statements with the logical AND or OR of several similar conditions using compare instructions that are themselves conditional.

6.6 Looping Constructs

Most routines critical to performance will contain a loop. We saw in Section 5.3 that on the ARM loops are fastest when they count down towards zero. This section describes how to implement these loops efficiently in assembly. We also look at examples of how to unroll loops for maximum performance.

6.6.1 Decremented Counted Loops

For a decrementing loop of N iterations, the loop counter i counts down from N to 1 inclusive. The loop terminates with $i = 0$. An efficient implementation is

```
        MOV i, N
loop
        ; loop body goes here and i=N,N-1,...,1
        SUBS i, i, #1
        BGT  loop
```

The loop overhead consists of a subtraction setting the condition codes followed by a conditional branch. On ARM7 and ARM9 this overhead costs four cycles per loop. If i is an array index, then you may want to count down from $N - 1$ to 0 inclusive instead so that you can access array element zero. You can implement this in the same way by using a different conditional branch:

```
        SUBS i, N, #1
loop
        ; loop body goes here and i=N-1,N-2,...,0
        SUBS i, i, #1
        BGE  loop
```

In this arrangement the *Z* flag is set on the last iteration of the loop and cleared for other iterations. If there is anything different about the last loop, then we can achieve this using the EQ and NE conditions. For example, if you preload data for the next loop (as discussed in Section 6.3.1.1), then you want to avoid the preload on the last loop. You can make all preload operations conditional on NE as in Section 6.3.1.1.

There is no reason why we must decrement by one on each loop. Suppose we require *N*/3 loops. Rather than attempting to divide *N* by three, it is far more efficient to subtract three from the loop counter on each iteration:

```
        MOV i, N
loop
        ; loop body goes here and iterates (round up)(N/3) times
        SUBS i, i, #3
        BGT loop
```

6.6.2 Unrolled Counted Loops

This brings us to the subject of loop unrolling. Loop unrolling reduces the loop overhead by executing the loop body multiple times. However, there are problems to overcome. What if the loop count is not a multiple of the unroll amount? What if the loop count is smaller than the unroll amount? We looked at these questions for C code in Section 5.3. In this section we look at how you can handle these issues in assembly.

We'll take the C library function memset as a case study. This function sets *N* bytes of memory at address *s* to the byte value *c*. The function needs to be efficient, so we will look at how to unroll the loop without placing extra restrictions on the input operands. Our version of memset will have the following C prototype:

```
void my_memset(char *s, int c, unsigned int N);
```

To be efficient for large *N*, we need to write multiple bytes at a time using STR or STM instructions. Therefore our first task is to align the array pointer *s*. However, it is only worth us doing this if *N* is sufficiently large. We aren't sure yet what "sufficiently large" means, but let's assume we can choose a threshold value T_1 and only bother to align the array when $N \geq T_1$. Clearly $T_1 \geq 3$ as there is no point in aligning if we don't have four bytes to write!

Now suppose we have aligned the array *s*. We can use store multiples to set memory efficiently. For example, we can use a loop of four store multiples of eight words each to set 128 bytes on each loop. However, it will only be worth doing this if $N \geq T_2 \geq 128$, where T_2 is another threshold to be determined later on.

Finally, we are left with $N < T_2$ bytes to set. We can write bytes in blocks of four using STR until $N < 4$. Then we can finish by writing bytes singly with STRB to the end of the array.

EXAMPLE
6.20

This example shows the unrolled memset routine. We've separated the three sections corresponding to the preceding paragraphs with rows of dashes. The routine isn't finished until we've decided the best values for T_1 and T_2.

```
s       RN 0    ; current string pointer
c       RN 1    ; the character to fill with
N       RN 2    ; the number of bytes to fill
c_1     RN 3    ; copies of c
c_2     RN 4
c_3     RN 5
c_4     RN 6
c_5     RN 7
c_6     RN 8
c_7     RN 12


        ; void my_memset(char *s, unsigned int c, unsigned int N)
my_memset
        ;-----------------------------------------------------
        ; First section aligns the array
        CMP     N, #T_1             ; We know that T_1>=3
        BCC     memset_1ByteBlk ; if (N<T_1) goto memset_1ByteBlk
        ANDS    c_1, s, #3          ; find the byte alignment of s
        BEQ     aligned             ; branch if already aligned
        RSB     c_1, c_1, #4        ; number of bytes until alignment
        SUB     N, N, c_1           ; number of bytes after alignment
        CMP     c_1, #2
        STRB    c, [s], #1
        STRGEB  c, [s], #1          ; if (c_1>=2) then output byte
        STRGTB  c, [s], #1          ; if (c_1>=3) then output byte
aligned                             ;the s array is now aligned
        ORR     c, c, c, LSL#8  ; duplicate the character
        ORR     c, c, c, LSL#16 ; to fill all four bytes of c
        ;-----------------------------------------------------
        ; Second section writes blocks of 128 bytes
        CMP     N, #T_2             ; We know that T_2 >= 128
        BCC     memset_4ByteBlk ; if (N<T_2) goto memset_4ByteBlk
        STMFD   sp!, {c_2-c_6}      ; stack scratch registers
        MOV     c_1, c
        MOV     c_2, c
        MOV     c_3, c
        MOV     c_4, c
        MOV     c_5, c
        MOV     c_6, c
```

```
        MOV    c_7, c
        SUB    N, N, #128       ; bytes left after next block
loop128 ; write 32 words = 128 bytes
        STMIA  s!, {c, c_1-c_6, c_7} ; write 8 words
        STMIA  s!, {c, c_1-c_6, c_7} ; write 8 words
        STMIA  s!, {c, c_1-c_6, c_7} ; write 8 words
        STMIA  s!, {c, c_1-c_6, c_7} ; write 8 words
        SUBS   N, N, #128       ; bytes left after next block
        BGE    loop128
        ADD    N, N, #128       ; number of bytes left
        LDMFD  sp!, {c_2-c_6}   ; restore corrupted registers
        ;--------------------------------------------------
        ; Third section deals with left over bytes
memset_4ByteBlk
        SUBS   N, N, #4         ; try doing 4 bytes
loop4   ; write 4 bytes
        STRGE  c, [s], #4
        SUBGES N, N, #4
        BGE    loop4
        ADD    N, N, #4         ; number of bytes left
memset_1ByteBlk
        SUBS   N, N, #1
loop1   ; write 1 byte
        STRGEB c, [s], #1
        SUBGES N, N, #1
        BGE    loop1
        MOV    pc, lr           ; finished so return
```

It remains to find the best values for the thresholds T_1 and T_2. To determine these we need to analyze the cycle counts for different ranges of N. Since the algorithm operates on blocks of size 128 bytes, 4 bytes, and 1 byte, respectively, we start by decomposing N with respect to these block sizes:

$$N = 128N_h + 4N_m + N_l, \quad \text{where } 0 \leq N_m < 32 \quad \text{and} \quad 0 \leq N_l < 4$$

We now partition into three cases. To follow the details of these cycle counts, you will need to refer to the instruction cycle timings in Appendix D.

- Case $0 \leq N < T_1$: The routine takes $5N + 6$ cycles on an ARM9TDMI including the return.

- Case $T_1 \leq N < T_2$: The first algorithm block takes 6 cycles if the s array is word aligned and 10 cycles otherwise. Assuming each alignment is equally likely, this averages to $(6 + 10 + 10 + 10)/4 = 9$ cycles. The second algorithm block takes 6 cycles. The final

Table 6.2   Cycles taken for each range of N values.

N range	Cycles taken
$0 \leq N < T_1$	$640N_h + 20N_m + 5N_l + 6$
$T_1 \leq N < T_2$	$160N_h + 5N_m + 5N_l + 17 + 5Z_l$
$T_2 \leq N$	$36N_h + 5N_m + 5N_l + 32 + 5Z_l + 5Z_m$

block takes $5(32N_h + N_m) + 5(N_l + Z_l) + 2$ cycles, where Z_l is 1 if $N_l = 0$, and 0 otherwise. The total cycles for this case is $5(32N_h + N_m + N_l + Z_l) + 17$.

- Case $N \geq T_2$: As in the previous case, the first algorithm block averages 9 cycles. The second algorithm block takes $36N_h + 21$ cycles. The final algorithm block takes $5(N_m + Z_m + N_l + Z_l) + 2$ cycles, where Z_m is 1 if N_m is 0, and 0 otherwise. The total cycles for this case is $36N_h + 5(N_m + Z_m + N_l + Z_l) + 32$.

Table 6.2 summarizes these results. Comparing the three table rows it is clear that the second row wins over the first row as soon as $N_m \geq 1$, unless $N_m = 1$ and $N_l = 0$. We set $T_1 = 5$ to choose the best cycle counts from rows one and two. The third row wins over the second row as soon as $N_h \geq 1$. Therefore take $T_2 = 128$.

This detailed example shows you how to unroll any important loop using threshold values and provide good performance over a range of possible input values.

6.6.3   MULTIPLE NESTED LOOPS

How many loop counters does it take to maintain multiple nested loops? Actually, one will suffice—or more accurately, one provided the sum of the bits needed for each loop count does not exceed 32. We can combine the loop counts within a single register, placing the innermost loop count at the highest bit positions. This section gives an example showing how to do this. We will ensure the loops count down from *max* − 1 to 0 inclusive so that the loop terminates by producing a negative result.

EXAMPLE 6.21   This example shows how to merge three loop counts into a single loop count. Suppose we wish to multiply matrix B by matrix C to produce matrix A, where A, B, C have the following constant dimensions. We assume that R, S, T are relatively large but less than 256.

Matrix A:	R rows × T columns
Matrix B:	R rows × S columns
Matrix C:	S rows × T columns

We represent each matrix by a lowercase pointer of the same name, pointing to an array of words organized by row. For example, the element at row i, column j, A[i, j], is at the byte address

```
&A[i,j] = a + 4*(i*T+j)
```

A simple C implementation of the matrix multiply uses three nested loops i, j, and k:

```
#define R 40
#define S 40
#define T 40

void ref_matrix_mul(int *a, int *b, int *c)
{
unsigned int i,j,k;
int sum;

for (i=0; i<R; i++)
{
  for (j=0; j<T; j++)
  {
    /* calculate a[i,j] */
    sum = 0;
    for (k=0; k<S; k++)
    {
      /* add b[i,k]*c[k,j] */
      sum += b[i*S+k]*c[k*T+j];
    }
    a[i*T+j] = sum;
  }
 }
}
```

There are many ways to improve the efficiency here, starting by removing the address indexing calculations, but we will concentrate on the looping structure. We allocate a register counter *count* containing all three loop counters i, j, k:

Bit 31	24 23	16 15	8 7	0
count =	0	S–1–k	T–1–j	R–1–i

Note that $S - 1 - k$ counts from $S - 1$ down to 0 rather than counting from 0 to $S - 1$ as k does. The following assembly implements the matrix multiply using this single counter in register *count*:

```
R          EQU 40
S          EQU 40
```

```
T           EQU 40

a           RN 0    ; points to an R rows × T columns matrix
b           RN 1    ; points to an R rows × S columns matrix
c           RN 2    ; points to an S rows × T columns matrix
sum         RN 3
bval        RN 4
cval        RN 12
count       RN 14

            ; void matrix_mul(int *a, int *b, int *c)
matrix_mul
            STMFD   sp!, {r4, lr}
            MOV     count, #(R-1)               ; i=0
loop_i
            ADD     count, count, #(T-1) << 8   ; j=0
loop_j
            ADD     count, count, #(S-1) << 16  ; k=0
            MOV     sum, #0
loop_k
            LDR     bval, [b], #4               ; bval = B[i,k], b=&B[i,k+1]
            LDR     cval, [c], #4*T             ; cval = C[k,j], c=&C[k+1,j]
            SUBS    count, count, #1 << 16      ; k++
            MLA     sum, bval, cval, sum        ; sum += bval*cval
            BPL     loop_k                      ; branch if k<=S-1
            STR     sum, [a], #4                ; A[i,j] = sum, a=&A[i,j+1]
            SUB     c, c, #4*S*T                ; c = &C[0,j]
            ADD     c, c, #4                    ; c = &C[0,j+1]
            ADDS    count, count, #(1 << 16)-(1 << 8)   ; zero (S-1-k), j++
            SUBPL   b, b, #4*S                  ; b = &B[i,0]
            BPL     loop_j                      ; branch if j<=T-1
            SUB     c, c, #4*T                  ; c = &C[0,0]
            ADDS    count, count, #(1 >> 8)-1   ; zero (T-1-j), i++
            BPL     loop_i                      ; branch if i<=R-1
            LDMFD   sp!, {r4, pc}
```

The preceding structure saves two registers over a naive implementation. First, we decrement the *count* at bits 16 to 23 until the result is negative. This implements the k loop, counting down from $S - 1$ to 0 inclusive. Once the result is negative, the code adds 2^{16} to clear bits 16 to 31. Then we subtract 2^8 to decrement the count stored at bits 8 to 15, implementing the j loop. We can encode the constant $2^{16} - 2^8 = 0xFF00$ efficiently using a single ARM instruction. Bits 8 to 15 now count down from $T - 1$ to 0. When the result of the combined add and subtract is negative, then we have finished the *j* loop. We repeat the same process for the *i* loop. ARM's ability to handle a wide range of rotated constants in addition and subtraction instructions makes this scheme very efficient.

6.6.4   OTHER COUNTED LOOPS

You may want to use the value of a loop counter as an input to calculations in the loop. It's not always desirable to count down from N to 1 or $N - 1$ to 0. For example, you may want to select bits out of a data register one at a time; in this case you may want a power-of-two mask that doubles on each iteration.

The following subsections show useful looping structures that count in different patterns. They use only a single instruction combined with a branch to implement the loop.

6.6.4.1   Negative Indexing

This loop structure counts from $-N$ to 0 (inclusive or exclusive) in steps of size *STEP*.

```
        RSB     i, N, #0        ; i=-N
loop
        ; loop body goes here and i=-N,-N+STEP,...,
        ADDS    i, i, #STEP
        BLT     loop            ; use BLT or BLE to exclude 0 or not
```

6.6.4.2   Logarithmic Indexing

This loop structure counts down from 2^N to 1 in powers of two. For example, if $N = 4$, then it counts 16, 8, 4, 2, 1.

```
        MOV     i, #1
        MOV     i, i, LSL N
loop
        ; loop body
        MOVS    i, i, LSR#1
        BNE     loop
```

The following loop structure counts down from an *N*-bit mask to a one-bit mask. For example, if $N = 4$, then it counts 15, 7, 3, 1.

```
        MOV     i, #1
        RSB     i, i, i, LSL N  ; i=(1<<N)-1
```

```
loop
        ; loop body
        MOVS    i, i, LSR#1
        BNE     loop
```

SUMMARY   **Looping Constructs**

- ARM requires two instructions to implement a counted loop: a subtract that sets flags and a conditional branch.

- Unroll loops to improve loop performance. Do not overunroll because this will hurt cache performance. Unrolled loops may be inefficient for a small number of iterations. You can test for this case and only call the unrolled loop if the number of iterations is large.

- Nested loops only require a single loop counter register, which can improve efficiency by freeing up registers for other uses.

- ARM can implement negative and logarithmic indexed loops efficiently.

6.7 BIT MANIPULATION

Compressed file formats pack items at a bit granularity to maximize the data density. The items may be of a fixed width, such as a length field or version field, or they may be of a variable width, such as a Huffman coded symbol. Huffman codes are used in compression to associate with each symbol a code of bits. The code is shorter for common symbols and longer for rarer symbols.

In this section we look at methods to handle a bitstream efficiently. First we look at fixed-width codes, then variable width codes. See Section 7.6 for common bit manipulation routines such as endianness and bit reversal.

6.7.1 FIXED-WIDTH BIT-FIELD PACKING AND UNPACKING

You can extract an unsigned bit-field from an arbitrary position in an ARM register in one cycle provided that you set up a mask in advance; otherwise you require two cycles. A signed bit-field always requires two cycles to unpack unless the bit-field lies at the top of a word (most significant bit of the bit-field is the most significant bit of the register). On the ARM we use logical operations and the barrel shifter to pack and unpack codes, as in the following examples.

EXAMPLE   The assembly code shows how to unpack bits 4 to 15 of register $r0$, placing the result in $r1$.
6.22

```
; unsigned unpack with mask set up in advance
; mask=0x00000FFF
```

```
AND     r1, mask, r0, LSR#4

; unsigned unpack with no mask
MOV     r1, r0, LSL#16  ; discard bits 16-31
MOV     r1, r1, LSR#20  ; discard bits 0-3 and zero extend

; signed unpack
MOV     r1, r0, LSL#16  ; discard bits 16-31
MOV     r1, r1, ASR#20  ; discard bits 0-3 and sign extend
```

EXAMPLE Packing the value *r1* into the bit-packed register *r0* requires one cycle if *r1* is already
6.23 restricted to the correct range and the corresponding field of *r0* is clear. In this example, *r1*
is a 12-bit number to be inserted at bit 4 of *r0*.

```
; pack r1 into r0
ORR     r0, r0, r1, LSL #4
```

Otherwise you need a mask register set up:

```
; pack r1 into r0
; mask=0x00000FFF set up in advance
AND     r1, r1, mask        ; restrict the r1 range
BIC     r0, r0, mask, LSL#4 ; clear the destination bits
ORR     r0, r0, r1, LSL#4   ; pack in the new data
```

6.7.2 VARIABLE-WIDTH BITSTREAM PACKING

Our task here is to pack a series of variable-length codes to create a bitstream. Typically
we are compressing a datastream and the variable-length codes represent Huffman or
arithmetic coding symbols. However, we don't need to make any assumptions about what
the codes represent to pack them efficiently.

We do need to be careful about the packing endianness. Many compressed file formats
use a big-endian bit-packing order where the first code is placed at the most significant bits
of the first byte. For this reason we will use a big-endian bit-packing order for our examples.
This is sometimes known as *network order*. Figure 6.5 shows how we form a bytestream out
of variable-length bitcodes using a big-endian packing order. *High* and *low* represent the
most and least significant bit ends of the byte.

To implement packing efficiently on the ARM we use a 32-bit register as a buffer to
hold four bytes, in big-endian order. In other words we place byte 0 of the bytestream in
the most significant 8 bits of the register. Then we can insert codes into the register one at
a time, starting from the most significant bit and working down to the least significant bit.

High   Low High   Low High   Low High   Low High   Low

Byte 0	Byte 1	Byte 2	Byte 3	...

Code 0	Code 1	Code 2	Code 3	Code 4		...

Figure 6.5   Big-endian bitcodes packed into a bytestream.

$$bitbuffer = \begin{array}{ccc} 31 & bitsfree & 0 \\ \hline \text{Code bits} & & 0 \\ \hline \end{array}$$

Figure 6.6   Format of *bitbuffer*.

Once the register is full we can store 32 bits to memory. For a big-endian memory system we can store the word without modification. For a little-endian memory system we need to reverse the byte order in the word before storing.

We call the 32-bit register we insert codes into *bitbuffer*. We need a second register *bitsfree* to record the number of bits that we haven't used in *bitbuffer*. In other words, *bitbuffer* contains $32 - bitsfree$ code bits, and *bitsfree* zero bits, as in Figure 6.6. To insert a code of k bits into *bitbuffer*, we subtract k from *bitsfree* and then insert the code with a left shift of *bitsfree*.

We also need to be careful about alignment. A bytestream need not be word aligned, and so we can't use word accesses to write it. To allow word accesses we will start by backing up to the last word-aligned address. Then we fill the 32-bit register *bitbuffer* with the backed-up data. From then on we can use word (32-bit) read and writes.

EXAMPLE
6.24

This example provides three functions bitstream_write_start, bitstream_write_code, and bitstream_write_flush. These are not ATPCS-compliant functions because they assume registers such as *bitbuffer* are preserved between calls. In practice you will inline this code for efficiency, and so this is not a problem.

The bitstream_write_start function aligns the bitstream pointer bitstream and initializes the 32-bit buffer bitbuffer. Each call to bitstream_write_code inserts a value code of bit-length codebits. Finally, the bitstream_write_flush function writes any remaining bytes to the bitstream to terminate the stream.

```
bitstream    RN 0  ; current byte address in the output bitstream
code         RN 4  ; current code
```

```
codebits        RN 5  ; length in bits of current code
bitbuffer       RN 6  ; 32-bit output big-endian bitbuffer
bitsfree        RN 7  ; number of bits free in the bitbuffer
tmp             RN 8  ; scratch register
mask            RN 12 ; endian reversal mask 0xFFFF00FF

bitstream_write_start
        MOV     bitbuffer, #0
        MOV     bitsfree, #32
align_loop
        TST     bitstream, #3
        LDRNEB  code, [bitstream, #-1]!
        SUBNE   bitsfree, bitsfree, #8
        ORRNE   bitbuffer, code, bitbuffer, ROR #8
        BNE     align_loop
        MOV     bitbuffer, bitbuffer, ROR #8
        MOV     pc, lr


bitstream_write_code
        SUBS    bitsfree, bitsfree, codebits
        BLE     full_buffer
        ORR     bitbuffer, bitbuffer, code, LSL bitsfree
        MOV     pc, lr
full_buffer
        RSB     bitsfree, bitsfree, #0
        ORR     bitbuffer, bitbuffer, code, LSR bitsfree
        IF {ENDIAN}="little"
          ; byte reverse the bit buffer prior to storing
          EOR   tmp, bitbuffer, bitbuffer, ROR #16
          AND   tmp, mask, tmp, LSR #8
          EOR   bitbuffer, tmp, bitbuffer, ROR #8
        ENDIF
        STR     bitbuffer, [bitstream], #4
        RSB     bitsfree, bitsfree, #32
        MOV     bitbuffer, code, LSL bitsfree
        MOV     pc, lr


bitstream_write_flush
        RSBS    bitsfree, bitsfree, #32
flush_loop
        MOVGT   bitbuffer, bitbuffer, ROR #24
        STRGTB  bitbuffer, [bitstream], #1
        SUBGTS  bitsfree, bitsfree, #8
        BGT     flush_loop
        MOV     pc, lr
```

6.7.3   Variable-Width Bitstream Unpacking

It is much harder to unpack a bitstream of variable-width codes than to pack it. The problem is that we usually don't know the width of the codes we are unpacking! For Huffman-encoded bitstreams you must derive the length of each code by looking at the next sequence of bits and working out which code it can be.

Here we will use a lookup table to speed up the unpacking process. The idea is to take the next N bits of the bitstream and perform a lookup in two tables, *look_codebits*[] and *look_code*[], each of size 2^N entries. If the next N bits are sufficient to determine the code, then the tables tell us the code length and the code value, respectively. If the next N bits are insufficient to determine the code, then the look_codebits table will return an *escape* value of 0xFF. An escape value is just a flag to indicate that this case is exceptional.

In a sequence of Huffman codes, common codes are short and rare codes are long. So, we expect to decode most common codes quickly, using the lookup tables. In the following example we assume that $N = 8$ and use 256-entry lookup tables.

EXAMPLE
6.25
This example provides three functions to unpack a big-endian bitstream stored in a bytestream. As with Example 6.24, these functions are not ATPCS compliant and will normally be inlined. The function bitstream_read_start initializes the process, starting to decode a bitstream at byte address bitstream. Each call to bitstream_read_code returns the next code in register code. The function only handles short codes that can be read from the lookup table. Long codes are trapped at the label long_code, but the implementation of this function depends on the codes you are decoding.

The code uses a register bitbuffer that contains $N + bitsleft$ code bits starting at the most significant bit (see Figure 6.7).

```
bitstream     RN 0   ; current byte address in the input bitstream
look_code     RN 2   ; lookup table to convert next N bits to a code
look_codebits RN 3   ; lookup table to convert next N bits to a code length
code          RN 4   ; code read
codebits      RN 5   ; length of code read
bitbuffer     RN 6   ; 32-bit input buffer (big endian)
bitsleft      RN 7   ; number of valid bits in the buffer - N
```

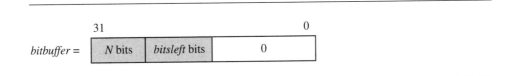

Figure 6.7   Format of bitbuffer.

```
tmp             RN 8   ; scratch
tmp2            RN 9   ; scratch
mask            RN 12 ; N-bit extraction mask (1<<N)-1

N               EQU 8  ; use a lookup table on 8 bits (N must be <= 9)

bitstream_read_start
        MOV     bitsleft, #32
read_fill_loop
        LDRB    tmp, [bitstream], #1
        ORR     bitbuffer, tmp, bitbuffer, LSL#8
        SUBS    bitsleft, bitsleft, #8
        BGT     read_fill_loop
        MOV     bitsleft, #(32-N)
        MOV     mask, #(1<<N)-1
        MOV     pc, lr


bitstream_read_code
        LDRB    codebits, [look_codebits, bitbuffer, LSR# (32-N)]
        AND     code, mask, bitbuffer, LSR#(32-N)
        LDR     code, [look_code, code, LSL#2]
        SUBS    bitsleft, bitsleft, codebits
        BMI     empty_buffer_or_long_code
        MOV     bitbuffer, bitbuffer, LSL codebits
        MOV     pc, lr
empty_buffer_or_long_code
        TEQ     codebits, #0xFF
        BEQ     long_code
        ; empty buffer - fill up with 3 bytes
        ; as N <= 9, we can fill 3 bytes without overflow
        LDRB    tmp, [bitstream], #1
        LDRB    tmp2, [bitstream], #1
        MOV     bitbuffer, bitbuffer, LSL codebits
        LDRB    codebits, [bitstream], #1
        ORR     tmp, tmp2, tmp, LSL#8
        RSB     bitsleft, bitsleft, #(8-N)
        ORR     tmp, codebits, tmp, LSL#8
        ORR     bitbuffer, bitbuffer, tmp, LSL bitsleft
        RSB     bitsleft, bitsleft, #(32-N)
        MOV     pc, lr


long_code
        ; handle the long code case depending on the application
        ; here we just return a code of -1
        MOV     code, #-1
        MOV     pc, lr
```

The counter `bitsleft` actually counts the number of bits remaining in the buffer `bitbuffer` less the N bits required for the next lookup. Therefore we can perform the next table lookup as long as `bitsleft` $\geq$ 0. As soon as `bitsleft` < 0 there are two possibilities. One possibility is that we found a valid code but then have insufficient bits to look up the next code. Alternatively, `codebits` contains the escape value 0xFF to indicate that the code was longer than N bits. We can trap both these cases at once using a call to `empty_buffer_or_long_code`. If the buffer is empty, then we fill it with 24 bits. If we have detected a long code, then we branch to the `long_code` trap.

The example has a best-case performance of seven cycles per code unpack on an ARM9TDMI. You can obtain faster results if you know the sizes of the packed bitfields in advance.

SUMMARY **Bit Manipulation**

- The ARM can pack and unpack bits efficiently using logical operations and the barrel shifter.

- To access bitstreams efficiently use a 32-bit register as a bitbuffer. Use a second register to keep track of the number of valid bits in the bitbuffer.

- To decode bitstreams efficiently, use a lookup table to scan the next N bits of the bitstream. The lookup table can return codes of length at most N bits directly, or return an escape character for longer codes.

6.8 EFFICIENT SWITCHES

A *switch* or *multiway branch* selects between a number of different actions. In this section we assume the action depends on a variable x. For different values of x we need to perform different actions. This section looks at assembly to implement a switch efficiently for different types of x.

6.8.1 SWITCHES ON THE RANGE $0 \leq x < N$

The example C function `ref_switch` performs different actions according to the value of x. We are only interested in x values in the range $0 \leq x < 8$.

```
int ref_switch(int x)
{
  switch (x)
  {
    case 0: return method_0();
```

```
       case 1: return method_1();
       case 2: return method_2();
       case 3: return method_3();
       case 4: return method_4();
       case 5: return method_5();
       case 6: return method_6();
       case 7: return method_7();
       default: return method_d();
   }
}
```

There are two ways to implement this structure efficiently in ARM assembly. The first method uses a table of function addresses. We load *pc* from the table indexed by *x*.

EXAMPLE
6.26

The switch_absolute code performs a switch using an inlined table of function pointers:

```
x       RN 0

        ; int switch_absolute(int x)
switch_absolute
        CMP     x, #8
        LDRLT   pc, [pc, x, LSL#2]
        B       method_d
        DCD     method_0
        DCD     method_1
        DCD     method_2
        DCD     method_3
        DCD     method_4
        DCD     method_5
        DCD     method_6
        DCD     method_7
```

The code works because the *pc* register is pipelined. The *pc* points to the method_0 word when the ARM executes the LDR instruction.

The method above is very fast, but has one drawback: The code is not position independent since it stores absolute addresses to the method functions in memory. Position-independent code is often used in modules that are installed into a system at run time. The next example shows how to solve this problem.

EXAMPLE
6.27

The code switch_relative is slightly slower compared to switch_absolute, but it is position independent:

```
        ; int switch_relative(int x)
switch_relative
```

```
CMP      x, #8
ADDLT    pc, pc, x, LSL#2
B        method_d
B        method_0
B        method_1
B        method_2
B        method_3
B        method_4
B        method_5
B        method_6
B        method_7
```

There is one final optimization you can make. If the method functions are short, then you can inline the instructions in place of the branch instructions.

EXAMPLE Suppose each nondefault method has a four-instruction implementation. Then you can
6.28   use code of the form

```
CMP      x, #8
ADDLT    pc, pc, x, LSL#4 ; each method is 16 bytes long
B        method_d
method_0
         ; the four instructions for method_0 go here
method_1
         ; the four instructions for method_1 go here
         ; ... continue in this way ...
```

6.8.2 SWITCHES ON A GENERAL VALUE x

Now suppose that x does not lie in some convenient range $0 \leq x < N$ for N small enough to apply the methods of Section 6.8.1. How do we perform the switch efficiently, without having to test x against each possible value in turn?

A very useful technique in these situations is to use a *hashing function*. A hashing function is any function $y = f(x)$ that maps the values we are interested in into a continuous range of the form $0 \leq y < N$. Instead of a switch on x, we can use a switch on $y = f(x)$. There is a problem if we have a collision, that is, if two x values map to the same y value. In this case we need further code to test all the possible x values that could have led to the y value. For our purposes a good hashing function is easy to compute and does not suffer from many collisions.

To perform the switch we apply the hashing function and then use the optimized switch code of Section 6.8.1 on the hash value y. Where two x values can map to the same hash, we need to perform an explicit test, but this should be rare for a good hash function.

EXAMPLE   Suppose we want to call method_k when $x = 2^k$ for eight possible methods. In other words
6.29   we want to switch on the values 1, 2, 4, 8, 16, 32, 64, 128. For all other values of x we need to
call the default method method_d. We look for a hash function formed out of multiplying
by powers of two minus one (this is an efficient operation on the ARM). By trying different
multipliers we find that $15 \times 31 \times x$ has a different value in bits 9 to 11 for each of the eight
switch values. This means we can use bits 9 to 11 of this product as our hash function.

The following switch_hash assembly uses this hash function to perform the switch.
Note that other values that are not powers of two will have the same hashes as the values
we want to detect. The switch has narrowed the case down to a single power of two that we
can test for explicitly. If x is not a power of two, then we fall through to the default case of
calling method_d.

```
x       RN 0
hash    RN 1

        ; int switch_hash(int x)
switch_hash
        RSB     hash, x, x, LSL#4        ; hash=x*15
        RSB     hash, hash, hash, LSL#5  ; hash=x*15*31
        AND     hash, hash, #7<<9        ; mask out the hash value
        ADD     pc, pc, hash, LSR#6
        NOP
        TEQ     x, #0x01
        BEQ     method_0
        TEQ     x, #0x02
        BEQ     method_1
        TEQ     x, #0x40
        BEQ     method_6
        TEQ     x, #0x04
        BEQ     method_2
        TEQ     x, #0x80
        BEQ     method_7
        TEQ     x, #0x20
        BEQ     method_5
        TEQ     x, #0x10
        BEQ     method_4
        TEQ     x, #0x08
        BEQ     method_3
        B       method_d
```

SUMMARY   **Efficient Switches**

- Make sure the switch value is in the range $0 \le x < N$ for some small N. To do this you
  may have to use a hashing function.

■ Use the switch value to index a table of function pointers or to branch to short
   sections of code at regular intervals. The second technique is position independent;
   the first isn't.

6.9 HANDLING UNALIGNED DATA

Recall that a load or store is *unaligned* if it uses an address that is not a multiple of the data
transfer width. For code to be portable across ARM architectures and implementations,
you must avoid unaligned access. Section 5.9 introduced unaligned accesses and ways of
handling them in C. In this section we look at how to handle unaligned accesses in assembly
code.

The simplest method is to use byte loads and stores to access one byte at a time. This
is the recommended method for any accesses that are not speed critical. The following
example shows how to access word values in this way.

EXAMPLE
6.30

This example shows how to read or write a 32-bit word using the unaligned address p. We
use three scratch registers t0, t1, t2 to avoid interlocks. All unaligned word operations
take seven cycles on an ARM9TDMI. Note that we need separate functions for 32-bit words
stored in big- or little-endian format.

```
p        RN 0
x        RN 1
t0       RN 2
t1       RN 3
t2       RN 12

         ; int load_32_little(char *p)
load_32_little
         LDRB    x,  [p]
         LDRB    t0, [p, #1]
         LDRB    t1, [p, #2]
         LDRB    t2, [p, #3]
         ORR     x, x, t0, LSL#8
         ORR     x, x, t1, LSL#16
         ORR     r0, x, t2, LSL#24
         MOV     pc, lr

         ; int load_32_big(char *p)
load_32_big
         LDRB    x,  [p]
         LDRB    t0, [p, #1]
         LDRB    t1, [p, #2]
```

```
            LDRB    t2, [p, #3]
            ORR     x, t0, x, LSL#8
            ORR     x, t1, x, LSL#8
            ORR     r0, t2, x, LSL#8
            MOV     pc, lr

            ; void store_32_little(char *p, int x)
store_32_little
            STRB    x,  [p]
            MOV     t0, x, LSR#8
            STRB    t0, [p, #1]
            MOV     t0, x, LSR#16
            STRB    t0, [p, #2]
            MOV     t0, x, LSR#24
            STRB    t0, [p, #3]
            MOV     pc, lr

            ; void store_32_big(char *p, int x)
store_32_big
            MOV     t0, x, LSR#24
            STRB    t0, [p]
            MOV     t0, x, LSR#16
            STRB    t0, [p, #1]
            MOV     t0, x, LSR#8
            STRB    t0, [p, #2]
            STRB    x,  [p, #3]
            MOV     pc, lr
```

If you require better performance than seven cycles per access, then you can write several variants of the routine, with each variant handling a different address alignment. This reduces the cost of the unaligned access to three cycles: the word load and the two arithmetic instructions required to join values together.

EXAMPLE
6.31

This example shows how to generate a checksum of N words starting at a possibly unaligned address data. The code is written for a little-endian memory system. Notice how we can use the assembler MACRO directive to generate the four routines checksum_0, checksum_1, checksum_2, and checksum_3. Routine checksum_a handles the case where data is an address of the form $4q + a$.

Using a macro saves programming effort. We need only write a single macro and instantiate it four times to implement our four checksum routines.

```
sum     RN 0    ; current checksum
N       RN 1    ; number of words left to sum
```

```
data    RN 2    ; word aligned input data pointer
w       RN 3    ; data word

        ; int checksum_32_little(char *data, unsigned int N)
checksum_32_little
        BIC     data, r0, #3        ; aligned data pointer
        AND     w, r0, #3          ; byte alignment offset
        MOV     sum, #0            ; initial checksum
        LDR     pc, [pc, w, LSL#2] ; switch on alignment
        NOP                        ; padding
        DCD     checksum_0
        DCD     checksum_1
        DCD     checksum_2
        DCD     checksum_3


        MACRO
        CHECKSUM $alignment
checksum_$alignment
        LDR     w, [data], #4      ; preload first value
10      ; loop
        IF $alignment<>0
          ADD   sum, sum, w, LSR#8*$alignment
          LDR   w, [data], #4
          SUBS  N, N, #1
          ADD   sum, sum, w, LSL#32-8*$alignment
        ELSE
          ADD   sum, sum, w
          LDR   w, [data], #4
          SUBS  N, N, #1
        ENDIF
        BGT     %BT10
        MOV     pc, lr
        MEND


        ; generate four checksum routines
        ; one for each possible byte alignment
        CHECKSUM 0
        CHECKSUM 1
        CHECKSUM 2
        CHECKSUM 3
```

You can now unroll and optimize the routines as in Section 6.6.2 to achieve the fastest speed. Due to the additional code size, only use the preceding technique for time-critical routines.

SUMMARY **Handling Unaligned Data**

- If performance is not an issue, access unaligned data using multiple byte loads and stores. This approach accesses data of a given endianness regardless of the pointer alignment and the configured endianness of the memory system.

- If performance is an issue, then use multiple routines, with a different routine optimized for each possible array alignment. You can use the assembler MACRO directive to generate these routines automatically.

6.10 SUMMARY

For the best performance in an application you will need to write optimized assembly routines. It is only worth optimizing the key routines that the performance depends on. You can find these using a profiling or cycle counting tool, such as the ARMulator simulator from ARM.

This chapter covered examples and useful techniques for optimizing ARM assembly. Here are the key ideas:

- Schedule code so that you do not incur processor interlocks or stalls. Use Appendix D to see how quickly an instruction result is available. Concentrate particularly on load and multiply instructions, which often take a long time to produce results.

- Hold as much data in the 14 available general-purpose registers as you can. Sometimes it is possible to pack several data items in a single register. Avoid stacking data in the innermost loop.

- For small if statements, use conditional data processing operations rather than conditional branches.

- Use unrolled loops that count down to zero for the maximum loop performance.

- For packing and unpacking bit-packed data, use 32-bit register buffers to increase efficiency and reduce memory data bandwidth.

- Use branch tables and hash functions to implement efficient switch statements.

- To handle unaligned data efficiently, use multiple routines. Optimize each routine for a particular alignment of the input and output arrays. Select between the routines at run time.

CHAPTER 7

OPTIMIZED PRIMITIVES

A *primitive* is a basic operation that can be used in a wide variety of different algorithms and programs. For example, addition, multiplication, division, and random number generation are all primitives. Some primitives are supported directly by the ARM instruction set, including 32-bit addition and multiplication. However, many primitives are not supported directly by instructions, and we must write routines to implement them (for example, division and random number generation).

This chapter provides optimized reference implementations of common primitives. The first three sections look at multiplication and division. Section 7.1 looks at primitives to implement extended-precision multiplication. Section 7.2 looks at normalization, which is useful for the division algorithms in Section 7.3.

The next two sections look at more complicated mathematical operations. Section 7.4 covers square root. Section 7.5 looks at the transcendental functions log, exp, sin, and cos. Section 7.6 looks at operations involving bit manipulation, and Section 7.7 at operations involving saturation and rounding. Finally, Section 7.8 looks at random number generation.

You can use this chapter in two ways. First, it is useful as a straight reference. If you need a division routine, go to the index and find the routine, or find the section on division. You can copy the assembly from the book's Web site. Second, this chapter provides the theory to explain why each implementation works, which is useful if you need to change or generalize the routine. For example, you may have different requirements about the precision or the format of the input and output operands. For this reason, the text necessarily contains many mathematical formulae and some tedious proofs. Please skip these as you see fit!

We have designed the code examples so that they are complete functions that you can lift directly from the Web site. They should assemble immediately using the toolkit supplied by ARM. For constancy we use the ARM toolkit ADS1.1 for all the examples of this chapter.

See Section A.4 in Appendix for help on the assembler format. You could equally well use the GNU assembler *gas*. See Section A.5 for help on the *gas* assembler format.

You will also notice that we use the C keyword `__value_in_regs`. On the ARM compiler *armcc* this indicates that a function argument, or return value, should be passed in registers rather than by reference. In practical applications this is not an issue because you will inline the operations for efficiency.

We use the notation Qk throughout this chapter to denote a fixed-point representation with binary point between bits $k-1$ and k. For example, 0.75 represented at Q15 is the integer value 0x6000. See Section 8.1 for more details of the Qk representation and fixed-point arithmetic. We say "$d < 0.5$ at Q15" to mean that d represents the value $d2^{-15}$ and that this is less than one half.

7.1   DOUBLE-PRECISION INTEGER MULTIPLICATION

You can multiply integers up to 32 bits wide using the UMULL and SMULL instructions. The following routines multiply 64-bit signed or unsigned integers, giving a 64-bit or 128-bit result. They can be extended, using the same ideas, to multiply any lengths of integer. Longer multiplication is useful for handling the `long long` C type, emulating double-precision fixed- or floating-point operations, and in the long arithmetic required by public-key cryptography.

We use a little-endian notation for multiword values. If a 128-bit integer is stored in four registers a_3, a_2, a_1, a_0, then these store bits [127:96], [95:64], [63:32], [31:0], respectively (see Figure 7.1).

7.1.1   `long long` MULTIPLICATION

Use the following three-instruction sequence to multiply two 64-bit values (signed or unsigned) b and c to give a new 64-bit `long long` value a. Excluding the ARM Thumb Procedure Call Standard (ATPCS) wrapper and with worst-case inputs, this operation takes 24 cycles on ARM7TDMI and 25 cycles on ARM9TDMI. On ARM9E the operation takes 8 cycles. One of these cycles is a pipeline interlock between the first UMULL and MLA, which you could remove by interleaving with other code.

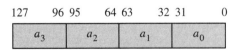

Figure 7.1   Representation of a 128-bit value as four 32-bit values.

```
b_0   RN 0    ; b bits [31:00]    (b low)
b_1   RN 1    ; b bits [63:32]    (b high)
c_0   RN 2    ; c bits [31:00]    (c low)
c_1   RN 3    ; c bits [63:32]    (c high)
a_0   RN 4    ; a bits [31:00]    (a low-low)
a_1   RN 5    ; a bits [63:32]    (a low-high)
a_2   RN 12   ; a bits [95:64]    (a high-low)
a_3   RN lr   ; a bits [127:96]   (a high-high)

      ; long long mul_64to64 (long long b, long long c)
mul_64to64
      STMFD  sp!, {r4,r5,lr}
      ; 64-bit a = 64-bit b * 64-bit c
      UMULL  a_0, a_1, b_0, c_0         ; low*low
      MLA    a_1, b_0, c_1, a_1         ; low*high
      MLA    a_1, b_1, c_0, a_1         ; high*low
      ; return wrapper
      MOV    r0, a_0
      MOV    r1, a_1
      LDMFD  sp!, {r4,r5,pc}
```

7.1.2 UNSIGNED 64-BIT BY 64-BIT MULTIPLY WITH 128-BIT RESULT

There are two slightly different implementations for an unsigned 64- by 64-bit multiply with 128-bit result. The first is faster on an ARM7M. Here multiply accumulate instructions take an extra cycle compared to the nonaccumulating version. The ARM7M version requires four long multiplies and six adds, a worst-case performance of 30 cycles.

```
      ; __value_in_regs struct { unsigned a0,a1,a2,a3; }
      ;   umul_64to128_arm7m(unsigned long long b,
      ;                      unsigned long long c)
umul_64to128_arm7m
      STMFD  sp!, {r4,r5,lr}
      ; unsigned 128-bit a = 64-bit b  * 64-bit c
      UMULL  a_0, a_1, b_0,  c_0   ; low*low
      UMULL  a_2, a_3, b_0,  c_1   ; low*high
      UMULL  c_1, b_0, b_1,  c_1   ; high*high
      ADDS   a_1, a_1, a_2
      ADCS   a_2, a_3, c_1
      ADC    a_3, b_0, #0
      UMULL  c_0, b_0, b_1,  c_0   ; high*low
```

```
ADDS    a_1,   a_1,   c_0
ADCS    a_2,   a_2,   b_0
ADC     a_3,   a_3,   #0
; return wrapper
MOV     r0,    a_0
MOV     r1,    a_1
MOV     r2,    a_2
MOV     r3,    a_3
LDMFD   sp!,    {r4,r5,pc}
```

The second method works better on the ARM9TDMI and ARM9E. Here multiply accumulates are as fast as multiplies. We schedule the multiply instructions to avoid result-use interlocks on the ARM9E (see Section 6.2 for a description of pipelines and interlocks).

```
; __value_in_regs struct { unsigned a0,a1,a2,a3; }
;   umul_64to128_arm9e(unsigned long long b,
;                        unsigned long long c)
umul_64to128_arm9e
        STMFD   sp!, {r4,r5,lr}
        ; unsigned 128-bit a = 64-bit b   * 64-bit c
        UMULL   a_0,   a_1,   b_0,   c_0   ; low*low
        MOV     a_2,   #0
        UMLAL   a_1,   a_2,   b_0,   c_1   ; low*high
        MOV     a_3,   #0
        UMLAL   a_1,   a_3,   b_1,   c_0   ; high*low
        MOV     b_0,   #0
        ADDS    a_2,   a_2,   a_3
        ADC     a_3,   b_0,   #0
        UMLAL   a_2,   a_3,   b_1,   c_1   ; high*high
        ; return wrapper
        MOV     r0,    a_0
        MOV     r1,    a_1
        MOV     r2,    a_2
        MOV     r3,    a_3
        LDMFD   sp!,    {r4,r5,pc}
```

Excluding the function call and return wrapper, this implementation requires 33 cycles on ARM9TDMI and 17 cycles on ARM9E. The idea is that the operation $ab + c + d$ cannot overflow an unsigned 64-bit integer if a, b, c, and d are unsigned 32-bit integers. Therefore you can achieve long multiplications with the normal schoolbook method of using the operation $ab + c + d$, where c and d are the horizontal and vertical carries.

7.1.3 Signed 64-Bit by 64-Bit Multiply with 128-Bit Result

A signed 64-bit integer breaks down into a signed high 32 bits and an unsigned low 32 bits. To multiply the high part of b by the low part of c requires a signed by unsigned multiply instruction. Although the ARM does not have such an instruction, we can synthesize one using macros.

The following macro USMLAL provides an unsigned-by-signed multiply accumulate operation. To multiply unsigned b by signed c, it first calculates the product bc considering both values as signed. If the top bit of b is set, then this signed multiply multiplied by the value $b - 2^{32}$. In this case it corrects the result by adding $c2^{32}$. Similarly, SUMLAL performs a signed-by-unsigned multiply accumulate.

```
MACRO
USMLAL $al, $ah, $b, $c
; signed $ah.$al += unsigned $b * signed $c
SMLAL   $al, $ah, $b, $c         ; a = (signed)b * c;
TST     $b, #1<<31               ; if ((signed)b<0)
ADDNE   $ah, $ah, $c             ; a += (c<<32);
MEND
MACRO
SUMLAL $al, $ah, $b, $c
; signed $ah.$al += signed $b * unsigned $c
SMLAL   $al, $ah, $b, $c         ; a = b * (signed)c;
TST     $c, #1<<31               ; if ((signed)c<0)
ADDNE   $ah, $ah, $b             ; a += (b<<32);
MEND
```

Using these macros it is relatively simple to convert the 64-bit multiply of Section 7.1.2 to a signed multiply. This signed version is four cycles longer than the corresponding unsigned version due to the signed-by-unsigned fix-up instructions.

```
; __value_in_regs struct { unsigned a0,a1,a2; signed a3; }
;    smul_64to128(long long b, long long c)
smul_64to128
        STMFD   sp!, {r4,r5,lr}
        ; signed 128-bit a = 64-bit b * 64-bit c
        UMULL   a_0,  a_1,  b_0,  c_0   ; low*low
        MOV     a_2,  #0
        USMLAL  a_1,  a_2,  b_0,  c_1   ; low*high
        MOV     a_3,  #0
        SUMLAL  a_1,  a_3,  b_1,  c_0   ; high*low
```

```
        MOV     b_0,    a_2,    ASR#31
        ADDS    a_2,    a_2,    a_3
        ADC     a_3,    b_0,    a_3,    ASR#31
        SMLAL   a_2,    a_3,    b_1,    c_1  ; high*high
        ; return wrapper
        MOV     r0, a_0
        MOV     r1, a_1
        MOV     r2, a_2
        MOV     r3, a_3
        LDMFD   sp!, {r4,r5,pc}
```

7.2 INTEGER NORMALIZATION AND COUNT LEADING ZEROS

An integer is normalized when the leading one, or most significant bit, of the integer is at a known bit position. We will need normalization to implement Newton-Raphson division (see Section 7.3.2) or to convert to a floating-point format. Normalization is also useful for calculating logarithms (see Section 7.5.1) and priority decoders used by some dispatch routines. In these applications, we need to know both the normalized value and the shift required to reach this value.

This operation is so important that an instruction is available from ARM architecture ARMv5E onwards to accelerate normalization. The CLZ instruction counts the number of leading zeros before the first significant one. It returns 32 if there is no one bit at all. The CLZ value is the left shift you need to apply to normalize the integer so that the leading one is at bit position 31.

7.2.1 NORMALIZATION ON ARMv5 AND ABOVE

On an ARMv5 architecture, use the following code to perform unsigned and signed normalization, respectively. Unsigned normalization shifts left until the leading one is at bit 31. Signed normalization shifts left until there is one sign bit at bit 31 and the leading bit is at bit 30. Both functions return a structure in registers of two values, the normalized integer and the left shift to normalize.

```
x       RN 0    ; input, output integer
shift   RN 1    ; shift to normalize

        ; __value_in_regs struct { unsigned x; int shift; }
        ;   unorm_arm9e(unsigned x)
unorm_arm9e
```

```
        CLZ     shift, x                ; left shift to normalize
        MOV     x, x, LSL shift         ; normalize
        MOV     pc, lr


        ; __value_in_regs struct { signed x; int shift; }
        ;   unorm_arm9e(signed x)
snorm_arm9e                             ; [ s s s 1-s x x ... ]
        EOR     shift, x, x, LSL#1      ; [ 0 0 1 x   x x ... ]
        CLZ     shift, shift            ; left shift to normalize
        MOV     x, x, LSL shift         ; normalize
        MOV     pc, lr
```

Note that we reduce the signed norm to an unsigned norm using a logical exclusive OR. If x is signed, then $x^\wedge(x \ll 1)$ has the leading one in the position of the first sign bit in x.

7.2.2 NORMALIZATION ON ARMv4

If you are using an ARMv4 architecture processor such as ARM7TDMI or ARM9TDMI, then there is no CLZ instruction available. Instead we can synthesize the same functionality. The simple divide-and-conquer method in unorm_arm7m gives a good trade-off between performance and code size. We successively test to see if we can shift x left by 16, 8, 4, 2, and 1 places in turn.

```
        ; __value_in_regs struct { unsigned x; int shift; }
        ;   unorm_arm7m(unsigned x)
unorm_arm7m
        MOV     shift, #0               ; shift=0;
        CMP     x, #1<<16               ; if (x < (1<<16))
        MOVCC   x, x, LSL#16            ;   { x = x<<16;
        ADDCC   shift, shift, #16       ;     shift+=16; }
        TST     x, #0xFF000000          ; if (x < (1<<24))
        MOVEQ   x, x, LSL#8             ;   { x = x<<8;
        ADDEQ   shift, shift, #8        ;     shift+=8; }
        TST     x, #0xF0000000          ; if (x < (1<<28))
        MOVEQ   x, x, LSL#4             ;   { x = x<<4;
        ADDEQ   shift, shift, #4        ;     shift+=4; }
        TST     x, #0xC0000000          ; if (x < (1<<30))
        MOVEQ   x, x, LSL#2             ;   { x = x<<2;
        ADDEQ   shift, shift, #2        ;     shift+=2; }
        TST     x, #0x80000000          ; if (x < (1<<31))
        ADDEQ   shift, shift, #1        ;   { shift+=1;
        MOVEQS  x, x, LSL#1             ;     x<<=1;
```

```
MOVEQ   shift, #32           ; if (x==0) shift=32; }
MOV     pc, lr
```

The final MOVEQ sets shift to 32 when x is zero and can often be omitted. The implementation requires 17 cycles on ARM7TDMI or ARM9TDMI and is sufficient for most purposes. However, it is not the fastest way to normalize on these processors. For maximum speed you can use a hash-based method.

The hash-based method first reduces the input operand to one of 33 different possibilities, without changing the CLZ value. We do this by iterating $x = x \mid (x \gg s)$ for shifts $s = 1, 2, 4, 8$. This replicates the leading one 16 positions to the right. Then we calculate $x = x \And {\sim}(x \gg 16)$. This clears the 16 bits to the right of the 16 replicated ones. Table 7.1 illustrates the combined effect of these operations. For each possible input binary pattern we show the 32-bit code produced by these operations. Note that the CLZ value of the input pattern is the same as the CLZ value of the code.

Now our aim is to get from the code value to the CLZ value using a hashing function followed by table lookup. See Section 6.8.2 for more details on hashing functions.

For the hashing function, we multiply by a large value and extract the top six bits of the result. Values of the form $2^a + 1$ and $2^a - 1$ are easy to multiply by on the ARM using the barrel shifter. In fact, multiplying by $(2^9 - 1)(2^{11} - 1)(2^{14} - 1)$ gives a different hash value for each distinct CLZ value. The authors found this multiplier using a computer search.

You can use the code here to implement a fast hash-based normalization on ARMv4 processors. The implementation requires 13 cycles on an ARM7TDMI excluding setting up the table pointer.

```
table   RN 2 ; address of hash lookup table

        ; _value_in_regs struct { unsigned x; int shift; }
        ;  unorm_arm7m_hash(unsigned x)
```

Table 7.1   Code and CLZ values for different inputs.

Input (in binary, x is a wildcard bit)	32-bit code	CLZ value
1xxxxxxx xxxxxxxx xxxxxxxx xxxxxxxx	0xFFFF0000	0
01xxxxxx xxxxxxxx xxxxxxxx xxxxxxxx	0x7FFF8000	1
001xxxxx xxxxxxxx xxxxxxxx xxxxxxxx	0x3FFFC000	2
...	...	...
00000000 00000000 00000000 000001xx	0x00000007	29
00000000 00000000 00000000 0000001x	0x00000003	30
00000000 00000000 00000000 00000001	0x00000001	31
00000000 00000000 00000000 00000000	0x00000000	32

```
unorm_arm7m_hash
        ORR     shift, x, x, LSR#1
        ORR     shift, shift, shift, LSR#2
        ORR     shift, shift, shift, LSR#4
        ORR     shift, shift, shift, LSR#8
        BIC     shift, shift, shift, LSR#16
        RSB     shift, shift, shift, LSL#9      ; *(2^9-1)
        RSB     shift, shift, shift, LSL#11     ; *(2^11-1)
        RSB     shift, shift, shift, LSL#14     ; *(2^14-1)
        ADR     table, unorm_arm7m_hash_table
        LDRB    shift, [table, shift, LSR#26]
        MOV     x, x, LSL shift
        MOV     pc, lr

unorm_arm7m_hash_table
        DCB     0x20, 0x14, 0x13, 0xff, 0xff, 0x12, 0xff, 0x07
        DCB     0x0a, 0x11, 0xff, 0xff, 0x0e, 0xff, 0x06, 0xff
        DCB     0xff, 0x09, 0xff, 0x10, 0xff, 0xff, 0x01, 0x1a
        DCB     0xff, 0x0d, 0xff, 0xff, 0x18, 0x05, 0xff, 0xff
        DCB     0xff, 0x15, 0xff, 0x08, 0x0b, 0xff, 0x0f, 0xff
        DCB     0xff, 0xff, 0xff, 0x02, 0x1b, 0x00, 0x19, 0xff
        DCB     0x16, 0xff, 0x0c, 0xff, 0xff, 0x03, 0x1c, 0xff
        DCB     0x17, 0xff, 0x04, 0x1d, 0xff, 0xff, 0x1e, 0x1f
```

7.2.3 COUNTING TRAILING ZEROS

Count trailing zeros is a related operation to count leading zeros. It counts the number of zeros below the least significant set bit in an integer. Equivalently, this detects the highest power of two that divides the integer. Therefore you can count trailing zeros to express an integer as a product of a power of two and an odd integer. If the integer is zero, then there is no lowest bit so the count trailing zeros returns 32.

There is a trick to finding the highest power of two dividing an integer n, for nonzero n. The trick is to see that the expression $(n \mathbin{\&} (-n))$ has a single bit set in position of the lowest bit set in n. Figure 7.2 shows how this works. The x represents wildcard bits.

$$n = xxxxxxxxxxxxxxxxxxx10000000000000$$
$$-n = yyyyyyyyyyyyyyyyyyy10000000000000 \quad \text{where } y = 1 - x$$
$$n \mathbin{\&} (-n) = 0000000000000000010000000000000$$

Figure 7.2   Identifying the least significant bit.

Using this trick, we can convert a count trailing zeros to a count leading zeros. The following code implements count trailing zeros on an ARM9E. We handle the zero-input case without extra overhead by using conditional instructions.

```
        ; unsigned ctz_arm9e(unsigned x)
ctz_arm9e
        RSBS    shift, x, #0      ; shift=-x
        AND     shift, shift, x   ; isolate trailing 1 of x
        CLZCC   shift, shift      ; number of zeros above last 1
        RSC     r0, shift, #32    ; number of zeros below last 1
        MOV     pc, lr
```

For processors without the CLZ instruction, a hashing method similar to that of Section 7.2.2 gives good performance:

```
        ; unsigned ctz_arm7m(unsigned x)
ctz_arm7m
        RSB     shift, x, #0
        AND     shift, shift, x                    ; isolate lowest bit
        ADD     shift, shift, shift, LSL#4         ; *(2^4+1)
        ADD     shift, shift, shift, LSL#6         ; *(2^6+1)
        RSB     shift, shift, shift, LSL#16        ; *(2^16-1)
        ADR     table, ctz_arm7m_hash_table
        LDRB    r0, [table, shift, LSR#26]
        MOV     pc, lr


ctz_arm7m_hash_table
        DCB     0x20, 0x00, 0x01, 0x0c, 0x02, 0x06, 0xff, 0x0d
        DCB     0x03, 0xff, 0x07, 0xff, 0xff, 0xff, 0xff, 0x0e
        DCB     0x0a, 0x04, 0xff, 0xff, 0x08, 0xff, 0xff, 0x19
        DCB     0xff, 0xff, 0xff, 0xff, 0xff, 0x15, 0x1b, 0x0f
        DCB     0x1f, 0x0b, 0x05, 0xff, 0xff, 0xff, 0xff, 0xff
        DCB     0x09, 0xff, 0xff, 0x18, 0xff, 0xff, 0x14, 0x1a
        DCB     0x1e, 0xff, 0xff, 0xff, 0xff, 0x17, 0xff, 0x13
        DCB     0x1d, 0xff, 0x16, 0x12, 0x1c, 0x11, 0x10
```

7.3 DIVISION

ARM cores don't have hardware support for division. To divide two numbers you must call a software routine that calculates the result using standard arithmetic operations. If you can't avoid a division (see Section 5.10 for how to avoid divisions and fast division by a repeated denominator), then you need access to very optimized division routines. This section provides some of these useful optimized routines.

With aggressive optimization the Newton-Raphson division routines on an ARM9E run as fast as one bit per cycle hardware division implementations. Therefore ARM does not need the complexity of a hardware division implementation.

This section describes the fastest division implementations that we know of. The section is unavoidably long as there are many different division techniques and precisions to consider. We will also prove that the routines actually work for all possible inputs. This is essential since we can't try all possible input arguments for a 32-bit by 32-bit division! If you are not interested in the theoretical details, skip the proof and just lift the code from the text.

Section 7.3.1 gives division implementations using trial subtraction, or binary search. Trial subtraction is useful when early termination is likely due to a small quotient, or on a processor core without a fast multiply instruction. Sections 7.3.2 and 7.3.3 give implementations using Newton-Raphson iteration to converge to the answer. Use Newton-Raphson iteration when the worst-case performance is important, or fast multiply instructions are available. The Newton-Raphson implementations use the ARMv5TE extensions. Finally Section 7.3.4 looks at signed rather than unsigned division.

We will need to distinguish between integer division and true mathematical division. Let's fix the following notation:

- n/d = the integer part of the result rounding towards zero (as in C)
- n%d = the integer remainder $n - d(n/d)$ (as in C)
- n//d = $nd^{-1} = \dfrac{n}{d}$ = the true mathematical result of n divided by d

7.3.1 UNSIGNED DIVISION BY TRIAL SUBTRACTION

Suppose we need to calculate the quotient $q = n/d$ and remainder $r = n \% d$ for unsigned integers n and d. Suppose also that we know the quotient q fits into N bits so that $n/d < 2^N$, or equivalently $n < (d \ll N)$. The trial subtraction algorithm calculates the N bits of q by trying to set each bit in turn, starting at the most significant bit, bit $N - 1$. This is equivalent to a binary search for the result. We can set bit k if we can subtract $(d \ll k)$ from the current remainder without giving a negative result. The example udiv_simple gives a simple C implementation of this algorithm:

```
unsigned udiv_simple(unsigned d, unsigned n, unsigned N)
{
  unsigned q=0, r=n;

  do
  {                              /* calculate next quotient bit */
```

```
    N--;                    /* move to next bit */
    if ( (r>>N) >= d )    /* if r>=d*(1<<N) */
    {
        r -= (d<<N);        /* update remainder */
        q += (1<<N);        /* update quotient */
    }
} while (N);

return q;
}
```

PROOF To prove that the answer is correct, note that before we decrement N, the invariants of
7.1   Equation (7.1) hold:

$$n = qd + r \quad \text{and} \quad 0 \le r < d2^N \tag{7.1}$$

At the start $q = 0$ and $r = n$, so the invariants hold by our assumption that the quotient fits into N bits. Assume now that the invariants hold for some N. If $r < d2^{N-1}$, then we need do nothing for the invariants to hold for $N - 1$. If $r \ge d2^{N-1}$, then we maintain the invariants by subtracting $d2^{N-1}$ from r and adding 2^{N-1} to q.

The preceding implementation is called a *restoring* trial subtraction implementation. In a *nonrestoring* implementation, the subtraction always takes place. However, if r becomes negative, then we use an addition of $(d \ll N)$ on the next round, rather than a subtraction, to give the same result. Nonrestoring division is slower on the ARM so we won't go into the details. The following subsections give you assembly implementations of the trial subtraction method for different numerator and denominator sizes. They run on any ARM processor.

7.3.1.1   Unsigned 32-Bit/32-Bit Divide by Trial Subtraction

This is the operation required by C compilers. It is called when the expression n/d or n%d occurs in C and d is not a power of 2. The routine returns a two-element structure consisting of the quotient and remainder.

```
d         RN 0    ; input denominator d, output quotient
r         RN 1    ; input numerator n, output remainder
t         RN 2    ; scratch register
q         RN 3    ; current quotient

          ; __value_in_regs struct { unsigned q, r; }
          ;   udiv_32by32_arm7m(unsigned d, unsigned n)
udiv_32by32_arm7m
```

```
        MOV     q, #0               ; zero quotient
        RSBS    t, d, r, LSR#3      ; if ((r>>3)>=d) C=1; else C=0;
        BCC     div_3bits           ; quotient fits in 3 bits
        RSBS    t, d, r, LSR#8      ; if ((r>>8)>=d) C=1; else C=0;
        BCC     div_8bits           ; quotient fits in 8 bits
        MOV     d, d, LSL#8         ; d = d*256
        ORR     q, q, #0xFF000000   ; make div_loop iterate twice
        RSBS    t, d, r, LSR#4      ; if ((r>>4)>=d) C=1; else C=0;
        BCC     div_4bits           ; quotient fits in 12 bits
        RSBS    t, d, r, LSR#8      ; if ((r>>8)>=d) C=1; else C=0;
        BCC     div_8bits           ; quotient fits in 16 bits
        MOV     d, d, LSL#8         ; d = d*256
        ORR     q, q, #0x00FF0000   ; make div_loop iterate 3 times
        RSBS    t, d, r, LSR#8      ; if ((r>>8)>=d)
        MOVCS   d, d, LSL#8         ; { d = d*256;
        ORRCS   q, q, #0x0000FF00   ; make div_loop iterate 4 times}
        RSBS    t, d, r, LSR#4      ; if ((r>>4)<d)
        BCC     div_4bits           ;    r/d quotient fits in 4 bits
        RSBS    t, d, #0            ; if (0 >= d)
        BCS     div_by_0            ;    goto divide by zero trap
        ; fall through to the loop with C=0
div_loop
        MOVCS   d, d, LSR#8         ; if (next loop) d = d/256
div_8bits                           ; calculate 8 quotient bits
        RSBS    t, d, r, LSR#7      ; if ((r>>7)>=d) C=1; else C=0;
        SUBCS   r, r, d, LSL#7      ; if (C) r -= d<<7;
        ADC     q, q, q             ; q=(q<<1)+C;
        RSBS    t, d, r, LSR#6      ; if ((r>>6)>=d) C=1; else C=0;
        SUBCS   r, r, d, LSL#6      ; if (C) r -= d<<6;
        ADC     q, q, q             ; q=(q<<1)+C;
        RSBS    t, d, r, LSR#5      ; if ((r>>5)>=d) C=1; else C=0;
        SUBCS   r, r, d, LSL#5      ; if (C) r -= d<<5;
        ADC     q, q, q             ; q=(q<<1)+C;
        RSBS    t, d, r, LSR#4      ; if ((r>>4)>=d) C=1; else C=0;
        SUBCS   r, r, d, LSL#4      ; if (C) r -= d<<4;
        ADC     q, q, q             ; q=(q<<1)+C;
div_4bits                           ; calculate 4 quotient bits
        RSBS    t, d, r, LSR#3      ; if ((r>>3)>=d) C=1; else C=0;
        SUBCS   r, r, d, LSL#3      ; if (C) r -= d<<3;
        ADC     q, q, q             ; q=(q<<1)+C;
div_3bits                           ; calculate 3 quotient bits
        RSBS    t, d, r, LSR#2      ; if ((r>>2)>=d) C=1; else C=0;
        SUBCS   r, r, d, LSL#2      ; if (C) r -= d<<2;
```

```
        ADC      q, q, q              ; q=(q<<1)+C;
        RSBS     t, d, r, LSR#1       ; if ((r>>1)>=d) C=1; else C=0;
        SUBCS    r, r, d, LSL#1       ; if (C) r -= d<<1;
        ADC      q, q, q              ; q=(q<<1)+C;
        RSBS     t, d, r              ; if (r>=d) C=1; else C=0;
        SUBCS    r, r, d              ; if (C) r -= d;
        ADCS     q, q, q              ; q=(q<<1)+C; C=old q bit 31;
div_next
        BCS      div_loop             ; loop if more quotient bits
        MOV      r0, q                ; r0 = quotient; r1=remainder;
        MOV      pc, lr               ; return { r0, r1 } structure;
div_by_0
        MOV      r0, #-1
        MOV      r1, #-1
        MOV      pc, lr               ; return { -1, -1 } structure;
```

To see how this routine works, first look at the code between the labels div_8bits and div_next. This calculates the 8-bit quotient r/d, leaving the remainder in r and inserting the 8 bits of the quotient into the lower bits of q. The code works by using a trial subtraction algorithm. It attempts to subtract $128d, 64d, 32d, 16d, 8d, 4d, 2d$, and d in turn from r. For each subtract it sets carry to one if the subtract is possible and zero otherwise. This carry forms the next bit of the result to insert into q.

Next note that we can jump into this code at div_4bits or div_3bits if we only want to perform a 4-bit or 3-bit divide, respectively.

Now look at the beginning of the routine. We want to calculate r/d, leaving the remainder in r and writing the quotient to q. We first check to see if the quotient q will fit into 3 or 8 bits. If so, we can jump directly to div_3bits or div_8bits, respectively to calculate the answer. This *early termination* is useful in C where quotients are often small. If the quotient requires more than 8 bits, then we multiply d by 256 until r/d fits into 8 bits. We record how many times we have multiplied d by 256 using the high bits of q, setting 8 bits for each multiply. This means that after we have calculated the 8-bit r/d, we loop back to div_loop and divide d by 256 for each multiply we performed earlier. In this way we reduce the divide to a series of 8-bit divides.

7.3.1.2   Unsigned 32/15-Bit Divide by Trial Subtraction

In the 32/32 divide of Section 7.3.1.1, each trial subtraction takes three cycles per bit of quotient. However, if we restrict the denominator and quotient to 15 bits, we can do a trial subtraction in only two cycles per bit of quotient. You will find this operation useful for 16-bit DSP, where the division of two positive Q15 numbers requires a 30/15-bit integer division (see Section 8.1.5).

In the following code, the numerator *n* is a 32-bit unsigned integer. The denominator *d* is a 15-bit unsigned integer. The routine returns a structure containing the 15-bit quotient *q* and remainder *r*. If $n \geq (d \ll 15)$, then the result overflows and we return the maximum possible quotient of 0x7fff.

```
m  RN 0    ; input denominator d then (-d << 14)
r  RN 1    ; input numerator n then remainder

   ; __value_in_regs struct { unsigned q, r; }
   ; udiv_32by16_arm7m(unsigned d, unsigned n)
udiv_32by16_arm7m
   RSBS   m, m, r, LSR#15          ; m = (n >> 15) - d
   BCS    overflow_15              ; overflow if (n >> 15)>=d
   SUB    m, m, r, LSR#15          ; m = -d
   MOV    m, m, LSL#14             ; m = -d << 14
   ; 15 trial division steps follow
   ADDS   r, m, r                  ; r=r-(d << 14); C=(r>=0);
   SUBCC  r, r, m                  ; if (C==0) r+=(d << 14)
   ADCS   r, m, r, LSL #1          ; r=(2*r+C)-(d << 14); C=(r>=0);
   SUBCC  r, r, m                  ; if (C==0) r+=(d << 14)
   ADCS   r, m, r, LSL #1          ; ... and repeat ...
   SUBCC  r, r, m
   ADCS   r, m, r, LSL #1
   SUBCC  r, r, m
   ADCS   r, m, r, LSL #1
   SUBCC  r, r, m
   ADCS   r, m, r, LSL #1
   SUBCC  r, r, m
   ADCS   r, m, r, LSL #1
   SUBCC  r, r, m
   ADCS   r, m, r, LSL #1
   SUBCC  r, r, m
   ADCS   r, m, r, LSL #1
   SUBCC  r, r, m
   ADCS   r, m, r, LSL #1
   SUBCC  r, r, m
   ADCS   r, m, r, LSL #1
   SUBCC  r, r, m
   ADCS   r, m, r, LSL #1
   SUBCC  r, r, m
   ADCS   r, m, r, LSL #1
   SUBCC  r, r, m
   ADCS   r, m, r, LSL #1
```

```
        SUBCC  r, r, m
        ADCS   r, m, r, LSL #1
        SUBCC  r, r, m
        ; extract answer and remainder (if required)
        ADC    r0, r, r           ; insert final answer bit
        MOV    r, r0, LSR #15     ; extract remainder
        BIC    r0, r0, r, LSL #15 ; extract quotient
        MOV    pc, lr             ; return { r0, r1 }
overflow_15                       ; quotient oveflows 15 bits
        LDR    r0, =0x7fff        ; maximum quotient
        MOV    r1, r0             ; maximum remainder
        MOV    pc, lr             ; return { 0x7fff, 0x7fff }
```

We start by setting $m = -d2^{14}$. Instead of subtracting a shifted version of the denominator from the remainder, we add the negated denominator to the shifted remainder. After the kth trial subtraction step, the bottom k bits of r hold the k top bits of the quotient. The upper $32 - k$ bits of r hold the remainder. Each ADC instruction performs three functions:

- It shifts the remainder left by one.
- It inserts the next quotient bit from the last trial subtraction.
- It subtracts $d \ll 14$ from the remainder.

After 15 steps the bottom 15 bits of r contain the quotient and the top 17 bits contain the remainder. We separate these into $r0$ and $r1$, respectively. Excluding the return, the division takes 35 cycles on ARM7TDMI.

7.3.1.3   Unsigned 64/31-Bit Divide by Trial Subtraction

This operation is useful when you need to divide Q31 fixed-point integers (see Section 8.1.5). It doubles the precision of the division in Section 7.3.1.2. The numerator n is an unsigned 64-bit integer. The denominator d is an unsigned 31-bit integer. The following routine returns a structure containing the 32-bit quotient q and remainder r. The result overflows if $n \geq d2^{32}$. In this case we return the maximum possible quotient of 0xffffffff. The routines takes 99 cycles on ARM7TDMI using a three-bit-per-cycle trial subtraction. In the code comments we use the notation $[r, q]$ to mean a 64-bit value with upper 32 bits r and lower 32 bits q.

```
m       RN 0      ; input denominator d, -d
r       RN 1      ; input numerator (low), remainder (high)
t       RN 2      ; input numerator (high)
q       RN 3      ; result quotient and remainder (low)
```

```
        ; __value_in_regs struct { unsigned q, r; }
        ;   udiv_64by32_arm7m(unsigned d, unsigned long long n)
udiv_64by32_arm7m
        CMP         t, m              ; if (n >= (d<<32))
        BCS         overflow_32       ;    goto overflow_32;
        RSB         m, m, #0          ; m = -d
        ADDS        q, r, r           ; { [r,q] = 2*[r,q]-[d,0];
        ADCS        r, m, t, LSL#1    ;   C = ([r,q]>=0); }
        SUBCC       r, r, m           ; if (C==0) [r,q] += [d,0]
        GBLA        k                 ; the next 32 steps are the same
k       SETA        1                 ; so we generate them using an
        WHILE       k<32              ; assembler while loop
          ADCS      q, q, q           ; { [r,q] = 2*[r,q]+C - [d,0];
          ADCS      r, m, r, LSL#1    ;   C = ([r,q]>=0); }
          SUBCC     r, r, m           ; if (C==0) [r,q] += [d,0]
k       SETA        k+1
        WEND
        ADCS        r0, q, q          ; insert final answer bit
        MOV         pc, lr            ; return { r0, r1 }
overflow_32
        MOV         r0, #-1
        MOV         r1, #-1
        MOV         pc, lr            ; return { -1, -1 }
```

The idea is similar to the 32/15-bit division. After the kth trial subtraction the 64-bit value $[r, q]$ contains the remainder in the top $64 - k$ bits. The bottom k bits contain the top k quotient bits. After 32 trial subtractions, r holds the remainder and q the quotient. The two ADC instructions shift $[r, q]$ left by one, inserting the last answer bit in the bottom and subtracting the denominator from the upper 32 bits. If the subtraction overflows, we correct r by adding back the denominator.

7.3.2 UNSIGNED INTEGER NEWTON-RAPHSON DIVISION

Newton-Raphson iteration is a powerful technique for solving equations numerically. Once we have a good approximation of a solution to an equation, the iteration converges very rapidly on that solution. In fact, convergence is usually quadratic with the number of valid fractional bits roughly doubling with each iteration. Newton-Raphson is widely used for calculating high-precision reciprocals and square roots. We will use the Newton-Raphson method to implement 16- and 32-bit integer and fractional divides, although the ideas we will look at generalize to any size of division.

The Newton-Raphson technique applies to any equation of the form $f(x) = 0$, where $f(x)$ is a differentiable function with derivative $f'(x)$. We start with an approximation x_n to a solution x of the equation. Then we apply the following iteration, to give us a better approximation x_{n+1}

$$x_{n+1} = x_n - \frac{f(x_n)}{f'(x_n)} \tag{7.2}$$

Figure 7.3 illustrates the Newton-Raphson iteration to solve $f(x) = 0.8 - x^{-1} = 0$, taking $x_0 = 1$ as our initial approximation. The first two steps are $x_1 = 1.2$ and $x_2 = 1.248$, converging rapidly to the solution 1.25.

For many functions f, the iteration converges rapidly to the solution x. Graphically, we place the estimate x_{n+1} where the tangent to the curve at estimate x_n meets the x-axis.

We will use Newton-Raphson iteration to calculate $2^N d^{-1}$ using only integer multiplication operations. We allow the factor of 2^N because this is useful when trying to estimate $2^{32}/d$ as used in Sections 7.3.2.1 and 5.10.2. Consider the following function:

$$f(x) = d - \frac{2^N}{x} \tag{7.3}$$

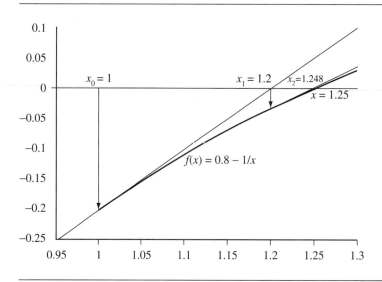

Figure 7.3   Newton-Raphson iteration for $f(x) = 0.8 - 1/x$.

The equation $f(x) = 0$ has a solution at $x = 2^N d^{-1}$ and derivative $f'(x) = 2^N x^{-2}$. By substitution, the Newton-Raphson iteration is given by

$$x_{n+1} = x_n - \frac{d - 2^N x_n^{-1}}{2^N x_n^{-2}} = 2x_n - \frac{dx_n^2}{2^N} \tag{7.4}$$

In one sense the iteration has turned our division upside-down. Instead of multiplying by 2^N and dividing by d, we are now multiplying by d and dividing by 2^N. There are two cases that are particularly useful:

- $N = 32$ and d is an integer. In this case we can approximate $2^{32} d^{-1}$ quickly and use this approximation to calculate n/d, the ratio of two unsigned 32-bit numbers. See Section 7.3.2.1 for iterations using $N = 32$.

- $N = 0$ and d is a fraction represented in fixed-point format with $0.5 \leq d < 1$. In this case we can calculate d^{-1} using the iteration, which is useful to calculate nd^{-1} for a range of fixed-point values n. See Section 7.3.3 for iterations using $N = 0$.

7.3.2.1   Unsigned 32/32-Bit Divide by Newton-Raphson

This section gives you an alterative to the routine of Section 7.3.1.1. The following routine has very good worst-case performance and makes use of the faster multiplier on ARM9E. We use Newton-Raphson iteration with $N = 32$ and integral d to approximate the integer $2^{32}/d$. We then multiply this approximation by n and divide by 2^{32} to get an estimate of the quotient $q = n/d$. Finally, we calculate the remainder $r = n - qd$ and correct quotient and remainder for any rounding error.

```
q       RN 0    ; input denominator d, output quotient q
r       RN 1    ; input numerator n, output remainder r
s       RN 2    ; scratch register
m       RN 3    ; scratch register
a       RN 12   ; scratch register

        ; __value_in_regs struct { unsigned q, r; }
        ;   udiv_32by32_arm9e(unsigned d, unsigned n)
udiv_32by32_arm9e ; instruction number : comment
        CLZ     s, q                    ; 01 : find normalizing shift
        MOVS    a, q, LSL s             ; 02 : perform a lookup on the
        ADD     a, pc, a, LSR#25        ; 03 : most significant 7 bits
        LDRNEB  a, [a, #t32-b32-64]     ; 04 : of divisor
b32     SUBS    s, s, #7                ; 05 : correct shift
        RSB     m, q, #0                ; 06 : m = -d
        MOVPL   q, a, LSL s             ; 07 : q approx (1<<32)/d
        ; 1st Newton iteration follows
        MULPL   a, q, m                 ; 08 : a = -q*d
```

```
        BMI       udiv_by_large_d        ; 09 : large d trap
        SMLAWT    q, q, a, q             ; 10 : q approx q-(q*q*d>>32)
        TEQ       m, m, ASR#1            ; 11 : check for d=0 or d=1
        ; 2nd Newton iteration follows
        MULNE     a, q, m                ; 12 : a = -q*d
        MOVNE     s, #0                  ; 13 : s = 0
        SMLALNE   s, q, a, q             ; 14 : q = q-(q*q*d>>32)
        BEQ       udiv_by_0_or_1         ; 15 : trap d=0 or d=1
        ; q now accurate enough for a remainder r, 0<=r<3*d
        UMULL     s, q, r, q             ; 16 : q = (r*q)>>32
        ADD       r, r, m                ; 17 : r = n-d
        MLA       r, q, m, r             ; 18 : r = n-(q+1)*d
        ; since 0 <= n-q*d < 3*d, thus -d <= r < 2*d
        CMN       r, m                   ; 19 : t = r-d
        SUBCS     r, r, m                ; 20 : if (t<-d || t>=0) r=r+d
        ADDCC     q, q, #1               ; 21 : if (-d<=t && t<0) q=q+1
        ADDPL     r, r, m, LSL#1         ; 22 : if (t>=0) { r=r-2*d
        ADDPL     q, q, #2               ; 23 :               q=q+2 }
        BX        lr                     ; 24 : return {q, r}
udiv_by_large_d
        ; at this point we know d >= 2^(31-6)=2^25
        SUB       a, a, #4               ; 25 : set q to be an
        RSB       s, s, #0               ; 26 : underestimate of
        MOV       q, a, LSR s            ; 27 : (1<<32)/d
        UMULL     s, q, r, q             ; 28 : q = (n*q)>>32
        MLA       r, q, m, r             ; 29 : r = n-q*d
        ; q now accurate enough for a remainder r, 0<=r<4*d
        CMN       m, r, LSR#1            ; 30 : if (r/2 >= d)
        ADDCS     r, r, m, LSL#1         ; 31 : { r=r-2*d;
        ADDCS     q, q, #2               ; 32 :   q=q+2; }
        CMN       m, r                   ; 33 : if (r >= d)
        ADDCS     r, r, m                ; 34 : { r=r-d;
        ADDCS     q, q, #1               ; 35 :   q=q+1; }
        BX        lr                     ; 36 : return {q, r}
udiv_by_0_or_1
        ; carry set if d=1, carry clear if d=0
        MOVCS     q, r                   ; 37 : if (d==1) { q=n;
        MOVCS     r, #0                  ; 38 :               r=0; }
        MOVCC     q, #-1                 ; 39 : if (d==0) { q=-1;
        MOVCC     r, #-1                 ; 40 :               r=-1; }
        BX        lr                     ; 41 : return {q,r}


        ; table for 32 by 32 bit Newton Raphson divisions
```

```
                ; table[0] = 255
                ; table[i] = (1<<14)/(64+i) for i=1,2,3,...,63
        t32     DCB 0xff, 0xfc, 0xf8, 0xf4, 0xf0, 0xed, 0xea, 0xe6
                DCB 0xe3, 0xe0, 0xdd, 0xda, 0xd7, 0xd4, 0xd2, 0xcf
                DCB 0xcc, 0xca, 0xc7, 0xc5, 0xc3, 0xc0, 0xbe, 0xbc
                DCB 0xba, 0xb8, 0xb6, 0xb4, 0xb2, 0xb0, 0xae, 0xac
                DCB 0xaa, 0xa8, 0xa7, 0xa5, 0xa3, 0xa2, 0xa0, 0x9f
                DCB 0x9d, 0x9c, 0x9a, 0x99, 0x97, 0x96, 0x94, 0x93
                DCB 0x92, 0x90, 0x8f, 0x8e, 0x8d, 0x8c, 0x8a, 0x89
                DCB 0x88, 0x87, 0x86, 0x85, 0x84, 0x83, 0x82, 0x81
```

PROOF
7.2
The proof that the code works is rather involved. To make the proof and explanation simpler, we comment each line with a line number for the instruction. Note that some of the instructions are conditional, and the comments only apply when the instruction is executed.

Execution follows several different paths through the code depending on the size of the denominator d. We treat these cases separately. We'll use Ik as shorthand notation for the instruction numbered k in the preceding code.

Case 1 $d = 0$: 27 cycles on ARM9E, including return

We check for this case explicitly. We avoid the table lookup at $I04$ by making the load conditional on $q \neq 0$. This ensures we don't read off the start of the table. Since $I01$ sets $s = 32$, there is no branch at $I09$. $I06$ sets $m = 0$, and so $I11$ sets the Z flag and clears the carry flag. We branch at $I15$ to special case code.

Case 2 $d = 1$: 27 cycles on ARM9E, including return

This case is similar to the $d = 0$ case. The table lookup at $I05$ does occur, but we ignore the result. $I06$ sets $m = -1$, and so $I11$ sets the Z and carry flags. The special code at $I37$ returns the trivial result of $q = n, r = 0$.

Case 3 $2 \leq d < 2^{25}$: 36 cycles on ARM9E, including return

This is the hardest case. First we use a table lookup on the leading bits of d to generate an estimate for $2^{32}/d$. $I01$ finds a shift s such that $2^{31} \leq d2^s < 2^{32}$. $I02$ sets $a = d2^s$. $I03$ and $I04$ perform a table lookup on the top seven bits of a, which we will call i_0. i_0 is an index between 64 and 127. Truncating d to seven bits introduces an error f_0:

$$i_0 = 2^{s-25}d - f_0, \quad \text{where } 0 \leq f_0 < 1 \tag{7.5}$$

We set a to the lookup value $a_0 = table[i_0 - 64] = 2^{14}i_0^{-1} - g_0$, where $0 \leq g_0 \leq 1$ is the table truncation error. Then,

$$a_0 = \frac{2^{14}}{i_0} - g_0 = \frac{2^{14}}{i_0}\left(1 - \frac{g_0 i_0}{2^{14}}\right) = \frac{2^{14}}{i_0 + f_0}\left(1 + \frac{f_0}{i_0} - g_0\frac{i_0 + f_0}{2^{14}}\right) \tag{7.6}$$

Noting that $i_0 + f_0 = 2^{s-25}d$ from Equation 7.5 and collecting the error terms into e_0:

$$a_0 = \frac{2^{39-s}}{d}(1 - e_0), \quad \text{where } e_0 = g_0 \frac{i_0 + f_0}{2^{14}} - \frac{f_0}{i_0} \tag{7.7}$$

Since $64 \leq i_0 \leq i_0 + f_0 < 128$ by the choice of s it follows that $-f_0 2^{-6} \leq e_0 \leq g_0 2^{-7}$. As $d < 2^{25}$, we know $s \geq 7$. $I05$ and $I07$ calculate the following value in register q:

$$q_0 = 2^{s-7}a_0 = \frac{2^{32}}{d}(1 - e_0) \tag{7.8}$$

This is a good initial approximation for $2^{32}d^{-1}$, and we now iterate Newton-Raphson twice to increase the accuracy of the approximation. $I08$ and $I10$ update the values of registers a and q to a_1 and q_1 according to Equation (7.9). $I08$ calculates a_1 using $m = -d$. Since $d \geq 2$, it follows that $q_0 < 2^{31}$ for when $d = 2$, then $f_0 = 0$, $i_0 = 64$, $g_0 = 1$, $e_0 = 2^{-8}$. Therefore we can use the signed multiply accumulate instruction SMLAWT at $I10$ to calculate q_1.

$$a_1 = 2^{32} - dq_0 = 2^{32}e_0 \quad \text{and} \quad q_1 = q_0 + (((a_1 \gg 16)q_0) \gg 16) \tag{7.9}$$

The right shifts introduce truncation errors $0 \leq f_1 < 1$ and $0 \leq g_1 < 1$, respectively:

$$q_1 = q_0 + (a_1 2^{-16} - f_1)q_0 2^{-16} - g_1 = \frac{2^{32}}{d}(1 - e_0^2 - f_1(1 - e_0)2^{-16}) - g_1 \tag{7.10}$$

$$q_1 = \frac{2^{32}}{d}(1 - e_1), \quad \text{where } e_1 = e_0^2 + f_1(1 - e_0)2^{-16} + g_1 d2^{-32} \tag{7.11}$$

The new estimate q_1 is more accurate with error $e_1 \approx e_0^2$. $I12$, $I13$, and $I14$ implement the second Newton-Raphson iteration, updating registers a and q to the values a_2 and q_2:

$$a_2 = 2^{32} - dq_1 = 2^{32}e_1 \quad \text{and} \quad q_2 = q_1 + ((a_2 q_1) \gg 32) \tag{7.12}$$

Again the shift introduces a truncation error $0 \leq g_2 < 1$:

$$q_2 = q_1 + a_2 q_1 2^{-32} - g_2 = \frac{2^{32}}{d}(1 - e_2), \quad \text{where}$$

$$e_2 = e_1^2 + g_2 d2^{-32} < e_1^2 + d2^{-32} \tag{7.13}$$

Our estimate of $2^{32}d^{-1}$ is now sufficiently accurate. $I16$ estimates n/d by setting q to the value q_3 in Equation (7.14). The shift introduces a rounding error $0 \leq g_3 < 1$.

$$q_3 = (nq_2) \gg 32 = nq_2 2^{-32} - g_3 = \frac{n}{d} - e_3, \quad \text{where}$$

$$e_3 = \frac{n}{d}e_2 + g_3 < \frac{n}{d}e_1^2 + 2 \tag{7.14}$$

The error e_3 is certainly positive and small, but how small? We will show that $0 \le e_3 < 3$, by showing that $e_1^2 < d2^{-32}$. We split into subcases:

Case 3.1 $2 \le d \le 16$

Then $f_0 = f_1 = g_1 = 0$ as the respective truncations do not drop any bits. So $e_1 = e_0^2$ and $e_0 = i_0 g_0 2^{-14}$. We calculate i_0 and g_0 explicitly in Table 7.2.

Case 3.2 $16 < d \le 256$

Then $f_0 \le 0.5$ implies $|e_0| \le 2^{-7}$. As $f_1 = g_1 = 0$, it follows that $e_1^2 \le 2^{-28} < d2^{-32}$.

Case 3.3 $256 < d < 512$

Then $f_0 \le 1$ implies $|e_0| \le 2^{-6}$. As $f_1 = g_1 = 0$, it follows that $e_1^2 \le 2^{-24} < d2^{-32}$.

Case 3.4 $512 \le d < 2^{25}$

Then $f_0 \le 1$ implies $|e_0| \le 2^{-6}$. Therefore, $e_1 < 2^{-12} + 2^{-15} + d2^{-32}$. Let $D = \sqrt{d2^{-32}}$. Then $2^{-11.5} \le D < 2^{-3.5}$. So, $e_1 < D(2^{-0.5} + 2^{-3.5} + 2^{-3.5}) < D$, the required result.

Now we know that $e_3 < 3$, $I16$ to $I23$ calculate which of the three possible results $q_3, q_3 + 1, q_3 + 2$, is the correct value for n/d. The instructions calculate the remainder $r = n - dq_3$, and subtract d from the remainder, incrementing q, until $0 \le r < d$.

Case 4 $2^{25} \le d$: 32 cycles on ARM9E including return

This case starts in the same way as Case 3. We have the same equation for i_0 and a_0. However, then we branch to $I25$, where we subtract four from a_0 and apply a right shift of $7 - s$. This gives the estimate q_0 in Equation (7.15). The subtraction of four forces q_0 to be an underestimate of $2^{32}d^{-1}$. For some truncation error $0 \le g_0 < 1$:

$$q_0 = \left(\frac{2^{14}}{i_0} - 4 \right) \gg (7 - s) = \frac{2^{s+7}}{i_0} - 2^{s-5} - g_0 \qquad (7.15)$$

Table 7.2   Error values for small d.

d	i_0	g_0	e_0	$2^{32} e_1^2$
2, 4, 8, 16	64	1	2^{-8}	1
3, 6, 12	96	$2//3$	2^{-8}	1
5, 10	80	$4//5$	2^{-8}	1
7, 14	112	$2//7$	2^{-9}	<1
9	72	$5//9$	$5 * 2^{-11}$	<1
11	88	$2//11$	2^{-10}	<1
13	104	$7//13$	$7 * 2^{-11}$	<1
15	120	$8//15$	2^{-8}	<1

$$q_0 = \frac{2^{32}}{d} - e_0, \quad \text{where } e_0 = 2^{s-5} + g_0 - \frac{2^{32}}{d}\frac{f_0}{i_0} \tag{7.16}$$

Since $(2^{32}d^{-1})(f_0 i_0^{-1}) \leq 2^{s+1}2^{-6} = 2^{s-5}$, it follows that $0 \leq e_0 < 3$. *I28* sets q to the approximated quotient g_1. For some truncation error $0 \leq g_1 < 1$:

$$q_1 = (nq_0) \gg 32 = \frac{nq_0}{2^{32}} - g_1 = \frac{n}{d} - \frac{n}{2^{32}}e_0 - g_1 \tag{7.17}$$

Therefore q_1 is an underestimate to n/d with error less than four. The final steps *I28* to *I35* use a two-step binary search to fix the exact answer. We have finished!

7.3.3   Unsigned Fractional Newton-Raphson Division

This section looks at Newton-Raphson techniques you can use to divide fractional values. Fractional values are represented using fixed-point arithmetic and are useful for DSP applications.

For a fractional division, we first scale the denominator to the range $0.5 \leq d < 1.0$. Then we use a table lookup to provide an estimate x_0 to d^{-1}. Finally we perform Newton-Raphson iterations with $N = 0$. From Section 7.3.2, the iteration is

$$x_{i+1} = 2x_i - dx_i^2 \tag{7.18}$$

As i increases, x_i becomes more accurate. For fastest implementation, we use low-precision multiplications when i is small, increasing the precision with each iteration.

The result is a short and fast routine. Section 7.3.3.3 gives a routine for 15-bit fractional division, and Section 7.3.3.4 a routine for 31-bit fractional division. Again, the hard part is to prove that we get the correct result for all possible inputs. For a 31-bit division we cannot test every combination of numerator and denominator. We must have a proof that the code works. Sections 7.3.3.1 and 7.3.3.2 cover the mathematical theory we require for the proofs in Sections 7.3.3.3 and 7.3.3.4. If you are not interested in this theory, then skip to Section 7.3.3.3.

Throughout the analysis, we stick to the following notation:

- d is a fractional value scaled so that $0.5 \leq d < 1$.
- i is the stage number of the iteration.
- k_i is the number of bits of precision used for x_i. We ensure that $k_{i+1} > k_i \geq 3$.
- x_i is a k_i-bit estimate to d^{-1} in the range $0 \leq x_i \leq 2 - 2^{2-k_i}$.
- x_i is a multiple of 2^{1-k_i}.
- $e_i = \dfrac{1}{d} - x_i$ is the error in the approximation x_i. We ensure $|e_i| \leq 0.5$.

With each iteration, we increase k_i and reduce the error e_i. First let's see how to calculate a good initial estimate x_0.

7.3.3.1   Theory: The Initial Estimate for Newton-Raphson Division

If you are not interested in Newton-Raphson theory, then skip the next two sections and jump to Section 7.3.3.3.

We use a lookup table on the most significant bits of d to determine the initial estimate x_0 to d^{-1}. For a good trade-off between table size and estimate accuracy, we index by the leading eight fractional bits of d, returning a nine-bit estimate x_0. Since the leading bits of d and x_0 are both one, we only need a lookup table consisting of 128 eight-bit entries.

Let a be the integer formed by the seven bits following the leading one of d. Then d is in the range $(128 + a)2^{-8} \le d < (129 + a)2^{-8}$. Choosing $c = (128.5 + a)2^{-8}$, the midpoint, we define the lookup table by

```
table[a] = round(256.0/c) - 256;
```

This is a floating-point formula, where round rounds to the nearest integer. We can reduce this to an integer formula that is easier to calculate if you don't have floating-point support:

```
table[a] = (511*(128-a))/(257+2*a);
```

Clearly, all the table entries are in the range 0 to 255. To start the Newton-Raphson iteration we set $x_0 = 1 + table[a]2^{-8}$ and $k_0 = 9$. Now we cheat slightly by looking ahead to Section 7.3.3.3. We will be interested in the value of the following error term:

$$E = d^2 e_0^2 + d2^{-16} \tag{7.19}$$

First let's look at $d|e_0|$. If $e_0 \le 0$, then

$$d|e_0| = x_0 d - 1 < x_0(129 + a)2^{-8} - 1 \tag{7.20}$$

$$d|e_0| < \left((256 + table[a])(129 + a) - 2^{-16}\right) 2^{-16} \tag{7.21}$$

If $e_0 \ge 0$, then

$$d|e_0| = 1 - x_0 d \le 1 - x_0(128 + a)2^{-8} \tag{7.22}$$

$$d|e_0| \le \left(2^{16} - (256 + table[a])(128 + a)\right) 2^{-16} \tag{7.23}$$

Running through the possible values of a, we find that $d|e_0| < 299 \times 2^{-16}$. This is the best possible bound. Take $d = (133 - e)2^{-16}$, and the smaller $e > 0$, the closer to the bound you will get! The same trick works for finding a sharp bound on E:

$$E2^{32} < \left((256 + table[a])(129 + a) - 2^{16}\right)^2 + (129 + a)2^8 \quad \text{if } e_0 \le 0 \tag{7.24}$$

$$E2^{32} < \left(2^{16} - (256 + table[a])(128 + a)\right)^2 + (129 + a)2^8 \quad \text{if } e_0 \ge 0 \tag{7.25}$$

Running over the possible values of a gives us the sharp bound $E < 2^{-15}$. Finally we need to check that $x_0 \le 2 - 2^{-7}$. This follows as the largest table entry is 254.

7.3.3.2 Theory: Accuracy of the Newton-Raphson Fraction Iteration

This section analyzes the error introduced by each fractional Newton-Raphson iteration:

$$x_{i+1} = 2x_i - dx_i^2 \qquad (7.26)$$

It is often slow to calculate this iteration exactly. As x_i is only accurate to at most k_i of precision, there is not much point in performing the calculation to more than $2k_i$ bits of precision. The following steps give a practical method of calculating the iteration. The iterations preserve the limits for x_i and e_i that we defined in Section 7.3.3.

1. Calculate x_i^2 exactly:

$$x_i^2 = \left(\frac{1}{d} - e_i\right)^2 \text{ and lies in the range } 0 \le x_i^2 \le 4 - 2^{4-k_i} + 2^{4-2k_i} \qquad (7.27)$$

2. Calculate an underestimate d_i to d, usually d to around $2k_i$ bits. We only actually require that

$$0.5 \le d_i = d - f_i \quad \text{and} \quad 0 \le f_i \le 2^{-4} \qquad (7.28)$$

3. Calculate, y_i, a $k_{i+1} + 1$ bit estimate to $d_i x_i^2$ in the range $0 \le y_i < 4$. Make y_i as accurate as possible. However, we only require that the error g_i satisfy

$$y_i = d_i x_i^2 - g_i \quad \text{and} \quad -2^{-2} \le g_i \le 2^{3-2k_i} - 2^{2-k_{i+1}} \qquad (7.29)$$

4. Calculate the new estimate $x_{i+1} = 2x_i - y_i$ using an exact subtraction. We will prove that $0 \le x_{i+1} < 2$ and so the result fits in k_{i+1} bits.

We must show that the new k_{i+1}–bit estimate x_{i+1} satisfies the properties mentioned prior to Section 7.3.3.1 and calculate a formula for the new error e_{i+1}. First, we check the range of x_{i+1}:

$$x_{i+1} = 2x_i - d_i x_i^2 + g_i \le 2x_i - 0.5x_i^2 + g_i \qquad (7.30)$$

The latter polynomial in x_i has positive gradient for $x_i \le 2$ and so reaches its maximum value when x_i is maximum. Therefore, using our bound on g_i,

$$x_{i+1} \le 2\left(2 - 2^{2-k_i}\right) - 0.5\left(4 - 2^{4-k_i} + 2^{4-2k_i}\right) + g_i \le 2 - 2^{2-k_{i+1}} \qquad (7.31)$$

On the other hand, since $|e_i| \le 0.5$ and $g_i \ge -0.25$, it follows that

$$x_{i+1} \ge 2x_i - 1.5x_i + g_i \ge 0 \qquad (7.32)$$

Finally, we calculate the new error:

$$e_{i+1} = \frac{1}{d} - x_{i+1} = \frac{1}{d} - 2x_i + (d - f_i)x_i^2 - g_i = de_i^2 - f_i x_i^2 - g_i \qquad (7.33)$$

It is easy to check that $|e_{i+1}| \le 0.5$.

7.3.3.3   Q15 Fixed-Point Division by Newton-Raphson

We calculate a Q15 representation of the ratio nd^{-1}, where n and d are 16-bit positive integers in the range $0 \le n < d < 2^{15}$. In other words, we calculate

```
q = (n << 15)/d;
```

You can use the routine `udiv_32by16_arm7m` in Section 7.3.1.2 to do this by trial subtraction. However, the following routine calculates exactly the same result but uses fewer cycles on an ARMv5E core. If you only need an estimate of the result, then you can remove instructions *I15* to *I18*, which correct the error of the initial estimate.

The routine veers perilously close to being inaccurate in many places, so it is followed by a proof that it is correct. The proof uses the theory of Section 7.3.3.2. The proof is a useful reference if the code requires adaptation or optimizing for another ARM core. The routine takes 24 cycles on an ARM9E including the return instruction. If $d \le n < 2^{15}$, then we return the saturated value `0x7fff`.

```
q         RN 0      ; input denominator d, quotient estimate q
r         RN 1      ; input numerator n, remainder r
s         RN 2      ; normalisation shift, scratch
d         RN 3      ; Q15 normalised denominator 2^14<=d<2^15

          ; unsigned udiv_q15_arm9e(unsigned d, unsigned q)
udiv_q15_arm9e ; instruction       number : comment
          CLZ     s, q               ; 01 : choose a shift s to
          SUB     s, s, #17          ; 02 : normalize d to the
          MOVS    d, q, LSL s        ; 03 : range 0.5<=d<1 at Q15
          ADD     q, pc, d, LSR#7    ; 04 : look up q, a Q8
          LDRNEB  q, [q, #t15-b15-128] ; 05 : approximation to 1//d
b15       MOV     r, r, LSL s        ; 06 : normalize numerator
          ADD     q, q, #256         ; 07 : part of table lookup
          ; q is now a Q8, 9-bit estimate to 1//d
          SMULBB  s, q, q            ; 08 : s = q*q at Q16
          CMP     r, d               ; 09 : check for overflow
          MUL     s, d, s            ; 10 : s = q*q*d at Q31
          MOV     q, q, LSL#9        ; 11 : change q to Q17
          SBC     q, q, s, LSR#15    ; 12 : q = 2*q-q*q*d at Q16
          ; q is now a Q16, 17-bit estimate to 1//d
          SMULWB  q, q, r            ; 13 : q approx n//d at Q15
          BCS     overflow_15        ; 14 : trap overflow case
          SMULBB  s, q, d            ; 15 : s = q*d at Q30
          RSB     r, d, r, LSL#15    ; 16 : r = n-d at Q30
          CMP     r, s               ; 17 : if (r>=s)
```

```
        ADDPL   q, q, #1              ; 18 :      q++
        BX      lr                    ; 19 : return q
overflow_15
        LDR     q, =0x7FFF            ; 20 : q = 0x7FFF
        BX      lr                    ; 21 : return q

        ; table for fractional Newton-Raphson division
        ; table[a] = (int)((511*(128-a))/(257+2*a)) 0<=a<128
t15     DCB 0xfe, 0xfa, 0xf6, 0xf2, 0xef, 0xeb, 0xe7, 0xe4
        DCB 0xe0, 0xdd, 0xd9, 0xd6, 0xd2, 0xcf, 0xcc, 0xc9
        DCB 0xc6, 0xc2, 0xbf, 0xbc, 0xb9, 0xb6, 0xb3, 0xb1
        DCB 0xae, 0xab, 0xa8, 0xa5, 0xa3, 0xa0, 0x9d, 0x9b
        DCB 0x98, 0x96, 0x93, 0x91, 0x8e, 0x8c, 0x8a, 0x87
        DCB 0x85, 0x83, 0x80, 0x7e, 0x7c, 0x7a, 0x78, 0x75
        DCB 0x73, 0x71, 0x6f, 0x6d, 0x6b, 0x69, 0x67, 0x65
        DCB 0x63, 0x61, 0x5f, 0x5e, 0x5c, 0x5a, 0x58, 0x56
        DCB 0x54, 0x53, 0x51, 0x4f, 0x4e, 0x4c, 0x4a, 0x49
        DCB 0x47, 0x45, 0x44, 0x42, 0x40, 0x3f, 0x3d, 0x3c
        DCB 0x3a, 0x39, 0x37, 0x36, 0x34, 0x33, 0x32, 0x30
        DCB 0x2f, 0x2d, 0x2c, 0x2b, 0x29, 0x28, 0x27, 0x25
        DCB 0x24, 0x23, 0x21, 0x20, 0x1f, 0x1e, 0x1c, 0x1b
        DCB 0x1a, 0x19, 0x17, 0x16, 0x15, 0x14, 0x13, 0x12
        DCB 0x10, 0x0f, 0x0e, 0x0d, 0x0c, 0x0b, 0x0a, 0x09
        DCB 0x08, 0x07, 0x06, 0x05, 0x04, 0x03, 0x02, 0x01
```

PROOF
7.3

The routine starts by normalizing d and n so that $2^{14} \le d < 2^{15}$ in instructions *I01, I02, I03, I06.* This doesn't affect the result since we shift the numerator and denominator left by the same number of places. Considering d as a Q15 format fixed-point fraction, $0.5 \le d < 1$. *I09* and *I14* are overflow traps that catch the case that $n \ge d$. This includes the case $d = 0$. Assuming from now on that there is no overflow, *I04, I05, I07* set q to the 9-bit Q8 initial estimate x_0 to d^{-1} as described in Section 7.3.1.1. Since d is in the range $0.5 \le d < 1$, we subtract 128 on the table lookup so that 0.5 corresponds to the first entry of the table.

Next we perform one Newton-Raphson iteration. *I08* sets a to the exact Q16 square of x_0, and *I10* sets a to the exact Q31 value of dx_0^2. There is a subtlety here. We need to check that this value will not overflow an unsigned Q31 representation. In fact:

$$dx_0^2 = \frac{x_0^2}{x_0 + e_0} = \left(1 + x_0 - \frac{e_0}{x_0 + e_0}\right) \tag{7.34}$$

This term reaches its maximum value when x_0 is as large as possible and e_0 as negative as possible, which occurs when $d = 0.5 + 2^{-8} - 2^{-15}$, where $x_0 = 2 - 2^{-7}$ and $dx_0^2 < 2 - 2^{-13} < 2$.

Finally *I11* and *I12* set q to a new Q16 estimate x_1. Since the carry flag is clear from *I09*, the SBC underestimates the reciprocal.

$$x_1 = 2x_0 - dx_0^2 + g_0 \quad \text{for some } -2^{-16} \le g_0 < 0 \tag{7.35}$$

Using Equation (7.33) for the new error:

$$0 \le e_1 = de_0^2 - g_0 \le de_0^2 + 2^{-16} \tag{7.36}$$

I13 calculates a Q15 estimate q_1 to the quotient nd^{-1}:

$$q_1 = nx_1 - h_1 = \frac{n}{d} - e_2 \tag{7.37}$$

where $0 \le h_1 < 2^{-15}$ is the truncation error and

$$e_2 = ne_1 + h_1 < de_1 + h_1 < E + h_1 < 2^{-14} \tag{7.38}$$

The bound on E is from Section 7.3.3.1. So, q_1 is an underestimate to nd^{-1} of error less than 2^{-14}. Finally *I15*, *I16*, *I17*, and *I18* calculate the remainder $n - qd$ and correct the estimate to Q15 precision.

7.3.3.4   Q31 Fixed-Point Division by Newton-Raphson

We calculate a Q31 representation of the ratio nd^{-1}, where n and d are 32-bit positive integers in the range $0 \le n < d < 2^{31}$. In other words we calculate

```
q = (unsigned int)(((unsigned long long)n<<31)/d);
```

You can use the routine udiv_64by32_arm7m in Section 7.3.1.3 to do this by trial subtraction. However, the following routine calculates exactly the same result but uses fewer cycles on an ARM9E. If you only need an estimate of the result, then you can remove the nine instructions *I21* to *I29*, which correct the error of the initial estimate.

As with the previous section, we show the assembly code followed by a proof of accuracy. The routine uses 46 cycles, including return, on an ARM9E. The routine uses the same lookup table as for the Q15 routine in Section 7.3.3.3.

```
q       RN 0     ; input denominator d, quotient estimate q
r       RN 1     ; input numerator n, remainder high r
s       RN 2     ; normalization shift, scratch register
d       RN 3     ; Q31 normalized denominator 2^30<=d<2^31
a       RN 12    ; scratch

        ; unsigned udiv_q31_arm9e(unsigned d, unsigned q)
udiv_q31_arm9e ;        instruction number : comment
```

```
          CLZ      s, q                    ; 01 : choose a shift s to
          CMP      r, q                    ; 02 : normalize d to the
          MOVCC    d, q, LSL s             ; 03 : range 0.5<=d<1 at Q32
          ADDCC    q, pc, d, LSR#24        ; 04 : look up q, a Q8
          LDRCCB   q, [q, #t15-b31-128]    ; 05 : approximation to 1//d
     b31  MOVCC    r, r, LSL s             ; 06 : normalize numerator
          ADDCC    q, q, #256              ; 07 : part of table lookup
          ; q is now a Q8, 9-bit estimate to 1//d
          SMULBBCC a, q, q                 ; 08 : a = q*q at Q16
          MOVCS    q, #0x7FFFFFFF          ; 09 : overflow case
          UMULLCC  s, a, d, a              ; 10 : a = q*q*d at Q16
          BXCS     lr                      ; 11 : exit on overflow
          RSB      q, a, q, LSL#9          ; 12 : q = 2*q-q*q*d at Q16
          ; q is now a Q16, 17-bit estimate to 1//d
          UMULL    a, s, q, q              ; 13 : [s,a] = q*q at Q32
          MOVS     a, a, LSR#1             ; 14 : now halve [s,a] and
          ADC      a, a, s, LSL#31         ; 15 : round so [N,a]=q*q at
          MOVS     s, s, LSL#30            ; 16 : Q31, C=0
          UMULL    s, a, d, a              ; 17 : a = a*d at Q31
          ADDMI    a, a, d                 ; 18 : if (N) a+=2*d at Q31
          RSC      q, a, q, LSL#16         ; 19 : q = 2*q-q*q*d at Q31
          ; q is now a Q31 estimate to 1/d
          UMULL    s, q, r, q              ; 20 : q approx n//d at Q31
          ; q is now a Q31 estimate to num/den, remainder<3*d
          UMULL    s, a, d, q              ; 21 : [a,s] = d*q at Q62
          RSBS     s, s, #0                ; 22 : [r,s] = n-d*q
          RSC      r, a, r, LSR#1          ; 23 : at Q62
          ; [r,s]=(r<<32)+s is now the positive remainder<3*d
          SUBS     s, s, d                 ; 24 : [r,s] = n-(d+1)*q
          SBCS     r, r, #0                ; 25 :   at Q62
          ADDPL    q, q, #1                ; 26 : if ([r,s]>=0) q++
          SUBS     s, s, d                 ; 27 : [r,s] = [r,s]-d
          SBCS     r, r, #0                ; 28 :   at Q62
          ADDPL    q, q, #1                ; 29 : if ([r,s]>=0) q++
          BX       lr                      ; 30 : return q
```

PROOF 7.4   We first check that $n < d$. If not, then a sequence of conditional instructions occur that return the saturated value 0x7fffffff at *I11*. Otherwise d and n are normalized to Q31 representations, $2^{30} \leq d < 2^{31}$. *I07* sets q to a Q8 representation of x_0, the initial approximation, as in Section 7.3.3.3.

   I08, *I10*, and *I12* implement the first Newton-Raphson iteration. *I08* sets a to the Q16 representation of x_0^2. *I10* sets a to the Q16 representation of $dx_0^2 - g_0$, where the rounding error satisfies $0 \leq g_0 < 2^{-16}$. $I12$ sets x to the Q16 representation of x_1, the new estimate to d^{-1}. Equation (7.33) tells us that the error in this estimate is $e_1 = de_0^2 - g_0$.

$I13$ to $I19$ implement the second Newton-Raphson iteration. $I13$ to $I15$ set a to the Q31 representation of $a_1 = x_1^2 + b_1$ for some error b_1. As we use the ADC instruction at $I15$, the calculation rounds up and so $0 \leq b_1 \leq 2^{-32}$. The ADC instruction cannot overflow since $2^{33} - 1$ and $2^{34} - 1$ are not squares. However, a_1 can overflow a Q31 representation. $I16$ clears the carry flag and records in the N flag if the overflow takes place so that $a_1 \geq 2$. $I17$ and $I18$ set a to the Q31 representation of $y_1 = da_1 - c_1$ for a rounding error $0 \leq c_1 < 2^{-31}$. As the carry flag is clear, $I19$ sets q to a Q31 representation of the new underestimate:

$$x_2 = 2x_1 - d(x_1^2 + b_1) + c_1 - 2^{-31} = \frac{1}{d} - e_2, \quad \text{where} \tag{7.39}$$

$$e_2 = de_1^2 - c_1 + 2^{-31} + db_1 < de_1^2 + d2^{-32} + 2^{-31} \tag{7.40}$$

$I20$ sets q to a Q31 representation of the quotient $q_2 = nx_2 - b_2$ for some rounding error $0 \leq b_2 < 2^{-31}$. So:

$$q_2 = \frac{n}{d} - e_3, \quad \text{where } e_3 = ne_2 + b_2 < d^2e_1^2 + d^22^{-32} + d2^{-31} + 2^{-31} \tag{7.41}$$

If $e_1 \geq 0$, then $d^2 e_1^2 \leq d^4 e_0^2 < (2^{-15} - d2^{-16})^2$, using the bound on E of Section 7.3.3.1.

$$e_3 < 2^{-30} - d2^{-31} + d^22^{-32} + 2^{-31} < 3 \times 2^{-31} \tag{7.42}$$

If $e_1 < 0$, then $d^2 e_1^2 \leq d^2 g_0^2 < 2^{-32}$. Again, $e_3 < 3 \times 2^{-31}$. In either case, q is an underestimate to the quotient of error less than 3×2^{-31}. $I21$ to $I23$ calculate the remainder, and $I24$ to $I29$ perform two conditional subtracts to correct the Q31 result q.

7.3.4   SIGNED DIVISION

So far we have only looked at unsigned division implementations. If you need to divide signed values, then reduce them to unsigned divides and add the sign back into the result. The quotient is negative if and only if the numerator and denominator have opposite sign. The sign of the remainder is the sign of the numerator. The following example shows how to reduce a signed integer division to an unsigned division and how to calculate the sign of the quotient and remainder.

```
d       RN 0     ; input denominator, output quotient
r       RN 1     ; input numerator , output remainder
sign    RN 12

        ; __value_in_regs struct { signed q, r; }
        ;   udiv_32by32_arm7m(signed d, signed n)
sdiv_32by32_arm7m
```

```
STMFD    sp!, {lr}
ANDS     sign, d, #1<<31       ; sign=(d<0 ? 1<<31 : 0);
RSBMI    d, d, #0              ; if (d<0) d=-d;
EORS     sign, sign, r, ASR#32 ; if (r<0) sign=~sign;
RSBCS    r, r, #0             ; if (r<0) r=-r;
BL       udiv_32by32_arm7m    ; (d,r)=(r/d,r%d)
MOVS     sign, sign, LSL#1    ; C=sign[31], N=sign[30]
RSBCS    d, d, #0             ; if (sign[31]) d=-d;
RSBMI    r, r, #0             ; if (sign[30]) r=-r;
LDMFD    sp!, {pc}
```

We use *r12* to hold the signs of the quotient and remainder as udiv_32by32_arm7m preserves *r12* (see Section 7.3.1.1).

7.4 SQUARE ROOTS

Square roots can be handled by the same techniques we used for division. You have a choice between trial subtraction and Newton-Raphson iteration based implementations. Use trial subtraction for a low-precision result less than 16 bits, but switch to Newton-Raphson for higher-precision results. Sections 7.4.1 and 7.4.2 cover trial subtraction and Newton-Raphson, respectively.

7.4.1 SQUARE ROOT BY TRIAL SUBTRACTION

We calculate the square root of a 32-bit unsigned integer d. The answer is a 16-bit unsigned integer q and a 17-bit unsigned remainder r such that

$$d = q^2 + r \quad \text{and} \quad 0 \le r \le 2q. \tag{7.43}$$

We start by setting $q = 0$ and $r = d$. Next we try and set each bit of q in turn, counting down from the highest possible bit, bit 15. We can set the bit if the new remainder is positive. Specifically if we set bit n by adding 2^n to q, then the new remainder is

$$r_{new} = d - (q + 2^n)^2 = (d - q^2) - 2^{n+1}q - 2^{2n} = r_{old} - 2^n(2q + 2^n) \tag{7.44}$$

So, to calculate the new remainder we try to subtract the value $2^n(2q + 2^n)$. If the subtraction succeeds with a nonnegative result, then we set bit n of q. The following C code illustrates the algorithm, calculating the N-bit square root q of a $2N$-bit input d:

```
unsigned usqr_simple(unsigned d, unsigned N)
{
```

```
unsigned t, q=0, r=d;

do
{                            /* calculate next quotient bit */
  N--;                       /* move down to next bit */
  t = 2*q+(1<<N);            /* new r = old r - (t<<N) */
  if ( (r>>N) >= t )         /* if (r >= (t<<N)) */
  {
    r -= (t<<N);             /* update remainder */
    q += (1<<N);             /* update root */
  }
} while (N);

return q;
}
```

Use the following optimized assembly to implement the preceding algorithm in only 50 cycles including the return. The trick is that register q holds the value $(1 << 30) \,|\, (q >> (N+1))$ before calculating bit N of the answer. If we rotate this value left by $2N + 2$ places, or equivalently right by $30 - 2N$ places, then we have the value $t \ll N$, used earlier for the trial subtraction.

```
q       RN 0        ; input value, current square root estimate
r       RN 1        ; the current remainder
c       RN 2        ; scratch register

usqr_32 ; unsigned usqr_32(unsigned q)
        SUBS    r, q, #1<<30        ; is q>=(1<<15)^2?
        ADDCC   r, r, #1<<30        ; if not restore
        MOV     c, #3<<30           ; c is a constant
        ADC     q, c, #1<<31        ; set bit 15 of answer
        ; calculate bits 14..0 of the answer
        GBLA    N
N       SETA    14
        WHILE   N<>-1
          CMP   r, q, ROR #(30-2*N) ; is r >= t<<N ?
          SUBCS r, r, q, ROR #(30-2*N) ; if yes then r -= t<<N;
          ADC   q, c, q, LSL#1      ; insert next bit of answer
N       SETA    (N-1)
        WEND
        BIC     q, q, #3<<30        ; extract answer
        MOV     pc, lr
```

7.4.2 SQUARE ROOT BY NEWTON-RAPHSON ITERATION

The Newton-Raphson iteration for a square root actually calculates the value of $d^{0.5}$. You may find this is a more useful result than the square root itself. For example, to normalize a vector (x, y) you will multiply by

$$\frac{1}{\sqrt{x^2 + y^2}} \tag{7.45}$$

If you do require $\sqrt{d}$, then simply multiply $d^{-0.5}$ by d. The equation $f(x) = d - x^{-2} = 0$ has positive solution $x = d^{-0.5}$. The Newton-Raphson iteration to solve this equation is (see Section 7.3.2)

$$x_{n+1} = 0.5x_n(3 - dx_n^2) \tag{7.46}$$

To implement this you can use the same methods we looked at in Section 7.3.2. First normalize d to the range $0.25 \le d < 1$. Then generate an initial estimate x_0 using a table lookup on the leading digits of d. Iterate the above formula until you've achieved the precision required for your application. Each iteration will roughly double the number of significant answer bits.

The following code calculates a Q31 representation of the value $d^{-0.5}$ for an input integer d. It uses a table lookup followed by two Newton-Raphson iterations and is accurate to a maximum error of 2^{-29}. On an ARM9E the code takes 34 cycles including the return.

```
q       RN 0       ; input value, estimated reciprocal root
b       RN 1       ; scratch register
s       RN 2       ; normalization shift
d       RN 3       ; normalized input value
a       RN 12      ; scratch register/accumulator


rsqr_32 ; unsigned rsqr_32(unsigned q)
        CLZ     s, q                    ; choose shift s which is
        BIC     s, s, #1                ; even such that d=(q<<s)
        MOVS    d, q, LSL s             ; is 0.25<=d<1 at Q32
        ADDNE   q, pc, d, LSR#25        ; table lookup on top 7 bits
        LDRNEB  q, [q, #tab-base-32]    ; of d in range 32 to 127
base    BEQ     div_by_zero             ; divide by zero trap
        ADD     q, q, #0x100            ; table stores only bottom 8 bits
        ; q is now a Q8, 9-bit estimate to 1/sqrt(d)
        SMULBB  a, q, q                 ; a = q*q at Q16
        MOV     b, d, LSR #17           ; b = d at Q15
        SMULWB  a, a, b                 ; a = d*q*q at Q15
        MOV     b, q, LSL #7            ; b = q at Q15
        RSB     a, a, #3<<15            ; a = (3-d*q*q) at Q15
```

```
        MUL       q, a, b              ; q = q*(3-d*q*q)/2 at Q31
        ; q is now a Q31 estimate to 1/sqrt(d)
        UMULL     b, a, d, q           ; a = d*q at Q31
        MOV       s, s, LSR #1         ; square root halves the shift
        UMULL     b, a, q, a           ; a = d*q*q at Q30
        RSB       s, s, #15            ; reciprocal inverts the shift
        RSB       a, a, #3<<30         ; a = (3-d*q*q) at Q30
        UMULL     b, q, a, q           ; q = q*(3-d*q*q)/2 at Q31
        ; q is now a good Q31 estimate to 1/sqrt(d)
        MOV       q, q, LSR s          ; undo the normalization shift
        BX        lr                   ; return q
div_by_zero
        MOV       q, #0x7FFFFFFF       ; maximum positive answer
        BX        lr                   ; return q

tab     ; tab[k] = round(256.0/sqrt((k+32.3)/128.0)) - 256
        DCB 0xfe, 0xf6, 0xef, 0xe7, 0xe1, 0xda, 0xd4, 0xce
        DCB 0xc8, 0xc3, 0xbd, 0xb8, 0xb3, 0xae, 0xaa, 0xa5
        DCB 0xa1, 0x9c, 0x98, 0x94, 0x90, 0x8d, 0x89, 0x85
        DCB 0x82, 0x7f, 0x7b, 0x78, 0x75, 0x72, 0x6f, 0x6c
        DCB 0x69, 0x66, 0x64, 0x61, 0x5e, 0x5c, 0x59, 0x57
        DCB 0x55, 0x52, 0x50, 0x4e, 0x4c, 0x49, 0x47, 0x45
        DCB 0x43, 0x41, 0x3f, 0x3d, 0x3b, 0x3a, 0x38, 0x36
        DCB 0x34, 0x32, 0x31, 0x2f, 0x2d, 0x2c, 0x2a, 0x29
        DCB 0x27, 0x26, 0x24, 0x23, 0x21, 0x20, 0x1e, 0x1d
        DCB 0x1c, 0x1a, 0x19, 0x18, 0x16, 0x15, 0x14, 0x13
        DCB 0x11, 0x10, 0x0f, 0x0e, 0x0d, 0x0b, 0x0a, 0x09
        DCB 0x08, 0x07, 0x06, 0x05, 0x04, 0x03, 0x02, 0x01
```

Similarly, to calculate $d^{\frac{-1}{k}}$ you can use the Newton-Raphson iteration for the equation $f(x) = d - x^{-k} = 0$.

7.5 TRANSCENDENTAL FUNCTIONS: LOG, EXP, SIN, COS

You can implement transcendental functions by using a combination of table lookup and series expansion. We examine how this works for the most common four transcendental operations: log, exp, sin, and cos. DSP applications use logarithm and exponentiation functions to convert between linear and logarithmic formats. The trigonometric functions sine and cosine are useful in 2D and 3D graphics and mapping calculations.

All the example routines of this section produce an answer accurate to 32 bits, which is excessive for many applications. You can accelerate performance by curtailing the series expansions with some loss in accuracy.

7.5.1   THE BASE-TWO LOGARITHM

Suppose we have a 32-bit integer n, and we want to find the base-two logarithm $s = \log_2(n)$ such that $n = 2^s$. Since s is in the range $0 \le s < 32$, we will actually find a Q26 representation q of the logarithm so that $q = s2^{26}$. We can easily calculate the integer part of s using CLZ or the alternatives of Section 7.2. This reduces us to a number in the range $1 \le n < 2$. First we perform a table lookup on an approximation a to n to find $\log_2(a)$ and a^{-1}. Since

$$\log_2(n) = \log_2(a) + \log_2\left(\frac{n}{a}\right) \tag{7.47}$$

we've reduced the problem to finding $\log_2(na^{-1})$. As na^{-1} is close to one, we can use the series expansion of $\log_2(1 + x)$ to improve the result accuracy:

$$\log_2(1 + x) = \frac{\ln(1 + x)}{\ln(2)} = \frac{1}{\ln(2)}\left(x - \frac{x^2}{2} + \frac{x^3}{3} - \cdots\right) \tag{7.48}$$

where *ln* is the natural logarithm to base e. To summarize, we calculate the logarithm in three stages as illustrated in Figure 7.4:

- We use CLZ to find bits [31:26] of the result.
- We use a table lookup of the first five fractional bits to find an estimate.
- We use series expansion to calculate the estimate error more accurately.

You can use the following code to implement this on an ARM9E processor using 31 cycles excluding the return. The answer is accurate to an error of 2^{-25}.

```
n       RN 0    ; Q0 input, Q26 log2 estimate
d       RN 1    ; normalize input Q32
r       RN 2
```

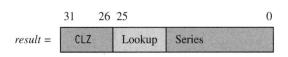

Figure 7.4   The three stages of the logarithm calculation.

```
q       RN 3
t       RN 12

        ; int ulog2_32(unsigned n)
ulog2_32
        CLZ     r, n
        MOV     d, n, LSL#1
        MOV     d, d, LSL r         ; 1<=d<2 at Q32
        RSB     n, r, #31           ; integer part of the log
        MOV     r, d, LSR#27        ; estimate e=1+(r/32)+(1/64)
        ADR     t, ulog2_table
        LDR     r, [t, r, LSL#3]!   ; r=log2(e) at Q26
        LDR     q, [t, #4]          ; q=1/e     at Q32
        MOV     t, #0
        UMLAL   t, r, d, r          ; r=(d/e)-1 at Q32
        LDR     t, =0x55555555      ; round(2^32/3)
        ADD     n, q, n, LSL#26     ; n+log2(e) at Q26
        SMULL   t, q, r, t          ; q = r/3    at Q32
        LDR     d, =0x05c551d9      ; round(2^26/ln(2))
        SMULL   t, q, r, q          ; q = r^2/3 at Q32
        MOV     t, #0
        SUB     q, q, r, ASR#1      ; q = -r/2+r^2/3 at Q32
        SMLAL   t, r, q, r          ; r - r^2/2 + r^3/3 at Q32
        MOV     t, #0
        SMLAL   t, n, d, r          ; n += r/log(2) at Q26
        MOV     pc, lr

ulog2_table
        ; table[2*i]   =round(2^32/a)      where a=1+(i+0.5)/32
        ; table[2*i+1]=round(2^26*log2(a)) and 0<=i<32
        DCD 0xfc0fc0fc, 0x0016e797, 0xf4898d60, 0x0043ace2
        DCD 0xed7303b6, 0x006f2109, 0xe6c2b448, 0x0099574f
        DCD 0xe070381c, 0x00c2615f, 0xda740da7, 0x00ea4f72
        DCD 0xd4c77b03, 0x0111307e, 0xcf6474a9, 0x0137124d
        DCD 0xca4587e7, 0x015c01a4, 0xc565c87b, 0x01800a56
        DCD 0xc0c0c0c1, 0x01a33761, 0xbc52640c, 0x01c592fb
        DCD 0xb81702e0, 0x01e726aa, 0xb40b40b4, 0x0207fb51
        DCD 0xb02c0b03, 0x0228193f, 0xac769184, 0x0247883b
        DCD 0xa8e83f57, 0x02664f8d, 0xa57eb503, 0x02847610
        DCD 0xa237c32b, 0x02a20231, 0x9f1165e7, 0x02bef9ff
        DCD 0x9c09c09c, 0x02db632d, 0x991f1a51, 0x02f7431f
        DCD 0x964fda6c, 0x03129ee9, 0x939a85c4, 0x032d7b5a
        DCD 0x90fdbc09, 0x0347dcfe, 0x8e78356d, 0x0361c825
```

```
DCD 0x8c08c08c, 0x037b40e4, 0x89ae408a, 0x03944b1c
DCD 0x8767ab5f, 0x03acea7c, 0x85340853, 0x03c52286
DCD 0x83126e98, 0x03dcf68e, 0x81020408, 0x03f469c2
```

7.5.2 BASE-TWO EXPONENTIATION

This is the inverse of the operation of Section 7.5.1. Given a Q26 representation of $0 \le x < 32$, we calculate the base-two exponent 2^x. We start by splitting x into an integer part, n, and fractional part, d. Then $2^x = 2^d \times 2^n$. To calculate 2^d, first find an approximation a to d and look up 2^a. Now,

$$2^d = 2^a \times \exp((d - a)\ln 2) \tag{7.49}$$

Calculate $x = (d - a)\ln 2$ and use the series expansion for $\exp(x)$ to improve the estimate:

$$\exp(x) = 1 + x + \frac{x^2}{2} + \frac{x^3}{6} + \cdots \tag{7.50}$$

You can use the following assembly code to implement the preceding algorithm. The answer has a maximum error of 4 in the result. The routine takes 31 cycles on an ARM9E excluding the return.

```
n       RN 0      ; input, integer part
d       RN 1      ; fractional part
r       RN 2
q       RN 3
t       RN 12

        ; unsigned uexp2_32(int n)
uexp2_32
        MOV     d, n, LSL#6       ; d = fractional part at Q32
        MOV     q, d, LSR#27      ; estimate a=(q+0.5)/32
        LDR     r, =0xb17217f8    ; round(2^32*log(2))
        BIC     d, d, q, LSL#27   ; d = d - (q/32) at Q32
        UMULL   t, d, r, d        ; d = d*log(2)   at Q32
        LDR     t, =0x55555555    ; round(2^32/3)
        SUB     d, d, r, LSR#6    ; d = d - log(2)/64 at Q32
        SMULL   t, r, d, t        ; r = d/3    at Q32
        MOVS    n, n, ASR#26      ; n = integer part of exponent
        SMULL   t, r, d, r        ; r = d^2/3 at Q32
        BMI     negative          ; catch negative exponent
        ADD     r, r, d           ; r = d+d^2/3
        SMULL   t, r, d, r        ; r = d^2+d^3/3
        ADR     t, uexp2_table
```

```
        LDR     q, [t, q, LSL#2]    ; q = exp2(a) at Q31
        ADDS    r, d, r, ASR#1      ; r = d+d^2/2+d^3/6 at Q32
        UMULL   t, r, q, r          ; r = exp2(a)*r    at Q31 if r<0
        RSB     n, n, #31           ; 31-(integer part of exponent)
        ADDPL   r, r, q             ; correct if r>0
        MOV     n, r, LSR n         ; result at Q0
        MOV     pc, lr
negative
        MOV     r0, #0              ; 2^(-ve)=0
        MOV     pc, lr
uexp2_table
        ; table[i]=round(2^31*exp2(a)) where a=(i+0.5)/32
        DCD 0x8164d1f4, 0x843a28c4, 0x871f6197, 0x8a14d575
        DCD 0x8d1adf5b, 0x9031dc43, 0x935a2b2f, 0x96942d37
        DCD 0x99e04593, 0x9d3ed9a7, 0xa0b05110, 0xa43515ae
        DCD 0xa7cd93b5, 0xab7a39b6, 0xaf3b78ad, 0xb311c413
        DCD 0xb6fd91e3, 0xbaff5ab2, 0xbf1799b6, 0xc346ccda
        DCD 0xc78d74c9, 0xcbec14ff, 0xd06333db, 0xd4f35aac
        DCD 0xd99d15c2, 0xde60f482, 0xe33f8973, 0xe8396a50
        DCD 0xed4f301f, 0xf281773c, 0xf7d0df73, 0xfd3e0c0d
```

7.5.3 TRIGONOMETRIC OPERATIONS

If you need low-precision trigonometric operations (typically the case when generating sine waves and other audio signals, or for graphics processing), use a lookup table. For high-precision graphics or global positioning, greater precision may be required. The routines we look at here generate sine and cosine accurate to 32 bits.

The standard C library functions sin and cos specify the angle in radians. Radians are an awkward choice of units when dealing with optimized fixed-point functions. First, on any angle addition you need to perform arithmetic modulo 2π. Second, it requires range checking involving π to find out which quadrant of the circle an angle lies in. Rather than operate modulo 2π, we will operate modulo 2^{32}, a very easy operation on any processor.

Let's define new base-two trigonometric functions s and c, where the angle is specified on a scale such that 2^{32} is one revolution (2π radians or 360 degrees). To add these angles we use standard modular integer addition:

$$s(x) = \sin(2\pi x 2^{-32}) = \sin(\pi x 2^{-31}) \quad \text{and} \quad c(x) = \cos(\pi x 2^{-31}) \tag{7.51}$$

In this form, x is the Q32 representation of the proportion of a revolution represented by the angle. The top two bits of x tell us which quadrant of the circle the angle lies in. First we use the top three bits of x to reduce $s(x)$ or $c(x)$ to the sine or cosine of an angle between zero and one eighth of a revolution. Then we choose an approximation a to x and use a table to look up $s(a)$ and $c(a)$. The addition formula for sine and cosine reduces the problem to finding the sine and cosine of a small angle:

$$s(x) = s(a)\cos\left(\pi(x-a)2^{-31}\right) + c(a)\sin\left(\pi(x-a)2^{-31}\right) \qquad (7.52)$$

$$c(x) = c(a)\cos\left(\pi(x-a)2^{-31}\right) - s(a)\sin\left(\pi(x-a)2^{-31}\right) \qquad (7.53)$$

Next, we calculate the small angle $n = \pi(x-a)2^{-31}$ in radians and use the following series expansions to improve accuracy further:

$$\sin(x) = x - \frac{x^3}{6} + \cdots \quad \text{and} \quad \cos(x) = 1 - \frac{x^2}{2} + \cdots \qquad (7.54)$$

You can use the following assembly to implement the preceding algorithm for sine and cosine. The answer is returned at Q30 and has a maximum error of 4×2^{-30}. The routine takes 31 cycles on an ARM9E excluding the return.

```
n       RN 0      ; the input angle in revolutions at Q32, result Q30
s       RN 1      ; the output sign
r       RN 2
q       RN 3
t       RN 12


cos_32 ; int cos_32(int n)
        EOR     s, n, n, LSL#1    ; cos is -ve in quadrants 1,2
        MOVS    n, n, LSL#1       ; angle in revolutions at Q33
        RSBMI   n, n, #0          ; in range 0-1/4 of a revolution
        CMP     n, #1<<30         ; if angle < 1/8 of a revolution
        BCC     cos_core          ; take cosine
        SUBEQ   n, n, #1          ; otherwise take sine of
        RSBHI   n, n, #1<<31      ; (1/4 revolution)-(angle)
sin_core                          ; take sine of Q33 angle n
        MOV     q, n, LSR#25      ; approximation a=(q+0.5)/32
        SUB     n, n, q, LSL#25   ; n = n-(q/32) at Q33
        SUB     n, n, #1<<24      ; n = n-(1/64) at Q33
        LDR     t, =0x6487ed51    ; round(2*PI*2^28)
        MOV     r, n, LSL#3       ; r = n at Q36
        SMULL   t, n, r, t        ; n = (x-a)*PI/2^31 at Q32
        ADR     t, cossin_tab
        LDR     q, [t, q, LSL#3]! ; c(a) at Q30
        LDR     t, [t, #4]        ; s(a) at Q30
        EOR     q, q, s, ASR#31   ; correct c(a) sign
        EOR     s, t, s, ASR#31   ; correct s(a) sign
        SMULL   t, r, n, n        ; n^2      at Q32
        SMULL   t, q, n, q        ; n*c(a)   at Q30
```

```
        SMULL    t, n, r, s       ; n^2*s(a)    at Q30
        LDR      t, =0xd5555556   ; round(-2^32/6)
        SUB      n, s, n, ASR#1   ; n = s(a)*(1-n^2/2) at Q30
        SMULL    t, s, r, t       ; s=-n^2/6         at Q32
        ADD      n, n, q          ; n += c(a)*n      at Q30
        MOV      t, #0
        SMLAL    t, n, q, s       ; n += -c(a)*n^3/6  at Q30
        MOV      pc, lr           ; return n

sin_32;int sin_32(int n)
        AND      s, n, #1<<31     ; sin is -ve in quadrants 2,3
        MOVS     n, n, LSL#1      ; angle in revolutions at Q33
        RSBMI    n, n, #0         ; in range 0-1/4 of a revolution
        CMP      n, #1<<30        ; if angle < 1/8 revolution
        BCC      sin_core         ; take sine
        SUBEQ    n, n, #1         ; otherwise take cosine of
        RSBHI    n, n, #1<<31     ; (1/4 revolution)-(angle)
cos_core                          ; take cosine of Q33 angle n
        MOV      q, n, LSR#25     ; approximation a=(q+0.5)/32
        SUB      n, n, q, LSL#25  ; n = n-(q/32) at Q33
        SUB      n, n, #1<<24     ; n = n-(1/64) at Q33
        LDR      t, =0x6487ed51   ; round(2*PI*2^28)
        MOV      r, n, LSL#3      ; r = n at Q26
        SMULL    t, n, r, t       ; n = (x-a)*PI/2^31 at Q32
        ADR      t, cossin_tab
        LDR      q, [t, q, LSL#3]!; c(a) at Q30
        LDR      t, [t, #4]       ; s(a) at Q30
        EOR      q, q, s, ASR#31  ; correct c(a) sign
        EOR      s, t, s, ASR#31  ; correct s(a) sign
        SMULL    t, r, n, n       ; n^2      at Q32
        SMULL    t, s, n, s       ; n*s(a)    at Q30
        SMULL    t, n, r, q       ; n^2*c(a) at Q30
        LDR      t, =0x2aaaaaab   ; round(+2^23/6)
        SUB      n, q, n, ASR#1   ; n = c(a)*(1-n^2/2) at Q30
        SMULL    t, q, r, t       ; n^2/6       at Q32
        SUB      n, n, s          ; n += -sin*n at Q30
        MOV      t, #0
        SMLAL    t, n, s, q       ; n += sin*n^3/6 at Q30
        MOV      pc, lr           ; return n

cossin_tab
        ; table[2*i]   =round(2^30*cos(a)) where a=(PI/4)*(i+0.5)/32
        ; table[2*i+1]=round(2^30*sin(a)) and 0 <= i < 32
```

```
DCD 0x3ffec42d, 0x00c90e90, 0x3ff4e5e0, 0x025b0caf
DCD 0x3fe12acb, 0x03ecadcf, 0x3fc395f9, 0x057db403
DCD 0x3f9c2bfb, 0x070de172, 0x3f6af2e3, 0x089cf867
DCD 0x3f2ff24a, 0x0a2abb59, 0x3eeb3347, 0x0bb6ecef
DCD 0x3e9cc076, 0x0d415013, 0x3e44a5ef, 0x0ec9a7f3
DCD 0x3de2f148, 0x104fb80e, 0x3d77b192, 0x11d3443f
DCD 0x3d02f757, 0x135410c3, 0x3c84d496, 0x14d1e242
DCD 0x3bfd5cc4, 0x164c7ddd, 0x3b6ca4c4, 0x17c3a931
DCD 0x3ad2c2e8, 0x19372a64, 0x3a2fcee8, 0x1aa6c82b
DCD 0x3983e1e8, 0x1c1249d8, 0x38cf1669, 0x1d79775c
DCD 0x3811884d, 0x1edc1953, 0x374b54ce, 0x2039f90f
DCD 0x367c9a7e, 0x2192e09b, 0x35a5793c, 0x22e69ac8
DCD 0x34c61236, 0x2434f332, 0x33de87de, 0x257db64c
DCD 0x32eefdea, 0x26c0b162, 0x31f79948, 0x27fdb2a7
DCD 0x30f8801f, 0x29348937, 0x2ff1d9c7, 0x2a650525
DCD 0x2ee3cebe, 0x2b8ef77d, 0x2dce88aa, 0x2cb2324c
```

7.6 ENDIAN REVERSAL AND BIT OPERATIONS

This section presents optimized algorithms for manipulating the bits within a register. Section 7.6.1 looks at endian reversal, a useful operation when you are reading data from a big-endian file on a little-endian memory system. Section 7.6.2 looks at permuting bits within a word, for example, reversing the bits. We show how to support a wide variety of bit permutations. See also Section 6.7 for a discussion on packing and unpacking bitstreams.

7.6.1 ENDIAN REVERSAL

To use the ARM core's 32-bit data bus to maximum efficiency, you will want to load and store 8- and 16-bit arrays four bytes at a time. However, if you load multiple bytes at once, then the processor endianness affects the order they will appear in the register. If this does not match the order you want, then you will need to reverse the byte order.

You can use the following code sequences to reverse the order of the bytes within a word. The first sequence uses two temporary registers and takes three cycles per word reversed after a constant setup cycle. The second code sequence only uses one temporary register and is useful for reversing a single word.

```
n       RN 0    ; input, output words
t       RN 1    ; scratch 1
m       RN 2    ; scratch 2

byte_reverse                    ; n = [ a , b , c , d ]
```

```
        MVN     m, #0x0000FF00    ; m = [0xFF,0xFF,0x00,0xFF  ]
        EOR     t, n, n, ROR #16  ; t = [ a^c, b^d, a^c, b^d ]
        AND     t, m, t, LSR#8    ; t = [ 0 , a^c,  0 , a^c ]
        EOR     n, t, n, ROR #8   ; n = [ d ,  c ,  b ,  a  ]
        MOV     pc, lr

byte_reverse_2reg                 ; n = [ a ,  b ,  c ,  d  ]
        EOR     t, n, n, ROR#16   ; t = [ a^c, b^d, a^c, b^d ]
        MOV     t, t, LSR#8       ; t = [ 0 , a^c, b^d, a^c ]
        BIC     t, t, #0xFF00     ; t = [ 0 , a^c,  0 , a^c ]
        EOR     n, t, n, ROR #8   ; n = [ d ,  c ,  b ,  a  ]
        MOV     pc, lr
```

Halfword reversing within a word is provided free by the ARM barrel shifter since it is the same as a rotate right by 16 places.

7.6.2 BIT PERMUTATIONS

The byte reversal of Section 7.6.1 is a special case of a bit permutation. There are many other important bit permutations that you might come across (see Table 7.3):

■ *Bit reversal.* Exchanging the value of bits k and $31 - k$.

■ *Bit spreading.* Spacing out the bits so that bit k moves to bit $2k$ for $k < 16$ and bit $2k - 31$ for $k \geq 16$.

■ *DES initial permutation.* DES stands for the Data Encryption Standard, a common algorithm for bulk data encryption. The algorithm applies a 64-bit permutation to the data before and after the encryption rounds.

Writing optimized code to implement such permutations is simple when you have at hand a toolbox of bit permutation primitives like the ones we will develop in this section (see Table 7.4). They are much faster than a loop that examines each bit in turn, since they process 32 bits at a time.

Table 7.3   Table of common permutations.

Permutation name	Permutation action
Byte reversal	$[b_4, b_3, b_2, b_1, b_0] \rightarrow [1 - b_4, 1 - b_3, b_2, b_1, b_0]$
Bit reversal	$[b_4, b_3, b_2, b_1, b_0] \rightarrow [1 - b_4, 1 - b_3, 1 - b_2, 1 - b_1, 1 - b_0]$
Bit spread	$[b_4, b_3, b_2, b_1, b_0] \rightarrow [b_3, b_2, b_1, b_0, b_4]$
DES permutation	$[b_5, b_4, b_3, b_2, b_1, b_0] \rightarrow [1 - b_0, b_2, b_1, 1 - b_5, 1 - b_4, 1 - b_3]$

Table 7.4   Permutation primitives.

Primitive name	Permutation action
A (bit index complement)	$[\ldots, b_k, \ldots] \to [\ldots, 1-b_k, \ldots]$
B (bit index swap)	$[\ldots, b_j, \ldots, b_k, \ldots] \to [\ldots, b_k, \ldots, b_j, \ldots]$
C (bit index complement+swap)	$[\ldots, b_j, \ldots, b_k, \ldots] \to [\ldots, 1-b_k, \ldots, 1-b_j, \ldots]$

Let's start with some notation. Suppose we are dealing with a 2^k-bit value n and we want to permute the bits of n. Then we can refer to each bit position in n using a k-bit index $b_{k-1}2^{k-1} + \cdots + b_1 2 + b_0$. So, for permuting the bits within 32-bit values, we take $k = 5$. We will look at permutations that move the bit at position $b_{k-1}2^{k-1} + \cdots + b_1 2 + b_0$ to position $c_{k-1}2^{k-1} + \cdots + c_1 2 + c_0$, where each c_i is either a b_j or a $1 - b_j$. We will denote this permutation by

$$[b_{k-1}, \ldots, b_1, b_0] \to [c_{k-1}, \ldots, c_1, c_0] \tag{7.55}$$

For example, Table 7.3 shows the notation and action for the permutations we've talked about so far.

What's the point of this? Well, we can achieve any of these permutations using a series of the three basic permutations in Table 7.4. In fact, we only need the first two since C is B followed by A twice. However, we can implement C directly for a faster result.

7.6.2.1   Bit Permutation Macros

The following macros implement the three permutation primitives for a 32-bit word n. They need only four cycles per permutation if the constant values are already set up in registers. For larger or smaller width permutations, the same ideas apply.

```
mask0    EQU    0x55555555    ; set bit positions with b0=0
mask1    EQU    0x33333333    ; set bit positions with b1=0
mask2    EQU    0x0F0F0F0F    ; set bit positions with b2=0
mask3    EQU    0x00FF00FF    ; set bit positions with b3=0
mask4    EQU    0x0000FFFF    ; set bit positions with b4=0

         MACRO
         PERMUTE_A $k
         ; [ ... b_k ... ]->[ ... 1-b_k ... ]
         IF $k=4
           MOV   n, n, ROR#16
         ELSE
           LDR   m, =mask$k
```

```
        AND     t, m, n, LSR#(1<<$k)    ; get bits with index b_k=1
        AND     n, n, m                 ; get bits with index b_k=0
        ORR     n, t, n, LSL#(1<<$k)    ; swap them over
    ENDIF
    MEND


    MACRO
    PERMUTE_B $j, $k
    ; [ .. b_j .. b_k .. ]->[ .. b_k .. b_j .. ] and j>k
    LDR     m, =(mask$j:AND::NOT:mask$k)     ; set when b_j=0 b_k=1
    EOR     t, n, n, LSR#(1<<$j)-(1<<$k)
    AND     t, t, m                         ; get bits where b_j!=b_k
    EOR     n, n, t, LSL#(1<<$j)-(1<<$k) ; change if bj=1 bk=0
    EOR     n, n, t                         ; change when b_j=0 b_k=1
    MEND


    MACRO
    PERMUTE_C $j, $k
    ; [ .. b_j .. b_k .. ]->[ .. 1-b_k .. 1-b_j .. ] and j>k
    LDR     m, =(mask$j:AND:mask$k)             ; set when b_j=0 b_k=0
    EOR     t, n, n, LSR#(1<<$j)+(1<<$k)
    AND     t, t, m                         ; get bits where b_j==b_k
    EOR     n, n, t, LSL#(1<<$j)+(1<<$k) ; change if bj=1 bk=1
    EOR     n, n, t                         ; change when b_j=0 b_k=0
    MEND
```

7.6.2.2 Bit Permutation Examples

Now, let's see how these macros will help us in practice. Bit reverse moves the bit at position b to position $31 - b$; in other words, it inverts each bit of the five-bit position index b. We can use five type A transforms to implement bit reversal, logically inverting each bit index position in turn.

```
bit_reverse                 ; n= [  b4    b3    b2    b1    b0  ]
        PERMUTE_A 0         ; -> [  b4    b3    b2    b1   1-b0 ]
        PERMUTE_A 1         ; -> [  b4    b3    b2   1-b1 1-b0 ]
        PERMUTE_A 2         ; -> [  b4    b3   1-b2 1-b1 1-b0 ]
        PERMUTE_A 3         ; -> [  b4   1-b3 1-b2 1-b1 1-b0 ]
        PERMUTE_A 4         ; -> [ 1-b4 1-b3 1-b2 1-b1 1-b0 ]
        MOV     pc, lr
```

We can implement the more difficult bit spreading permutation using four type B transforms. This is only 16 cycles ignoring the constant setups—much faster than any loop testing each bit one at a time.

```
bit_spread                      ; n= ⌈ b4 b3 b2 b1 b0 ⌉
        PERMUTE_B 4,3           ; -> [ b3 b4 b2 b1 b0 ]
        PERMUTE_B 3,2           ; -> [ b3 b2 b4 b1 b0 ]
        PERMUTE_B 2,1           ; -> [ b3 b2 b1 b4 b0 ]
        PERMUTE_B 1,0           ; -> [ b3 b2 b1 b0 b4 ]
        MOV    pc, lr
```

Finally, type C permutations allow us to perform bit reversal and bit spreading at the same time and with the same number of cycles.

```
bit_rev_spread                  ; n= [  b4   b3   b2   b1   b0 ]
        PERMUTE_C 4,3           ; -> [ 1-b3 1-b4  b2   b1   b0 ]
        PERMUTE_C 3,2           ; -> [ 1-b3 1-b2  b4   b1   b0 ]
        PERMUTE_C 2,1           ; -> [ 1-b3 1-b2 1-b1 1-b4  b0 ]
        PERMUTE_C 1,0           ; -> [ 1-b3 1-b2 1-b1 1-b0  b4 ]
        MOV    pc, lr
```

7.6.3   Bit Population Count

A bit population count finds the number of bits set within a word. For example, this is useful if you need to find the number of interrupts set in an interrupt mask. A loop testing each bit is slow, since ADD instructions can be used to sum bits in parallel provided that the sums do not interfere with each other. The idea of the *divide by three and conquer* method is to split the 32-bit word into bit triplets. The sum of each bit triplet is a 2-bit number in the range 0 to 3. We calculate these in parallel and then sum them in a logarithmic fashion.

Use the following code for bit population counts of a single word. The operation is 10 cycles plus 2 cycles for setup of constants.

```
bit_count              ; input n = xyzxyzxyzxyzxyzxyzxyzxyzxyzxyzxy
        LDR    m, =0x49249249  ; 01001001001001001001001001001001
        AND    t, n, m, LSL #1 ; x00x00x00x00x00x00x00x00x00x00x0
        SUB    n, n, t, LSR #1 ; uuzuuzuuzuuzuuzuuzuuzuuzuuzuuzuu
        AND    t, n, m, LSR #1 ; 00z00z00z00z00z00z00z00z00z00z00
        ADD    n, n, t         ; vv0vv0vv0vv0vv0vv0vv0vv0vv0vv0vv
        ; triplets summed, uu=x+y, vv=x+y+z
        LDR    m, =0xC71C71C7  ; 11000111000111000111000111000111
        ADD    n, n, n, LSR #3 ; ww0vvwww0vvwww0vvwww0vvwww0vvwww
        AND    n, n, m         ; ww000www000www000www000www000www
```

```
; each www is the sum of six adjacent bits
ADD     n, n, n, LSR #6  ; sum the w's
ADD     n, n, n, LSR #12
ADD     n, n, n, LSR #24
AND     n, n, #63        ; mask out irrelevant bits
MOV     pc, lr
```

7.7 SATURATED AND ROUNDED ARITHMETIC

Saturation clips a result to a fixed range to prevent overflow. You are most likely to need 16- and 32-bit saturation, defined by the following operations:

- *saturate16(x)* = x clipped to the range −0x00008000 to +0x00007fff inclusive
- *saturate32(x)* = x clipped to the range −0x80000000 to +0x7fffffff inclusive

We'll concentrate on these operations although you can easily convert the 16-bit saturation examples to 8-bit saturation or any other length. The following sections give standard implementations of basic saturating and rounding operations you may need. They use a standard trick: for a 32-bit signed integer x,

$$x \gg 31 = sign(x) = -1 \text{ if } x < 0 \text{ and } 0 \text{ if } x \geq 0$$

7.7.1 SATURATING 32 BITS TO 16 BITS

This operation crops up frequently in DSP applications. For example, sound samples are often saturated to 16 bits before storing to memory. This operation takes three cycles, provided a constant m is set up beforehand in a register.

```
; b=saturate16(b)
LDR     m, =0x00007FFF       ; m = 0x7FFF maximum +ve
MOV     a, b, ASR#15         ; a = (b >> 15)
TEQ     a, b, ASR#31         ; if (a!=sign(b))
EORNE   b, m, b, ASR#31      ; b = 0x7FFF ^ sign(b)
```

7.7.2 SATURATED LEFT SHIFT

In signal processing left shifts that could overflow need to saturate the result. This operation requires three cycles for a constant shift or five cycles for a variable shift c.

```
; a=saturate32(b << c)
MOV     m, #0x7FFFFFFF       ; m = 0x7FFFFFFF max +ve
MOV     a, b, LSL c          ; a = b << c
```

```
TEQ    b, a, ASR c        ; if (b != (a>>c))
EORNE  a, m, b, ASR#31    ; a = 0x7FFFFFFF^sign(b)
```

7.7.3 ROUNDED RIGHT SHIFT

A rounded shift right requires two cycles for a constant shift or three cycles for a nonzero variable shift. Note that a zero variable shift will only work properly if carry is clear.

```
; a=round(b>>c)
MOVS   a, b, ASR c        ; a = b>>c, carry=b bit c-1
ADC    a, a, #0           ; if (carry) a++ to round
```

7.7.4 SATURATED 32-BIT ADDITION AND SUBTRACTION

On ARMv5TE cores, new instructions QADD and QSUB provide saturated addition and subtraction. If you have an ARMv4T or earlier core, then use the following code sequences instead. The code requires two cycles and a register held constant.

```
; a = saturate32(b+c)
MOV    m, #0x80000000     ; m = 0x80000000 max -ve
ADDS   a, b, c            ; a = b+c, V records overflow
EORVS  a, m, a, ASR#31    ; if (V) a=0x80000000^sign(a)

; a = saturate32(b-c)
MOV    m, #0x80000000     ; m = 0x80000000 max -ve
SUBS   a, b, c            ; a = b-c, V records overflow
EORVS  a, m, a, ASR#31    ; if (V) a=0x80000000^sign(a)
```

7.7.5 SATURATED ABSOLUTE

The absolute function overflows if the input argument is −0x80000000. The following two-cycle code sequence handles this case:

```
; a = saturate32(abs(b))
SUB    a, b, b, LSR #31   ; a = b - (b<0)
EOR    a, a, a, ASR #31   ; a = a ^ sign(a)
```

On a similar theme, an accumulated, unsaturated absolute also takes two cycles:

```
; a = b+abs(c)
EORS   a, c, c, ASR#32    ; a = c^sign(c) = abs(c)-(c<0)
ADC    a, b, a            ; a = b + a + (c<0)
```

7.8 RANDOM NUMBER GENERATION

To generate truly random numbers requires special hardware to act as a source of random noise. However, for many computer applications, such as games and modeling, speed of generation is more important than statistical purity. These applications usually use *pseudorandom* numbers.

Pseudorandom numbers aren't actually random at all; a repeating sequence generates the numbers. However, the sequence is so long, and so scattered, that the numbers appear to be random. Typically we obtain R_k, the kth element of a pseudorandom sequence, by iterating a simple function of R_{k-1}:

$$R_k = f(R_{k-1}) \tag{7.56}$$

For a fast pseudorandom number generator we need to pick a function $f(x)$ that is easy to compute and gives random-looking output. The sequence must also be very long before it repeats. For a sequence of 32-bit numbers the longest length achievable is clearly 2^{32}.

A linear congruence generator uses a function of the following form.

```
f(x) = (a*x+c) % m;
```

These functions are studied in detail in Knuth, *Seminumerical Algorithms*, Sections 3.2.1 and 3.6. For fast computation, we would like to take $m = 2^{32}$. The theory in Knuth assures us that if a % 8 = 5 and $c = a$, then the sequence generated has maximum length of 2^{32} and is likely to appear random. For example, suppose that a $= $ 0x91e6d6a5. Then the following iteration generates a pseudorandom sequence:

```
MLA     r, a, r, a      ; r_k = (a*r_(k-1) + a) mod 2^32
```

Since m is a power of two, the low-order bits of the sequence are not very random. Use the high-order bits to derive pseudorandom numbers of a smaller range. For example, set $s = r \gg 28$ to generate a four-bit random number s in the range 0–15. More generally, the following code generates a pseudorandom number between 0 and n:

```
; r is the current random seed
; a is the multiplier (eg 0x91E6D6A5)
; n is the random number range (0...n-1)
; t is a scratch register
MLA     r, a, r, a      ; iterate random number generator
UMULL   t, s, r, n      ; s = (r*n)/2^32
; r is the new random seed
; s is the random result in range 0 ... n-1
```

7.9 SUMMARY

ARM instructions only implement simple primitives such as addition, subtraction, and multiplication. To perform more complex operations such as division, square root, and trigonometric functions, you need to use software routines. There are many useful tricks and algorithms to improve the performance of these complex operations. This chapter covered the algorithms and code examples for a number of standard operations.

Standard tricks include

- using binary search or trial subtraction to calculate small quotients

- using Newton-Raphson iteration for fast calculation of reciprocals and extraction of roots

- using a combination of table lookup followed by series expansion to calculate transcendental functions such as exp, log, sin, and cos

- using logical operations with barrel shift to perform bit permutations, rather than testing bits individually

- using multiply accumulate instructions to generate pseudorandom numbers

CHAPTER 8

DIGITAL SIGNAL PROCESSING

Microprocessors now wield enough computational power to process real-time digitized signals. You are probably familiar with mp3 audio players, digital cameras, and digital mobile/cellular telephones. Processing digitized signals requires high memory bandwidths and fast multiply accumulate operations. In this chapter we will look at ways you can maximize the performance of the ARM for *digital signal processing* (DSP) applications.

Traditionally an embedded or portable device would contain two types of processor: A microcontroller would handle the user interface, and a separate DSP processor would manipulate digitized signals such as audio. However, now you can often use a single microprocessor to perform both tasks because of the higher performance and clock frequencies available on microprocessors today. A single-core design can reduce cost and power consumption over a two-core solution.

Additions to the ARM architecture mean that ARM is well suited for many DSP applications. The ARMv5TE extensions available in the ARM9E and later cores provide efficient multiply accumulate operations. With careful coding, the ARM9E processor will perform decently on the DSP parts of an application while outperforming a DSP on the control parts of the application.

DSP applications are typically multiply and load-store intensive. A basic operation is a multiply accumulate multiplying two 16-bit signed numbers and accumulating onto a 32-bit signed accumulator. Table 8.1 shows the increase in performance available on different generations of the ARM core. The second column gives cycles for a signed 16-bit by 16-bit multiply with 32-bit accumulate; the third column, cycles for a signed 32-bit by 32-bit multiply with a 64-bit accumulate. The latter is especially useful for high-quality audio algorithms such as mp3.

Table 8.1 assumes that you use the most efficient instruction for the task and that you can avoid any postmultiply interlocks. We cover this in detail in Section 8.2.

259

Table 8.1   Multiply accumulate timings by processor.

Processor (architecture)	16- × 16-bit multiply with 32-bit accumulate (cycles)	32- × 32-bit multiply with 64-bit accumulate (cycles)
ARM7 (ARMv3)	~12	~44
ARM7TDMI (ARMv4T)	4	7
ARM9TDMI (ARMv4T)	4	7
StrongARM (ARMv4)	2 or 3	4 or 5
ARM9E (ARMv5TE)	1	3
XScale (ARMv5TE)	1	2–4
ARM1136 (ARMv6)	0.5	2 (result top half)

Due to their high data bandwidth and performance requirements, you will often need to code DSP algorithms in hand-written assembly. You need fine control of register allocation and instruction scheduling to achieve the best performance. We cannot cover implementations of all DSP algorithms in this chapter, so we will concentrate on common examples and general rules that can be applied to a whole range of DSP algorithms.

Section 8.1 looks at the basic problem of how to represent a signal on the ARM so that we can process it. Section 8.2 looks at general rules on writing DSP algorithms for the ARM.

Filtering is probably the most commonly used signal processing operation. It can be used to remove noise, to analyze signals, or in signal compression. We look at audio filtering in detail in Sections 8.3 and 8.4. Another very common algorithm is the Discrete Fourier Transform (DFT), which converts a signal from a time representation to a frequency representation or vice versa. We look at the DFT in Section 8.5.

8.1   REPRESENTING A DIGITAL SIGNAL

Before you can process a digital signal, you need to choose a representation of the signal. How can you describe a signal using only the integer types available on ARM processors? This is an important problem that will affect the design of the DSP software. Throughout this chapter we will use the notations x_t and $x[t]$ to denote the value of a signal x at time t. The first notation is often clearer in equations and formulae. The second notation is used in programming examples as it is closer to the C style of array notation.

8.1.1   CHOOSING A REPRESENTATION

In an analogue signal $x[t]$, the index t and the value x are both continuous real variables. To convert an analogue signal to a digital signal, we must choose a finite number of sampling points t_i and a digital representation for the sample values $x[t_i]$.

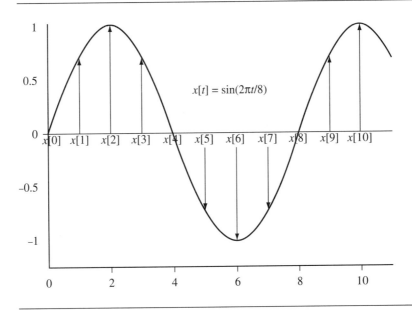

$x[t] = \sin(2\pi t/8)$

Figure 8.1   Digitizing an analogue signal.

Figure 8.1 shows a sine wave signal digitized at the sampling points 0, 1, 2, 3, and so on. Signals like this are typical in audio processing, where $x[t]$ represents the tth audio sample.

For example, in a CD player, the sampling rate is 44,100 Hz (that is, 44,100 samples per second). Therefore t represents the time in units of a sample period of 1/44,100 Hz = 22.7 microseconds. In this application $x[t]$ represents the signed voltage applied to the loudspeaker at time t.

There are two things to worry about when choosing a representation of $x[t]$:

1. The *dynamic range* of the signal—the maximum fluctuation in the signal defined by Equation (8.1). For a signed signal we are interested in the maximum absolute value M possible. For this example, let's take $M = 1$ volt.

$$M = max|x[t]| \text{ over all } t = 0, 1, 2, 3 \dots \qquad (8.1)$$

2. The *accuracy* required in the representation, sometimes given as a proportion of the maximum range. For example, an accuracy of 100 parts per million means that each $x[t]$ needs to be represented within an error of

$$E = M \times 0.0001 = 0.0001 \text{ volts} \qquad (8.2)$$

Let's work out the best way of storing $x[t]$ subject to the given dynamic range and accuracy constraints.

We could use a floating-point representation for $x[t]$. This would certainly meet our dynamic range and accuracy constraints, and it would also be easy to manipulate using the C type float. However, most ARM cores do not support floating point in hardware, and so a floating-point representation would be very slow.

A better choice for fast code is a *fixed-point* representation. A fixed-point representation uses an integer to represent a fractional value by scaling the fraction. For example, for a maximum error of 0.0001 volts, we only require a step of 0.0002 volts between each representable value. This suggests that we represent $x[t]$ by the integer $X[t]$ defined as

$$X[t] = round\_to\_nearest\_integer(5000 \times x[t]) \tag{8.3}$$

In practice we would rather scale by a power of two. Then we can implement multiplication and division by the scale using shifts. In this case, the smallest power of two greater than 5000 is $2^{13} = 8192$. We say that $X[t]$ is a Qk *fixed-point representation* of $x[t]$ if

$$X[t] = round\_to\_nearest\_integer(2^k x[t]) \tag{8.4}$$

In our example we can use a Q13 representation to meet the accuracy required. Since $x[t]$ ranges between -1 and $+1$ volt, $X[t]$ will range between the integers -8192 and $+8192$. This range will fit in a 16-bit C variable of type short. Signals that vary between -1 and $+1$ are often stored as Q15 values because this scales them to the maximum range of a short type integer: $-32,768$ to $+32,767$. Note that $+1$ does not have an exact representation, and we approximate it by $+32,767$ representing $1 - 2^{-15}$. However, we will see in Section 8.1.2 that scaling up to the maximum range is not always a good idea. It increases the probability of overflow when manipulating the fixed-point representations.

In a fixed-point representation we represent each signal value by an integer and use the same scaling for the whole signal. This differs from a floating-point representation, where each signal value $x[t]$ has its own scaling called the *exponent* dependent upon t.

A common error is to think that floating point is more accurate than fixed point. This is false! For the same number of bits, a fixed-point representation gives greater accuracy. The floating-point representation gives higher dynamic range at the expense of lower absolute accuracy. For example, if you use a 32-bit integer to hold a fixed-point value scaled to full range, then the maximum error in a representation is 2^{-32}. However, single-precision 32-bit floating-point values give a relative error of 2^{-24}. The single-precision floating-point mantissa is 24 bits. The leading 1 of the mantissa is not stored, so 23 bits of storage are actually used. For values near the maximum, the fixed-point representation is $2^{32-24} = 256$ times more accurate! The 8-bit floating-point exponent is of little use when you are interested in maximum error rather than relative accuracy.

To summarize, a fixed-point representation is best when there is a clear bound to the strength of the signal and when maximum error is important. When there is no clear bound and you require a large dynamic range, then floating point is better. You can also use the other following representations, which give more dynamic range than fixed point while still being more efficient to implement than floating point.

8.1.1.1   Saturating Fixed-Point Representation

Suppose the maximum value of the signal is not known, but there is a clear range in which the vast majority of samples lie. In this case you can use a fixed-point representation based on the common range. You then *saturate* or *clip* any out-of-range samples to the closest available sample in the normal range. This approach gives greater accuracy at the expense of some distortion of very loud signals. See Section 7.7 for hints on efficient saturation.

8.1.1.2   Block-Floating Representation

When small sample values are close to large sample values, they are usually less important. In this case, you can divide the signal into blocks or *frames* of samples. You can use a different fixed-point scaling on each block or frame according to the strength of the signal in that block or frame.

   This is similar to floating point except that we associate a single exponent with a whole frame rather than a single sample. You can use efficient fixed-point operations to operate on the samples within the frame, and you only need costly, exponent-related operations when comparing values among frames.

8.1.1.3   Logarithmic Representation

Suppose your signal $x[t]$ has a large dynamic range. Suppose also that multiplication operations are far more frequent than addition. Then you can use a base-two logarithmic representation. For this representation we consider the related signal $y[t]$:

$$y[t] = \log_2(x[t]) \tag{8.5}$$

Represent $y[t]$ using a fixed-point format. Replace operations of the form

$$x[a] = x[b] \times x[c] \text{ by } y[a] = y[b] + y[c] \tag{8.6}$$

and operations of the form

$$x[a] = x[b] + x[c] \text{ by } y[a] = y[b] + \log_2\left(1 + 2^{y[c]-y[b]}\right) \tag{8.7}$$

In the second case we arrange that $y[c] \leq y[b]$. Calculate the function $f(x) = \log_2(1 + 2^x)$ by using lookup tables and/or interpolation. See Section 7.5 for efficient implementations of $\log_2(x)$ and 2^x.

8.1.2 OPERATING ON VALUES STORED IN FIXED-POINT FORMAT

Suppose now that we have chosen a Qk fixed point representation for the signal $x[t]$. In other words, we have an array of integers $X[t]$ such that

$$X[t] - \text{the closet integer to } \left(2^k x[t]\right) \qquad (8.8)$$

Equivalently, if we write the integer $X[t]$ in binary notation, and insert a binary point between bits k and $k-1$, then we have the value of $x[t]$. For example, in Figure 8.2, the fixed-point value 0x6000 at Q15 represents 0.11 in binary, or $3/4 = 0.75$ in decimal.

The following subsections cover the basic operations of addition, subtraction, multiplication, division, and square root as applied to fixed-point signals. There are several concepts that apply to all fixed-point operations:

- *Rounding on right shift.* When you perform a right shift to divide by a power of two, the shift rounds towards $-\infty$ rather than rounding to the nearest integer. For a more accurate answer use the operation $y = (x + (1 \ll (shift - 1))) \gg shift$ instead. This will round to the nearest integer with 0.5 rounded up. To implement this efficiently, see Section 7.7.3.

- *Rounding on divide.* For an unsigned divide, calculate $y = (x + (d \gg 1))/d$ rather than $y = x/d$. This gives a rounded result.

- *Headroom.* The *headroom* of a fixed point representation is the ratio of the maximum magnitude that can be stored in the integer to the maximum magnitude that will occur. For example, suppose you use a 16-bit integer to store a Q13 representation of an audio signal that can range between -1 and $+1$. Then there is a headroom of four times or two bits. You can double a sample value twice without risk of overflowing the 16-bit container integer.

- *Conversion of Q representation.* If $X[t]$ is a Qn representation of $x[t]$, then

$$X[t] \ll k \text{ is a } Q(n+k) \text{ representation of } x[t] \qquad (8.9)$$

$$X[t] \gg k \text{ is a } Q(n-k) \text{ representation of } x[t] \qquad (8.10)$$

For the following sections we fix signals $x[t]$, $c[t]$, and $y[t]$. Let $X[t]$, $C[t]$, $Y[t]$ denote their Qn, Qm, Qd fixed-point representations, respectively.

Bit	15	14	13	12	11	10	9	8	7	6	5	4	3	2	1	0
0x6000 =	0.	1	1	0	0	0	0	0	0	0	0	0	0	0	0	0

Figure 8.2   Representation of 3/4 in Q15 fixed-point arithmetic.

8.1.3 ADDITION AND SUBTRACTION OF FIXED-POINT SIGNALS

The general case is to convert the signal equation

$$y[t] = x[t] + c[t] \qquad (8.11)$$

into fixed-point format; that is, approximately:

$$Y[t] = 2^d y[t] = 2^d (x[t] + c[t]) = 2^{d-n} X[t] + 2^{d-m} C[t] \qquad (8.12)$$

or in integer C:

```
Y[t] = (X[t] << (d-n)) + (C[t] << (d-m));
```

Here we use the convention that you should interpret a negative left shift value as a rounded right shift. In other words, we first convert $x[t]$ and $c[t]$ to Qd representations, then add to give $Y[t]$.

We know the values of d, n, and m, at compile time, and so there is no problem in determining the shift direction, or whether there is a shift at all! In practice we usually arrange that $n = m = d$. Therefore normal integer addition gives a fixed-point addition:

```
Y[t] = X[t] + C[t];
```

Provided $d = m$ or $d = n$, we can perform the operation in a single cycle using the ARM barrel shifter:

```
Y[t] = X[t] + (C[t] << (d-m));    /* d==n case */
Y[t] = C[t] + (X[t] << (d-n));    /* d==m case */
```

We must be careful though. The preceding equations are only meaningful if the shifted values and the result do not overflow. For example, if $Y[t] = X[t] + C[t]$, then the dynamic range of $Y[t]$ is the sum of the dynamic ranges of $X[t]$ and $C[t]$. This is liable to overflow the integer container.

There are four common ways you can prevent overflow:

1. Ensure that the $X[t]$ and $C[t]$ representations have one bit of spare headroom each; in other words, each use up only half the range of their integer container. Then there can be no overflow on the addition.

2. Use a larger container type for Y than for X and C. For example, if $X[t]$ and $C[t]$ are stored as 16-bit integers, use a 32-bit integer for $Y[t]$. This will ensure that there can be no overflow. In fact, $Y[t]$ then has 15 bits of headroom, so you can add many 16-bit values to $Y[t]$ without the possibility of overflow.

3. Use a smaller Q representation for $y[t]$. For example, if $d = n - 1 = m - 1$, then the operation becomes

```
Y[t] = (X[t] + X[t-1]) >> 1;
```

This operation takes two cycles rather than one since the shift follows the add. However, the operation result cannot overflow.

4. Use saturation. If the value of $X[t] + C[t]$ is outside the range of the integer storing $Y[t]$, then clip it to the nearest possible value that is in range. Section 7.7 shows how to implement saturating arithmetic efficiently.

8.1.4 MULTIPLICATION OF FIXED-POINT SIGNALS

The general case is to convert the signal equation

$$y[t] = x[t]c[t] \tag{8.13}$$

into fixed point format; that is, approximately:

$$Y[t] = 2^d y[t] = 2^d x[t]c[t] = 2^{d-n-m} X[t]C[t] \tag{8.14}$$

or in integer C:

```
Y[t] = (X[t]*C[t]) >> (n+m-d);
```

You should interpret a negative right shift as a left shift. The product $X[t]C[t]$ is a $Q(n + m)$ representation of $Y[t]$ and the shift converts representation. There are two common uses:

1. We want to accumulate a whole series of products. In this case we set $d = n + m$, using a wider integer to store $Y[t]$ than $X[t]$ and $C[t]$. The multiply and multiply accumulate operations are then just

```
Y[t]  = X[t] * C[t];    /* multiply */
Y[t] += X[t] * C[t];    /* multiply accumulate */
```

2. The signal $Y[t]$ is the signal $X[t]$ with pointwise multiplication by some scaling coefficients. In this case, use $d = n$ so that the operation is

```
Y[t] = (X[t] * C[t]) >> m;
```

For audio DSP applications, a 16-bit × 16-bit multiply is usually used. Common values for n and m are 14 and 15. As with addition and subtraction it is important to check each operation to make sure that it cannot overflow.

EXAMPLE   Suppose $X[t]$ is a 16-bit signed representation for an audio signal $x[t]$. Suppose we need to
8.1   reduce the power of the signal by a half. To do this we must scale each sample by $1/(\sqrt{2})$,
so $c[t] = 2^{-0.5} = 0.70710678\ldots$

Since we are using a 16-bit representation for $X[t]$, a 16-bit multiply will suffice. The
largest power of two that we can multiply $c[t]$ by and have it remain a 16-bit integer is 15.
So take $n = d$, $m = 15$, and $C[t] = 2^{15}/(\sqrt{2}) = 23,710 = \text{0x5A82}$. Therefore we can scale
using the integer operation

```
X[t] = (X[t] * 0x5A82) >> 15;
```

8.1.5   DIVISION OF FIXED-POINT SIGNALS

The general case is to convert the signal equation

$$y[t] = \frac{x[t]}{c[t]} \tag{8.15}$$

into fixed point format; that is, approximately:

$$Y[t] = 2^d y[t] = \frac{2^d x[t]}{c[t]} = 2^{d-n+m} \frac{X[t]}{C[t]} \tag{8.16}$$

or in integer C:

```
Y[t] = (X[t] << (d-n+m)) / C[t];
```

Again a negative left shift indicates a right shift. You must take care that the left shift does
not cause an overflow. In typical applications, $n = m$. Then the preceding operation gives
a Qd result accurate to d places of binary fraction:

```
Y[t] = (X[t] << d) / C[t];
```

See Section 7.3.3 for efficient implementations of fixed-point division.

8.1.6   SQUARE ROOT OF A FIXED-POINT SIGNAL

The general case is to convert the signal equation

$$y[t] = \sqrt{x[t]} \tag{8.17}$$

into fixed point format; that is, approximately:

$$Y[t] = 2^d y[t] = 2^d \sqrt{x[t]} = \sqrt{2^{2d-n} X[t]} \tag{8.18}$$

or in integer C:

```
Y[t] = isqrt( X[t] << (2*d-n) );
```

The function isqrt finds the nearest integer to the square root of the integer. See Section 7.4 for efficient implementation of square root operations.

8.1.7 SUMMARY: HOW TO REPRESENT A DIGITAL SIGNAL

To choose a representation for a signal value, use the following criteria:

- Use a floating-point representation for prototyping algorithms. Do not use floating point in applications where speed is critical. Most ARM implementations do not include hardware floating-point support.

- Use a fixed-point representation for DSP applications where speed is critical with moderate dynamic range. The ARM cores provide good support for 8-, 16- and 32-bit fixed-point DSP.

- For applications requiring speed and high dynamic range, use a block-floating or logarithmic representation.

Table 8.2 summarizes how you can implement standard operations in fixed-point arithmetic. It assumes there are three signals $x[t]$, $c[t]$, $y[t]$, that have Qn, Qm, Qd representations $X[t]$, $C[t]$, $Y[t]$, respectively. In other words:

$$X[t] = 2^n x[t], C[t] = 2^m c[t], Y[t] = 2^d y[t] \qquad (8.19)$$

to the nearest integer.

To make the table more concise, we use <<< as shorthand for an operation that is either a left or right shift according to the sign of the shift amount. Formally:

```
x <<< s :=
    x << s          if s>=0
```

Table 8.2   Summary of standard fixed-point operations.

Signal operation	Integer fixed-point equivalent
y[t]=x[t]	Y[t]=X[t] <<< (d-n);
y[t]=x[t]+c[t]	Y[t]=(X[t] <<< (d-n))+(C[t] <<< (d-m));
y[t]=x[t]-c[t]	Y[t]=(X[t] <<< (d-n))-(C[t] <<< (d-m));
y[t]=x[t]*c[t]	Y[t]=(X[t]*C[t]) <<< (d-n-m);
y[t]=x[t]/c[t]	Y[t]=(X[t] <<< (d-n+m))/C[t];
y[t]=sqrt(x[t])	Y[t]=isqrt(X[t] <<< (2*d-n));

```
     x >> (-s)          if s<0 and rounding is not required
    (x+round) >> (-s)   if s<0 and rounding is required

round  :=  (1 << (-1-s))    if 0.5 should round up
           (1 << (-1-s))-1  if 0.5 should round down
```

You must always check the precision and dynamic range of the intermediate and output values. Ensure that there are no overflows or unacceptable losses of precision. These considerations determine the representations and size to use for the container integers.

These equations are the most general form. In practice, for addition and subtraction we usually take $d = n = m$. For multiplication we usually take $d = n + m$ or $d = n$. Since you know d, n, and m, at compile time, you can eliminate shifts by zero.

8.2   INTRODUCTION TO DSP ON THE ARM

This section begins by looking at the features of the ARM architecture that are useful for writing DSP applications. We look at each common ARM implementation in turn, highlighting its strengths and weaknesses for DSP.

The ARM core is not a dedicated DSP. There is no single instruction that issues a multiply accumulate and data fetch in parallel. However, by reusing loaded data you can achieve a respectable DSP performance. The key idea is to use block algorithms that calculate several results at once, and thus require less memory bandwidth, increase performance, and decrease power consumption compared with calculating single results.

The ARM also differs from a standard DSP when it comes to precision and saturation. In general, ARM does not provide operations that saturate automatically. Saturating versions of operations usually cost additional cycles. Section 7.7 covered saturating operations on the ARM. On the other hand, ARM supports extended-precision 32-bit multiplied by 32-bit to 64-bit operations very well. These operations are particularly important for CD-quality audio applications, which require intermediate precision at greater than 16 bits.

From ARM9 onwards, ARM implementations use a multistage execute pipeline for loads and multiplies, which introduces potential processor interlocks. If you load a value and then use it in either of the following two instructions, the processor may stall for a number of cycles waiting for the loaded value to arrive. Similarly if you use the result of a multiply in the following instruction, this may cause stall cycles. It is particularly important to schedule code to avoid these stalls. See the discussion in Section 6.3 on instruction scheduling.

SUMMARY   **Guidelines for Writing DSP Code for ARM**

- Design the DSP algorithm so that saturation is not required because saturation will cost extra cycles. Use extended-precision arithmetic or additional scaling rather than saturation.

- Design the DSP algorithm to minimize loads and stores. Once you load a data item, then perform as many operations that use the datum as possible. You can often do this by calculating several output results at once. Another way of increasing reuse is to concatenate several operations. For example, you could perform a dot product and signal scale at the same time, while only loading the data once.

- Write ARM assembly to avoid processor interlocks. The results of load and multiply instructions are often not available to the next instruction without adding stall cycles. Sometimes the results will not be available for several cycles. Refer to Appendix D for details of instruction cycle timings.

- There are 14 registers available for general use on the ARM, *r0* to *r12* and *r14*. Design the DSP algorithm so that the inner loop will require 14 registers or fewer.

In the following sections we look at each of the standard ARM cores in turn. We implement a *dot-product* example for each core. A dot-product is one of the simplest DSP operations and highlights the difference among different ARM implementations. A dot-product combines N samples from two signals x_t and c_t to produce a correlation value a:

$$a = \sum_{i=0}^{N-1} c_i x_i \qquad (8.20)$$

The C interface to the dot-product function is

```
int dot_product(sample *x, coefficient *c, unsigned int N);
```

where

- *sample* is the type to hold a 16-bit audio sample, usually a `short`
- *coefficient* is the type to hold a 16-bit coefficient, usually a `short`
- $x[i]$ and $c[i]$ are two arrays of length N (the data and coefficients)
- the function returns the accumulated 32-bit integer dot product a

8.2.1 DSP ON THE ARM7TDMI

The ARM7TDMI has a 32-bit by 8-bit per cycle multiply array with early termination. It takes four cycles for a 16-bit by 16-bit to 32-bit multiply accumulate. Load instructions take three cycles and store instructions two cycles for zero-wait-state memory or cache. See Section D.2 in Appendix D for details of cycle timings for ARM7TDMI instructions.

SUMMARY **Guidelines for Writing DSP Code for the ARM7TDMI**

- Load instructions are slow, taking three cycles to load a single value. To access memory efficiently use load and store multiple instructions LDM and STM. Load and store multiples only require a single cycle for each additional word transferred after the first word. This often means it is more efficient to store 16-bit data values in 32-bit words.

- The multiply instructions use early termination based on the second operand in the product *Rs*. For predictable performance use the second operand to specify constant coefficients or multiples.

- Multiply is one cycle faster than multiply accumulate. It is sometimes useful to split an MLA instruction into separate MUL and ADD instructions. You can then use a barrel shift with the ADD to perform a scaled accumulate.

- You can often multiply by fixed coefficients faster using arithmetic instructions with shifts. For example, $240x = (x \ll 8) - (x \ll 4)$. For any fixed coefficient of the form $\pm 2^a \pm 2^b \pm 2^c$, ADD and SUB with shift give a faster multiply accumulate than MLA.

EXAMPLE This example shows a 16-bit dot-product optimized for the ARM7TDMI. Each MLA takes
8.2 a worst case of four cycles. We store the 16-bit input samples in 32-bit words so that we can use the LDM instruction to load them efficiently.

```
x        RN 0     ; input array x[]
c        RN 1     ; input array c[]
N        RN 2     ; number of samples (a multiple of 5)
acc      RN 3     ; accumulator
x_0      RN 4     ; elements from array x[]
x_1      RN 5
x_2      RN 6
x_3      RN 7
x_4      RN 8
c_0      RN 9     ; elements from array c[]
c_1      RN 10
c_2      RN 11
c_3      RN 12
c_4      RN 14


         ; int dot_16by16_arm7m(int *x, int *c, unsigned N)
dot_16by16_arm7m
         STMFD   sp!, {r4-r11, lr}
         MOV     acc, #0
loop_7m ; accumulate 5 products
         LDMIA   x!, {x_0, x_1, x_2, x_3, x_4}
         LDMIA   c!, {c_0, c_1, c_2, c_3, c_4}
         MLA     acc, x_0, c_0, acc
         MLA     acc, x_1, c_1, acc
         MLA     acc, x_2, c_2, acc
         MLA     acc, x_3, c_3, acc
```

```
MLA      acc, x_4, c_4, acc
SUBS     N, N, #5
BGT      loop_7m
MOV      r0, acc
LDMFD    sp!, {r4-r11, pc}
```

This code assumes that the number of samples N is a multiple of five. Therefore we can use a five-word load multiple to increase data bandwidth. The cost per load is $7/4 = 1.4$ cycles compared to 3 cycles per load if we had used LDR or LDRSH. The inner loop requires a worst case of $7 + 7 + 5 * 4 + 1 + 3 = 38$ cycles to process each block of 5 products from the sum. This gives the ARM7TDMI a DSP rating of $38/5 = 7.6$ cycles per tap for a 16-bit dot-product. The block filter algorithm of Section 8.3 gives a much better performance per tap if you are calculating multiple products.

8.2.2 DSP ON THE ARM9TDMI

The ARM9TDMI has the same 32-bit by 8-bit per cycle multiplier array with early termination as the ARM7TDMI. However, load and store operations are much faster compared to the ARM7TDMI. They take one cycle provided that you do not attempt to use the loaded value for two cycles after the load instruction. See Section D.3 in Appendix D for cycle timings of ARM9TDMI instructions.

SUMMARY   **Writing DSP Code for the ARM9TDMI**

- Load instructions are fast as long as you schedule the code to avoid using the loaded value for two cycles. There is no advantage to using load multiples. Therefore you should store 16-bit data in 16-bit short type arrays. Use the LDRSH instruction to load the data.

- The multiply instructions use early termination based on the second operand in the product Rs. For predictable performance use the second operand to specify constant coefficients or multiples.

- Multiply is the same speed as multiply accumulate. Try to use the MLA instruction rather than a separate multiply and add.

- You can often multiply by fixed coefficients faster using arithmetic instructions with shifts. For example, $240x = (x \ll 8) - (x \ll 4)$. For any fixed coefficient of the form $\pm 2^a \pm 2^b \pm 2^c$, ADD and SUB with shift give a faster multiply accumulate than using MLA.

EXAMPLE   This example shows a 16-bit dot-product optimized for the ARM9TDMI. Each MLA takes
8.3   a worst case of four cycles. We store the 16-bit input samples in 16-bit short integers, since there is no advantage in using LDM rather than LDRSH, and using LDRSH reduces the memory size of the data.

```
x        RN 0    ; input array x[]
c        RN 1    ; input array c[]
N        RN 2    ; number of samples (a multiple of 4)
acc      RN 3    ; accumulator
x_0      RN 4    ; elements from array x[]
x_1      RN 5
c_0      RN 9    ; elements from array c[]
c_1      RN 10

         ; int dot_16by16_arm9m(short *x, short *c, unsigned N)
dot_16by16_arm9m
         STMFD   sp!, {r4-r5, r9-r10, lr}
         MOV     acc, #0
         LDRSH   x_0, [x], #2
         LDRSH   c_0, [c], #2
loop_9m ; accumulate 4 products
         SUBS    N, N, #4
         LDRSH   x_1, [x], #2
         LDRSH   c_1, [c], #2
         MLA     acc, x_0, c_0, acc
         LDRSH   x_0, [x], #2
         LDRSH   c_0, [c], #2
         MLA     acc, x_1, c_1, acc
         LDRSH   x_1, [x], #2
         LDRSH   c_1, [c], #2
         MLA     acc, x_0, c_0, acc
         LDRGTSH x_0, [x], #2
         LDRGTSH c_0, [c], #2
         MLA     acc, x_1, c_1, acc
         BGT     loop_9m
         MOV     r0, acc
         LDMFD   sp!, {r4-r5, r9-r10, pc}
```

We have assumed that the number of samples N is a multiple of four. Therefore we can unroll the loop four times to increase performance. The code is scheduled so that there are four instructions between a load and the use of the loaded value. This uses the preload tricks of Section 6.3.1.1:

- The loads are double buffered. We use x_0, c_0 while we are loading x_1, c_1 and vice versa.

- We load the initial values x_0, c_0, before the inner loop starts. This initiates the double buffer process.

- We are always loading one pair of values ahead of the ones we are using. Therefore we must avoid the last pair of loads or we will read off the end of the arrays. We do this by having a loop counter that counts down to zero on the last loop. Then we can make the final loads conditional on $N > 0$.

The inner loop requires 28 cycles per loop, giving $28/4 = 7$ cycles per tap. See Section 8.3 for more efficient block filter implementations.

8.2.3 DSP ON THE STRONGARM

The StrongARM core SA-1 has a 32-bit by 12-bit per cycle signed multiply array with early termination. If you attempt to use a multiply result in the following instruction, or start a new multiply, then the core will stall for one cycle. Load instructions take one cycle, except for signed byte and halfword loads, which take two cycles. There is a one-cycle delay before you can use the loaded value. See Section D.4 in Appendix D for details of the StrongARM instruction cycle timings.

SUMMARY **Writing DSP Code for the StrongARM**

- Avoid signed byte and halfword loads. Schedule the code to avoid using the loaded value for one cycle. There is no advantage to using load multiples.

- The multiply instructions use early termination based on the second operand in the product *Rs*. For predictable performance use the second operand to specify constant coefficients or multiples.

- Multiply is the same speed as multiply accumulate. Try to use the MLA instruction rather than a separate multiply and add.

EXAMPLE This example shows a 16-bit dot-product. Since a signed 16-bit load requires two cycles, it 8.4 is more efficient to use 32-bit data containers for the StrongARM. To schedule StrongARM code, one trick is to interleave loads and multiplies.

```
x       RN 0    ; input array x[]
c       RN 1    ; input array c[]
N       RN 2    ; number of samples (a multiple of 4)
acc     RN 3    ; accumulator
x_0     RN 4    ; elements from array x[]
x_1     RN 5
c_0     RN 9    ; elements from array c[]
c_1     RN 10

        ; int dot_16by16_SA1(int *x, int *c, unsigned N)
dot_16by16_SA1
        STMFD   sp!, {r4-r5, r9-r10, lr}
```

```
          MOV     acc, #0
          LDR     x_0, [x], #4
          LDR     c_0, [c], #4
loop_sa ; accumulate 4 products
          SUBS    N, N, #4
          LDR     x_1, [x], #4
          LDR     c_1, [c], #4
          MLA     acc, x_0, c_0, acc
          LDR     x_0, [x], #4
          LDR     c_0, [c], #4
          MLA     acc, x_1, c_1, acc
          LDR     x_1, [x], #4
          LDR     c_1, [c], #4
          MLA     acc, x_0, c_0, acc
          LDRGT   x_0, [x], #4
          LDRGT   c_0, [c], #4
          MLA     acc, x_1, c_1, acc
          BGT     loop_sa
          MOV     r0, acc
          LDMFD   sp!, {r4-r5, r9-r10, pc}
```

We have assumed that the number of samples N is a multiple of four and so have unrolled by four times. For worst-case 16-bit coefficients, each multiply requires two cycles. We have scheduled to remove all load and multiply use interlocks. The inner loop uses 19 cycles to process 4 taps, giving a rating of $19/4 = 4.75$ cycles per tap.

8.2.4 DSP on the ARM9E

The ARM9E core has a very fast pipelined multiplier array that performs a 32-bit by 16-bit multiply in a single issue cycle. The result is not available on the next cycle unless you use the result as the accumulator in a multiply accumulate operation. The load and store operations are the same speed as on the ARM9TDMI. See Section D.5 in Appendix D for details of the ARM9E instruction cycle times.

To access the fast multiplier, you will need to use the multiply instructions defined in the ARMv5TE architecture extensions. For 16-bit by 16-bit products use SMULxy and SMLAxy. See Appendix A for a full list of ARM multiply instructions.

SUMMARY **Writing DSP Code for the ARM9E**

■ The ARMv5TE architecture multiply operations are capable of unpacking 16-bit halves from 32-bit words and multiplying them. For best load bandwidth you should use word load instructions to load packed 16-bit data items. As for the ARM9TDMI you should schedule code to avoid load use interlocks.

- The multiply operations do not early terminate. Therefore you should only use MUL and MLA for multiplying 32-bit integers. For 16-bit values use SMULxy and SMLAxy.

- Multiply is the same speed as multiply accumulate. Try to use the SMLAxy instruction rather than a separate multiply and add.

EXAMPLE
8.5

This example shows the dot-product for the ARM9E. It assumes that the ARM is configured for a little-endian memory system. If the ARM is configured for a big-endian memory system, then you need to swap the B and T instruction suffixes. You can use macros to do this for you automatically as in Example 8.11. We use the naming convention x_10 to mean that the top 16 bits of the register holds x_1 and the bottom 16 bits x_0.

```
x       RN 0    ; input array x[]
c       RN 1    ; input array c[]
N       RN 2    ; number of samples (a multiple of 8)
acc     RN 3    ; accumulator
x_10    RN 4    ; packed elements from array x[]
x_32    RN 5
c_10    RN 9    ; packed elements from array c[]
c_32    RN 10

        ; int dot_16by16_arm9e(short *x, short *c, unsigned N)
dot_16by16_arm9e
        STMFD   sp!, {r4-r5, r9-r10, lr}
        MOV     acc, #0
        LDR     x_10, [x], #4
        LDR     c_10, [c], #4
loop_9e ; accumulate 8 products
        SUBS    N, N, #8
        LDR     x_32, [x], #4
        SMLABB  acc, x_10, c_10, acc
        LDR     c_32, [c], #4
        SMLATT  acc, x_10, c_10, acc
        LDR     x_10, [x], #4
        SMLABB  acc, x_32, c_32, acc
        LDR     c_10, [c], #4
        SMLATT  acc, x_32, c_32, acc
        LDR     x_32, [x], #4
        SMLABB  acc, x_10, c_10, acc
        LDR     c_32, [c], #4
        SMLATT  acc, x_10, c_10, acc
        LDRGT   x_10, [x], #4
        SMLABB  acc, x_32, c_32, acc
        LDRGT   c_10, [c], #4
```

```
SMLATT   acc, x_32, c_32, acc
BGT      loop_9e
MOV      r0, acc
LDMFD    sp!, {r4-r5, r9-r10, pc}
```

We have unrolled eight times, assuming that N is a multiple of eight. Each load instruction reads two 16-bit values, giving a high memory bandwidth. The inner loop requires 20 cycles to accumulate 8 products, a rating of $20/8 = 2.5$ cycles per tap. A block filter gives even greater efficiency.

8.2.5   DSP ON THE ARM10E

Like ARM9E, the ARM10E core also implements ARM architecture ARMv5TE. The range and speed of multiply operations is the same as for the ARM9E, except that the 16-bit multiply accumulate requires two cycles rather than one. For details of the ARM10E core cycle timings, see Section D.6 in Appendix D.

The ARM10E implements a background loading mechanism to accelerate load and store multiples. A load or store multiple instruction issues in one cycle. The operation will run in the background, and if you attempt to use the value before the background load completes, then the core will stall. ARM10E uses a 64-bit-wide data path that can transfer two registers on every background cycle. If the address isn't 64-bit aligned, then only 32 bits can be transferred on the first cycle.

SUMMARY   **Writing DSP Code for the ARM10E**

- Load and store multiples run in the background to give a high memory bandwidth. Use load and store multiples whenever possible. Be careful to schedule the code so that it does not use data before the background load has completed.

- Ensure data arrays are 64-bit aligned so that load and store multiple operations can transfer two words per cycle.

- The multiply operations do not early terminate. Therefore you should only use MUL and MLA for multiplying 32-bit integers. For 16-bit values use SMULxy and SMLAxy.

- The SMLAxy instruction takes one cycle more than SMULxy. It may be useful to split a multiply accumulate into a separate multiply and add.

EXAMPLE   In the example code the number of samples N is a multiple of 10.
8.6

```
x     RN 0    ; input array x[]
c     RN 1    ; input array c[]
N     RN 2    ; number of samples (a multiple of 10)
acc   RN 3    ; accumulator
```

```
        x_10      RN 4     ; packed elements from array x[]
        x_32      RN 5
        x_54      RN 6
        x_76      RN 7
        x_98      RN 8
        c_10      RN 9     ; packed elements from array c[]
        c_32      RN 10
        c_54      RN 11
        c_76      RN 12
        c_98      RN 14

              ; int dot_16by16_arm10(short *x, short *c, int n)
        dot_16by16_arm10
              STMFD    sp!, {r4-r11, lr}
              LDMIA    x!, {x_10, x_32}
              MOV      acc, #0
              LDMIA    c!, {c_10, c_32}
        loop_10 ; accumulate 10 products
              SUBS     N, N, #10
              LDMIA    x!, {x_54, x_76, x_98}
              SMLABB   acc, x_10, c_10, acc
              SMLATT   acc, x_10, c_10, acc
              LDMIA    c!, {c_54, c_76, c_98}
              SMLABB   acc, x_32, c_32, acc
              SMLATT   acc, x_32, c_32, acc
              LDMGTIA  x!, {x_10, x_32}
              SMLABB   acc, x_54, c_54, acc
              SMLATT   acc, x_54, c_54, acc
              SMLABB   acc, x_76, c_76, acc
              LDMGTIA  c!, {c_10, c_32}
              SMLATT   acc, x_76, c_76, acc
              SMLABB   acc, x_98, c_98, acc
              SMLATT   acc, x_98, c_98, acc
              BGT      loop_10
              MOV      r0, acc
              LDMFD    sp!, {r4-r11, pc}
```

The inner loop requires 25 cycles to process 10 samples, or 2.5 cycles per tap.

8.2.6   DSP ON THE INTEL XSCALE

The Intel XScale implements version ARMv5TE of the ARM architecture like ARM9E and ARM10E. The timings of load and multiply instructions are similar to the ARM9E, and code you've optimized for the ARM9E should run efficiently on XScale. See Section D.7 in Appendix D for details of the XScale core cycle timings.

SUMMARY   **Writing DSP Code for the Intel XScale**

- The load double word instruction LDRD can transfer two words in a single cycle. Schedule the code so that you do not use the first loaded register for two cycles and the second for three cycles.

- Ensure data arrays are 64-bit aligned so that you can use the 64-bit load instruction LDRD.

- The result of a multiply is not available immediately. Following a multiply with another multiply may introduce stalls. Schedule code so that multiply instructions are interleaved with load instructions to prevent processor stalls.

- The multiply operations do not early terminate. Therefore you should only use MUL and MLA for multiplying 32-bit integers. For 16-bit values use SMULxy and SMLAxy.

EXAMPLE   In this example we use LDRD instructions to improve load bandwidth. The input arrays
8.7   must be 64-bit aligned. The number of samples N is a multiple of eight.

```
x        RN 0     ; input array x[] (64-bit aligned)
c        RN 1     ; input array c[] (64-bit aligned)
N        RN 2     ; number of samples (a multiple of 8)
acc0     RN 3     ; accumulators
acc1     RN 14
x_10     RN 4     ; packed elements from array x[]
x_32     RN 5
x_54     RN 6
x_76     RN 7
c_10     RN 8     ; packed elements from array c[]
c_32     RN 9
c_54     RN 10
c_76     RN 11


dot_16by16_xscale
         STMFD    sp!, {r4-r11, lr}
         LDRD     x_10, [x], #8    ; preload x_10, x_32
         LDRD     c_10, [c], #8    ; preload c_10, c_32
         MOV      acc0, #0
         MOV      acc1, #0
loop_xscale
         ; accumulate 8 products
         SUBS     N, N, #8
```

```
LDRD    x_54, [x], #8    ; load x_54, x_76
SMLABB  acc0, x_10, c_10, acc0
SMLATT  acc1, x_10, c_10, acc1
LDRD    c_54, [c], #8    ; load c_54, c_76
SMLABB  acc0, x_32, c_32, acc0
SMLATT  acc1, x_32, c_32, acc1
LDRGTD  x_10, [x], #8    ; load x_10, x_32
SMLABB  acc0, x_54, c_54, acc0
SMLATT  acc1, x_54, c_54, acc1
LDRGTD  c_10, [c], #8    ; load c_10, c_32
SMLABB  acc0, x_76, c_76, acc0
SMLATT  acc1, x_76, c_76, acc1
BGT     loop_xscale
ADD     r0, acc0, acc1
LDMFD   sp!, {r4-r11, pc}
```

The inner loop requires 14 cycles to accumulate 8 products, a rating of 1.75 cycles per tap.

8.3 FIR FILTERS

The finite impulse response (FIR) filter is a basic building block of many DSP applications and worth investigating in some detail. You can use a FIR filter to remove unwanted frequency ranges, boost certain frequencies, or implement special effects. We will concentrate on efficient implementation of the filter on the ARM. The FIR filter is the simplest type of digital filter. The filtered sample y_t depends linearly on a fixed, finite number of unfiltered samples x_t. Let M be the length of the filter. Then for some filter coefficients, c_i:

$$y_t = \sum_{i=0}^{M-1} c_i x_{t-i} \tag{8.21}$$

Some books refer to the coefficients c_i as the impulse response. If you feed the impulse signal $x = (1, 0, 0, 0, \ldots)$ into the filter, then the output is the signal of filter coefficients $y = (c_0, c_1, c_2, \ldots)$.

Let's look at the issue of dynamic range and possible overflow of the output signal. Suppose that we are using Qn and Qm fixed-point representations $X[t]$ and $C[i]$ for x_t and c_i, respectively. In other words:

$$X[t] = \text{round}(2^n x_t) \quad \text{and} \quad C[i] = \text{round}(2^m c_i) \tag{8.22}$$

We implement the filter by calculating accumulated values $A[t]$:

$$A[t] = C[0]X[t] + C[1]X[t-1] + \cdots + C[M-1]X[t-M+1] \tag{8.23}$$

Then $A[t]$ is a $Q(n+m)$ representation of y_t. But, how large is $A[t]$? How many bits of precision do we need to ensure that $A[t]$ does not overflow its integer container and give a meaningless filter result? There are two very useful inequalities that answer these questions:

$$|A[t]| \le max\{|X[t-i]|, 0 \le i < M\} \times \sum_{i=0}^{M-1} |C[i]| \qquad (8.24)$$

$$|A[t]| \le \sqrt{\sum_{i=0}^{M-1} |X[t-i]|^2} \times \sqrt{\sum_{i=0}^{M-1} |C[i]|^2} \qquad (8.25)$$

Equation (8.24) says that if you know the dynamic range of $X[t]$, then the maximum gain of dynamic range is bounded by the sum of the absolute values of the filter coefficients $C[i]$. Equation (8.25) says that if you know the power of the signal $X[t]$, then the dynamic range of $A[t]$ is bounded by the product of the input signal and coefficient powers. Both inequalities are the best possible. Given fixed $C[t]$, we can choose $X[t]$ so that there is equality. They are special cases of the more general Holder inequalities. Let's illustrate with an example.

EXAMPLE **8.8**   Consider the simple, crude, high-pass filter defined by Equation (8.26). The filter allows through high-frequency signals, but attenuates low-frequency ones.

$$y_t = -0.45x_t + 0.9x_{t-1} - 0.45x_{t-2} \qquad (8.26)$$

Suppose we represent x_i and c_i by Qn, Qm 16-bit fixed-point signals $X[t]$ and $C[i]$. Then,

$$C[0] = -0.45 \times 2^m, \quad C[1] = 0.90 \times 2^m, \quad C[2] = -0.45 \times 2^m \qquad (8.27)$$

Since $X[t]$ is a 16-bit integer, $|X[t]| \le 2^{15}$, and so, using the first inequality above,

$$|A[t]| \le 2^{15} \times 1.8 \times 2^m = 1.8 \times 2^{15+m} \qquad (8.28)$$

$A[t]$ will not overflow a 32-bit integer, provided that $m \le 15$. So, take $m = 15$ for greatest coefficient accuracy. The following integer calculation implements the filter with 16-bit Qn input $X[t]$ and 32-bit $Q(n+15)$ output $A[t]$:

```
A[t] = -0x399A*X[t] + 0x7333*X[t-1] - 0x399A*X[t-2];
```

For a Qn output $Y[t]$ we need to set $Y[t] = A[t] \gg 15$. However, this could overflow a 16-bit integer. Therefore you either need to saturate the result, or store the result using a $Q(n-1)$ representation.

8.3.1   BLOCK FIR FILTERS

Example 8.8 shows that we can usually implement filters using integer sums of products, without the need to check for saturation or overflow:

```
A[t] = C[0]*X[t] + C[1]*X[t-1] + ... + C[M-1]*X[t-M+1];
```

Generally $X[t]$ and $C[i]$ are k-bit integers and $A[t]$ is a $2k$-bit integer, where $k = 8$, 16, or 32. Table 8.3 shows the precision for some typical applications.

We will look at detailed examples of long 16-bit and 32-bit filters. By a long filter, we mean that M is so large that you can't hold the filter coefficients in registers. You should optimize short filters such as Example 8.8 on a case-by-case basis. For these you can hold many coefficients in registers.

For a long filter, each result $A[t]$ depends on M data values and M coefficients that we must read from memory. These loads are time consuming, and it is inefficient to calculate just a single result $A[t]$. While we are loading the data and coefficients, we can calculate $A[t + 1]$ and possibly $A[t + 2]$ at the same time.

An R-way block filter implementation calculates the R values $A[t], A[t + 1], \ldots,$ $A[t + R - 1]$ using a single pass of the data $X[t]$ and coefficients $C[i]$. This reduces the number of memory accesses by a factor of R over calculating each result separately. So R should be as large as possible. On the other hand, the larger R is, the more registers we require to hold accumulated values and data or coefficients. In practice we choose R to be the largest value such that we do not run out of registers in the inner loop. On ARM R can range from 2 to 6, as we will show in the following code examples.

An $R \times S$ block filter is an R-way block filter where we read S data and coefficient values at a time for each iteration of the inner loop. On each loop we accumulate $R \times S$ products onto the R accumulators.

Figure 8.3 shows a typical 4×3 block filter implementation. Each accumulator on the left is the sum of products of the coefficients on the right multiplied by the signal value heading each column. The diagram starts with the oldest sample X_{t-M+1} since the filter routine will load samples in increasing order of memory address. Each inner loop of a 4×3 filter accumulates the 12 products in a 4×3 parallelogram. We've shaded the first parallelogram and the first sample of the third parallelogram.

As you can see from Figure 8.3, an $R \times S$ block filter implementation requires R accumulator registers and a history of $R - 1$ input samples. You also need a register to hold the

Table 8.3   Filter precision for different applications.

Application	$X[t]$ precision (bits)	$C[t]$ precision (bits)	$A[t]$ precision (bits)
Video	8	8	16
Telecoms audio	16	16	32
High-quality audio	32	32	64

	X_{t-M+1}	X_{t-M+2}	X_{t-M+3}	X_{t-M+4}	X_{t-M+5}	X_{t-M+6}	X_{t-M+7}
A_t	C_{M-1}	C_{M-2}	C_{M-3}	C_{M-4}	C_{M-5}	C_{M-6}	C_{M-7}
A_{t+1}		C_{M-1}	C_{M-2}	C_{M-3}	C_{M-4}	C_{M-5}	C_{M-6}
A_{t+2}			C_{M-1}	C_{M-2}	C_{M-3}	C_{M-4}	C_{M-5}
A_{t+3}				C_{M-1}	C_{M-2}	C_{M-3}	C_{M-4}

Figure 8.3 A 4 × 3 block filter implementation.

next coefficient. The loop repeats after adding S products to each accumulator. Therefore we must allocate $X[t]$ and $X[t-S]$ to the same register. We must also keep the history of length at least $R-1$ samples in registers. Therefore $S \geq R-1$. For this reason, block filters are usually of size $R \times (R-1)$ or $R \times R$.

The following examples give optimized block FIR implementations. We select the best values for R and S for different ARM implementations. Note that for these implementations, we store the coefficients in reverse order in memory. Figure 8.3 shows that we start from coefficient $C[M-1]$ and work backwards.

EXAMPLE 8.9 As with the ARM7TDMI dot product, we store 16-bit and 32-bit data items in 32- bit words. Then we can use load multiples for maximum load efficiency. This example implements a 4 × 3 block filter for 16-bit input data. The array pointers *a*, *x*, and *c* point to output and input arrays of the formats given in Figure 8.4.

Note that the *x* array holds a history of $M-1$ samples and that we reverse the coefficient array. We hold the coefficient array pointer *c* and length M in a structure, which limits the function to four register arguments. We also assume that N is a multiple of four and M a multiple of three.

Array name	First element	Second element	Third element	...	Last element	Array length
a	A_t	A_{t+1}	A_{t+2}	...	A_{t+N-1}	N
x	X_{t-M+1}	X_{t-M+2}	X_{t-M+3}	...	X_{t+N-1}	$N+M-1$
c	C_{M-1}	C_{M-2}	C_{M-3}	...	C_0	M

Figure 8.4 Formats of arrays a, x, and c.

```
a       RN 0     ; array for output samples a[]
x       RN 1     ; array of input samples x[]
c       RN 2     ; array of coefficients c[]
N       RN 3     ; number of outputs (a multiple of 4)
M       RN 4     ; number of coefficients (a multiple of 3)
c_0     RN 3     ; coefficient registers
c_1     RN 12
c_2     RN 14
x_0     RN 5     ; data registers
x_1     RN 6
x_2     RN 7
a_0     RN 8     ; output accumulators
a_1     RN 9
a_2     RN 10
a_3     RN 11

        ; void fir_16by16_arm7m
        ;  (int *a,
        ;   int *x,
        ;   struct { int *c; unsigned int M; } *c,
        ;   unsigned int N)
fir_16by16_arm7m
        STMFD   sp!, {r4-r11, lr}
        LDMIA   c, {c, M}        ; load coefficient array and length
next_sample_arm7m
        STMFD   sp!, {N, M}
        LDMIA   x!, {x_0, x_1, x_2}
        MOV     a_0, #0          ; zero accumulators
        MOV     a_1, #0
        MOV     a_2, #0
        MOV     a_3, #0
next_tap_arm7m
        ; perform next block of 4x3=12 taps
        LDMIA   c!, {c_0, c_1, c_2}
        MLA     a_0, x_0, c_0, a_0
        MLA     a_0, x_1, c_1, a_0
        MLA     a_0, x_2, c_2, a_0
        MLA     a_1, x_1, c_0, a_1
        MLA     a_1, x_2, c_1, a_1
        MLA     a_2, x_2, c_0, a_2
        LDMIA   x!, {x_0, x_1, x_2}
        MLA     a_1, x_0, c_2, a_1
        MLA     a_2, x_0, c_1, a_2
```

```
        MLA     a_2, x_1, c_2, a_2
        MLA     a_3, x_0, c_0, a_3
        MLA     a_3, x_1, c_1, a_3
        MLA     a_3, x_2, c_2, a_3
        SUBS    M, M, #3         ; processed 3 coefficents
        BGT     next_tap_arm7m
        LDMFD   sp!, {N, M}
        STMIA   a!, {a_0, a_1, a_2, a_3}
        SUB     c, c, M, LSL#2   ; restore coefficient pointer
        SUB     x, x, M, LSL#2   ; restore data pointer
        ADD     x, x, #(4-3)*4   ; advance data pointer
        SUBS    N, N, #4         ; filtered four samples
        BGT     next_sample_arm7m
        LDMFD   sp!, {r4-r11, pc}
```

Each iteration of the inner loop processes the next three coefficients and updates four filter outputs. Assuming the coefficients are 16-bit, each multiply accumulate requires 4 cycles. Therefore it processes 12 filter taps in 62 cycles, giving a block FIR rating of 5.17 cycles/tap.

Note that it is cheaper to reset the coefficient and input pointers c and x using a subtraction, rather than save their values on the stack.

EXAMPLE 8.10   This example gives an optimized block filter for the ARM9TDMI. First, the ARM9TDMI has a single-cycle 16-bit load, so there is no advantage in using load multiples. We can save memory by storing the data and coefficients in 16-bit halfwords. Second, we can use a 4×4 block filter implementation rather than a 4×3 implementation. This reduces the loop overhead and is useful if the number of coefficients is a multiple of four rather than a multiple of three.

The input and output arrays have the same format as Example 8.9, except that the input arrays are now 16-bit. The number of outputs and coefficients, N and M, must be multiples of four.

```
a       RN 0     ; array for output samples a[]
x       RN 1     ; array of input samples x[]
c       RN 2     ; array of coefficients c[]
N       RN 3     ; number of outputs (a multiple of 4)
M       RN 4     ; number of coefficients (a multiple of 4)
c_0     RN 3     ; coefficient registers
c_1     RN 12
x_0     RN 5     ; data registers
x_1     RN 6
x_2     RN 7
x_3     RN 14
```

```
a_0      RN 8     ; output accumulators
a_1      RN 9
a_2      RN 10
a_3      RN 11
         ; void fir 16by16 arm9m
         ;   (int *a,
         ;     short *x,
         ;     struct { short *c; unsigned int M; } *c,
         ;     unsigned int N)
fir_16by16_arm9m
         STMFD    sp!, {r4-r11, lr}
         LDMIA    c, {c, M}
next_sample_arm9m
         STMFD    sp!, {N, M}
         LDRSH    x_0, [x], #2
         LDRSH    x_1, [x], #2
         LDRSH    x_2, [x], #2
         LDRSH    x_3, [x], #2
         MOV      a_0, #0
         MOV      a_1, #0
         MOV      a_2, #0
         MOV      a_3, #0
next_tap_arm9m
         ; perform next block of 4x4=16 taps
         LDRSH    c_0, [c], #2
         LDRSH    c_1, [c], #2
         SUBS     M, M, #4
         MLA      a_0, x_0, c_0, a_0
         LDRSH    x_0, [x], #2
         MLA      a_1, x_1, c_0, a_1
         MLA      a_2, x_2, c_0, a_2
         MLA      a_3, x_3, c_0, a_3
         LDRSH    c_0, [c], #2
         MLA      a_0, x_1, c_1, a_0
         LDRSH    x_1, [x], #2
         MLA      a_1, x_2, c_1, a_1
         MLA      a_2, x_3, c_1, a_2
         MLA      a_3, x_0, c_1, a_3
         LDRSH    c_1, [c], #2
         MLA      a_0, x_2, c_0, a_0
         LDRSH    x_2, [x], #2
         MLA      a_1, x_3, c_0, a_1
         MLA      a_2, x_0, c_0, a_2
```

```
        MLA     a_3, x_1, c_0, a_3
        MLA     a_0, x_3, c_1, a_0
        LDRSH   x_3, [x], #2
        MLA     a_1, x_0, c_1, a_1
        MLA     a_2, x_1, c_1, a_2
        MLA     a_3, x_2, c_1, a_3
        BGT     next_tap_arm9m
        LDMFD   sp!, {N, M}
        STMIA   a!, {a_0, a_1, a_2, a_3}
        SUB     c, c, M, LSL#1  ; restore coefficient pointer
        SUB     x, x, M, LSL#1  ; advance data pointer
        SUBS    N, N, #4        ; filtered four samples
        BGT     next_sample_arm9m
        LDMFD   sp!, {r4-r11, pc}
```

The code is scheduled so that we don't use a loaded value on the following two cycles. We've moved the loop counter decrement to the start of the loop to fill a load delay slot.

Each iteration of the inner loop processes the next four coefficients and updates four filter outputs. Assuming the coefficients are 16 bits, each multiply accumulate requires 4 cycles. Therefore it processes 16 filter taps in 76 cycles, giving a block FIR rating of 4.75 cycles/tap.

This code also works well for other ARMv4 architecture processors such as the StrongARM. On StrongARM the inner loop requires 61 cycles, or 3.81 cycles/tap.

EXAMPLE
8.11
The ARM9E has a faster multiplier than previous ARM processors. The ARMv5TE 16-bit multiply instructions also unpack 16-bit data when two 16-bit values are packed into a single 32-bit word. Therefore we can store more data and coefficients in registers and use fewer load instructions.

This example implements a 6×6 block filter for ARMv5TE processors. The routine is rather long because it is optimized for maximum speed. If you don't require as much performance, you can reduce code size by using a 4×4 block implementation.

The input and output arrays have the same format as Example 8.9, except that the input arrays are now 16-bit values. The number of outputs and coefficients, N and M, must be multiples of six. The input arrays must be 32-bit aligned and the memory system little-endian. If you need to write endian-neutral routines, then you should replace SMLAxy instructions by macros that change the T and B settings according to endianness. For example the following macro, SMLA00, evaluates to SMLABB or SMLATT for little- or big-endian memory systems, respectively. If b and c are read as arrays of 16-bit values, then SMLA00 always multiplies $b[0]$ by $c[0]$ regardless of endianness.

```
        MACRO
        SMLA00  $a, $b, $c, $d
```

```
          IF {ENDIAN}="big"
            SMLATT $a, $b, $c, $d
          ELSE
            SMLABB $a, $b, $c, $d
          ENDIF
          MEND
```

To keep the example simple, we haven't used macros like this. The following code only works on a little-endian memory system.

```
a         RN 0    ; array for output samples a[]
x         RN 1    ; array of input samples x[] (32-bit aligned)
c         RN 2    ; array of coefficients c[] (32-bit aligned)
N         RN 3    ; number of outputs (a multiple of 6)
M         RN 4    ; number of coefficients (a multiple of 6)
c_10      RN 0    ; coefficient pairs
c_32      RN 3
x_10      RN 5    ; sample pairs
x_32      RN 6
x_54      RN 7
a_0       RN 8    ; output accumulators
a_1       RN 9
a_2       RN 10
a_3       RN 11
a_4       RN 12
a_5       RN 14


          ; void fir_16by16_arm9e
          ; (int *a,
          ;   short *x,
          ;   struct { short *c; unsigned int M; } *c,
          ;   unsigned int N)
fir_16by16_arm9e
          STMFD   sp!, {r4-r11, lr}
          LDMIA   c, {c, M}
next_sample_arm9e
          STMFD   sp!, {a, N, M}
          LDMIA   x!, {x_10, x_32, x_54} ; preload six samples
          MOV     a_0, #0                ; zero accumulators
          MOV     a_1, #0
          MOV     a_2, #0
          MOV     a_3, #0
          MOV     a_4, #0
```

```
        MOV     a_5, #0
next_tap_arm9e
        ; perform next block of 6x6=36 taps
        LDMIA   c!, {c_10, c_32}        ; load four coefficients
        SUBS    M, M, #6
        SMLABB  a_0, x_10, c_10, a_0
        SMLATB  a_1, x_10, c_10, a_1
        SMLABB  a_2, x_32, c_10, a_2
        SMLATB  a_3, x_32, c_10, a_3
        SMLABB  a_4, x_54, c_10, a_4
        SMLATB  a_5, x_54, c_10, a_5
        SMLATT  a_0, x_10, c_10, a_0
        LDR     x_10, [x], #4           ; load two coefficients
        SMLABT  a_1, x_32, c_10, a_1
        SMLATT  a_2, x_32, c_10, a_2
        SMLABT  a_3, x_54, c_10, a_3
        SMLATT  a_4, x_54, c_10, a_4
        SMLABT  a_5, x_10, c_10, a_5
        LDR     c_10, [c], #4
        SMLABB  a_0, x_32, c_32, a_0
        SMLATB  a_1, x_32, c_32, a_1
        SMLABB  a_2, x_54, c_32, a_2
        SMLATB  a_3, x_54, c_32, a_3
        SMLABB  a_4, x_10, c_32, a_4
        SMLATB  a_5, x_10, c_32, a_5
        SMLATT  a_0, x_32, c_32, a_0
        LDR     x_32, [x], #4
        SMLABT  a_1, x_54, c_32, a_1
        SMLATT  a_2, x_54, c_32, a_2
        SMLABT  a_3, x_10, c_32, a_3
        SMLATT  a_4, x_10, c_32, a_4
        SMLABT  a_5, x_32, c_32, a_5
        SMLABB  a_0, x_54, c_10, a_0
        SMLATB  a_1, x_54, c_10, a_1
        SMLABB  a_2, x_10, c_10, a_2
        SMLATB  a_3, x_10, c_10, a_3
        SMLABB  a_4, x_32, c_10, a_4
        SMLATB  a_5, x_32, c_10, a_5
        SMLATT  a_0, x_54, c_10, a_0
        LDR     x_54, [x], #4
        SMLABT  a_1, x_10, c_10, a_1
        SMLATT  a_2, x_10, c_10, a_2
        SMLABT  a_3, x_32, c_10, a_3
```

Table 8.4   ARMv5TE 16-bit block filter timings.

Processor	Inner loop cycles	Filter rating cycles/tap
ARM9E	46	$46/36 = 1.28$
ARM10E	78	$78/36 = 2.17$
XScale	46	$46/36 = 1.28$

```
        SMLATT  a_4, x_32, c_10, a_4
        SMLABT  a_5, x_54, c_10, a_5
        BGT     next_tap_arm9e
        LDMFD   sp!, {a, N, M}
        STMIA   a!, {a_0, a_1, a_2, a_3, a_4, a_5}
        SUB     c, c, M, LSL#1      ; restore coefficient pointer
        SUB     x, x, M, LSL#1      ; advance data pointer
        SUBS    N, N, #6
        BGT     next_sample_arm9e
        LDMFD   sp!, {r4-r11, pc}
```

Each iteration of the inner loop updates the next six filter outputs, accumulating six products to each output. Table 8.4 shows the cycle timings for ARMv5TE architecture processors.

EXAMPLE
8.12

Sometimes 16-bit data items do not give a large enough dynamic range. The ARMv5TE architecture adds an instruction SMLAWx that allows for efficient filtering of 32-bit data by 16-bit coefficients. The instruction multiplies a 32-bit data item by a 16-bit coefficient, extracts the top 32 bits of the 48-bit result, and adds it to a 32-bit accumulator.

This example implements a 5×4 block FIR filter with 32-bit data and 16-bit coefficients. The input and output arrays have the same format as Example 8.9, except that the coefficient array is 16-bit. The number of outputs must be a multiple of five and the number of coefficients a multiple of four. The input coefficient array must be 32-bit aligned and the memory system little-endian. As described in Example 8.11, you can write endian-neutral code by using macros.

If the input samples and coefficients use Qn and Qm representations, respectively, then the output is $Q(n + m - 16)$. The SMLAWx shifts down by 16 to prevent overflow.

```
a      RN 0    ; array for output samples a[]
x      RN 1    ; array of input samples x[]
c      RN 2    ; array of coefficients c[] (32-bit aligned)
N      RN 3    ; number of outputs (a multiple of 5)
M      RN 4    ; number of coefficients (a multiple of 4)
c_10   RN 0    ; coefficient pair
```

```
c_32      RN 3
x_0       RN 5      ; input samples
x_1       RN 6
x_2       RN 7
x_3       RN 14
a_0       RN 8      ; output accumulators
a_1       RN 9
a_2       RN 10
a_3       RN 11
a_4       RN 12


          ; void fir_32by16_arm9e
          ;  (int *a,
          ;   int *x,
          ;   struct { short *c; unsigned int M; } *c,
          ;   unsigned int N)
fir_32by16_arm9e
          STMFD  sp!, {r4-r11, lr}
          LDMIA  c, {c, M}
next_sample32_arm9e
          STMFD  sp!, {a, N, M}
          LDMIA  x!, {x_0, x_1, x_2, x_3}
          MOV    a_0, #0
          MOV    a_1, #0
          MOV    a_2, #0
          MOV    a_3, #0
          MOV    a_4, #0
next_tap32_arm9e
          ; perform next block of 5x4=20 taps
          LDMIA  c!, {c_10, c_32}
          SUBS   M, M, #4
          SMLAWB a_0, x_0, c_10, a_0
          SMLAWB a_1, x_1, c_10, a_1
          SMLAWB a_2, x_2, c_10, a_2
          SMLAWB a_3, x_3, c_10, a_3
          SMLAWT a_0, x_1, c_10, a_0
          LDMIA  x!, {x_0, x_1}
          SMLAWT a_1, x_2, c_10, a_1
          SMLAWT a_2, x_3, c_10, a_2
          SMLAWB a_0, x_2, c_32, a_0
          SMLAWB a_1, x_3, c_32, a_1
          SMLAWT a_0, x_3, c_32, a_0
          LDMIA  x!, {x_2, x_3}
```

Table 8.5   ARMv5TE 32 × 16 filter timings.

Processor	Inner loop cycles	Filter rating cycles/tap
ARM9E	30	30/20 = 1.5
ARM10E	44	44/20 = 2.2
XScale	34	34/20 = 1.7

```
SMLAWB   a_4, x_0, c_10, a_4
SMLAWT   a_3, x_0, c_10, a_3
SMLAWT   a_4, x_1, c_10, a_4
SMLAWB   a_2, x_0, c_32, a_2
SMLAWB   a_3, x_1, c_32, a_3
SMLAWB   a_4, x_2, c_32, a_4
SMLAWT   a_1, x_0, c_32, a_1
SMLAWT   a_2, x_1, c_32, a_2
SMLAWT   a_3, x_2, c_32, a_3
SMLAWT   a_4, x_3, c_32, a_4
BGT      next_tap32_arm9e
LDMFD    sp!, {a, N, M}
STMIA    a!, {a_0, a_1, a_2, a_3, a_4}
SUB      c, c, M, LSL#1
SUB      x, x, M, LSL#2
ADD      x, x, #(5-4)*4
SUBS     N, N, #5
BGT      next_sample32_arm9e
LDMFD    sp!, {r4-r11, pc}
```

Each iteration of the inner loop updates five filter outputs, accumulating four products to each. Table 8.5 gives cycle counts for architecture ARMv5TE processors.

EXAMPLE 8.13   High-quality audio applications often require intermediate sample precision at greater than 16-bit. On the ARM we can use the long multiply instruction SMLAL to implement an efficient filter with 32-bit input data and coefficients. The output values are 64-bit. This makes the ARM very competitive for CD audio quality applications.

The output and input arrays have the same format as in Example 8.9. We implement a 3 × 2 block filter so N must be a multiple of three and M a multiple of two. The filter works well on any ARMv4 implementation.

```
a        RN 0    ; array for output samples a[]
x        RN 1    ; array of input samples x[]
c        RN 2    ; array of coefficients c[]
```

```
N       RN 3    ; number of outputs (a multiple of 3)
M       RN 4    ; number of coefficients (a multiple of 2)
c_0     RN 3    ; coefficient registers
c_1     RN 12
x_0     RN 5    ; data registers
x_1     RN 6
a_0l    RN 7    ; accumulators (low 32 bits)
a_0h    RN 8    ; accumulators (high 32 bits)
a_1l    RN 9
a_1h    RN 10
a_2l    RN 11
a_2h    RN 14

        ; void fir_32by32
        ;   (long long *a,
        ;    int *x,
        ;    struct { int *c; unsigned int M; } *c,
        ;    unsigned int N)
fir_32by32
        STMFD   sp!, {r4-r11, lr}
        LDMIA   c, {c, M}
next_sample32
        STMFD   sp!, {N, M}
        LDMIA   x!, {x_0, x_1}
        MOV     a_0l, #0
        MOV     a_0h, #0
        MOV     a_1l, #0
        MOV     a_1h, #0
        MOV     a_2l, #0
        MOV     a_2h, #0
next_tap32
        ; perform next block of 3x2=6 taps
        LDMIA   c!, {c_0, c_1}
        SMLAL   a_0l, a_0h, x_0, c_0
        SMLAL   a_1l, a_1h, x_1, c_0
        SMLAL   a_0l, a_0h, x_1, c_1
        LDMIA   x!, {x_0, x_1}
        SUBS    M, M, #2
        SMLAL   a_2l, a_2h, x_0, c_0
        SMLAL   a_1l, a_1h, x_0, c_1
        SMLAL   a_2l, a_2h, x_1, c_1
        BGT     next_tap32
        LDMFD   sp!, {N, M}
```

Table 8.6   32-bit by 32-bit filter timing.

Processor	Inner loop cycles	Filter rating cycles/tap
ARM7TDMI	54	54/6 = 9
ARM9TDMI	50	50/6 − 8.3
StrongARM	31	31/6 = 5.2
ARM9E	26	26/6 = 4.3
ARM10E	22	22/6 = 3.7
XScale	22	22/6 = 3.7

```
STMIA    a!, {a_0l, a_0h, a_1l, a_1h, a_2l, a_2h}
SUB      c, c, M, LSL#2
SUB      x, x, M, LSL#2
ADD      x, x, #(3-2)*4
SUBS     N, N, #3
BGT      next_sample32
LDMFD    sp!, {r4-r11, pc}
```

Each iteration of the inner loop processes the next two coefficients and updates three filter outputs. Assuming the coefficients use the full 32-bit range, the multiply does not terminate early. The routine is optimal for most ARM implementations. Table 8.6 gives the cycle timings for a range of processors.

SUMMARY   **Writing FIR Filters on the ARM**

■ If the number of FIR coefficients is small enough, then hold the coefficients and history samples in registers. Often coefficients are repeated. This will save on the number of registers you need.

■ If the FIR filter length is long, then use a block filter algorithm of size $R \times (R-1)$ or $R \times R$. Choose the largest R possible given the 14 available general purpose registers on the ARM.

■ Ensure that the input arrays are aligned to the access size. This will be 64-bit when using LDRD. Ensure that the array length is a multiple of the block size.

■ Schedule to avoid all load-use and multiply-use interlocks.

8.4   IIR FILTERS

An infinite impulse response (IIR) filter is a digital filter that depends linearly on a finite number of input samples and a finite number of previous filter outputs. In other words, it combines a FIR filter with feedback from previous filter outputs. Mathematically, for some coefficients b_i and a_j:

$$y_t = \sum_{i=0}^{M} b_i x_{t-i} - \sum_{j=1}^{L} a_j y_{t-j} \tag{8.29}$$

If you feed in the impulse signal $x = (1, 0, 0, 0, \ldots)$, then y_t may oscillate forever. This is why it has an infinite impulse response. However, for a stable filter, y_t will decay to zero. We will concentrate on efficient implementation of this filter.

You can calculate the output signal y_t directly, using Equation (8.29). In this case the code is similar to the FIR of Section 8.3. However, this calculation method may be numerically unstable. It is often more accurate, and more efficient, to factorize the filter into a series of *biquads*—an IIR filter with $M = L = 2$:

$$y_t = b_0 x_t + b_1 x_{t-1} + b_2 x_{t-2} - a_1 y_{t-1} - a_2 y_{t-2} \tag{8.30}$$

We can implement any IIR filter by repeatedly filtering the data by a number of biquads. To see this, we use the *z-transform*. This transform associates with each signal x_t, a polynomial $x(z)$ defined as

$$x(z) = \sum_t x_t z^{-t} \tag{8.31}$$

If we transform the IIR equation into z-coordinates, we obtain

$$\left(1 + a_1 z^{-1} + \cdots + a_L z^{-L}\right) y(z) = \left(b_0 + b_1 z^{-1} + \cdots + b_M z^{-M}\right) x(z) \tag{8.32}$$

Equivalently,

$$y(z) = H(z)x(z), \text{ where } H(z) = \frac{b_0 + b_1 z^{-1} + \cdots + b_M z^{-M}}{1 + a_1 z^{-1} + \cdots + a_L z^{-L}} \tag{8.33}$$

Next, consider $H(z)$ as the ratio of two polynomials in z^{-1}. We can factorize the polynomials into quadratic factors. Then we can express $H(z)$ as a product of quadratic ratios $H_i(z)$, each $H_i(z)$ representing a biquad.

So, now we only have to implement biquads efficiently. On the face of it, to calculate y_t for a biquad, we need the current sample x_t and four history elements $x_{t-1}, x_{t-2}, y_{t-1}, y_{t-2}$. However, there is a trick to reduce the number of history or state values we require from four to two. We define an intermediate signal s_t by

$$s_t = x_t - a_1 s_{t-1} - a_2 s_{t-2} \tag{8.34}$$

Then

$$y_t = b_0 s_t + b_1 s_{t-1} + b_2 s_{t-2} \tag{8.35}$$

In other words, we perform the feedback part of the filter before the FIR part of the filter. Equivalently we apply the denominator of $H(z)$ before the numerator. Now each biquad filter requires a state of only two values, s_{t-1} and s_{t-2}.

The coefficient b_0 controls the amplitude of the biquad. We can assume that $b_0 = 1$ when performing a series of biquads, and use a single multiply or shift at the end to correct the signal amplitude. So, to summarize, we have reduced an IIR to filtering by a series of biquads of the form

$$s_t = x_t - a_1 s_{t-1} - a_2 s_{t-2}, \quad y_t = s_t + b_1 s_{t-1} + b_2 s_{t-2} \tag{8.36}$$

To implement each biquad, we need to store fixed-point representations of the six values $-a_1, -a_2, b_1, b_2, s_{t-1}, s_{t-2}$ in ARM registers. To load a new biquad requires six loads; to load a new sample, only one load. Therefore it is much more efficient for the inner loop to loop over samples rather than loop over biquads.

For a block IIR, we split the input signal x_t into large frames of N samples. We make multiple passes over the signal, filtering by as many biquads as we can hold in registers on each pass. Typically for ARMv4 processors we filter by one biquad on each pass; for ARMv5TE processors, by two biquads. The following examples give IIR code for different ARM processors.

EXAMPLE
8.14

This example implements a 1×2 block IIR filter on the ARM7TDMI. Each inner loop applies one biquad filter to the next two input samples. The input arrays have the format given in Figure 8.5.

Each biquad B_k is a list of six values $(-a_1, -a_2, b_1, b_2, s_{t-1}, s_{t-2})$. As with previous implementations for the ARM7TDMI, we store the 16-bit input values in 32-bit integers so we can use load multiples. We store the biquad coefficients at Q14 fixed-point format. The number of samples N must be even.

```
y       RN 0    ; address for output samples y[]
x       RN 1    ; address of input samples x[]
b       RN 2    ; address of biquads
N       RN 3    ; number of samples to filter (a multiple of 2)
M       RN 4    ; number of biquads to apply
x_0     RN 2    ; input samples
```

Array name	First element	Second element	Third element		Last element	Array length
x	X_t	X_{t+1}	X_{t+2}	...	X_{t+N-1}	N
y	Y_t	Y_{t+1}	Y_{t+2}	...	Y_{t+N-1}	N
b	B_0	B_1	B_2	...	B_{M-1}	M

Figure 8.5   Formats of the arrays x, y, and b.

```
x_1      RN 4
a_1      RN 6    ; biquad coefficient -a[1] at Q14
a_2      RN 7    ; biquad coefficient -a[2] at Q14
b_1      RN 8    ; biquad coefficient +b[1] at Q14
b_2      RN 9    ; biquad coefficient +b[2] at Q14
s_1      RN 10   ; s[t-1] then s[t-2] (alternates)
s_2      RN 11   ; s[t-2] then s[t-1] (alternates)
acc0     RN 12   ; accumulators
acc1     RN 14

         ; typedef struct {
         ;   int a1,a2;  /* coefficients -a[1],-a[2] at Q14 */
         ;   int b1,b2;  /* coefficients +b[1],+b[2] at Q14 */
         ;   int s1,s2;  /* s[t-1], s[t-2] */
         ; } biquad;
         ;
         ; void iir_q14_arm7m
         ; (int *y,
         ;   int *x,
         ;   struct { biquad *b; unsigned int M; } *b,
         ;   unsigned int N);
iir_q14_arm7m
         STMFD   sp!, {r4-r11, lr}
         LDMIA   b, {b, M}
next_biquad_arm7m
         LDMIA   b!, {a_1, a_2, b_1, b_2, s_1, s_2}
         STMFD   sp!, {b, N, M}
next_sample_arm7m
         ; use a 2x1 block IIR
         LDMIA   x!, {x_0, x_1}
         ; apply biquad to sample 0 (x_0)
         MUL     acc0, s_1, a_1
         MLA     acc0, s_2, a_2, acc0
         MUL     acc1, s_1, b_1
         MLA     acc1, s_2, b_2, acc1
         ADD     s_2, x_0, acc0, ASR #14
         ADD     x_0, s_2, acc1, ASR #14
         ; apply biquad to sample 1 (x_1)
         MUL     acc0, s_2, a_1
         MLA     acc0, s_1, a_2, acc0
         MUL     acc1, s_2, b_1
         MLA     acc1, s_1, b_2, acc1
         ADD     s_1, x_1, acc0, ASR #14
```

```
        ADD     x_1, s_1, acc1, ASR #14
        STMIA   y!, {x_0, x_1}
        SUBS    N, N, #2
        BGT     next_sample_arm7m
        LDMFD   sp!, {b, N, M}
        STMDB   b, {s_1, s_2}
        SUB     y, y, N, LSL#2
        MOV     x, y
        SUBS    M, M, #1
        BGT     next_biquad_arm7m
        LDMFD   sp!, {r4-r11, pc}
```

Each inner loop requires a worst case of 44 cycles to apply one biquad to two samples. This gives the ARM7TDMI an IIR rating of 22 cycles/biquad-sample for a general biquad. ◾

EXAMPLE
8.15

On the ARM9TDMI we can use halfword load instructions rather than load multiples. Therefore we can store samples in 16-bit short integers. This example implements a load scheduled IIR suitable for the ARM9TDMI. The interface is the same as in Example 8.14, except that we use 16-bit data items.

```
y       RN 0    ; address for output samples y[]
x       RN 1    ; address of input samples x[]
b       RN 2    ; address of biquads
N       RN 3    ; number of samples to filter (a multiple of 2)
M       RN 4    ; number of biquads to apply
x_0     RN 2    ; input samples
x_1     RN 4
round   RN 5    ; rounding value (1 << 13)
a_1     RN 6    ; biquad coefficient -a[1] at Q14
a_2     RN 7    ; biquad coefficient -a[2] at Q14
b_1     RN 8    ; biquad coefficient +b[1] at Q14
b_2     RN 9    ; biquad coefficient +b[2] at Q14
s_1     RN 10   ; s[t-1] then s[t-2] (alternates)
s_2     RN 11   ; s[t-2] then s[t-1] (alternates)
acc0    RN 12   ; accumulators
acc1    RN 14
        ; typedef struct {
        ;   short a1,a2; /* coefficients -a[1],-a[2] at Q14 */
        ;   short b1,b2; /* coefficients +b[1],+b[2] at Q14 */
        ;   short s1,s2; /* s[t-1], s[t-2] */
        ; } biquad;
        ;
        ; void iir_q14_arm9m
```

```
        ; (short *y,
        ;   short *x,
        ;   struct { biquad *b; unsigned int M; } *b,
        ;   unsigned int N);
iir_q14_arm9m
        STMFD   sp!, {r4-r11, lr}
        LDMIA   b, {b, M}
        MOV     round, #1 << 13
iir_next_biquad
        LDRSH   a_1, [b], #2
        LDRSH   a_2, [b], #2
        LDRSH   b_1, [b], #2
        LDRSH   b_2, [b], #2
        LDRSH   s_1, [b], #2
        LDRSH   s_2, [b], #2
        STMFD   sp!, {b, N, M}
iir_inner_loop
        ; use a 2x1 block IIR
        ; apply biquad to x_0
        MLA     acc0, s_1, a_1, round
        LDRSH   x_0, [x], #2
        MLA     acc0, s_2, a_2, acc0
        MLA     acc1, s_1, b_1, round
        MLA     acc1, s_2, b_2, acc1
        ADD     s_2, x_0, acc0, ASR #14
        ADD     x_0, s_2, acc1, ASR #14
        STRH    x_0, [y], #2
        ; apply biquad to x_1
        MLA     acc0, s_2, a_1, round
        LDRSH   x_1, [x], #2
        MLA     acc0, s_1, a_2, acc0
        MLA     acc1, s_2, b_1, round
        MLA     acc1, s_1, b_2, acc1
        ADD     s_1, x_1, acc0, ASR #14
        ADD     x_1, s_1, acc1, ASR #14
        STRH    x_1, [y], #2
        SUBS    N, N, #2
        BGT     iir_inner_loop
        LDMFD   sp!, {b, N, M}
        STRH    s_1, [b, #-4]
        STRH    s_2, [b, #-2]
        SUB     y, y, N, LSL#1
        MOV     x, y
        SUBS    M, M, #1
        BGT     iir_next_biquad
        LDMFD   sp!, {r4-r11, pc}
```

Table 8.7   ARMv4T IIR timings.

Processor	Cycles per loop	Cycles per biquad-sample
ARM9TDMI	44	22
StrongARM	33	16.5

The timings on ARM9TDMI and StrongARM are shown in Table 8.7.

EXAMPLE
8.16 With ARMv5TE processors, we can pack two 16-bit values into each register. This means we can store the state and coefficients for two biquads in registers at the same time. This example implements a 2×2 block IIR filter. Each iteration of the inner loop applies two biquad filters to the next two input samples.

The format of the input arrays is the same as for Example 8.14, except that we use 16-bit arrays. The biquad array must be 32-bit aligned. The number of samples N and number of biquads M must be even.

As with the ARM9E FIR, the routine only works for a little-endian memory system. See the discussion in Example 8.11 on how to write endian-neutral DSP code using macros.

```
y       RN 0    ; address for output samples y[]
x       RN 1    ; address of input samples x[]
b       RN 2    ; address of biquads (32-bit aligned)
N       RN 3    ; number of samples to filter (a multiple of 2)
M       RN 4    ; number of biquads to apply (a multiple of 2)
x_0     RN 2    ; input samples
x_1     RN 4
s_0     RN 5    ; new state
b0_a21  RN 6    ; biquad 0, packed -a[2], -a[1]
b0_b21  RN 7    ; biquad 0, packed +b[2], +b[1]
b0_s_1  RN 8    ; biquad 0, s[t-1]
b0_s_2  RN 9    ; biquad 0, s[t-2]
b1_a21  RN 10   ; biquad 1, packed -a[2], -a[1]
b1_b21  RN 11   ; biquad 1, packed +b[2], +b[1]
b1_s_1  RN 12   ; biquad 1, s[t-1]
b1_s_2  RN 14   ; biquad 1, s[t-2]

        ; typedef struct {
        ;   short a1,a2; /* coefficients -a[1],-a[2] at Q14 */
        ;   short b1,b2; /* coefficients +b[1],+b[2] at Q14 */
        ;   short s1,s2; /* s[t-1], s[t-2] */
        ; } biquad;
        ;
```

```
        ; void iir_q14_arm9e
        ;   (short *y,
        ;    short *x,
        ;    struct { biquad *b; unsigned int M; } *b,
        ;    unsigned int N);
iir_q14_arm9e
        STMFD   sp!, {r4-r11, lr}
        LDMIA   b, {b, M}
next_biquad_arm9e
        LDMIA   b!, {b0_a21, b0_b21}
        LDRSH   b0_s_1, [b], #2
        LDRSH   b0_s_2, [b], #2
        LDMIA   b!, {b1_a21, b1_b21}
        LDRSH   b1_s_1, [b], #2
        LDRSH   b1_s_2, [b], #2
        STMFD   sp!, {b, N, M}
next_sample_arm9e
        ; use a 2x2 block IIR
        LDRSH   x_0, [x], #2
        LDRSH   x_1, [x], #2
        SUBS    N, N, #2
        MOV     x_0, x_0, LSL #14
        MOV     x_1, x_1, LSL #14
        ; apply biquad 0 to sample 0
        SMLABB  x_0, b0_s_1, b0_a21, x_0
        SMLABT  s_0, b0_s_2, b0_a21, x_0
        SMLABB  x_0, b0_s_1, b0_b21, s_0
        SMLABT  x_0, b0_s_2, b0_b21, x_0
        MOV     b0_s_2, s_0, ASR #14
        ; apply biquad 0 to sample 1
        SMLABB  x_1, b0_s_2, b0_a21, x_1
        SMLABT  s_0, b0_s_1, b0_a21, x_1
        SMLABB  x_1, b0_s_2, b0_b21, s_0
        SMLABT  x_1, b0_s_1, b0_b21, x_1
        MOV     b0_s_1, s_0, ASR #14
        ; apply biquad 1 to sample 0
        SMLABB  x_0, b1_s_1, b1_a21, x_0
        SMLABT  s_0, b1_s_2, b1_a21, x_0
        SMLABB  x_0, b1_s_1, b1_b21, s_0
        SMLABT  x_0, b1_s_2, b1_b21, x_0
        MOV     b1_s_2, s_0, ASR #14
        ; apply biquad 1 to sample 1
        SMLABB  x_1, b1_s_2, b1_a21, x_1
```

Table 8.8 ARMv5E IIR timings.

Processor	Cycles per loop	Cycles per biquad-sample
ARM9E	32	8.0
ARM10E	45	11.2
XScale	30	7.7

```
SMLABT  s_0, b1_s_1, b1_a21, x_1
SMLABB  x_1, b1_s_2, b1_b21, s_0
SMLABT  x_1, b1_s_1, b1_b21, x_1
MOV     b1_s_1, s_0, ASR #14
MOV     x_0, x_0, ASR #14
MOV     x_1, x_1, ASR #14
STRH    x_0, [y], #2
STRH    x_1, [y], #2
BGT     next_sample_arm9e
LDMFD   sp!, {b, N, M}
STRH    b0_s_1, [b, #-12-4]
STRH    b0_s_2, [b, #-12-2]
STRH    b1_s_1, [b, #-4]
STRH    b1_s_2, [b, #-2]
SUB     y, y, N, LSL#1
MOV     x, y
SUBS    M, M, #2
BGT     next_biquad_arm9e
LDMFD   sp!, {r4-r11, pc}
```

The timings on ARM9E, ARM10E, and XScale are shown in Table 8.8.

SUMMARY **Implementing 16-bit IIR Filters**

- Factorize the IIR into a series of *biquads*. Choose the data precision so there can be no overflow during the IIR calculation. To compute the maximum gain of an IIR, apply the IIR to an impulse to generate the impulse response. Apply the equations of Section 8.3 to the impulse response $c[j]$.

- Use a block IIR algorithm, dividing the signal to be filtered into large frames.

- On each pass of the sample frame, filter by M biquads. Choose M to be the largest number of biquads so that you can hold the state and coefficients in the 14 available registers on the ARM. Ensure that the total number of biquads is a multiple of M.

- As always, schedule code to avoid load and multiply use interlocks.

8.5 THE DISCRETE FOURIER TRANSFORM

The *Discrete Fourier Transform* (DFT) converts a time domain signal x_t to a frequency domain signal y_k. The associated inverse transform (IDFT) reconstructs the time domain signal from the frequency domain signal. This tool is heavily used in signal analysis and compression. It is particularly powerful because there is an algorithm, the *Fast Fourier Transform* (FFT), that implements the DFT very efficiently. In this section we will look at some efficient ARM implementations of the FFT.

The DFT acts on a frame of N complex time samples, converting them into N complex frequency coefficients. We will use Equations (8.37) and (8.38) as the definition. You may see slightly different equations in different texts because some authors may use a different scaling or a different definition of which is the forward and which the inverse transform. This doesn't affect any of the important properties of the transform.

$$y = DFT_N(x) \text{ means } y_k = \sum_{t=0}^{N-1} x_t w_N^{kt}, \quad \text{where } w_N = e^{-2\pi i/N} \qquad (8.37)$$

$$x = IDFT_N(y) \text{ means } x_t = \frac{1}{N}\sum_{k=0}^{N-1} y_k w_N^{kt}, \quad \text{where } w_N = e^{2\pi i/N} \qquad (8.38)$$

As you can see, the transforms are the same except for scaling and choice of w_N. Therefore we'll only look at the forward transform. In fact the Fast Fourier Transform algorithm works for any w_N such that $w_N^N = 1$. The algorithm is only invertible for principal roots of unity where $w_N^k \neq 1$ for $k < N$.

8.5.1 THE FAST FOURIER TRANSFORM

The idea of the FFT is to break down the transform by factorizing N. Suppose for example that $N = R \times S$. Split the output into S blocks of size R and the input into R blocks of size S. In other words:

$$k = nR + m \quad \text{for } n = 0, 1, \ldots, S-1 \quad \text{and} \quad m = 0, 1, \ldots, R-1 \qquad (8.39)$$

$$t = rS + s \quad \text{for } r = 0, 1, \ldots, R-1 \quad \text{and} \quad s = 0, 1, \ldots, S-1 \qquad (8.40)$$

Then,

$$y[nR + m] = \sum_{r=0}^{R-1}\sum_{s=0}^{S-1} x[rS + s]w_N^{(nR+m)(rS+s)} \qquad (8.41)$$

$$y[nR + m] = \sum_{s=0}^{S-1} w_S^{ns} w_N^{ms} \left(\sum_{r=0}^{R-1} x[rS + s]w_R^{mr} \right) \qquad (8.42)$$

Equation (8.42) reduces the N-point DFT to S sets of R-point DFTs, N multiplications by coefficients of the form w_N^{ms}, and R sets of S-point DFTs. Specifically, if we set in turn:

$$(u[sR], u[sR + 1], \ldots, u[sR + R - 1]) = DFT_R(x[s], x[s + S], \ldots, x[s + (R - 1)S]) \tag{8.43}$$

$$v[sR + m] = w_N^{ms} u[sR + m] \tag{8.44}$$

Then $y[nR + m] = \displaystyle\sum_{s=0}^{S-1} w_S^{ns} v[sR + m]$, and so

$$(y[m], y[R + m], \ldots, y[(S - 1)R + m]) = DFT_S(v[m], v[R + m], \ldots, v[(S - 1)R + m]) \tag{8.45}$$

In practice we then repeat this process to calculate the R- and S-point DFTs efficiently. This works well when N has many small factors. The most useful case is when N is a power of 2.

8.5.1.1 The Radix-2 Fast Fourier Transform

Suppose $N = 2^a$. Take $R = 2^{a-1}$ and $S = 2$ and apply the reduction of the DFT. Since $DFT_2(v[m], v[R + m]) = (v[m] + v[R + m], v[m] - v[R + m])$, we have

$$y[m] = u[m] + w_N^m u[R + m] \quad \text{and} \quad y[R + m] = u[m] - w_N^m u[R + m] \tag{8.46}$$

This pair of operations is called the *decimation-in-time radix-2 butterfly*. The N-point DFT reduces to two R-point DFTs followed by $N/2$ butterfly operations. We repeat the process decomposing $R = 2^{a-2} \times 2$, and so on for each factor of 2. The result is an algorithm consisting of a stages, each stage calculating $N/2$ butterflies.

You will notice that the data order must be changed when we calculate $u[sR + m]$ from $x[rS + s]$. We can avoid this if we store $x[t]$ in a transposed order. For a radix-2 Fast Fourier Transform, all the butterfly operations may be performed in place provided that the input array $x[t]$ is stored in *bit-reversed* order—store $x[t]$ at $x[s]$, where the a bits of the index s are the reverse of the a bits of the index t.

There is another way to apply the FFT reduction. We could choose $R = 2$ and $S = 2^{a-1}$ and iterate by decomposing the second factor instead. This generates the *decimation-in-frequency radix-2 transform*. For the decimation-in-frequency transformation, the butterfly is

$$v[2s] = x[s] + x[S + s] \quad \text{and} \quad v[2s + 1] = w_N^s(x[s] - x[S + s]) \tag{8.47}$$

From an ARM optimization point of view, the important difference is the position of the complex multiply. The decimation-in-time algorithm multiplies by w_N^m before the addition and subtraction. The decimation-in-frequency algorithm multiplies by w_N^s after the addition and subtraction. A fixed-point multiply involves a multiply followed by a right shift.

The ARM barrel shifter is positioned before the add or subtract in ARM instruction operations, so the ARM is better suited to the decimation-in-time algorithm.

We won't go into the details of coding a radix-2 FFT, since a radix-4 FFT gives better performance. We look at this in the next section.

8.5.1.2   The Radix-4 Fast Fourier Transform

This is very similar to the radix-2 transform except we treat N as a power of four, $N = 4^b$. We use the decimation-in-time decomposition, $R = 4^{b-1}$ and $S = 4$. Then the radix-4 butterfly is

$$(y[m], y[R + m], y[2R + m], y[3R + m])$$

$$= DFT_4(u[m], w_N^m u[R + m], w_N^{2m} u[2R + m], w_N^{3m} u[3R + m]) \qquad (8.48)$$

The four-point DFT does not require any complex multiplies. Therefore, the decimation-in-time radix-4 algorithm requires $bN/4$ radix-4 butterflies with three complex multiplies in each. The radix-2 algorithm requires $2bN/2$ radix-2 butterflies with one complex multiply in each. Therefore, the radix-4 algorithm saves 25% of the multiplies.

It is tempting to consider a radix-8 transform. However, you can only save a small percentage of the multiplies. This gain will usually be outweighed by the extra load and store overhead required. The ARM has too few registers to support the general radix-8 butterfly efficiently. The radix-4 butterfly is at a sweet spot: It saves a large number of multiplies and will fit neatly into the 14 available ARM registers.

To implement the radix-4 butterfly efficiently, we use a radix-2 FFT to calculate DFT_4. Provided that the input is bit-reversed, we can calculate a four-point DFT in place, in eight ARM registers. The following C_FFT4 macro lies at the heart of our FFT implementations. It performs the four-point DFT and input scale at the same time, which makes good use of the ARM barrel shifter. To prevent overflow, we also divide the answer by four.

```
x0_r    RN 4     ; data register (real part)
x0_i    RN 5     ; data register (imaginary part)
x1_r    RN 6
x1_i    RN 7
x2_r    RN 8
x2_i    RN 9
x3_r    RN 10
x3_i    RN 11
y3_r    RN x3_i
y3_i    RN x3_r

        ; Four-point complex Fast Fourier Transform
        ;
        ; (x0,x1,x2,y3)=DFT4(x0,x2 >> s,x1 >> s,x3 >> s)/4
```

```
;
; x0 = (x0 +   (x2>>s) + (x1>>s) +   (x3>>s))/4
; x1 = (x0 - i*(x2>>s) - (x1>>s) + i*(x3>>s))/4
; x2 = (x0 -   (x2>>s) + (x1>>s) -   (x3>>s))/4
; y3 = (x0 + i*(x2>>s) - (x1>>s) - i*(x3>>s))/4
;
MACRO
C_FFT4  $s
; (x2,x3) = (x2+x3, x2-x3)
ADD     x2_r, x2_r, x3_r
ADD     x2_i, x2_i, x3_i
SUB     x3_r, x2_r, x3_r, LSL#1
SUB     x3_i, x2_i, x3_i, LSL#1
; (x0,x1) = (x0+(x1>>s), x0-(x1>>s))/4
MOV     x0_r, x0_r, ASR#2
MOV     x0_i, x0_i, ASR#2
ADD     x0_r, x0_r, x1_r, ASR#(2+$s)
ADD     x0_i, x0_i, x1_i, ASR#(2+$s)
SUB     x1_r, x0_r, x1_r, ASR#(1+$s)
SUB     x1_i, x0_i, x1_i, ASR#(1+$s)
; (x0,x2) = (x0+(x2>>s)/4, x0-(x2>>s)/4)
ADD     x0_r, x0_r, x2_r, ASR#(2+$s)
ADD     x0_i, x0_i, x2_i, ASR#(2+$s)
SUB     x2_r, x0_r, x2_r, ASR#(1+$s)
SUB     x2_i, x0_i, x2_i, ASR#(1+$s)
; (x1,y3) = (x1-i*(x3>>s)/4, x1+i*(x3>>s)/4)
ADD     x1_r, x1_r, x3_i, ASR#(2+$s)
SUB     x1_i, x1_i, x3_r, ASR#(2+$s)
SUB     y3_r, x1_r, x3_i, ASR#(1+$s)
ADD     y3_i, x1_i, x3_r, ASR#(1+$s)
MEND
```

We will also use the following macros, C_LDR and C_STR, to load and store complex values. This will clarify the FFT code listing in Examples 8.17 and 8.18.

```
; complex load, x=[a], a+=offset
MACRO
C_LDR   $x, $a, $offset
LDRSH   $x._i, [$a, #2]
LDRSH   $x._r, [$a], $offset
MEND

; complex store, [a]=x, a+=offset
```

```
MACRO
C_STR    $x, $a, $offset
STRH     $x._i, [$a, #2]
STRH     $x._r, [$a], $offset
MEND
```

EXAMPLE
8.17

This example implements a 16-bit radix-4 FFT for any ARMv4 architecture processor. We assume that the number of points is $n = 4^b$. If N is an odd power of two, then you will need to alter the routine to start with a radix-2 stage, or a radix-8 stage, rather than the radix-4 stage we show.

The code uses a trick to perform a complex multiply using only three real multiplies. If $a + ib$ is a complex data item, and $c + is$ a complex coefficient, then

$$(a + ib)(c - is) = [(b - a)s + a(c + s)] + i[(b - a)s + b(c - s)] \tag{8.49}$$

$$(a + ib)(c + is) = [(a - b)s + a(c - s)] + i[(a - b)s + b(c + s)] \tag{8.50}$$

When $c + is = e^{2\pi i/N}$, these are the complex multiplies required for the forward and inverse transform radix-4 butterflies, respectively. Given inputs $c - s, s, c + s, a, b$, you can calculate either of the above using a subtract, multiply, and two multiply accumulates. In the coefficient lookup table we store $(c - s, s)$ and calculate $c + s$ on the fly. We can use the same table for both forward and inverse transforms.

Use the following code to perform the radix-4 transform on ARMv4. The number of points N must be a power of four. The algorithm actually calculates $DFT_N(x)/N$, the extra scaling by N preventing overflow. The algorithm uses the C_FFT4 and load-store macros defined previously.

```
; Complex conjugate multiply a=(xr+i*xi)*(cr-i*ci)
;    x = xr + i*xi
;    w = (cr-ci) + i*ci
MACRO
C_MUL9m $a, $x, $w
SUB     t1, $x._i, $x._r          ; (xi-xr)
MUL     t0, t1, $w._i             ; (xi-xr)*ci
ADD     t1, $w._r, $w._i, LSL#1   ; (cr+ci)
MLA     $a._i, $x._i, $w._r, t0   ; xi*cr-xr*ci
MLA     $a._r, $x._r, t1, t0      ; xr*cr+xi*ci
MEND
```

```
y    RN 0    ; output complex array y[]
c    RN 0    ; coefficient array
x    RN 1    ; input complex array x[]
N    RN 2    ; number of samples (a power of 2)
S    RN 2    ; the number of blocks
```

```
R         RN 3    ; the number of samples in each block
x0_r      RN 4    ; data register (real part)
x0_i      RN 5    ; data register (complex part)
x1_r      RN 6
x1_i      RN 7
x2_r      RN 8
x2_i      RN 9
x3_r      RN 10
x3_i      RN 11
y3_r      RN x3_i
y3_i      RN x3_r
t0        RN 12   ; scratch register
t1        RN 14


          ; void fft_16_arm9m(short *y, short *x, unsigned int N)
fft_16_arm9m
          STMFD   sp!, {r4-r11, lr}
          MOV     t0, #0              ; bit reversed counter
first_stage_arm9m
          ; first stage load and bit reverse
          ADD     t1,  x, t0, LSL#2
          C_LDR   x0, t1, N
          C_LDR   x2, t1, N
          C_LDR   x1, t1, N
          C_LDR   x3, t1, N
          C_FFT4  0
          C_STR   x0, y, #4
          C_STR   x1, y, #4
          C_STR   x2, y, #4
          C_STR   y3, y, #4
          EOR     t0, t0, N, LSR#3   ; increment third bit
          TST     t0, N, LSR#3       ; from the top
          BNE     first_stage_arm9m
          EOR     t0, t0, N, LSR#4   ; increment fourth bit
          TST     t0, N, LSR#4       ; from the top
          BNE     first_stage_arm9m
          MOV     t1, N, LSR#5       ; increment fifth
bit_reversed_count_arm9m             ; bits downward
          EOR     t0, t0, t1
          TST     t0, t1
          BNE     first_stage_arm9m
          MOVS    t1, t1, LSR#1
          BNE     bit_reversed_count_arm9m
```

```
        ; finished the first stage
        SUB     x, y, N, LSL#2      ; x = working buffer
        MOV     R, #16
        MOVS    S, N, LSR#4
        LDMEQFD sp!, {r4-r11, pc}
        ADR     c, fft_table_arm9m
next_stage_arm9m
        ; S = the number of blocks
        ; R = the number of samples in each block
        STMFD   sp!, {x, S}
        ADD     t0, R, R, LSL#1
        ADD     x, x, t0
        SUB     S, S, #1<<16
next_block_arm9m
        ADD     S, S, R, LSL#(16-2)
next_butterfly_arm9m
        ; S=((number butterflies left-1)<<16)
        ;    + (number of blocks left)
        C_LDR   x0, x, -R
        C_LDR   x3, c, #4
        C_MUL9m x3, x0, x3
        C_LDR   x0, x, -R
        C_LDR   x2, c, #4
        C_MUL9m x2, x0, x2
        C_LDR   x0, x, -R
        C_LDR   x1, c, #4
        C_MUL9m x1, x0, x1
        C_LDR   x0, x, #0
        C_FFT4  14                  ; coefficients are Q14
        C_STR   x0, x, R
        C_STR   x1, x, R
        C_STR   x2, x, R
        C_STR   y3, x, #4
        SUBS    S, S, #1<<16
        BGE     next_butterfly_arm9m
        ADD     t0, R, R, LSL#1
        ADD     x, x, t0
        SUB     S, S, #1
        MOVS    t1, S, LSL#16
        SUBNE   c, c, t0
        BNE     next_block_arm9m
        LDMFD   sp!, {x, S}
        MOV     R, R, LSL#2         ; quadruple block size
```

```
        MOVS    S, S, LSR#2      ; quarter number of blocks
        BNE     next_stage_arm9m
        LDMFD   sp!, {r4-r11, pc}

fft_table_arm9m
        ; FFT twiddle table of triplets E(3t), E(t), E(2t)
        ; Where E(t)=(cos(t)-sin(t))+i*sin(t) at Q14
        ; N=16 t=2*PI*k/N for k=0,1,2,..,N/4-1
        DCW 0x4000,0x0000, 0x4000,0x0000, 0x4000,0x0000
        DCW 0xdd5d,0x3b21, 0x22a3,0x187e, 0x0000,0x2d41
        DCW 0xa57e,0x2d41, 0x0000,0x2d41, 0xc000,0x4000
        DCW 0xdd5d,0xe782, 0xdd5d,0x3b21, 0xa57e,0x2d41
        ; N=64 t=2*PI*k/N for k=0,1,2,..,N/4-1
        DCW 0x4000,0x0000, 0x4000,0x0000, 0x4000,0x0000
        DCW 0x2aaa,0x1294, 0x396b,0x0646, 0x3249,0x0c7c
        DCW 0x11a8,0x238e, 0x3249,0x0c7c, 0x22a3,0x187e
        DCW 0xf721,0x3179, 0x2aaa,0x1294, 0x11a8,0x238e
        DCW 0xdd5d,0x3b21, 0x22a3,0x187e, 0x0000,0x2d41
        DCW 0xc695,0x3fb1, 0x1a46,0x1e2b, 0xee58,0x3537
        DCW 0xb4be,0x3ec5, 0x11a8,0x238e, 0xdd5d,0x3b21
        DCW 0xa963,0x3871, 0x08df,0x289a, 0xcdb7,0x3ec5
        DCW 0xa57e,0x2d41, 0x0000,0x2d41, 0xc000,0x4000
        DCW 0xa963,0x1e2b, 0xf721,0x3179, 0xb4be,0x3ec5
        DCW 0xb4be,0x0c7c, 0xee58,0x3537, 0xac61,0x3b21
        DCW 0xc695,0xf9ba, 0xe5ba,0x3871, 0xa73b,0x3537
        DCW 0xdd5d,0xe782, 0xdd5d,0x3b21, 0xa57e,0x2d41
        DCW 0xf721,0xd766, 0xd556,0x3d3f, 0xa73b,0x238e
        DCW 0x11a8,0xcac9, 0xcdb7,0x3ec5, 0xac61,0x187e
        DCW 0x2aaa,0xc2c1, 0xc695,0x3fb1, 0xb4be,0x0c7c
        ; N=256 t=2*PI*k/N for k=0,1,2,..,N/4-1
        ;... continue as necessary ...
```

The code is in two parts. The first stage does not require any complex multiplies. We read the data in a bit reversed order from the source array *x*, and then we apply the radix-4 butterfly and write to the destination array *y*. We perform the remaining stages in place in the destination buffer.

It is possible to implement the FFT without bit reversal, by alternating between the source and destination buffers at each stage. However, this requires more registers in the general stage loop, and there are none available. The bit-reversed increment is very cheap, costing less than 1.5 cycles per input sample in total.

See Section 8.6 for the benchmark results for the preceding code.

EXAMPLE
8.18   This example implements a radix-4 FFT on an ARMv5TE architecture processor such as the ARM9E. For the ARM9E we do not need to avail ourselves of the trick used in

Example 8.17 to reduce a complex multiply to three real multiplies. With the single-cycle 16-bit × 16-bit multiplier it is faster to implement the complex multiply in the normal way. This also means that we can use a Q15 coefficient table of (c, s) values, and so the transform is slightly more accurate than in Example 8.17. We have omitted the register allocation because it is the same as for Example 8.17.

```
        ; Complex conjugate multiply a=(xr+i*xi)*(cr-i*ci)
        ;  x = xr + i*xi (two 16-bits packed in 32-bit)
        ;  w = cr + i*ci (two 16-bits packed in 32-bit)
        MACRO
        C_MUL9e $a, $x, $w
        SMULBT  t0, $x, $w               ; xr*ci
        SMULBB  $a._r, $x, $w            ; xr*cr
        SMULTB  $a._i, $x, $w            ; xi*cr
        SMLATT  $a._r, $x, $w, $a._r     ; xr*cr+xi*ci
        SUB     $a._i, $a._i, t0         ; xi*cr-xr*ci
        MEND


        ; void fft_16_arm9e(short *y, short *x, unsigned int N)
fft_16_arm9e
        STMFD   sp!, {r4-r11, lr}
        MOV     t0, #0               ; bit-reversed counter
        MVN     R, #0x80000000       ; R=0x7FFFFFFF
first_stage_arm9e
        ; first stage load and bit reverse
        ADDS    t1,  x, t0, LSL#2 ; t1=&x[t0] and clear carry
        C_LDR   x0, t1, N
        C_LDR   x2, t1, N
        C_LDR   x1, t1, N
        C_LDR   x3, t1, N
        C_FFT4  0
        C_STR   x0, y, #4
        C_STR   x1, y, #4
        C_STR   x2, y, #4
        C_STR   y3, y, #4
        ; bit reversed increment modulo (N/4)
        RSC     t0, t0, N, LSR #2 ; t0 = (N/4)-t0-1
        CLZ     t1, t0               ; find leading 1
        EORS    t0, t0, R, ASR t1 ; toggle bits below leading 1
        BNE     first_stage_arm9e ; loop if count nonzero
        ; finished the first stage
        SUB     x, y, N, LSL #2   ; x = working buffer
        MOV     R, #16
```

```
                MOVS    S, N, LSR#4
                LDMEQFD sp!, {r4-r11, pc}
                ADR     c, fft_table_arm9e
next_stage_arm9e
                ; S = the number of blocks
                ; R = the number of samples in each block
                STMFD   sp!, {x, S}
                ADD     t0, R, R, LSL#1
                ADD     x, x, t0
                SUB     S, S, #1 << 16
next_block_arm9e
                ADD     S, S, R, LSL#(16-2)
next_butterfly_arm9e
                ; S=((number butterflies left-1) << 16)
                ;   + (number of blocks left)
                LDR     x2_r, [x], -R   ; packed data
                LDR     x2_i, [c], #4   ; packed coefficients
                LDR     x1_r, [x], -R
                LDR     x1_i, [c], #4
                LDR     x0_r, [x], -R
                LDR     x0_i, [c], #4
                C_MUL9e x3, x2_r, x2_i
                C_MUL9e x2, x1_r, x1_i
                C_MUL9e x1, x0_r, x0_i
                C_LDR   x0, x, #0
                C_FFT4  15                  ; coefficients are Q15
                C_STR   x0, x, R
                C_STR   x1, x, R
                C_STR   x2, x, R
                C_STR   y3, x, #4
                SUBS    S, S, #1 << 16
                BGE     next_butterfly_arm9e
                ADD     t0, R, R, LSL#1
                ADD     x, x, t0
                SUB     S, S, #1
                MOVS    t1, S, LSL#16
                SUBNE   c, c, t0
                BNE     next_block_arm9e
                LDMFD   sp!, {x, S}
                MOV     R, R, LSL#2      ; quadruple block size
                MOVS    S, S, LSR#2      ; quarter number of blocks
                BNE     next_stage_arm9e
                LDMFD   sp!, {r4-r11, pc}
```

```
fft_table_arm9e
        ; FFT twiddle table of triplets E(3t), E(t), E(2t)
        ; Where E(t)=cos(t)+i*sin(t) at Q15
        ; N=16 t=2*PI*k/N for k=0,1,2,..,N/4-1
        DCW 0x7fff,0x0000, 0x7fff,0x0000, 0x7fff,0x0000
        DCW 0x30fc,0x7642, 0x7642,0x30fc, 0x5a82,0x5a82
        DCW 0xa57e,0x5a82, 0x5a82,0x5a82, 0x0000,0x7fff
        DCW 0x89be,0xcf04, 0x30fc,0x7642, 0xa57e,0x5a82
        ; N=64 t=2*PI*k/N for k=0,1,2,..,N/4-1
        DCW 0x7fff,0x0000, 0x7fff,0x0000, 0x7fff,0x0000
        DCW 0x7a7d,0x2528, 0x7f62,0x0c8c, 0x7d8a,0x18f9
        DCW 0x6a6e,0x471d, 0x7d8a,0x18f9, 0x7642,0x30fc
        DCW 0x5134,0x62f2, 0x7a7d,0x2528, 0x6a6e,0x471d
        DCW 0x30fc,0x7642, 0x7642,0x30fc, 0x5a82,0x5a82
        DCW 0x0c8c,0x7f62, 0x70e3,0x3c57, 0x471d,0x6a6e
        DCW 0xe707,0x7d8a, 0x6a6e,0x471d, 0x30fc,0x7642
        DCW 0xc3a9,0x70e3, 0x62f2,0x5134, 0x18f9,0x7d8a
        DCW 0xa57e,0x5a82, 0x5a82,0x5a82, 0x0000,0x7fff
        DCW 0x8f1d,0x3c57, 0x5134,0x62f2, 0xe707,0x7d8a
        DCW 0x8276,0x18f9, 0x471d,0x6a6e, 0xcf04,0x7642
        DCW 0x809e,0xf374, 0x3c57,0x70e3, 0xb8e3,0x6a6e
        DCW 0x89be,0xcf04, 0x30fc,0x7642, 0xa57e,0x5a82
        DCW 0x9d0e,0xaecc, 0x2528,0x7a7d, 0x9592,0x471d
        DCW 0xb8e3,0x9592, 0x18f9,0x7d8a, 0x89be,0x30fc
        DCW 0xdad8,0x8583, 0x0c8c,0x7f62, 0x8276,0x18f9
        ; N=256 t=2*PI*k/N for k=0,1,2,..,N/4-1
        ; .... continue as required ....
```

Once again, the routine actually calculates $DFT_N(x)/N$, so that there is no possibility of overflow. Section 8.6 gives benchmark results for the preceding code.

Note that we use the CLZ instruction in ARMv5E to accelerate the bit-reversed count required for the bit reversal.

SUMMARY   **DFT Implementations**

- Use a radix-4, decimation-in-time-based FFT implementation. If the number of points is not a power of four, then use radix-2 or radix-8 first stage.

- Perform bit reversal at the start of the algorithm, as you read data for the first stage. Although you can perform an FFT without bit reversal, this often requires more registers in the inner loop than are available.

- If a scalar multiply requires more than one cycle, then reduce a complex multiply to three scalar multiplies using the trick of Example 8.17. This is the case for a 16-bit FFT on ARM9TDMI or a 32-bit FFT on ARM9E.

■ To prevent overflow, scale down by *k* in each radix-*k* stage. Alternatively ensure that the inputs to an *N*-point DFT have room to grow by *N* times. This is often the case when implementing a 32-bit FFT.

8.6 SUMMARY

Tables 8.9 and 8.10 summarize the performance obtained using the code examples of this chapter. It's always possible to tune these routines further by unrolling, or coding for a specific application. However, these figures should give you a good idea of the sustained DSP performance obtainable in practice on an ARM system. The benchmarks include all load, store, and loop overheads assuming zero-wait-state memory or cache hits in the case of a cached core.

In this chapter we have looked at efficient ways of implementing fixed-point DSP algorithms on the ARM. We've looked in detail at four common algorithms: dot-product, block FIR filter, block IIR filter, and Discrete Fourier Transform. We've also considered the differences between different ARM architectures and implementations.

Table 8.9   ARM filtering benchmarks.

Processor core	16-bit dot-product (cycles/tap)	16-bit block FIR filter (cycles/tap)	32-bit block FIR filter (cycles/tap)	16-bit block IIR filter (cycles/biquad)
ARM7TDMI	7.6	5.2	9.0	22.0
ARM9TDMI	7.0	4.8	8.3	22.0
StrongARM	4.8	3.8	5.2	16.5
ARM9E	2.5	1.3	4.3	8.0
XScale	1.8	1.3	3.7	7.7

Table 8.10   ARM FFT benchmarks.

16-bit complex FFT (radix-4)	ARM9TDMI (cycles/FFT)	ARM9E (cycles/FFT)
64 point	3,524	2,480
256 point	19,514	13,194
1,024 point	99,946	66,196
4,096 point	487,632	318,878

CHAPTER 9

EXCEPTION AND INTERRUPT HANDLING

At the heart of an embedded system lie the exception handlers. They are responsible for handling errors, interrupts, and other events generated by the external system. Efficient handlers can dramatically improve system performance. The process of determining a good handling method can be complicated, challenging, and fun.

In this chapter we will cover the theory and practice of handling exceptions, and specifically the handling of interrupts on the ARM processor. The ARM processor has seven exceptions that can halt the normal sequential execution of instructions: Data Abort, Fast Interrupt Request, Interrupt Request, Prefetch Abort, Software Interrupt, Reset, and Undefined Instruction.

This chapter is divided into three main sections:

- *Exception handling.* Exception handling covers the specific details of how the ARM processor handles exceptions.

- *Interrupts.* ARM defines an interrupt as a special type of exception. This section discusses the use of interrupt requests, as well as introducing some of the common terms, features, and mechanisms surrounding interrupt handling.

- *Interrupt handling schemes.* The final section provides a set of interrupt handling methods. Included with each method is an example implementation.

9.1 EXCEPTION HANDLING

An exception is any condition that needs to halt the normal sequential execution of instructions. Examples are when the ARM core is reset, when an instruction fetch or memory access fails, when an undefined instruction is encountered, when a software interrupt instruction is executed, or when an external interrupt has been raised. Exception handling is the method of processing these exceptions.

Most exceptions have an associated software *exception handler*—a software routine that executes when an exception occurs. For instance, a Data Abort exception will have a Data Abort handler. The handler first determines the cause of the exception and then services the exception. Servicing takes place either within the handler or by branching to a specific service routine. The Reset exception is a special case since it is used to initialize an embedded system.

This section covers the following exception handling topics:

- ARM processor mode and exceptions
- Vector table
- Exception priorities
- Link register offsets

9.1.1 ARM PROCESSOR EXCEPTIONS AND MODES

Table 9.1 lists the ARM processor exceptions. Each exception causes the core to enter a specific mode. In addition, any of the ARM processor modes can be entered manually by changing the *cpsr*. *User* and *system* mode are the only two modes that are not entered by a corresponding exception, in other words, to enter these modes you must modify the *cpsr*.

When an exception causes a mode change, the core automatically

- saves the *cpsr* to the *spsr* of the exception mode
- saves the *pc* to the *lr* of the exception mode

Table 9.1   ARM processor exceptions and associated modes.

Exception	Mode	Main purpose
Fast Interrupt Request	*FIQ*	fast interrupt request handling
Interrupt Request	*IRQ*	interrupt request handling
SWI and Reset	*SVC*	protected mode for operating systems
Prefetch Abort and Data Abort	*abort*	virtual memory and/or memory protection handling
Undefined Instruction	*undefined*	software emulation of hardware coprocessors

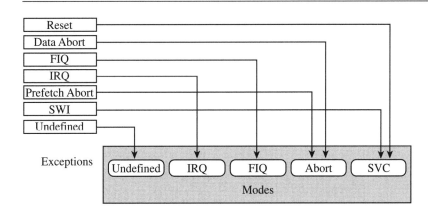

Figure 9.1   Exceptions and associated modes.

- sets the *cpsr* to the exception mode
- sets *pc* to the address of the exception handler

Figure 9.1 shows a simplified view of exceptions and associated modes. Note that when an exception occurs the ARM processor always switches to ARM state.

9.1.2 VECTOR TABLE

Chapter 2 introduced the *vector table*—a table of addresses that the ARM core branches to when an exception is raised. These addresses commonly contain branch instructions of one of the following forms:

- B <address>—This *branch instruction* provides a branch relative from the *pc*.
- LDR pc, [pc, #offset]—This *load register instruction* loads the handler address from memory to the *pc*. The address is an absolute 32-bit value stored close to the vector table. Loading this absolute literal value results in a slight delay in branching to a specific handler due to the extra memory access. However, you can branch to any address in memory.
- LDR pc, [pc, #-0xff0]—This *load register instruction* loads a specific interrupt service routine address from address 0xffff030 to the *pc*. This specific instruction is only used when a vector interrupt controller is present (VIC PL190).

Table 9.2   Vector table and processor modes.

Exception	Mode	Vector table offset
Reset	SVC	+0x00
Undefined Instruction	UND	+0x04
Software Interrupt (SWI)	SVC	+0x08
Prefetch Abort	ABT	+0x0c
Data Abort	ABT	+0x10
Not assigned	—	+0x14
IRQ	IRQ	+0x18
FIQ	FIQ	+0x1c

- MOV pc, #immediate—This *move instruction* copies an immediate value into the *pc*. It lets you span the full address space but at limited alignment. The address must be an 8-bit immediate rotated right by an even number of bits.

You can also have other types of instructions in the vector table. For example, the FIQ handler might start at address offset +0x1c. Thus, the FIQ handler can start immediately at the FIQ vector location, since it is at the end of the vector table. The branch instructions cause the *pc* to jump to a specific location that can handle the specific exception.

Table 9.2 shows the exception, mode, and vector table offset for each exception.

EXAMPLE   Figure 9.2 shows a typical vector table. The Undefined Instruction entry is a branch instruc-
9.1   tion to jump to the undefined handler. The other vectors use an indirect address jump with the LDR load to *pc* instruction.

Notice that the FIQ handler also uses the LDR load to *pc* instruction and does not take advantage of the fact that the handler can be placed at the FIQ vector entry location.

```
0x00000000: 0xe59ffa38  RESET: > ldr  pc, [pc, #reset]
0x00000004: 0xea000502  UNDEF:   b    undInstr
0x00000008: 0xe59ffa38  SWI  :   ldr  pc, [pc, #swi]
0x0000000c: 0xe59ffa38  PABT :   ldr  pc, [pc, #prefetch]
0x00000010: 0xe59ffa38  DABT :   ldr  pc, [pc, #data]
0x00000014: 0xe59ffa38   -   :   ldr  pc, [pc, #notassigned]
0x00000018: 0xe59ffa38  IRQ  :   ldr  pc, [pc, #irq]
0x0000001c: 0xe59ffa38  FIQ  :   ldr  pc, [pc, #fiq]
```

Figure 9.2   Example vector table.

9.1.3 EXCEPTION PRIORITIES

Exceptions can occur simultaneously, so the processor has to adopt a priority mechanism. Table 9.3 shows the various exceptions that occur on the ARM processor and their associated priority level. For instance, the Reset exception is the highest priority and occurs when power is applied to the processor. Thus, when a reset occurs, it takes precedence over all other exceptions. Similarly, when a Data Abort occurs, it takes precedence over all other exceptions apart from a Reset exception. The lowest priority level is shared by two exceptions, the Software Interrupt and Undefined Instruction exceptions. Certain exceptions also disable interrupts by setting the *I* or *F* bits in the *cpsr*, as shown in Table 9.3.

Each exception is dealt with according to the priority level set out in Table 9.3. The following is a summary of the exceptions and how they should be handled, starting with the highest.

The Reset exception is the highest priority exception and is always taken whenever it is signaled. The reset handler initializes the system, including setting up memory and caches. External interrupt sources should be initialized before enabling IRQ or FIQ interrupts to avoid the possibility of spurious interrupts occurring before the appropriate handler has been set up. The reset handler must also set up the stack pointers for all processor modes.

During the first few instructions of the handler, it is assumed that no exceptions or interrupts will occur. The code should be designed to avoid SWIs, undefined instructions, and memory accesses that may abort, that is, the handler is carefully implemented to avoid further triggering of an exception.

Data Abort exceptions occur when the memory controller or MMU indicates that an invalid memory address has been accessed (for example, if there is no physical memory for an address) or when the current code attempts to read or write to memory without the correct access permissions. An FIQ exception can be raised within a Data Abort handler since FIQ exceptions are not disabled. When the FIQ is completely serviced, control is returned back to the Data Abort handler.

A Fast Interrupt Request (FIQ) exception occurs when an external peripheral sets the FIQ pin to *nFIQ*. An FIQ exception is the highest priority interrupt. The core disables

Table 9.3 Exception priority levels.

Exceptions	Priority	*I* bit	*F* bit
Reset	1	1	1
Data Abort	2	1	—
Fast Interrupt Request	3	1	1
Interrupt Request	4	1	—
Prefetch Abort	5	1	—
Software Interrupt	6	1	—
Undefined Instruction	6	1	—

both IRQ and FIQ exceptions on entry into the FIQ handler. Thus, no external source can interrupt the processor unless the IRQ and/or FIQ exceptions are reenabled by software. It is desirable that the FIQ handler (and also the abort, SWI, and IRQ handlers) is carefully designed to service the exception efficiently.

An Interrupt Request (IRQ) exception occurs when an external peripheral sets the IRQ pin to *nIRQ*. An IRQ exception is the second-highest priority interrupt. The IRQ handler will be entered if neither an FIQ exception nor Data Abort exception occurs. On entry to the IRQ handler, the IRQ exceptions are disabled and should remain disabled until the current interrupt source has been cleared.

A Prefetch Abort exception occurs when an attempt to fetch an instruction results in a memory fault. This exception is raised when the instruction is in the execute stage of the pipeline and if none of the higher exceptions have been raised. On entry to the handler, IRQ exceptions will be disabled, but the FIQ exceptions will remain unchanged. If FIQ is enabled and an FIQ exception occurs, it can be taken while servicing the Prefetch Abort.

A Software Interrupt (SWI) exception occurs when the SWI instruction is executed and none of the other higher-priority exceptions have been flagged. On entry to the handler, the *cpsr* will be set to *supervisor* mode.

If the system uses nested SWI calls, the link register *r14* and *spsr* must be stored away before branching to the nested SWI to avoid possible corruption of the link register and the *spsr*.

An Undefined Instruction exception occurs when an instruction not in the ARM or Thumb instruction set reaches the execute stage of the pipeline and none of the other exceptions have been flagged. The ARM processor "asks" the coprocessors if they can handle this as a coprocessor instruction. Since coprocessors follow the pipeline, instruction identification can take place in the execute stage of the core. If none of the coprocessors claims the instruction, an Undefined Instruction exception is raised.

Both the SWI instruction and Undefined Instruction have the same level of priority, since they cannot occur at the same time (in other words, the instruction being executed cannot both be an SWI instruction and an undefined instruction).

9.1.4   LINK REGISTER OFFSETS

When an exception occurs, the link register is set to a specific address based on the current *pc*. For instance, when an IRQ exception is raised, the link register *lr* points to the last executed instruction plus 8. Care has to be taken to make sure the exception handler does not corrupt *lr* because *lr* is used to return from an exception handler. The IRQ exception is taken only after the current instruction is executed, so the return address has to point to the next instruction, or *lr* − 4. Table 9.4 provides a list of useful addresses for the different exceptions.

The next three examples show different methods of returning from an IRQ or FIQ exception handler.

Table 9.4 Useful link-register-based addresses.

Exception	Address	Use
Reset	—	*lr* is not defined on a Reset
Data Abort	*lr* − 8	points to the instruction that caused the Data Abort exception
FIQ	*lr* − 4	return address from the FIQ handler
IRQ	*lr* − 4	return address from the IRQ handler
Prefetch Abort	*lr* − 4	points to the instruction that caused the Prefetch Abort exception
SWI	*lr*	points to the next instruction after the SWI instruction
Undefined Instruction	*lr*	points to the next instruction after the undefined instruction

EXAMPLE
9.2

This example shows that a typical method of returning from an IRQ and FIQ handler is to use a SUBS instruction:

```
handler
        <handler code>
        ...
        SUBS    pc, r14, #4              ; pc=r14-4
```

Because there is an S at the end of the SUB instruction and the *pc* is the destination register, the *cpsr* is automatically restored from the *spsr* register.

EXAMPLE
9.3

This example shows another method that subtracts the offset from the link register *r14* at the beginning of the handler.

```
handler
        SUB     r14, r14, #4            ; r14-=4
        ...
        <handler code>
        ...
        MOVS    pc, r14                 ; return
```

After servicing is complete, return to normal execution occurs by moving the link register *r14* into the *pc* and restoring *cpsr* from the *spsr*.

EXAMPLE
9.4

The final example uses the interrupt stack to store the link register. This method first subtracts an offset from the link register and then stores it onto the interrupt stack.

```
handler
        SUB     r14, r14, #4            ; r14-=4
```

```
STMFD    r13!,{r0-r3, r14}              ; store context
...
<handler code>
...
LDMFD    r13!,{r0-r3, pc}^              ; return
```

To return to normal execution, the LDM instruction is used to load the *pc*. The ^ symbol in the instruction forces the *cpsr* to be restored from the *spsr*.

9.2   INTERRUPTS

There are two types of interrupts available on the ARM processor. The first type of interrupt causes an exception raised by an external peripheral—namely, IRQ and FIQ. The second type is a specific instruction that causes an exception—the SWI instruction. Both types suspend the normal flow of a program.

In this section we will focus mainly on IRQ and FIQ interrupts. We will cover these topics:

- Assigning interrupts
- Interrupt latency
- IRQ and FIQ exceptions
- Basic interrupt stack design and implementation

9.2.1   ASSIGNING INTERRUPTS

A system designer can decide which hardware peripheral can produce which interrupt request. This decision can be implemented in hardware or software (or both) and depends upon the embedded system being used.

An *interrupt controller* connects multiple external interrupts to one of the two ARM interrupt requests. Sophisticated controllers can be programmed to allow an external interrupt source to cause either an IRQ or FIQ exception.

When it comes to assigning interrupts, system designers have adopted a standard design practice:

- Software Interrupts are normally reserved to call privileged operating system routines. For example, an SWI instruction can be used to change a program running in *user* mode to a privileged mode. For an SWI handler example, take a look at Chapter 11.
- Interrupt Requests are normally assigned for general-purpose interrupts. For example, a periodic timer interrupt to force a context switch tends to be an IRQ exception. The IRQ exception has a lower priority and higher interrupt latency (to be discussed in the next section) than the FIQ exception.

■ Fast Interrupt Requests are normally reserved for a single interrupt source that requires a fast response time—for example, direct memory access specifically used to move blocks of memory. Thus, in an embedded operating system design, the FIQ exception is used for a specific application, leaving the IRQ exception for more general operating system activities.

9.2.2 INTERRUPT LATENCY

Interrupt-driven embedded systems have to fight a battle with *interrupt latency*—the interval of time from an external interrupt request signal being raised to the first fetch of an instruction of a specific interrupt service routine (ISR).

Interrupt latency depends on a combination of hardware and software. System architects must balance the system design to handle multiple simultaneous interrupt sources and minimize interrupt latency. If the interrupts are not handled in a timely manner, then the system will exhibit slow response times.

Software handlers have two main methods to minimize interrupt latency. The first method is to use a *nested interrupt handler*, which allows further interrupts to occur even when currently servicing an existing interrupt (see Figure 9.3). This is achieved by reenabling the interrupts as soon as the interrupt source has been serviced (so it won't generate more interrupts) but before the interrupt handling is complete. Once a nested interrupt has been serviced, then control is relinquished to the original interrupt service routine.

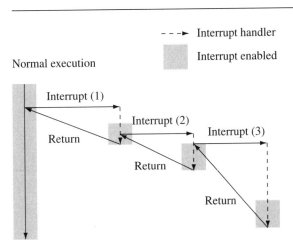

Figure 9.3   A three-level nested interrupt.

The second method involves *prioritization*. You program the interrupt controller to ignore interrupts of the same or lower priority than the interrupt you are handling, so only a higher-priority task can interrupt your handler. You then reenable interrupts.

The processor spends time in the lower-priority interrupts until a higher-priority interrupt occurs. Therefore higher-priority interrupts have a lower average interrupt latency than the lower-priority interrupts, which reduces latency by speeding up the completion time on the critical time-sensitive interrupts.

9.2.3 IRQ AND FIQ EXCEPTIONS

IRQ and FIQ exceptions only occur when a specific interrupt mask is cleared in the *cpsr*. The ARM processor will continue executing the current instruction in the execution stage of the pipeline before handling the interrupt—an important factor in designing a deterministic interrupt handler since some instructions require more cycles to complete the execution stage.

An IRQ or FIQ exception causes the processor hardware to go through a standard procedure (provided the interrupts are not masked):

1. The processor changes to a specific interrupt request mode, which reflects the interrupt being raised.

2. The previous mode's *cpsr* is saved into the *spsr* of the new interrupt request mode.

3. The *pc* is saved in the *lr* of the new interrupt request mode.

4. *Interrupt/s are disabled*—either the IRQ or both IRQ and FIQ exceptions are disabled in the *cpsr*. This immediately stops another interrupt request of the same type being raised.

5. The processor branches to a specific entry in the vector table.

The procedure varies slightly depending upon the type of interrupt being raised. We will illustrate both interrupts with an example. The first example shows what happens when an IRQ exception is raised, and the second example shows what happens when an FIQ exception is raised.

EXAMPLE 9.5   Figure 9.4 shows what happens when an IRQ exception is raised when the processor is in *user* mode. The processor starts in state 1. In this example both the IRQ and FIQ exception bits in the *cpsr* are enabled.

When an IRQ occurs the processor moves into state 2. This transition automatically sets the IRQ bit to one, disabling any further IRQ exceptions. The FIQ exception, however, remains enabled because FIQ has a higher priority and therefore does not get disabled when a low-priority IRQ exception is raised. The *cpsr* processor mode changes to *IRQ* mode. The *user* mode *cpsr* is automatically copied into *spsr_irq*.

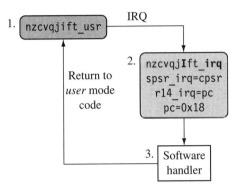

Figure 9.4   Interrupt Request (IRQ).

Register *r14_irq* is assigned the value of the *pc* when the interrupt was raised. The *pc* is then set to the IRQ entry +0x18 in the vector table.

In state 3 the software handler takes over and calls the appropriate interrupt service routine to service the source of the interrupt. Upon completion, the processor mode reverts back to the original *user* mode code in state 1.

EXAMPLE 9.6   Figure 9.5 shows an example of an FIQ exception. The processor goes through a similar procedure as with the IRQ exception, but instead of just masking further IRQ exceptions from occurring, the processor also masks out further FIQ exceptions. This means that both interrupts are disabled when entering the software handler in state 3.

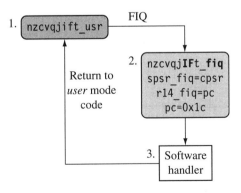

Figure 9.5   Fast Interrupt Request (FIQ).

Changing to *FIQ* mode means there is no requirement to save registers *r8* to *r12* since these registers are banked in *FIQ* mode. These registers can be used to hold temporary data, such as buffer pointers or counters. This makes *FIQ* ideal for servicing a single-source, high-priority, low-latency interrupt.

9.2.3.1   Enabling and Disabling FIQ and IRQ Exceptions

The ARM processor core has a simple procedure to manually enable and disable interrupts that involves modifying the *cpsr* when the processor is in a privileged mode.

Table 9.5 shows how IRQ and FIQ interrupts are enabled. The procedure uses three ARM instructions.

The first instruction MRS copies the contents of the *cpsr* into register *r1*. The second instruction clears the IRQ or FIQ mask bit. The third instruction then copies the updated contents in register *r1* back into the *cpsr*, enabling the interrupt request. The postfix _c identifies that the bit field being updated is the control field bit [7:0] of the *cpsr*. (For more details see Chapter 2.) Table 9.6 shows a similar procedure to disable or mask an interrupt request.

It is important to understand that the interrupt request is either enabled or disabled only once the MSR instruction has completed the execution stage of the pipeline. Interrupts can still be raised or masked prior to the MSR completing this stage.

Table 9.5   Enabling an interrupt.

cpsr value	IRQ	FIQ
Pre	*nzcvqj**I**F**t_SVC*	*nzcvqj**IF**t_SVC*
Code	enable_irq	enable_fiq
	MRS r1, cpsr	MRS r1, cpsr
	BIC r1, r1, #0x80	BIC r1, r1, #0x40
	MSR cpsr_c, r1	MSR cpsr_c, r1
Post	*nzcvqji**F**t_SVC*	*nzcvqj**I**ft_SVC*

Table 9.6   Disabling an interrupt.

cpsr	IRQ	**FIQ**
Pre	*nzcvqjift_SVC*	*nzcvqjift_SVC*
Code	disable_irq	disable_fiq
	MRS r1, cpsr	MRS r1, cpsr
	ORR r1, r1, #0x80	ORR r1, r1, #0x40
	MSR cpsr_c, r1	MSR cpsr_c, r1
Post	*nzcvqj**I**ft_SVC*	*nzcvqji**F**t_SVC*

To enable and disable both the IRQ and FIQ exceptions requires a slight modification to the second instruction. The immediate value on the data processing BIC or ORR instruction has to be changed to 0xc0 to enable or disable both interrupts.

9.2.4 BASIC INTERRUPT STACK DESIGN AND IMPLEMENTATION

Exceptions handlers make extensive use of stacks, with each mode having a dedicated register containing the stack pointer. The design of the exception stacks depends upon these factors:

- *Operating system requirements*—Each operating system has its own requirements for stack design.

- *Target hardware*—The target hardware provides a physical limit to the size and positioning of the stack in memory.

Two design decisions need to be made for the stacks:

- The *location* determines where in the memory map the stack begins. Most ARM-based systems are designed with a stack that descends downwards, with the top of the stack at a high memory address.

- *Stack size* depends upon the type of handler, nested or nonnested. A nested interrupt handler requires more memory space since the stack will grow with the number of nested interrupts.

A good stack design tries to avoid *stack overflow*—where the stack extends beyond the allocated memory—because it causes instability in embedded systems. There are software techniques that identify overflow and that allow corrective measures to take place to repair the stack before irreparable memory corruption occurs. The two main methods are (1) to use memory protection and (2) to call a stack check function at the start of each routine.

The *IRQ* mode stack has to be set up before interrupts are enabled—normally in the initialization code for the system. It is important that the maximum size of the stack is known in a simple embedded system, since the stack size is reserved in the initial stages of boot-up by the firmware.

Figure 9.6 shows two typical memory layouts in a linear address space. The first layout, *A*, shows a traditional stack layout with the interrupt stack stored underneath the code segment. The second layout, *B*, shows the interrupt stack at the top of the memory above the user stack. The main advantage of layout *B* over *A* is that *B* does not corrupt the vector table when a stack overflow occurs, and so the system has a chance to correct itself when an overflow has been identified.

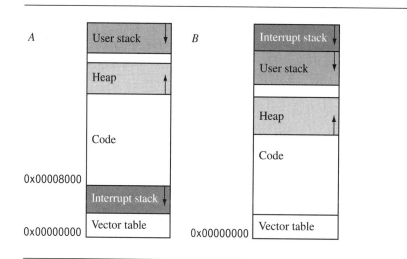

Figure 9.6   Typical memory layouts.

EXAMPLE
9.7   For each processor mode a stack has to be set up. This is carried out every time the processor is reset. Figure 9.7 shows an implementation using layout *A*. To help set up the memory layout, a set of defines are declared that map the memory region names with an absolute address.

For instance, the User stack is given the label USR_Stack and is set to address 0x20000. The Supervisor stack is set to an address that is 128 bytes below the IRQ stack.

```
USR_Stack      EQU 0x20000
IRQ_Stack      EQU 0x8000
SVC_Stack      EQU IRQ_Stack-128
```

To help change to the different processor modes, we declare a set of defines that map each processor mode with a particular mode bit pattern. These labels can then be used to set the *cpsr* to a new mode.

```
Usr32md        EQU 0x10          ; User mode
FIQ32md        EQU 0x11          ; FIQ mode
IRQ32md        EQU 0x12          ; IRQ mode
SVC32md        EQU 0x13          ; Supervisor mode
Abt32md        EQU 0x17          ; Abort mode
Und32md        EQU 0x1b          ; Undefined instruction mode
Sys32md        EQU 0x1f          ; System mode
```

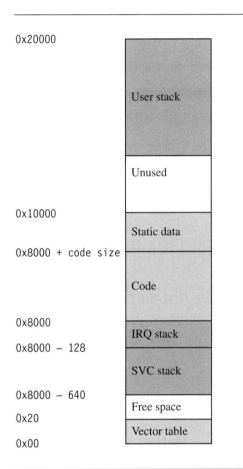

0x20000

User stack

Unused

0x10000

Static data

0x8000 + code size

Code

0x8000

IRQ stack

0x8000 − 128

SVC stack

0x8000 − 640

Free space

0x20

Vector table

0x00

Figure 9.7   Example implementation using layout *A*.

For safety reasons a define is declared to disable both the IRQ and FIQ exceptions in the *cpsr*:

```
NoInt         EQU 0xc0              ; Disable interrupts
```

NoInt masks both interrupts by setting the masks to one.

Initialization code starts by setting up the stack registers for each processor mode. The stack register *r13* is one of the registers that is always banked when a mode change occurs. The code first initializes the IRQ stack. For safety reasons, it is always best to make sure that interrupts are disabled by using a bitwise OR between NoInt and the new mode.

Each mode stack must be set up. Here is an example of how to set up three different stacks when the processor core comes out of *reset*. Note that, since this is a basic example, we do not implement a stack for the *abort*, *FIQ*, and *undefined instruction* modes. If these stacks are required, then very similar code is used.

- *Supervisor mode stack*—The processor core starts in *supervisor* mode so the SVC stack setup involves loading register *r13_svc* with the address pointed to by SVC_NewStack. For this example the value is SVC_Stack.

```
            LDR      r13, SVC_NewStack        ; r13_svc
            ...
SVC_NewStack
            DCD      SVC_Stack
```

- *IRQ mode stack*—To set up the IRQ stack, the processor mode has to change to *IRQ* mode. This is achieved by storing a *cpsr* bit pattern into register *r2*. Register *r2* is then copied into the *cpsr*, placing the processor into *IRQ* mode. This action immediately makes register *r13_irq* viewable, and it can then be assigned the IRQ_Stack value.

```
            MOV      r2, #NoInt|IRQ32md
            MSR      cpsr_c, r2
            LDR      r13, IRQ_NewStack        ; r13_irq
            ...
IRQ_NewStack
            DCD      IRQ_Stack
```

- *User mode stack*—It is common for the *user* mode stack to be the last to be set up because when the processor is in *user* mode there is no direct method to modify the *cpsr*. An alternative is to force the processor into *system* mode to set up the *user* mode stack since both modes share the same registers.

```
            MOV      r2, #Sys32md
            MSR      cpsr_c, r2
            LDR      r13, USR_NewStack        ; r13_usr
            ...
USR_NewStack
            DCD      USR_Stack
```

Using separate stacks for each mode rather than processing using a single stack has one main advantage: errant tasks can be debugged and isolated from the rest of the system.

9.3 INTERRUPT HANDLING SCHEMES

In this final section we will introduce a number of different interrupt handling schemes, ranging from the simple nonnested interrupt handler to the more complex grouped prioritized interrupt handler. Each scheme is presented as a reference with a general description plus an example implementation.

The schemes covered are the following:

- A *nonnested interrupt handler* handles and services individual interrupts sequentially. It is the simplest interrupt handler.

- A *nested interrupt handler* handles multiple interrupts without a priority assignment.

- A *reentrant interrupt handler* handles multiple interrupts that can be prioritized.

- A *prioritized simple interrupt handler* handles prioritized interrupts.

- A *prioritized standard interrupt handler* handles higher-priority interrupts in a shorter time than lower-priority interrupts.

- A *prioritized direct interrupt handler* handles higher-priority interrupts in a shorter time and goes directly to a specific service routine.

- A *prioritized grouped interrupt handler* is a mechanism for handling interrupts that are grouped into different priority levels.

- A *VIC PL190 based interrupt service routine* shows how the vector interrupt controller (VIC) changes the design of an interrupt service routine.

9.3.1 NONNESTED INTERRUPT HANDLER

The simplest interrupt handler is a handler that is nonnested: the interrupts are disabled until control is returned back to the interrupted task or process. Because a nonnested interrupt handler can only service a single interrupt at a time, handlers of this form are not suitable for complex embedded systems that service multiple interrupts with differing priority levels.

Figure 9.8 shows the various stages that occur when an interrupt is raised in a system that has implemented a simple nonnested interrupt handler:

1. *Disable interrupt/s*—When the IRQ exception is raised, the ARM processor will disable further IRQ exceptions from occurring. The processor mode is set to the appropriate interrupt request mode, and the previous *cpsr* is copied into the newly available *spsr_{interrupt request mode}*. The processor will then set the *pc* to point to the correct entry in the vector table and execute the instruction. This instruction will alter the *pc* to point to the specific interrupt handler.

2. *Save context*—On entry the handler code saves a subset of the current processor mode nonbanked registers.

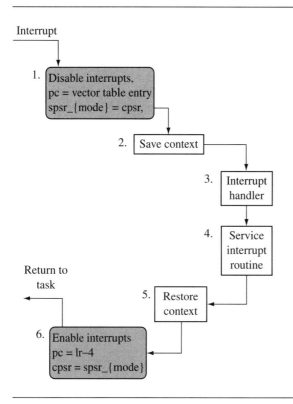

Figure 9.8   Simple nonnested interrupt handler.

3. *Interrupt handler*—The handler then identifies the external interrupt source and executes the appropriate interrupt service routine (ISR).

4. *Interrupt service routine*—The ISR services the external interrupt source and resets the interrupt.

5. *Restore context*—The ISR returns back to the interrupt handler, which restores the context.

6. *Enable interrupts*—Finally, to return from the interrupt handler, the *spsr_{interrupt request mode}* is restored back into the *cpsr*. The *pc* is then set to the next instruction after the interrupt was raised.

EXAMPLE   This IRQ handler example assumes that the IRQ stack has been correctly set up by the
9.8   initialization code.

```
interrupt_handler
        SUB     r14,r14,#4                          ; adjust lr
        STMFD   r13!,{r0-r3,r12,r14}                ; save context
        <interrupt service routine>
        LDMFD   r13!,{r0-r3,r12,pc}^                ; return
```

The first instruction sets the link register *r14_irq* to return back to the correct location in the interrupted task or process. As described in Section 9.1.4, due to the pipeline, on entry to an IRQ handler the link register points four bytes beyond the return address, so the handler must subtract four from the link register to account for this discrepancy. The link register is stored on the stack. To return to the interrupted task, the link register contents are restored from the stack and moved into the *pc*.

Notice registers *r0* to *r3* and register *r12* are also preserved because of the ATPCS. This allows an ATPCS-compliant subroutine to be called within the handler.

The STMFD instruction saves the context by placing a subset of the registers onto the stack. To reduce interrupt latency we save a minimum number of registers because the time taken to execute an STMFD or LDMFD instruction is proportional to the number of registers being transferred. The registers are saved to the stack pointed to by the register *r13_{interrupt request mode}*.

If you are using a high-level language within your system it is important to understand the compiler's procedure calling convention because it will influence both the registers saved and the order they are saved onto the stack. For instance, the ARM compilers preserves registers *r4* to *r11* within a subroutine call so there is no need to preserve them unless they will be used by the interrupt handler. If no C routines are called, it may not be necessary to save all of the registers. It is safe to call a C function only when the registers have been saved onto the interrupt stack.

Within a nonnested interrupt handler, it is not necessary to save the *spsr* because it will not be destroyed by any subsequent interrupt.

At the end of the handler the LDMFD instruction will restore the context and return from the interrupt handler. The ^ at the end of the LDMFD instruction means that the *cpsr* will be restored from the *spsr*, which is only valid if the *pc* is loaded at the same time. If the *pc* is not loaded, then ^ will restore the *user* bank registers.

In this handler all processing is handled within the interrupt handler, which returns directly to the application.

Once the interrupt handler has been entered and the context has been saved, the handler must determine the interrupt source. The following code shows a simple example of how to determine the interrupt source. IRQStatus is the address of the interrupt status register. If the interrupt source is not determined, then control can pass to another handler. In this example we pass control to the debug monitor. Alternatively we could just ignore the interrupt.

```
interrupt_handler
        SUB     r14,r14,#4              ; r14-=4
```

```
STMFD    sp!,{r0-r3,r12,r14}    ; save context
LDR      r0,=IRQStatus          ; interrupt status addr
LDR      r0,[r0]                ; get interrupt status
TST      r0,#0x0080             ; if counter timer
BNE      timer_isr              ;   then branch to ISR
TST      r0,#0x0001             ; else if button press
BNE      button_isr             ;   then call button ISR
LDMFD    sp!,{r0-r3,r12,r14}    ; restore context
LDR      pc,=debug_monitor      ; else debug monitor
```

In the preceding code there are two ISRs: `timer_isr` and `button_isr`. They are mapped to specific bits in the `IRQStatus` register, 0x0080 and 0x0001, respectively.

SUMMARY   **Simple Nonnested Interrupt Handler**

- Handles and services individual interrupts sequentially.

- High interrupt latency; cannot handle further interrupts occurring while an interrupt is being serviced.

- Advantages: relatively easy to implement and debug.

- Disadvantage: cannot be used to handle complex embedded systems with multiple priority interrupts.

9.3.2 NESTED INTERRUPT HANDLER

A nested interrupt handler allows for another interrupt to occur within the currently called handler. This is achieved by reenabling the interrupts before the handler has fully serviced the current interrupt.

For a real-time system this feature increases the complexity of the system but also improves its performance. The additional complexity introduces the possibility of subtle timing issues that can cause a system failure, and these subtle problems can be extremely difficult to resolve. A nested interrupt method is designed carefully so as to avoid these types of problems. This is achieved by protecting the context restoration from interruption, so that the next interrupt will not fill the stack (cause stack overflow) or corrupt any of the registers.

The first goal of any nested interrupt handler is to respond to interrupts quickly so the handler neither waits for asynchronous exceptions, nor forces them to wait for the handler. The second goal is that execution of regular synchronous code is not delayed while servicing the various interrupts.

The increase in complexity means that the designers have to balance efficiency with safety, by using a defensive coding style that assumes problems will occur. The handler has to check the stack and protect against register corruption where possible.

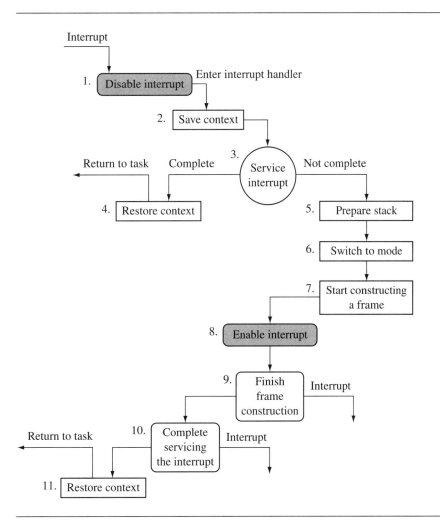

Figure 9.9   Nested interrupt handler.

Figure 9.9 shows a nested interrupt handler. As can been seen from the diagram, the handler is quite a bit more complicated than the simple nonnested interrupt handler described in Section 9.3.1.

The nested interrupt handler entry code is identical to the simple nonnested interrupt handler, except that on exit, the handler tests a flag that is updated by the ISR. The flag indicates whether further processing is required. If further processing is not required, then the interrupt service routine is complete and the handler can exit. If further processing is required, the handler may take several actions: reenabling interrupts and/or performing a context switch.

Reenabling interrupts involves switching out of *IRQ* mode to either *SVC* or *system* mode. Interrupts cannot simply be reenabled when in *IRQ* mode because this would lead to possible link register *r14_irq* corruption, especially if an interrupt occurred after the execution of a BL instruction. This problem will be discussed in more detail in Section 9.3.3.

Performing a context switch involves flattening (emptying) the IRQ stack because the handler does not perform a context switch while there is data on the IRQ stack. All registers saved on the IRQ stack must be transferred to the task's stack, typically on the SVC stack. The remaining registers must then be saved on the task stack. They are transferred to a reserved block of memory on the stack called a *stack frame*.

EXAMPLE
9.9

This nested interrupt handler example is based on the flow diagram in Figure 9.9. The rest of this section will walk through the handler and describe in detail the various stages.

```
Maskmd          EQU 0x1f                   ; processor mode mask
SVC32md         EQU 0x13                   ; SVC mode
I_Bit           EQU 0x80                   ; IRQ bit

FRAME_R0        EQU 0x00
FRAME_R1        EQU FRAME_R0+4
FRAME_R2        EQU FRAME_R1+4
FRAME_R3        EQU FRAME_R2+4
FRAME_R4        EQU FRAME_R3+4
FRAME_R5        EQU FRAME_R4+4
FRAME_R6        EQU FRAME_R5+4
FRAME_R7        EQU FRAME_R6+4
FRAME_R8        EQU FRAME_R7+4
FRAME_R9        EQU FRAME_R8+4
FRAME_R10       EQU FRAME_R9+4
FRAME_R11       EQU FRAME_R10+4
FRAME_R12       EQU FRAME_R11+4
FRAME_PSR       EQU FRAME_R12+4
FRAME_LR        EQU FRAME_PSR+4
FRAME_PC        EQU FRAME_LR+4
FRAME_SIZE      EQU FRAME_PC+4

IRQ_Entry ; instruction                             state : comment
        SUB     r14,r14,#4                  ; 2 :
        STMDB   r13!,{r0-r3,r12,r14}        ; 2 : save context
        <service interrupt>
        BL      read_RescheduleFlag         ; 3 : more processing
```

```
        CMP     r0,#0                           ; 3 : if processing?
        LDMNEIA r13!,{r0-r3,r12,pc}^            ; 4 :   else return
        MRS     r2,spsr                         ; 5 : copy spsr_irq
        MOV     r0,r13                          ; 5 : copy r13_irq
        ADD     r13,r13,#6*4                    ; 5 : reset stack
        MRS     r1,cpsr                         ; 6 : copy cpsr
        BIC     r1,r1,#Maskmd                   ; 6 :
        ORR     r1,r1,#SVC32md                  ; 6 :
        MSR     cpsr_c,r1                       ; 6 : change to SVC
        SUB     r13,r13,#FRAME_SIZE-FRAME_R4    ; 7 : make space
        STMIA   r13,{r4-r11}                    ; 7 : save r4-r11
        LDMIA   r0,{r4-r9}                      ; 7 : restore r4-r9
        BIC     r1,r1,#I_Bit                    ; 8 :
        MSR     cpsr_c,r1                       ; 8 : enable IRA
        STMDB   r13!,{r4-r7}                    ; 9 : save r4-r7 SVC
        STR     r2,[r13,#FRAME_PSR]             ; 9 : save PSR
        STR     r8,[r13,#FRAME_R12]             ; 9 : save r12
        STR     r9,[r13,#FRAMF_PC]              ; 9 : save pc
        STR     r14,[r13,#FRAME_LR]             ; 9 : save lr
        <complete interrupt service routine>
        LDMIA   r13!,{r0-r12,r14}               ; 11 : restore context
        MSR     spsr_cxsf,r14                   ; 11 : restore spsr
        LDMIA   r13!,{r14,pc}^                  ; 11 : return
```

This example uses a stack frame structure. All registers are saved onto the frame except for the stack register *r13*. The order of the registers is unimportant except that FRAME_LR and FRAME_PC should be the last two registers in the frame because we will return with a single instruction:

```
        LDMIA r13!, {r14, pc}^
```

There may be other registers that are required to be saved onto the stack frame, depending upon the operating system or application being used. For example:

- Registers *r13_usr* and *r14_usr* are saved when there is a requirement by the operating system to support both *user* and *SVC* modes.
- Floating-point registers are saved when the system uses hardware floating point.

There are a number of defines declared in this example. These defines map various *cpsr/spsr* changes to a particular label (for example, the *I_Bit*).

A set of defines is also declared that maps the various frame register references with frame pointer offsets. This is useful when the interrupts are reenabled and registers have to be stored into the stack frame. In this example we store the stack frame on the SVC stack.

The entry point for this example handler uses the same code as for the simple nonnested interrupt handler. The link register *r14* is first modified so that it points to the correct return address, and then the context plus the link register *r14* are saved onto the IRQ stack.

An interrupt service routine then services the interrupt. When servicing is complete or partially complete, control is passed back to the handler. The handler then calls a function called `read_RescheduleFlag`, which determines whether further processing is required. It returns a nonzero value in register *r0* if no further processing is required; otherwise it returns a zero. Note we have not included the source for `read_RescheduleFlag` because it is implementation specific.

The return flag in register *r0* is then tested. If the register is not equal to zero, the handler restores context and returns control back to the suspended task.

Register *r0* is set to zero, indicating that further processing is required. The first operation is to save the *spsr*, so a copy of the *spsr_irq* is moved into register *r2*. The *spsr* can then be stored in the stack frame by the handler later on in the code.

The IRQ stack address pointed to by register *r13_irq* is copied into register *r0* for later use. The next step is to flatten (empty) the IRQ stack. This is done by adding 6 * 4 bytes to the top of the stack because the stack grows downwards and an ADD instruction can be used to set the stack.

The handler does not need to worry about the data on the IRQ stack being corrupted by another nested interrupt because interrupts are still disabled and the handler will not reenable the interrupts until the data on the IRQ stack has been recovered.

The handler then switches to *SVC* mode; interrupts are still disabled. The *cpsr* is copied into register *r1* and modified to set the processor mode to *SVC*. Register *r1* is then written back into the *cpsr*, and the current mode changes to *SVC* mode. A copy of the new *cpsr* is left in register *r1* for later use.

The next stage is to create a stack frame by extending the stack by the stack frame size. Registers *r4* to *r11* can be saved onto the stack frame, which will free up enough registers to allow us to recover the remaining registers from the IRQ stack still pointed to by register *r0*.

At this stage the stack frame will contain the information shown in Table 9.7. The only registers that are not in the frame are the registers that are stored upon entry to the IRQ handler.

Table 9.8 shows the registers in SVC mode that correspond to the existing IRQ registers. The handler can now retrieve all the data from the IRQ stack, and it is safe to reenable interrupts.

IRQ exceptions are reenabled, and the handler has saved all the important registers. The handler can now complete the stack frame. Table 9.9 shows a completed stack frame that can be used either for a context switch or to handle a nested interrupt.

At this stage the remainder of the interrupt servicing may be handled. A context switch may be performed by saving the current value of register *r13* in the current task's control block and loading a new value for register *r13* from the new task's control block.

It is now possible to return to the interrupted task/handler, or to another task if a context switch occurred.

Table 9.7   SVC stack frame.

Label	Offset	Register
FRAME_R0	+0	—
FRAME_R1	+4	—
FRAME_R2	+8	—
FRAME_R3	+12	—
FRAME_R4	+16	*r4*
FRAME_R5	+20	*r5*
FRAME_R6	+24	*r6*
FRAME_R7	+28	*r7*
FRAME_R8	+32	*r8*
FRAME_R9	+36	*r9*
FRAME_R10	+40	*r10*
FRAME_R11	+44	*r11*
FRAME_R12	+48	—
FRAME_PSR	+52	—
FRAME_LR	+56	—
FRAME_PC	+60	—

Table 9.8   Data retrieved from the IRQ stack.

Registers (SVC)	Retrieved IRQ registers
r4	*r0*
r5	*r1*
r6	*r2*
r7	*r3*
r8	*r12*
r9	*r14* (return address)

SUMMARY   **Nested Interrupt Handler**

- Handles multiple interrupts without a priority assignment.
- Medium to high interrupt latency.
- Advantage—can enable interrupts before the servicing of an individual interrupt is complete reducing interrupt latency.
- Disadvantage—does not handle prioritization of interrupts, so lower priority interrupts can block higher priority interrupts.

Table 9.9   Complete frame stack.

Label	Offset	Register
FRAME_R0	+0	r0
FRAME_R1	+4	r1
FRAME_R2	+8	r2
FRAME_R3	+12	r3
FRAME_R4	+16	r4
FRAME_R5	+20	r5
FRAME_R6	+24	r6
FRAME_R7	+28	r7
FRAME_R8	+32	r8
FRAME_R9	+36	r9
FRAME_R10	+40	r10
FRAME_R11	+44	r11
FRAME_R12	+48	r12
FRAME_PSR	+52	spsr_irq
FRAME_LR	+56	r14
FRAME_PC	+60	r14_irq

9.3.3   REENTRANT INTERRUPT HANDLER

A reentrant interrupt handler is a method of handling multiple interrupts where interrupts are filtered by priority, which is important if there is a requirement that interrupts with higher priority have a lower latency. This type of filtering cannot be achieved using the conventional nested interrupt handler.

The basic difference between a reentrant interrupt handler and a nested interrupt handler is that the interrupts are reenabled early on in the reentrant interrupt handler, which can reduce interrupt latency. There are a number of issues relating to reenabling interrupts early, which will be described in more detail later on in this section.

All interrupts in a reentrant interrupt handler must be serviced in *SVC, system, undefined instruction,* or *abort* mode on the ARM processor.

If interrupts are reenabled in an interrupt mode and the interrupt routine performs a BL subroutine call instruction, the subroutine return address will be set in the register *r14_irq*. This address would be subsequently destroyed by an interrupt, which would overwrite the return address into register *r14_irq*. To avoid this, the interrupt routine should swap into *SVC* or *system* mode. The BL instruction can then use register *r14_svc* to store the subroutine return address. The interrupts must be disabled at the source by setting a bit in the interrupt controller before reenabling interrupts via the *cpsr*.

If interrupts are reenabled in the *cpsr* before processing is complete and the interrupt source is not disabled, an interrupt will be immediately regenerated, leading to an infinite interrupt sequence or *race condition*. Most interrupt controllers have an interrupt mask

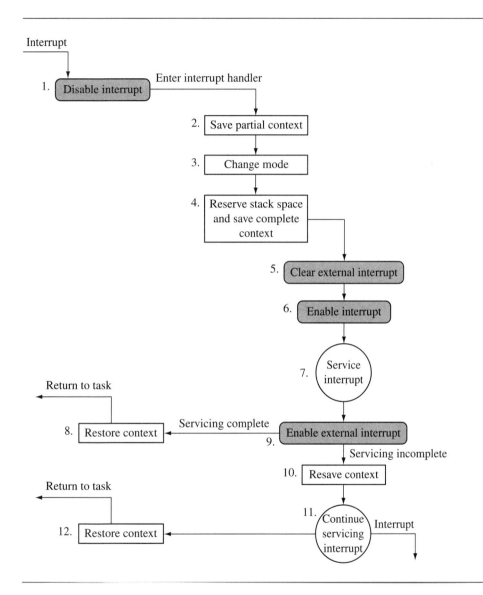

Figure 9.10   Reentrant interrupt handler.

register that allows you to mask out one or more interrupts, but the remaining interrupts are still enabled.

The interrupt stack is unused since interrupts are serviced in *SVC* mode (for example, on the task's stack). Instead the IRQ stack register *r13* is used to point to a 12-byte structure that will be used to store some registers temporarily on interrupt entry.

It is paramount to prioritize interrupts in a reentrant interrupt handler. If the interrupts are not prioritized, the system latency degrades to that of a nested interrupt handler because lower-priority interrupts will be able to preempt the servicing of a higher-priority interrupt. This in turn leads to the locking out of higher-priority interrupts for the duration of the servicing of a lower-priority interrupt.

EXAMPLE
9.10

It is assumed that register *r13_irq* has been set up to point to a 12-byte data structure and does not point to a standard IRQ stack. Offsets such as IRQ_SPSR are used to point into the data structure. As with all interrupt handlers, there are some standard definitions that are required to modify the *cpsr* and *spsr* registers.

```
IRQ_R0          EQU 0
IRQ_spsr        EQU 4
IRQ_R14         EQU 8

Maskmd          EQU 0x1f            ; mask mode
SVC32md         EQU 0x13            ; SVC mode
I_Bit           EQU 0x80            ; IRQ bit

ic_Base         EQU 0x80000000
IRQStatus       EQU 0x0
IRQRawStatus    EQU 0x4
IRQEnable       EQU 0x8
IRQEnableSet    EQU 0x8
IRQEnableClear  EQU 0xc

IRQ_Entry ; instruction                      state : comment
        SUB     r14, r14, #4          ; 2 : r14_irq-=4
        STR     r14, [r13, #IRQ_R14]  ; 2 : save r14_irq
        MRS     r14, spsr             ; 2 : copy spsr
        STR     r14, [r13, #IRQ_spsr] ; 2 : save spsr
        STR     r0, [r13, #IRQ_R0]    ; 2 : save r0
        MOV     r0, r13               ; 2 : copy r13_irq
        MRS     r14, cpsr             ; 3 : copy cpsr
        BIC     r14, r14, #Maskmd     ; 3 :
        ORR     r14, r14, #SVC32md    ; 3 :
        MSR     cpsr_c, r14           ; 3 : enter SVC mode
        STR     r14, [r13, #-8]!      ; 4 : save r14
        LDR     r14, [r0, #IRQ_R14]   ; 4 : r14_svc=r14_irq
        STR     r14, [r13, #4]        ; 4 : save r14_irq
        LDR     r14, [r0, #IRQ_spsr]  ; 4 : r14_svc=spsr_irq
        LDR     r0, [r0, #IRQ_R0]     ; 4 : restore r0
        STMDB   r13!, {r0-r3,r8,r12,r14} ; 4 : save context
```

```
LDR      r14, =ic_Base               ; 5 : int crtl address
LDR      r8, [r14, #IRQStatus]       ; 5 : get int status
STR      r8, [r14, #IRQEnableClear]  ; 5 : clear interrupts
MRS      r14, cpsr                   ; 6 : r14_svc=cpsr
BIC      r14, r14, #I_Bit            ; 6 : clear I-Bit
MSR      cpsr_c, r14                 ; 6 : enable IRQ int
BL       process_interrupt           ; 7 : call ISR
LDR      r14, =ic_Base               ; 9 : int ctrl address
STR      r8, [r14, #IRQEableSet]     ; 9 : enable ints
BL       read_RescheduleFlag         ; 9 : more processing
CMP      r0, #0                      ; 8 : if processing
LDMNEIA  r13!, {r0-r3,r8,r12,r14}    ; 8 : then load context
MSRNE    spsr_cxsf, r14              ; 8 :    update spsr
LDMNEIA  r13!, {r14, pc}^            ; 8 :    return
LDMIA    r13!, {r0-r3, r8}           ; 10 : else load reg
STMDB    r13!, {r0-r11}              ; 10 :    save context
BL       continue_servicing          ; 11 : continue service
LDMIA    r13!, {r0-r12, r14}         ; 12 : restore context
MSR      spsr_cxsf, r14              ; 12 : update spsr
LDMIA    r13!, {r14, pc}^            ; 12 : return
```

The start of the handler includes a normal interrupt entry point, with four being subtracted from the register *r14_irq*.

It is now important to assign values to the various fields in the data structure pointed to by register *r13_irq*. The registers that are recorded are *r14_irq*, *spsr_irq*, and *r0*. The register *r0* is used to transfer a pointer to the data structure when swapping to *SVC* mode since register *r0* will not be banked. This is why register *r13_irq* cannot be used for this purpose: it is not visible from *SVC* mode.

The pointer to the data structure is saved by copying register *r13_irq* into *r0*.

Offset (from *r13_irq*)	Value
+0	*r0* (on entry)
+4	*spsr_irq*
+8	*r14_irq*

The handler will now set the processor into *SVC* mode using the standard procedure of manipulating the *cpsr*. The link register *r14* for *SVC* mode is saved on the SVC stack. Subtracting 8 provides room on the stack for two 32-bit words.

Register *r14_irq* is then recovered and stored on the SVC stack. Now both the link registers *r14* for IRQ and SVC are stored on the SVC stack.

The rest of the IRQ context is recovered from the data structure passed into the *SVC* mode. Register *r14_svc* will now contain the *spsr* for *IRQ* mode.

Registers are then saved onto the SVC stack. Register *r8* is used to hold the interrupt mask for the interrupts that have been disabled in the interrupt handler. They will be reenabled later.

The interrupt source(s) are then disabled. An embedded system would at this point prioritize the interrupts and disable all interrupts lower than the current priority to prevent a low-priority interrupt from locking out a high-priority interrupt. Interrupt prioritizing will be discussed later on in this chapter.

Since the interrupt source has been cleared, it is now safe to reenable IRQ exceptions. This is achieved by clearing the *i* bit in the *cpsr*. Note that the interrupt controller still has external interrupts disabled.

It is now possible to process the interrupt. The interrupt processing should not attempt to do a context switch because the external source interrupt is disabled. If during the interrupt processing a context switch is needed, it should set a flag that could be picked up later by the interrupt handler. It is now safe to reenable external interrupts.

The handler needs to check if further processing is required. If the returned value is nonzero in register *r0*, then no further processing is required. If zero, the handler restores the context and then returns control back to the suspended task.

A stack frame now has to be created so that the service routine can complete. This is achieved by restoring parts of the context and then storing the complete context back on to the SVC stack.

The subroutine `continue_servicing`, which will complete the servicing of the interrupt, is called. This routine is not provided because it is specific to an implementation.

After the interrupt routine has been serviced, control can be given back to the suspended task.

SUMMARY   **Reentrant Interrupt Handler**

- Handles multiple interrupts that can be prioritized.

- Low interrupt latency.

- Advantage: handles interrupts with differing priorities.

- Disadvantage: tends to be more complex.

9.3.4   PRIORITIZED SIMPLE INTERRUPT HANDLER

Both the nonnested interrupt handler and the nested interrupt handler service interrupts on a first-come-first-served basis. In comparison, the prioritized interrupt handler will associate a priority level with a particular interrupt source. The priority level is used to dictate the order that the interrupts will be serviced. Thus, a higher-priority interrupt will take precedence over a lower-priority interrupt, which is a particularly desirable characteristic in many embedded systems.

Methods of handling prioritization can either be achieved in hardware or software. For hardware prioritization, the handler is simpler to design since the interrupt controller will provide the current highest-priority interrupt that requires servicing. These systems require more initialization code at startup since the interrupts and associated priority level tables have to be constructed before the system can be switched on; software prioritization, on the other hand, requires the additional assistance of an external interrupt controller. This interrupt controller has to provide a minimal set of functions that include being able to set and un-setmasks, and to read the interrupt status and source.

The rest of this section will cover a software prioritization technique chosen because it is a general method and does not rely on a specialized interrupt controller. To help describe the priority interrupt handler, we will introduce a fictional interrupt controller based upon a standard interrupt controller from ARM. The controller takes multiple interrupt sources and generates an IRQ and/or FIQ signal depending upon whether a particular interrupt source is enabled or disabled.

Figure 9.11 shows a flow diagram of a simple priority interrupt handler, based on a reentrant interrupt handler.

EXAMPLE
9.11

The interrupt controller has a register (*IRQRawStatus*) that holds the *raw interrupt status*—the state of the interrupt signals prior to being masked by the controller. The *IRQEnable* register determines which interrupts are masked from the processor. This register can only be set or cleared using *IRQEnableSet* and *IRQEnableClear*. Table 9.10 shows the interrupt controller register names, offsets from the controller's base address, read/write operations, and a description of the registers.

```
I_Bit          EQU 0x80

PRIORITY_0     EQU 2                    ; Comms Rx
PRIORITY_1     EQU 1                    ; Comms Tx
PRIORITY_2     EQU 0                    ; Timer 1
PRIORITY_3     EQU 3                    ; Timer 2

BINARY_0       EQU 1 << PRIORITY_0      ; 1 << 2 0x00000004
BINARY_1       EQU 1 << PRIORITY_1      ; 1 << 1 0x00000002
BINARY_2       EQU 1 << PRIORITY_2      ; 1 << 0 0x00000001
BINARY_3       EQU 1 << PRIORITY_3      ; 1 << 3 0x00000008

MASK_3         EQU BINARY_3
MASK_2         EQU MASK_3+BINARY_2
MASK_1         EQU MASK_2+BINARY_1
MASK_0         EQU MASK_1+BINARY_0

ic_Base        EQU 0x80000000
IRQStatus      EQU 0x0
```

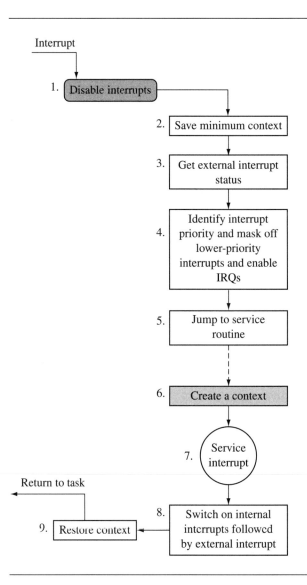

Figure 9.11 Priority interrupt handler.

```
IRQRawStatus    EQU 0x4
IRQEnable       EQU 0x8
IRQEnableSet    EQU 0x8
IRQEnableClear  EQU 0xc
```

Table 9.10   Interrupt controller registers.

Register	Offset	R/W	Description
IRQRawStatus	+0x04	r	represents status of the interrupt sources
IRQEnable	+0x08	r	masks the interrupt sources that generate IRQ/FIQ to the CPU
IRQStatus	+0x00	r	represents interrupt sources after masking
IRQEnableSet	+0x08	w	sets bits in the interrupt enable register
IRQEnableClear	+0x0c	w	clears bits in the interrupt enable register

```
IRQ_Handler          ; instruction                  state : comment
       SUB     r14, r14, #4                   ; 2 : r14_irq -= 4
       STMFD   r13!, {r14}                    ; 2 : save r14_irq
       MRS     r14, spsr                      ; 2 : copy spsr_irq
       STMFD   r13!, {r10,r11,r12,r14}        ; 2 : save context
       LDR     r14, =ic_Base                  ; 3 : int crtl addr
       MOV     r11, #PRIORITY_3               ; 3 : default priority
       LDR     r10, [r14, #IRQStatus]         ; 3 : load IRQ status
       TST     r10, #BINARY_3                 ; 4 : if Timer 2
       MOVNE   r11, #PRIORITY_3               ; 4 :    then P3(lo)
       TST     r10, #BINARY_2                 ; 4 : if Timer 1
       MOVNE   r11, #PRIORITY_2               ; 4 :    then P2
       TST     r10, #BINARY_1                 ; 4 : if Comm Tx
       MOVNE   r11, #PRIORITY_1               ; 4 :    then P1
       TST     r10, #BINARY_0                 ; 4 : if Comm Rx
       MOVNE   r11, #PRIORITY_0               ; 4 :    then P0(hi)
       LDR     r12, [r14,#IRQEnable]          ; 4 : IRQEnable reg
       ADR     r10, priority_masks            ; 4 : mask address
       LDR     r10, [r10,r11,LSL #2]          ; 4 : priority value
       AND     r12, r12,r10                   ; 4 : AND enable reg
       STR     r12, [r14,#IRQEnableClear]     ; 4 : disable ints
       MRS     r14, cpsr                      ; 4 : copy cpsr
       BIC     r14, r14, #I_Bit               ; 4 : clear I-bit
       MSR     cpsr_c, r14                    ; 4 : enable IRQ ints
       LDR     pc, [pc, r11, LSL#2]           ; 5 : jump to an ISR
       NOP                                    ;
       DCD     service_timer1                 ; timer1 ISR
       DCD     service_commtx                 ; commtx ISR
       DCD     service_commrx                 ; commrx ISR
       DCD     service_timer2                 ; timer2 ISR

priority_masks
       DCD     MASK_2                         ; priority mask 2
```

```
          DCD     MASK_1                      ; priority mask 1
          DCD     MASK_0                      ; priority mask 0
          DCD     MASK_3                      ; priority mask 3
          ...
service_timer1
          STMFD   r13!, {r0-r9}               ; 6 : save context
          <service routine>
          LDMFD   r13!, {r0-r10}              ; 7 : restore context
          MRS     r11, cpsr                   ; 8 : copy cpsr
          ORR     r11, r11, #I_Bit            ; 8 : set I-bit
          MSR     cpsr_c, r11                 ; 8 : disable IRQ
          LDR     r11, =ic_Base               ; 8 : int ctrl addr
          STR     r12, [r11, #IRQEnableSet]   ; 8 : enable ints
          LDMFD   r13!, {r11, r12, r14}       ; 9 : restore context
          MSR     spsr_cxsf, r14              ; 9 : set spsr
          LDMFD   r13!, {pc}^                  ; 9 : return
```

Most interrupt controllers also have a corresponding set of registers for the FIQ exceptions and even allow individual interrupt sources to be attached to a particular interrupt signal going to the core. Thus, by programming the controller, a particular interrupt source can be made to cause either an IRQ or FIQ exception.

The registers are offset from a base address in memory. Table 9.10 shows all the offsets for the various registers from interrupt controller base address ic_Base. Note that offset 0x08 is used for both IRQEnable and IRQEnableSet.

In the interrupt controller each bit is associated with a particular interrupt source (see Figure 9.12). For example, bit 2 is associated with a receive interrupt source for serial communication.

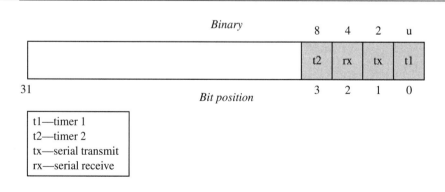

Figure 9.12   32-bit interrupt control register.

The PRIORITY_x defines the four interrupt sources, used in the example, to a corresponding set of priority levels, where PRIORITY_0 is the highest-priority interrupt and PRIORITY_3 is the lowest-priority interrupt.

The BINARY_x defines provide the bit patterns for each of the priority levels. For instance, for a PRIORITY_0 interrupt the binary pattern would be 0x00000004 (or 1 ≪ 2). For each priority level there is a corresponding mask that masks out all interrupts that are equal or lower in priority. For instance, MASK_2 will mask out interrupts from Timer2 (priority = 3) and CommRx (priority = 2).

The defines for the interrupt controller registers are also listed. ic_Base is the base address, and the remaining defines (for instance, IRQStatus) are all offsets from that base address.

The priority interrupt handler starts with a standard entry, but at first only the IRQ link register is stored onto the IRQ stack.

Next the handler obtains the *spsr* and places the contents into register *r14_irq* and frees up a group of registers for use in processing the prioritization.

The handler needs to obtain the status of the interrupt controller. This is achieved by loading in the base address of the interrupt controller into register *r14* and loading register *r10* with ic_Base (register *r14*) offset by IRQStatus (0x00).

The handler now needs to determine the highest-priority interrupt by testing the status information. If a particular interrupt source matches a priority level, then the priority level is set in register *r11*. The method compares the interrupt source with all the set priority levels, starting first with the lowest priority and working to the highest priority.

After this code fragment, register *r14_irq* will contain the base address of the interrupt controller, and register *r11* will contain the bit number of the highest-priority interrupt. It is now important to disable the lower- and equal-priority interrupts so that the higher-priority interrupts can still interrupt the handler.

Notice that this method is more deterministic since the time taken to discover the priority is always the same.

To set the interrupt mask in the controller, the handler must determine the current IRQ enable register and also obtain the start address of the priority mask table. The priority_masks are defined at the end of the handler.

Register *r12* will now contain the current IRQ enable register, and register *r10* will contain the start address of the priority table. To obtain the correct mask, register *r11* is shifted left by two (using the barrel shifter LSL #2). This will multiply the address by four and add that to the start address of the priority table.

Register *r10* contains the new mask. The next step is to clear the lower-priority interrupts using the mask, by performing a binary AND with the mask and register *r12* (*IRQEnable* register) and then clearing the bits by storing the new mask into *IRQEnableClear* register. It is now safe to enable IRQ exceptions by clearing the *i* bit in the *cpsr*.

Lastly the handler needs to jump to the correct service routine, by modifying register *r11* (which still contains the highest-priority interrupt) and the *pc*. Shifting register *r11* left by two (multiplying by four) and adding it to the *pc* allows the handler to jump to the correct routine by loading the address of the service routine directly into the *pc*.

The jump table has to follow the instruction that loads the *pc*. There is an NOP in between the jump table and the instruction that manipulates the *pc* because the *pc* will be pointing two instructions ahead (or eight bytes). The *priority mask table* is in interrupt source bit order.

Each ISR follows the same entry style. The example given is for the timer1 interrupt service routine.

The ISR is then inserted after the header above. Once the ISR is complete, the interrupt sources must be reset and control passed back to the interrupted task.

The handler must disable the IRQs before the interrupts can be switched back on. The external interrupts can now be restored to their original value, which is possible because the service routine did not modify register *r12* and so it still contains the original value.

To return back to the interrupted task, context is restored and the original *spsr* is copied back into the *spsr_irq*.

SUMMARY   **Prioritized Simple Interrupt Handler**

■   Handles prioritized interrupts.

■   Low interrupt latency.

■   Advantage: deterministic interrupt latency since the priority level is identified first and then the service is called after the lower-priority interrupts are masked.

■   Disadvantage: the time taken to get to a low-priority service routine is the same as for a high-priority routine.

9.3.5   PRIORITIZED STANDARD INTERRUPT HANDLER

Following on from the prioritized simple interrupt handler, the next handler adds an additional level of complexity. The prioritized simple interrupt handler tested all the interrupts to establish the highest priority—an inefficient method of establishing the priority level but it does have the advantage of being deterministic since each interrupt priority will take the same length of time to be identified.

An alternative approach is to jump early when the highest-priority interrupt has been identified (see Figure 9.13), by setting the *pc* and jumping immediately once the priority level has been established. This means that the identification section of the code for the prioritized standard interrupt handler is more involved than for the prioritized simple interrupt handler. The identification section will determine the priority level and jump immediately to a routine that will handle the masking of the lower-priority interrupts and then jump again via a jump table to the appropriate ISR.

EXAMPLE   A prioritized standard interrupt handler starts the same as a prioritized simple interrupt
9.12   handler but intercepts the interrupts with a higher-priority earlier. Register *r14* is assigned to point to the base of the interrupt controller and load register *r10* with the interrupt controller status register. To allow the handler to be relocatable, the current address pointed to by the *pc* is recorded into register *r11*.

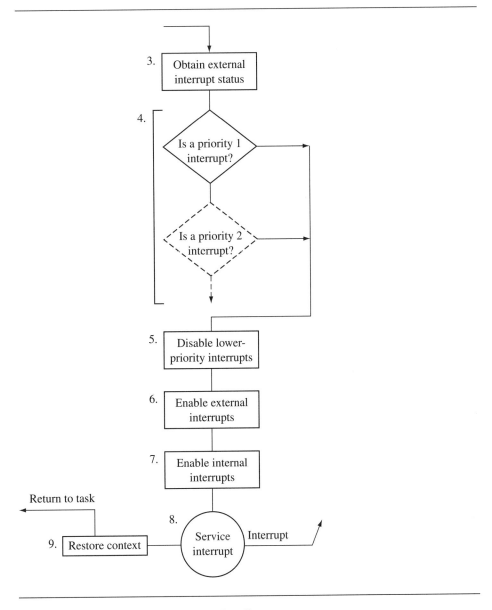

Figure 9.13   Part of a prioritized standard interrupt handler.

```
        I_Bit               EQU 0x80

        PRIORITY_0          EQU 2                       ; Comms Rx
        PRIORITY_1          EQU 1                       ; Comms Tx
        PRIORITY_2          EQU 0                       ; Timer 1
        PRIORITY_3          EQU 3                       ; Timer 2

        BINARY_0            EQU 1 << PRIORITY_0          ; 1<<2 0x00000004
        BINARY_1            EQU 1 << PRIORITY_1          ; 1<<1 0x00000002
        BINARY_2            EQU 1 << PRIORITY_2          ; 1<<0 0x00000001
        BINARY_3            EQU 1 << PRIORITY_3          ; 1<<3 0x00000008

        MASK_3              EQU BINARY_3
        MASK_2              EQU MASK_3+BINARY_2
        MASK_1              EQU MASK_2+BINARY_1
        MASK_0              EQU MASK_1+BINARY_0

        ic_Base             EQU 0x80000000
        IRQStatus           EQU 0x0
        IRQRawStatus        EQU 0x4
        IRQEnable           EQU 0x8
        IRQEnableSet        EQU 0x8
        IRQEnableClear      EQU 0xc

        IRQ_Handler         ; instruction                state : comment
                SUB         r14, r14, #4                 ; 2 : r14_irq -= 4
                STMFD       r13!, {r14}                  ; 2 : save r14_irq
                MRS         r14, spsr                    ; 2 : copy spsr_irq
                STMFD       r13!,{r10,r11,r12,r14}       ; 2 : save context
                LDR         r14, =ic_Base                ; 3 : int crtl addr
                LDR         r10, [r14, #IRQStatus]       ; 3 : load IRQ status
                MOV         r11, pc                      ; 4 : copy pc
                TST         r10, #BINARY_0               ; 5 : if CommRx
                BLNE        disable_lower                ; 5 :   then branch
                TST         r10, #BINARY_1               ; 5 : if CommTx
                BLNE        disable_lower                ; 5 :   then branch
                TST         r10, #BINARY_2               ; 5 : if Timer1
                BLNE        disable_lower                ; 5 :   then branch
                TST         r10, #BINARY_3               ; 5 : if Timer2
                BLNE        disable_lower                ; 5 :   then branch
        disable_lower
                SUB         r11, r14, r11                ; 5 : r11=r14-copy of pc
                LDR         r12,=priority_table          ; 5 : priority table
```

```
        LDRB    r11,[r12,r11,LSR #3]      ; 5 : mem8[tbl+(r11>>3)]
        ADR     r10, priority_masks       ; 5 : priority mask
        LDR     r10, [r10,r11,LSL #2]     ; 5 : load mask
        LDR     r14, =ic_Base             ; 6 : int crtl addr
        LDR     r12, [r14,#IRQEnable]     ; 6 : IRQ enable reg
        AND     r12, r12, r10             ; 6 : AND enable reg
        STR     r12, [r14,#IRQEnableClear] ; 6 : disable ints
        MRS     r14, cpsr                 ; 7 : copy cpsr
        BIC     r14, r14, #I_Bit          ; 7 : clear I-bit
        MSR     cpsr_c, r14               ; 7 : enable IRQ
        LDR     pc, [pc, r11, LSL#2]      ; 8 : jump to an ISR
        NOP                               ;

        DCD     service_timer1            ; timer1 ISR
        DCD     service_commtx            ; commtx ISR
        DCD     service_commrx            ; commrx ISR
        DCD     service_timer2            ; timer2 ISR

priority_masks
        DCD     MASK_2                    ; priority mask 2
        DCD     MASK_1                    ; priority mask 1
        DCD     MASK_0                    ; priority mask 0
        DCD     MASK_3                    ; priority mask 3

priority_table
        DCB     PRIORITY_0                ; priority 0
        DCB     PRIORITY_1                ; priority 1
        DCB     PRIORITY_2                ; priority 2
        DCB     PRIORITY_3                ; priority 3
        ALIGN
```

The interrupt source can now be tested by comparing the highest to the lowest priority. The first priority level that matches the interrupt source determines the priority level of the incoming interrupt because each interrupt has a preset priority level. Once a match is achieved, then the handler can branch to the routine that masks off the lower-priority interrupts.

To disable the equal- or lower-priority interrupts, the handler enters a routine that first calculates the priority level using the base address in register *r11* and link register *r14*.

Following the SUB instruction register *r11* will now contain the value 4, 12, 20, or 28. These values correspond to the priority level of the interrupt multiplied by eight plus four. Register *r11* is then divided by eight and added to the address of the *priority_table*. Following the LDRB register *r11* will equal one of the priority interrupt numbers (0, 1, 2, or 3).

The priority mask can now be determined, using the technique of shifting left by two and adding that to the register *r10*, which contains the address of the *priority_mask*.

The base address for the interrupt controller is copied into register *r14_irq* and is used to obtain the *IRQEnable* register in the controller and place it into register *r12*.

Register *r10* contains the new mask. The next step is to clear the lower-priority interrupts using this mask by performing a binary AND with the mask and *r12* (*IRQEnable* register) and storing the result into the *IRQEnableClear* register. It is now safe to enable IRQ exceptions by clearing the *i* bit in the *cpsr*.

Lastly the handler needs to jump to the correct service routine, by modifying *r11* (which still contains the highest-priority interrupt) and the *pc*. Shifting register *r11* left by two (multiplying *r11* by four) and adding it to the *pc* allows the handler to jump to the correct routine by loading the address of the service routine directly into the *pc*. The jump table must follow the instruction that loads the *pc*. There is an NOP between the jump table and the LDR instruction that modifies the *pc* because the *pc* is pointing two instructions ahead (or eight bytes).

Note that the priority mask table is in interrupt bit order, and the priority table is in priority order.

SUMMARY   **Prioritized Standard Interrupt Handler**

- Handles higher-priority interrupts in a shorter time than lower-priority interrupts.

- Low interrupt latency.

- Advantage: higher-priority interrupts treated with greater urgency with no duplication of code to set external interrupt masks.

- Disadvantage: there is a time penalty since this handler requires two jumps, resulting in the pipeline being flushed each time a jump occurs.

9.3.6 PRIORITIZED DIRECT INTERRUPT HANDLER

One difference between the prioritized direct interrupt handler and the prioritized standard interrupt handler is that some of the processing is moved out of the handler into the individual ISRs. The moved code masks out the lower-priority interrupts. Each ISR will have to mask out the lower-priority interrupts for the particular priority level, which can be a fixed number since the priority level has already been previously determined.

The second difference is that the prioritized direct interrupt handler jumps directly to the appropriate ISR. Each ISR is responsible for disabling the lower-priority interrupts before modifying the *cpsr* to reenable interrupts. This type of handler is relatively simple since the masking is done by the individual ISR, but there is a small amount of code duplication since each interrupt service routine is effectively carrying out the same task.

EXAMPLE
9.13   The bit_*x* defines associate an interrupt source with a bit position within the interrupt controller, which will be used to help mask the lower-priority interrupts within an ISR.

Once the context is saved, the base address of the ISR table has to be loaded into register *r12*. This register is used to jump to the correct ISR once the priority has been established for the interrupt source.

```
I_Bit             EQU 0x80

PRIORITY_0        EQU 2                        ; Comms Rx
PRIORITY_1        EQU 1                        ; Comms Tx
PRIORITY_2        EQU 0                        ; Timer 1
PRIORITY_3        EQU 3                        ; Timer 2

BINARY_0          EQU 1 << PRIORITY_0          ; 1 << 2 0x00000004
BINARY_1          EQU 1 << PRIORITY_1          ; 1 << 1 0x00000002
BINARY_2          EQU 1 << PRIORITY_2          ; 1 << 0 0x00000001
BINARY_3          EQU 1 << PRIORITY_3          ; 1 << 3 0x00000008

MASK_3            EQU BINARY_3
MASK_2            EQU MASK_3+BINARY_2
MASK_1            EQU MASK_2+BINARY_1
MASK_0            EQU MASK_1+BINARY_0

ic_Base           EQU 0x80000000
IRQStatus         EQU 0x0
IRQRawStatus      EQU 0x4
IRQEnable         EQU 0x8
IRQEnableSet      EQU 0x8
IRQEnableClear    EQU 0xc

bit_timer1        EQU 0
bit_commtx        EQU 1
bit_commrx        EQU 2
bit_timer2        EQU 3

IRQ_Handler       ; instruction                comment
        SUB       r14, r14, #4                 ; r14_irq-=4
        STMFD     r13!, {r14}                  ; save r14_irq
        MRS       r14, spsr                    ; copy spsr_irq
        STMFD     r13!,{r10,r11,r12,r14}       ; save context
        LDR       r14, =ic_Base                ; int crtl addr
        LDR       r10, [r14, #IRQStatus]       ; load IRQ status
        ADR       r12, isr_table               ; obtain ISR table
        TST       r10, #BINARY_0               ; if CommRx
        LDRNE     pc, [r12, #PRIORITY_0 << 2]  ;   then CommRx ISR
```

```
        TST     r10, #BINARY_1              ; if CommTx
        LDRNE   pc, [r12, #PRIORITY_1 << 2] ;   then CommTx ISR
        TST     r10, #BINARY_2              ; if Timer1
        LDRNE   pc, [r12, #PRIORITY_2 << 2] ;   then Timer1 ISR
        TST     r10, #BINARY_3              ; if Timer2
        LDRNE   pc, [r12, #PRIORITY_3 << 2] ;   then Timer2 ISR
        B       service_none

isr_table
        DCD     service_timer1              ; timer1 ISR
        DCD     service_commtx              ; commtx ISR
        DCD     service_commrx              ; commrx ISR
        DCD     service_timer2              ; timer2 ISR

priority_masks
        DCD     MASK_2                      ; priority mask 2
        DCD     MASK_1                      ; priority mask 1
        DCD     MASK_0                      ; priority mask 0
        DCD     MASK_3                      ; priority mask 3
        ...
service_timer1
        MOV     r11, #bit_timer1            ; copy bit_timer1
        LDR     r14, =ic_Base               ; int ctrl addr
        LDR     r12, [r14,#IRQEnable]       ; IRQ enable register
        ADR     r10, priority_masks         ; obtain priority addr
        LDR     r10, [r10,r11,LSL#2]        ; load priority mask
        AND     r12, r12, r10               ; AND enable reg
        STR     r12, [r14, #IRQEnableClear] ; disable ints
        MRS     r14, cpsr                   ; copy cpsr
        BIC     r14, r14, #I_Bit            ; clear I-bit
        MSR     cpsr_c, r14                 ; enable IRQ
        <rest of the ISR>
```

The priority interrupt is established by checking the highest-priority interrupt first and then working down to the lowest. Once a priority interrupt is identified, the *pc* is then loaded with the address of the appropriate ISR. The indirect address is stored at the address of the *isr_table* plus the priority level shifted two bits to the left (multiplied by four). Alternatively you could use a conditional branch BNE.

The ISR jump table *isr_table* is ordered with the highest-priority interrupt at the beginning of the table.

The *service_timer1* entry shows an example of an ISR used in a priority direct interrupt handler. Each ISR is unique and depends upon the particular interrupt source.

A copy of the base address for the interrupt controller is placed into register *r14_irq*. This address plus an offset is used to copy the *IRQEnable* register into register *r12*.

The address of the priority mask table has to be copied into register *r10* so it can be used to calculate the address of the actual mask. Register *r11* is shifted left two positions, which gives an offset of 0, 4, 8, or 12. The offset plus the address of the priority mask table address is used to load the mask into register *r10*. The priority mask table is the same as for the priority interrupt handler in the previous section.

Register *r10* will contain the ISR mask, and register *r12* will contain the current mask. A binary AND is used to merge the two masks. Then the new mask is used to configure the interrupt controller using the *IRQEnableClear* register. It is now safe to enable IRQ exceptions by clearing the *i* bit in the *cpsr*.

The handler can continue servicing the current interrupt unless an interrupt with a higher priority occurs, in which case that interrupt will take precedence over the current interrupt.

SUMMARY   **Prioritized Direct Interrupt Handler**

- Handles higher-priority interrupts in a shorter time. Goes directly to the specific ISR.
- Low interrupt latency.
- Advantage: uses a single jump and saves valuable cycles to go to the ISR.
- Disadvantage: each ISR has a mechanism to set the external interrupt mask to stop lower-priority interrupts from halting the current ISR, which adds extra code to each ISR.

9.3.7 PRIORITIZED GROUPED INTERRUPT HANDLER

Lastly, the prioritized grouped interrupt handler differs from the other prioritized interrupt handlers since it is designed to handle a large set of interrupts. This is achieved by grouping interrupts together and forming a subset, which can then be given a priority level.

The designer of an embedded system must identify each subset of interrupt sources and assign a group priority level to that subset. It is important to be careful when selecting the subsets of interrupt sources since the groups can determine the characteristics of the system. Grouping the interrupt sources together tends to reduce the complexity of the handler since it is not necessary to scan through every interrupt to determine the priority level. If a prioritized grouped interrupt handler is well designed, it will dramatically improve overall system response times.

EXAMPLE
9.14
This handler has been designed to have two priority groups. Timer sources are grouped into group 0, and communication sources are grouped into group 1 (see Table 9.11.) Group 0 interrupts are given a higher priority than group 1 interrupts.

```
I_Bit           EQU 0x80

PRIORITY_0      EQU 2                   ; Comms Rx
```

Table 9.11   Group interrupt sources.

Group	Interrupts
0	timer1, timer2
1	commtx, commrx

```
        PRIORITY_1      EQU 1                   ; Comms Tx
        PRIORITY_2      EQU 0                   ; Timer 1
        PRIORITY_3      EQU 3                   ; Timer 2

        BINARY_0        EQU 1 << PRIORITY_0     ; 1 << 2  0x00000004
        BINARY_1        EQU 1 << PRIORITY_1     ; 1 << 1  0x00000002
        BINARY_2        EQU 1 << PRIORITY_2     ; 1 << 0  0x00000001
        BINARY_3        EQU 1 << PRIORITY_3     ; 1 << 3  0x00000008

        GROUP_0         EQU BINARY_2|BINARY_3
        GROUP_1         EQU BINARY_0|BINARY_1

        GMASK_1         EQU GROUP_1
        GMASK_0         EQU GMASK_1+GROUP_0

        MASK_TIMER1     EQU GMASK_0
        MASK_COMMTX     EQU GMASK_1
        MASK_COMMRX     EQU GMASK_1
        MASK_TIMER2     EQU GMASK_0

        ic_Base         EQU 0x80000000
        IRQStatus       EQU 0x0
        IRQRawStatus    EQU 0x4
        IRQEnable       EQU 0x8
        IRQEnableSet    EQU 0x8
        IRQEnableClear  EQU 0xc

interrupt_handler
        SUB     r14, r14,#4                 ; r14_irq-=4
        STMFD   r13!, {r14}                 ; save r14_irq
        MRS     r14, spsr                   ; copy spsr_irq
        STMFD   r13!, {r10,r11,r12,r14}     ; save context
        LDR     r14, =ic_Base               ; int ctrl addr
        LDR     r10, [r14, #IRQStatus]      ; load IRQ status
        ANDS    r11, r10, #GROUP_0          ; belong to GROUP_0
        ANDEQS  r11, r10, #GROUP_1          ; belong to GROUP_1
```

```
        AND     r10, r11, #0xf              ; mask off top 24-bit
        ADR     r11, lowest_significant_bit ; load LSB addr
        LDRB    r11, [r11, r10]             ; load byte
        B       disable_lower_priority      ; jump to routine

lowest_significant_bit
        ;       0   1 2 3 4 5 6 7 8 9 a b c d e f
        DCB     0xff,0,1,0,2,0,1,0,3,0,1,0,2,0,1,0

disable_lower_priority
        CMP     r11, #0xff                  ; if unknown
        BEQ     unknown_condition           ;    then jump
        LDR     r12, [r14, #IRQEnable]      ; load IRQ enable reg
        ADR     r10, priority_mask          ; load priority addr
        LDR     r10, [r10, r11, LSL #2]     ; mem32[r10+r11<<2]
        AND     r12, r12, r10               ; AND enable reg
        STR     r12, [r14, #IRQEnableClear] ; disable ints
        MRS     r14, cpsr                   ; copy cpsr
        BIC     r14, r14, #I_Bit            ; clear I-bit
        MSR     cpsr_c, r14                 ; enable IRQ ints
        LDR     pc, [pc, r11, LSL #2]       ; jump to an ISR
        NOP
        DCD     service_timer1              ; timer1 ISR
        DCD     service_commtx              ; commtx ISR
        DCD     service_commrx              ; commrx ISR
        DCD     service_timer2              ; timer2 ISR

priority_mask
        DCD     MASK_TIMER1                 ; mask GROUP 0
        DCD     MASK_COMMTX                 ; mask GROUP 1
        DCD     MASK_COMMRX                 ; mask GROUP 1
        DCD     MASK_TIMER2                 ; mask GROUP 0
```

The GROUP_x defines assign the various interrupt sources to their specific priority level by using a binary OR operation on the binary patterns. The GMASK_x defines assign the masks for the grouped interrupts. The MASK_x defines connect each GMASK_x to a specific interrupt source, which can then be used in the priority mask table.

After the context has been saved the interrupt handler loads the IRQ status register using an offset from the interrupt controller base address.

The handler then identifies the group to which the interrupt source belongs by using the binary AND operation on the source. The letter *S* postfixed to the instructions means update condition flags in the *cpsr*.

Register *r11* will now contain the highest-priority group 0 or 1. The handler now masks out the other interrupt sources by applying a binary AND operation with 0xf.

Table 9.12   Lowest significant bit table.

Binary pattern	Value
0000	unknown
0001	0
0010	1
0011	0
0100	2
0101	0
0110	1
0111	0
1000	3
1001	0
1010	1
1011	0
1100	2
1101	0
1110	1
1111	0

The address of the lowest significant bit table is then loaded into register *r11*. A byte is loaded from the start of the table using the value in register *r10* (0, 1, 2, or 3, see Table 9.12). Once the lowest significant bit position is loaded into register *r11*, the handler branches to a routine.

The *disable_lower_priority* interrupt routine first checks for a spurious (no longer present) interrupt. If the interrupt is spurious, then the *unknown_condition* routine is called. The handler then loads the *IRQEnable* register and places the result in register *r12*.

The priority mask is found by loading in the address of the priority mask table and then shifting the data in register *r11* left by two. The result, 0, 4, 8, or 12, is added to the priority mask address. Register *r10* then contains a mask to disable the lower-priority group interrupts from being raised.

The next step is to clear the lower-priority interrupts using the mask by performing a binary AND with the mask in registers *r10* and *r12* (IRQEnable register) and then clearing the bits by saving the result into the IRQEnableClear register. At this point it is now safe to enable IRQ exceptions by clearing the *i* bit in the *cpsr*.

Lastly the handler jumps to the correct interrupt service routine by modifying register *r11* (which still contains the highest-priority interrupt) and the *pc*. By shifting register *r11* left by two and adding the result to the *pc* the address of the ISR is determined. This address is then loaded directly into the *pc*. Note that the jump table must follow the LDR instruction. The NOP is present due to the ARM pipeline.

SUMMARY   **Prioritized Grouped Interrupt Handler**

- Mechanism for handling interrupts that are grouped into different priority levels.

- Low interrupt latency.

- Advantage: useful when the embedded system has to handle a large number of interrupts, and also reduces the response time since the determining of the priority level is shorter.

- Disadvantage: determining how the interrupts are grouped together.

9.3.8 VIC PL190 Based Interrupt Service Routine

To take advantage of the vector interrupt controller, the IRQ vector entry has to be modified.

```
0x00000018   LDR     pc,[pc,#-0xff0]   ; IRQ pc=mem32[0xfffff030]
```

This instruction loads an ISR address from the memory mapped location 0xffffff030 into the *pc* which bypasses any software interrupt handler since the interrupt source can be obtained directly from the hardware. It also reduces interrupt latency since there is only a single jump to a specific ISR.

Here is an example of VIC service routine:

```
INTON          EQU 0x0000                 ; enable interrupts
SYS32md        EQU 0x1f                   ; system mode
IRQ32md        EQU 0x12                   ; IRQ mode
I_Bit          EQU 0x80
VICBaseAddr    EQU 0xfffff000             ; addr of VIC ctrl
VICVectorAddr  EQU VICBaseAddr+0x30       ; isr address of int

vector_service_routine
        SUB     r14,r14,#4               ; r14-=4
        STMFD   r13!, {r0-r3,r12,r14}    ; save context
        MRS     r12, spsr                ; copy spsr
        STMFD   r13!,{r12}               ; save spsr
        <clear the interrupt source>
        MSR     cpsr_c, #INTON|SYS32md   ; cpsr_c=ift_sys
        <interrupt service code>
        MSR     cpsr_c, #I_Bit|IRQ32md   ; cpsr_c=Ift_irq
        LDMFD   r13!, {r12}              ; restore (spsr_irq)
        MSR     spsr_cxsf, r12           ; restore spsr
        LDR     r1,=VICVectorAddr        ; load VectorAddress
        STR     r0, [r1]                 ; servicing complete
        LDMFD   r13!, {r0-r3,r12,pc}^    ; return
```

This routine saves the context and *s psr_irq* before clearing the interrupt source. Once this is complete, the IRQ exceptions can be reenabled by clearing the *i* bit, and the processor mode is set to *system* mode. The service routine can then process the interrupt in *system* mode. Once complete, the IRQ exceptions are disabled by setting the *i* bit, and the processor mode is switched back to *IRQ* mode.

The *spsr_irq* is restored from the IRQ stack, preparing the routine to return to the interrupted task.

The service routine then writes to the `VICVectorAddr` register in the controller. Writing to this address indicates to the priority hardware that the interrupt has been serviced.

Note that since the VIC is basically a hardware interrupt handler, the array of ISR addresses must be preprogrammed into the VIC before it is activated.

9.4 SUMMARY

An exception changes the normal sequential execution of instructions. There are seven exceptions: Data Abort, Fast Interrupt Request, Interrupt Request, Prefetch Abort, Software Interrupt, Reset, and Undefined Instruction. Each exception has an associated ARM processor mode. When an exception is raised, the processor goes into a specific mode and branches to an entry in the vector table. Each exception also has a priority level.

Interrupts are a special type of exception that are caused by an external peripheral. The IRQ exception is used for general operating system activities. The FIQ exception is normally reserved for a single interrupt source. *Interrupt latency* is the interval of time from an external interrupt request signal being raised to the first fetch of an instruction of a specific interrupt service routine (ISR).

We covered eight interrupt handling schemes, from a very simple nonnested interrupt handler that handles and services individual interrupts, to an advanced prioritized grouped interrupt handler that handles interrupts that are grouped into different priority levels.

CHAPTER

FIRMWARE 10

This chapter discusses firmware for ARM-based embedded systems. Firmware is an important part of any embedded system since it is frequently the first code to be ported and executed on a new platform. Firmware can vary from being a complete software embedded system to just a simple initialization and bootloader routine. We have divided this chapter into two sections.

The first section introduces firmware. In this section we define the term *firmware* and describe two popular industry standard firmware packages available for the ARM processor—ARM Firmware Suite and Red Hat's RedBoot. These firmware packages are general purpose and can be ported to different ARM platforms relatively easily and quickly.

The second section focuses on just the initialization and bootloader process. To help with this, we have developed a simple example called Sandstone. Sandstone is designed to initialize hardware, load an image into memory, and relinquish control of the *pc* over to that image.

We start by first discussing firmware and introduce the two common ARM firmware packages.

10.1 FIRMWARE AND BOOTLOADER

We realize that the use of terms may differ among engineers, but we will use the following definitions:

- The *firmware* is the deeply embedded, low-level software that provides an interface between the hardware and the application/operating system level software. It resides in the ROM and executes when power is applied to the embedded hardware system. Firmware can remain active after system initialization and supports basic system operations. The choice of which firmware to use for a particular ARM-based system depends upon the specific application, which can range from loading and executing a sophisticated operating system to simply relinquishing control to a small microkernel. Consequently, requirements can vary greatly from one firmware implementation to another. For example, a small system may require just minimal firmware support to boot a small operating system. One of the main purposes of firmware is to provide a stable mechanism to load and boot an operating system.

■ The *bootloader* is a small application that installs the operating system or application onto a hardware target. The bootloader only exists up to the point that the operating system or application is executing, and it is commonly incorporated into the firmware.

To help understand the features of different firmware implementations, we have a common execution flow (see Table 10.1). Each stage is now discussed in more detail.

The first stage is to set up the target platform—in other words, prepare the environment to boot an operating system since an operating system expects a particular type of environment before it can operate. This step involves making sure that the platform is correctly initialized (for example, making sure that the control registers of a particular microcontroller are placed at a known address or changing the memory map to an expected layout).

It is common for the same executable to operate on different cores and platforms. In this case, the firmware has to identify and discover the exact core and platform it is operating on. The core is normally recognized by reading register 0 in coprocessor 15, which holds both the processor type and the manufacturer name. There are multiple ways to identify the platform, from checking for the existence of a set of particular peripherals to simply reading a preprogrammed chip.

Table 10.1   Firmware execution flow.

Stage	Features
Set up target platform	Program the hardware system registers
	Platform identification
	Diagnostics
	Debug interface
	Command line interpreter
Abstract the hardware	Hardware Abstraction Layer
	Device driver
Load a bootable image	Basic filing system
Relinquish control	Alter the *pc* to point into the new image

Diagnostics software provides a useful way for quickly identifying basic hardware malfunctions. Because of the nature of this type of software, it tends to be specific to a particular piece of hardware.

Debug capabiliy is provided in the form of a module or monitor that provides software assistance for debugging code running on a hardware target. This assistance includes the following:

- Setting up breakpoints in RAM. A breakpoint allows a program to be interrupted and the state of the processor core to be examined.

- Listing and modifying memory (using peek and poke operations).

- Showing current processor register contents.

- Disassembling memory into ARM and Thumb instruction mnemonics.

These are interactive functions: you can either send the commands through a command line interpreter (CLI) or through a dedicated host debugger attached to the target platform. Unless the firmware has access to the internal hardware debug circuitry, only RAM images can be debugged through a software debug mechanism.

The CLI is commonly available on the more advanced firmware implementations. It allows you to change the operating system to be booted by altering the default configurations through typing commands at a command prompt. For embedded systems, the CLI is commonly controlled through a host terminal application. Communication between the host and the target is normally over a serial or network connection.

The second stage is to abstract the hardware. The *Hardware Abstraction Layer* (HAL) is a software layer that hides the underlying hardware by providing a set of defined programming interfaces. When you move to a new target platform, these programming interfaces remain constant but the underlying implementation changes. For instance, two target platforms might use a different timer peripheral. Each peripheral would require new code to initialize and configure the device. The HAL programming interface would remain unaltered even though both the hardware and software may differ greatly between implementations.

The HAL software that communicates with specific hardware peripherals is called a *device driver*. A device driver provides a standard application programming interface (API) to read and write to a specific peripheral.

The third stage is to load a bootable image. The ability of firmware to carry out this activity depends upon the type of media used to store the image. Note that not all operating system images or application images need to be copied into RAM. The operating system image or application image can simply execute directly from ROM.

ARM processors are normally found in small devices that include flash ROM. A common feature is a simple flash ROM filing system (FFS), which allows multiple executable images to be stored.

Other media devices, such as hard drives, require that the firmware incorporates a device driver that is suitable for accessing the hardware. Accessing the hardware requires that the firmware has knowledge of the underlying filing system format, which gives the firmware the ability to read the filing system, find the file that contains the image, and copy the image into memory. Similarly, if the image is on the network, then the firmware must also understand the network protocol as well as the Ethernet hardware.

The load process has to take into account the image format. The most basic image format is plain binary. A plain binary image does not contain any header or debug information. A popular image format for ARM-based systems is Executable and Linking Format (ELF). This format was originally developed for UNIX systems and replaced the older format called Common Object File Format (COFF). ELF files come in three forms: relocatable, executable, and shared object.

Most firmware systems must deal with the executable form. Loading an ELF image involves deciphering the standard ELF header information (that is, execution address, type, size, and so on). The image may also be encrypted or compressed, in which case the load process would involve performing decryption or decompression on the image.

The fourth stage is to relinquish control. This is where the firmware hands over control of the platform to an operating system or application. Note that not all firmware hands over control; instead the firmware can remain the controlling software on the platform.

Firmware designed to pass control to an operating system may become inactive once the operating system has control. Alternatively, the Machine Independent Layer (MIL) or Hardware Abstraction Layer (HAL) part of the firmware can remain active. This layer exposes, through the SWI mechanism, a standard application interface for specific hardware devices.

Relinquishing control on an ARM system means updating the vector table and modifying the *pc*. Updating the vector table involves modifying particular exception and interrupt vectors so that they point to specialized operating system handlers. The *pc* has to be modified so that it points to the operating system entry point address.

For more sophisticated operating systems, such as Linux, relinquishing control requires that a standard data structure be passed to the kernel. This data structure explains the environment that the kernel will be running in. For example, one field may include the amount of available RAM on the platform, while another field includes the type of MMU being used.

We use these definitions to describe two common firmware suites.

10.1.1 ARM FIRMWARE SUITE

ARM has developed a firmware package called the ARM Firmware Suite (AFS). AFS is designed purely for ARM-based embedded systems. It provides support for a number of boards and processors including the Intel XScale and StrongARM processors. The package includes two major pieces of technology, a Hardware Abstraction Layer called μHAL (pronounced micro-HAL) and a debug monitor called Angel.

μHAL provides a low-level device driver framework that allows it to operate over different communication devices (for example, USB, Ethernet, or serial). It also provides a standard API. Consequently, when a port takes place, the various hardware-specific parts must be implemented in accordance with the various μHAL API functions.

This has the advantage of making the porting process relatively straightforward since you have a standard function framework to work within. Once the firmware is ported, the task of moving an operating system over to the new target platform can take place. The speed of this activity depends upon whether the OS takes advantage of the ported μHAL API call to access the hardware.

μHAL supports these main features:

- *System initialization*—setting up the target platform and processor core. Depending upon the complexity of the target platform, this can either be a simple or complicated task.

- *Polled serial driver*—used to provide a basic method of communication with a host.

- *LED support*—allows control over the LEDs for simple user feedback. This provides an application the ability to display operational status.

- *Timer support*—allows a periodic interrupt to be set up. This is essential for preemptive context switching operating systems that require this mechanism.

- *Interrupt controllers*—support for different interrupt controllers.

The boot monitor in μHAL contains a CLI.

The second technology, Angel, allows communication between a host debugger and a target platform. It allows you to inspect and modify memory, download and execute images, set breakpoints, and display processor register contents. All this control is through the host debugger. The Angel debug monitor must have access to the SWI and IRQ or FIQ vectors.

Angel uses SWI instructions to provides a set of APIs that allow a program to open, read, and write to a host filing system. IRQ/FIQ interrupts are used for communication purposes with the host debugger.

10.1.2 RED HAT REDBOOT

RedBoot is a firmware tool developed by Red Hat. It is provided under an open source license with no royalties or up front fees. RedBoot is designed to execute on different CPUs (for instance, ARM, MIPS, SH, and so on). It provides both debug capability through GNU Debugger (GDB), as well as a bootloader. The RedBoot software core is based on a HAL.

RedBoot supports these main features:

- *Communication*—configuration is over serial or Ethernet. For serial, X-Modem protocol is used to communicate with the GNU Debugger (GDB). For Ethernet, TCP is used to communicate with GDB. RedBoot supports a range of network standards, such as *bootp*, *telnet*, and *tftp*.

- *Flash ROM memory management*—provides a set of filing system routines that can download, update, and erase images in flash ROM. In addition, the images can either be compressed or uncompressed.

- *Full operating system support*—supports the loading and booting of Embedded Linux, Red Hat eCos, and many other popular operating systems. For Embedded Linux, RedBoot supports the ability to define parameters that are passed directly to the kernel upon booting.

10.2 EXAMPLE: SANDSTONE

We have designed Sandstone to be a minimal system. It carries out only the following tasks: set up target platform environment, load a bootable image into memory, and relinquish control to an operating system. It is, however, still a real working example.

The implementation is specific to the ARM Evaluator-7T platform, which includes an ARM7TDMI processor. This example shows you exactly how a simple platform can be set up and a software payload can be loaded into memory and booted. The payload can either be an application or operating system image. Sandstone is a static design and cannot be configured after the build process is complete. Table 10.2 lists the basic characteristics of Sandstone.

We will walk you through the directory layout and code structure. The directory layout shows you where the source code is located and where the different build files are placed. The code structure focuses more on the actual initialization and boot process.

Note that Sandstone is written entirely in ARM assembler and is a working piece of code that can be used to intialize target hardware and boot any piece of software, within reason, on the ARM Evaluator-7T.

10.2.1 SANDSTONE DIRECTORY LAYOUT

Sandstone can be found on our Web site. If you take a look at Sandstone, you will see that the directory structure is as shown in Figure 10.1. The structure follows a standard style

Table 10.2 Summary of Sandstone.

Feature	Configuration
Code	ARM instructions only
Tool chain	ARM Developer Suite 1.2
Image size	700 bytes
Source	17 KB
Memory	remapped

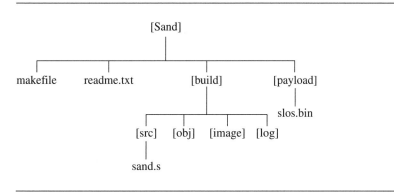

Figure 10.1 Standstone directory layout.

that we will continue to use in further chapters. The sandstone source file sand.s is located under the sand/build/src directory.

The object file produced by the assembler is placed under the build/obj directory. The object file is then linked, and the final Sandstone image is placed under the sand/build/image directory. This image includes both the Sandstone code and the payload. The payload image, the image that is loaded and booted by Sandstone, is found under the sand/payload directory.

For information about the Sandstone build procedure, take a look at the readme.txt file under the sand directory. This file contains a description of how to build the example binary image for the ARM Evaluator-7T.

10.2.2 SANDSTONE CODE STRUCTURE

Sandstone consists of a single assembly file. The file structure is broken down into a number of steps, where each step corresponds to a stage in the execution flow of Sandstone (see Table 10.3).

Table 10.3 Sandstone execution flow.

Step	Description
1	Take the Reset exception
2	Start initializing the hardware
3	Remap memory
4	Initialize communication hardware
5	Bootloader—copy payload and relinquish control

We will take you through these steps, trying to avoid as much as possible the platform-specific parts. You should note that some specific parts are unavoidable (for example, configuring system registers and memory remapping).

The initial goal of Sandstone is to set up the target platform environment so that it can provide some form of feedback to indicate that the firmware is running and has control of the platform.

10.2.2.1   Step 1: Take the Reset Exception

Execution begins with a Reset exception. Only the reset vector entry is required in the default vector table. It is the very first instruction executed. You can see from the code here that all the vectors, apart from the reset vector, branch to a unique *dummy handler*—a branch instruction that causes an infinite loop. It is assumed that no exception or interrupt will occur during the operation of Sandstone. The reset vector is used to move the execution flow to the second stage.

```
        AREA start,CODE,READONLY
        ENTRY


sandstone_start
        B       sandstone_init1     ; reset vector
        B       ex_und              ; undefined vector
        B       ex_swi              ; swi vector
        B       ex_pabt             ; prefetch abort vector
        B       ex_dabt             ; data abort vector
        NOP                         ; not used...
        B       int_irq             ; irq vector
        B       int_fiq             ; fiq vector


ex_und  B       ex_und              ; loop forever
ex_swi  B       ex_swi              ; loop forever
ex_dabt B       ex_dabt             ; loop forever
ex_pabt B       ex_pabt             ; loop forever
int_irq B       int_irq             ; loop forever
int_fiq B       int_fiq             ; loop forever
```

`sandstone_start` is located at address 0x00000000.

The results of executing step 1 are the following:

- Dummy handlers are set up.

- Control is passed to code to initialize the hardware.

10.2.2.2   Step 2: Start Initializing the Hardware

The primary phase in initializing hardware is setting up system registers. These registers have to be set up before accessing the hardware. For example, the ARM Evaluator-7T has a seven-segment display, which we have chosen to be used as a feedback tool to indicate that the firmware is active. Before we can set up the segment display, we have to position the base address of the system registers to a known location. In this case, we have picked the default address 0x03ff0000, since this places all the hardware system registers away from both ROM and RAM, separating the peripherals and memory.

Consequently, all the microcontroller memory-mapped registers are located as an offset from 0x03ff0000. This is achieved using the following code:

```
sandstone_init1
        LDR     r3, =SYSCFG        ; where SYSCFG=0x03ff0000
        LDR     r4, =0x03ffffa0
        STR     r4, [r3]
```

Register *r3* contains the default system register base address and is used to set the new default address, as well as other specific attributes such as the cache. Register *r4* contains the new configuration. The top 16 bits contain the high address of the new system register base address 0x03ff, and the lower 16 bits contain the new attribute settings 0xffa0.

After setting up the system register base address, the segment display can be configured. The segment display hardware is used to show Sandstone's progress. Note that the segment display is not shown since it is hardware specific.

The results of executing step 2 are the following:

- The system registers are set from a known base address—0x03ff0000.
- The segment display is configured, so that it can be used to display progress.

10.2.2.3   Step 3: Remap Memory

One of the major activities of hardware initialization is to set up the memory environment. Sandstone is designed to initialize SRAM and remap memory. This process occurs fairly early on in the initialization of the system. The platform starts in a known memory state, as shown in Table 10.4.

As you can see, when the platform is powered up, only flash ROM is assigned a location in the memory map. The two SRAM banks (0 and 1) have not been initialized and are not available. The next stage is to bring in the two SRAM banks and remap flash ROM to a new location. This is achieved using the following code:

```
        LDR     r14, =sandstone_init2
        LDR     r4, =0x01800000          ; new flash ROM location
```

Table 10.4   Initial memory state.

Memory type	Start address	End address	Size
Flash ROM	0x00000000	0x00080000	512K
SRAM bank 0	Unavailable	unavailable	256K
SRAM bank 1	Unavailable	unavailable	256K

```
        ADD     r14, r14, r4
        ADRL    r0, memorymaptable_str
        LDMIA   r0, {r1-r12}
        LDR     r0, =EXTDBWTH              ; =(SYSCFG + 0x3010)
        STMIA   r0, {r1-r12}
        MOV     pc, r14                    ; jump to remapped memory

sandstone_init2
        ; Code after sandstone_init2 executes @ +0x1800000
```

The first part of the code calculates the absolute address of the routine *sandstone_init2* before remapping takes place. This address is used by Sandstone to jump to the next routine in the new remapped environment.

The second part carries out the memory remapping. The new memory map data is loaded into registers *r1* to *r12*, from a structure pointed by memorymaptable_str. This structure, using the registers, is then written to the memory controller offset 0x3010 from system configuration register. Once this is complete, the new memory map as shown in Table 10.5 is active.

You can see that the SRAM banks are now available, and the flash ROM is set to a higher address. The final part is to jump to the next routine, or stage, of the firmware.

This jump is achieved by taking advantage of the ARM pipeline. Even though the new memory environment is active, the next instruction has already been loaded into the pipeline. The next routine can be called by moving the contents of register *r14* (the address sandstone_init2) into the *pc*. We achieve this by using a single MOV instruction that follows immediately after the remap code.

Table 10.5   Remapping.

Type	Start address	End address	Size
Flash ROM	0x01800000	0x01880000	512K
SRAM bank 0	0x00000000	0x00040000	256K
SRAM bank 1	0x00040000	0x00080000	256K

The results of executing step 3 are the following:

- Memory has been remapped as shown in Table 10.5.

- *pc* now points to the next step. This address is located in the newly remapped flash ROM.

10.2.2.4   Step 4: Initialize Communication Hardware

Communication initialization involves configuring a serial port and outputting a standard banner. The banner is used to show that the firmware is fully functional and memory has been successfully remapped. Again, because the code for initializing the serial port on the ARM Evaluator-7T is hardware specific, it is not shown.

The serial port is set to 9600 baud, no parity, one stop bit, and no flow control. If a serial cable is attached to the board, then the host terminal has to be configured with these settings.

The results of executing step 4 are the following:

- Serial port initialized—9600 baud, no parity, one stop bit, and no flow control.

- Sandstone banner sent out through the serial port:

```
Sandstone Firmware (0.01)
- platform ........ e7t
- status .......... alive
- memory .......... remapped

+ booting payload ...
```

10.2.2.5   Step 5: Bootloader—Copy Payload and Relinquish Control

The final stage involves copying a payload and relinquishing control of the *pc* over to the copied payload. This is achieved using the code shown here. The first part of the code sets up the registers *r12*, *r13*, and *r14* used in the block copy. The bootloader code assumes that the payload is a plain binary image that requires no deciphering or uncompressing.

```
sandstone_load_and_boot
        MOV     r13,#0                  ; destination addr
        LDR     r12,payload_start_address ; start addr
        LDR     r14,payload_end_address   ; end addr
```

```
_copy
        LDMIA   r12!,{r0-r11}
        STMIA   r13!,{r0-r11}
        CMP     r12,r14
        BLT     _copy
        MOV     pc,#0


payload_start_address
        DCD     startAddress
payload_end_address
        DCD     endAddress
```

Destination register *r13* points to the beginning of SRAM, in this case 0x00000000. The source register *r12* points to the start of the payload, and the source end register *r14* points to the end of the payload. Using these registers, the payload is then copied into SRAM.

Control of the *pc* is then relinquished to the payload by forcing the *pc* to the entry address of the copied payload. For this particular payload the entry point is address 0x00000000. The payload now has control of the system.

The results of executing step 5 are the following:

- Payload copied into SRAM, address 0x00000000.

- Control of the *pc* is relinquished to the payload; *pc* = 0x00000000.

- The system is completely booted. The following output is shown on the serial port:

```
Sandstone Firmware (0.01)

- platform ........ e7t

- status .......... alive

- memory .......... remapped


+ booting payload ...


Simple Little OS (0.09)

- initialized ...... ok

- running on ....... e7t


e7t:
```

10.3 SUMMARY

This chapter covered the firmware. We defined *firmware* as the low-level code that interfaces the hardware with an application or operating system. We also defined the *bootloader* as the software that loads an operating system or application into memory and relinquishes control of the *pc* to that software.

We introduced the ARM Firmware Suite and RedBoot. The ARM Firmware Suite is designed only for ARM-based systems. RedBoot, however, is more generic and can be used on other, non-ARM processors.

Next we looked at a firmware example called Sandstone. Sandstone initializes the hardware and then loads and boots an image following this procedure:

- Takes the Reset exception.
- Starts initializing the hardware; sets the system register's base address and initializes segment display hardware.
- Remaps memory; ROM address = high addr and SRAM addr = 0x00000000.
- Initializes the communication hardware output on the serial port.
- Bootloader—loads an image into SRAM and relinquishes control of the *pc* to the image (*pc* = 0x00000000).

We now have a fully initialized ARM7TDMI embedded system.

EMBEDDED OPERATING SYSTEMS

This chapter discusses the implementation of embedded operating systems (OS). Because embedded operating systems are designed for a specific purpose, historically embedded operating systems were simple, time constrained, and operated in limited memory. This distinction has changed over time as the sophistication of embedded hardware has increased. Features, traditionally found on desktop computers, such as virtual memory, have migrated into the embedded system world.

Since this is a large subject, we have limited our scope to just the fundamental components that make up an embedded operating system. We also build on the firmware example shown in Chapter 10.

This chapter is divided into two sections: The first section takes you through the fundamental components that make up an embedded operating system and notes issues specific to ARM processors. The second section takes you through an example operating system called the Simple Little Operating System (SLOS). SLOS is designed to show an implementation of the fundamental components.

11.1 FUNDAMENTAL COMPONENTS

There is a common set of low-level components, each carrying out a prescribed action, that form an operating system. It is how these components interact and function that determines the characteristics of a specific operating system.

Initialization is the first code of the operating system to execute and involves setting up internal data structures, global variables, and the hardware. Initialization starts after the firmware hands over control. For hardware initialization an operating system sets up various control registers, initializes the device drivers, and, if the operating system is preemptive, sets up a periodic interrupt.

Memory handling involves setting up the system and task stacks. The positioning of the stacks determines how much memory is available for either the tasks or the system. The decision as to where the system stack is placed is normally carried out during operating system initialization. Setting up the task stack depends upon whether the task is static or dynamic.

A static task is defined at build time and is included in the operating system image. For these tasks the stack can be set up during operating system initialization. For example, SLOS is a static-task-based operating system.

A dynamic task loads and executes after the operating system is installed and executing and is not part of the operating system image. The stack is set up when the task is created (for example, as in Linux). Memory handling varies in complexity from one operating system to another. It depends upon a number of factors, such as the ARM processor core selected, the capabilities of the microcontroller, and the physical memory layout of the end target hardware.

The example operating system, SLOS, in Section 11.2 uses a static memory design. It simply configures a set of registers within the microcontroller and positions the stacks. Because there is no form of dynamic memory management, you will not find an implementation of `malloc()` and `free()`. These functions are normally found in the standard C library.

The method for *handling interrupts and exceptions* is part of the architecture design of the operating system. You have to decide how to handle the various exceptions: Data Abort, Fast Interrupt Request, Interrupt Request, Prefetch Abort, Reset, and Software Interrupt (SWI).

Not all of the exceptions require a handler. For instance, if you have a target board that does not use the FIQ interrupt, then a specific FIQ handler is not required. It is always safer to provide an infinite loop as a default handler for unused exceptions. This approach makes it easy to debug: when you break, it is clear that you have trapped at a specific handler. It also protects the system from unexpected exceptions.

A preemptive operating system like SLOS requires a *periodic interrupt*, which is normally produced by a counter/timer device on the target hardware. As part of the initialization stage, an operating system sets the periodic interrupt frequency. This is normally achieved by setting a specified value into one of the counter/timer memory-mapped registers.

When activated, the counter/timer will start to decrement this value. Once the value reaches zero, an interrupt is raised. This interrupt is then handled by the appropriate ISR for periodic interrupts. The ISR first reinitializes the counter/timer with a new start value and then calls either a scheduler or another specialized routine.

In contrast, a nonpreemptive operating system does not require a periodic interrupt and will use a different technique, for example, *polling*—the continuous checking for a state change in a device. If the device state changes, then a specific action can be connected to a particular state change.

The *scheduler* is an algorithm that determines which task is to be executed next. There are many scheduling algorithms available. One of the simplest is called a *round-robin algorithm*—it activates tasks in a fixed cyclic order. Scheduling algorithms have to balance efficiency and size with complexity.

Once the scheduler is complete, the new and old tasks have to be swapped with a *context switch*. A context switch saves all the old task registers from the processor into a data structure. Data for the new task is then loaded into the processor's registers. (For more details on this procedure, take a look at Section 11.2.6.)

The last component is the *device driver framework*—the mechanism an operating system uses to provide a consistent interface between different hardware peripherals. The framework allows a standard and easy way of integrating new support for a particular peripheral into the operating system. For an application to access a particular peripheral there has to be a specific device driver available. The framework must provide a safe method of accessing the peripheral (for example, not allowing the simultaneous access of the same peripheral by more than one application).

11.2 EXAMPLE: SIMPLE LITTLE OPERATING SYSTEM

We have developed a small operating system we call the Simple Little Operating System (SLOS). It shows how the fundamental components discussed earlier come together in a complete operating system. We have chosen the ARM7TDMI since it is the simplest core in the ARM family. For a development environment we use the ARM Developers' Suite version 1.2, and for a target the Evaluator-7T from ARM. It should be relatively easy to modify SLOS to build in other development environments. SLOS is loaded and executed using the Sandstone firmware described in Chapter 10.

SLOS is a preemptive operating system. A periodic interrupt activates a dormant task. For simplicity, all the tasks and device drivers are static; that is, they are created at build time and not while the system is running. SLOS also provides a device driver framework, discussed in Section 11.2.7.

SLOS is designed to execute on an ARM7TDMI core with no memory management unit or protection unit. It is assumed that the memory map has already been configured by the initialization code (in this case, Sandstone, found in Chapter 10). SRAM is required to be located between 0x00000000 to 0x00080000, and the base configuration registers must be set to address 0x03ff0000.

SLOS is loaded at address 0x00000000, where the vector table is located. This is the same address as the entry point into SLOS. It is important that the ARM processor is in *SVC* mode when the firmware hands over control because *SVC* mode is a privileged mode and hence allows the initialization code to change modes by accessing the *cpsr*. We take advantage of this to set up the stacks in *IRQ* and *system* mode.

In this current configuration, SLOS includes three tasks and two service routines. Tasks 1 and 2 provide an example of mutual exclusion using a binary semaphore. The two service routines implemented are the periodic timer (which is essential) and a push-button interrupt (which is optional). Task 3 provides a simple command line interface through one of the ARM Evaluator-7T's serial ports.

Each task in SLOS requires its own stack. All the tasks operate in *user* mode; thus, a task can read but not write to the *cpsr*. The only way a task can change to a privileged mode is to use an SWI instruction call. This is the mechanism used to call a device driver function, since a device driver may require full access to the *cpsr*.

The *cpsr* can be modified in a task, but only indirectly using an instruction that updates the condition flags.

11.2.1 SLOS DIRECTORY LAYOUT

SLOS can be found on our Web site under the Chapter 11 directory. The directory layout for SLOS is similar to the Sandstone firmware layout (see Figures 10.1 and 11.1).

There are six subdirectories under *slos/build/src* that hold all the operating system source files. The *slos/build/src/core* directory includes the miscellaneous utility files, as well as the command line interpreter (CLI) sources.

Specific code for a platform is stored under a directory with the name of that platform. For instance, the code for the Evaluator-7T is stored under directory *e7t*.

The slos/build/src/e7t/devices directory holds all the device driver files, and the slos/build/src/e7t/events directory holds the files that handle services, exceptions, and interrupts.

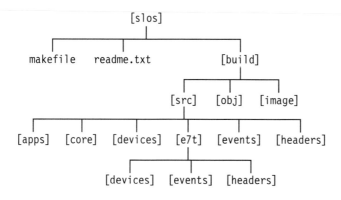

Figure 11.1   SLOS directory layout.

Finally, the `slos/build/src/apps` directory holds all the applications/tasks for a particular configuration. For instance, for the Evaluator-7T implementation, there are three applications/tasks.

11.2.2 INITIALIZATION

There are three main stages of initializing SLOS—startup, executing process control block (PCB) setup code, and executing the C initialization code. The startup code sets up the FIQ registers and the *system*, *SVC*, and *IRQ* mode stacks. In the next stage, the PCB, which contains the state of each task, is set up, including all the ARM registers. It is used to store and restore task state during a context switch. The setup code sets the process control block to an initial start state. The final C initialization stage calls the device driver, event handler, and periodic timer initialization routines. Once complete, the first task can be invoked.

Control is passed to SLOS through the reset vector. The `vectorReset` is a location in memory that holds the start address of the initialization code. It is assumed that the firmware has left the processor in *SVC* mode, which allows the operating system initialization code to have full access to the *cpsr*. The first operating system instruction loads the *pc* with the start address of the initialization code, or `coreInitialization`. You can see from the vector table, shown here, that this instruction loads a word using the load *pc*-relative instruction. The assembler tool has already calculated the offset value using the difference between the *pc* and the address of the `vectorReset`.

```
    AREA ENTRYSLOS,CODE,READONLY
    ENTRY

    LDR     pc, vectorReset
    LDR     pc, vectorUndefined
    LDR     pc, vectorSWI
    LDR     pc, vectorPrefetchAbort
    LDR     pc, vectorDataAbort
    LDR     pc, vectorReserved
    LDR     pc, vectorIRQ
    LDR     pc, vectorFIQ

vectorReset             DCD     coreInitialize
vectorUndefined         DCD     coreUndefinedHandler
vectorSWI               DCD     coreSWIHandler
vectorPrefetchAbort     DCD     corePrefetchAbortHandler
vectorDataAbort         DCD     coreDataAbortHandler
vectorReserved          DCD     coreReservedHandler
vectorIRQ               DCD     coreIRQHandler
vectorFIQ               DCD     coreFIQHandler
```

As part of the initialization process we have implemented a low-level debug system using the banked *FIQ* mode registers, as shown here. These registers are used to store status information. It is not always possible to use FIQ registers since they may be used for another purpose.

```
bringupInitFIQRegisters
        MOV     r2,r14                  ; save r14
        BL      switchToFIQMode         ; change FIQ mode
        MOV     r8,#0                   ; r8_fiq=0
        MOV     r9,#0                   ; r9_fiq=0
        MOV     r10,#0                  ; r10_fiq=0
        BL      switchToSVCMode         ; change SVC mode
        MOV     pc,r2                   ; return


coreInitialize
        BL      bringupInitFIQRegisters
```

The next stage is to set up the SVC, IRQ, and System base stack registers. For the SVC stack, this is straightforward since the processor is already in *SVC* mode. The code is

```
        MOV     sp,#0x80000                     ; SVC stack
        MSR     cpsr_c,#NoInt|SYS32md
        MOV     sp,#0x40000                     ; user/system stack
        MSR     cpsr_c,#NoInt|IRQ32md
        MOV     sp,#0x9000                      ; IRQ stack
        MSR     cpsr_c,#NoInt|SVC32md
```

As you can see from the code, once the stacks are set up, the processor is switched back into *SVC* mode, which allows the rest of the initialization process to continue. Being in privileged mode allows the final initialization stage to unmask the IRQ interrupt by clearing the *I* bit and changing the processor to *user* mode.

The results of executing the startup code are the following:

- Low-level debug mechanism is initialized.
- SVC, IRQ, and System base stacks are set.

To start SLOS running, the PCB for each task has to be initialized. A PCB is a reserved data structure and holds a copy of the entire ARM register set (see Table 11.1). A task is made active by copying the appropriate task's PCB data into the processor registers.

The PCB of each task has to be set up prior to a context switch occurring since the switch will transfer the PCB data into registers *r0* to *r15* and *cpsr*. Left uninitialized, the context switch will copy garbage data into these registers.

Table 11.1   Process control block.

Offset	Registers
0	—
−4	*r14*
−8	*r13*
−12	*r12*
−16	*r11*
−20	*r10*
−24	*r9*
−28	*r8*
−32	*r7*
−36	*r6*
−40	*r5*
−44	*r4*
−48	*r3*
−52	*r2*
−56	*r1*
−60	*r0*
−64	*pc* + 4
−68	*spsr*

There are four major parts of the PCB that have to be initialized: the program counter, the link register, the *user* mode stack, and the saved processor status register (in other words registers *r13*, *r14*, *r15*, and the *spsr*) for each task.

```
        ; void pcbSetUp(void *entryAddr, void *PCB, UINT offset);
pcbSetUp
        STR    r0,[r1,#-4]      ; PCB[-4]=C_TaskEntry
        STR    r0,[r1,#-64]     ; PCB[-64]=C_TaskEntry
        SUB    r0,sp,r2
        STR    r0,[r1,#-8]      ; PCB[-8]=sp-<offset>
        MOV    r0,#0x50         ; cpsr_c
        STR    r0,[r1,#-68]     ; PCB[-68]=iFt_User
        MOV    pc,lr
```

To help illustrate this, we have extracted the routine for initializing PCBs. The routine *pcbSetUp* is called to set up tasks 2 and 3. Register *r0* is the task entry address—label *entryAddr*. This is the execution address for a task. Register *r1* is the PCB data structure address—label *pcbAddr*. This address points into a block of memory that stores the

PCB for a task. Register *r2* is the stack offset and is used to position the stack in the memory map. Note that task 1 does not require initialization since it is the first task to be executed.

The final part of setting up the PCBs is to set up the current task identifier, which is used by the scheduling algorithm to determine which task is to be executed.

```
LDR     r0,=PCB_CurrentTask
MOV     r1,#0
STR     r1,[r0]
LDR     lr,=C_Entry
MOV     pc,lr  ; enter the CEntry world
```

At the end of the code fragment the first C routine—*C_Entry*—is called by setting the *pc* to the start address of the routine.

The results of executing the PCB setup code are the following:

- Initialize the PCB for all three tasks.
- Set the current PCB to be executed as task 1 (identifier 0).

Initialization is now handed over to the C_Entry() routine, which can be found in build/src/core/cinit.c file. The C_Entry routine calls another routine, cinit_init(). This routine, shown here, initializes the device drivers, services, and finally the periodic interrupt tick. The C code has been designed so it does not require the standard C library to be initialized because it does not call any standard C library functions such as printf(), fopen(), and so on.

```
void cinit_init(void)
{
    eventIODeviceInit();
    eventServicesInit();
    eventTickInit(2);
}
```

The functions eventIODeviceInit, eventServicesInit, and eventTickInit are all called to initialize the various specific parts of the operating system. You will notice that eventTickInit has a single parameter with the value 2. This is used to set the number of milliseconds between periodic tick events.

After initialization is complete, the periodic timer can be started, as shown here. This means that task 1 needs to be called before the first timer interrupt. To allow for the periodic event to interrupt the processor, the IRQ has to be enabled and the processor has to be placed into *user* mode. Once this is accomplished, the address of the entry point for task 1, C_EntryTask1, is then called.

```
int C_Entry(void)
{
  cinit_init();
  eventTickStart();
  __asm
  {
  MSR       cpsr_c,#0x50
  }

  C_EntryTask1();
  return 0;
}
```

If everything is working correctly, the return at the end of C_Entry routine will never be executed. At this point all initialization is complete and the operating system is fully functional.

The results of executing all the C initialization code are the following:

- The device drivers are initialized.

- The services are initialized.

- The periodic timer tick is initialized and started.

- The IRQ interrupts are enabled in the *cpsr*.

- The processor is placed in *user* mode.

- The entry point to task 1 is called (i.e., C_EntryTask1).

11.2.3 MEMORY MODEL

We have adopted a simple memory model for SLOS. Figure 11.2 shows that the code portion of SLOS, including the tasks, are located in low memory, and the stacks for the IRQ and for each task are located in higher memory. The SVC stack is set at the top of memory. The arrows in the memory map show the direction of stack growth.

11.2.4 INTERRUPTS AND EXCEPTIONS HANDLING

In this implementation of the operating system only three exceptions are actually used. The other exceptions are ignored by going to specific dummy handlers, which for safety reasons are implemented as infinite loops. For a complete implementation these dummy handlers should be replaced with full handlers. Table 11.2 shows the three exceptions and how they are used within the operating system.

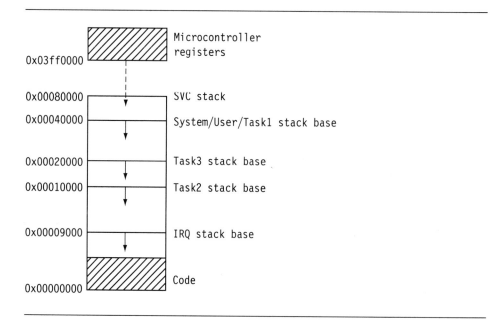

Figure 11.2   Memory map.

Table 11.2   Exception assignment.

Exception	Purpose
Reset	initialize the operating system
SWI	mechanism to access device drivers
IRQ	mechanism to service events

11.2.4.1   Reset Exception

The reset vector is only called once during the initialization phase. In theory, it could be called again to reinitialize the system—for example, in response to a watchdog timer event resetting the processor. Watchdog timers are used to reset a system when prolonged inactivity occurs.

11.2.4.2   SWI Exception

Whenever a device driver is called from an application, the call goes through the SWI handler mechanism. The SWI instruction forces the processor to change from *user* to *SVC* mode.

The core SWI handler is shown here. The first action of the handler is to store registers *r0* to *r12* to the SVC stack.

The next action calculates the address of the SWI instruction and loads that instruction into register *r10*. The SWI number is obtained by masking the top 8 bits. The address of the SVC stack is then copied into register *r1* and is used as the second parameter when calling the SWI C handler.

The *spsr* is then copied to register *r2* and stored on the stack. This is only required when a nested SWI call occurs. The handler then jumps to the code that calls the C handler routine.

```
coreSWIHandler
        STMFD   sp!,{r0-r12,r14}    ; save context
        LDR     r10,[r14,#-4]       ; load SWI instruction
        BIC     r10,r10,#0xff000000 ; mask off the MSB 8 bits
        MOV     r1,r13              ; copy r13_svc to r1
        MRS     r2,spsr             ; copy spsr to r2
        STMFD   r13!,{r2}           ; save r2 onto the stack
        BL      swi_jumptable       ; branch to the swi_jumptable
```

The code that follows the BL instruction returns back to the callee program as shown here. This is achieved by restoring the *spsr* from the stack and loading all the user banked registers back, including the *pc*.

```
        LDMFD   r13!,{r2}           ; restore the r2 (spsr)
        MSR     spsr_cxsf,r2        ; copy r2 back to spsr
        LDMFD   r13!,{r0-r12,pc}^   ; restore context and return
```

The link register has been set in the BL instruction. This code is executed when the SWI C handler is complete.

```
swi_jumptable
        MOV     r0,r10              ; move the SWI number to r0
        B       eventsSWIHandler    ; branch to SWI handler
```

The C handler, `eventsSWIHandler`, shown in Figure 11.3, is called with register *r0* containing the SWI number and register *r1* pointing to the registers stored on the SVC stack.

```
void eventsSWIHandler(int swi_number, SwiRegs *r)
{
  if (swi_number==SLOS)
  {
    if (r->r[0]==Event_IODeviceInit)
    {
    /* do not enable IRQ interrupts .... */
    io_initialize_drivers ();
    }
    else
    {
      /* if not initializing change to system mode
         and enable IRQs */
      if (STATE!=1) {modifyControlCPSR (SYSTEM|IRQoN);}

      switch (r->r[0])
      {
      case /* SWI */ Event_IODeviceOpen:
        r->r[0] =
          (unsigned int) io_open_driver
          (
          /*int *ID */ (UID *)r->r[1],
          /*unsigned major_device */ r->r[2],
          /*unsigned minor_device */ r->r[3]
          );
        break;
      case /* SWI */ Event_IODeviceClose:
        /* call io_open_driver */
        break;
      case /* SWI */ Event_IODeviceWriteByte:
        /* call io_writebyte_driver */
        break;
      case /* SWI */ Event_IODeviceReadByte:
        /* call io_readbyte_driver */
        break;
      case /* SWI */ Event_IODeviceWriteBit:
        /* call io_writebit_driver */
        break;
      case /* SWI */ Event_IODeviceReadBit:
        /* call io_readbit_driver */
        break;
```

Figure 11.3   SWI C handler.

```
      case /* SWI */ Event_IODeviceWriteBlock:
        /* call io_writeblock_driver */
        break;
      case /* SWI */ Event_IODeviceReadBlock:
        /* call io_readblock_driver */
        break;
    }
    /* if not initializing change back to svc mode
       and disable IRQs */
    if (STATE!=1) {modifyControlCPSR (SVC|IRQoFF);}
    }
  }
 }
}
```

Figure 11.3   SWI C handler. (*Continued.*)

11.2.4.3   IRQ Exception

The IRQ handler is a lot simpler than the SWI handler. It is implemented as a basic nonnested interrupt handler. The handler first saves the context and then copies the contents of the interrupt controller status register, INTPND, into register *r0*. Each service routine then compares register *r0* with a particular interrupt source. If the source and interrupt match, then the service routine is called; otherwise the interrupt is treated as being a phantom interrupt and ignored.

```
TICKINT   EQU 0x400
BUTTONINT EQU 0x001

eventsIRQHandler
        SUB     r14, r14, #4                ; r14_irq-=4
        STMFD   r13!, {r0-r3, r12, r14}     ; save context
        LDR     r0,INTPND                   ; r0=int pending reg
        LDR     r0,[r0]                     ; r0=memory[r0]
        TST     r0,#TICKINT                 ; if tick int
        BNE     eventsTickVeneer            ;   then tick ISR
        TST     r0,#BUTTONINT               ; if button interrupt
        BNE     eventsButtonVeneer          ;   then button ISR
        LDMFD   r13!, {r0-r3, r12, pc}^     ; return to task
```

For a known interrupt source an interrupt veneer is called to service the event. The following code shows an example timer veneer. You can see from the example that the veneer includes calling two routines: The first resets the timer, `eventsTickService` (platform-specific call), and the second, `kernelScheduler`, calls the scheduler, which in turn calls a context switch.

```
eventsTickVeneer
        BL      eventsTickService       ; reset tick hardware
        B       kernelScheduler         ; branch to scheduler
```

There is no requirement to have registers *r4* to *r12* on the IRQ stack, since the scheduling algorithm and the context switch handle all the register details.

11.2.5 SCHEDULER

The low-level scheduler, or dispatcher, used in SLOS is a simple static round-robin algorithm as illustrated in the following pseudocode. "Static" in this case means that the tasks are only created when the operating system is initialized. Tasks in SLOS can neither be created nor destroyed when the operating system is active.

```
task t=0,t';

scheduler()
{
  t' = t + 1;
  if t' = MAX_NUMBER_OF_TASKS then
    t' = 0 // the first task.
  end;

  ContextSwitch(t,t')
}
```

As stated previously, the current active task *t*, *PCB_CurrentTask*, is set to 0 during the initialization phase. When the periodic tick interrupt occurs, the new task *t'* is calculated from the current task *t* plus 1. If this task number equals the task limit, `MAX_NUMBER_OF_TASKS`, then task *t'* is reset to the start 0.

Table 11.3 is a list of the labels used by the scheduler and a description of how they are used in the algorithm. These labels are used in the following procedure and code for the scheduler:

1. Obtain the current task ID by loading the contents of `PCB_CurrentTask`.

2. Find the corresponding PCB address of the current task by using the `PCB_CurrentTask` as the index into the `PCB_Table`.

3. Use the address obtained in stage 2 to update the value in the `PCB_PtrCurrentTask`.

Table 11.3   Labels used by the scheduler.

Label	Description
PCB_CurrentTask	contains the current task t
PCB_Table	table of address pointers to each task PCB
PCB_PtrCurrentTask	pointer to the current task t
PCB_PtrNextTask	pointer to the next task t'
PCB_IRQStack	temporary storage for the IRQ stack (context switch)

4. Calculate the new task t' ID using the round-robin algorithm.

5. Store the new task t' ID into PCB_CurrentTask.

6. Find the address of the next task PCB by indexing into the PCB_Table using the updated PCB_CurrentTask.

7. Store the next task PCB into PCB_PtrNextTask.

The code scheduling the next task t' is:

```
MaxNumTasks EQU 3
FirstTask   EQU 0

CurrentTask
        LDR     r3,=PCB_CurrentTask    ; [1] r3=PCB_CurrentTask
        LDR     r0,[r3]                ; r0= current Task ID
        LDR     r1,=PCB_Table          ; [2] r1=PCB_Table address
        LDR     r1,[r1,r0,LSL#2]       ; r1=mem32[r1+r0<<2]
        LDR     r2,=PCB_PtrCurrentTask ; [3] r2=PCB_PtrCurrentTask
        STR     r1,[r2]                ; mem32[r2]=r1 : task addr

; ** PCB_PtrCurrentTask - updated with the addr of the current task
; ** r2 = PCB_PtrCurrentTask address
; ** r1 = current task PCB address
; ** r0 = current task ID

NextTask
        ADD     r0,r0,#1               ; [4] r0 = (CurrentTaskID)+1
        CMP     r0,#MaxNumTasks        ; if r0==MaxNumTasks
        MOVEQ   r0,#FirstTask          ;    then r0 = FirstTask (0)
        STR     r0,[r3]                ; [5] mem32[r3]=next Task ID
        LDR     r1,=PCB_Table          ; [6] r1=PCB_Table addr
        LDR     r1,[r1,r0,LSL#2]       ; r1=memory[r1+r0<<2]
```

```
LDR    r0,=PCB_PtrNextTask    ; [7] r0=PCB_PtrNextTask
STR    r1,[r0]                ; memory[r0]=next task addr
```

The results of executing the scheduler are the following:

- PCB_PtrCurrentTask points to the address of the current active PCB.
- PCB_PtrNextTask points to the address of the next active PCB.
- PCB_CurrentTask holds the value of the next task identifier.

11.2.6 CONTEXT SWITCH

Using the updated information produced by the scheduler, the context switch then swaps the active task *t* with the next task *t′*. To achieve this, a context switch splits the activity into two stages, as shown in Figure 11.4. The first stage involves saving the processor registers into the current task *t* PCB pointed by PCB_PtrCurrentTask. The second stage loads the registers with data from the next *t′* PCB pointed by PCB_PtrNextTask.

We will now take you through the procedure and code of the two stages of the context switch, detailing the saving of the current context first, followed by loading a new context.

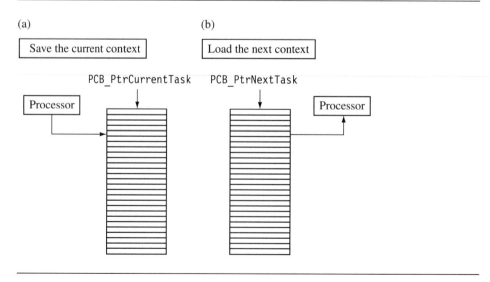

Figure 11.4   Context switch. (a) Save the Current Context (b) Load the Next Context

11.2.6.1   Save the Current Context

The first stage is to save the current registers of the active task *t*. All tasks execute in *user* mode, so the *user* mode registers have to be saved. Here is the procedure:

1. We must restore registers *r0* to *r3* and *r14* from the stack. These registers belong to the current task.
2. Register *r13* is then used to point into the PCB of the current task *PCB_CurrentTask* offset by −60. This offset allows two instructions to update the entire PCB.
3. The final action of the first stage is to store all the user bank registers *r0* to *r14*. This occurs in a single instruction. Remember that the ˆ symbol means that the store multiple acts on the *user* mode registers. The second store instruction saves the *spsr* and the returning link register.

The code for saving the registers to a PCB is

```
Offset15Regs EQU 15*4

handler_contextswitch
        LDMFD   r13!,{r0-r3,r12,r14}    ; [1.1] restore registers
        LDR     r13,=PCB_PtrCurrentTask ; [1.2]
        LDR     r13,[r13]               ; r13=mem32[r13]
        SUB     r13,r13,#Offset15Regs   ; r13-=15*Reg:place r13
        STMIA   r13,{r0-r14}ˆ           ; [1.3] save user mode registers
        MRS     r0, spsr                ; copy spsr
        STMDB   r13,{r0,r14}            ; save r0(spsr) & r14(lr)
```

The results of saving the current context are the following:

- The IRQ stack is reset and saved to *PCB_IRQStack*.
- The *user* mode registers for task *t* are saved to the current PCB.

11.2.6.2   Load the Next Context

The second stage of the context switch involves transferring the PCB for *t'* into the banked *user* mode registers. Once complete, the routine then must hand over control to the new task *t'*. Here is the procedure:

1. Load and position register *r13* at offset −60 from the start of the new PCB.
2. Load register *spsr* and the link register first. Then the next task registers *r0* to *r14* are loaded. Register *r14* is the user bank register *r14*, not the IRQ register *r14* shown by ˆ in the instruction.

3. The IRQ stack is then restored from *PCB_IRQStack.*

4. The new task is resumed by copying the address held in register *r14* into the *pc* and updating the *cpsr.*

The code for loading the registers from a PCB is

```
LDR     r13,=PCB_PtrNextTask  ; [2.1] r13=PCB_PtrNextTask
LDR     r13,[r13]             ; r13=mem32[r13] : next PCB
SUB     r13,r13,#Offset15Regs ; r13-=15*Registers
LDMDB   r13,{r0,r14}          ; [2.2] load r0 & r14
MSR     spsr_cxsf, r0         ; spsr = r0
LDMIA   r13,{r0-r14}^         ; load r0_user-r14_user
LDR     r13,=PCB_IRQStack     ; [2.3] r13=IRQ stack addr
LDR     r13,[r13]             ; r13=mem32[r13] : reset IRQ
MOVS    pc,r14                ; [2.4] return to next task
```

The results of loading the next context are the following:

■ The context switch is complete.

■ The next task's registers are loaded into the *user* mode registers.

■ The IRQ stack is restored to the original setting before entering the IRQ handler.

11.2.7 DEVICE DRIVER FRAMEWORK

The device driver framework (DDF) is implemented using SWI instructions. The DDF protects the operating system from applications accessing hardware directly and provides a uniform standard interface for the tasks. For a task to access a particular device it must first obtain a unique identification number (UID). This is achieved by calling the open macro, or *eventsIODeviceOpen.* This macro is translated directly into a device driver *SWI* instruction. The UID is used to check that another task has not already accessed the same device.

The task code for opening a device driver is

```
device_treestr *host;
UID serial;
```

```
host = eventIODeviceOpen(&serial,DEVICE_SERIAL_E7T,COM1);

  if (host==0)
  {
    /* ...error device driver not found...*/
  }

  switch (serial)
  {
  case DEVICE_IN_USE:
  case DEVICE_UNKNOWN:
   /* ...problem with device... */
  }
```

The example shows a serial device being opened using the device driver framework.

A set of macros translates the arguments into registers *r1* to *r3*. These registers are then passed through the SWI mechanism to the device driver function. In the example, only the value pointed to by *r1*, &serial, is actually updated. This value is used to return the UID. If the value returned is zero, then an error has occurred.

The following code shows how the macro eventIODeviceOpen is transformed into a single SWI instruction call:

```
PRE     r0 = Event_IODeviceOpen (unsigned int)
        r1 = &serial (UID *u)
        r2 = DEVICE_SERIAL_E7T (unsigned int major)
        r3 = COM1 (unsigned int minor)

        SWI     5075

POST    r1 = The data pointed to by the UID pointer is updated
```

The SWI interface is used as a method of changing to a privileged mode when the task executes in a nonprivileged mode. This allows the device driver to gain full access to the *cpsr*. Figure 11.5 shows the actual mode changes when a device driver function is called. You can see from the diagram that the device driver itself executes in *system* mode (which is privileged).

Once an SWI instruction is executed, the processor enters *SVC* mode and IRQ interrupts are automatically disabled. Interrupts are only reenabled when the processor changes to *system* mode. The only exception to this is when a device driver function is called during the initialization phase; in this case, interrupts will remain disabled.

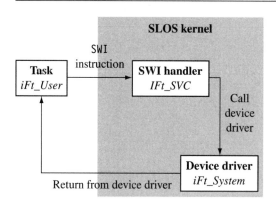

Figure 11.5   Calling a device driver.

11.3 SUMMARY

The fundamental components that make up an embedded operating system executing on an ARM processor are the following:

- The *initialization* sets up all of the internal variables, data structures, and hardware devices used by the operating system.

- *Memory handling* organizes the memory to accommodate the kernel plus the various applications to be executed.

- All interrupts and exceptions require a *handler*. For unused interrupts and exceptions, a dummy handler must be installed.

- A *periodic timer* is required for preemptive operating systems. The timer produces an interrupt that causes the scheduler to be called.

- A *scheduler* is an algorithm that determines the new task to be executed.

- A *context switch* saves the state of the current task and loads the state of the next task.

These components are exemplified in the operating system called the Simple Little Operating System (SLOS):

- *Initialization*—The initialization sets up all the functions of SLOS, including the bank mode stacks, process control blocks (PCB) for each application, device drivers, and so on.

- *Memory model*—The SLOS kernel is placed in lower memory, and each application has its own storage area and stack. The microcontroller system registers are placed away from the ROM and SRAM.

- *Interrupts and exceptions*—SLOS makes use of only three events. These events are Reset, SWI, and IRQ. All the other unused interrupts and exceptions have a dummy handler installed.

- *Scheduler*—SLOS implements a simple round-robin scheduler.

- *Context switch*—First the current context is saved into a PCB, and then the next task context is loaded from a PCB.

- *Device driver framework*—This protects the operating system from applications accessing hardware directly.

CHAPTER 12
CACHES

A *cache* is a small, fast array of memory placed between the processor core and main memory that stores portions of recently referenced main memory. The processor uses cache memory instead of main memory whenever possible to increase system performance. The goal of a cache is to reduce the memory access bottleneck imposed on the processor core by slow memory.

Often used with a cache is a *write buffer*—a very small first-in-first-out (FIFO) memory placed between the processor core and main memory. The purpose of a write buffer is to free the processor core and cache memory from the slow write time associated with writing to main memory.

The word *cache* is a French word meaning "a concealed place for storage." When applied to ARM embedded systems, this definition is very accurate. The cache memory and write buffer hardware when added to a processor core are designed to be transparent to software code execution, and thus previously written software does not need to be rewritten for use on a cached core. Both the cache and write buffer have additional control hardware that automatically handles the movement of code and data between the processor and main memory. However, knowing the details of a processor's cache design can help you create programs that run faster on a specific ARM core.

Since the majority of this chapter is about the wonderful things a cache can do to make programs run faster, the question arises, "Are there any drawbacks created by having a cache in your system?" The answer is yes. The main drawback is the difficulty of determining the execution time of a program. Why this is a problem will become evident shortly.

Since cache memory only represents a very small portion of main memory, the cache fills quickly during program execution. Once full, the cache controller frequently evicts existing code or data from cache memory to make more room for the new code or data. This eviction process tends to occur randomly, leaving some data in cache and removing others. Thus, at any given instant in time, a value may or may not be stored in cache memory.

Because data may or may not be present in cache at any given point in time, the execution time of a routine may vary slightly from run to run due to the difference between the time it takes to use data immediately out of cache memory and the time it takes to load a cache line from main memory.

So, with that caveat, we begin by showing where caches fit in a standard memory hierarchy and introduce the principle of locality of reference to explain why a cache improves system performance. We then describe cache architectures in general and define a set of terms used by the ARM community. We end the chapter with example code showing how to clean and flush caches and to lock code and data segments in cache.

12.1 The Memory Hierarchy and Cache Memory

In Chapter 1 we introduced the memory hierarchy in a computer system. Figure 12.1 reviews some of this information to show where a cache and write buffer fit in the hierarchy.

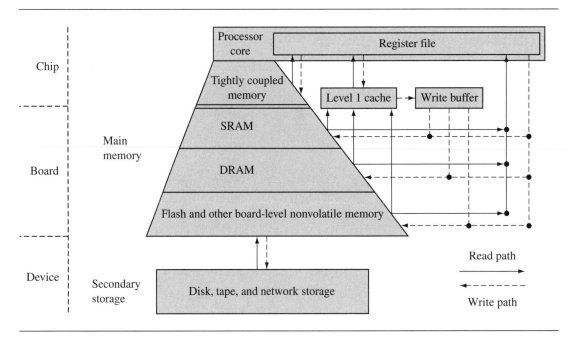

Figure 12.1   Memory hierarchy.

The innermost level of the hierarchy is at the processor core. This memory is so tightly coupled to the processor that in many ways it is difficult to think of it as separate from the processor. This memory is known as a *register file*. These registers are integral to the processor core and provide the fastest possible memory access in the system.

At the primary level, memory components are connected to the processor core through dedicated on-chip interfaces. It is at this level we find tightly coupled memory (TCM) and level 1 cache. We talk more about caches in a moment.

Also at the primary level is main memory. It includes volatile components like SRAM and DRAM, and nonvolatile components like flash memory. The purpose of main memory is to hold programs while they are running on a system.

The next level is secondary storage—large, slow, relatively inexpensive mass storage devices such as disk drives or removable memory. Also included in this level is data derived from peripheral devices, which are characterized by their extremely long access times. Secondary memory is used to store unused portions of very large programs that do not fit in main memory and programs that are not currently executing.

It is useful to note that a memory hierarchy depends as much on architectural design as on the technology surrounding it. For example, TCM and SRAM are of the same technology yet differ in architectural placement: TCM is located on the chip, while SRAM is located on a board.

A cache may be incorporated between any level in the hierarchy where there is a significant access time difference between memory components. A cache can improve system performance whenever such a difference exists. A cache memory system takes information stored in a lower level of the hierarchy and temporarily moves it to a higher level.

Figure 12.1 includes a level 1 (L1) cache and write buffer. The L1 cache is an array of high-speed, on-chip memory that temporarily holds code and data from a slower level. A cache holds this information to decrease the time required to access both instructions and data. The write buffer is a very small FIFO buffer that supports writes to main memory from the cache.

Not shown in the figure is a level 2 (L2) cache. An L2 cache is located between the L1 cache and slower memory. The L1 and L2 caches are also known as the *primary* and *secondary* caches.

Figure 12.2 shows the relationship that a cache has with main memory and the processor core. The upper half of the figure shows a block diagram of a system without a cache. Main memory is accessed directly by the processor core using the datatypes supported by the processor core. The lower half of the diagram shows a system with a cache. The cache memory is much faster than main memory and thus responds quickly to data requests by the core. The cache's relationship with main memory involves the transfer of small blocks of data between the slower main memory to the faster cache memory. These blocks of data are known as cache lines. The write buffer acts as a temporary buffer that frees available space in the cache memory. The cache transfers a cache line to the write buffer at high speed and then the write buffer drains it to main memory at slow speed.

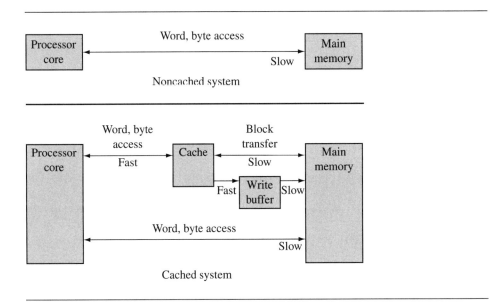

Figure 12.2   Relationship that a cache has between the processor core and main memory.

12.1.1   CACHES AND MEMORY MANAGEMENT UNITS

If a cached core supports virtual memory, it can be located between the core and the memory management unit (MMU), or between the MMU and physical memory. Placement of the cache before or after the MMU determines the addressing realm the cache operates in and how a programmer views the cache memory system. Figure 12.3 shows the difference between the two caches.

A *logical cache* stores data in a virtual address space. A logical cache is located between the processor and the MMU. The processor can access data from a logical cache directly without going through the MMU. A logical cache is also known as a *virtual cache.*

A *physical cache* stores memory using physical addresses. A physical cache is located between the MMU and main memory. For the processor to access memory, the MMU must first translate the virtual address to a physical address before the cache memory can provide data to the core.

ARM cached cores with an MMU use logical caches for processor families ARM7 through ARM10, including the Intel StrongARM and Intel XScale processors. The ARM11 processor family uses a physical cache. See Chapter 14 for additional information on the operation of the MMU.

The improvement a cache provides is possible because computer programs execute in nonrandom ways. Predictable program execution is the key to the success of cached systems. If a program's accesses to memory were random, a cache would provide little

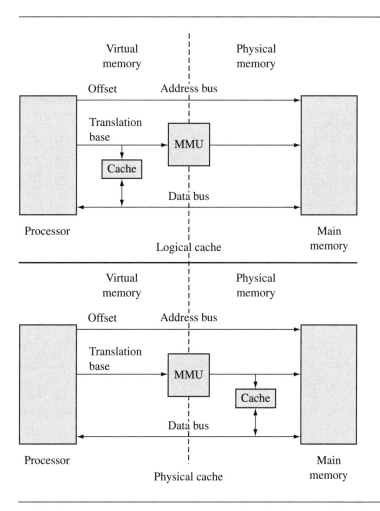

Figure 12.3 Logical and physical caches.

improvement to overall system performance. The principle of *locality of reference* explains the performance improvement provided by the addition of a cache memory to a system. This principle states that computer software programs frequently run small loops of code that repeatedly operate on local sections of data memory.

The repeated use of the same code or data in memory, or those very near, is the reason a cache improves performance. By loading the referenced code or data into faster memory when first accessed, each subsequent access will be much faster. It is the repeated access to the faster memory that improves performance.

The cache makes use of this repeated local reference in both time and space. If the reference is in time, it is called *temporal locality*. If it is by address proximity, then it is called *spatial locality*.

12.2   CACHE ARCHITECTURE

ARM uses two bus architectures in its cached cores, the Von Neumann and the Harvard. The Von Neumann and Harvard bus architectures differ in the separation of the instruction and data paths between the core and memory. A different cache design is used to support the two architectures.

In processor cores using the Von Neumann architecture, there is a single cache used for instruction and data. This type of cache is known as a *unified cache*. A unified cache memory contains both instruction and data values.

The Harvard architecture has separate instruction and data buses to improve overall system performance, but supporting the two buses requires two caches. In processor cores using the Harvard architecture, there are two caches: an instruction cache (I-cache) and a data cache (D-cache). This type of cache is known as a *split cache*. In a split cache, instructions are stored in the instruction cache and data values are stored in the data cache.

We introduce the basic architecture of caches by showing a unified cache in Figure 12.4. The two main elements of a cache are the cache *controller* and the cache *memory*. The cache memory is a dedicated memory array accessed in units called *cache lines*. The cache controller uses different portions of the address issued by the processor during a memory request to select parts of cache memory. We will present the architecture of the cache memory first and then proceed to the details of the cache controller.

12.2.1   BASIC ARCHITECTURE OF A CACHE MEMORY

A simple cache memory is shown on the right side of Figure 12.4. It has three main parts: a directory store, a data section, and status information. All three parts of the cache memory are present for each cache line.

The cache must know where the information stored in a cache line originates from in main memory. It uses a directory store to hold the address identifying where the cache line was copied from main memory. The directory entry is known as a *cache-tag*.

A cache memory must also store the data read from main memory. This information is held in the data section (see Figure 12.4).

The size of a cache is defined as the actual code or data the cache can store from main memory. Not included in the cache size is the cache memory required to support cache-tags or status bits.

There are also status bits in cache memory to maintain state information. Two common status bits are the valid bit and dirty bit. A *valid* bit marks a cache line as active, meaning it contains live data originally taken from main memory and is currently available to the

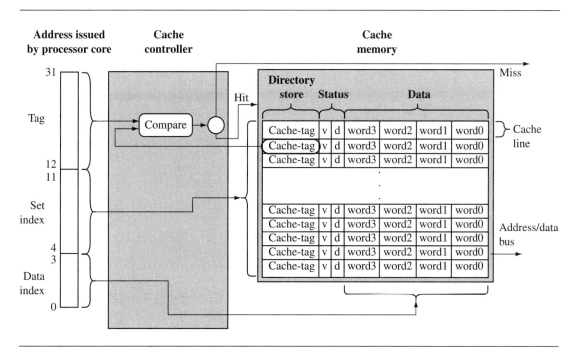

Figure 12.4   A 4 KB cache consisting of 256 cache lines of four 32-bit words.

processor core on demand. A *dirty* bit defines whether or not a cache line contains data that is different from the value it represents in main memory. We explain dirty bits in more detail in Section 12.3.1.

12.2.2 BASIC OPERATION OF A CACHE CONTROLLER

The *cache controller* is hardware that copies code or data from main memory to cache memory automatically. It performs this task automatically to conceal cache operation from the software it supports. Thus, the same application software can run unaltered on systems with and without a cache.

The cache controller intercepts read and write memory requests before passing them on to the memory controller. It processes a request by dividing the address of the request into three fields, the *tag* field, the *set index* field, and the *data index* field. The three bit fields are shown in Figure 12.4.

First, the controller uses the set index portion of the address to locate the cache line within the cache memory that might hold the requested code or data. This cache line contains the cache-tag and status bits, which the controller uses to determine the actual data stored there.

The controller then checks the valid bit to determine if the cache line is active, and compares the cache-tag to the tag field of the requested address. If both the status check and comparison succeed, it is a cache *hit*. If either the status check or comparison fails, it is a cache *miss*.

On a cache miss, the controller copies an entire cache line from main memory to cache memory and provides the requested code or data to the processor. The copying of a cache line from main memory to cache memory is known as a *cache line fill*.

On a cache hit, the controller supplies the code or data directly from cache memory to the processor. To do this it moves to the next step, which is to use the data index field of the address request to select the actual code or data in the cache line and provide it to the processor.

12.2.3 THE RELATIONSHIP BETWEEN CACHE AND MAIN MEMORY

Having a general understanding of basic cache memory architecture and how the cache controller works provides enough information to discuss the relationship that a cache has with main memory.

Figure 12.5 shows where portions of main memory are temporarily stored in cache memory. The figure represents the simplest form of cache, known as a *direct-mapped* cache. In a direct-mapped cache each addressed location in main memory maps to a single location in cache memory. Since main memory is much larger than cache memory, there are many addresses in main memory that map to the same single location in cache memory. The figure shows this relationship for the class of addresses ending in 0x824.

The three bit fields introduced in Figure 12.4 are also shown in this figure. The set index selects the one location in cache where all values in memory with an ending address of 0x824 are stored. The data index selects the word/halfword/byte in the cache line, in this case the second word in the cache line. The tag field is the portion of the address that is compared to the cache-tag value found in the directory store. In this example there are one million possible locations in main memory for every one location in cache memory. Only one of the possible one million values in the main memory can exist in the cache memory at any given time. The comparison of the tag with the cache-tag determines whether the requested data is in cache or represents another of the million locations in main memory with an ending address of 0x824.

During a cache line fill the cache controller may forward the loading data to the core at the same time it is copying it to cache; this is known as *data streaming*. Streaming allows a processor to continue execution while the cache controller fills the remaining words in the cache line.

If valid data exists in this cache line but represents another address block in main memory, the entire cache line is evicted and replaced by the cache line containing the requested address. This process of removing an existing cache line as part of servicing a cache miss is known as *eviction*—returning the contents of a cache line to main memory from the cache to make room for new data that needs to be loaded in cache.

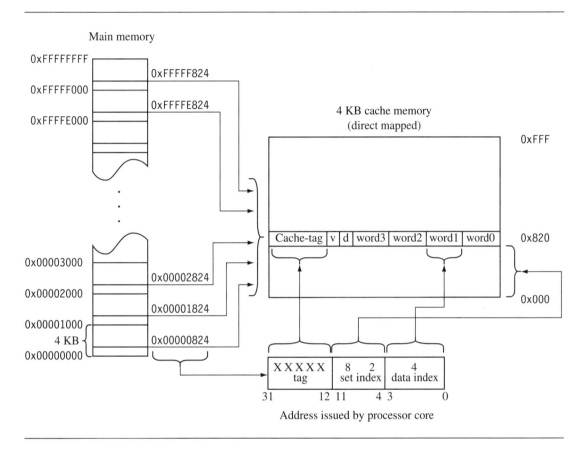

Figure 12.5   How main memory maps to a direct-mapped cache.

A direct-mapped cache is a simple solution, but there is a design cost inherent in having a single location available to store a value from main memory. Direct-mapped caches are subject to high levels of *thrashing*—a software battle for the same location in cache memory. The result of thrashing is the repeated loading and eviction of a cache line. The loading and eviction result from program elements being placed in main memory at addresses that map to the same cache line in cache memory.

Figure 12.6 takes Figure 12.5 and overlays a simple, contrived software procedure to demonstrate thrashing. The procedure calls two routines repeatedly in a do while loop. Each routine has the same set index address; that is, the routines are found at addresses in physical memory that map to the same location in cache memory. The first time through the loop, routine A is placed in the cache as it executes. When the procedure calls routine B, it evicts routine A a cache line at a time as it is loaded into cache and executed. On the second time through the loop, routine A replaces routine B, and then routine B replaces routine A.

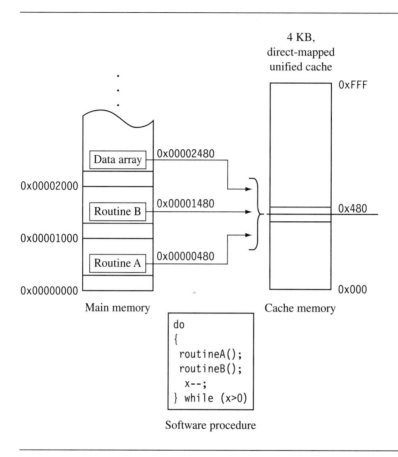

Figure 12.6   Thrashing: two functions replacing each other in a direct-mapped cache.

Repeated cache misses result in continuous eviction of the routine that not running. This
is cache thrashing.

12.2.4 SET ASSOCIATIVITY

Some caches include an additional design feature to reduce the frequency of thrashing (see
Figure 12.7). This structural design feature is a change that divides the cache memory into
smaller equal units, called *ways*. Figure 12.7 is still a four KB cache; however, the set index
now addresses more than one cache line—it points to one cache line in each way. Instead
of one way of 256 lines, the cache has four ways of 64 lines. The four cache lines with the
same set index are said to be in the same *set*, which is the origin of the name "set index."

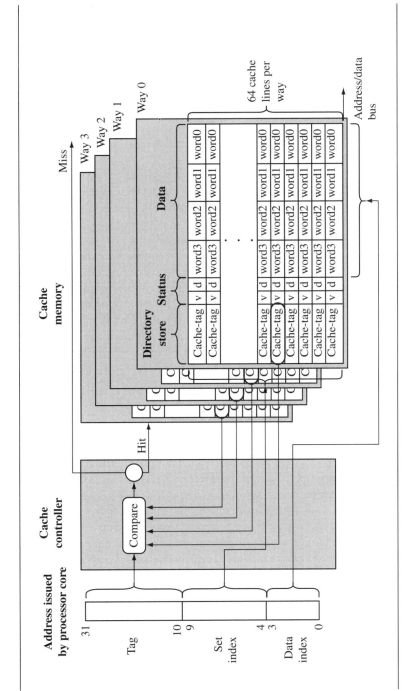

Figure 12.7   A 4 KB, four-way set associative cache. The cache has 256 total cache lines, which are separated into four ways, each containing 64 cache lines. The cache line contains four words.

The set of cache lines pointed to by the set index are *set associative*. A data or code block from main memory can be allocated to any of the four ways in a set without affecting program behavior; in other words the storing of data in cache lines within a set does not affect program execution. Two sequential blocks from main memory can be stored as cache lines in the same way or two different ways. The important thing to note is that the data or code blocks from a specific location in main memory can be stored in any cache line that is a member of a set. The placement of values within a set is exclusive to prevent the same code or data block from simultaneously occupying two cache lines in a set.

The mapping of main memory to a cache changes in a four-way set associative cache. Figure 12.8 shows the differences. Any single location in main memory now maps to four different locations in the cache. Although Figures 12.5 and 12.8 both illustrate 4 KB caches, here are some differences worth noting.

The bit field for the tag is now two bits larger, and the set index bit field is two bits smaller. This means four million main memory addresses now map to one set of four cache lines, instead of one million addresses mapping to one location.

The size of the area of main memory that maps to cache is now 1 KB instead of 4 KB. This means that the likelihood of mapping cache line data blocks to the same set is now four times higher. This is offset by the fact that a cache line is one fourth less likely to be evicted.

If the example code shown in Figure 12.6 were run in the four-way set associative cache shown in Figure 12.8, the incidence of thrashing would quickly settle down as routine A, routine B, and the data array would establish unique places in the four available locations in a set. This assumes that the size of each routine and the data are less than the new smaller 1 KB area that maps from main memory.

12.2.4.1 Increasing Set Associativity

As the associativity of a cache controller goes up, the probability of thrashing goes down. The ideal goal would be to maximize the set associativity of a cache by designing it so any main memory location maps to any cache line. A cache that does this is known as a *fully associative* cache. However, as the associativity increases, so does the complexity of the hardware that supports it. One method used by hardware designers to increase the set associativity of a cache includes a *content addressable memory* (CAM).

A CAM uses a set of comparators to compare the input tag address with a cache-tag stored in each valid cache line. A CAM works in the opposite way a RAM works. Where a RAM produces data when given an address value, a CAM produces an address if a given data value exists in the memory. Using a CAM allows many more cache-tags to be compared simultaneously, thereby increasing the number of cache lines that can be included in a set.

Using a CAM to locate cache-tags is the design choice ARM made in their ARM920T and ARM940T processor cores. The caches in the ARM920T and ARM940T are 64-way set associative. Figure 12.9 shows a block diagram of an ARM940T cache. The cache controller uses the address tag as the input to the CAM and the output selects the way containing the valid cache line.

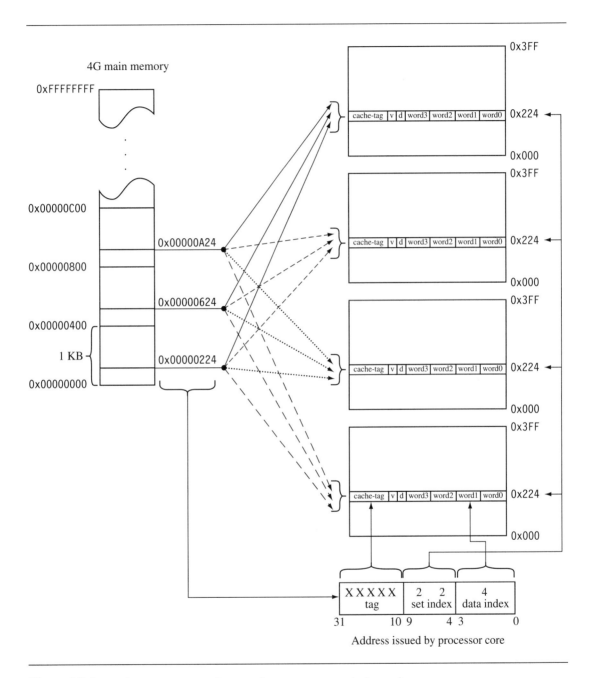

Figure 12.8   Main memory mapping to a four-way set associative cache.

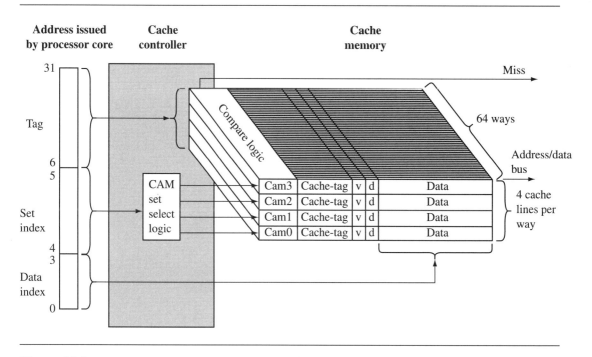

Figure 12.9 ARM940T—4 KB 64-way set associative D-cache using a CAM.

The tag portion of the requested address is used as an input to the four CAMs that simultaneously compare the input tag with all cache-tags stored in the 64 ways. If there is a match, cache data is provided by the cache memory. If no match occurs, a miss signal is generated by the memory controller.

The controller enables one of four CAMs using the set index bits. The indexed CAM then selects a cache line in cache memory and the data index portion of the core address selects the requested word, halfword, or byte within the cache line.

12.2.5 Write Buffers

A write buffer is a very small, fast FIFO memory buffer that temporarily holds data that the processor would normally write to main memory. In a system without a write buffer, the processor writes directly to main memory. In a system with a write buffer, data is written at high speed to the FIFO and then emptied to slower main memory. The write buffer reduces the processor time taken to write small blocks of sequential data to main memory. The FIFO memory of the write buffer is at the same level in the memory hierarchy as the L1 cache and is shown in Figure 12.1.

The efficiency of the write buffer depends on the ratio of main memory writes to the number of instructions executed. Over a given time interval, if the number of writes to main memory is low or sufficiently spaced between other processing instructions, the write buffer will rarely fill. If the write buffer does not fill, the running program continues to execute out of cache memory using registers for processing, cache memory for reads and writes, and the write buffer for holding evicted cache lines while they drain to main memory.

A write buffer also improves cache performance; the improvement occurs during cache line evictions. If the cache controller evicts a dirty cache line, it writes the cache line to the write buffer instead of main memory. Thus the new cache line data will be available sooner, and the processor can continue operating from cache memory.

Data written to the write buffer is not available for reading until it has exited the write buffer to main memory. The same holds true for an evicted cache line: it too cannot be read while it is in the write buffer. This is one of the reasons that the FIFO depth of a write buffer is usually quite small, only a few cache lines deep.

Some write buffers are not strictly FIFO buffers. The ARM10 family, for example, supports *coalescing*—the merging of write operations into a single cache line. The write buffer will merge the new value into an existing cache line in the write buffer if they represent the same data block in main memory. Coalescing is also known as *write merging*, *write collapsing*, or *write combining*.

12.2.6 MEASURING CACHE EFFICIENCY

There are two terms used to characterize the cache efficiency of a program: the cache hit rate and the cache miss rate. The *hit rate* is the number of cache hits divided by the total number of memory requests over a given time interval. The value is expressed as a percentage:

$$hit\ rate = \left(\frac{cache\ hits}{memory\ requests}\right) \times 100$$

The *miss rate* is similar in form: the total cache misses divided by the total number of memory requests expressed as a percentage over a time interval. Note that the miss rate also equals 100 minus the hit rate.

The hit rate and miss rate can measure reads, writes, or both, which means that the terms can be used to describe performance information in several ways. For example, there is a hit rate for reads, a hit rate for writes, and other measures of hit and miss rates.

Two other terms used in cache performance measurement are the *hit time*—the time it takes to access a memory location in the cache and the *miss penalty*—the time it takes to load a cache line from main memory into cache.

12.3   CACHE POLICY

There are three policies that determine the operation of a cache: the write policy, the replacement policy, and the allocation policy. The cache write policy determines where data is stored during processor write operations. The replacement policy selects the cache line in a set that is used for the next line fill during a cache miss. The allocation policy determines when the cache controller allocates a cache line.

12.3.1   WRITE POLICY—WRITEBACK OR WRITETHROUGH

When the processor core writes to memory, the cache controller has two alternatives for its write policy. The controller can write to both the cache and main memory, updating the values in both locations; this approach is known as *writethrough*. Alternatively, the cache controller can write to cache memory and not update main memory, this is known as *writeback* or *copyback*.

12.3.1.1   Writethrough

When the cache controller uses a writethrough policy, it writes to both cache and main memory when there is a cache hit on write, ensuring that the cache and main memory stay coherent at all times. Under this policy, the cache controller performs a write to main memory for each write to cache memory. Because of the write to main memory, a writethrough policy is slower than a writeback policy.

12.3.1.2   Writeback

When a cache controller uses a writeback policy, it writes to valid cache data memory and not to main memory. Consequently, valid cache lines and main memory may contain different data. The cache line holds the most recent data, and main memory contains older data, which has not been updated.

Caches configured as writeback caches must use one or more of the dirty bits in the cache line status information block. When a cache controller in writeback writes a value to cache memory, it sets the dirty bit true. If the core accesses the cache line at a later time, it knows by the state of the dirty bit that the cache line contains data not in main memory. If the cache controller evicts a dirty cache line, it is automatically written out to main memory. The controller does this to prevent the loss of vital information held in cache memory and not in main memory.

One performance advantage a writeback cache has over a writethrough cache is in the frequent use of temporary local variables by a subroutine. These variables are transient in nature and never really need to be written to main memory. An example of one of these transient variables is a local variable that overflows onto a cached stack because there are not enough registers in the register file to hold the variable.

12.3.2 CACHE LINE REPLACEMENT POLICIES

On a cache miss, the cache controller must select a cache line from the available set in cache memory to store the new information from main memory. The cache line selected for replacement is known as a *victim*. If the victim contains valid, dirty data, the controller must write the dirty data from the cache memory to main memory before it copies new data into the victim cache line. The process of selecting and replacing a victim cache line is known as *eviction*.

The strategy implemented in a cache controller to select the next victim is called its *replacement policy*. The replacement policy selects a cache line from the available associative member set; that is, it selects the way to use in the next cache line replacement. To summarize the overall process, the set index selects the set of cache lines available in the ways, and the replacement policy selects the specific cache line from the set to replace.

ARM cached cores support two replacement policies, either pseudorandom or round-robin.

- Round-robin or cyclic replacement simply selects the next cache line in a set to replace. The selection algorithm uses a sequential, incrementing victim counter that increments each time the cache controller allocates a cache line. When the victim counter reaches a maximum value, it is reset to a defined base value.

- Pseudorandom replacement randomly selects the next cache line in a set to replace. The selection algorithm uses a nonsequential incrementing victim counter. In a pseudorandom replacement algorithm the controller increments the victim counter by randomly selecting an increment value and adding this value to the victim counter. When the victim counter reaches a maximum value, it is reset to a defined base value.

Most ARM cores support both policies (see Table 12.1 for a comprehensive list of ARM cores and the policies they support). The round-robin replacement policy has greater predictability, which is desirable in an embedded system. However, a round-robin replacement policy is subject to large changes in performance given small changes in memory access. To show this change in performance, we provide Example 12.1.

EXAMPLE 12.1   This example determines the time it takes to execute a software routine using the round-robin and random replacement policies. The test routine cache_RRtest collects timings using the clock function available in the C library header time.h. First, it enables a round robin policy and runs a timing test, and then enables the random policy and runs the same test.

The test routine readSet is written specifically for an ARM940T and intentionally shows a worst-case abrupt change in cache behavior using a round-robin replacement policy.

Table 12.1   ARM cached core policies.

Core	Write policy	Replacement policy	Allocation policy
ARM720T	writethrough	random	read-miss
ARM740T	writethrough	random	read-miss
ARM920T	writethrough, writeback	random, round-robin	read-miss
ARM940T	writethrough, writeback	random	read-miss
ARM926EJS	writethrough, writeback	random, round-robin	read-miss
ARM946E	writethrough, writeback	random, round-robin	read-miss
ARM10202E	writethrough, writeback	random, round-robin	read-miss
ARM1026EJS	writethrough, writeback	random, round-robin	read-miss
Intel StrongARM	writeback	round-robin	read-miss
Intel XScale	writethrough, writeback	round-robin	read-miss, write-miss

```
#include <stdio.h>
#include <time.h>

void cache_RRtest(int times,int numset)
{
    clock_t count;

    printf("Round Robin test size = %d\r\n", numset);
    enableRoundRobin();
    cleanFlushCache();
    count = clock();
    readSet(times,numset);
    count = clock() - count;
    printf("Round Robin enabled = %.2f seconds\r\n",
                        (float)count/CLOCKS_PER_SEC);

    enableRandom();
    cleanFlushCache();
    count = clock();
    readSet(times, numset);
    count = clock() - count;
    printf("Random enabled = %.2f seconds\r\n\r\n",
                        (float)count/CLOCKS_PER_SEC);
}

int readSet( int times, int numset)
{
```

```
int setcount, value;
volatile int *newstart;
volatile int *start = (int *)0x20000;

  __asm
  {
    timesloop:
        MOV     newstart, start
        MOV     setcount, numset
    setloop:
        LDR     value,[newstart,#0];
        ADD     newstart,newstart,#0x40;
        SUBS    setcount, setcount, #1;
        BNE     setloop;
        SUBS    times, times, #1;
        BNE     timesloop;
  }
  return value;
}
```

We wrote the readSet routine to fill a single set in the cache. There are two arguments to the function. The first, times, is the number of times to run the test loop; this value increases the time it takes to run the test. The second, numset, is the number of set values to read; this value determines the number of cache lines the routine loads into the same set. Filling the set with values is done in a loop using an LDR instruction that reads a value from a memory location and then increments the address by 16 words (64 bytes) in each pass through the loop. Setting the value of numset to 64 will fill all the available cache lines in a set in an ARM940T. There are 16 words in a way and 64 cache lines per set in the ARM940T.

Here are two calls to the round-robin test using two set sizes. The first reads and fills a set with 64 entries; the second attempts to fill the set with 65 entries.

```
unsigned int times = 0x10000;
unsigned int numset = 64;

cache_RRtest(times, numset);
numset = 65;
cache_RRtest(times, numset);
```

The console output of the two tests follows. The tests were run on an ARM940T core module simulated using the ARM ADS1.2 ARMulator with a core clock speed of 50 MHz and a memory read access time of 100 ns nonsequential and 50 ns sequential. The thing to notice is the change in timing for the round-robin test reading 65 set values.

```
Round Robin test size = 64
Round Robin enabled = 0.51 seconds
Random enabled = 0.51 seconds
Round Robin test size = 65
Round Robin enabled = 2.56 seconds
Random enabled = 0.58 seconds
```

This is an extreme example, but it does shows a difference between using a round-robin policy and a random replacement policy.

Another common replacement policy is *least recently used* (LRU). This policy keeps track of cache line use and selects the cache line that has been unused for the longest time as the next victim.

ARM's cached cores do not support a least recently used replacement policy, although ARM's semiconductor partners have taken noncached ARM cores and added their own cache to the chips they produce. So there are ARM-based products that use an LRU replacement policy.

12.3.3   ALLOCATION POLICY ON A CACHE MISS

There are two strategies ARM caches may use to allocate a cache line after a the occurrence of a cache miss. The first strategy is known as *read-allocate*, and the second strategy is known as *read-write-allocate*.

A read allocate on cache miss policy allocates a cache line only during a read from main memory. If the victim cache line contains valid data, then it is written to main memory before the cache line is filled with new data.

Under this strategy, a write of new data to memory does not update the contents of the cache memory unless a cache line was allocated on a previous read from main memory. If the cache line contains valid data, then a write updates the cache and may update main memory if the cache write policy is writethrough. If the data is not in cache, the controller writes to main memory only.

A read-write allocate on cache miss policy allocates a cache line for either a read or write to memory. Any load or store operation made to main memory, which is not in cache memory, allocates a cache line. On memory reads the controller uses a read-allocate policy.

On a write, the controller also allocates a cache line. If the victim cache line contains valid data, then it is first written back to main memory before the cache controller fills the victim cache line with new data from main memory. If the cache line is not valid, it simply does a cache line fill. After the cache line is filled from main memory, the controller writes the data to the corresponding data location within the cache line. The cached core also updates main memory if it is a writethrough cache.

The ARM7, ARM9, and ARM10 cores use a read-allocate on miss policy; the Intel XScale supports both read-allocate and write-allocate on miss. Table 12.1 provides a listing of the policies supported by each core.

12.4 Coprocessor 15 and Caches

There are several coprocessor 15 registers used to specifically configure and control ARM cached cores. Table 12.2 lists the coprocessor 15 registers that control cache configuration. Primary CP15 registers *c7* and *c9* control the setup and operation of cache. Secondary CP15:c7 registers are write only and clean and flush cache. The CP15:c9 register defines the victim pointer base address, which determines the number of lines of code or data that are locked in cache. We discuss these commands in more detail in the sections that follow. To review the general use of coprocessor 15 instructions and syntax, see Section 3.5.2.

There are other CP15 registers that affect cache operation; the definition of these registers is core dependent. These other registers are explained in Chapter 13 in Sections 13.2.3 and 13.2.4 on initializing the MPU, and in Chapter 14 in Section 14.3.6 on initializing the MMU.

In the next several sections we use the CP15 registers listed in Table 12.2 to provide example routines to clean and flush caches, and to lock code or data in cache. The control system usually calls these routines as part of its memory management activities.

12.5 Flushing and Cleaning Cache Memory

ARM uses the terms *flush* and *clean* to describe two basic operations performed on a cache.

To "flush a cache" is to clear it of any stored data. Flushing simply clears the valid bit in the affected cache line. All or just portions of a cache may need flushing to support changes in memory configuration. The term *invalidate* is sometimes used in place of the term *flush*. However, if some portion of the D-cache is configured to use a writeback policy, the data cache may also need cleaning.

To "clean a cache" is to force a write of dirty cache lines from the cache out to main memory and clear the dirty bits in the cache line. Cleaning a cache reestablishes coherence between cached memory and main memory, and only applies to D-caches using a writeback policy.

Table 12.2   Coprocessor 15 registers that configure and control cache operation.

Function	Primary register	Secondary registers	Opcode 2
Clean and flush cache	c7	c5, c6, c7, c10, c13, c14	0, 1, 2
Drain write buffer	c7	c10	4
Cache lockdown	c9	c0	0, 1
Round-robin replacement	c15	c0	0

Changing the memory configuration of a system may require cleaning or flushing a cache. The need to clean or flush a cache results directly from actions like changing the access permission, cache, and buffer policy, or remapping virtual addresses.

The cache may also need cleaning or flushing before the execution of self-modifying code in a split cache. Self-modifying code includes a simple copy of code from one location to another. The need to clean or flush arises from two possible conditions: First, the self-modifying code may be held in the D-cache and therefore be unavailable to load from main memory as an instruction. Second, existing instructions in the I-cache may mask new instructions written to main memory.

If a cache is using a writeback policy and self-modifying code is written to main memory, the first step is to write the instructions as a block of data to a location in main memory. At a later time, the program will branch to this memory and begin executing from that area of memory as an instruction stream. During the first write of code to main memory as data, it may be written to cache memory instead; this occurs in an ARM cache if valid cache lines exist in cache memory representing the location where the self-modifying code is written. The cache lines are copied to the D-cache and not to main memory. If this is the case, then when the program branches to the location where the self-modifying code should be, it will execute old instructions still present because the self-modifying code is still in the D-cache. To prevent this, clean the cache, which forces the instructions stored as data into main memory, where they can be read as an instruction stream.

If the D-cache has been cleaned, new instructions are present in main memory. However, the I-cache may have valid cache lines stored for the addresses where the new data (code) was written. Consequently, a fetch of the instruction at the address of the copied code would retrieve the old code from the I-cache and not the new code from main memory. Flush the I-cache to prevent this from happening.

12.5.1 FLUSHING ARM CACHED CORES

Flushing a cache invalidates the contents of a cache. If the cache is using a writeback policy, care should be taken to clean the cache before flushing so data is not lost as a result of the flushing process.

There are three CP15:c7 commands that perform flush operations on a cache. The first flushes the entire cache, the second flushes just the I-cache, and the third just the D-cache. The commands and cores that support them are shown in Table 12.3. The value of the processor core register *Rd* should be zero for all three MCR instructions.

We provide Example 12.2 to show how to flush caches using these instructions. The example can be used "as is" or customized to suit the requirements of the system. The example contains a macro that produces three routines (for information on using macros, see Appendix A):

- flushICache flushes the I-cache.
- flushDCache flushes the D-cache.

Table 12.3   CP15:c7:Cm commands to flush the entire cache.

Command	MCR instruction	Core support
Flush cache	MCR p15, 0, Rd, c7, c7, 0	ARM720T, ARM920T, ARM922T, ARM926EJ-S, ARM1022E, ARM1026EJ-S, StrongARM, XScale
Flush data cache	MCR p15, 0, Rd, c7, c6, 0	ARM920T, ARM922T, ARM926EJ-S, ARM940T, ARM946E-S, ARM1022E, ARM1026EJ-S, StrongARM, XScale
Flush instruction cache	MCR p15, 0, Rd, c7, c5, 0	ARM920T, ARM922T, ARM926EJ-S, ARM940T, ARM946E-S, ARM1022E, ARM1026EJ-S, StrongARM, XScale

- flushCache flushes both the I-cache and D-cache.

The routines have no input parameters and are called from C with the following prototypes:

```
void flushCache(void);    /* flush all cache */
void flushDCache(void);   /* flush D-cache */
void flushICache(void);   /* flush I-cache */
```

EXAMPLE **12.2**   This example begins by filtering the cores into groups based on the commands that they support.

We use a macro called CACHEFLUSH to help in the creation of the routines. The macro starts by setting the core register written to the CP15:c7:Cm to zero. Then it inserts the specific MCR instruction depending on the type of cache operation needed and its availability within each core.

```
        IF   {CPU} = "ARM720T"     :LOR: \
             {CPU} = "ARM920T"     :LOR: \
             {CPU} = "ARM922T"     :LOR: \
             {CPU} = "ARM926EJ-S"  :LOR: \
             {CPU} = "ARM940T"     :LOR: \
             {CPU} = "ARM946E-S"   :LOR: \
             {CPU} = "ARM1022E"    :LOR: \
             {CPU} = "ARM1026EJ-S" :LOR: \
             {CPU} = "SA-110"      :LOR: \
             {CPU} = "XSCALE"

c7f     RN 0 ; register in CP17:c7 format
```

```
            MACRO
            CACHEFLUSH $op

            MOV     c7f, #0
            IF      "$op" = "Icache"
              MCR     p15,0,c7f,c7,c5,0      ; flush I-cache
            ENDIF
            IF      "$op" = "Dcache"
              MCR     p15,0,c7f,c7,c6,0      ; flush D-cache
            ENDIF
            IF      "$op" = "IDcache"
              IF {CPU} = "ARM940T" :LOR: \
                 {CPU} = "ARM946E-S"
                MCR     p15,0,c7f,c7,c5,0    ; flush I-cache
                MCR     p15,0,c7f,c7,c6,0    ; flush D-cache
              ELSE
                MCR     p15,0,c7f,c7,c7,0    ; flush I-cache & D-cache
              ENDIF
            ENDIF
            MOV     pc, lr
            MEND


            IF  {CPU} = "ARM720T"
              EXPORT flushCache
flushCache
              CACHEFLUSH IDcache
            ELSE
              EXPORT flushCache
              EXPORT flushICache
              EXPORT flushDCache
flushCache
              CACHEFLUSH IDcache
flushICache
              CACHEFLUSH Icache
flushDCache
              CACHEFLUSH Dcache
            ENDIF
```

Finally, we use the macro several times to create the routines. The ARM720T has a unified cache so only the flushCache routine is available; otherwise, the routine uses the macro three times to create the routines.

This example contains a little more code than most implementations require. However, it is provided as an exhaustive routine that supports all current ARM processor cores.

You can use Example 12.2 to create simpler routines dedicated to the specific core you are using. We use an ARM926EJ-S as a model to show how the three routines can be extracted from Example 12.2. The rewritten version is

```
        EXPORT flushCache926
        EXPORT flushICache926
        EXPORT flushDCache926
c7f     RN 0 ; register in CP15:c7 format

flushCache926
        MCR     p15,0,c7f,c7,c7,0     ; flush I-cache & D-cache
        MOV     pc, lr
flushICache926
        MCR     p15,0,c7f,c7,c5,0     ; flush I-cache
        MOV     pc, lr
flushDCache926
        MCR     p15,0,c7f,c7,c6,0     ; flush D-cache
        MOV     pc, lr
```

If you are writing in C, you might simplify this code even further and make them inline functions that can be collected and placed in an include file. The inline functions are

```
__inline void flushCache926(void)
{
  unsigned int c7format = 0;
  __asm{ MCR p15,0,c7format,c7,c7,0 }; /* flush I&D-cache */
}


__inline void flushDcache926(void)
{
  unsigned int c7format = 0;
  __asm{MCR p15,0,c7format,c7,c6,0 } /* flush D-cache */
}


__inline void flushIcache926(void)
{
  unsigned int c7format = 0;
  __asm{MCR p15,0,c7format,c7,c5,0 } /* flush I-cache */
}
```

The remainder of the examples in this chapter are presented in ARM assembler and support all current cores. The same extraction procedures can be applied to the routines provided.

12.5.2   CLEANING ARM CACHED CORES

To *clean* a cache is to issue commands that force the cache controller to write all dirty D-cache lines out to main memory. In the process the dirty status bits in the cache line are cleared. Cleaning a cache reestablishes coherence between cached memory and main memory and can only apply to D-caches using a writeback policy.

The terms *writeback* and *copyback* are sometimes used in place of the term *clean*. So to force a *writeback* or *copyback* of cache to main memory is the same as cleaning the cache. The terms are similar to the adjectives used to describe cache write policy; however, in this case they describe an action performed on cache memory. In the non-ARM world the term *flush* may be used to mean what ARM calls *clean*.

12.5.3   CLEANING THE D-CACHE

At the time of writing this book there are three methods used to clean the D-cache (see Table 12.4); the method used is processor dependent because different cores have different command sets to clean the D-cache.

Although the method used to clean the cache may vary, in the examples we provide the same procedure call to provide a consistent interface across all cores. To do this we provide the same three procedures to clean the entire cache written once for each method:

- `cleanDCache` cleans the entire D-cache.
- `cleanFlushDCache` cleans and flushes the entire D-cache.
- `cleanFlushCache` cleans and flushes both the I-cache and D-cache.

The `cleanDCache`, `cleanFlushDCache`, and `cleanFlushCache` procedures do not take any input parameters and can be called from C using the following prototypes:

```
void cleanDCache(void);        /* clean D-cache */
void cleanFlushDCache(void);   /* clean-and-flush D-cache */
void cleanFlushCache(void);    /* clean-and-flush I&D-cache */
```

Table 12.4   Procedural methods to clean the D-cache.

Method	Example	Processor
Way and set index addressing	Example 12.3	ARM920T, ARM922T, ARM926EJ-S, ARM940T, ARM946E-S, ARM1022E, ARM1026EJ-S
Test-clean	Example 12.4	ARM926EJ-S, ARM1026EJ-S
Special allocate command reading a dedicated block of memory	Example 12.5	XScale, SA-110

The macros in these examples were written to support as many ARM cores as possible without major modification. This effort produced a common header file used in this example and several other examples presented in this chapter. The header file is named `cache.h` and is shown in Figure 12.10.

```
        IF {CPU} = "ARM920T"
CSIZE   EQU 14  ; cache size as 1<<CSIZE (16 K assumed)
CLINE   EQU  5  ; cache line size in bytes as 1<<CLINE
NWAY    EQU  6  ; set associativity = 1<<NWAY (64 way)
I7SET   EQU  5  ; CP15 c7 set incrementer as 1<<ISET
I7WAY   EQU 26  ; CP15 c7 way incrementer as 1<<SSET
I9WAY   EQU 26  ; CP15 c9 way incrementer as 1<<SSET
        ENDIF
        IF {CPU} = "ARM922T"
CSIZE   EQU 14  ; cache size as 1<<CSIZE (16 K assumed)
CLINE   EQU  5  ; cache line size in bytes as 1<<CLINE
NWAY    EQU  6  ; set associativity = 1<<NWAY (64 way)
I7SET   EQU  5  ; CP15 c7 set incrementer as 1<<ISET
I7WAY   EQU 26  ; CP15 c7 way incrementer as 1<<SSET
I9WAY   EQU 26  ; CP15 c9 way incrementer as 1<<SSET
    ENDIF
        IF {CPU} = "ARM926EJ-S"
CSIZE   EQU 14  ; cache size as 1<<CSIZE (16 K assumed)
CLINE   EQU  5  ; cache line size in bytes as 1<<CLINE
NWAY    EQU  2  ; set associativity = 1<<NWAY (4 way)
I7SET   EQU  4  ; CP15 c7 set incrementer as 1<<ISET
I7WAY   EQU 30  ; CP15 c7 way incrementer as 1<<IWAY
    ENDIF
        IF {CPU} = "ARM940T"
CSIZE   EQU 12  ; cache size as 1<<CSIZE (4K)
CLINE   EQU  4  ; cache line size in bytes as 1<<CLINE
NWAY    EQU  6  ; set associativity = 1<<NWAY (64 way)
I7SET   EQU  4  ; CP15 c7 set incrementer = 1<<ISET
I7WAY   EQU 26  ; CP15 c7 way incrementer = 1<<IWAY
I9WAY   EQU  0  ; CP15 c9 way incrementer = 1<<IWAY
    ENDIF
```

Figure 12.10 The header file *cache.h*.

```
        IF {CPU} = "ARM946E-S"
CSIZE   EQU 12  ; cache size as 1<<CSIZE (4 K assumed)
CLINE   EQU 5   ; cache line size in bytes as 1<<CLINE
NWAY    EQU 2   ; set associativity = 1<<NWAY (4 way)
I7SET   EQU 4   ; CP15 c7 set incrementer = 1<<ISET
I7WAY   EQU 30  ; CP15 c7 way incrementer = 1<<IWAY
I9WAY   EQU 0   ; CP15 c7 way incrementer = 1<<IWAY
    ENDIF
        IF {CPU} = "ARM1022E"
CSIZE   EQU 14  ; cache size as 1<<CSIZE (16 K)
CLINE   EQU 5   ; cache line size in bytes as 1<<CLINE
NWAY    EQU 6   ; set associativity = 1<<NWAY (64 way)
I7SET   EQU 5   ; CP15 c7 set incrementer as 1<<ISET
I7WAY   EQU 26  ; CP15 c7 way incrementer as 1<<SSET
I9WAY   EQU 26  ; CP15 c7 way incrementer = 1<<IWAY
    ENDIF
        IF {CPU} = "ARM1026EJ-S"
CSIZE   EQU 14  ; cache size as 1<<CSIZE (16 K assumed)
CLINE   EQU 5   ; cache line size in bytes as 1<<CLINE
NWAY    EQU 2   ; set associativity = 1<<NWAY (4 way)
I7SET   EQU 5   ; CP15 c7 set incrementer as 1<<ISET
I7WAY   EQU 30  ; CP15 c7 way incrementer as 1<<IWAY
    ENDIF
        IF {CPU} = "SA-110"
CSIZE   EQU 14  ; cache size as 1<<CSIZE (16 K)
CLINE   EQU 5   ; cache line size in bytes as 1<<CLINE
NWAY    EQU 5   ; set associativity = 1<<NWAY (4 way)
CleanAddressDcache   EQU 0x8000
    ENDIF
    IF {CPU} = "XSCALE"
CSIZE   EQU 15  ; cache size as 1<<CSIZE (32 K)
CLINE   EQU 5   ; cache line size in bytes as 1<<CLINE
NWAY    EQU 5   ; set associativity = 1<<NWAY (32 way)
MNWAY   EQU 1   ; set assoc mini D-cache = 1<<NWAY (2 way)
MCSIZE  EQU 11  ; mini cache size  as 1<<CSIZE (2 K)
    ENDIF

; ----------------
SWAY    EQU (CSIZE-NWAY)        ; size of way = 1<<SWAY
NSET    EQU (CSIZE-NWAY-CLINE) ; cache lines per way = 1<<NSET
```

Figure 12.10 The header file *cache.h*. (*Continued.*)

All values in the header file are either a size expressed in log base two or a field locator. If the value is a locator, it represents the lowest bit in a bit field in a CP15 register. For example, the constant *I7WAY* points to the lowest bit in the way selection field in the CP15:c7:c5 register. Just to be clear, the value of *I7WAY* is 26 in an ARM920T, ARM922T, ARM940T, and ARM1022E, and the value is 30 in the ARM926EJ-S, ARM946E-S, and ARM1026EJ-S (see Figure 12.11). The values are stored in this format to support bit manipulation of the core register (*Rm*) moved into a CP15:Cd:Cm register when a clean command is issued using an MCR instruction.

The six constants in the header file that depend on the core architecture are the following:

- *CSIZE* is the log base two of the size of the cache in bytes; in other words, the cache size is $(1 \ll CSIZE)$ bytes.

- *CLINE* is the log base two of the length of a cache line in bytes; the cache line length would be $(1 \ll CLINE)$ bytes.

- *NWAY* is the number of ways and is the same as the set associativity.

- *I7SET* is the number of bits that the set index is shifted to the left in the CP15:c7 command register. This value is also used to increment or decrement the set index portion of the CP15:c7 register when sequentially accessing the cache.

- *I7WAY* is the number of bits that the way index is shifted to the left in the CP15:c7 command register. This value is also used to increment or decrement the way index portion of the CP15:c7 register when sequentially accessing the cache.

- *I9WAY* is the number of bits that the way index is shifted to the left in the CP15:c9 command register. This value is also used to increment or decrement the way index portion of the CP15:c9 register when sequentially accessing the cache.

There are two constants calculated from the core specific data:

- *SWAY* is the log base two of the size of a way in bytes. The size of a way would be $(1 \ll SWAY)$ bytes.

- *NSET* is the number of cache lines per way. This is the log base two of the size of the set index. The number of sets would be $(1 \ll NSET)$.

12.5.4 CLEANING THE D-CACHE USING WAY AND SET INDEX ADDRESSING

Some ARM cores support cleaning and flushing a single cache line using the way and set index to address its location in cache. The commands available to clean and flush a cache line by way are shown as MCR instructions in Table 12.5. Two commands flush a cache line, one flushes an instruction cache line, and another flushes a data cache line. The remaining two commands clean the D-cache: one cleans a cache line and another cleans and flushes a cache line.

Table 12.5   CP15:c7 Commands to clean cache using way and set index addressing.

Command	MCR instruction	Core support
Flush instruction cache line	MCR p15, 0, Rd, c7, c5, 2	ARM926EJ-S, ARM940T, ARM1026EJ-S
Flush data cache line	MCR p15, 0, Rd, c7, c6, 2	ARM926EJ-S, ARM940T, ARM1026EJ-S
Clean data cache line	MCR p15, 0, Rd, c7, c10, 2	ARM920T, ARM922T, ARM926EJ-S, ARM940T, ARM946E-S, ARM1022E, ARM1026EJ-S
Clean and flush data cache line	MCR p15, 0, Rd, c7, c14, 2	ARM920T, ARM922T ARM926EJ-S, ARM940T, ARM946E-S, ARM1022E, ARM1026EJ-S

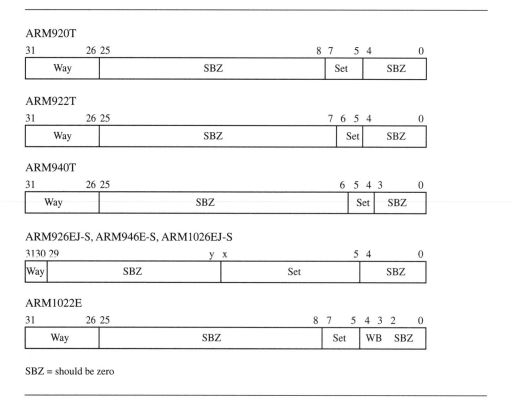

SBZ = should be zero

Figure 12.11 Format of CP15:c7:Cm register *Rd* when cleaning cache by way and set index addressing.

Each core listed selects an individual cache line by its way and set index address. When using these instructions the value in core register *Rd* is the same for all four commands within a single processor core; however, the format of the bit fields within the register varies from processor to processor. The CP15:c7:Cm register format for cores that support cleaning and flushing a cache line by way is shown in Figure 12.11. To execute the command, create a value in a core register (*Rd*) in the desired CP15:c7 register format. The general form of the register includes two bit fields: one selects the way and the other selects the set in the way. Once the register is created, execute the desired MCR instruction to move the core register (*Rd*) to the CP15:c7 register.

The cleanDCache, cleanFlushDCache, and cleanFlushCache procedures for the ARM920T, ARM922T, ARM940T, ARM946E-S, and ARM1022E processors are shown in the following example.

EXAMPLE
12.3

We use a macro called CACHECLEANBYWAY to create the three procedures that clean, flush, or clean and flush the cache using way and set index addressing.

The macro uses constants in the header file cache.h to build a processor register in CP15:C7 register format (*c7f*) for the selected core. The first step is to set the *c7f* register to zero, which is used as the *Rd* input value in the MCR instruction to execute the selected operation. The macro then increments the *c7f* register according to the format in Figure 12.11, once for each written cache line. It increments the set index in the inner loop and the way index in the outer loop. Using these nested loops, it steps through and cleans all the cache lines in all the ways.

```
        AREA cleancachebyway , CODE, READONLY ; Start of Area block
        IF  {CPU} = "ARM920T"      :LOR: \
            {CPU} = "ARM922T"      :LOR: \
            {CPU} = "ARM940T"      :LOR: \
            {CPU} = "ARM946E-S"    :LOR: \
            {CPU} = "ARM1022E"
        EXPORT cleanDCache
        EXPORT cleanFlushDCache
        EXPORT cleanFlushCache
        INCLUDE cache.h

c7f     RN  0   ; cp15:c7  register format

        MACRO
        CACHECLEANBYWAY $op

        MOV     c7f, #0                     ; create c7 format
5
        IF      "$op" = "Dclean"
          MCR   p15, 0, c7f, c7, c10, 2   ; clean D-cline
```

```
                   ENDIF
                   IF      "$op" = "Dcleanflush"
                     MCR     p15, 0, c7f, c7, c14, 2     ; cleanflush D-cline
                   ENDIF

                   ADD     c7f, c7f, #1 << I7SET        ; +1 set index
                   TST     c7f, #1 << (NSET+I7SET)      ; test index overflow
                   BEQ     %BT5

                   BIC     c7f, c7f, #1 << (NSET+I7SET) ; clear index overflow
                   ADDS    c7f, c7f, #1 << I7WAY        ; +1 victim pointer
                   BCC     %BT5                         ; test way overflow
                   MEND

cleanDCache
           CACHECLEANBYWAY Dclean
           MOV     pc, lr
cleanFlushDCache
           CACHECLEANBYWAY Dcleanflush
           MOV     pc, lr
cleanFlushCache
           CACHECLEANBYWAY Dcleanflush
           MCR     p15,0,r0,c7,c5,0     ; flush I-cache
           MOV     pc, lr
           ENDIF
```

12.5.5   CLEANING THE D-CACHE USING THE TEST-CLEAN COMMAND

Two of the newer ARM cores, the ARM926EJ-S and ARM1026EJ-S, have commands to clean cache lines using a test-clean CP15:c7 register. The test clean command is a special clean instruction that can efficiently clean a cache when used in a software loop. The ARM926EJ-S and ARM1026EJ-S also support cleaning using set and way indexing; however, using the test clean command method of cleaning the D-cache is more efficient.

We use the commands shown in Table 12.6 in the following routines to clean the ARM926EJ-S and ARM1026EJ-S cores. The cleanDCache, cleanFlushDCache, and

Table 12.6   Commands to test clean a single D-cache line.

Command	MCR instruction	Core Support
Test, clean D-cache line by loop	MCR p15, 0, r15, c7, c10, 3	ARM926EJ-S, ARM1026EJ-S
Test, clean, and flush D-cache by loop	MCR p15, 0, r15, c7, c14, 3	ARM926EJ-S, ARM1026EJ-S

cleanFlushCache procedures for the ARM926EJ-S and ARM1026EJ-S processors are shown in Example 12.4.

EXAMPLE 12.4   The test clean command finds the first dirty cache line and cleans it by transferring its contents to main memory. If another dirty cache exists in cache memory, then the *Z* flag will be zero.

```
IF  {CPU} = "ARM926EJ-S" :LOR: {CPU} = "ARM1026EJ-S"
  EXPORT cleanDCache
  EXPORT cleanFlushDCache
  EXPORT cleanFlushCache

cleanDCache
        MRC     p15, 0, pc, c7, c10, 3   ; test/clean D-cline
        BNE     cleanDCache
        MOV     pc, lr
cleanFlushDCache
        MRC     p15, 0, pc, c7, c14, 3   ; test/cleanflush D-cline
        BNE     cleanFlushDCache
        MOV     pc, lr
cleanFlushCache
        MRC     p15, 0, pc, c7, c14, 3   ; test/cleanflush D-cline
        BNE     cleanFlushCache
        MCR     p15, 0, r0, c7, c5, 0    ; flush I-cache
        MOV     pc, lr
ENDIF
```

To clean the cache, a software loop is created that uses the test clean command. By testing the *Z* flag and branching back to repeat the test, the processor loops through the test until the D-cache is clean. Note that the test clean command uses the program counter (*r15*) as the *Rd* register input to the MCR instruction.

12.5.6 CLEANING THE D-CACHE IN INTEL XSCALE SA-110 AND INTEL STRONGARM CORES

The Intel XScale and Intel StrongARM processors use a third method to clean their D-caches. The Intel XScale processors have a command to allocate a line in the D-cache without doing a line fill. When the processor executes the command, it sets the valid bit and fills the directory entry with the cache-tag provided in the *Rd* register. No data is transferred from main memory when the command executes. Thus, the data in the cache is not initialized until it is written to by the processor. The allocate command, shown in Table 12.7, has the beneficial feature of evicting a cache line if it is dirty.

Table 12.7   Intel XScale CP15:c7 commands to allocate a D-cache line.

Command	MCR instruction	Core supported
Allocate line in data cache	`MCR p15, 0, Rd, c7, c2, 5`	XScale

The Intel StrongARM and Intel XScale processors require an additional technique to clean their caches. They need a dedicated area of unused cached main memory to clean the cache. By software design the memory block is dedicated to cleaning the cache only.

The Intel StrongARM and Intel XScale processors can be cleaned by reading this fixed block of memory because they use a round-robin replacement policy. If a routine is executed that forces the core to sequentially read an area of cached main data memory equal to the size of the cache, then the series of reads will evict all current cache lines and replace them with data blocks from the dedicated scratch read area. When the read sequence completes, the cache will contain no important data because the dedicated read block has no useful information in it. At this point, the cache can be flushed without fear of losing valued cached data.

We use this technique to clean the Intel StrongARM D-cache and the Intel XScale mini D-cache. The `cleanDCache`, `cleanFlushDCache`, and `cleanFlushCache` procedures for the Intel XScale and Intel StrongARM processors are shown in the following example. There is one additional procedure, called `cleanMiniDCache`, provided to clean the mini D-cache in the Intel XScale processor.

EXAMPLE
12.5

This example uses two macros, CPWAIT and CACHECLEANXSCALE. The CPWAIT macro is a three-instruction sequence used on Intel XScale processors to guarantee that CP15 operations execute without side effects. The macro executes these instructions so that enough processor cycles have completed to ensure that the CP15 command has completed and that the pipeline is clear of instructions. The CPWAIT macro is

```
MACRO
CPWAIT
MRC     p15, 0, r12, c2, c0, 0 ; read any CP15
MOV     r12, r12
SUB     pc, pc, #4 ; branch to next instruction
MEND
```

The macro CACHECLEANXSCALE creates the procedures `cleanDCache`, `cleanFlushD-Cache`, and `cleanFlushCache`. The first part of the macro sets physical parameters for the routine. The first parameter, `adr`, is the starting virtual memory address of the dedicated area of memory used to clean the cache. The second parameter, `nl` is the total number of cache lines in the cache.

```
           IF  {CPU} = "XSCALE" :LOR: {CPU} = "SA-110"
             EXPORT cleanDCache
             EXPORT cleanFlushDCache
             EXPORT cleanFlushCache
             INCLUDE cache.h


CleanAddressDcache  EQU 0x8000  ;(32K block 0x8000-0x10000)
CleanAddressMiniDcache  EQU 0x10000 ;(2K block 0x10000-0x10800)


adr        RN  0   ; start address
nl         RN  1   ; number of cache lines to process
tmp        RN  12  ; scratch register



           MACRO
           CACHECLEANXSCALE $op

           IF "$op" - "Dclean"
             LDR     adr, =CleanAddressDcache
             MOV     nl, #(1 << (NWAY+NSET))
           ENDIF
           IF "$op" = "DcleanMini"
             LDR     adr, =CleanAddressMiniDcache
             MOV     nl, #(1 << (MNWAY+NSET))
           ENDIF
5
           IF  {CPU} = "XSCALE" :LAND: "$op" = "Dclean"
             MCR     p15, 0, adr, c7, c2, 5 ; allocate d-cline
             ADD     adr, adr, #32          ; +1 d-cline
           ENDIF
           IF  {CPU} = "SA-110" :LOR: "$op"= "DcleanMini"
             LDR     tmp,[adr],#32      ; Load data, +1 d-cline
           ENDIF
           SUBS    nl, nl, #1                ; -1 loop count
           BNE     %BT5
           IF  {CPU} = "XSCALE"
             CPWAIT
           ENDIF
           MEND

cleanDCache
           CACHECLEANXSCALE Dclean
           MOV pc, lr
```

```
cleanFlushDCache
        STMFD   sp!, {lr}
        BL cleanDCache
        IF  {CPU} = "XSCALE"
          BL cleanMiniDCache
        ENDIF
        MOV     r0, #0
        MCR     p15,0,r0,c7,c6,0    ; flush D-cache
        IF  {CPU} = "XSCALE"
          CPWAIT
        ENDIF
        LDMFD   sp!, {pc}
cleanFlushCache
        STMFD   sp!, {lr}
        BL cleanDCache
        IF  {CPU} = "XSCALE"
          BL cleanMiniDCache
        ENDIF
        MOV     r0, #0
        MCR     p15,0,r0,c7,c7,0    ; flush I-cache & D-cache
        IF  {CPU} = "XSCALE"
          CPWAIT
        ENDIF
        LDMFD   sp!, {pc}
      ENDIF

      IF  {CPU} = "XSCALE"
      EXPORT cleanMiniDCache

cleanMiniDCache
        CACHECLEANXSCALE DcleanMini
        MOV pc, lr
      ENDIF
```

The macro then filters the needed commands to execute the clean operation for the two processor cores. The Intel XScale uses the allocate CP15:c7 command to clean the D-cache and reads a dedicated cached memory block to clean the mini D-cache. The Intel StrongARM reads from a dedicated area of memory to clean its D-cache.

Finally, we use the macro several times to create the cleanDCache, cleanFlushDCache, cleanFlushCache, and cleanMiniDCache procedures.

12.5.7 CLEANING AND FLUSHING PORTIONS OF A CACHE

ARM cores support cleaning and flushing a single cache line by reference to the location it represents in main memory. We show these commands as MCR instructions in Table 12.8.

Table 12.8 Commands to clean and flush a cache line referenced by its location in main memory.

Command	MCR instruction	Core support
Flush instruction cache line	MCR p15, 0, Rd, c7, c5, 1	ARM920T, ARM922T, ARM926EJ-S, ARM946E-S, ARM1022E, ARM1026EJ-S, XScale
Flush data cache line	MCR p15, 0, Rd, c7, c6, 1	ARM920T, ARM922T, ARM926EJ-S, ARM946E-S, ARM1022E, ARM1026EJ-S, StrongARM, XScale
Clean data cache line	MCR p15, 0, Rd, c7, c10, 1	ARM920T, ARM922T, ARM926EJ-S, ARM946E-S, ARM1022E, ARM1026EJ-S, StrongARM, XScale
Clean and flush data cache line	MCR p15, 0, Rd, c7, c14, 1	ARM920T, ARM922T, ARM926EJ-S, ARM946E-S, ARM1022E, ARM1026EJ-S, XScale

Two of the commands flush a single cache line, one flushes the instruction cache, and the other flushes the data cache. There are also two commands to clean the data cache: one that cleans a single cache line and another that cleans and flushes a single cache line.

When using these instructions the value in core register *Rd* is the same for all four commands within the same processor, and its contents must be the value needed to set the CP15:c7 register. However, the format of the bit values in the CP15:c7 register vary slightly from processor to processor. Figure 12.12 shows the register format for cores that support cleaning and flushing a cache line by its modified virtual address if the core has an MMU, or its physical address if it has an MPU.

We use the four commands to create six routines, which clean and/or flush the cache lines in the cache that represent a region of memory:

- flushICacheRegion flushes the cache lines from the I-cache representing a region of main memory.
- flushDCacheRegion flushes the cache lines from the D-cache representing a region of main memory.
- cleanDCacheRegion cleans the cache lines from the D-cache representing a region of main memory.
- cleanFlushDcacheRegion cleans and flushes the cache lines from the D-cache representing a region of main memory.
- flushCacheRegion flushes the cache lines representing a region of main memory from both the I-cache and D-cache.
- cleanFlushCacheRegion cleans and flushes the D-cache and then flushes the I-cache.

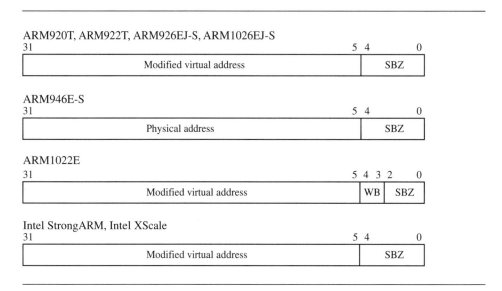

ARM920T, ARM922T, ARM926EJ-S, ARM1026EJ-S

Modified virtual address	SBZ

ARM946E-S

Physical address	SBZ

ARM1022E

Modified virtual address	WB	SBZ

Intel StrongARM, Intel XScale

Modified virtual address	SBZ

Figure 12.12 CP15:c7 Register Format when cleaning and flushing a cache line referenced by its origin in main memory.

All the procedures have two arguments passed to them, the starting address in main memory (adr) and the size of the region in bytes (b). The C function prototypes are

```
void flushICacheRegion(int * adr, unsigned int b);
void flushDCacheRegion(int * adr, unsigned int b);

void cleanDCacheRegion(int * adr, unsigned int b);
void cleanFlushDcacheRegion(int * adr, unsigned int b);

void flushCacheRegion(int * adr, unsigned int b);
void cleanFlushCacheRegion(int * adr, unsigned int b);
```

Care should be taken when using the clean cache region procedures. The use of these procedures is most successful on small memory regions. If the size of the region is several times larger than the cache itself, it is probably more efficient to clean the entire cache using one of the clean cache procedures provided in Sections 12.5.4, 12.5.5, and 12.5.6.

The region procedures are available on a limited set of ARM cores. Figure 12.12 lists the cores that support cleaning and flushing by address. They are also listed at the start of the code in the following example.

EXAMPLE
12.6
The macro takes the input address and truncates it to a cache line boundary. This truncation always addresses the first double word in the cache line of an ARM1022E (see Figure 12.12). The macro then takes the size argument and converts it from bytes to cache lines. The macro uses the number of cache lines as a counter variable to loop through the selected flush or clean operation, incrementing the address by a cache line size at the end of each loop. It exits when the counter reaches zero.

```
        IF  {CPU} = "ARM920T"      :LOR: \
            {CPU} = "ARM922T"      :LOR: \
            {CPU} = "ARM946E-S"    :LOR: \
            {CPU} = "ARM926EJ-S"   :LOR: \
            {CPU} = "ARM1022E"     :LOR: \
            {CPU} = "ARM1026EJ-S"  :LOR: \
            {CPU} = "XSCALE"       :LOR: \
            {CPU} = "SA-110"

        INCLUDE cache.h

adr     RN  0   ; active address
size    RN  1   ; size of region in bytes
nl      RN  1   ; number of cache lines to clean or flush

        MACRO
        CACHEBYREGION $op

        BIC     adr, adr, #(1<<CLINE)-1    ; clip 2 cline adr
        MOV     nl, size, lsr #CLINE       ; bytes to cline
10
        IF "$op" = "IcacheFlush"
          MCR   p15, 0, adr, c7, c5, 1     ; flush I-cline@adr
        ENDIF
        IF "$op" = "DcacheFlush"
          MCR   p15, 0, adr, c7, c6, 1     ; flush D-cline@adr
        ENDIF
        IF "$op" = "IDcacheFlush"
          MCR   p15, 0, adr, c7, c5, 1     ; flush I-cline@adr
          MCR   p15, 0, adr, c7, c6, 1     ; flush D-cline@adr
        ENDIF
        IF "$op" = "DcacheClean"
          MCR   p15, 0, adr, c7, c10, 1    ; clean D-cline@adr
        ENDIF
        IF "$op" = "DcacheCleanFlush"
          IF {CPU} = "XSCALE" :LOR: \
```

```
          {CPU} = "SA-110"
    MCR    p15, 0, adr, c7, c10, 1   ; clean D-cline@adr
    MCR    p15, 0, adr, c7, c6, 1    ; flush D-cline@adr
  ELSE
    MCR    p15, 0, adr, c7, c14, 1 ; cleanflush D-cline@adr
  ENDIF
ENDIF
IF "$op" = "IDcacheCleanFlush"
  IF {CPU} = "ARM920T"    :LOR: \
     {CPU} = "ARM922T"    :LOR: \
     {CPU} = "ARM946E-S"  :LOR: \
     {CPU} = "ARM926EJ-S" :LOR: \
     {CPU} = "ARM1022E"   :LOR: \
     {CPU} = "ARM1026EJ-S"
    MCR    p15, 0, adr, c7, c14, 1 ;cleanflush D-cline@adr
    MCR    p15, 0, adr, c7, c5, 1    ; flush I-cline@adr
  ENDIF
  IF {CPU} = "XSCALE"
    MCR    p15, 0, adr, c7, c10, 1   ; clean D-cline@adr
    MCR    p15, 0, adr, c7, c6, 1    ; flush D-cline@adr
    MCR    p15, 0, adr, c7, c5, 1    ; flush I-cline@adr
  ENDIF
ENDIF

ADD    adr, adr, #1<<CLINE         ; +1 next cline adr
SUBS   nl, nl, #1                  ; -1 cline counter
BNE    %BT10                       ; flush # lines +1
IF {CPU} = "XSCALE"
  CPWAIT
ENDIF
MOV    pc, lr
MEND


IF {CPU} = "SA-110"
  EXPORT cleanDCacheRegion
  EXPORT flushDCacheRegion
  EXPORT cleanFlushDCacheRegion
cleanDCacheRegion
  CACHEBYREGION DcacheClean
flushDCacheRegion
  CACHEBYREGION DcacheFlush
cleanFlushDCacheRegion
  CACHEBYREGION DcacheCleanFlush
```

```
        ELSE
          EXPORT flushICacheRegion
          EXPORT flushDCacheRegion
          EXPORT flushCacheRegion
          EXPORT cleanDCacheRegion
          EXPORT cleanFlushDCacheRegion
          EXPORT cleanFlushCacheRegion
flushICacheRegion
          CACHEBYREGION IcacheFlush
flushDCacheRegion
          CACHEBYREGION DcacheFlush
flushCacheRegion
          CACHEBYREGION IDcacheFlush
cleanDCacheRegion
          CACHEBYREGION DcacheClean
cleanFlushDCacheRegion
          CACHEBYREGION DcacheCleanFlush
cleanFlushCacheRegion
          CACHEBYREGION IDcacheCleanFlush
        ENDIF
      ENDIF
```

Finally, using the CACHEBYREGION macro, we either create three procedures if the core is an Intel StrongARM, which has a limited command set, or all six procedures for the remainder of the processors that have split caches.

12.6 Cache Lockdown

Cache lockdown is a feature that enables a program to load time-critical code and data into cache memory and mark it as exempt from eviction. Code or data in lockdown provides faster system response because it is held in the cache memory. Cache lockdown avoids the problem of unpredictable execution times that result from the cache line eviction process, a normal part of cache operation.

The purpose of locking information in cache is to avoid the cache miss penalty. However, because any cache memory used for lockdown is unavailable for caching other parts of main memory, the useful cache size is reduced.

The ARM core allocates fixed units of the cache for lockdown. The unit size that ARM cores allocate in lockdown is a way. For example, a four-way set associative cache allows locking code or data in units that are 1/4th of the cache size. The cached core always reserves at least one way for normal cache operation.

Some instructions that are candidates for locking in cache are the vector interrupt table, interrupt service routines, or code for a critical algorithm that the system uses extensively. On the data side, frequently used global variables are good candidates for lockdown.

Data or code locked in an ARM cache core is immune from replacement. However, when the cache is flushed, the information in lockdown is lost and the area remains unavailable as cache memory. The cache lockdown routine must be rerun to restore the lockdown information.

12.6.1 LOCKING CODE AND DATA IN CACHE

This section presents a procedure to lock code and data in cache. A typical sequence of C calls to lock code and data in cache is the following:

```
int interrupt_state;   /* saves the state of the FIQ and IRQ bits */
int globalData[16];
unsigned int *vectortable = (unsigned int *)0x0;
int wayIndex;
int vectorCodeSize = 212;  /* vector table & FIQ handler in bytes*/

  interrupt_state = disable_interrupts();    /* no code provided */
  enableCache();                 /* see Chapters 13(MPU) and 14(MMU) */
  flushCache();                        /* see code Example 12.2  */

  /* Lock Global Data Block */
  wayIndex = lockDcache((globalData, sizeof globalData);
  /* Lock Vector table and FIQ Handler */
  wayIndex = lockIcache((vectortable, vectorCodeSize);}

  enable_interrupts(interrupt_state);          /* no code provided */
```

To begin, interrupts are disabled and the cache enabled. The procedure that disables interrupts is not shown. The flushCache procedure is one selected from the previous examples; the actual call used depends on the cache configuration and may also include cleaning the cache.

The function lockDCache locks a block of data in the D-cache; similarly, the function lockIcache locks a code block in the I-cache.

The lockdown software routines themselves must be located in noncached main memory. The code and data locked in cache must be located in cached main memory. It is important that the code and data locked in cache does not exist elsewhere in cache; in other words, if the contents of the cache are unknown, then flush the cache before loading. If the core is using a writeback D-cache, then clean the D-cache. Once the code and data are loaded in cache, reenable interrupts.

We present the code for the two functions lockDCache and lockIcache three different times because there are three different lockdown methods used to lock code in cache, depending on the architectural implementation. The first method locks code and data in the cache using way addressing techniques. The second uses a set of lock bits. In the third,

Table 12.9   Methods of cache lockdown.

Example	Procedural method	Processor core
Example 12.7	way addressing	ARM920T, ARM926EJ-S, ARM940T, ARM946E-S, ARM1022E, ARM1026EJ-S
Example 12.8	lock bits	ARM926EJ-S, ARM1026EJ-S
Example 12.9	special allocate command	XScale

code and data are locked in cache using a combination of a special allocate command and reading a dedicated block of main memory.

Table 12.9 lists the three examples that implement the two procedures lockDcache and lockIcache, the methods used, and the associated processors.

12.6.2 LOCKING A CACHE BY INCREMENTING THE WAY INDEX

The ARM920T, ARM926EJ-S, ARM940T, ARM946E-S, ARM1022E, and ARM1026EJ-S use way and set index addressing for lockdown. Two CP15:c9:c0 registers contain the victim counter reset registers described in Section 12.3.2. One of the registers controls the I-cache, and the other controls the D-cache. These registers are used to select the cache line within the way in which to lock the code or data.

The value written to the CP15:c7 register sets the *victim reset value*—the value that the victim counter is reset to when it increments beyond the number of ways in the core. The reset value is zero at power-up and is only changed by software if some portion of the cache is used for lockdown. When a portion of the cache is used for lockdown, the number of cache lines for caching information decreases by the number of cache lines locked down. Reading the register returns the current victim reset value. The MRC and MCR instructions to read and write to the two registers are shown in Table 12.10.

Table 12.10   Commands that lock data in cache by referencing its way.

Command	MRC and MCR instructions	Processor core
Read D-cache lockdown base	MRC p15, 0, Rd, c9, c0, 0	ARM920T, ARM926EJ-S, ARM940T, ARM946E-S, ARM1022E, ARM1026EJ-S
Write D-cache lockdown base	MCR p15, 0, Rd, c9, c0, 0	ARM920T, ARM926EJ-S, ARM940T, ARM946E-S, ARM1022E, ARM1026EJ-S
Read I-cache lockdown base	MRC p15, 0, Rd, c9, c0, 1	ARM920T, ARM926EJ-S, ARM940T, ARM946E-S, ARM1022E, ARM1026EJ-S
Write I-cache lockdown base	MCR p15, 0, Rd, c9, c0, 1	ARM920T, ARM926EJ-S, ARM940T, ARM946E-S, ARM1022E, ARM1026EJ-S

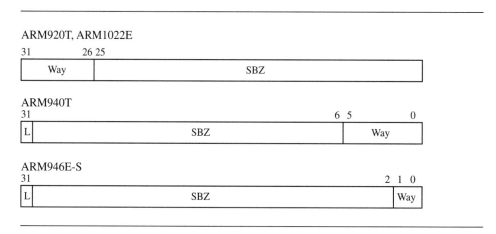

ARM920T, ARM1022E

ARM940T

ARM946E-S

Figure 12.13 CP15:c9 register format used when locking data in cache by reference to its way.

When reading or writing the lockdown base address, the format of the core register *Rd* used in the *MCR* and *MRC* instructions varies slightly from processor to processor. For each processor that uses these instructions, the format of the processor core *Rd* register is shown in Figure 12.13. To ensure that the command executes properly, be sure that the *Rd* register format matches that shown in the figure.

A special load command is also needed to lock instructions in cache. This special load command copies a cache-line-sized block of main memory to a cache line in the I-cache. The command and the format for the *Rd* register used in the instruction are shown in Table 12.11 and Figure 12.14.

The following example shows lockDCache and lockICache routines for processors supporting lockdown using incremented way addressing. The return value for the two routines is the next available victim pointer base address.

EXAMPLE
12.7

The first part of the routine defines the registers used in the macro CACHELOCKBYWAY. The macro also uses constants in the header file *cache.h* shown in Figure 12.10.

Table 12.11   Command to lock a cache line in the I-cache.

Command	MCR instruction	Processor core
Prefetch I-cache line by address	MCR p15, 0, Rd, c7, c13, 1	ARM920T, ARM922T, ARM926EJ-S, ARM940T, ARM946E-S, ARM1022E, ARM1026EJ-S, StrongARM, XScale

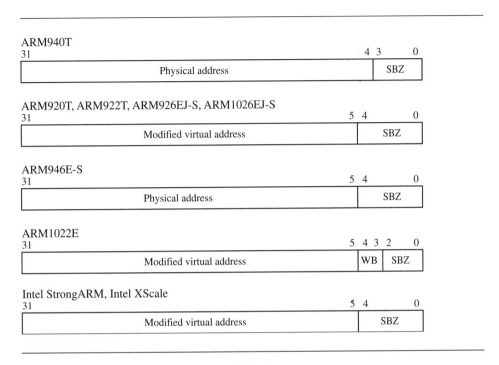

Figure 12.14 CP15:c7:c13 register format to lock a cache line in I-cache.

The first line in the macro aligns the address (*adr*) to a cache line. The next three lines use the code size in bytes to determine the number of ways it takes to hold the code. Then the I-cache or D-cache current victim pointer is read from CP15:c9:c0.

The next few lines do some error checking to test for overfilling the cache and if the size of the code to load is zero.

To lock code or data in the cache of an ARM940T or ARM946E-S, there is a lock bit that must be set before locking a memory block in a cache line. The next instruction sets this bit and writes the data back to CP15:c9:c0.

At this point the code enters a nested loop, the outer loop selects the way, and the inner loop increments the cache lines within the way.

At the center of the two loops a prefetch instruction or load data command is used to lock a cache line in cache memory. To lock instructions, the macro writes to a special CP15:c7:c13 register that preloads the code segment from main memory. To lock data, a read of the data using an LDR instruction is all that is required.

The macro exits by clearing the lock bit in the CP15:c9:c0 register if it is an ARM940T or ARM946E-S. On all cores it sets the victim pointer to the next available way after the locked code or data.

```
        IF  {CPU} = "ARM920T"        :LOR: \
            {CPU} = "ARM922T"        :LOR: \
            {CPU} = "ARM940T"        :LOR: \
            {CPU} = "ARM946E-S"      :LOR: \
            {CPU} = "ARM1022E"
        EXPORT lockDCache
        EXPORT lockICache
        INCLUDE cache.h


adr     RN 0     ; current address of code or data
size    RN 1     ; memory size in bytes
nw      RN 1     ; memory size in ways
count   RN 2
tmp     RN 2     ; scratch register
tmp1    RN 3     ; scratch register
c9f     RN 12    ; CP15:c9 register format

        MACRO
        CACHELOCKBYWAY $op

        BIC    adr, adr, #(1<<CLINE)-1 ; align to cline
        LDR    tmp, =(1<<SWAY)-1    ; scratch = size of way
        TST    size, tmp           ; way end fragment ?
        MOV    nw, size, lsr #SWAY ; convert bytes to ways
        ADDNE  nw, nw, #1          ; add way if fragment
        CMP    nw, #0              ; no lockdown requested
        BEQ    %FT2                ; exit return victim base

        IF "$op" = "Icache"
          MRC    p15, 0, c9f, c9, c0, 1  ; get i-cache victim
        ENDIF
        IF "$op" = "Dcache"
          MRC    p15, 0, c9f, c9, c0, 0  ; get d-cache victim
        ENDIF

        AND    c9f, c9f, tmp       ; mask high bits c9f = victim
        ADD    tmp, c9f, nw        ; temp = victim + way count
        CMP    tmp, #(1<<NWAY)-1   ; > total ways ?
        MOVGT  r0, #-1             ; return -1 if to many ways
        BGT    %FT1                ; Error: cache way overrun

        IF {CPU} = "ARM940T" :LOR: {CPU} = "ARM946E-S"
          ORR    c9f, c9f, #1<<31  ; put cache in lockdown mode
```

```
          ENDIF
10
          IF "$op" = "Icache"
            MCR     p15, 0, c9f, c9, c0, 1 ; set victim
          ENDIF
          IF "$op" = "Dcache"
            MCR     p15, 0, c9f, c9, c0, 0 ; set victim
          ENDIF

          MOV     count, #(1 << NSET)-1
5
          IF "$op" = "Icache"
            MCR     p15, 0, adr, c7, c13, 1    ; load code cacheline
            ADD     adr, adr, #1 << CLINE      ; cline addr =+ 1
          ENDIF
          IF "$op" = "Dcache"
            LDR     tmp1, [adr], #1 << CLINE ; load data cacheline
          ENDIF

          SUBS    count, count, #1
          BNE     %BT5
          ADD     c9f, c9f, #1 << I9WAY      ; victim pointer =+ 1
          SUBS    nw, nw, #1                 ; way counter =- 1
          BNE     %BT10                      ; repeat for # of ways
2
          IF {CPU} = "ARM940T" :LOR: {CPU} = "ARM946E-S"
            BIC     r0, c9f, #1 << 31 ; clear lock bit & r0=victim
          ENDIF
          IF "$op" = "Icache"
            MCR     p15, 0, r0, c9, c0, 1 ; set victim counter
          ENDIF
          IF "$op" = "Dcache"
            MCR     p15, 0, r0, c9, c0, 0 ; set victim counter
          ENDIF
1
          MOV     pc, lr
          MEND

lockDCache
          CACHELOCKBYWAY Dcache
lockICache
          CACHELOCKBYWAY Icache
          ENDIF
```

Finally, the macro is used twice to create the lockDCache and lockICache functions.

12.6.3 LOCKING A CACHE USING LOCK BITS

The ARM926EJ-S and ARM1026EJ-S lock code and data in cache using a set of lock bits, as shown in Figure 12.15. These two processors have a different *Rd* format for the CP15:c9 instructions, shown in Table 12.12. The four bits from zero to three represent each way in the four-way set associative cache in the two processors. If the bit's set, the way is locked and contains either code if it is the I-cache or data if it is the D-cache. A locked way does not evict a cache line until it is unlocked. Clearing one of the *L* bits unlocks its way. This form of locking the cache allows the system code to individually select the way to lock or unlock.

The ability to individually select a way to lock allows code to be more easily locked and unlocked in a system. The example code in this section implements a procedure that has the same programming interface used to lock data in the other cached cores.

The example lockDCache and lockICache procedures for the ARM926EJ-S and ARM1026EJ-S processors have the same input parameters. However, the code size is limited to a maximum of the way size, and it can be called up to three times. In the example, *L* bit 3 is always dedicated to cache. This is not a limitation of the processor hardware, but simply a limit placed on the procedure call to meet the needs of the programming interface.

The example procedure returns the *L* bit of the locked way if the size argument is one byte or greater. The procedure returns the next available *L* bit if the size is zero, and eight if there are no available ways for lockdown.

ARM926EJ-S, ARM1026EJ-S

31	16 15	4 3	0
SBZ	SBO	L bits	

Figure 12.15 CP15:c9 register format when locking cache using lockdown bits.

Table 12.12 CP15:c9 Commands to lock cache using lockdown bits.

Command	MRC and MCR instructions	
Read I-cache lock page register	MRC	p15, 0, Rd, c9, c0, 1
Read D-cache lock page register	MRC	p15, 0, Rd, c9, c0, 0
Write I-cache lock page register	MCR	p15, 0, Rd, c9, c0, 1
Write D-cache lock page register	MCR	p15, 0, Rd, c9, c0, 0
Load code cache line at address	MCR	p15, 0, Rd, c7, c13, 1

EXAMPLE
12.8

A macro called CACHELOCKBYLBIT generates both the lockDCache and lockICache functions. The macro also uses constants in the header file cache.h shown in Figure 12.10.

The macro starts by checking if the number of bytes to lock in cache is zero. Then it aligns the address adr to a cache line while determining the number of cache lines it takes to contain the code.

If the procedure is locking data in the D-cache, then it reads the lock register CP15:c9:c0:0. If the procedure is locking code in the I-cache, then it reads the lock register CP15:c9:c0:1. The resulting value is placed in the core *c9f* register. The *L* bits are also stored in the *tmp* register for later use.

```
        IF  {CPU} = "ARM926EJ-S"   :LOR: \
            {CPU} = "ARM1026EJ-S"
        EXPORT lockDCache
        EXPORT lockICache
        EXPORT bittest
        INCLUDE cache.h


adr     RN 0    ; current address of code or data
size    RN 1    ; memory size in bytes
tmp     RN 2    ; scratch register
tmp1    RN 3    ; scratch register
c9f     RN 12   ; CP15:c9 register format


        MACRO
        CACHELOCKBYLBIT $op

        ADD     size, adr, size         ; size = end address
        BIC     adr, adr, #(1<<CLINE)-1 ; align to CLINE
        MOV     tmp,  #(1<<CLINE)-1     ; scratch CLINE mask
        TST     size, tmp               ; CLINE end fragment ?
        SUB     size, size, adr         ; add alignment bytes
        MOV     size, size, lsr #CLINE  ; convert size 2 # CLINE
        ADDNE   size, size, #1          ; add CLINE for fragment
        CMP     size, #(1<<NSET)-1      ; size to large ?
        BHI     %FT1                    ; exit return victim base

        IF "$op" = "Icache"
          MRC     p15, 0, c9f, c9, c0, 1 ; get i-cache lock bits
        ENDIF
        IF "$op" = "Dcache"
          MRC     p15, 0, c9f, c9, c0, 0 ; get d-cache lock bits
        ENDIF

        AND     tmp, c9f, #0xf          ; tmp = state of Lbits
```

```
         MOV     tmp1, #1
         TST     c9f, tmp1                ; test lock bit 0
         MOVNE   tmp1, tmp1, LSL #1
         TSTNE   c9f, tmp1                ; test lock bit 1
         MOVNE   tmp1, tmp1, LSL #1
         TSTNE   c9f, tmp1                ; test lock bit 2
         MOVNE   tmp1, tmp1, LSL #1
         BNE     %FT1                     ; ERROR: no available ways
         CMP     size, #0                  ; no lockdown requested
         BEQ     %FT1                      ; exit return size =0

         MVN     tmp1, tmp1               ; select L bit
         AND     tmp1, tmp1, #0xf         ; mask off non L bits
         BIC     c9f, c9f, #0xf           ; construct c9f
         ADD     c9f, c9f, tmp1

   IF "$op" = "Icache"
     MCR     p15, 0, c9f, c9, c0, 1 ; set lock I page
   ENDIF
   IF "$op" = "Dcache"
     MCR     p15, 0, c9f, c9, c0, 0 ; set lock D page
   ENDIF

   IF "$op" = "Icache"
     MCR     p15, 0, adr, c7, c13, 1    ; load code cacheline
     ADD     adr, adr, #1<<CLINE        ; cline addr =+ 1
   ENDIF
   IF "$op" = "Dcache"
     LDR     tmp1, [adr], #1<<CLINE ; load data cacheline
   ENDIF

         SUBS    size, size, #1           ; cline =- 1
         BNE     %BT5                     ; loop thru clines

         MVN     tmp1, c9f                ; lock selected L-bit
         AND     tmp1, tmp1, #0xf         ; mask off non L-bits
         ORR     tmp, tmp, tmp1           ; merge with orig L-bits
         BIC     c9f, c9f, #0xf           ; clear all L-bits
         ADD     c9f, c9f, tmp            ; set L-bits in c9f

   IF "$op" = "Icache"
     MCR     p15, 0, adr, c9, c0, 1 ; set i-cache lock bits
   ENDIF
```

5

```
            IF "$op" = "Dcache"
              MCR    p15, 0, adr, c9, c0, 0 ; set d-cache lock bits
            ENDIF
1
            MOV    r0, tmp1              ; return allocated way
            MOV    pc, lr
            MEND

lockDCache
            CACHELOCKBYLBIT Dcache
lockICache
            CACHELOCKBYLBIT Icache
            ENDIF
```

The next seven lines check the *c9f* register to see if there is a way available to store code or data; if not, the routine exits. If there is an available way, then the *c9f* format is modified in the next four lines to select the way in which to lock data. The *c9f* register is then used in the MCR instruction to select the way.

At this point the code enters a loop that fills the cache with locked code or data. If the procedure is locking code in the I-cache, it executes a prefetch I-cache line command. If locking data from external memory, it cleans, flushes, and loads a new cache line into the D-cache.

The macro exits by merging the saved *L* bits with the newly locked page and uses the result to create a new *c9f* register. The macro uses the *c9f* register in an MCR instruction to set the *L* bits in the CP15:c9:c0 cache lockdown register.

Finally, the CACHELOCKBYLBIT macro is used twice to create the lockDCache and lockICache functions.

12.6.4 LOCKING CACHE LINES IN THE INTEL XSCALE SA-110

The Intel XScale processor also has the capability to lock code and data into cache. This method requires the use of a set of CP15:c9 cache lockdown commands, shown in Table 12.13. The format of the CP15:c9:c2 register is shown in Figure 12.16. It also requires the CP15:c7 allocate D-cache line command we used to clean the D-cache in Example 12.5; this command is shown in Table 12.7.

In the Intel XScale processor, each set in the cache has a dedicated round-robin pointer that is increased sequentially each time an additional cache line in the cache is locked. Up to 28 of the 32 cache lines within a set can be locked in cache. Attempting to lock more than 28 cache lines in a set results in the line being allocated but not locked in cache.

The Intel XScale processor supports two uses for locking data in the D-cache. The first use simply locks main memory locations into the D-cache. In the second use, the allocate cache line command is used to reconfigure a portion of the cache as data RAM; in that case,

Table 12.13   Fetch and Allocate commands to lock code or data in cache on an
Intel XScale processor.

Command	MRC and MCR instructions
Fetch and lock I-cache line VA	MCR p15, 0, Rd, c9, c1, 0
Unlock instruction cache	MCR p15, 0, Rd, c9, c1, 1
Read data cache lock register	MRC p15, 0, Rd, c9, c2, 0
Write data cache lock register and set/clear lock mode	MCR p15, 0, Rd, c9, c2, 0
Unlock D-cache	MCR p15, 0, Rd, c9, c2, 1

31	1 0
SBZ	L

Figure 12.16   Format of the CP15:c9:c2 D-cache lock register.

the portion of cache allocated is not initialized and needs a write from the processor core
to contain valid data. In our example we initialize the memory to zero.

EXAMPLE
12.9

The first part of the routine defines the registers used in the macro CACHELOCKREGION. The
macro also uses constants in the header file *cache.h* shown in Figure 12.10.

The macro starts by aligning the address (*adr*) to a cache line and determining the
number of cache lines it takes to contain the code.

If the procedure is locking data in the D-cache, then the next few lines drain the write
buffer and unlock the D-cache. Locking data in the D-cache requires an unlock command
that must be issued prior to locking a D-cache line. The macro sets this bit by writing a one
to the CP15:c9:c2:0 register.

At this point the code enters a loop that fills the cache with locked code or data. If the
procedure is locking code in the I-cache, it executes a lock I-cache line command. If it
is locking data from external memory, it cleans, flushes, and loads a new cache line into
the D-cache. If creating data RAM, it allocates a D-cache line and drains the write buffer
to protect against errors that might result from trying to lock more than 28 sets. It then
initializes the cache line to zero using STRD instructions.

The macro exits by clearing the lock bit on cache load CP15 register if it is locking
D-cache data.

```
            IF  {CPU} = "XSCALE"
              EXPORT lockICache
              EXPORT lockDCache
              EXPORT lockDCacheRAM
              INCLUDE cache.h

adr    RN 0    ; current address of code or data
size   RN 1    ; memory size in bytes
tmp    RN 2    ; cp15:c9:c2 format & STRD reg 0
tmp1   RN 3    ; scratch reg for LDR & STRD reg 1
            MACRO
            CACHELOCKREGION $op

            ADD    size, adr, size        ; size = end address
            BIC    adr, adr, #(1<<CLINE)-1 ; align to CLINE
            MOV    tmp, #(1<<CLINE)-1     ; scratch CLINE mask
            TST    size, tmp             ; CLINE end fragment ?
            SUB    size, size, adr        ; add alignment bytes
            MOV    size, size, lsr #CLINE ; convert size 2 # CLINE
            ADDNE  size, size, #1         ; add CLINE to hold fragment

            CMP    size, #0              ; no lockdown requested
            BEQ    %FT1                  ; exit return size =0

            IF     "$op" = "Dcache" :LOR: "$op" = "DcacheRAM"
              MCR    p15, 0, adr, c7, c10, 4 ; drain write buffer
              MOV    tmp, #1
              MCR    p15, 0, tmp, c9, c2, 0 ; unlock data cache
              CPWAIT
              MOV    tmp, #0              ; even words to zero
            ENDIF
            IF     "$op" = "DcacheRAM"
              MOV    tmp1, #0             ; init odd words to zero
            ENDIF
  5
            IF     "$op" = "Icache"
              MCR    p15, 0, adr, c9, c1, 0; lock ICache line
              ADD    adr, adr, #1<<CLINE
            ENDIF
            IF     "$op" = "Dcache"
              MCR    p15, 0, adr, c7, c10, 1   ; clean dirty line
              MCR    p15, 0, adr, c7, c6, 1    ; Flush d-cache line
              LDR    tmp1, [adr], #1<<CLINE ; load data cache line
```

```
        ENDIF

        IF      "$op" = "DcacheRAM"
          MCR     p15, 0, adr, c7, c2, 5  ; Allocate d-cache line
          MCR     p15, 0, adr, c7, c10, 4 ; drain write buffer
          STRD    tmp, [adr], #8     ; init 2 zero & adr=+2
          STRD    tmp, [adr], #8     ; init 2 zero & adr=+2
          STRD    tmp, [adr], #8     ; init 2 zero & adr=+2
          STRD    tmp, [adr], #8     ; init 2 zero & adr=+2
        ENDIF
        SUBS    size, size, #1
        BNE     %BT5

        IF "$op" = "Dcache" :LOR: "$op" = "DcacheRAM"
          MCR     p15, 0, adr, c7, c10, 4    ; drain write buffer
          MCR     p15, 0, tmp, c9, c2, 0     ; lock data cache
          CPWAIT
        ENDIF
1
        MOV     r0, #0
        MOV     pc, lr
        MEND
lockICache
        CACHELOCKREGION Icache
lockDCache
        CACHELOCKREGION Dcache
lockDCacheRAM
        CACHELOCKREGION DcacheRAM
        ENDIF
```

Finally, the macro is used three times to create the lockICache, lockDCache, and lockDCacheRAM functions.

12.7   CACHES AND SOFTWARE PERFORMANCE

Here are a few simple rules to help write code that takes advantage of cache architecture.

Most regions in a memory system are configured to have both the caches and write buffer enabled, taking maximum advantage of the cache architecture to reduce average memory access time. For more information on regions and the configuration of cache and write buffers operation within them, refer to Chapter 13 if you are using an ARM processor core with a memory protection unit and Chapter 14 if you are using an ARM processor core with a memory management unit.

Memory-mapped peripherals frequently fail if they are configured to use cache or the write buffer. It is best to configure them as noncached and nonbuffered memory, which forces the processor to read the peripheral device on every memory access, rather than use what would be stale data from cache.

Try to place frequently accessed data sequentially in memory, remembering that the cost of fetching a new data value from main memory requires a cache line fill. If the data in the cache line is used only once before it is evicted, performance will be poor. Placing data in the same cache line has the effect of actively forcing more cache hits by packing data close together to take advantage of spatial locality. It is most important to keep the data accessed by a common routine close together in main memory.

Try to organize data so reading, processing, and writing is done in cache-line-sized blocks whose lower main memory address matches the starting address of the cache line.

The best general approach is to keep code routines small and to group related data close together. The smaller the code, the more likely it is to be cache efficient.

Linked lists can reduce program performance when using a cache because searching the list results in a high number of cache misses. When accessing data from a linked list, a program fetches data in a more random fashion than it would if it were accessing the data from a sequential array. This hint really applies to searching any unordered list. The way you choose to search for data may require a performance analysis of your system.

However, it is important to remember that there are other factors that play a greater role in system performance than writing code to efficiently use cache. See Chapters 5 and 6 for efficient programming techniques.

12.8 SUMMARY

A cache is a small, fast array of memory placed between the processor and main memory. It is a holding buffer that stores portions of recently referenced system memory. The processor uses cache memory in preference to system memory whenever possible to increase average system performance.

A write buffer is a very small FIFO memory placed between the processor core and main memory, which helps free the processor core and cache memory from the slow write time associated with writing to main memory.

The principle of *locality of reference* states that computer software programs frequently run small loops of code that repeatedly operate on local sections of data memory and explains why the average system performance increases significantly when using a cached processor core.

There are many terms used by the ARM community to describe features of cache architecture. As a convenience we have created Table 12.14, which lists the features of all current ARM cached cores.

The *cache line* is a fundamental component in a cache and contains three parts: a directory store, a data section, and status information. The *cache-tag* is a directory entry

Table 12.14   ARM cached core features.

Core	Cache type	Cache size (kilobytes)	Cache line size (words)	Associativity	Location	Cache lockdown support	Write buffer size (words)
ARM720T	unified	8	4	4-way	logical	no	8
ARM740T	unified	4 or 8	4	4-way		yes 1/4	8
ARM920T	split	16/16 D + I	8	64-way	logical	yes 1/64	16
ARM922T	split	8/8 D + I	8	64-way	logical	yes 1/64	16
ARM940T	split	4/4 D + I	4	64-way		yes 1/64	8
ARM926EJ-S	split	4–128/4–128 D + I	8	4-way	logical	yes 1/4	16
ARM946E-S	split	4–128/4–128 D + I	4	4-way		yes 1/4	4
ARM1022E	split	16/16 D + I	8	64-way	logical	yes 1/64	16
ARM1026EJ-S	split	4–128/4–128 D + I	8	4-way	logical	yes 1/4	8
Intel StrongARM	split	16/16 D + I	4	32-way	logical	no	32
Intel XScale	split	32/32 D + I	8	32-way	logical	yes 1/32	32
		2 D	8	2-way	logical	no	

indicating where a cache line was loaded from main memory. There are two common status bits within the cache: the valid bit and the dirty bit. The *valid* bit is set when the associated cache line contains active memory. The *dirty* bit is active when the cache is using a writeback policy and new data has been written to cache memory.

The placement of a cache before or after the MMU is either physical or logical. A *logical* cache is placed between the processor core and the MMU, and references code and data in a virtual address space. A *physical* cache is placed between the MMU and main memory, and references code and data memory using physical addresses.

A direct-mapped cache is a very simple cache architecture where there is a single location in cache for a given main memory location. A direct-mapped cache is subject to *thrashing*. To reduce thrashing, a cache is divided into smaller equal units called *ways*. The use of ways provides multiple storage locations in cache for a single main memory address. These caches are known as *set associative* caches.

The core bus architecture helps determine the design of a cached system. A Von Neumann architecture uses a *unified* cache to store code and data. A Harvard architecture uses a *split* cache: it has one cache for instructions and a separate cache for data.

The cache replacement policy determines which cache line is selected for replacement on a cache miss. The configured policy defines the algorithm a cache controller uses to select a cache line from the available set in cache memory. The cache line selected for replacement is a *victim*. The two replacement policies available in ARM cached cores are *pseudorandom* and *round-robin*.

There are two policies available when writing data to cache memory. If the controller only updates cache memory, it is a *writeback* policy. If the cache controller writes to both the cache and main memory, it is a *writethrough* policy.

There are two policies a cache controller uses to allocate a cache line on a cache miss. A *read-allocate* policy allocates a cache line when data is read from main memory. A *write-allocate* policy allocates a cache line on a write to main memory.

ARM uses the term *clean* to mean forcing a copyback of data in the D-cache to main memory. ARM uses the term *flush* to mean invalidating the contents of a cache.

Cache lockdown is a feature provided by some ARM cores. The lockdown feature allows code and data to be loaded into cache and marked as exempt from eviction.

We also provided example code showing how to clean and flush ARM cached cores, and to lock code and data in cache.

C H A P T E R **13**

MEMORY
PROTECTION
UNITS

Some embedded systems use a multitasking operating or control system and must ensure that a running task does not disrupt the operation of other tasks. The shielding of system resources and other tasks from unwanted access is called protection and is the subject of this chapter.

There are two methods to control access to system resources, *unprotected* and *protected*. An unprotected system relies solely on software to protect the system resources. A protected system relies on both hardware and software to protect the system resources. The choice of method used by the control system depends on the capability of the processor and the requirements of the control system.

An unprotected embedded system has no hardware dedicated to enforcing the use of memory and peripheral devices during operation. In these systems, each task must cooperate with all other tasks when accessing system resources because any task could corrupt the state of another task. This cooperative scheme may result in task failure when one task ignores the access limits of another task's environment.

An example of a task failure that might occur in an unprotected system involves reading and writing to a serial port register for communication. If one task is using the port, there is no way to prevent another task from using the same port. Successful use of the port must be coordinated through a system call that provides access to the port. An unauthorized access by a task working around these calls can easily disrupt communications through the port. The undesirable use of the resource could be unintentional, or it could be hostile in nature.

In contrast, a protected system has dedicated hardware to check and restrict access to system resources. It can enforce resource ownership. Tasks are required to behave by a set of rules defined by the operating environment and enforced by hardware, which grants special privileges to the programs that monitor and control resources at the hardware level. A protected system is proactive in preventing one task from using the resources of another. The use of hardware to actively monitor the system provides better protection than cooperatively enforced software routines.

ARM provides several processors equipped with hardware that actively protects system resources, either through a memory protection unit (MPU) or a memory management unit (MMU). A processor core with an MPU, the subject of this chapter, provides hardware protection over several software-designated regions. A processor core with an MMU, the subject of the next chapter, provides hardware protection and adds a virtual memory capability.

In a protected system, there are two major classes of resource that need monitoring: the memory system and peripheral devices. Since ARM peripherals are generally memory mapped, the MPU uses the same method to protect both resources.

An ARM MPU uses regions to manage system protection. A *region* is a set of attributes associated with an area of memory. The processor core holds these attributes in several CP15 registers and identifies each region by a number, which ranges between zero and seven.

A region's memory boundaries are configured using two attributes, the starting address and its length, which can be any power of two between 4 KB and 4 GB. In addition, the operation system assigns additional attributes to these regions: access rights and the cache and write buffer policies. The access to a region in memory is set as read-write, read-only, or no access and is subject to additional rights based on the current processor mode, which is either privileged or user. A region also has a cache write policy, which controls cache and write buffer attributes. For example, one region can be set to access memory using a writethrough policy, while another operates as noncached and nonbuffered.

When the processor accesses a region in main memory, the MPU compares the region's access permission attributes with the current processor mode to determine what action it will take. If the request satisfies the region access criteria, the core is allowed to read or write to main memory. However, if the memory request results in a memory access violation, the MPU will generate an abort signal.

The abort signal is routed to the processor core, where it responds to the abort signal by taking an exception and vectoring to the abort handler. The abort handler then determines the abort type as either a prefetch or data abort, and based on the abort type the handler branches to the appropriate service routine.

To implement a protected system, the control system assigns several regions to different areas in main memory. A region may be created once and last for the life of the embedded system or may be created temporarily to satisfy the needs of a specific operation and then removed. How to assign and create regions is the subject of the next section.

13.1 PROTECTED REGIONS

There are currently four ARM cores that contain an MPU; the ARM740T, ARM940T, ARM946E-S, and the ARM1026EJ-S. The ARM740T, ARM946E-S, and ARM1026EJ-S each contain 8 protection regions; the ARM940T contains 16 (see Table 13.1).

The ARM740T, ARM946E-S, and ARM1026EJ-S have *unified* instruction and data regions—the data region and instruction region are defined using the same register that sets the size and starting address. The memory access permission and cache policies are configured independently for instruction and data access in the ARM946E-S and ARM1026EJ-S cores; in the ARM740T the same access permission and cache policies are assigned to both instruction and data memory. Regions are independent of whether the core has a Von Neumann or Harvard architecture. Each region is referenced by an identifying number between zero and seven.

Because the ARM940T has separate regions to control instruction and data memory, the core can maintain different region sizes and starting addresses for instruction and data regions. The separation of instruction and data regions results in eight additional regions in this cached core. Although the identifying region numbers in an ARM940T still range from zero to seven, each region number has a pair of regions, one data region and one instruction region.

There are several rules that govern regions:

1. Regions can overlap other regions.

2. Regions are assigned a priority number that is independent of the privilege assigned to the region.

3. When regions overlap, the attributes of the region with the highest priority number take precedence over the other regions. The priority only applies over the addresses within the areas that overlap.

4. A region's starting address must be a multiple of its size.

5. A region's size can be any power of two between 4 KB and 4 GB—in other words, any of the following values: 4 KB, 8 KB, 16 KB, 32 KB, 64 KB, . . . , 2 GB, 4 GB.

Table 13.1   Summary of ARM cores with protection units.

ARM core	Number of regions	Separate instruction and data regions	Separate configuration of instruction and data regions
ARM740T	8	no	no
ARM940T	16	yes	yes
ARM946E-S	8	no	yes
ARM1026EJ-S	8	no	yes

6. Accessing an area of main memory outside of a defined region results in an abort. The MPU generates a prefetch abort if the core was fetching an instruction or a data abort if the memory request was for data.

13.1.1   OVERLAPPING REGIONS

Overlapping regions occur when some portion of the memory space assigned to one region is also in the memory space assigned to another region. Overlapping regions provide a greater flexibility when assigning access permission than nonoverlapping regions.

For an example of overlapping regions, suppose a small embedded system has 256 KB of available memory starting at address 0x00000000 and must protect a privileged system area from *user* mode reads and writes. The privileged area code, data, and stacks fit in a 32 KB region starting, with the vector table, at 0x00000000. The remaining memory is assigned to user space.

With overlapping regions, the system uses two regions, a 256 KB user region and a 32 KB privileged region (see Figure 13.1). The privileged region 1 is given the higher number because its attributes must take precedence over the user region 0.

13.1.2   BACKGROUND REGIONS

Another useful feature provided by overlapping regions is a background region—a low-priority region used to assign the same attributes to a large memory area. Other regions with higher priority are then placed over this background region to change the attributes of a smaller subset of the defined background region. So the higher-priority region is changing a subset of the background region attributes. A background region can shield several dormant

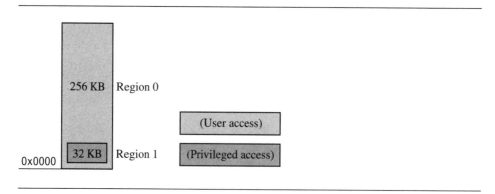

Figure 13.1   Creating regions that overlap.

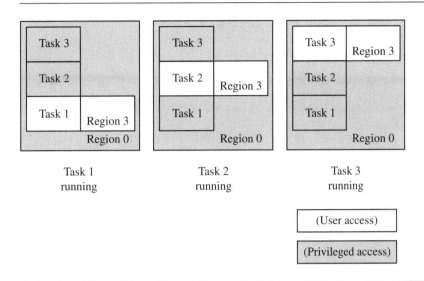

Figure 13.2   Using a background region to control task access.

memory areas from unwanted access while another part of the background region is active under a different region's control.

For example, if an embedded system defines a large privileged background region, it can lay a smaller unprivileged region over this background. The location of the smaller region can be moved over different areas of the background region to reveal different user spaces. When the system moves the smaller user region from one location to another, the previously covered area becomes protected by the background region. So the user region is acting as a window allowing access to different parts of the privileged background but has user-level attributes (see Figure 13.2).

Figure 13.2 shows a simple three-task protection scheme. Region 3 defines the protection attributes of the active task, and the background region 0 controls access to the other tasks when they are dormant. When task 1 is running, the background region protects tasks 2 and 3 from task 1. When task 2 is running, tasks 1 and 3 are protected. Finally, when Task 3 is running, tasks 1 and 2 are protected. The reason this works is that region 3 has higher priority than region 0, even though region 0 has higher privilege.

We use a background region in the example code at the end of this chapter to demonstrate a simple multitasking protection scheme.

13.2 INITIALIZING THE MPU, CACHES, AND WRITE BUFFER

In order to initialize the MPU, caches, and write buffer, the control system must define the protection regions required during the target operation.

Table 13.2   Coprocessor registers that control the MPU.

Function	Primary register	Secondary registers
System control	*c1*	*c0*
Region cache attributes	*c2*	*c0*
Region write buffer attributes	*c3*	*c0*
Region access permissions	*c5*	*c0*
Region size and location	*c6*	*c0* to *c7*

At a minimum the control system must define at least one data region and one instruction region before it can enable the protection unit. The protection unit must be enabled before or at the same time as the caches and write buffer are enabled.

The control system configures the MPU by setting primary CP15 registers *c1*, *c2*, *c3*, *c5*, and *c6*. Table 13.2 lists the primary registers needed to control the operation of the MPU. Register *c1* is the primary control register.

Configuring registers *c2* and *c3* sets the cache and write buffer attributes of regions. Register *c5* controls region access permissions. There are 8 or 16 secondary registers in register *c6* that define the location and size of each region. There are other configuration registers in the ARM740T, ARM940T, ARM946E-S, and ARM1026EJ-S, but their use does not involve the basic operation of the MPU. To review the use of coprocessor 15 registers, refer to Section 3.5.2.

The following steps are required to initialize the MPU, caches, and write buffer:

1. Define the size and location of the instruction and data regions using CP15:c6.

2. Set the access permission for each region using CP15:c5.

3. Set the cache and write buffer attributes for each region using CP15:c2 for cache and CP15:c3 for the write buffer.

4. Enable the caches and the MPU using CP15:c1.

For each of these steps, there is a chapter section that follows describing the coprocessor 15 commands needed to configure each register. There is also example code showing the commands used in a routine that completes the step in the initialization process.

13.2.1 DEFINING REGION SIZE AND LOCATION

To define the size and address range of each region, the embedded system writes to one of the eight secondary registers, CP15:c6:c0:0 to CP15:c6:c7:0. Each secondary coprocessor register number maps to the corresponding region number identifier.

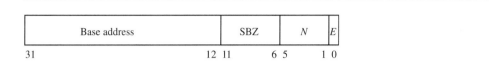

Figure 13.3   CP15:c6 register format setting size and location of a region.

Table 13.3   Bit field description of registers CP15:c6:c0 to CP15:c6:c7.

Field name	Bit fields	Comments
Base address	[31:12]	Address greater than 4 KB must be a multiple of the size represented in [5:1]
SBZ	[11:6]	Value "should be zero"
N	[5:1]	Size of region is 2^{N+1}, where $11 \leq N \leq 31$
E	[0]	Region enable, 1 – enable, 0 = disable

The starting address for each region must be aligned on an address that is a multiple of its size. For example, if a region is 128 KB in size, it can start at any address multiple of 0x20000. The size of a region can be any power of two from 4 KB to 4 GB.

The bit fields and the format of the eight secondary registers CP15:c6:c0 to CP15:c6:c7 are shown in Figure 13.3 and Table 13.3. The starting address is stored in the top bit field [31:20] and must be a multiple of the size bit field [5:1]. The *E* field bit [0] enables or disables the region; that is, a region can be defined and disabled so that its attributes are not enforced until the enable bit is set. The unused bits in the CP15:c6 secondary registers should be set to zero.

To define the size of a region, you can use the formula, $size = 2^{N+1}$ or look up the value in Table 13.4 . To set the size, place the exponent value *N* in the size bit field of the CP15:c6 register. The value of *N* is limited by the hardware design to be any integer between 11 and 31, representing 4 KB to 4 GB. The binary value provides the exact bit field for the size entry. Once you have determined the size of a region, the starting address of the region can be any integer value times the size calculated from the formula, or if you like, taken from Table 13.4. The region size and starting address are determined by the memory map of your system and the areas the control system must protect. The demonstration system at the end of this chapter shows how to set up regions given a system memory map.

The ARM740T, ARM946E-S, and ARM1026EJ-S processors each have eight regions. To set the size and location of a region requires a write to a secondary register in CP15:c6:cX. For example, the instruction syntax needed to set the location and size of region 3 to start

Table 13.4   Region size encoding.

Size	Decimal value	Binary value
4 KB	11	01011
8 KB	12	01100
16 KB	13	01101
32 KB	14	01110
64 KB	15	01111
128 KB	16	10000
256 KB	17	10001
512 KB	18	10010
1 MB	19	10011
2 MB	20	10100
4 MB	21	10101
8 MB	22	10110
16 MB	23	10111
32 MB	24	11000
64 MB	25	11001
128 MB	26	11010
256 MB	27	11011
512 MB	28	11100
1 GB	29	11101
2 GB	30	11110
4 GB	31	11111

at 0x300000 with a size of 256 KB is

```
MOV    r1, #0x300000        ; set starting address
ORR    r1, r1, #0x11<<1     ; set size to 256 KB
MCR    p15, 0, r1, c6, c3, 0
```

The core register *r1* is filled with the required bit field data; then it is written to the CP15 secondary register using an MCR instruction.

The ARM940T has eight instruction regions and eight data regions. The regions require an additional opcode2 modifier to select either the instruction or data region. Opcode2 is zero for data regions and one for instruction regions.

For example, to read the size and location of data and instruction region 5 requires two MRC instructions, one for the instruction region and one for the data region. The instructions needed to read the size and starting location of the regions are

```
MRC    p15, 0, r2, c6, c5, 0  ; r2 = base/size Data Region 5
MRC    p15, 0, r3, c6, c5, 1  ; r3 = base/size Inst Region 5
```

The first instruction loads core register *r2* with the size and starting address of data region 5, and the second instruction loads core register *r3* with the size and starting address of instruction region 5. The ARM940T is the only processor core that has separate instruction and data regions.

EXAMPLE The following example code shows how to set the starting address, size of a region, and the
13.1 enable bit. The routine regionSet has the following C prototype:

```
void regionSet(unsigned region, unsigned address,
                unsigned sizeN, unsigned enable);
```

The routine has four unsigned integer inputs: the region to configure, the starting address of the region, the encoded sizeN of the region, and whether the region is enabled or disabled. It is a good idea to disable a region while changing its attributes and then reenabling it when the changes are complete.

To make the routine work for all four available versions of an MPU processor, we unified the ARM940T region space by configuring the instruction and data regions with the size and starting address information. To do this, we wrote a macro called SET_REGION with two parts, one for the ARM940T and one for the other cores. This allows the same routine to support the four MPU cores.

```
#if defined( __TARGET_CPU_ARM940T)
#define SET_REGION(REGION) \
            /* set Data region base & size */ \
  __asm{MCR p15, 0, c6f, c6, c ## REGION, 0 } \
            /* set Instruction region base & size */ \
  __asm{MCR p15, 0, c6f, c6, c ## REGION, 1 }
#endif

#if defined(__TARGET_CPU_ARM946E_S) | \
   defined(__TARGET_CPU_ARM1026EJ_S)
#define SET_REGION(REGION_NUMBER) \
            /* set region base & size */ \
  __asm{MCR p15, 0, c6f, c6, c ## REGION_NUMBER, 0 }
#endif

void regionSet(unsigned region, unsigned address,
                unsigned sizeN, unsigned enable)
{
  unsigned int c6f;
  c6f = enable | (sizeN << 1) | address;
  switch (region)
```

```
{
    case 0: { SET_REGION(0); break;}
    case 1: { SET_REGION(1); break;}
    case 2: { SET_REGION(2); break;}
    case 3: { SET_REGION(3); break;}
    case 4: { SET_REGION(4); break;}
    case 5: { SET_REGION(5); break;}
    case 6: { SET_REGION(6); break;}
    case 7: { SET_REGION(7); break;}
    default: { break; }
    }
}
```

The code starts by merging the `region` attributes of starting `address`, `sizeN`, and `enable` into an unsigned integer named *c6f*. The routine then branches to one of eight `regionSet` routines created using the macro `SET_REGION`, which sets the region's starting address, size, and enable state by writing to CP15:c6 secondary register for the region defined.

13.2.2 ACCESS PERMISSION

There are two sets of access permission schemes available, a standard set and an extended set. All four cores support the standard set, which provides four levels of permission. The newer ARM946E-S and ARM1026EJ-S support an extended set, which adds an additional two levels of permission (see Table 13.5). The extended set AP (access permission) bit field encoding supports 12 additional permission values. Only two of these bits have been allocated to date. Using an undefined encoding results in unpredictable behavior.

Table 13.5   CP15 register 5 access permissions.

Supervisor	User	Standard AP value encoding	Extended AP value encoding
No access	no access	00	0000
Read/write	no access	01	0001
Read/write	read only	10	0010
Read/write	read/write	11	0011
Unpredictable	unpredictable	—	0100
Read only	no access	—	0101
Read only	read only	—	0110
Unpredictable	unpredictable	—	0111
Unpredictable	unpredictable	—	1000 to 1111

Table 13.6   Bit field assignments for the standard and extended access permission registers CP15:c5.

Region	Standard AP		Extended AP	
	Field name	Bit field	Field name	Bit field
0	AP0	[1:0]	eAP0	[3:0]
1	AP1	[3:2]	eAP1	[7:4]
2	AP2	[5:4]	eAP2	[11:8]
3	AP3	[7:6]	eAP3	[15:12]
4	AP4	[9:8]	eAP4	[19:16]
5	AP5	[11:10]	eAP5	[23:20]
6	AP6	[13:12]	eAP6	[27:24]
7	AP7	[15:14]	eAP7	[31:28]

CP15:c5:c0 standard instruction region AP
CP15:c5:c1 standard data region AP

	AP7	AP6	AP5	AP4	AP3	AP2	AP1	AP0
31	1615	1413	1211	109	8 7	6 5	4 3	2 1 0

CP15:c5:c2 extended instruction region AP
CP15:c5:c3 extended data region AP

eAP7	eAP6	eAP5	eAP4	eAP3	eAP2	eAP1	eAP0
31 28	27 24	23 20	19 16	15 12	11 8	7 4	3 0

Figure 13.4   CP15 register 5 access permission register formats.

To assign access permission to a region requires a write to a secondary register in CP15:c5. Secondary registers CP15:c5:c0:0 and CP15:c5:c0:1 configure standard AP, and secondary registers CP15:c5:c0:2 or CP15:c5:c0:3 configure extended AP. Table 13.6 and Figure 13.4 show the register's permission bit assignments for the AP registers.

Processors that support extended permission can also run software written for standard permission. The type of permission in effect depends on the last write to a CP15 AP register: If the last written AP register was a standard AP register, then the core is using standard permission; if the last written AP register was an extended AP register, then the core uses extended permission. This works because a write to the standard AP registers also updates the extended AP registers, meaning that the high bits [2:3] of the extended AP region entry are cleared.

When using standard AP, each region has two bits in registers CP15:c5:c0:0 and CP15:c5:c0:1. CP15:c5:c0:0 sets the AP for data, and CP15:c5:c0:1 sets the instruction region.

To read the standard AP for instruction and data memory requires reading two registers. The following two MRC instruction sequence places AP information for data region memory in core register *r1* and AP information for instruction region in register *r2*:

```
MRC    p15, 0, r1, c5, c0, 0 ; Std AP Data Regions
MRC    p15, 0, r2, c5, c0, 1 ; Std AP Inst Regions
```

When using extended AP, each region uses four bits in registers CP15:c5:c0:2 and CP15:c5:c0:3. The core stores instruction information for the eight regions in a single register and the data information in another register. CP15:c5:c0:2 sets the AP for the data region, and CP15:c5:c0:3 sets the AP for the instruction region.

Obtaining the instruction and data region extended AP requires reading two registers. The following two-instruction sequence places region data AP in core register *r3* and region instruction AP in register *r4*:

```
MRC    p15, 0, r3, c5, c0, 2    ; Extended AP Data Regions
MRC    p15, 0, r4, c5, c0, 3    ; Extended AP Inst Regions
```

We supply two examples to demonstrate using access permissions, one for standard AP and the other for extended AP. These examples use the inline assembler to read and write to the CP15 registers.

We provide two standard AP routines, regionSetISAP and regionSetDSAP, to set the standard AP bits for a region. They are called from C using the following function prototype:

```
void regionSetISAP(unsigned region, unsigned ap);
void regionSetDSAP(unsigned region, unsigned ap);
```

The first parameter is the region number, and the second is the two-bit value defining the standard AP for the instruction or data memory controlled by the region.

EXAMPLE
13.2

The two routines are identical with the exception that they read and write to different CP15:c5 secondary registers; one writes to the instruction register, and the other to the data register. The routine does a simple read-modify-write operation on the CP15:c5 register to set the AP of the specified region, leaving the remaining regions intact.

```
void regionSetISAP(unsigned region, unsigned ap)
{
    unsigned c5f, shift;

    shift = 2*region;
    __asm{ MRC p15, 0, c5f, c5, c0, 1 }    /* load standard D AP */
```

```
    c5f = c5f &~  (0x3<<shift);             /* clear old AP bits */
    c5f = c5f | (ap<<shift);                /* set new AP bits */
    __asm{MCR p15, 0, c5f, c5, c0, 1 }      /* store standard D AP */
}

void regionSetDSAP(unsigned region, unsigned ap)
{
    unsigned c5f, shift;

    shift = 2*region;                       /* set bit field width */
    __asm {MRC p15, 0, c5f, c5, c0, 0 }     /* load standard I AP */
    c5f = c5f &~  (0x3<<shift);             /* clear old AP bits */
    c5f = c5f | (ap<<shift);                /* set new AP bits */
    __asm {MCR p15, 0, c5f, c5, c0, 0 }     /* store standard I AP */
}
```

The routine sets the specified region permissions by clearing its AP bits using a shifted mask value and then setting the AP bit field with the ap input parameter. The AP bit field location is calculated as the region number times the number of bits in the permission bit field; this is the shift variable. The value of the bit field is set by shifting the ap value and using an OR to modify the *c5f* core register.

We provide two extended AP routines, regionSetIEAP and regionSetDEAP, to set the extended AP bits for a region. They have the following C function prototypes:

```
void regionSetIEAP(unsigned region, unsigned ap);
void regionSetDEAP(unsigned region, unsigned ap);
```

The first parameter is the region number, and the second is the four-bit value representing the extended AP for the instruction or data memory controlled by the region.

EXAMPLE
13.3
The two routines are identical to the standard AP routines with the exception that they read and write to different CP15:c5 secondary registers and they have a four-bit-wide AP bit field.

```
void regionSetIEAP(unsigned region, unsigned ap)
{
    unsigned c5f, shift;

    shift = 4*region;                       /* set bit field width */
    __asm{ MRC p15, 0, c5f, c5, c0, 3 }     /* load extended D AP */
    c5f = c5f &~ (0xf<<shift);              /* clear old AP bits */
    c5f = c5f | (ap<<shift);                /* set new AP bits */
    __asm{ MCR p15, 0, c5f, c5, c0, 3 }     /* store extended D AP */
}
```

```
void regionSetDEAP(unsigned region, unsigned ap)
{
    unsigned c5f, shift;

    shift = 4*region;                        /* set bit field width */
    __asm{ MRC p15, 0, c5f, c5, c0, 2 }      /* load extended I AP */
    c5f = c5f &~  (0xf<<shift);              /* clear old AP bits */
    c5f = c5f | (ap<<shift);                 /* set new AP bits */
    __asm{ MCR p15, 0, c5f, c5, c0, 2 }      /* store extended I AP */
}
```

Each routine sets the specified region permissions by clearing its AP bits using a shifted mask value and then setting the AP bit field with the ap input parameter. The AP bit field location is calculated as the region number times the number of bits in the permission bit field; this is the shift variable. The value of the bit field is set by shifting the ap value and using an OR to modify the *c5f* core register.

13.2.3 SETTING REGION CACHE AND WRITE BUFFER ATTRIBUTES

Three CP15 registers control the cache and write buffer attributes for each core. Two registers, CP15:c2:c0:0 and CP15:c2:c0:1, hold the D-cache and I-cache region attributes. A third, CP15:c3:c0:0, holds the region write buffer attributes and applies to memory data regions. (Refer to Figure 13.5 and Table 13.7 for details.)

Register CP15:c2:c0:1 contains the cache configuration data for all eight instruction regions, and register CP15:c2:c0:0 contains all eight data regions. Both registers use the same bit field encoding.

The cache bit determines if the cache is enabled for a given address within the region. In the ARM740T and ARM940T, the cache is always searched, regardless of the state of the

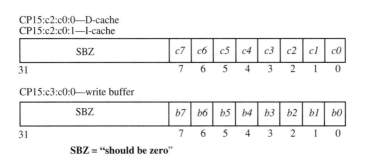

Figure 13.5   CP15:c2 cache and CP15:c3 write buffer region registers.

Table 13.7   Bit field assignments for CP15:c2 and CP15:c3 registers.

	Region cache fields		Region write buffer fields	
Region	Field name	Bit fields	Field name	Bit fields
0	*c0*	[0]	*b0*	[0]
1	*c1*	[1]	*b1*	[1]
2	*c2*	[2]	*b2*	[2]
3	*c3*	[3]	*b3*	[3]
4	*c4*	[4]	*b4*	[4]
5	*c5*	[5]	*b5*	[5]
6	*c6*	[6]	*b6*	[6]
7	*c7*	[7]	*b7*	[7]

cache bit. If the controller finds a valid cache entry, it will use the cached data over data in external memory.

Because of this cache behavior, you need to flush and possibly clean the cache in a region where the cache policy changes from cached to noncached. Consequently, the MPU control system must always flush the cache when changing the cache policy from writethrough to noncached. It must always clean and flush the cache when changing the cache policy from writeback to noncached. It must also clean the cache when changing the cache policy from writeback to writethrough. See Chapter 12 for routines to clean and/or flush the cache.

In the ARM946E-S, if the cache bit is clear, information physically in cache will not be returned from the cache, and an external memory access is performed instead. This design lightens the requirement to flush the cache when it is disabled. However, the cleaning rules for the old region still apply.

The eight region write buffer bits in the register CP15:c3:c0:0 enable or disable the write buffer for each region (again see Figure 13.5).

When configuring data regions, the region cache and write buffer bits together determine the policy of the region. The write buffer bit has two uses; it enables or disables the write buffer for a region and sets the region cache write policy. The region cache bit controls the purpose of the write buffer bit. When the cache bit is zero, the buffer bit enables the write buffer when its value is one and disables the write buffer when its value is zero. When the cache bit is set to one, the cache and write buffer are both enabled and the buffer bit determines the cache write policy. The region uses a writethrough policy if the buffer bit is zero and a writeback policy if the buffer bit is set. Table 13.8 gives a tabular view of the various states of the cache and write buffer bits and their meanings. For more details on writeback and writethrough policies, see Section 12.3.1.

We supply two routines to demonstrate enabling and disabling the caches and write buffer. The two routines use the inline assembler to read and write to the CP15 registers.

We combine control of the cache and write buffer into a single routine call to simplify system configuration. We reference both the data cache and write buffer bits by the write

Table 13.8   Control of the cache and write buffer.

Instruction cache		Data cache		
Cache bit CP15:c2:c0:1	Region attribute	Cache bit CP15:c2:c0:0	Buffer bit CP15:c3:c0:0	Region attribute
0	not cached	0	0	NCNB (not cached, not buffered)
1	cached	0	1	NCB (not cached, buffered)
		1	0	WT (cached, writethrough)
		1	1	WB (cached, writeback)

policy they control, and the instruction cache bit stands alone. From a system view, merging the state of the caches and write buffer into a single value for each region makes it easier to group region information into a region control block (discussed in Section 13.3.3).

The set cache and buffer routine, called `regionSetCB`, is shown in Example 13.4 and has the following C function prototype:

```
void regionSetCB(unsigned region, unsigned CB);
```

The routine has two input parameters. The first parameter, `region`, is the region number, and the second, `CB`, combines the region instruction cache attributes and the data cache and write buffer attributes. The second parameter has a format that uses the lower three bits of the unsigned integer: the instruction cache bit in bit [2], the data cache bit in bit [1], and the data buffer bit in bit [0].

EXAMPLE 13.4   The routine sequentially sets the data write buffer bit, the data cache bit, and the instruction cache bit. To do this, for each bit it reads the CP15 register, clears the old bit value, sets the new bit value, and writes the value back into the CP15 register.

```
void regionSetCB(unsigned region, unsigned CB)
{
    unsigned c3f, tempCB;

    tempCB = CB;
    __asm{MRC p15, 0, c3f, c3, c0, 0 }    /* load buffer register */
    c3f = c3f &~ (0x1 << region);         /* clear old buffer bit */
    c3f = c3f | ((tempCB & 0x1) << region); /* set new buffer bit */
    __asm{MCR p15, 0, c3f, c3, c0, 0 }    /* store buffer info */

    tempCB = CB >> 0x1;                    /* shift to D-cache bit */
    __asm{MRC p15, 0, c3f, c2, c0, 0 }    /* load D-cache register */
```

```
    c3f = c3f &~  (0x1 << region);        /* clear old D-cache bit */
    c3f = c3f | ((tempCB & 0x1) << region); /* set new D-cache bit */
    __asm{MCR p15, 0, c3f, c2, c0, 0 }    /* store D-cache info */

  tempCB = CB >> 0x2;                      /* shift to I-cache bit */
    __asm{MRC p15, 0, c3f, c2, c0, 1 }    /* load I-cache register */
    c3f = c3f &~  (0x1 << region);        /* clear old I-cache bit */
    c3f = c3f | ((tempCB & 0x1) << region); /* set new I-cache bit */
    __asm{MCR p15, 0, c3f, c2, c0, 1 }    /* store I-cache info */
}
```

13.2.4 ENABLING REGIONS AND THE MPU

There are two steps left in the initialization process. The first is to enable active regions, and the second is to turn on the protection unit hardware by enabling the MPU, caches, and write buffer.

To enable a region, the control system can reuse the routine regionSet presented in Section 13.2.1. The multiple use of regionSet is shown in Example 13.6 at the end of the chapter.

To enable the MPU, caches, and write buffer requires modifying bit values in CP15:c1:c0:0, the system control register. The location of the MPU, cache, and write buffer bits in CP15:c1:c0 are the same in the ARM940T, ARM946E-S, and ARM1026EJ-S processors, which makes enabling a configured MPU the same for the three cores. The enable bit locations are shown in Figure 13.6 and Table 13.9. The CP15:c1:c0 register has configuration bits not shown in Figure 13.6; the purpose and location of these bits are processor specific and are not a part of the protection system.

We use the routine changeControl, shown in Example 13.5, to enable the MPU and caches. However, the routine changeControl can change any set of values in the CP15:c1:c0:0 register. It has the following C function prototype:

void controlSet(unsigned value, unsigned mask);

The first parameter passed is an unsigned integer containing the bit values to change. The second parameter is used to select the bits you want changed: A bit value of 1 changes the

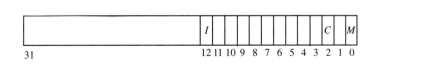

Figure 13.6   Memory protection unit control bits in the CP15:c1:c0 control register.

Table 13.9   Protection unit enable bits in CP15 control register 1.

Bit	Function enabled	Value
0	MPU	0 = disabled, 1 = enabled
2	data cache	0 = disabled, 1 = enabled
12	instruction cache	0 = disabled, 1 = enabled

bit in the control register, and a 0 leaves the bit value unchanged, regardless of the bit state in the first parameter.

For example, to enable the MPU and I-cache, and disable the D-cache, set bit [12] to 1, bit [2] to 0, and bit [0] to 1. The value of the first parameter should be 0x00001001; the remaining unchanged bits should be zero. To select only bit [12], bit [2], and bit [0] as the values to change, set the mask value to 0x00001005.

EXAMPLE
13.5

This routine reads the control register and places the value in a holding register. Then it clears all the changing bits using the mask input and assigns them the desired state using the *value* input. The routine completes by writing the new control values to the CP15:c1:c0 register.

```
void controlSet(unsigned value, unsigned mask)
{
  unsigned int clf;

  __asm{ MRC p15, 0, clf, c1, c0, 0  }     /* read control register */
  clf = clf &~ mask;                       /* mask off bit that change */
  clf = clf | value;                       /* set bits that change */
  __asm{ MCR p15, 0, clf, c1, c0, 0  }     /* write control register */
}
```

13.3 DEMONSTRATION OF AN MPU SYSTEM

We have provided a set of routines to use as building blocks to initialize and control a protected system. This section uses the routines described to initialize and control a simple protected system using a fixed memory map.

Here is a demonstration that uses the examples presented in the previous sections of this chapter to create a functional protection system. It provides an infrastructure that enables the running of three tasks in a simple protected multi-tasking system. We believe it provides a suitable demonstration of the concepts underlying the ARM MPU hardware. It is written in C and uses standard access permission.

13.3.1 SYSTEM REQUIREMENTS

The demonstration system has the following hardware characteristics:

- An ARM core with an MPU
- 256 KB of physical memory starting at 0x0 and ending at 0x40000
- Several memory-mapped peripherals spaced over several megabytes from 0x10000000 to 0x12000000

In this demonstration, all the memory-mapped peripherals are considered a single area of memory that needs protection (see Table 13.10).

The demonstration system has the following software components:

- The system software is less than 64 KB in size. It includes the vector table, exception handlers, and data stacks to support the exceptions. The system software must be inaccessible from *user* mode; that is, a *user* mode task must make a system call to run code or access data in this region.
- There is shared software that is less than 64 KB in size. It contains commonly used libraries and data space for messaging between user tasks.
- There are three user tasks that control independent functions in the system. These tasks are less than 32 KB in size. When these tasks are running, they must be protected from access by the other two tasks.

The software is linked to place the software components within the regions assigned to them. Table 13.10 shows the software memory map for the example. The system software has system-level access permission. The shared software area is accessible by the entire system. The task software areas contain user-level tasks.

Table 13.10 Memory map of example protection system.

Function	Access level	Starting address	Size	Region
Protect memory-mapped peripheral devices	system	0x10000000	2 MB	4
Protected system	system	0x00000000	4 GB	1
Shared system	user	0x00010000	64 KB	2
User task 1	user	0x00020000	32 KB	3
User task 2	user	0x00028000	32 KB	3
User task 3	user	0x00030000	32 KB	3

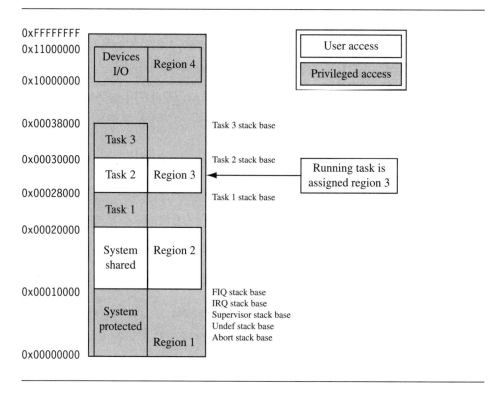

Figure 13.7   Region assignment and memory map of demonstration protection system.

13.3.2   ASSIGNING REGIONS USING A MEMORY MAP

The last column of Table 13.10 shows the four regions we assigned to the memory areas. The regions are defined using the starting address listed in the table and the size of the code and data blocks. A memory map showing the region layout is provided in Figure 13.7.

Region 1 is a background region that covers the entire addressable memory space. It is a privileged region (i.e., no *user* mode access is permitted). The instruction cache is enabled, and the data cache operates with a writethrough policy. This region has the lowest region priority because it is the region with the lowest assigned number.

The primary function of region 1 is to restrict access to the 64 KB space between 0x0 and 0x10000, the protected system area. Region 1 has two secondary functions: it acts as a background region and as a protection region for dormant user tasks. As a background region it ensures the entire memory space by default is assigned system-level access; this is done to prevent a user task from accessing spare or unused memory locations. As a user task protection region, it protects dormant tasks from misconduct by the running task (see Figure 13.7).

Region 2 controls access to shared system resources. It has a starting address of 0x10000 and is 64 KB in length. It maps directly over the shared memory space of the shared system code. Region 2 lies on top of a portion of protected region 1 and will take precedence over protected region 1 because it has a higher region number. Region 2 permits both user and system level memory access.

Region 3 controls the memory area and attributes of a running task. When control transfers from one task to another, as during a context switch, the operating system redefines region 3 so that it overlays the memory area of the running task. When region 3 is relocated over the new task, it exposes the previous task to the attributes of region 1. The previous task becomes part of region 1, and the running task is a new region 3. The running task cannot access the previous task because it is protected by the attributes of region 1.

Region 4 is the memory-mapped peripheral system space. The primary purpose of this region is to establish the area as not cached and not buffered. We don't want input, output, or control registers subject to the stale data issues caused by caching, or the time or sequence issues involved when using buffered writes (see Chapter 12 for details on using I/O devices with caches and write buffers).

13.3.3 INITIALIZING THE MPU

To organize the initialization process we created a datatype called Region; it is a structure whose members hold the attributes of a region used during system operation. This Region structure is not required when using the MPU; it is simply a design convenience created to support the demonstration software. For this demonstration, we call the set of these data structures a region control block (RCB).

The initialization software uses the information stored in the RCB to configure the regions in the MPU. Note that there can be more Region structures defined in the RCB than physical regions. For example, region 3 is the only region used for tasks, yet there are three Region structures that use region 3, one for each user task. The typedef for the structure is

```
typedef struct {
            unsigned int number;
            unsigned int type;
            unsigned int baseaddress;
            unsigned int size;
            unsigned int IAP;
            unsigned int DAP;
            unsigned int CB;
        } Region;
```

There are eight values in the Region structure. The first two values describe characteristics of the Region itself: they are the MPU region number assigned to the Region, and the type of access permission used, either STANDARD or EXTENDED. The remaining four members of the structure are attributes of the specified region: the region starting address, baseaddress; region size, SIZE; access permissions, IAP and DAP; and cache and buffer configuration, CB.

The six Region structures in the RCB are

```
/*                       REGION NUMBER, APTYPE */
/*                  START ADDRESS,  SIZE,     IAP,  DAP,  CB */

Region peripheralRegion = {PERIPH, STANDARD,
                      0x10000000, SIZE_1M,   RONA, RWNA, ccb};
Region kernelRegion =    {KERNEL, STANDARD,
                      0x00000000, SIZE_4G,   RONA, RWNA, CWT};
Region sharedRegion =    {SHARED, STANDARD,
                      0x00010000, SIZE_64K, RORO, RWRW, CWT};
Region task1Region  =    {TASK, STANDARD,
                      0x00020000, SIZE_32K, RORO, RWRW, CWT};
Region task2Region  =    {TASK, STANDARD,
                      0x00028000, SIZE_32K, RORO, RWRW, CWT};
Region task3Region  =    {TASK, STANDARD,
                      0x00030000, SIZE_32K, RORO, RWRW, CWT};
```

We created a set of macros to make entries in the RCB more humanly readable; they are shown in Figure 13.8. Most notably, we enter access permission to data and instruction memory using a simple combination of four letters. The first two letters represent system access permission, and the second two letters represent user access. The two letters for system and user access can be read/write (RW), read-only (RO), or no access (NA).

We also mapped the cache and buffer information to an instruction cache and a data cache policy attribute. The first letter is C or c and enables or disables the instruction cache for the region. The last two letters determine the data cache policy and write buffer control. The values can be WT for writethrough or WB for writeback. The letters c and b are also supported and are manual configurations of the cache and buffer bits. Cb is an alias of WT, and CB is an alias of WB. cB means not cached and buffered, and finally cb means not cached and not buffered.

13.3.4 INITIALIZING AND CONFIGURING A REGION

Next we provide the routine configRegion, which takes a single Region structure entry in the RCB to populate the CP15 registers with data describing the region.

The routine follows the initialization steps listed in Section 13.3.3. The input to the routine is a pointer to the RCB of a region. Within the routine, members of the Region are

```
/* Region Number Assignment */
#define   BACKGROUND 0
#define   KERNEL 1
#define   TASK   2
#define   SHARED 3
#define   PERIPH  4

/* Region Type Assignment */
#define   STANDARD 0
#define   EXTENDED 1
#define   DISABLE 0

/* Access Permissions */
#define NANA 0
#define RWNA 1
#define RWRO 2
#define RWRW 3
#define RONA 5
#define RORO 6

/* Region Size */
#define SIZE_4G    31
#define SIZE_2G    30
#define SIZE_1G    29
#define SIZE_512M 28
#define SIZE_256M 27
#define SIZE_128M 26
#define SIZE_64M   25
#define SIZE_32M   24
#define SIZE_16M   23
#define SIZE_8M    22
#define SIZE_4M    21
#define SIZE_2M    20
#define SIZE_1M    19
#define SIZE_512K 18
#define SIZE_256K 17
#define SIZE_128K 16
#define SIZE_64K   15
#define SIZE_32K   14
```

Figure 13.8   Defined macros used in the demonstration example.

```
#define SIZE_16K   13
#define SIZE_8K    12
#define SIZE_4K    11

/* CB - ICache[2], DCache[1], Write Buffer[0] */
/* ICache[2], WB[1:0] = writeback, WT[1:0] = writethrough */
#define CCB 7
#define CWB 7
#define CCb 6
#define CWT 6
#define CcB 5
#define Ccb 4
#define cCB 3
#define cWB 3
#define cCb 2
#define cWT 2
#define ccB 1
#define ccb 0

/* Region enable */
#define R_ENABLE 1
#define R_DISABLE 0
```

Figure 13.8   Defined macros used in the demonstration example. (*Continued.*)

used as data inputs in the initialization process. The routine has the following C function prototype:

```
void configRegion(Region *region);
```

EXAMPLE   This example initializes the MPU, caches, and write buffer for the protected system. The
   13.6   routines presented earlier in this chapter are used in the initialization process. We imple-
            ment the steps first listed in Section 13.2 to initialize the MPU, caches, and write buffer.
            The steps are labeled as comments in the example code. Executing this example initializes
            the MPU.

```
void configRegion(Region *region)
{
/* Step 1 - Define the size and location of the instruction */
/*          and data regions using CP15:c6 */
```

```
        regionSet(region->number, region->baseaddress,
                  region->size, R_DISABLE);

/* Step 2 - Set access permission for each region using CP15:c5 */

    if (region->type == STANDARD)
    {
        regionSetISAP(region->number, region->IAP);
        regionSetDSAP(region->number, region->DAP);
    }
    else if (region->type == EXTENDED)
    {
        regionSetIEAP(region->number, region->IAP);
        regionSetDEAP(region->number, region->DAP);
    }

    /* Step 3 - Set the cache and write buffer attributes */
    /*          for each region using CP15:c2 for cache */
    /*          and CP15:c3 for the write buffer. */

        regionSetCB(region->number, region->CB);

    /* Step 4 - Enable the caches, write buffer and the MPU */
    /*          using CP15:c6 and CP15:c1 */

        regionSet(region->number, region->baseaddress,
                  region->size, region->enable);
}
```

13.3.5 PUTTING IT ALL TOGETHER, INITIALIZING THE MPU

For the demonstration, we use the RCB to store data describing all regions. To initialize the MPU we use a top-level routine named initActiveRegions. The routine is called once for each active region when the system starts up. To complete the initialization, the routine also enables the MPU. The routine has the following C function prototype:

```
void initActiveRegions();
```

The routine has no input parameters.

EXAMPLE 13.7   The routine first calls configRegion once for each region that is active at system startup: the kernelRegion, the sharedRegion, the peripheralRegion, and the task1Region. In this demonstration task 1 is the first task entered. The last routine called is controlSet, which enables the caches and MPU.

```
#define ENABLEMPU    (0x1)
#define ENABLEDCACHE (0x1 << 2)
#define ENABLEICACHE (0x1 << 12)
#define MASKMPU      (0x1)
#define MASKDCACHE   (0x1 << 2)
#define MASKICACHE   (0x1 << 12)

void initActiveRegions()
{
    unsigned value,mask;
    configRegion(&kernelRegion);
    configRegion(&sharedRegion);
    configRegion(&peripheralRegion);
    configRegion(&task1Region);

    value = ENABLEMPU | ENABLEDCACHE | ENABLEICACHE;
    mask = MASKMPU | MASKDCACHE | MASKICACHE;
    controlSet(value, mask);
}
```

13.3.6 A PROTECTED CONTEXT SWITCH

The demonstration system is now initialized, and the control system has launched its first task. At some point, the system will make a context switch to run another task. The RCB contains the current task's region context information, so there is no need to save region data from the CP15 registers during the context switch.

To switch to the next task, for example task 2, the operating system would move region 3 over the task 2 memory area (see Figure 13.7). We reuse the routine configRegion to perform this function as part of the setup just prior to executing the code that performs the context switch between the current task and the next task. The input to configRegion would be a pointer to the task2Region. See the following assembly code sample:

```
STMFD   sp!, {r0-r3,r12,lr}
BL      configRegion
LDMFD   sp!, {r0-r3,r12,pc}        ; return
```

The same call in C is

```
configRegion(&task2Region);
```

13.3.7   MPUSLOS

Many of the concepts and the code examples have been incorporated into a functional control system we call mpuSLOS.

mpuSLOS is the memory protection unit variant of SLOS that was described in Chapter 11. It can be found on the publisher's Web site and implements the same functions as the base SLOS with a number of important differences.

- mpuSLOS takes full advantage of the MPU.

- Applications are compiled and built separately from the kernel and then combined as a single binary file. Each application is linked to execute out of a different memory area.

- Each of the three applications are loaded into separate fixed regions 32 KB in size by a routine called the Static Application Loader. This address is the execution address of the application. The stack pointer is set at the top of the 32 KB since each region is 32 KB in size.

- Applications can only access hardware via a device driver call. If an application attempts to access hardware directly, a data abort is raised. This differs from the base SLOS variant since a data abort will not be raised when a device is accessed directly from an application.

- Jumping to an application involves setting up the *spsr* and then changing the *pc* to point to the entry point to task 1 using a MOVS instruction.

- Each time the scheduler is called, the active task region is changed to reflect the new executing application.

13.4   SUMMARY

There are two methods to handle memory protection. The first method is known as *unprotected* and uses voluntarily enforced software control routines to manage rules for task interaction. The second method is known as *protected* and uses hardware and software to enforce rules for task interaction. In a protected system the hardware protects areas of memory by generating an abort when access permission is violated and software responds to handle the abort routines and manage control to memory-based resources.

An ARM MPU uses regions as the primary construct for system protection. A *region* is a set of attributes associated with an area of memory. Regions can overlap, allowing the use of a background region to shield a dormant task's memory areas from unwanted access by the current running task.

Several steps are required to initialize the MPU, included are routines to set various region attributes. The first step sets the size and location of the instruction and data regions using CP15:c6. The second step sets the access permission for each region using CP15:c5. The third step sets the cache and write buffer attributes for each region using CP15:c2 for cache and CP15:c3 for the write buffer. The last step enables active regions using CP15:c6 and the caches, write buffer, and MPU using CP15:c1.

In closing, a demonstration system showed three tasks, each protected from the other, in a simple multitasking environment. The demonstration system defined a protected system and then showed how to initialize it. After initialization, the last step needed to run a protected system is to change the region assignments to the next task during a task switch. This demonstration system is incorporated into mpuSLOS to provide a functional example of a protected operating system.

C H A P T E R 14

MEMORY MANAGEMENT UNITS

When creating a multitasking embedded system, it makes sense to have an easy way to write, load, and run independent application tasks. Many of today's embedded systems use an operating system instead of a custom proprietary control system to simplify this process. More advanced operating systems use a hardware-based memory management unit (MMU).

One of the key services provided by an MMU is the ability to manage tasks as independent programs running in their own private memory space. A task written to run under the control of an operating system with an MMU does not need to know the memory requirements of unrelated tasks. This simplifies the design requirements of individual tasks running under the control of an operating system.

In Chapter 13 we introduced processor cores with memory protection units. These cores have a single addressable physical memory space. The addresses generated by the processor core while running a task are used directly to access main memory, which makes it impossible for two programs to reside in main memory at the same time if they are compiled using addresses that overlap. This makes running several tasks in an embedded system difficult because each task must run in a distinct address block in main memory.

The MMU simplifies the programming of application tasks because it provides the resources needed to enable *virtual memory*—an additional memory space that is independent of the physical memory attached to the system. The MMU acts as a translator, which converts the addresses of programs and data that are compiled to run in virtual memory to the actual physical addresses where the programs are stored in physical main memory. This translation process allows programs to run with the same virtual addresses while being held in different locations in physical memory.

This dual view of memory results in two distinct address types: virtual addresses and physical addresses. *Virtual addresses* are assigned by the compiler and linker when locating a program in memory. *Physical addresses* are used to access the actual hardware components of main memory where the programs are physically located.

ARM provides several processor cores with integral MMU hardware that efficiently support multitasking environments using virtual memory. The goal of this chapter is to learn the basics of ARM memory management units and some basic concepts that underlie the use of virtual memory.

We begin with a review of the protection features of an MPU and then present the additional features provided by an MMU. We introduce relocation registers, which hold the conversion data to translate virtual memory addresses to physical memory addresses, and the Translation Lookaside Buffer (TLB), which is a cache of recent address relocations. We then explain the use of pages and page tables to configure the behavior of the relocation registers.

We then discuss how to create regions by configuring blocks of pages in virtual memory. We end the overview of the MMU and its support of virtual memory by showing how to manipulate the MMU and page tables to support multitasking.

Next we present the details of configuring the MMU hardware by presenting a section for each of the following components in an ARM MMU: page tables, the Translation Lookaside Buffer (TLB), access permission, caches and write buffer, the CP15:c1 control register, and the Fast Context Switch Extension (FCSE).

We end the chapter by providing demonstration software that shows how to set up an embedded system using virtual memory. The demonstration supports three tasks running in a multitasking environment and shows how to protect each task from the others running in the system by compiling the tasks to run at a common virtual memory execution address and placing them in different locations in physical memory. The key part of the demonstration is showing how to configure the MMU to translate the virtual address of a task to the physical address of a task, and how to switch between tasks.

The demonstration has been integrated into the SLOS operating system presented in Chapter 11 as a variant known as mmuSLOS.

14.1   MOVING FROM AN MPU TO AN MMU

In Chapter 13, we introduced the ARM cores with a memory protection unit (MPU). More importantly, we introduced *regions* as a convenient way to organize and protect memory. Regions are either active or dormant: An *active* region contains code or data in current use by the system; a *dormant* region contains code or data that is not in current use, but is likely to become active in a short time. A dormant region is protected and therefore inaccessible to the current running task.

Table 14.1   Region attributes from the MPU example.

Region attributes	Configuration options
Type	instruction, data
Start address	multiple of size
Size	4 KB to 4 GB
Access permissions	read, write, execute
Cache	copyback, writethrough
Write buffer	enabled, disabled

The MPU has dedicated hardware that assigns attributes to regions. The attributes assigned to a region are shown in Table 14.1.

In this chapter, we assume the concepts introduced in Chapter 13 regarding memory protection are understood and simply show how to configure the protection hardware on an MMU.

The primary difference between an MPU and an MMU is the addition of hardware to support virtual memory. The MMU hardware also expands the number of available regions by moving the region attributes shown in Table 14.1 from CP15 registers to tables held in main memory.

14.2 HOW VIRTUAL MEMORY WORKS

In Chapter 13 we introduced the MPU and showed a multitasking embedded system that compiled and ran each task at distinctly different, fixed address areas in main memory. Each task ran in only one of the process regions, and none of the tasks could have overlapping addresses in main memory. To run a task, a protection region was placed over the fixed address program to enable access to an area of memory defined by the region. The placement of the protection region allowed the task to execute while the other tasks were protected.

In an MMU, tasks can run even if they are compiled and linked to run in regions with overlapping addresses in main memory. The support for virtual memory in the MMU enables the construction of an embedded system that has multiple virtual memory maps and a single physical memory map. Each task is provided its own virtual memory map for the purpose of compiling and linking the code and data, which make up the task. A kernel layer then manages the placement of the multiple tasks in physical memory so they have a distinct location in physical memory that is different from the virtual location it is designed to run in.

To permit tasks to have their own virtual memory map, the MMU hardware performs *address relocation*, translating the memory address output by the processor core before it reaches main memory. The easiest way to understand the translation process is to imagine a relocation register located in the MMU between the core and main memory.

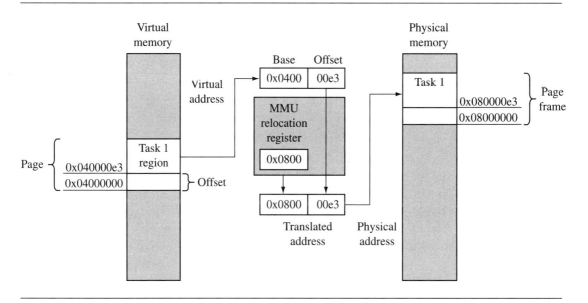

Figure 14.1   Mapping a task in virtual memory to physical memory using a relocation register.

When the processor core generates a virtual address, the MMU takes the upper bits of the virtual address and replaces them with the contents of the relocation register to create a physical address, shown in Figure 14.1

The lower portion of the virtual address is an offset that translates to a specific address in physical memory. The range of addresses that can be translated using this method is limited by the maximum size of this offset portion of the virtual address.

Figure 14.1 shows an example of a task compiled to run at a starting address of 0x04000000 in virtual memory. The relocation register translates the virtual addresses of Task 1 to physical addresses starting at 0x08000000.

A second task compiled to run at the same virtual address, in this case 0x04000000, can be placed in physical memory at any other multiple of 0x010000 (64 KB) and mapped to 0x04000000 simply by changing the value in the relocation register.

A single relocation register can only translate a single area of memory, which is set by the number of bits in the offset portion of the virtual address. This area of virtual memory is known as a *page*. The area of physical memory pointed to by the translation process is known as a *page frame*.

The relationship between pages, the MMU, and page frames is shown in Figure 14.2. The ARM MMU hardware has multiple relocation registers supporting the translation of virtual memory to physical memory. The MMU needs many relocation registers to effectively support virtual memory because the system must translate many pages to many page frames.

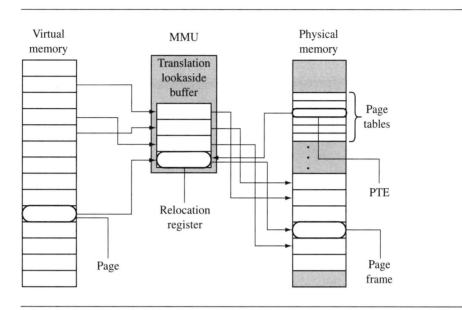

Figure 14.2   The components of a virtual memory system.

The set of relocation registers that temporarily store the translations in an ARM MMU are really a fully associative cache of 64 relocation registers. This cache is known as a Translation Lookaside Buffer (TLB). The TLB caches translations of recently accessed pages.

In addition to having relocation registers, the MMU uses tables in main memory to store the data describing the virtual memory maps used in the system. These tables of translation data are known as *page tables*. An entry in a page table represents all the information needed to translate a page in virtual memory to a page frame in physical memory.

A *page table entry* (PTE) in a page table contains the following information about a virtual page: the physical base address used to translate the virtual page to the physical page frame, the access permission assigned to the page, and the cache and write buffer configuration for the page. If you refer to Table 14.1, you can see that most of the region configuration data in an MPU is now held in a page table entry. This means access permission and cache and write buffer behavior are controlled at a granularity of the page size, which provides finer control over the use of memory. Regions in an MMU are created in software by grouping blocks of virtual pages in memory.

14.2.1   DEFINING REGIONS USING PAGES

In Chapter 13 we explained the use of regions to organize and control areas of memory used for specific functions such as task code and data, or memory input/output. In that explanation we showed regions as a hardware component of the MPU architecture. In an MMU, regions are defined as groups of page tables and are controlled completely in software as sequential pages in virtual memory.

Since a page in virtual memory has a corresponding entry in a page table, a block of virtual memory pages map to a set of sequential entries in a page table. Thus, a region can be defined as a sequential set of page table entries. The location and size of a region can be held in a software data structure while the actual translation data and attribute information is held in the page tables.

Figure 14.3 shows an example of a single task that has three regions: one for text, one for data, and a third to support the task stack. Each region in virtual memory is mapped to different areas in physical memory. In the figure, the executable code is located in flash memory, and the data and stack areas are located in RAM. This use of regions is typical of operating systems that support sharing code between tasks.

With the exception of the master level 1 (L1) page table, all page tables represent 1 MB areas of virtual memory. If a region's size is greater than 1 MB or crosses over the 1 MB boundary addresses that separate page tables, then the description of a region must also

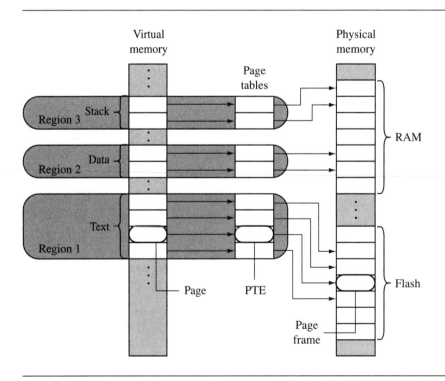

Figure 14.3   An example mapping pages to page frames in an ARM with an MMU.

include a list of page tables. The page tables for a region will always be derived from sequential page table entries in the master L1 page table. However, the locations of the L2 page tables in physical memory do not need to be located sequentially. Page table levels are explained more fully in Section 14.4.

14.2.2 MULTITASKING AND THE MMU

Page tables can reside in memory and not be mapped to MMU hardware. One way to build a multitasking system is to create separate sets of page tables, each mapping a unique virtual memory space for a task. To activate a task, the set of page tables for the specific task and its virtual memory space are mapped into use by the MMU. The other sets of inactive page tables represent dormant tasks. This approach allows all tasks to remain resident in physical memory and still be available immediately when a context switch occurs to activate it.

By activating different page tables during a context switch, it is possible to execute multiple tasks with overlapping virtual addresses. The MMU can relocate the execution address of a task without the need to move it in physical memory. The task's physical memory is simply mapped into virtual memory by activating and deactivating page tables. Figure 14.4 shows three views of three tasks with their own sets of page tables running at a common execution virtual address of 0x0400000.

In the first view, Task 1 is running, and Task 2 and Task 3 are dormant. In the second view, Task 2 is running, and Task 1 and Task 3 are dormant. In the third view, Task 3 is running, and Task 1 and Task 2 are dormant. The virtual memory in each of the three views represents memory as seen by the running task. The view of physical memory is the same in all views because it represents the actual state of real physical memory.

The figure also shows active and dormant page tables where only the running task has an active set of page tables. The page tables for the dormant tasks remain resident in privileged physical memory and are simply not accessible to the running task. The result is that dormant tasks are fully protected from the active task because there is no mapping to the dormant tasks from virtual memory.

When the page tables are activated or deactivated, the virtual-to-physical address mappings change. Thus, accessing an address in virtual memory may suddenly translate to a different address in physical memory after the activation of a page table. As mentioned in Chapter 12, the ARM processor cores have a logical cache and store cached data in virtual memory. When this translation occurs, the caches will likely contain invalid virtual data from the old page table mapping. To ensure memory coherency, the caches may need cleaning and flushing. The TLB may also need flushing because it will have cached old translation data.

The effect of cleaning and flushing the caches and the TLB will slow system operation. However, cleaning and flushing stale code or data from cache and stale translated physical addresses from the TLB keep the system from using invalid data and breaking.

During a context switch, page table data is not moved in physical memory; only pointers to the locations of the page tables change.

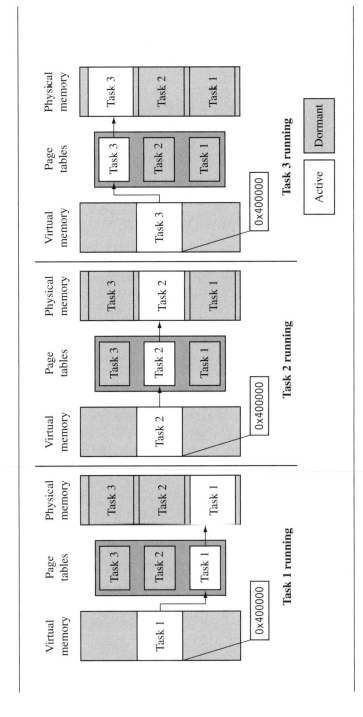

Figure 14.4   Virtual memory from a user task context.

To switch between tasks requires the following steps:

1. Save the active task context and place the task in a dormant state.
2. Flush the caches; possibly clean the D-cache if using a writeback policy.
3. Flush the TLB to remove translations for the retiring task.
4. Configure the MMU to use new page tables translating the virtual memory execution area to the awakening task's location in physical memory.
5. Restore the context of the awakening task.
6. Resume execution of the restored task.

Note: to reduce the time it takes to perform a context switch, a writethrough cache policy can be used in the ARM9 family. Cleaning the data cache can require hundreds of writes to CP15 registers. By configuring the data cache to use a writethrough policy, there is no need to clean the data cache during a context switch, which will provide better context switch performance. Using a writethrough policy distributes these writes over the life of the task. Although a writeback policy will provide better overall performance, it is simply easier to write code for small embedded systems using a writethrough policy.

This simplification applies because most systems use flash memory for nonvolatile storage, and copy programs to RAM during system operation. If your system has a file system and uses dynamic paging then it is time to switch to a write-back policy because the access time to file system storage are tens to hundreds of thousands of times slower than access to RAM memory.

If, after some performance analysis, the efficiency of a writethrough system is not adequate, then performance can be improved using a writeback cache. If you are using a disk drive or other very slow secondary storage, a writeback policy is almost mandatory.

This argument only applies to ARM cores that use logical caches. If a physical cache is present, as in the ARM11 family, the information in cache remains valid when the MMU changes its virtual memory map. Using a physical cache eliminates the need to perform cache management activities when changing virtual memory addresses. For further information on caches, refer to Chapter 12.

14.2.3 MEMORY ORGANIZATION IN A VIRTUAL MEMORY SYSTEM

Typically, page tables reside in an area of main memory where the virtual-to-physical address mapping is fixed. By "fixed," we mean data in a page table doesn't change during normal operation, as shown in Figure 14.5. This fixed area of memory also contains the operating system kernel and other processes. The MMU, which includes the TLB shown in Figure 14.5, is hardware that operates outside the virtual or physical memory space; its function is to translate addresses between the two memory spaces.

The advantage of this fixed mapping is seen during a context switch. Placing system software at a fixed virtual memory location eliminates some memory management tasks

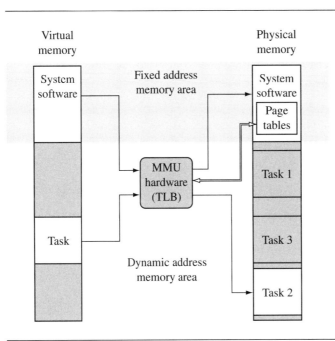

Figure 14.5 A general view of memory organization in a system using an MMU.

and the pipeline effects that result if a processor is executing in a region of virtual memory that is suddenly remapped to a different location in physical memory.

When a context switch occurs between two application tasks, the processor in reality makes many context switches. It changes from a user mode task to a kernel mode task to perform the actual movement of context data in preparation for running the next application task. It then changes from the kernel mode task to the new user mode task of the next context.

By sharing the system software in a fixed area of virtual memory that is seen across all user tasks, a system call can branch directly to the system area and not worry about needing to change page tables to map in a kernel process. Making the kernel code and data map to the same virtual address in all tasks eliminates the need to change the memory map and the need to have an independent kernel process that consumes a time slice.

Branching to a fixed kernel memory area also eliminates an artifact inherent in the pipeline architecture. If the processor core is executing code in a memory area that changes addresses, the core will have prefetched several instructions from the old physical memory space, which will be executed as the new instructions fill the pipeline from the newly mapped memory space. Unless special care is taken, executing the instructions still in the pipeline from the old memory map may corrupt program execution.

We recommend activating page tables while executing system code at a fixed address region where the virtual-to-physical memory mapping never changes. This approach ensures a safe switch between user tasks.

Many embedded systems do not use complex virtual memory but simply create a "fixed" virtual memory map to consolidate the use of physical memory. These systems usually collect blocks of physical memory spread over a large address space into a contiguous block of virtual memory. They commonly create a "fixed" map during the initialization process, and the map remains the same during system operation.

14.3 DETAILS OF THE ARM MMU

The ARM MMU performs several tasks: It translates virtual addresses into physical addresses, it controls memory access permission, and it determines the individual behavior of the cache and write buffer for each page in memory. When the MMU is disabled, all virtual addresses map one-to-one to the same physical address. If the MMU is unable to translate an address, it generates an abort exception. The MMU will only abort on translation, permission, and domain faults.

The main software configuration and control components in the MMU are

- Page tables
- The Translation Lookaside Buffer (TLB)
- Domains and access permission
- Caches and write buffer
- The CP15:c1 control register
- The Fast Context Switch Extension

We provide the details of operation and how to configure these components in the following sections.

14.4 PAGE TABLES

The ARM MMU hardware has a multilevel page table architecture. There are two levels of page table: level 1 (L1) and level 2 (L2).

There is a single level 1 page table known as the L1 *master* page table that can contain two types of page table entry. It can hold pointers to the starting address of level 2 page tables, and page table entries for translating 1 MB pages. The L1 master table is also known as a *section* page table.

The master L1 page table divides the 4 GB address space into 1 MB sections; hence the L1 page table contains 4096 page table entries. The master table is a hybrid table that acts

Table 14.2   Page tables used by the MMU.

Name	Type	Memory consumed by page table (KB)	Page sizes supported (KB)	Number of page table entries
Master/section	level 1	16	1024	4096
Fine	level 2	4	1, 4, or 64	1024
Coarse	level 2	1	4 or 64	256

as both a page directory of L2 page tables and a page table translating 1 MB virtual pages called *sections*. If the L1 table is acting as a directory, then the PTE contains a pointer to either an L2 *coarse* or L2 *fine* page table that represents 1 MB of virtual memory. If the L1 master table is translating a 1 MB section, then the PTE contains the base address of the 1 MB page frame in physical memory. The directory entries and 1 MB section entries can coexist in the master page table.

A coarse L2 page table has 256 entries consuming 1 KB of main memory. Each PTE in a coarse page table translates a 4 KB block of virtual memory to a 4 KB block in physical memory. A coarse page table supports either 4 or 64 KB pages. The PTE in a coarse page contains the base address to either a 4 or 64 KB page frame; if the entry translates a 64 KB page, an identical PTE must be repeated in the page table 16 times for each 64 KB page.

A fine page table has 1024 entries consuming 4 KB of main memory. Each PTE in a fine page translates a 1 KB block of memory. A fine page table supports 1, 4, or 64 KB pages in virtual memory. These entries contain the base address of a 1, 4, or 64 KB page frame in physical memory. If the fine table translates a 4 KB page, then the same PTE must be repeated 4 consecutive times in the page table. If the table translates a 64 KB page, then the same PTE must be repeated 64 consecutive times in the page table.

Table 14.2 summarizes the characteristics of the three kinds of page table used in ARM memory management units.

14.4.1 LEVEL 1 PAGE TABLE ENTRIES

The level 1 page table accepts four types of entry:

- A 1 MB section translation entry
- A directory entry that points to a fine L2 page table
- A directory entry that points to a coarse L2 page table
- A fault entry that generates an abort exception

The system identifies the type of entry by the lower two bits [1:0] in the entry field. The format of the PTE requires the address of an L2 page table to be aligned on a multiple of its page size. Figure 14.6 shows the format of each entry in the L1 page table.

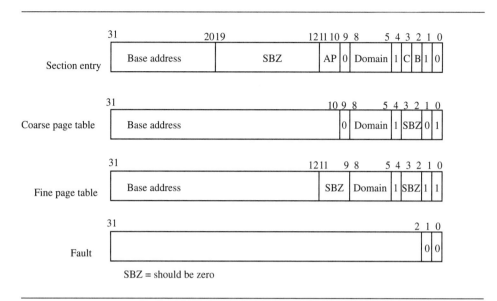

Figure 14.6 L1 page table entries.

A section page table entry points to a 1 MB section of memory. The upper 12 bits of the page table entry replace the upper 12 bits of the virtual address to generate the physical address. A section entry also contains the domain, cached, buffered, and access permission attributes, which we discuss in Section 14.6.

A coarse page entry contains a pointer to the base address of a second-level coarse page table. The coarse page table entry also contains domain information for the 1 MB section of virtual memory represented by the L1 table entry. For coarse pages, the tables must be aligned on an address multiple of 1 KB.

A fine page table entry contains a pointer to the base address of a second-level fine page table. The fine page table entry also contains domain information for the 1 MB section of virtual memory represented by the L1 table entry. Fine page tables must be aligned on an address multiple of 4 KB.

A fault page table entry generates a memory page fault. The fault condition results in either a prefetch or data abort, depending on the type of memory access attempted.

The location of the L1 master page table in memory is set by writing to the CP15:c2 register.

14.4.2 THE L1 TRANSLATION TABLE BASE ADDRESS

The CP15:c2 register holds the *translation table base address* (TTB)—an address pointing to the location of the master L1 table in virtual memory. Figure 14.7 shows the format of CP15:c2 register.

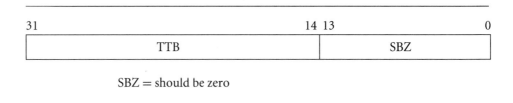

31   14 13   0

TTB	SBZ

SBZ = should be zero

Figure 14.7   Translation table base address CP15 register 2.

EXAMPLE 14.1

Here is a routine named `ttbSet` that sets the TTB of the master L1 page table. The `ttbSet` routine uses an MRC instruction to write to CP15:c2:c0:0. The routine is defined using the following function prototype:

```
void ttbSet(unsigned int ttb);
```

The only argument passed to the procedure is the base address of the translation table. The TTB address must be aligned on a 16 KB boundary in memory.

```
void ttbSet(unsigned int ttb)
{
  ttb &= 0xffffc000;
  __asm{MRC p15, 0, ttb, c2, c0, 0 } /* set translation table base */
}
```

14.4.3   LEVEL 2 PAGE TABLE ENTRIES

There are four possible entries used in L2 page tables:

- A *large* page entry defines the attributes for a 64 KB page frame.
- A *small* page entry defines a 4 KB page frame.
- A *tiny* page entry defines a 1 KB page frame.
- A *fault* page entry generates a page fault abort exception when accessed.

Figure 14.8 shows the format of the entries in an L2 page table. The MMU identifies the type of L2 page table entry by the value in the lower two bits of the entry field.

A large PTE includes the base address of a 64 KB block of physical memory. The entry also has four sets of permission bit fields, as well as the cache and write buffer attributes for the page. Each set of access permission bit fields represents one-fourth of the page in virtual memory. These entries may be thought of as 16 KB subpages providing finer control of access permission within the 64 KB page.

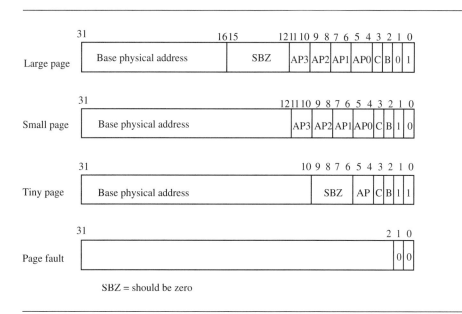

Figure 14.8   L2 page table entries.

A small PTE holds the base address of a 4 KB block of physical memory. The entry also includes four sets of permission bit fields and the cache and write buffer attributes for the page. Each set of permission bit fields represents one-fourth of the page in virtual memory. These entries may be thought of as 1 KB subpages providing finer control of access permission within the 4 KB page.

A tiny PTE provides the base address of a 1 KB block of physical memory. The entry also includes a single access permission bit field and the cache and write buffer attributes for the page. The tiny page has not been incorporated in the ARMv6 architecture. If you are planning to create a system that is easily portable to future architectures, we recommend avoiding the use of tiny 1 KB pages in your system.

A fault PTE generates a memory page access fault. The fault condition results in either a prefetch or data abort, depending on the type of memory access.

14.4.4 SELECTING A PAGE SIZE FOR YOUR EMBEDDED SYSTEM

Here are some tips and suggestions for setting the page size in your system:

- The smaller the page size, the more page frames there will be in a given block of physical memory.

- The smaller the page size, the less the internal fragmentation. Internal fragmentation is the unused memory area in a page. For example, a task 9 KB in size can fit in three 4 KB pages or one 64 KB page. In the first case, using 4 KB pages, there are 3 KB of unused space. In the case using 64 KB pages, there are 55 KB of unused page space.

- The larger the page size, the more likely the system will load referenced code and data.

- Large pages are more efficient as the access time to secondary storage increases.

- As the page size increases, each TLB entry represents more area in memory. Thus, the system can cache more translation data, and the faster the TLB is loaded with all translation data for a task.

- Each page table consumes 1 KB of memory if you use L2 coarse pages. Each L2 fine page table consumes 4 KB. Each L2 page table translates 1 MB of address space. Your maximum page table memory use, per task, is

$$((\text{task size}/1 \text{ megabyte}) + 1) * (\text{L2 page table size}) \qquad (14.1)$$

14.5 THE TRANSLATION LOOKASIDE BUFFER

The TLB is a special cache of recently used page translations. The TLB maps a virtual page to an active page frame and stores control data restricting access to the page. The TLB is a cache and therefore has a victim pointer and a TLB line replacement policy. In ARM processor cores the TLB uses a round-robin algorithm to select which relocation register to replace on a TLB miss.

The TLB in ARM processor cores does not have many software commands available to control its operation. The TLB supports two types of commands: you can flush the TLB, and you can lock translations in the TLB.

During a memory access, the MMU compares a portion of the virtual address to all the values cached in the TLB. If the requested translation is available, it is a TLB *hit*, and the TLB provides the translation of the physical address.

If the TLB does not contain a valid translation, it is a TLB *miss*. The MMU automatically handles TLB misses in hardware by searching the page tables in main memory for valid translations and loading them into one of the 64 lines in the TLB. The search for valid translations in the page tables is known as a *page table walk*. If there is a valid PTE, the hardware copies the translation address from the PTE to the TLB and generates the physical address to access main memory. If, at the end of the search, there is a fault entry in the page table, then the MMU hardware generates an abort exception.

During a TLB miss, the MMU may search up to two page tables before loading data to the TLB and generating the needed address translation. The cost of a miss is generally one or two main memory access cycles as the MMU translation table hardware searches the page tables. The number of cycles depends on which page table the translation data is found in. A single-stage page table walk occurs if the search ends with the L1 master page table; there is a two-stage page table walk if the search ends with an L2 page table.

A TLB miss may take many extra cycles if the MMU generates an abort exception. The extra cycles result as the abort handler maps in the requested virtual memory. The ARM720T has a single TLB because it has a unified bus architecture. The ARM920T, ARM922T, ARM926EJ-S, and ARM1026EJ-S have two Translation Lookaside Buffers because they use a Harvard bus architecture: one TLB for instruction translation and one TLB for data translation.

14.5.1 SINGLE-STEP PAGE TABLE WALK

If the MMU is searching for a 1 MB section page, then the hardware can find the entry in a single-step search because 1 MB page table entries are found in the master L1 page table.

Figure 14.9 shows the table walk of an L1 table for a 1 MB section page translation. The MMU uses the base portion of the virtual address, bits [31:20], to select one of the 4096

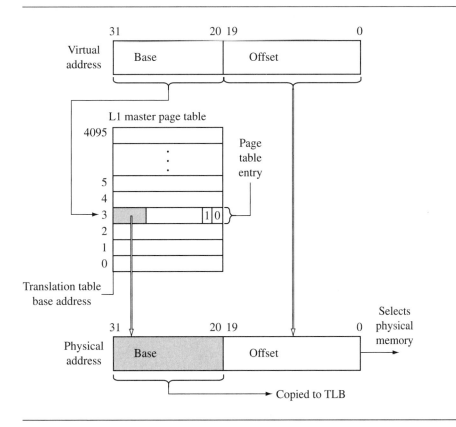

Figure 14.9 L1 Page table virtual-to-physical memory translation using 1 MB sections.

entries in the L1 master page table. If the value in bits [1:0] is binary 10, then the PTE has a valid 1 MB page available. The data in the PTE is transferred to the TLB, and the physical address is translated by combining it with the offset portion of the virtual address.

If the lower two bits are 00, then a fault is generated. If it is either of the other two values, the MMU performs a two-stage search.

14.5.2 TWO-STEP PAGE TABLE WALK

If the MMU ends its search for a page that is 1, 4, 16, or 64 KB in size, then the page table walk will have taken two steps to find the address translation. Figure 14.10 details

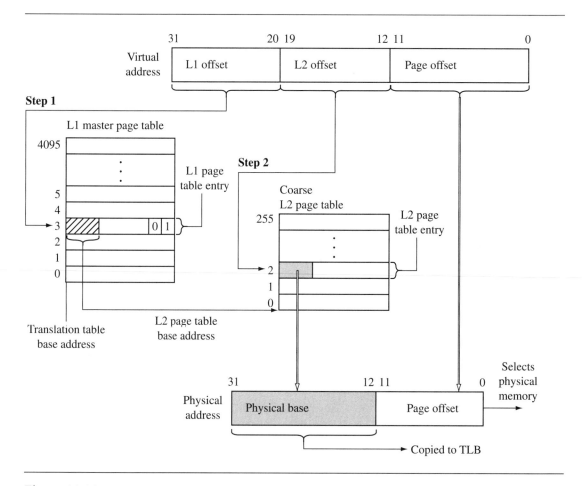

Figure 14.10   Two-level virtual-to-physical address translation using coarse page tables and 4 KB pages.

the two-stage process for a translation held in a coarse L2 page table. Note that the virtual address is divided into three parts.

In the first step, the L1 offset portion is used to index into the master L1 page table and find the L1 PTE for the virtual address. If the lower two bits of the PTE contain the binary value 01, then the entry contains the L2 page table base address to a coarse page (see Figure 14.6).

In the second step, the L2 offset is combined with the L2 page table base address found in the first stage; the resulting address selects the PTE that contains the translation for the page. The MMU transfers the data in the L2 PTE to the TLB, and the base address is combined with the offset portion of the virtual address to generate the requested address in physical memory.

14.5.3 TLB OPERATIONS

If the operating system changes data in the page tables, translation data cached in the TLB may no longer be valid. To invalidate data in the TLB, the core has CP15 commands to flush the TLB. There are several commands available (see Table 14.3): one to flush all TLB data, one to flush the Instruction TLB, and another to flush the Data TLB. The TLB can also be flushed a line at a time.

Table 14.3   CP15:c7 commands to flush the TLB.

Command	MCR instruction	Value in *Rd*	Core support
Invalidate all TLBs	`MCR p15, 0, Rd, c8, c7, 0`	should be zero	ARM720T, ARM920T, ARM922T, ARM926EJ-S, ARM1022E, ARM1026EJ-S, StrongARM, XScale
Invalidate TLB by line	`MCR p15, 0, Rd, c8, c7, 1`	virtual address to invalidate	ARM720T
Invalidate I TLB	`MCR p15, 0, Rd, c8, c5, 0`	virtual address to invalidate	ARM920T, ARM922T, ARM926EJ-S, ARM1022E, ARM1026EJ-S, StrongARM, XScale
Invalidate I TLB by line	`MCR p15, 0, Rd, c8, c5, 1`	virtual address to invalidate	ARM920T, ARM922T, ARM926EJ-S, ARM1022E, ARM1026EJ-S, StrongARM, XScale
Invalidate D TLB	`MCR p15, 0, Rd, c8, c6, 0`	virtual address to invalidate	ARM920T, ARM922T, ARM926EJ-S, ARM1022E, ARM1026EJ-S, StrongARM, XScale
Invalidate D TLB by line	`MCR p15, 0, Rd, c8, c6, 1`	virtual address to invalidate	ARM920T, ARM922T, ARM926EJ-S, ARM1022E, ARM1026EJ-S, StrongARM, XScale

EXAMPLE   Here is a small C routine that invalidates the TLB.
14.2

```
void flushTLB(void)
{
  unsigned int c8format = 0;
  __asm{MCR p15, 0, c8format, c8, c7, 0 }   /* flush TLB */
}
```

14.5.4   TLB LOCKDOWN

The ARM920T, ARM922T, ARM926EJ-S, ARM1022E, and ARM1026EJ-S support locking translations in the TLB. If a line is locked in the TLB, it remains in the TLB when a TLB flush command is issued. We list the available lockdown commands for the various ARM cores in Table 14.4. The format of the core register *Rd* used in the MCR instruction that locks data in the TLB in shown in Figure 14.11.

14.6   DOMAINS AND MEMORY ACCESS PERMISSION

There are two different controls to manage a task's access permission to memory: The primary control is the *domain*, and a secondary control is the *access permission* set in the page tables.

Domains control basic access to virtual memory by isolating one area of memory from another when sharing a common virtual memory map. There are 16 different domains that

Table 14.4   Commands to access the TLB lockdown registers.

Command	MCR instruction	Value in *Rd*	Core support
Read D TLB lockdown	MRC p15,0,Rd,c10,c0,0	TLB lockdown	ARM920T, ARM922T, ARM926EJ-S, ARM1022E, ARM1026EJ-S, StrongARM, XScale
Write D TLB lockdown	MCR p15,0,Rd,c10,c0,0	TLB lockdown	ARM920T, ARM922T, ARM926EJ-S, ARM1022E, ARM1026EJ-S, StrongARM, XScale
Read I TLB lockdown	MRC p15,0,Rd,c10,c0,1	TLB lockdown	ARM920T, ARM922T, ARM926EJ-S, ARM1022E, ARM1026EJ-S, StrongARM, XScale
Write I TLB lockdown	MCR p15,0,Rd,c10,c0,1	TLB lockdown	ARM920T, ARM922T,ARM926EJ-S, ARM1022E,ARM1026EJ-S, StrongARM, XScale

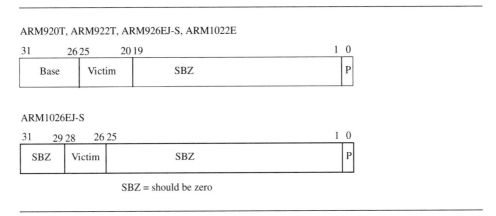

Figure 14.11 Format of the CP15:c10:c0 register.

can be assigned to 1 MB sections of virtual memory and are assigned to a section by setting the domain bit field in the master L1 PTE (see Figure 14.6).

When a domain is assigned to a section, it must obey the domain access rights assigned to the domain. Domain access rights are assigned in the CP15:c3 register and control the processor core's ability to access sections of virtual memory.

The CP15:c3 register uses two bits for each domain to define the access permitted for each of the 16 available domains. Table 14.5 shows the value and meaning of a domain access bit field. Figure 14.12 gives the format of the CP15:c3:c0 register, which holds the domain access control information. The 16 available domains are labeled from D0 to D15 in the figure.

Even if you don't use the virtual memory capabilities provided by the MMU, you can still use these cores as simple memory protection units: first, by mapping virtual memory directly to physical memory, assigning a different domain to each task, then using domains to protect dormant tasks by assigning their domain access to "no access."

Table 14.5 Domain access bit assignments.

Access	Bit field value	Comments
Manager	11	access is uncontrolled, no permission aborts generated
Reserved	10	unpredictable
Client	01	access controlled by permission values set in PTE
No access	00	generates a domain fault

30	28	26	24	22	20	18	16	14	12	10	8	6	4	2	0
D15	D14	D13	D12	D11	D10	D9	D8	D7	D6	D5	D4	D3	D2	D1	D0

Figure 14.12 Format of the domain access control register CP15:c3.

Table 14.6 Access permission and control bits.

Privileged mode	User mode	AP bit field	System bit	Rom bit
Read and write	read and write	11	ignored	ignored
Read and write	read only	10	ignored	ignored
Read and write	no access	01	ignored	ignored
No access	no access	00	0	0
Read only	read only	00	0	1
Read only	no access	00	1	0
Unpredictable	unpredictable	00	1	1

14.6.1 PAGE-TABLE-BASED ACCESS PERMISSIONS

The AP bits in a PTE determine the access permission for a page. The AP bits are shown in Figures 14.6 and 14.8. Table 14.6 shows how the MMU interprets the two bits in the AP bit field.

In addition to the AP bits located in the PTE, there are two bits in the CP15:c1 control register that act globally to modify access permission to memory: the *system* (S) bit and the *rom* (R) bit. These bits can be used to reveal large blocks of memory from the system at different times during operation.

Setting the S bit changes all pages with "no access" permission to allow read access for privileged mode tasks. Thus, by changing a single bit in CP15:c1, all areas marked as no access are instantly available without the cost of changing every AP bit field in every PTE.

Changing the R bit changes all pages with "no access" permission to allow read access for both privileged and user mode tasks. Again, this bit can speed access to large blocks of memory without needing to change lots of PTEs.

14.7 THE CACHES AND WRITE BUFFER

We presented the basic operation of caches and write buffers in Chapter 12. You configure the caches and write buffer for each page in memory using two bits in a PTE (see Figures 14.6 and 14.8). When configuring a page of instructions, the write buffer bit is ignored and the

Table 14.7   Configuring the cache and write buffer for a page.

Instruction cache		Data cache		
Cache bit	Page attribute	Cache bit	Buffer bit	Page attribute
0	not cached	0	0	not cached, not buffered
1	cached	0	1	not cached, buffered
		1	0	cached, writethrough
		1	1	cached, writeback

cache bit determines cache operation. When the bit is set, the page is cached, and when the bit is clear, the page is not cached.

When configuring data pages, the write buffer bit has two uses: it enables or disables the write buffer for a page, and it sets the page cache write policy. The page cache bit controls the meaning of the write buffer bit. When the cache bit is zero, the buffer bit enables the write buffer when the buffer bit value is one, and disables the write buffer when the buffer bit value is zero. When the cache bit is set to one, the write buffer is enabled, and the state of the buffer bit determines the cache write policy. The page uses a writethrough policy if the buffer bit is zero and a writeback policy if the buffer bit is set; refer to Table 14.7, which gives a tabular view of the various states of the cache and write buffer bits and their meaning.

14.8 Coprocessor 15 and MMU Configuration

We first introduced the procedure *changeControl* in Chapter 12. Example 14.3 revisits the procedure *changeControl*, which we use to enable the MMU, caches, and write buffer.

The control register values that control MMU operation are shown in Table 14.8 and Figure 14.13. The ARM720T, ARM920T, and the ARM926EJ-S all have the MMU enable bit[0] and cache enable bit[2] in the same location in the control register. The ARM720T and ARM1022E have a write buffer enable, bit[3]. The ARM920T, ARM922T, and ARM926EJS have split instruction and data caches, requiring an extra bit to enable the I-cache, bit[12]. All processor cores with an MMU support changing the vector table to high memory at address 0xffff0000, bit[13].

Enabling a configured MMU is very similar for the three cores. To enable the MMU, caches, and write buffer, you need to change bit[12], bit[3], bit[2], and bit[0] in the control register.

The procedure, changeControl, operates on register CP15:c1:c0:0 to change the values in the control register *c1*. Example 14.3 gives a small C routine that sets bits in the control register; it is called using the following function prototype:

```
void controlSet(unsigned int value, unsigned int mask)
```

Table 14.8 Description of the bit fields in the control register CP15:c1 that control MMU operation.

Bit	Letter designator	Function enabled	Control
0	M	MMU	0 = disabled, 1 = enabled
2	C	(data) cache	0 = disabled, 1 = enabled
3	W	write buffer	0 = disabled, 1 = enabled
8	S	system	shown in Table 14.6
9	R	rom	shown in Table 14.6
12	I	instruction cache	0 = disabled, 1 = enabled
13	V	high vector table	0 = vector table at 0x00000000 1 = vector table at 0xFFFF0000

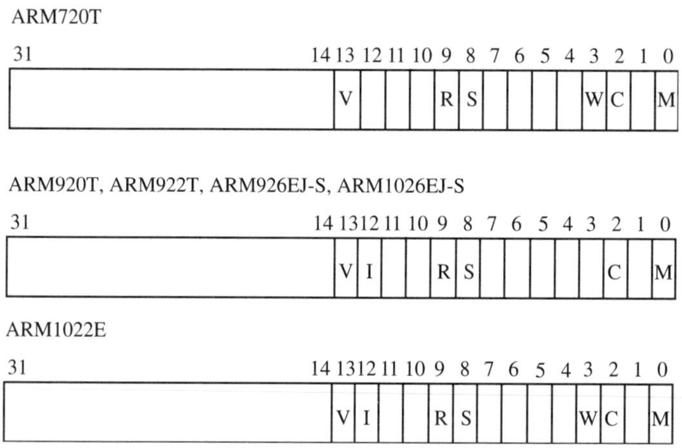

ARM720T

ARM920T, ARM922T, ARM926EJ-S, ARM1026EJ-S

ARM1022E

Figure 14.13 CP15:c1 register control bits in the MMU.

The first parameter passed to the procedure is an unsigned integer containing the state of the control values you want to change. The second parameter, mask, is a bit pattern that selects the bits that need changing. A bit set to one in the mask variable changes the bit in the CP15:c1c0 register to the value of the same bit in the value input parameter. A zero leaves the bit in the control register unchanged, regardless of the bit state in the value parameter.

EXAMPLE
14.3

The routine `controlSet` sets the control bits register in CP15:c1. The routine first reads the CP15:c1 register and places it in the variable `c1format`. The routine then uses the input `mask` value to clear the bits in `c1format` that need updating. The update is done by ORing `c1format` with the `value` input parameter. The updated `c1format` is finally written back out to the CP15:c1 register to enable the MMU, caches, and write buffer.

```
void controlSet(unsigned int value, unsigned int mask)
{
  unsigned int c1format;

  __asm{MRC p15, 0, c1format, c1, c0, 0 }   /* read control register */
  c1format &= ~mask;                        /* clear bits that change */
  c1format |= value;                        /* set bits that change */
  __asm{MCR p15, 0, c1format, c1, c0, 0 }   /* write control register */
}
```

Here is a code sequence that calls the `controlSet` routine to enable the I-cache, D-cache, and the MMU in an ARM920T:

```
#define ENABLEMMU      0x00000001
#define ENABLEDCACHE   0x00000004
#define ENABLEICACHE   0x00001000

#define CHANGEMMU      0x00000001
#define CHANGEDCACHE   0x00000004
#define CHANGEICACHE   0x00001000
```

```
  unsigned int enable, change;
  #if defined(__TARGET_CPU_ARM920T)
    enable = ENABLEMMU | ENABLEICACHE | ENABLEDCACHE;
    change = CHANGEMMU | CHANGEICACHE | CHANGEDCACHE;
  #endif
  controlSet(enable, change);
```

14.9 THE FAST CONTEXT SWITCH EXTENSION

The Fast Context Switch Extension (FCSE) is additional hardware in the MMU that is considered an enhancement feature, which can improve system performance in an ARM embedded system. The FCSE enables multiple independent tasks to run in a fixed overlapping area of memory without the need to clean or flush the cache, or flush the TLB during a context switch. The key feature of the FCSE is the elimination of the need to flush the cache and TLB.

Without the FCSE, switching from one task to the next requires a change in virtual memory maps. If the change involves two tasks with overlapping address ranges, the information stored in the caches and TLB become invalid, and the system must flush the caches and TLB. The process of flushing these components adds considerable time to the task switch because the core must not only clear the caches and TLB of invalid data, but it must also reload data to the caches and TLB from main memory.

With the FCSE there is an additional address translation when managing virtual memory. The FCSE modifies virtual addresses before it reaches the cache and TLB using a special relocation register that contains a value known as the *process ID*. ARM refers to the addresses in virtual memory before the first translation as a *virtual address* (VA), and those addresses after the first translation as a *modified virtual address*(MVA), shown in Figure 14.4. When using the FCSE, all modified virtual addresses are active. Tasks are protected by using the domain access facilities to block access to dormant tasks. We discuss this in more detail in the next section.

Switching between tasks does not involve changing page tables; it simply requires writing the new task's process ID into the FCSE process ID register located in CP15. Because a task switch does not require changing the page tables, the caches and TLB remain valid after the switch and do not need flushing.

When using the FCSE, each task must execute in the fixed virtual address range from 0x00000000 to 0x1FFFFFFF and must be located in a different 32 MB area of modified virtual memory. The system shares all memory addresses above 0x2000000, and uses domains to protect tasks from each other. The running task is identified by its current process ID.

To utilize the FCSE, compile and link all tasks to run in the first 32 MB block of virtual memory (VA) and assign a unique process ID. Then place each task in a different 32 MB *partition* of modified virtual memory using the following relocation formula:

$$MVA = VA + (0x2000000 * process\ ID) \tag{14.2}$$

To calculate the starting address of a task partition in modified virtual memory, take a value of zero for the VA and the task's process ID, and use these values in Equation (14.2).

The value held in the CP15:c13:c0 register contains the current process ID. The process ID bit field in the register is seven bits wide and supports 128 process IDs. The format of the register is shown in Figure 14.15.

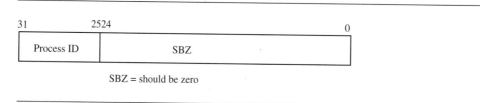

Figure 14.15 Fast context switch register CP15 register 13.

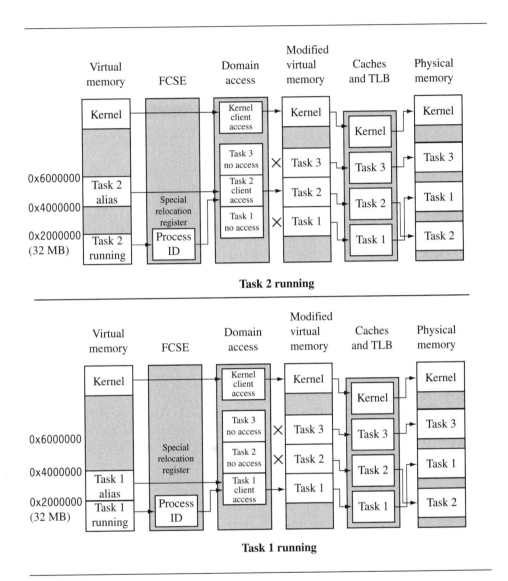

Figure 14.14 Fast Context Switch Extension example showing task 1 before a context switch and task 2 running after a context switch in a three-task multitasking environment.

Example 14.4 shows a small routine processIDSet that sets the process ID in the FCSE. It can be called using the following function prototype:

```
void processIDSet(unsigned value);
```

EXAMPLE   This routine takes an unsigned integer as an input, clips it to seven bits, mod 128, by
14.4   multiplying the value by 0x2000000 (32 MB), and then writing the result to the process
ID register using an MCR instruction.

```
void processIDSet(unsigned int value)
{
  unsigned int PID;
  PID = value<<25;
  __asm{MCR p15, 0, PID, c13, c0, 0 } /* write Process ID register */
}
```

14.9.1   HOW THE FCSE USES PAGE TABLES AND DOMAINS

To use the FCSE efficiently, the system uses page tables to control region configuration
and operation, and domains to isolate tasks from each other. Refer again to Figure 14.14,
which shows the memory layout before and after a context switch from Task 1 to Task 2.
Table 14.9 shows the numerical details used to create Figure 14.14.

Figure 14.16 shows how to change the value in the domain access register of CP15:c3:c0
to switch from Task 1 to Task 2. Switching between tasks requires a change in the process
ID and a new entry in the domain access register.

Table 14.9 shows that Task 1 is assigned Domain 1, and Task 2 is assigned Domain 2.
When changing from Task 1 to Task 2, change the domain access register to allow client
access to Domain 2, and no access to Domain 1. This prevents Task 2 from accessing the
memory space of Task 1. Note that client access remains the same for the kernel, Domain 0.
This allows the page tables to control access to the system area of memory.

Sharing memory between tasks can be accomplished by using a "sharing" domain,
shown as Domain 15 in Figure 14.16 and Table 14.9. The sharing domain is not shown
in Figure 14.15. Tasks can share a domain that allows client access to a partition in modified

Table 14.9   Domain assignment in a simple three-task multiprogramming environment using the
FSCE.

Region	Domain	Privileged AP	User AP	Partition starting address in modified virtual memory	Process ID
Kernel	0	read write	no access	0xFE000000	not assigned
Task 3	3	read write	read write	0x06000000	0x03
Task 2	2	read write	read write	0x04000000	0x02
Task 1	1	read write	read write	0x02000000	0x01
Shared	15	read write	read write	0xF8000000	not assigned

Pre

	D15	D14	D13	D12	D11	D10	D9	D8	D7	D6	D5	D4	D3	D2	D1	D0
Task 1 running	01	00	00	00	00	00	00	00	00	00	00	00	00	00	01	01

Post

	D15	D14	D13	D12	D11	D10	D9	D8	D7	D6	D5	D4	D3	D2	D1	D0
Task 2 running	01	00	00	00	00	00	00	00	00	00	00	00	00	01	00	01

Figure 14.16 Pre- and post-view of CP15 register 3 changing from Task 1 to Task 2 in a three-task multiprogramming environment.

virtual memory. This shared memory can be seen by both tasks, and access is determined by the page table entries that map the memory space.

Here are the steps needed to perform a context switch when using the FCSE:

1. Save the active task context and place the task in a dormant state.
2. Write the awakening task's process ID to CP15:c13:c0.
3. Set the current task's domain to no access, and the awakening task's domain to client access, by writing to CP15:c3:c0.
4. Restore the context of the awakening task.
5. Resume execution of the restored task.

14.9.2 HINTS FOR USING THE FCSE

- A task has a fixed 32 MB maximum limit on size.
- The memory manager must use fixed 32 MB partitions with a fixed starting address that is a multiple of 32 MB.
- Unless you want to manage an exception vector table for each task, place the exception vector table at virtual address 0xffff0000, using the V bit in CP15 register 1.
- You must define and use an active domain control system.
- The core fetches the two instructions following a change in process ID from the previous process space, if execution is taking place in the first 32 MB block. Therefore, it is wise to switch tasks from a "fixed" region in memory.

- If you use domains to control task access, the running task also appears as an alias at VA + (0x2000000 ∗ process ID) in virtual memory.

- If you use domains to protect tasks from each other, you are limited to a maximum of 16 concurrent tasks, unless you are willing to modify the domain fields in the level 1 page table and flush the TLB on a context switch.

14.10   DEMONSTRATION: A SMALL VIRTUAL MEMORY SYSTEM

Here is a little demonstration that shows the fundamentals of a small embedded system using virtual memory. It is designed to run on an ARM720T or ARM920T core. The demonstration provides a static multitasking system showing the infrastructure needed to run three concurrent tasks. We wrote the demonstration using the ARM ADS1.2 developer suite. There are many ways to improve the demonstration, but its primary purpose is as an aid in understanding the underlying ARM MMU hardware. Paging or swapping to secondary storage is not demonstrated.

The demonstration uses the same execution region for all user tasks, which simplifies the compiling and linking of those tasks. Each task is compiled as a standalone program containing text, data, and stack information in a single region.

The hardware requirements are an ARM-based evaluation board, which includes an ARM720T or ARM920T processor core. The example requires 256 KB of RAM starting at address 0x00000000 and a method of loading code and data into memory. In addition there are also several memory-mapped peripherals spread over 256 MB from address 0x10000000 to 0x20000000.

The software requirements are an operating system infrastructure such as SLOS, provided in earlier chapters. The system must support fixed partition multitasking.

The example uses only 1 MB and 4 KB pages. However, the coded examples support all page sizes. Tasks are limited to less than 1 MB and therefore fit in a single L2 page table. Thus, a task switch can be performed by changing a single L2 PTE in the master L1 page table.

This approach is much simpler than trying to create and maintain full sets of page tables for each task, and changing the TTB address during each context switch. Changing the TTB to change between task memory maps would require creating a master table and all the L2 system tables in three different sets of page tables. This would also require additional memory to store these additional page tables. The purpose for swapping out a single L2 table is to eliminate the duplication of system information in the multiple sets of page tables. The reduction in the number of duplicated page tables reduces the required memory to run the system.

We use seven steps to set up the MMU for the demonstration:

1. Define the fixed system software regions; this fixed area is shown in Figure 14.5.

2. Define the three virtual memory maps for the three tasks; the general layout of these maps is shown in Figure 14.4.

3. Locate the regions listed in steps 1 and 2 into the physical memory map; this is an implementation of what is shown on the right side of Figure 14.5.

4. Define and locate the page tables within the page table region.

5. Define the data structures needed to create and manage the regions and page tables. These structures are implementation dependent and are defined specifically for the example. However, the general form of the structures is a good starting point for most simple systems.

6. Initialize the MMU, caches, and write buffer.

7. Set up a context switch routine to gracefully transition from one task to the next.

We present these steps in detail in the following sections.

14.10.1   STEP 1: DEFINE THE FIXED SYSTEM SOFTWARE REGIONS

There are four fixed system software regions used by the operating system: a dedicated 32 KB *kernel* region at 0x00000, a 32 KB *shared memory* region at 0x8000, a dedicated 32 KB *page table* region at 0x10000, and a 256 MB *peripheral* region at 0x10000000 (see Figure 14.17). We define these regions during the initialization process and never change their page tables again.

The privileged kernel region stores the system software; it contains the operating system kernel code and data. The region uses fixed addressing to avoid the complexity of remapping when changing to a system mode context. It also contains the vector table and the stacks for handling FIQ, IRQ, SWI, UND, and ABT exceptions.

The shared memory region is located at a fixed address in virtual memory. All tasks use this region to access shared system resources. The shared memory region contains shared libraries and the transition routines for switching from privileged mode to user mode during a context switch.

The page table region contains five page tables. Although the page table region is 32 KB in size, the system uses only 20 KB: 16 KB for the master table and 1 KB each for the four L2 tables.

The peripheral region controls the system device I/O space. The primary purpose of this region is to establish this area as a noncached, nonbuffered region. You don't want to have input, output, or control registers subject to the stale data issues of caching or the time sequence delays involved in using the write buffer.

This region also prevents user mode access to peripheral devices; thus, access to the devices must be made through device drivers. This region permits privileged access only; no user access is allowed. In the demonstration, this is a single region, but in a more refined system, there would be more regions defined to provide finer control over individual devices.

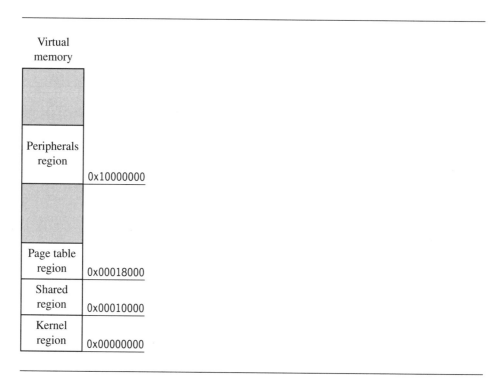

Figure 14.17 Fixed regions in virtual memory.

14.10.2 STEP 2: DEFINE VIRTUAL MEMORY MAPS FOR EACH TASK

There are three user tasks that run during three time slice intervals. Each task has an identical virtual memory map.

Each task sees two regions in its memory map: a dedicated 32 KB *task* region at 0x400000, and a 32 KB *shared memory* region at 0x8000 (see Figure 14.18).

The task region contains the text, data, and stack of the running user task. When the scheduler transfers control from one task to another, it must remap the task region by changing the L1 page table entry to point to the upcoming task's L2 page table. After the entry is made, the task region points to the physical location of the next running task.

The shared region is a fixed system software region. Its function is described in Section 14.10.1.

14.10.3 STEP 3: LOCATE REGIONS IN PHYSICAL MEMORY

The regions we defined for the demonstration must be located in physical memory at addresses that do not overlap or conflict. Table 14.10 shows where we located all the

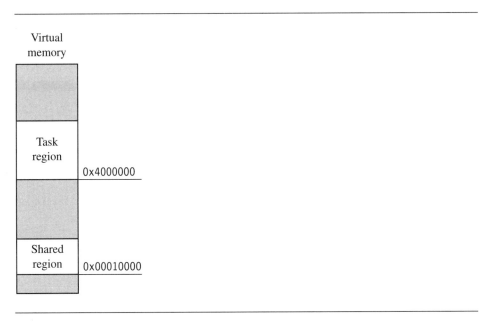

Figure 14.18 Virtual memory as seen by the running task.

Table 14.10 Region placement in the MMU example.

Region	Addressing	Region size	Virtual base address	Page size	Number of pages	Physical base address
Kernel	fixed	64 KB	0x00000000	4 KB	16	0x00000000
Shared	fixed	32 KB	0x00010000	4 KB	8	0x00010000
Page table	fixed	32 KB	0x00018000	4 KB	8	0x00018000
Peripheral	fixed	256 MB	0x10000000	1 MB	256	0x10000000
Task 1	dynamic	32 KB	0x00400000	4 KB	8	0x00020000
Task 2	dynamic	32 KB	0x00400000	4 KB	8	0x00028000
Task 3	dynamic	32 KB	0x00400000	4 KB	8	0x00030000

regions in physical memory as well as their virtual addresses and size. The table also lists our choice of page size for each region and the number of pages that need to be translated to support the size of each region.

Table 14.10 lists the four regions that use fixed page tables during system operation: the kernel, shared memory, page table, and peripheral regions.

The task region dynamically changes page tables during system operation. The task region translates the same virtual address to a different physical address that depends on the running task.

Figure 14.19 shows the placement of the regions in virtual and physical memory graphically. The kernel, shared and page table regions map directly to physical memory as blocks

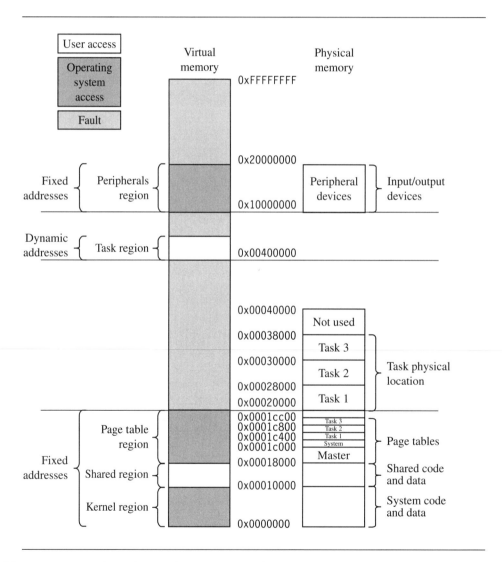

Figure 14.19 Memory map of simple virtual memory example.

of sequential page frames. Above this area are the page frames dedicated to the three user tasks. The tasks in physical memory are 32 KB fixed partitions, also sequential page frames. Sparsely scattered over 256 MB of physical memory are the memory-mapped peripheral I/O devices.

14.10.4 STEP 4: DEFINE AND LOCATE THE PAGE TABLES

We previously dedicated a region to hold the page tables in the system. The next step is to locate the actual page table within the region to physical memory. Figure 14.20 shows a close-up detail of where the page table region maps to physical memory. It is a blow-up of the page tables shown in Figure 14.19. We spread the memory out a little to show the relationship between the L1 master page table and the four L2 page tables. We also show where the translation data is located in the page tables.

The one master L1 page table locates the L2 tables and translates the 1 MB sections of the peripheral region. The system L2 page table contains translation address data for three system regions: the kernel region, shared memory region, and page table region. There are three task L2 page tables that map to the physical addresses of the three concurrent tasks.

Only three of the five page tables are active simultaneously during run time: the L1 master table, the L2 system table, and one of the three L2 task page tables.

The scheduler controls which task is active and which tasks are dormant by remapping the task region during a context switch. Specifically, the master L1 page table entry at address 0x18010 is changed during the context switch to point to the L2 page table base address of the next active task.

14.10.5 STEP 5: DEFINE PAGE TABLE AND REGION DATA STRUCTURES

For the example, we define two data structures used to configure and control the system. These two data structures represent the actual code used to define and initialize the page tables and regions discussed in previous sections. We define two data types, a Pagetable type that contains the page table data, and a Region type that defines and controls each region in the system.

The type definition for the Pagetable structure, with a description of the members in the Pagetable structure, is:

```
typedef struct {
            unsigned int vAddress;
            unsigned int ptAddress;
            unsigned int masterPtAddress;
            unsigned int type;
            unsigned int dom;
          } Pagetable;
```

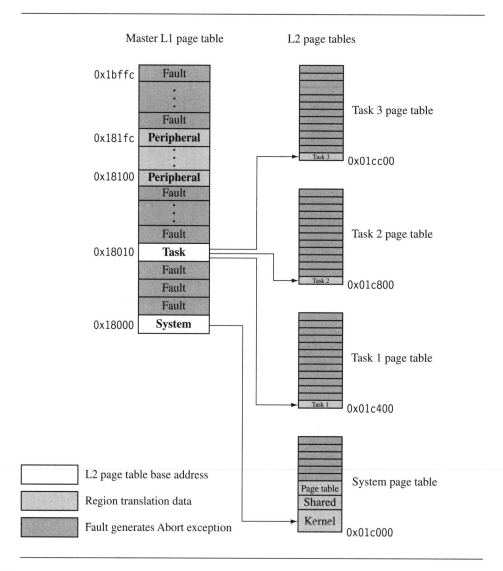

Figure 14.20 Page table content in the simple virtual memory demonstration.

- vAddress identifies the starting address of a 1 MB section of virtual memory controlled by either a section entry or an L2 page table.
- ptAddress is the address where the page table is located in virtual memory.
- masterPtAddress is the address of the parent master L1 page table. If the table is an L1 table, then the value is the same as ptAddress.

- type identifies the type of the page table, it can be COARSE, FINE, or MASTER.

- dom sets the domain assigned to the 1 MB memory blocks of an L1 table entry.

We use the Pagetable type to define the five page tables used in the system. Together the Pagetable structures form a block of page table data that we use to manage, fill, locate, identify, and set the domain for all active and nonactive page tables. We refer to this block of Pagetables as the *page table control block* (PTCB) for the remainder of this demonstration.

The five Pagetables described in previous sections and shown in Figure 14.20 with their initialization values, are

```
#define FAULT 0
#define COARSE 1
#define MASTER 2
#define FINE 3

/* Page Tables */
/* VADDRESS, PTADDRESS, MasterPTADDRESS, PTTYPE, DOM */
Pagetable masterPT   = {0x00000000, 0x18000, 0x18000, MASTER, 3};
Pagetable systemPT   = {0x00000000, 0x1c000, 0x18000, COARSE, 3};
Pagetable task1PT    = {0x00400000, 0x1c400, 0x18000, COARSE, 3};
Pagetable task2PT    = {0x00400000, 0x1c800, 0x18000, COARSE, 3};
Pagetable task3PT    = {0x00400000, 0x1cc00, 0x18000, COARSE, 3};
```

The type definition for the Region structure, with a description of the members in the Region structure, is

```
typedef struct {
            unsigned int vAddress;
            unsigned int pageSize;
            unsigned int numPages;
            unsigned int AP;
            unsigned int CB;
            unsigned int pAddress;
            Pagetable *PT;
        } Region;
```

- vAddress is the starting address of the region in virtual memory.

- pageSize is the size of a virtual page.

- numPages is the number of pages in the region.

- AP is the region access permissions.

- CB is the cache and write buffer attributes for the region.

- pAddress is the starting address of the region in physical memory.

- *PT is a pointer to the Pagetable in which the region resides.

All of the `Region` data structures together form a second block of data that we use to define the size, location, access permission, cache and write buffer operation, and page table location for the regions used in the system. We refer to this block of regions as the region control block (RCB) for the remainder of this demonstration.

There are the seven `Region` structures that define the regions described in previous sections and shown in Figure 14.19. Here are the initialization values for each of the four system software and three task `Regions` in the RCB:

```
#define NANA 0x00
#define RWNA 0x01
#define RWRO 0x02
#define RWRW 0x03
/* NA = no access, RO = read only, RW = read/write */

#if defined(__TARGET_CPU_ARM920T)
  #define cb 0x0
  #define cB 0x1
  #define WT 0x2
  #define WB 0x3
#endif
 /* 720 */
#if defined(__TARGET_CPU_ARM720T)
  #define cb 0x0
  #define cB 0x1
  #define Cb 0x2
  #define WT 0x3
#endif
/* cb = not cached/not buffered */
/* cB = not Cached/Buffered */
/* Cb = Cached/not Buffered */
/* WT = write through cache */
/* WB = write back cache */

/* REGION TABLES */
/*        VADDRESS, PAGESIZE, NUMPAGES, AP, CB, PADDRESS, &PT */
Region kernelRegion
    = {0x00000000, 4, 16, RWNA, WT, 0x00000000, &systemPT};
Region sharedRegion
    = {0x00010000, 4,  8, RWRW, WT, 0x00010000, &systemPT};
Region pageTableRegion
    = {0x00018000, 4,  8, RWNA, WT, 0x00018000, &systemPT};
Region peripheralRegion
    = {0x10000000, 1024, 256, RWNA, cb, 0x10000000, &masterPT};
```

```
/* Task Process Regions */
Region t1Region
    = {0x00400000, 4, 8, RWRW, WT, 0x00020000, &task1PT};
Region t2Region
    = {0x00400000, 4, 8, RWRW, WT, 0x00028000, &task2PT};
Region t3Region
    = {0x00400000, 4, 8, RWRW, WT, 0x00030000, &task3PT}
```

14.10.6 STEP 6: INITIALIZE THE MMU, CACHES, AND WRITE BUFFER

Before the MMU and the caches and write buffer are activated, they must be initialized. The PTCB and RCB hold the configuration data for the three components. There are five parts to initialize the MMU:

1. Initialize the page tables in main memory by filling them with FAULT entries.
2. Fill in the page tables with translations that map regions to physical memory.
3. Activate the page tables.
4. Assign domain access rights.
5. Enable the memory management unit and cache hardware.

The first four parts configure the system and the last part enables it. In the following sections we provide routines to perform the five parts to the initialization process; the routines are listed by function and example number in Figure 14.21.

14.10.6.1 Initializing the Page Tables in Memory

The first part in initializing the MMU is to set the page tables to a known state. The easiest way to do this is to fill the page tables with FAULT page table entries. Using a FAULT entry makes sure that no valid translations exist outside those defined by the PTCB. By setting all the page table entries in all the active page tables to a FAULT, the system will generate an abort exception for an entry not later filled in using the PTCB.

EXAMPLE
14.5

The routine mmuInitPT initializes a page table by taking the memory area allocated for a page table and setting it with FAULT values. It is called using the following function prototype:

```
void mmuInitPT(Pagetable *pt);
```

The routine takes a single argument, which is a pointer to a Pagetable in the PTCB.

1. Initialize the page tables in memory by filling them with FAULT entries.

```
mmuInitPT(Pagetable *); Example 14.5
```

2. Fill in the page tables with translations that map regions to physical memory.

```
mmuMapRegion(Region *);   Example 14.6
  mmuMapSectionTableRegion(Region *region); Example 14.7
  mmuMapCoarseTableRegion(Region *region); Example 14.8
  mmuMapFineTableRegion(Region *region); Example 14.9
```

3. Activate the page tables.

```
int mmuAttachPT(Pagetable *pt);   Example 14.10
```

4. Assign domain access rights.

```
domainAccessSet(unsigned int value, unsigned int mask); Example 14.11
```

5. Enable the memory management unit and cache hardware.

```
controlSet (unsigned int, unsigned int);   Example 14.3
```

Figure 14.21 List of MMU initialization routines.

```
void mmuInitPT(Pagetable *pt)
{
    int  index;     /* number of lines in PT/entries written per loop*/
    unsigned int PTE, *PTEptr;   /* points to page table entry in PT */
    PTEptr = (unsigned int *)pt->ptAddress;   /* set pointer base PT */
    PTE = FAULT;

    switch (pt->type)
    {
      case COARSE: {index =  256/32; break;}
      case MASTER: {index = 4096/32; break;}
      #if defined(__TARGET_CPU_ARM920T)
      case FINE: {index = 1024/32; break;}     /* no FINE PT in 720T */
      #endif
      default:
      {
        printf("mmuInitPT: UNKNOWN pagetable type\n");
```

```
        return -1;
    }
}
__asm
{
  mov     r0, PTE
  mov     r1, PTE
  mov     r2, PTE
  mov     r3, PTE
}
for (; index != 0; index--)
{
  __asm
  {
    STMIA PTEptr!, {r0-r3}        /* write 32 entries to table */
    STMIA PTEptr!, {r0-r3}
    STMIA PTEptr!, {r0-r3}
    STMIA PTEptr!, {r0-r3}
    STMIA PTEptr!, {r0-r3}
    STMIA PTEptr!, {r0-r3}
    STMIA PTEptr!, {r0-r3}
    STMIA PTEptr!, {r0-r3}
  }
}
return 0;
}
```

mmuInitPT starts with the base page table address PTEptr and fills the page table with
FAULT entries. The size of the table is determined by reading the type of Pagetable defined
in pt->type. The table type can be the master L1 page table with 4096 entries, a coarse L2
page table with 256 entries, or a fine L2 page table with 1024 entries.

The routine fills the table by writing small blocks to memory using a loop. The routine
determines the number of blocks to write index from the number of entries in the page table
divided by the number of entries written per loop. A switch statement selects the Pagetable
type and branches to the case that sets the index size for the table. The procedure completes
by executing the loop that fills the table. Note the __asm keyword to invoke the inline
assembler; this reduces the execution time of the loop by using the stmia store multiple
instruction.

14.10.6.2   Filling Page Tables with Translations

The second part in initializing the MMU is to convert the data held in the RCB into
page table entries and to copy them into the page tables. We provide several routines

to convert the data in the RCB to entries in a page table. The first high-level routine mmuMapRegion determines the type of page table and then calls one of three routines to create the page table entries: mmuMapSectionTableRegion, mmuMapCoarseTableRegion, or mmuMapFineTableRegion.

To ease future porting of code, we advise not using tiny pages and the mmuMapFineTableRegion routine because the ARMv6 architecture doesn't use the tiny page. The fine page table type has also been removed in the ARMv6 architecture because the need for it disappears without tiny pages.

Here is a description of the four routines:

- The mmuMapRegion routine determines the page table type and branches to one of the routines listed below; it is presented in Example 14.6.

- mmuMapSectionTableRegion fills an L1 master table with section entries; it is presented in Example 14.7.

- mmuMapCoarseTableRegion fills an L2 coarse page table with region entries; it is presented in Example 14.8 .

- mmuMapFineTableRegion fills an L2 fine page table with region entries; it is presented in Example 14.9.

Here is a list of the C function prototypes for the four routines:

```
int mmuMapRegion(Region *region);
void mmuMapSectionTableRegion(Region *region);
int mmuMapCoarseTableRegion(Region *region);
int mmuMapFineTableRegion(Region *region);
```

The four procedures all have a single input parameter, which is a pointer to a Region structure that contains the configuration data needed to generate page table entries.

EXAMPLE
14.6

Here is the high-level routine that selects the page table type:

```
int mmuMapRegion(Region *region)
{
  switch (region->PT->type)
  {
    case SECTION:                              /* map section in L1 PT */
    {
      mmuMapSectionTableRegion(region);
      break;
    }
    case COARSE:                    /* map PTE to point to COARSE L2 PT */
```

```
    {
      mmuMapCoarseTableRegion(region);
      break;
    }
    #if defined(__TARGET_CPU_ARM920T)
    case FINE:                      /* map PTE to point to FINE L2 PT */
    {
      mmuMapFineTableRegion(region);
      break;
    }
    #endif
    default:
    {
      printf("UNKNOWN page table type\n");
      return -1;
    }
  }
  return 0;
}
```

Within the Region is a pointer to a Pagetable in which the region translation data resides. The routine determines the page table type region->PT->type and calls a routine that maps the Region into the page table in the format of the specified page table type.

There is a separate procedure for each of the three types of page table, section (L1 master), coarse, and fine (refer to Section 14.4).

EXAMPLE 14.7

Here is the first of the three routines that convert the region data to page table entries:

```
void mmuMapSectionTableRegion(Region *region)
{
  int i;
  unsigned int *PTEptr, PTE;

  PTEptr = (unsigned int *)region->PT->ptAddress;  /* base addr PT */
  PTEptr += region->vAddress >> 20;   /* set to first PTE in region */
  PTEptr += region->numPages - 1;     /* set to last PTE in region */

  PTE = region->pAddress & 0xfff00000;    /* set physical address */
  PTE |= (region->AP & 0x3) << 10;        /* set Access Permissions */
  PTE |= region->PT->dom   << 5;          /* set Domain for section */
  PTE |= (region->CB & 0x3) << 2;         /* set Cache & WB attributes */
  PTE |= 0x12;                            /* set as section entry */

  for (i = region->numPages - 1; i >= 0; i--) /* fill PTE in region */
```

```
  {
    *PTEptr-- = PTE + (i << 20);              /* i = 1 MB section */
  }
}
```

The `mmuMapSectionTableRegion` procedure begins by setting a local pointer variable `PTEptr` to the base address of the master L1 page table. It then uses the virtual starting address of the region to create an index into the page table where the region page table entries begin. This index is added to the variable `PTEptr`. The variable `PTEptr` now points to the start of the region entries in the page table. The next line calculates the size of the region and adds this value to `PTEptr`. The variable `PTEptr` now points to the last PTE for the region. The `PTEptr` variable is set to the end of the region so we can use a count-down counter in the loop that fills the page table with entries.

Next the routine constructs a section page table entry using the values in the `Region` structure; the entry is held in the local variable PTE. A series of ORs constructs this PTE from the starting physical address, the access permission, the domain, and cache and write buffer attributes. The format of the PTE is shown in Figure 14.6.

The PTE now contains a pointer to the first physical address of the region and its attributes. The counter variable i is used for two purposes: It is an offset into the page table, and it is added to the PTE variable to increment the physical address translation for the page frame. Remember, all regions in the demonstration map to sequential page frames in physical memory. The procedure concludes by writing all the PTEs for the region into the page table. It starts from the last translation entry and counts down to the first translation entry.

EXAMPLE
14.8   The next two routines, `mmuMapCoarseTableRegion` and `mmuMapFineTableRegion`, are very similar, which makes the descriptive text of the routines very similar; after reading the coarse page table example, you can skip the other example if you are not using tiny pages.

```
int mmuMapCoarseTableRegion(Region *region)
{
  int i,j;
  unsigned int *PTEptr, PTE;
  unsigned int tempAP = region->AP & 0x3;

  PTEptr = (unsigned int *)region->PT->ptAddress;  /* base addr PT */

  switch (region->pageSize)
  {
    case LARGEPAGE:
    {
      PTEptr += (region->vAddress & 0x000ff000) >> 12;  /* 1st PTE */
      PTEptr += (region->numPages*16) - 1;       /* region last PTE */
```

```
        PTE = region->pAddress & 0xffff0000; /* set physical address */
        PTE |= tempAP << 10;    /* set Access Permissions subpage 3 */
        PTE |= tempAP << 8;                            /* subpage 2 */
        PTE |= tempAP << 6;                            /* subpage 1 */
        PTE |= tempAP << 4;                            /* subpage 0 */
        PTE |= (region->CB & 0x3) << 2; /* set cache & WB attributes */
        PTE |= 0x1;                            /* set as LARGE PAGE */

                              /* fill in table entries for region */
        for (i = region->numPages-1; i >= 0; i--)
        {
          for (j = 15 ; j >= 0; j--)
            *PTEptr-- = PTE + (i << 16);    /* i = 64 KB large page */
        }
        break;
      }
    case SMALLPAGE:
      {
        PTEptr += (region->vAddress & 0x000ff000) >> 12;   /* first  */
        PTEptr += (region->numPages - 1);          /* last PTEptr */

        PTE = region->pAddress & 0xfffff000; /* set physical address */
        PTE |= tempAP << 10;    /* set Access Permissions subpage 3 */
        PTE |= tempAP << 8;                            /* subpage 2 */
        PTE |= tempAP << 6;                            /* subpage 1 */
        PTE |= tempAP << 4;                            /* subpage 0 */
        PTE |= (region->CB & 0x3) << 2;    /* set cache & WB attrib */
        PTE |= 0x2;                            /* set as SMALL PAGE */
                              /* fill in table entries for region */
        for (i = region->numPages - 1; i >= 0; i--)
        {
          *PTEptr-- = PTE + (i << 12);        /* i = 4 KB small page */
        }
        break;
      }
    default:
      {
      printf("mmuMapCoarseTableRegion: Incorrect page size\n");
      return -1;
      }
    }
  return 0;
}
```

The routine begins by setting a local variable *tempAP* that holds the access permission for pages or subpages in the region. Next, it sets the variable PTEptr to point to the base address of the page table that will hold the mapped region.

The procedure then switches to handle either the case of a large or small page. The algorithms for the two cases are the same; only the format of the PTE and the way values are written into the page table are different.

At this point the variable PTEptr contains the starting address of the L2 page table. The routine then uses the starting address of the region *region->vAddress* to calculate an index to the first entry of the region in the page table. This index value is added to the PTEptr. The next line calculates the size of the region and adds this value to PTEptr. PTEptr now points to the last PTE for the region.

Next the routine constructs a page table entry variable PTE for either a large or a small entry from the values in the region passed into the routine. The routine uses a series of ORs to construct the PTE from the starting physical address, the access permission, and cache and write buffer attributes. See Figure 14.8 to review the formats of a large and small PTE.

The PTE now contains a pointer to the physical address of the first page frame for the region. The counter variable i is used for two purposes: First, it is an offset into the page table. Second it is added to the PTE variable to modify the address translation bit field to point to the next lower page frame in physical memory. The routine finishes by writing all the PTEs for the region into the page table. Note that there is a nested loop in the LARGEPAGE case: the j loop writes the required identical PTE to map a large page in a coarse page table (refer to Section 14.4 for details).

EXAMPLE
14.9
This example fills a fine page table with region translation information. Fine page tables are not available in the ARM720T and have been discontinued in the v6 architecture. For compatibility with these changes we would advise avoiding their use in new projects.

```
#if defined(__TARGET_CPU_ARM920T)
int mmuMapFineTableRegion(Region *region)
{
  int i,j;
  unsigned int *PTEptr, PTE;
  unsigned int tempAP = region->AP & 0x3;

  PTEptr = (unsigned int *)region->PT->ptAddress; /* base addr PT */

  switch (region->pageSize)
  {
    case LARGEPAGE:
    {
      PTEptr += (region->vAddress & 0x000ffc00) >> 10;  /* first PTE*/
      PTEptr += (region->numPages*64) - 1;              /* last PTE */
```

```
      PTE = region->pAddress & 0xffff0000; /* get physical address */
      PTE |= tempAP << 10;      /* set Access Permissions subpage 3 */
      PTE |= tempAP << 8;                            /* subpage 2 */
      PTE |= tempAP << 6;                            /* subpage 1 */
      PTE |= tempAP << 4;                            /* subpage 0 */
      PTE |= (region->CB & 0x3) << 2;       /* set cache & WB attrib */
      PTE |= 0x1;                           /* set as LARGE PAGE */
                              /* fill in table entries for region */
      for (i = region->numPages-1; i >= 0; i--)
      {
        for (j = 63 ; j >= 0; j--)
          *PTEptr-- = PTE + (i << 16);       /* i = 64 KB large page */
      }
      break;
    }
    case SMALLPAGE:
    {
      PTEptr += (region->vAddress & 0x000ffc00) >> 10;   /* first PTE*/
      PTEptr += (region->numPages*4) - 1;              /* last PTE */

      PTE = region->pAddress & 0xfffff000; /* get physical address */
      PTE |= tempAP << 10;      /* set Access Permissions subpage 3 */
      PTE |= tempAP << 8;                           /* subpage 2 */
      PTE |= tempAP << 6;                           /* subpage 1 */
      PTE |= tempAP << 4;                           /* subpage 0 */
      PTE |= (region->CB & 0x3) << 2;       /* set cache & WB attrib */
      PTE |= 0x2;                           /* set as SMALL PAGE */

                              /* fill in table entries for region */
      for (i = region->numPages-1; i >= 0; i--)
      {
        for (j = 3 ; j >= 0; j--)
          *PTEptr-- = PTE + (i << 12);       /* i = 4 KB small page */
      }
      break;
    }
    case TINYPAGE:
    {
      PTEptr += (region->vAddress & 0x000ffc00) >> 10;    /* first */
      PTEptr += (region->numPages - 1);             /* last PTEptr */

      PTE = region->pAddress & 0xfffffc00; /* get physical address */
      PTE |=  tempAP << 4;                 /* set Access Permissions */
```

```
      PTE |= (region->CB & 0x3) << 2;      /* set cache & WB attribu */
      PTE |= 0x3;                                /* set as TINY PAGE */

            /* fill table with PTE for region; from last to first */
   for (i =(region->numPages) - 1; i >= 0; i--)
   {
      *PTEptr-- = PTE + (i << 10);            /* i = 1 KB tiny page */
   }
   break;
   }
   default:
   {
      printf("mmuMapFineTableRegion: Incorrect page size\n");
      return -1;
   }
  }
  return 0;
}
#endif
```

The routine begins by setting a local variable tempAP that holds the access permission for pages or subpages in the region. This routine does not support subpages with different access permissions. Next, the routine sets the variable PTEptr to point to the base of the page table that will hold the mapped fine-paged region.

The routine then switches to handle the three cases of a large, small, or tiny page. The algorithm for each of the three cases is the same; only the format of the PTE and the way values are written into the page table differ.

At this point the variable PTEptr contains the starting address of the L2 page table. The routine then takes the starting address of the region region->vAddress and calculates an index to the first region entry in the page table. This index value is added to the PTEptr. The next line determines the size of the region and adds this value to PTEptr. PTEptr now points to the last PTE for the region.

Next the routine constructs the PTE for a either a large, small, or tiny entry from the values in the region. A series of ORs constructs the PTE from the starting physical address, the access permission, and cache and write buffer attributes. Figure 14.8 shows the formats for large, small, and tiny page table entries.

The PTE now contains a pointer to the physical address of the first page frame and attributes for the region. A counter variable i is used for two purposes: It is an offset into the page table, and it is added to the PTE variable to change the address translation so it points to the next lower page frame in physical memory. The procedure concludes by looping until all the PTEs for the region are mapped in the page table. Note the nested loop in the LARGEPAGE and SMALLPAGE cases: the j loop writes the required identical PTE to properly map the given page in a fine page table.

14.10.6.3 Activating a Page Table

A page table can reside in memory and not be used by the MMU hardware. This happens when a task is dormant and its page tables are mapped out of active virtual memory. However, the task remains resident in physical memory, so it is immediately available for use when a context switch occurs to activate it.

The third part in initializing the MMU is to activate the page tables needed to execute code located in the fixed regions.

EXAMPLE
14.10

The routine mmuAttachPT either activates an L1 master page table by placing its address into the TTB in the CP15:c2:c0 register, or activates an L2 page table by placing its base address into an L1 master page table entry.

It can be called using the following function prototype:

```
int mmuAttachPT(Pagetable *pt);
```

The procedure takes a single argument, a pointer to the Pagetable to activate and add new translations from virtual to physical virtual memory.

```
int mmuAttachPT(Pagetable *pt)      /* attach L2 PT to L1 master PT */
{
  unsigned int *ttb, PTE, offset;

  ttb = (unsigned int *)pt->masterPtAddress;   /* read ttb from PT */
  offset = (pt->vAddress) >> 20;     /* determine PTE from vAddress */

  switch (pt->type)
  {
    case MASTER:
    {
      __asm{ MCR p15, 0, ttb, c2, c0, 0 } ;   /* TTB -> CP15:c2:c0 */
      break;
    }
    case COARSE:
    {
                      /* PTE = addr L2 PT | domain | COARSE PT type*/
      PTE = (pt->ptAddress & 0xfffffc00);
      PTE |= pt->dom << 5;
      PTE |= 0x11;
      ttb[offset] = PTE;
      break;
    }
```

```
    #if defined(__TARGET_CPU_ARM920T)
    case FINE:
    {
                            /* PTE = addr L2 PT | domain | FINE PT type*/
      PTE = (pt->ptAddress & 0xfffff000);
      PTE |= pt->dom<<5;
      PTE |= 0x13;
      ttb[offset] = PTE;
      break;
    }
    #endif
    default:
    {
      printf("UNKNOWN page table type\n");
      return -1;
    }
  }
  return 0;
}
```

The first thing the routine does is prepare two variables, the base address of the master L1 page table, *ttb*, and an offset into the L1 page table, *offset*. The offset variable is created from the virtual address of the page table. To calculate the offset, it takes the virtual address and divides it by 1 MB by shifting the virtual address right by 20 bits. Adding this offset to the master L1 base address generates a pointer to the address within the L1 master table that represents the translation for the 1 MB section.

The procedure attaches the page table to the MMU hardware using the *Pagetable* type *pt->type* variable to switch to the case that attaches the page table. The three possible cases are described below.

The *Master* case attaches the master L1 page table. The routine attaches this special table using an assembly language MCR instruction to set the CP15:c2:c0 register.

The *Coarse* case attaches a coarse page table to the master L1 page table. This case takes the address of the L2 page table stored in the Pagetable structure and combines it with the Domain and the coarse table type, to build a PTE. The PTE is then written into the L1 page table using the previously calculated offset. The format of the coarse PTE is shown in Figure 14.6.

The *Fine* case attaches a fine L2 page table to the master L1 page table. This routine takes the address of the L2 page table stored in the *Pagetable* structure and combines it with the *Domain* and fine table type to build a PTE. The PTE is then written into the L1 page table using the previously calculated offset.

The previous sections presented the routines that condition, load, and activate the page tables while initializing the MMU. The last two parts set the domain access rights and enable the MMU.

14.10.6.4   Assigning Domain Access and Enabling the MMU

The fourth part in initializing the MMU is to configure the domain access for the system. The demonstration does not use the FCSE, nor does it need to quickly expose and hide large blocks of memory, which eliminates the need to use the S and R access control bits in the CP15:c1:c0 register. This means that the access permissions defined in the page tables are enough to protect the system, and there is no reason to use Domains.

However, the hardware requires all active memory areas to have a domain assignment and be granted domain access privileges. The minimum domain configuration places all regions in the same domain and sets the domain access to client access. This domain configuration makes the access permission entries in the page tables the only permission system active.

In this demo, all regions are assigned Domain 3 and have client domain access. The other domains are unused and masked by the fault entry in the unused page table entries of the L1 master page table. Domains are assigned in the master L1 page table, and domain access is defined in the CP15:c3:c0 register.

EXAMPLE
14.11

domainAccessSet is a routine that sets the access rights for the 16 domains in the domain access control register CP15:c3:c0:0. It can be called from C using the following function prototype:

```
void domainAccessSet(unsigned int value, unsigned int mask);
```

The first argument passed to the procedure is an unsigned integer containing bit fields that set the Domain access for the 16 domains. The second parameter defines which domains need their access rights changed. The routine first reads the CP15:c3 register and places it in the variable *c3format*. The routine then uses the input *mask* value to clear the bits in *c3format* that need updating. The update is done by ORing *c3format* with *value* input parameter. The updated *c3format* is finally written back out to the CP15:c3 register to set the domain access.

```
void domainAccessSet(unsigned int value, unsigned int mask)
{
  unsigned int c3format;

  __asm{MRC p15, 0, c3format, c3, c0, 0 }  /* read domain register */
  c3format &= ~mask;                       /* clear bits that change */
  c3format |= value;                       /* set bits that change */
  __asm{MCR p15, 0, c3format, c3, c0, 0 }  /* write domain register */
}
```

Enabling the MMU is the fifth and final last part in the MMU initialization process. The routine controlSet, shown as Example 14.3, enables the MMU. It is advisable to call the controlSet procedure from a "fixed" address area.

14.10.6.5 Putting It All Together: Initializing the MMU for the Demonstration.

The routine mmuInit calls the routines described in previous sections to initialize the MMU for the demonstration. While reading this section of code it will be helpful to review the control blocks shown in Section 14.10.5.

The routine can be called using the following C function prototype:

```
void mmuInit(void)
```

EXAMPLE
14.12

This example calls the routines previously described as the five parts in the process of initializing the MMU. The five parts are labeled as comments in the example code.

The mmuInit begins by initializing the page tables and mapping regions in the privileged system area. The first part initalizes the fixed system area with calls to the routine mmuInitPT. These calls fill the L1 master and the L2 page tables with FAULT values. The routine calls mmuInitPT five times: once to initialize the L1 master page table, once to initialize the system L2 page table, and then calls mmuInitPT three more time to initialize the three task page tables:

```
#define DOM3CLT        0x00000040
#define CHANGEALLDOM 0xffffffff

#define ENABLEMMU      0x00000001
#define ENABLEDCACHE 0x00000004
#define ENABLEICACHE  0x00001000
#define CHANGEMMU 0x00000001
#define CHANGEDCACIIC   0x00000004
#define CHANGEICACHE 0x00001000
#define ENABLEWB        0x00000008
#define CHANGEWB 0x00000008

void mmuInit()
{
  unsigned int enable, change;

  /* Part 1 Initialize system (fixed) page tables */
  mmuInitPT(&masterPT);          /* init master L1 PT with FAULT PTE */
```

```
mmuInitPT(&systemPT);        /* init system L2 PT with FAULT PTE */
mmuInitPT(&task3PT);         /*  init task 3 L2 PT with FAULT PTE */
mmuInitPT(&task2PT);         /*  init task 2 L2 PT with FAULT PTE */
mmuInitPT(&task1PT);         /*  init task 1 L2 PT with FAULT PTE */

/* Part 2 filling page tables with translation & attribute data */
mmuMapRegion(&kernelRegion);        /* Map kernelRegion SystemPT */
mmuMapRegion(&sharedRegion);        /* Map sharedRegion SystemPT */
mmuMapRegion(&pageTableRegion);  /* Map pagetableRegion SystemPT */
mmuMapRegion(&peripheralRegion);/* Map peripheralRegion MasterPT */
mmuMapRegion(&t3Region);         /* Map task3 PT with Region data */
mmuMapRegion(&t2Region);         /* Map task3 PT with Region data */
mmuMapRegion(&t1Region);         /* Map task3 PT with Region data */

/* Part 3 activating page tables */
mmuAttachPT(&masterPT);    /* load L1 TTB to cp15:c2:c0 register */
mmuAttachPT(&systemPT);      /* load L2 system PTE into L1 PT */
mmuAttachPT(&task1PT);       /*  load L2 task 1 PTE into L1 PT */

/* Part 4 Set Domain Access */
domainAccessSet(DOM3CLT , CHANGEALLDOM); /* set Domain Access */

/* Part 5 Enable MMU, caches and write buffer */
#if defined(__TARGET_CPU_ARM720T)
  enable = ENABLEMMU | ENABLECACHE | ENABLEWB ;
  change = CHANGEMMU | CHANGECACHE | CHANGEWB ;
#endif
#if defined(__TARGET_CPU_ARM920T)
  enable = ENABLEMMU | ENABLEICACHE | ENABLEDCACHE ;
  change = CHANGEMMU | CHANGEICACHE | CHANGEDCACHE ;
#endif
controlSet(enable, change);            /* enable cache and MMU */
}
```

The second part then maps the seven Regions in the system into their page tables by calling mmuMapRegion seven times: four times to map the kernel, shared, page table, and peripheral regions, and three times to map the three task regions. mmuMapRegion converts the data from the control blocks into page table entries that are then written to a page table.

The third part in initalizing the MMU is to activate the page tables necessary to start the system. This is done by calling mmuAttachPT three times. First, it activates the master L1 page table by loading its base address into the TTB entry in CP15:c2:c0. The routine then activates the L2 system page table. The peripheral region is comprised of 1 MB pages residing in the L1 master page table and is activated when the master L1 table is actived. The third part is completed by activating the first task that runs after the system is enabled with a call to mmuAttachPT. In the demo, the first task to run is Task 1.

The fourth part in initializing the MMU is to set domain access by calling domainAccessSet. All regions are assigned to Domain 3 and the domain access for Domain 3 set to client access.

The mmuInit completes part five by calling controlSet to enable the MMU and caches.

When the routine mmuInit completes, the MMU is initialized and enabled. The final task in setting up the multitasking demonstration system is to define the procedural steps needed to perform a context switch between two tasks.

14.10.7 STEP 7: ESTABLISH A CONTEXT SWITCH PROCEDURE

A context switch in the demonstration system is relatively simple. There are six parts to performing a context switch:

1. Save the active task context and place the task in a dormant state.
2. Flush the caches; possibly clean the D-cache if using a writeback policy.
3. Flush the TLB to remove translations for the retiring task.
4. Configure the MMU to use new page tables translating the common virtual memory execution area to the awakening task's location in physical memory.
5. Restore the context of the awakening task.
6. Resume execution of the restored task.

The routines to perform all the parts just listed have been presented in previous sections. We list the procedure here. Parts 1, 5, and 6 were provided in Chapter 11; refer to that chapter for more details. Parts 2, 3, and 4 are the additions needed to support a context switch using an MMU and are shown here with the arguments needed to switch from task 1 to task 2 in the demonstration.

```
SAVE retiring task context;        /* part 1 shown in Chapter 11 */
flushCache();                      /* part 2 shown in Chapter 12 */
flushTLB();                        /* part 3 shown in Example 14.2 */
mmuAttachPT(&task2PT);             /* part 4 shown in Example 14.10 */
RESTORE awakening task context     /* part 5 shown in Chapter 11 */
RESUME execution of restored task  /* part 6 shown in Chapter 11 */
```

14.11 THE DEMONSTRATION AS MMUSLOS

Many of the concepts and the examples from the MMU demonstration code have been incorporated into a functional control system we call mmuSLOS. It is an extension of the control system called SLOS presented in Chapter 11.

mpuSLOS is the memory protection unit extension to SLOS, and was described in Chapter 13. We use the mpuSLOS variant as the base source code for mmuSLOS. All three variants can be found on the publisher's Web site. We changed three major parts of the mpuSLOS code:

- The MMU tables are created during the mmuSLOS initialization stage.
- The application tasks are built to execute at 0x400000, but are loaded at a different physical addresses. Each application task executes in a virtual memory starting at the execution address. The top of the stack is located as an 32 KB offset from the execution address.
- Each time the scheduler is called, the active 32 KB page in the MMU table is changed to reflect the new active application/task.

14.12 SUMMARY

The chapter presented the basics of memory management and virtual memory systems. A key service of an MMU is the ability to manage tasks as independent programs running in their own private virtual memory space.

An important feature of a virtual memory system is address relocation. Address relocation is the translation of the address issued by the processor core to a different address in main memory. The translation is done by the MMU hardware.

In a virtual memory system, virtual memory is commonly divided into parts as fixed areas and dynamic areas. In fixed areas the translation data mapped in a page table does not change during normal operation; in dynamic areas the memory mapping between virtual and physical memory frequently changes.

Page tables contain descriptions of virtual page information. A page table entry (PTE) translates a page in virtual memory to a page frame in physical memory. Page table entries are organized by virtual address and contain the translation data to map a page to a page frame.

The functions of an ARM MMU are to:

- read level 1 and level 2 page tables and load them into the TLB
- store recent virtual-to-physical memory address translations in the TLB
- perform virtual-to-physical address translation
- enforce access permission and configure the cache and write buffer

An additional special feature in an ARM MMU is the Fast Context Switch Extension. The Fast Context Switch Extension improves performance in a multitasking environment because it does not require flushing the caches or TLB during a context switch.

A working example of a small virtual memory system provided in-depth details to set up the MMU to support multitasking. The steps in setting up the demonstration are to define the regions used in the fixed system software of virtual memory, define the virtual memory maps for each task, locate the fixed and task regions into the physical memory map, define and locate the page tables within the page table region, define the data structures needed to create and manage the regions and page tables, initialize the MMU by using the defined region data to create page table entries and write them to the page tables, and establish a context switch procedure to transition from one task to the next.

JOHN RAYFIELD

In October 1999, ARM began to consider the future direction of the architecture that would eventually become ARMv6, first implemented in a new product called ARM1136J-S. By this time, ARM already had designs for many different applications, and the future requirements of each of those designs needed to be evaluated, as well as the new application areas for which ARM would be used in the future.

As system-on-chip designs have become more sophisticated, ARM processors have become the central processors in systems with multiple processing elements and subsystems. In particular, the portable and mobile computing markets were introducing new software and performance challenges for ARM. Areas that needed addressing were digital signal processing (DSP) and video performance for portable devices, interworking mixed-endian systems such as TCP/IP, and efficient synchronization in multiprocessing environments. The challenge for ARM was to address all of these market requirements and yet maintain its competitive advantage in computational efficiency (computing power per mW) as the best in the industry.

This chapter describes the components within ARMv6 introduced by ARM to address these market requirements, including enhanced DSP support and support for a multi-processing environment. The chapter also introduces the first high-performance ARMv6 implementations and, in addition to the ARMv6 technologies, one of ARM's latest technologies—TrustZone.

15.1   Advanced DSP and SIMD Support in ARMv6

Early in the ARMv6 project, ARM considered how to improve the DSP and media processing capabilities of the architecture beyond the ARMv5E extensions described in Section 3.7. This work was carried out very closely with the ARM1136J-S engineering team, which was in the early stages of developing the microarchitecture for the product. SIMD (Single Instruction Multiple Data) is a popular technique used to garner considerable data parallelism and is particularly effective in very math-intensive routines that are commonly used in DSP, video and graphics processing algorithms. SIMD is attractive for high code density and low power since the number of instructions executed (and hence memory system accesses) is kept low. The price for this efficiency is the reduced flexibility of having to compute things arranged in certain blocked data patterns; this, however, works very well in many image and signal processing algorithms.

Using the standard ARM design philosophy of computational efficiency with very low power, ARM came up with a simple and elegant way of slicing up the existing ARM 32-bit datapath into four 8-bit and two 16-bit slices. Unlike many existing SIMD architectures that add separate datapaths for the SIMD operations, this method allows the SIMD to be added to the base ARM architecture with very little extra hardware cost.

The ARMv6 architecture includes this "lightweight" SIMD approach that costs virtually nothing in terms of extra complexity (gate count) and therefore power. At the same time the new instructions can improve the processing throughput of some algorithms by up to two times for 16-bit data or four times for 8-bit data. In common with most operations in the ARM instruction set architecture, all of these new instructions are executed conditionally, as described in Section 2.2.6.

You can find a full description of all ARMv6 instructions in the instruction set tables of Appendix A.

15.1.1   SIMD Arithmetic Operations

Table 15.1 shows a summary of the 8-bit SIMD operations. Each byte result is formed from the arithmetic operation on each of the corresponding byte slices through the source operands.

The results of these 8-bit operations may require that up to 9 bits be represented, which either causes a wraparound or a saturation to take place, depending on the particular instruction used.

In addition to the 8-bit SIMD operations, there are an extensive range of dual 16-bit operations, shown in Table 15.2. Each halfword (16-bit) result is formed from the arithmetic operation on each of the corresponding 16-bit slices through the source operands.

The results may need 17 bits to be stored, and in this case they can either wrap around or are saturated to within the range of a 16-bit signed result with the saturating version of the instruction.

Table 15.1   8-bit SIMD arithmetic operations.

Instruction	Description
SADD8{<cond>} Rd, Rn, Rm	Signed 8-bit SIMD add
SSUB8{<cond>} Rd, Rn, Rm	Signed 8-bit SIMD subtract
UADD8{<cond>} Rd, Rn, Rm	Unsigned 8-bit SIMD add
USUB8{<cond>} Rd, Rn, Rm	Unsigned 8-bit SIMD subtract
QADD8{<cond>} Rd, Rn, Rm	Signed saturating 8-bit SIMD add
QSUB8{<cond>} Rd, Rn, Rm	Signed saturating 8-bit SIMD subtract
UQADD8{<cond>} Rd, Rn, Rm	Unsigned saturating 8-bit SIMD add
UQSUB8{<cond>} Rd, Rn, Rm	Unsigned saturating 8-bit SIMD subtract

Table 15.2   16-bit SIMD arithmetic operations.

Instruction	Description
SADD16{<cond>} Rd, Rn, Rm	Signed add of the 16-bit pairs
SSUB16{<cond>} Rd, Rn, Rm	Signed subtract of the 16-bit pairs
UADD16{<cond>} Rd, Rn, Rm	Unsigned add of the 16-bit pairs
USUB16{<cond>} Rd, Rn, Rm	Unsigned subtract of the 16-bit pairs
QADD16{<cond>} Rd, Rn, Rm	Signed saturating add of the 16-bit pairs
QSUB16{<cond>} Rd, Rn, Rm	Signed saturating subtract of the 16-bit pairs
UQADD16{<cond>} Rd, Rn, Rm	Unsigned saturating add of the 16-bit pairs
UQSUB16{<cond>} Rd, Rn, Rm	Unsigned saturating subtract of the 16-bit pairs

Operands for the SIMD instructions are not always found in the correct order within the source registers; to improve the efficiency of dealing with these situations, there are 16-bit SIMD operations that perform swapping of the 16-bit words of one operand register. These operations allow a great deal of flexibility in dealing with halfwords that may be aligned in different ways in memory and are particularly useful when working with 16-bit complex number pairs that are packed into 32-bit registers. There are signed, unsigned, saturating signed, and saturating unsigned versions of these operations, as shown in Table 15.3.

The X in the instruction mnemonic signifies that the two halfwords in *Rm* are swapped before the operations are applied so that operations like the following take place:

```
Rd[15:0]  = Rn[15:0] - Rm[31:16]
Rd[31:16] = Rn[31:16] + Rm[15:0]
```

The addition of the SIMD operations means there is now a need for some way of showing an overflow or a carry from each SIMD slice through the datapath. The *cpsr* as originally

Table 15.3   16-bit SIMD arithmetic operations with swap.

Instruction	Description
SADDSUBX{<cond>} Rd, Rn, Rm	Signed upper add, lower subtract, with a swap of halfwords in *Rm*
UADDSUBX{<cond>} Rd, Rn, Rm	Unsigned upper add, lower subtract, with swap of halfwords in *Rm*
QADDSUBX{<cond>} Rd, Rn, Rm	Signed saturating upper add, lower subtract, with swap of halfwords in *Rm*
UQADDSUBX{<cond>} Rd, Rn, Rm	Unsigned saturating upper add, lower subtract, with swap of halfwords in *Rm*
SSUBADDX{<cond>} Rd, Rn, Rm	Signed upper subtract, lower add, with a swap of halfwords in *Rm*
USUBADDX{<cond>} Rd, Rn, Rm	Unsigned upper subtract, lower add, with swap of halfwords in *Rm*
QSUBADDX{<cond>} Rd, Rn, Rm	Signed saturating upper subtract, lower add, with swap of halfwords in *Rm*
UQSUBADDX{<cond>} Rd, Rn, Rm	Unsigned saturating upper subtract, lower add, with swap of halfwords in *Rm*

described in Section 2.2.5 is modified by adding four additional flag bits to represent each 8-bit slice of the data path. The newly modified *cpsr* register with the *GE* bits is shown in Figure 15.1 and Table 15.4. The functionality of each *GE* bit is that of a "greater than or equal" flag for each slice through the datapath.

Operating systems already save the *cpsr* register on a context switch. Adding these bits to the *cpsr* has little effect on OS support for the architecture.

In addition to basic arithmetic operations on the SIMD data slices, there is considerable use for operations that allow the picking of individual data elements within the datapath and forming new ensembles of these elements. A select instruction SEL can independently select each eight-bit field from one source register *Rn* or another source register *Rm*, depending on the associated *GE* flag.

31 30 29 28	27	26 25 24 23 22 21 20	19 18 17 16	15 14 13 12 11 10 9 8 7	6 5	4 3 2 1 0
N Z C V *Q*	Res *J*	Res	*GE* [3:0]	Res	*E A* *I F T*	mode

Figure 15.1   *cpsr* layout for ARMv6.

Table 15.4   *cpsr* fields for ARMv6.

Field	Use
N	Negative flag. Records bit 31 of the result of flag-setting operations.
Z	Zero flag. Records if the result of a flag-setting operation is zero.
C	Carry flag. Records unsigned overflow for addition, not-borrow for subtraction, and is also used by the shifting circuit. See Table A.3.
V	Overflow flag. Records signed overflows for flag-setting operations.
Q	Saturation flag. Certain saturating operations set this flag on saturation. See for example QADD in Appendix A (ARMv5E and above).
J	$J = 1$ indicates Java execution (must have $T = 0$). Use the BXJ instruction to change this bit (ARMv5J and above).
Res	These bits are reserved for future expansion. Software should preserve the values in these bits.
GE[3:0]	The SIMD greater-or-equal flags. See SADD in Appendix A (ARMv6).
E	Controls the data endianness. See SETEND in Appendix A (ARMv6).
A	$A = 1$ disables imprecise data aborts (ARMv6).
I	$I = 1$ disables IRQ interrupts.
F	$F = 1$ disables FIQ interrupts.
T	$T = 1$ indicates Thumb state. $T = 0$ indicates ARM state. Use the BX or BLX instructions to change this bit (ARMv4T and above).
mode	The current processor mode. See Table B.4.

```
SEL Rd, Rn, Rm
Rd[31:24] = GE[3] ? Rn[31:24] : Rm[31:24]
Rd[23:16] = GE[2] ? Rn[23:16] : Rm[23:16]
Rd[15:08] = GE[1] ? Rn[15:08] : Rm[15:08]
Rd[07:00] = GE[0] ? Rn[07:00] : Rm[07:00]
```

These instructions, together with the other SIMD operations, can be used very effectively to implement the core of the Viterbi algorithm, which is used extensively for symbol recovery in communication systems. Since the Viterbi algorithm is essentially a statistical maximum likelihood selection algorithm, it is also used in such areas as speech and handwriting recognition engines. The core of Viterbi is an operation that is commonly known as add-compare-select (ACS), and in fact many DSP processors have customized ACS instructions. With its parallel (SIMD) add, subtract (which can be used to compare), and selection instructions, ARMv6 can implement an extremely efficient add-compare-select:

```
ADD8    Rp1, Rs1, Rb1   ; path 1 = state 1 + branch 1  (metric update)
ADD8    Rp2, Rs2, Rb2   ; path 2 = state 2 + branch 2  (metric update)
```

Table 15.5   Packing instructions.

Instruction	Description
PKHTB{<cond>} Rd, Rn, Rm {, ASR #<shift_imm>}	Pack the top 16 bits of *Rn* with the bottom 16 bits of the shifted *Rm* into the destination *Rd*
PKHBT{<cond>} Rd, Rn, Rm {, LSL #<shift_imm>}	Pack the top 16 bits of the shifted *Rm* with the bottom 16 bits of *Rn* into the destination *Rd*

```
USUB8   Rt, Rp1, Rp2   ; compare metrics - setting the SIMD flags
SEL     Rd, Rp2, Rp1   ; choose best (smallest) metric
```

This kernel performs the ACS operation on four paths in parallel and takes a total of 4 cycles on the ARM1136J-S. The same sequence coded for the ARMv5TE instruction set must perform each of the operations serially, taking at least 16 cycles. Thus the add-compare-select function is four times faster on ARM1136J-S for eight-bit metrics.

15.1.2 PACKING INSTRUCTIONS

The ARMv6 architecture includes a new set of packing instructions, shown in Table 15.5, that are used to construct new 32-bit packed data from pairs of 16-bit values in different source registers. The second operand can be optionally shifted. Packing instructions are particularly useful for pairing 16-bit values so that you can make use of the 16-bit SIMD processing instructions described earlier.

15.1.3 COMPLEX ARITHMETIC SUPPORT

Complex arithmetic is commonly used in communication signal processing, and in particular in the implementations of transform algorithms such as the Fast Fourier Transform as described in Chapter 8. Much of the implementation detail examined in that chapter concerns the efficient implementation of the complex multiplication using ARMv4 or ARMv5E instruction sets.

ARMv6 adds new multiply instructions to accelerate complex multiplication, shown in Table 15.6. Both of these operations optionally swap the order of the two 16-bit halves of source operand *Rs* if you specify the X suffix.

EXAMPLE
15.1   In this example *Ra* and *Rb* hold complex numbers with 16-bit coefficients packed with their real parts in the lower half of a register and their imaginary part in the upper half.

Table 15.6 Instructions to support 16-bit complex multiplication.

Instruction	Description
SMUAD{X}{<cond>} Rd, Rm, Rs	Dual 16-bit signed multiply and add
SMUSD{X}{<cond>} Rd, Rm, Rs	Dual 16-bit signed multiply and subtract

We multiply *Ra* and *Rb* to produce a new complex number *Rc*. The code assumes that the 16-bit values represent Q15 fractions. Here is the code for ARMv6:

```
SMUSD   Rt, Ra, Rb    ; real*real−imag*imag at Q30
SMUADX  Rc, Ra, Rb    ; real*imag+imag*real at Q30
QADD    Rt, Rt, Rt    ; convert to Q31 & saturate
QADD    Rc, Rc, Rc    ; convert to Q31 & saturate
PKHTB   Rc, Rc, Rt, ASR #16 ; pack results
```

Compare this with an ARMv5TE implementation:

```
SMULBB  Rc, Ra, Rb    ; real*real
SMULTT  Rt, Ra, Rb    ; imag*imag
QSUB    Rt, Rc, Rt    ; real*real-imag*imag at Q30
SMULTB  Rc, Ra, Rb    ; imag*real
SMLABT  Rc, Ra, Rb    ; + real*imag at Q30
QADD    Rt, Rt, Rt    ; convert to Q31 & saturate
QADD    Rc, Rc, Rc    ; convert to Q31 & saturate
MOV     Rc, Rc, LSR #16
MOV     Rt, Rt, LSR #16
ORR     Rt, Rt, Rc, LSL#16   ; pack results
```

There are 10 cycles for ARMv5E versus 5 cycles for ARMv6. Clearly with any algorithm doing very intense complex maths, a two times improvement in performance can be gained for the complex multiply.

15.1.4 SATURATION INSTRUCTIONS

Saturating arithmetic was first addressed with the E extensions that were added to the ARMv5TE architecture, which was introduced with the ARM966E and ARM946E products. ARMv6 takes this further with individual and more flexible saturation instructions that can operate on 32-bit words and 16-bit halfwords. In addition to these instructions, shown in Table 15.7, there are the new saturating arithmetic SIMD operations that have already been described in Section 15.1.1.

Table 15.7   Saturation instructions.

Instruction	Description
SSAT Rd, #<BitPosition>, Rm,{<Shift>}	Signed 32-bit saturation at an arbitrary bit position. Shift can be an LSL or ASR.
SSAT16{<cond>} Rd, #<immed>, Rm	Dual 16-bit saturation at the same position in both halves.
USAT Rd, #<BitPosition>, Rm,{<Shift>}	Unsigned 32-bit saturation at an arbitrary bit position. Shift can be LSL or ASR.
USAT16{<cond>} Rd, #<immed>, Rm	Unsigned dual 16-bit saturation at the same position in both halves.

Note that in the 32-bit versions of these saturation operations there is an optional arithmetic shift of the source register *Rm* before saturation, allowing scaling to take place in the same instruction.

15.1.5   SUM OF ABSOLUTE DIFFERENCES INSTRUCTIONS

These two new instructions are probably the most application specific within the ARMv6 architecture—USAD8 and USADA8. They are used to compute the absolute difference between eight-bit values and are particularly useful in motion video compression algorithms such as MPEG or H.263, including motion estimation algorithms that measure motion by comparing blocks using many sum-of-absolute-difference operations (see Figure 15.2). Table 15.8 lists these instructions.

Table 15.8   Sum of absolute differences.

Instruction	Description
USAD8{<cond>} Rd, Rm, Rs	Sum of absolute differences
USADA8{<cond>} Rd, Rm, Rs, Rn	Accumulated sum of absolute differences

To compare an $N \times N$ square at (x, y) in image p_1 with an $N \times N$ square p_2, we calculate the accumulated sum of absolute differences:

$$a(x, y) = \sum_{i=0}^{N-1} \sum_{j=0}^{N-1} \left| p_1(x + i, y + j) - p_2(i, j) \right|$$

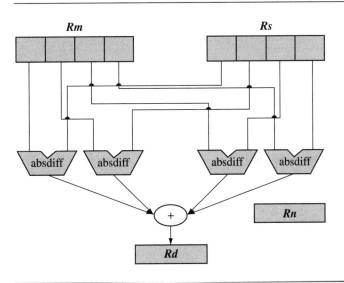

Figure 15.2   Sum-of-absolute-differences operation.

To implement this using the new instructions, use the following sequence to compute the sum-of-absolute differences of four pixels:

```
LDR     p1,[p1Ptr],#4    ; load 4 pixels from p1
LDR     p2,[p2Ptr],#4    ; load 4 pixels from p2
;load delay-slot
;load delay-slot
USADA8  acc, p1,  p2     ; accumlate sum abs diff
```

There is a tremendous performance advantage for this algorithm over an ARMv5TE implementation. There is a four times improvement in performance from the eight-bit SIMD alone. Additionally the USADA8 operation includes the accumulation operation. The USAD8 operation will typically be used to carry out the setup into the loop before there is an existing accumulated value.

15.1.6   DUAL 16-BIT MULTIPLY INSTRUCTIONS

ARMv5TE introduced considerable DSP performance to ARM, but ARMv6 takes this much further. Implementations of ARMv6 (such as ARM1136J) have a dual 16 × 16 multiply capability, which is comparable with many high-end dedicated DSP devices. Table 15.9 lists these instructions.

Table 15.9   Dual 16-bit multiply operations.

Instruction	Description
SMLAD{X}{<cond>} Rd, Rm, Rs, Rn	Dual signed multiply accumulate with 32-bit accumulation
SMLALD{X}{<cond>} RdLo, RdHi, Rm, Rs	Dual signed multiply accumulate with 64-bit accumulation
SMLSD{X}{<cond>} Rd, Rm, Rs, Rn	Dual signed multiply subtract with 32-bit accumulation
SMLSLD{X}{<cond>} RdLo, RdHi, Rm, Rs	Dual signed multiply subtract with 64-bit accumulation

We demonstrate the use of SMLAD as a signed dual multiply in a dot-product inner loop:

```
        MOV     R0, #0                  ; zero accumulator
Loop
        LDMIA   R2!,{R4,R5,R6,R7}       ; load 8 16-bit data items
        LDMIA   R1!,{R8,R9,R10,R11}     ; load 8 16-bit coefficients
        SUBS    R3,R3,#8                ; subtract 8 from the loop counter
        SMLAD   R0,R4,R8,R0             ; 2 multiply accumulates
        SMLAD   R0,R5,R9,R0
        SMLAD   R0,R6,R10,R0
        SMLAD   R0,R7,R11,R0
        BGT     Loop                    ; loop if more coefficients
```

This loop delivers eight 16×16 multiply accumulates in 10 cycles without using any data-blocking techniques. If a set of the operands for the dot-product is stored in registers, then performance approaches the true dual multiplies per cycle.

15.1.7 MOST SIGNIFICANT WORD MULTIPLIES

ARMv5TE added arithmetic operations that are used extensively in a very broad range of DSP algorithms including control and communications and that were designed to use the Q15 data format. However, in audio processing applications it is common for 16-bit processing to be insufficient to describe the quality of the signals. Typically 32-bit values are used in these cases, and ARMv6 adds some new multiply instructions that operate on Q31 formatted values. (Recall that Q-format arithmetic is described in detail in Chapter 8.) These new instructions are listed in Table 15.10.

Table 15.10   Most significant word multiplies.

Instruction	Description
`SMMLA{R}{<cond>} Rd, Rm, Rs, Rn`	Signed 32 × 32 multiply with accumulation of the high 32 bits of the product to the 32-bit accumulator *Rn*
`SMMLS{R}{<cond>} Rd, Rm, Rs, Rn`	Signed 32 × 32 multiply subtracting from (*Rn* << 32) and then taking the high 32 bits of the result
`SMMUL{R}{<cond>} Rd, Rm, Rs`	Signed 32 × 32 multiply with upper 32 bits of product only

The optional {R} in the mnemonic allows the addition of the fixed constant 0x80000000 to the 64-bit product before producing the upper 32 bits. This allows for biased rounding of the result.

15.1.8   CRYPTOGRAPHIC MULTIPLICATION EXTENSIONS

In some cryptographic algorithms, very long multiplications are quite common. In order to maximize their throughput, a new $64 + 32 \times 32 \rightarrow 64$ multiply accumulate operation has been added to complement the already existing 32×32 multiply operation UMULL (see Table 15.11).

Here is an example of a very efficient 64-bit × 64-bit multiply using the new instructions:

```
; inputs: First 64-bit multiply operand in (RaHi,RaLo)
; Second 64-bit multiply operand in (RbHi, RbLo)

umull64x64
      UMULL    R0, R2, RaLo, RbLo
      UMULL    R1, R3, RaHi, RbLo
      UMAAL    R1, R2, RaLo, RbHi
      UMAAL    R2, R3, RaHi, RbHi

; output: 128-bit result in (R3, R2, R1, R0)
```

Table 15.11   Cryptographic multiply.

`UMAAL{<cond>} RdLo, RdHi, Rm, Rs`	Special crypto multiply ($RdHi : RdLo$) = $Rm * Rs + RdHi + RdLo$

15.2   System and Multiprocessor Support Additions to ARMv6

As systems become more complicated, they incorporate multiple processors and processing engines. These engines may share different views of memory and even use different endiannesses (byte order). To support communication in these systems, ARMv6 adds support for mixed-endian systems, fast exception processing, and new synchronization primitives.

15.2.1   Mixed-Endianness Support

Traditionally the ARM architecture has had a little-endian view of memory with a big-endian mode that could be switched at reset. This big-endian mode sets the memory system up as big-endian ordered instructions and data.

As mentioned in the introduction to this chapter, ARM has found its cores integrated into very sophisticated system-on-chip devices dealing with mixed endianess, and often has to deal with both little- and big-endian data in software. ARMv6 adds a new instruction to set the data endianness for large code sequences (see Table 15.12), and also some individual manipulation instructions to increase the efficiency of dealing with mixed-endian environments.

The endian_specifier is either BE for big-endian or LE for little endian. A program would typically use SETEND when there is a considerable chunk of code that is carrying out operations on data with a particular endianness. Figure 15.3 shows individual byte manipulation instructions.

Table 15.12   Setting data-endianness operation.

SETEND <endian_specifier>	Change the default data endianness based on the <endian_specifier> argument.

15.2.2   Exception Processing

It is common for operating systems to save the return state of an interrupt or exception on a stack. ARMv6 adds the instructions in Table 15.13 to improve the efficiency of this operation, which can occur very frequently in interrupt/scheduler driven systems.

15.2.3   Multiprocessing Synchronization Primitives

As system-on-chip (SoC) architectures have become more sophisticated, ARM cores are now often found in devices with many processing units that compete for shared resources.

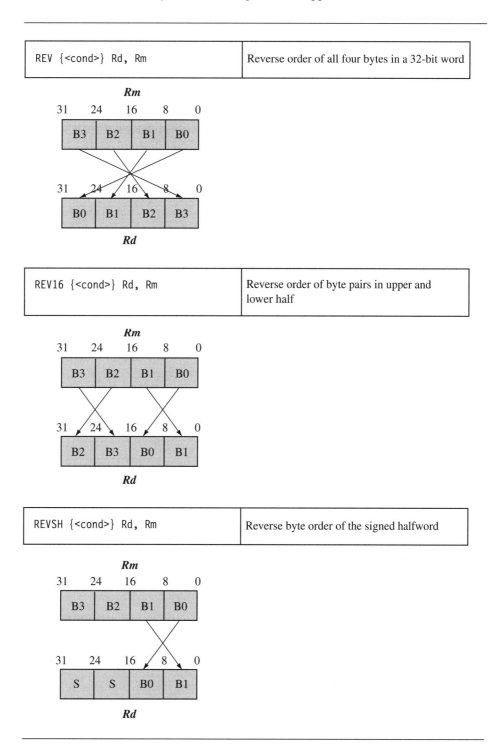

| REV {<cond>} Rd, Rm | Reverse order of all four bytes in a 32-bit word |

| REV16 {<cond>} Rd, Rm | Reverse order of byte pairs in upper and lower half |

| REVSH {<cond>} Rd, Rm | Reverse byte order of the signed halfword |

Figure 15.3   Reverse instructions in ARMv6.

Table 15.13   Exception processing operations.

Instruction	Description
SRS<addressing_mode>, #mode{!}	Save return state (*lr* and *spsr*) on the stack addressed by *sp* in the specified mode.
RFE <addressing_mode>, Rn{!}	Return from exception. Loads the *pc* and *cpsr* from the stack pointed to by *Rn*.
CPS<effect> <iflags> {,#<mode>}	Change processor state with interrupt enable or disable.
CPS #<mode>	Change processor state only.

The ARM architecture has always had the SWP instruction for implementing semaphores to ensure consistency in such environments. As the SoC has become more complex, however, certain aspects of SWP cause a performance bottleneck in some instances. Recall that SWP is basically a "blocking" primitive that locks the external bus of the processor and uses most of its bandwidth just to wait for a resource to be released. In this sense the SWP instruction is considered "pessimistic"—no computation can continue until SWP returns with the freed resource.

New instructions LDREX and STREX (load and store exclusive) were added to the ARMv6 architecture to solve this problem. These instructions, listed in Table 15.14, are very straightforward in use and are implemented by having a system monitor out in the memory system. LDREX optimistically loads a value from memory into a register assuming that nothing else will change the value in memory while we are working on it. STREX stores a value back out to memory and returns an indication of whether the value in memory was changed or not between the original LDREX operation and this store. In this way the primitives are "optimistic"—you continue processing the data you loaded with LDREX even though some external device may also be modifying the value. Only if a modification actually took place externally is the value thrown away and reloaded.

The big difference for the system is that the processor no longer waits around on the system bus for a semaphore to be free, and therefore leaves most of the system bus bandwidth available for other processes or processors.

Table 15.14   Load and store exclusive operations.

Instructions	Description
LDREX{<cond>} Rd, [Rn]	Load from address in *Rn* and set memory monitor
STREX{<cond>} Rd, Rm, [Rn]	Store to address in *Rn* and flag if successful in *Rd* (*Rd* = 0 if successful)

15.3 ARMv6 Implementations

ARM completed development of ARM1136J in December 2002, and at this writing consumer products are being designed with this core. The ARM1136J pipeline is the most sophisticated ARM implementation to date. As shown in Figure 15.4, it has an eight-stage pipeline with separate parallel pipelines for load/store and multiply/accumulate.

The parallel load/store unit (LSU) with hit-under-miss capability allows load and store operations to be issued and execution to continue while the load or store is completing with the slower memory system. By decoupling the execution pipeline from the completion of loads or stores, the core can gain considerable extra performance since the memory system is typically many times slower than the core speed. Hit-under-miss extends this decoupling out to the L1-L2 memory interface so that an L1 cache miss can occur and an L2 transaction can be completing while other L1 hits are still going on.

Another big change in microarchitecture is the move from virtually tagged caches to physically tagged caches. Traditionally, ARM has used virtually tagged caches where the MMU is between the caches and the outside L2 memory system. With ARMv6, this changes so that the MMU is now between the core and the L1 caches, so that all cache memory accesses are using physical (already translated) addresses. One of the big benefits of this approach is considerably reduced cache flushing on context switches when the ARM is running large operating systems. This reduced flushing will also reduce power consumption in the end system since cache flushing directly implies more external memory accesses. In some cases it is expected that this architectural change will deliver up to a 20% performance improvement.

15.4 Future Technologies beyond ARMv6

In 2003, ARM made further technology announcements including TrustZone and Thumb-2. While these technologies are very new, at this writing, they are being included in new microprocessor cores. The next sections briefly introduce these new technologies.

15.4.1 TrustZone

TrustZone is an architectural extension targeting the security of transactions that may be carried out using consumer products such as cell phones and, in the future, perhaps online transactions to download music or video for example. It was first introduced in October 2003 when ARM announced the ARM1176JZ-S.

The fundamental idea is that operating systems (even on embedded devices) are now so complex that it is very hard to verify security and correctness in the software. The ARM solution to this problem is to add new operating "states" to the architecture where only a small verifiable software kernel will run, and this will provide services to the larger operating system. The microprocessor core then takes a role in controlling system peripherals that

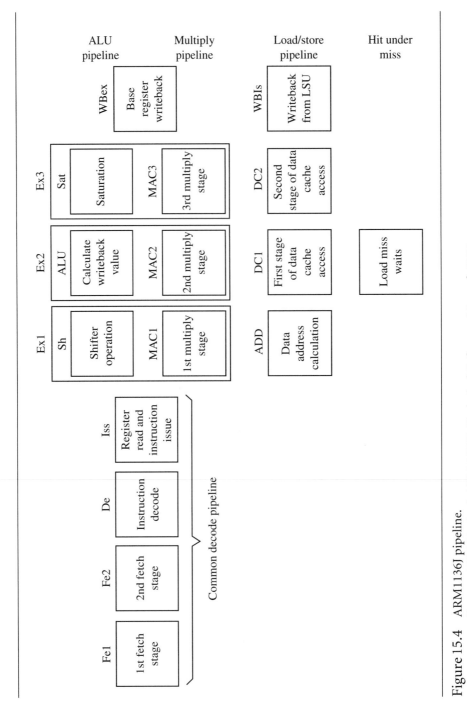

Figure 15.4   ARM1136J pipeline.
Source: ARM Limited, ARM 1136J, Technical Reference Manual, 2003.

may be only available to the secure "state" through some new exported signals on the bus interface. The system states are shown in Figure 15.5.

TrustZone is most useful in devices that will be carrying out content downloads such as cell phones or other portable devices with network connections. Details of this architecture are not public at the time of writing.

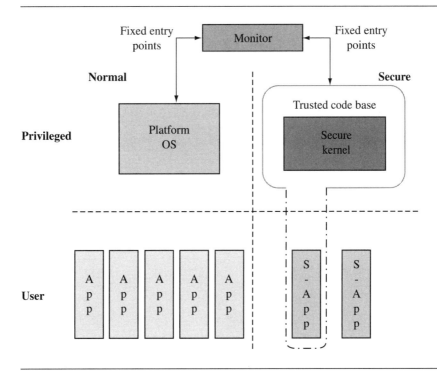

Figure 15.5   Modified security structure using TrustZone technology.
Source: Richard York, *A New Foundation for CPU Systems Security: Security Extensions to the ARM Architecture*, 2003.

15.4.2 THUMB-2

Thumb-2 is an architectural extension designed to increase performance at high code density. It allows for a blend of 32-bit ARM-like instructions with 16-bit Thumb instructions. This combination enables you to have the code density benefits of Thumb with the additional performance benefits of access to 32-bit instructions.

Thumb-2 was announced in October 2003 and will be implemented in the ARM1156T2-S processor. Details of this architecture are not public at the time of writing.

15.5 SUMMARY

The ARM architecture is not a static constant but is being developed and improved to suit the applications required by today's consumer devices. Although the ARMv5TE architecture was very successful at adding some DSP support to the ARM, the ARMv6 architecture extends the DSP support as well as adding support for large multiprocessor systems. Table 15.15 shows how these new technologies map to different processor cores.

ARM still concentrates on one of its key benefits—code density—and has recently announced the Thumb-2 extension to its popular Thumb architecture. The new focus on security with TrustZone gives ARM a leading edge in this area.

Expect many more innovations over the years to come!

Table 15.15   Recently announced cores.

Processor core	Architecture version
ARM1136J-S	ARMv6J
ARM1156T2-S	ARMv6 + Thumb-2
ARM1176JZ-S	ARMv6J + TrustZone

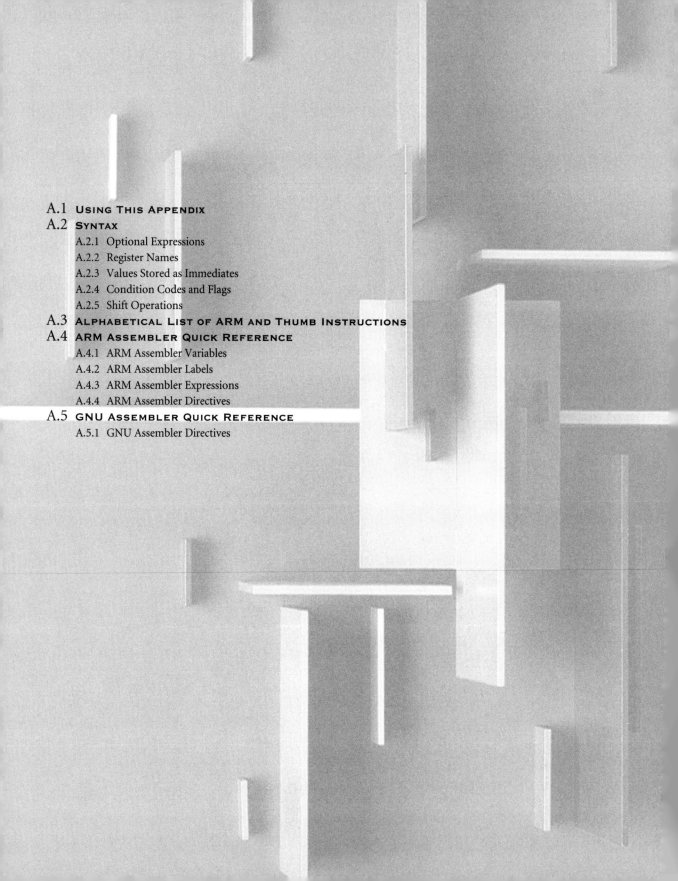

ARM AND THUMB ASSEMBLER INSTRUCTIONS

This appendix lists the ARM and Thumb instructions available up to, and including, ARM architecture ARMv6, which was just released at the time of writing. We list the operations in alphabetical order for easy reference. Sections A.4 and A.5 give quick reference guides to the ARM and GNU assemblers *armasm* and *gas*.

We have designed this appendix for practical programming use, both for writing assembly code and for interpreting disassembly output. It is not intended as a definitive architectural ARM reference. In particular, we do not list the exhaustive details of each instruction bitmap encoding and behavior. For this level of detail, see the *ARM Architecture Reference Manual*, edited by David Seal, published by Addison Wesley. We do give a summary of ARM and Thumb instruction set encodings in Appendix B.

A.1 USING THIS APPENDIX

Each appendix entry begins by enumerating the available instructions formats for the given instruction class. For example, the first entry for the instruction class ADD reads

```
1. ADD<cond>{S} Rd, Rn, #<rotated_immed>                        ARMv1
```

The fields <cond> and <rotated_immed> are two of a number of standard fields described in Section A.2. Rd and Rn denote ARM registers. The instruction is only executed if the

569

Table A.1   Instruction types.

Type	Meaning
ARMvX	32-bit ARM instruction first appearing in ARM architecture version X
THUMBvX	16-bit Thumb instruction first appearing in Thumb architecture version X
MACRO	Assembler pseudoinstruction

condition <cond> is passed. Each entry also describes the action of the instruction if it is executed.

The {S} denotes that you may apply an optional S suffix to the instruction. Finally, the right-hand column specifies that the instruction is available from the listed ARM architecture version onwards. Table A.1 shows the entries possible for this column.

Note that there is no direct correlation between the Thumb architecture number and the ARM architecture number. The THUMBv1 architecture is used in ARMv4T processors; the THUMBv2 architecture, in ARMv5T processors; and the THUMBv3 architecture, in ARMv6 processors.

Each instruction definition is followed by a notes section describing restrictions on the use of the instruction. When we make a statement such as "*Rd* must not be *pc*," we mean that the description of the function only applies when this condition holds. If you break the condition, then the instruction may be unpredictable or have predictable effects that we haven't had space to describe here. Well-written programs should not need to break these conditions.

A.2 SYNTAX

We use the following syntax and abbreviations throughout this appendix.

A.2.1 OPTIONAL EXPRESSIONS

- *{<expr>}* is an optional expression. For example, LDR{B} is shorthand for LDR or LDRB.
- *{<exp1>|<exp2>|...|<expN>}*, including at least one "|" divider, is a list of expressions. One of the listed expressions must appear. For example LDR{B|H} is shorthand for LDRB or LDRH. It does not include LDR. We would represent these three possibilities by LDR{|B|H}.

A.2.2 REGISTER NAMES

- *Rd, Rn, Rm, Rs, RdHi, RdLo* represent ARM registers in the range *r0* to *r15*.
- *Ld, Ln, Lm, Ls* represent low-numbered ARM registers in the range *r0* to *r7*.

- *Hd, Hn, Hm, Hs* represent high-numbered ARM registers in the range *r8* to *r15*.

- *Cd, Cn, Cm* represent coprocessor registers in the range *c0* to *c15*.

- *sp, lr, pc* are names for *r13, r14, r15*, respectively.

- *Rn*[*a*] denotes bit *a* of register *Rn*. Therefore $Rn[a] = (Rn \gg a)$ & 1.

- *Rn*[*a:b*] denotes the $a + 1 - b$ bit value stored in bits *a* to *b* of *Rn* inclusive.

- *RdHi:RdLo* represents the 64-bit value with high 32 bits *RdHi* and low 32 bits *RdLo*.

A.2.3 VALUES STORED AS IMMEDIATES

- `<immedN>` is any unsigned *N*-bit immediate. For example, `<immed8>` represents any integer in the range 0 to 255. `<immed5>*4` represents any integer in the list 0, 4, 8, ..., 124.

- `<addressN>` is an address or label stored as a relative offset. The address must be in the range $pc - 2^N \leq address < pc + 2^N$. Here, *pc* is the address of the instruction plus eight for ARM state, or the address of the instruction plus four for Thumb state. The address must be four-byte aligned if the destination is an ARM instruction or two-byte aligned if the destination is a Thumb instruction.

- `<A-B>` represents any integer in the range *A* to *B* inclusive.

- `<rotated_immed>` is any 32-bit immediate that can be represented as an eight-bit unsigned value rotated right (or left) by an even number of bit positions. In other words, `<rotated_immed>` = `<immed8>` ROR (2*`<immed4>`). For example 0xff, 0x104, 0xe0000005, and 0x0bc00000 are possible values for `<rotated_immed>`. However, 0x101 and 0x102 are not. When you use a rotated immediate, `<shifter_C>` is set according to Table A.3 (discussed in Section A.2.5). A nonzero rotate may cause a change in the carry flag. For this reason, you can also specify the rotation explicitly, using the assembly syntax `<immed8>`, 2*`<immed4>`.

A.2.4 CONDITION CODES AND FLAGS

- `<cond>` represents any of the standard ARM condition codes. Table A.2 shows the possible values for `<cond>`.

- `<SignedOverflow>` is a flag indicating that the result of an arithmetic operation suffered from a signed overflow. For example, 0x7fffffff + 1 = 0x80000000 produces a signed overflow because the sum of two positive 32-bit signed integers is a negative 32- bit signed integer. The *V* flag in the *cpsr* typically records signed overflows.

- `<UnsignedOverflow>` is a flag indicating that the result of an arithmetic operation suffered from an unsigned overflow. For example, 0xffffffff + 1 = 0 produces an overflow in unsigned 32-bit arithmetic. The *C* flag in the *cpsr* typically records unsigned overflows.

Table A.2   ARM condition mnemonics.

\<cond\>	Instruction is executed when	*cpsr* condition
{|AL}	ALways	TRUE
EQ	EQual (last result zero)	Z==1
NE	Not Equal (last result nonzero)	Z==0
{CS|HS}	Carry Set, unsigned Higher or Same (following a compare)	C==1
{CC|LO}	Carry Clear, unsigned LOwer (following a comparison)	C==0
MI	MInus (last result negative)	N==1
PL	PLus (last result greater than or equal to zero)	N==0
VS	V flag Set (signed overflow on last result)	V==1
VC	V flag Clear (no signed overflow on last result)	V==0
HI	unsigned HIgher (following a comparison)	C==1 && Z==0
LS	unsigned Lower or Same (following a comparison)	C==0 || Z==1
GE	signed Greater than or Equal	N==V
LT	signed Less Than	N!=V
GT	signed Greater Than	N==V && Z==0
LE	signed Less than or Equal	N!=V || Z==1
NV	NeVer—ARMv1 and ARMv2 only—*DO NOT USE*	FALSE

- \<NoUnsignedOverflow\> is the same as $1 - $ \<UnsignedOverflow\>.

- \<Zero\> is a flag indicating that the result of an arithmetic or logical operation is zero. The *Z* flag in the *cpsr* typically records the zero condition.

- \<Negative\> is a flag indicating that the result of an arithmetic or logical operation is negative. In other words, \<Negative\> is bit 31 of the result. The *N* flag in the *cpsr* typically records this condition.

A.2.5 SHIFT OPERATIONS

- \<imm_shift\> represents a shift by an immediate specified amount. The possible shifts are LSL #\<0-31\>, LSR #\<1-32\>, ASR #\<1-32\>, ROR #\<1-31\>, and RRX. See Table A.3 for the actions of each shift.

- \<reg_shift\> represents a shift by a register-specified amount. The possible shifts are LSL Rs, LSR Rs, ASR Rs, and ROR Rs. *Rs* must not be *pc*. The bottom eight bits of *Rs* are used as the shift value *k* in Table A.3. Bits *Rs*[31:8] are ignored.

- \<shift\> is shorthand for \<imm_shift\> or \<reg_shift\>.

- \<shifted_Rm\> is shorthand for the value of *Rm* after the specified shift has been applied. See Table A.3.

Table A.3   Barrel shifter circuit outputs for different shift types.

Shift	k range	<shifted_Rm>	<shifter_C>
LSL k	$k = 0$	Rm	C (from *cpsr*)
LSL k	$1 \leq k \leq 31$	Rm << k	Rm[32-k]
LSL k	$k = 32$	0	Rm[0]
LSL k	$k \geq 33$	0	0
LSR k	$k = 0$	Rm	C
LSR k	$1 \leq k \leq 31$	(unsigned)Rm >> k	Rm[k-1]
LSR k	$k = 32$	0	Rm[31]
LSR k	$k \geq 33$	0	0
ASR k	$k = 0$	Rm	C
ASR k	$1 \leq k \leq 31$	(signed)Rm >> k	Rm[k-1]
ASR k	$k \geq 32$	-Rm[31]	Rm[31]
ROR k	$k = 0$	Rm	C
ROR k	$1 \leq k \leq 31$	((unsigned)Rm >> k) | (Rm << (32-k))	Rm[k-1]
ROR k	$k \geq 32$	Rm ROR (k & 31)	Rm[(k-1)&31]
RRX		(C << 31) | ((unsigned)Rm >> 1)	Rm[0]

- <shifter_C> is shorthand for the carry value output by the shifting circuit. See Table A.3.

A.3 ALPHABETICAL LIST OF ARM AND THUMB INSTRUCTIONS

Instructions are listed in alphabetical order. However, where signed and unsigned variants of the same operation exist, the main entry is under the signed variant.

ADC	Add two 32-bit values and carry	
	1. ADC<cond>{S} Rd, Rn, #<rotated_immed>	ARMv1
	2. ADC<cond>{S} Rd, Rn, Rm {, <shift>}	ARMv1
	3. ADC Ld, Lm	THUMBv1
	Action	Effect on the *cpsr*
	1. Rd = Rn + <rotated_immed> + C	Updated if S suffix specified

    2. Rd = Rn + <shifted_Rm> + C   Updated if S suffix specified

    3. Ld = Ld + Lm + C   Updated (see Notes below)

Notes

- If the operation updates the *cpsr* and *Rd* is not *pc*, then N = <Negative>, Z = <Zero>, C = <UnsignedOverflow>, V = <SignedOverflow>.
- If *Rd* is *pc*, then the instruction effects a jump to the calculated address. If the operation updates the *cpsr*, then the processor mode must have an *spsr*; in this case, the *cpsr* is set to the value of the *spsr*.
- If *Rn* or *Rm* is *pc*, then the value used is the address of the instruction plus eight bytes.

Examples

```
ADDS    r0, r0, r2    ; first half of a 64-bit add
ADC     r1, r1, r3    ; second half of a 64-bit add
ADCS    r0, r0, r0    ; shift r0 left, inserting carry (RLX)
```

ADD   Add two 32-bit values

1. ADD<cond>S Rd, Rn, #<rotated_immed>		ARMv1
2. ADD<cond>S Rd, Rn, Rm {, <shift>}		ARMv1
3. ADD	Ld, Ln, #<immed3>	THUMBv1
4. ADD	Ld, #<immed8>	THUMBv1
5. ADD	Ld, Ln, Lm	THUMBv1
6. ADD	Hd, Lm	THUMBv1
7. ADD	Ld, Hm	THUMBv1
8. ADD	Hd, Hm	THUMBv1
9. ADD	Ld, pc, #<immed8>*4	THUMBv1
10. ADD	Ld, sp, #<immed8>*4	THUMBv1
11. ADD	sp, #<immed7>*4	THUMBv1

Action   Effect on the *cpsr*

    1. Rd = Rn + <rotated_immed>   Updated if S suffix specified

```
 2. Rd = Rn + <shifted_Rm>          Updated if S suffix specified

 3. Ld = Ln + <immed3>              Updated (see Notes below)

 4. Ld = Ld + <immed8>              Updated (see Notes below)

 5. Ld = Ln + Lm                    Updated (see Notes below)

 6. Hd = Hd + Lm                    Preserved

 7. Ld = Ld + Hm                    Preserved

 8. Hd = Hd + Hm                    Preserved

 9. Ld = pc + 4*<immed8>            Preserved

10. Ld = sp + 4*<immed8>            Preserved

11. sp = sp + 4*<immed7>            Preserved
```

Notes

- If the operation updates the *cpsr* and *Rd* is not *pc*, then N = <*Negative*>, Z = <*Zero*>, C = <*UnsignedOverflow*>, V = <*SignedOverflow*>.

- If *Rd* or *Hd* is *pc*, then the instruction effects a jump to the calculated address. If the operation updates the *cpsr*, then the processor mode must have an *spsr*; in this case, the *cpsr* is set to the value of the *spsr*.

- If *Rn* or *Rm* is *pc*, then the value used is the address of the instruction plus eight bytes.

- If *Hd* or *Hm* is *pc*, then the value used is the address of the instruction plus four bytes.

Examples

```
ADD    r0, r1, #4          ; r0 = r1 + 4
ADDS   r0, r2, r2          ; r0 = r2 + r2 and flags updated
ADD    r0, r0, r0, LSL #1  ; r0 = 3*r0
ADD    pc, pc, r0, LSL #2  ; skip r0+1 instructions
ADD    r0, r1, r2, ROR r3  ; r0 = r1 + ((r2 >> r3)|(r2 << (32-r3)))
ADDS   pc, lr, #4          ; jump to lr+4, restoring the cpsr
```

ADR   Address relative

```
1. ADR{L}<cond> Rd, <address>              MACRO
```

This is not an ARM instruction, but an assembler macro that attempts to set *Rd* to the value <address> using a *pc*-relative calculation. The ADR instruction macro always uses a single ARM (or Thumb) instruction. The long-version ADRL always uses two ARM instructions and so can access a wider range of addresses. If the assembler cannot generate an instruction sequence reaching the address, then it will generate an error.

The following example shows how to call the function pointed to by *r9*. We use ADR to set *lr* to the return address; in this case, it will assemble to ADD lr, pc, #4. Recall that *pc* reads as the address of the current instruction plus eight in this case.

```
        ADR     lr, return_address    ; set return address
        MOV     r0, #0                ; set a function argument
        BX      r9                    ; call the function
return_address                        ; resume
```

AND Logical bitwise AND of two 32-bit values

1. AND<cond>{S} Rd, Rn, #<rotated_immed>   ARMv1

2. AND<cond>{S} Rd, Rn, Rm {, <shift>}   ARMv1

3. AND   Ld, Lm   THUMBv1

Action	Effect on the *cpsr*
1. Rd = Rn & <rotated_immed>	Updated if S suffix specified
2. Rd = Rn & <shifted_Rm>	Updated if S suffix specified
3. Ld = Ld & Lm	Updated (see Notes below)

Notes

- If the operation updates the *cpsr* and *Rd* is not *pc*, then N = <Negative>, Z = <Zero>, C = <shifter_C> (see Table A.3), V is preserved.

- If *Rd* is *pc*, then the instruction effects a jump to the calculated address. If the operation updates the *cpsr*, then the processor mode must have an *spsr*; in this case, the *cpsr* is set to the value of the *spsr*.

- If *Rn* or *Rm* is *pc*, then the value used is the address of the instruction plus eight bytes.

Examples

```
AND     r0, r0, #0xFF     ; extract the lower 8 bits of a byte
ANDS    r0, r0, #1<<31    ; extract sign bit
```

ASR Arithmetic shift right for Thumb (see MOV for the ARM equivalent)

1. ASR Ld, Lm, #<1-32>   THUMBv1

2. ASR Ld, Ls   THUMBv1

Action	Effect on the *cpsr*
1. Ld = Lm ASR #<1-32>	Updated (see Notes below)
2. Ld = Ld ASR Ls[7:0]	Updated

Note

■ The *cpsr* is updated: N = <*Negative*>, Z = <*Zero*>, C = <*shifter_C*> (see Table A.3).

B   Branch relative

1. B<cond> <address25>	ARMv1
2. B<cond> <address8>	THUMBv1
3. B <address11>	THUMBv1

Branches to the given address or label. The address is stored as a relative offset.
Examples

```
B       label       ; branch unconditionally to a label
BGT     loop        ; conditionally continue a loop
```

BIC   Logical bit clear (AND NOT) of two 32-bit values

1. BIC<cond>{S} Rd, Rn, #<rotated_immed>	ARMv1
2. BIC<cond>{S} Rd, Rn, Rm {, <shift>}	ARMv1
3. BIC Ld, Lm	THUMBv1

Action	Effect on the *cpsr*
1. Rd = Rn & ~<rotated_immed>	Updated if S suffix specified
2. Rd = Rn & ~<shifted_Rm>	Updated if S suffix specified
3. Ld = Ld & ~Lm	Updated (see Notes below)

Notes

■ If the operation updates the *cpsr* and *Rd* is not *pc*, then N = <*Negative*>, Z = <*Zero*>, C = <*shifter_C*> (see Table A.3), V is preserved.

- If *Rd* is *pc*, then the instruction effects a jump to the calculated address. If the operation updates the *cpsr*, then the processor mode must have an *spsr*; in this case, the *cpsr* is set to the value of the *spsr*.

- If *Rn* or *Rm* is *pc*, then the value used is the address of the instruction plus eight bytes.

Examples

```
BIC    r0, r0, #1<<22        ; clear bit 22 of r0
```

BKPT   Breakpoint instruction

    1.   BKPT <immed16>   ARMv5

    2.   BKPT <immed8>   THUMBv2

The breakpoint instruction causes a prefetch data abort, unless overridden by debug hardware. The ARM ignores the immediate value. This immediate can be used to hold debug information such as the breakpoint number.

BL   Relative branch with link (subroutine call)

    1.   BL<cond> <address25>   ARMv1

    2.   BL   <address22>   THUMBv1

Action	Effect on the *cpsr*
1. lr = ret+0; pc = <address25>	None
2. lr = ret+1; pc = <address22>	None

Note

- These instructions set *lr* to the address of the following instruction ret plus the current *cpsr* *T*-bit setting. Therefore you can return from the subroutine using BX lr to resume execution address and ARM or Thumb state.

Examples

```
BL     subroutine   ; call subroutine (return with MOV pc,lr)
BLVS   overflow     ; call subroutine on an overflow
```

BLX	Branch with link and exchange (subroutine call with possible state switch)	
	1. BLX <address25>	ARMv5
	2. BLX<cond> Rm	ARMv5
	3. BLX <address22>	THUMBv2
	4. BLX Rm	THUMBv2

Action	Effect on the *cpsr*
1. lr = ret+0; pc = <address25>	T=1 (switch to Thumb state)
2. lr = ret+0; pc = Rm & 0xfffffffe	T=Rm & 1
3. lr = ret+1; pc = <address22>	T=0 (switch to ARM state)
4. lr = ret+1; pc = Rm & 0xfffffffe	T=Rm & 1

Notes

- These instructions set *lr* to the address of the following instruction ret plus the current *cpsr* T-bit setting. Therefore you can return from the subroutine using BX lr to resume execution address and ARM or Thumb state.
- *Rm* must not be *pc*.
- *Rm* & 3 must not be 2. This would cause a branch to an unaligned ARM instruction.

Example

```
BLX     thumb_code   ; call a Thumb subroutine from ARM state
BLX     r0           ; call the subroutine pointed to by r0
                     ; ARM code if r0 even, Thumb if r0 odd
```

BX BXJ	Branch with exchange (branch with possible state switch)	
	1. BX<cond> Rm	ARMv4T
	2. BX Rm	THUMBv1
	3. BXJ<cond> Rm	ARMv5J

Action	Effect on the *cpsr*
1. pc = Rm & 0xfffffffe	T=Rm & 1

```
2.  pc = Rm & 0xfffffffe            T=Rm & 1
3.  Depends on JE configuration bit  J,T affected
```

Notes

- If *Rm* is *pc* and the instruction is word aligned, then *Rm* takes the value of the current instruction plus eight in ARM state or plus four in Thumb state.
- *Rm* & 3 must not be 2. This would cause a branch to an unaligned ARM instruction.
- If the JE (Java Enable) configuration bit is clear, then BXJ behaves as a BX. Otherwise, the behavior is defined by the architecture of the Java Extension hardware. Typically it sets $J = 1$ in the *cpsr* and starts executing Java instructions from a general purpose register designated as the Java program counter *jpc*.

Examples

```
BX      lr      ; return from ARM or Thumb subroutine
BX      r0      ; branch to ARM or Thumb function pointer r0
```

CDP   Coprocessor data processing operation

```
1.  CDP<cond> <copro>, <op1>, Cd, Cn, Cm, <op2>      ARMv2
2.  CDP2      <copro>, <op1>, Cd, Cn, Cm, <op2>      ARMv5
```

These instructions initiate a coprocessor-dependent operation. *<copro>* is the number of the coprocessor in the range *p0* to *p15*. The core takes an undefined instruction trap if the coprocessor is not present. The coprocessor operation specifiers *<op1>* and *<op2>*, and the coprocessor register numbers *Cd, Cn, Cm*, are interpreted by the coprocessor and ignored by the ARM. CDP2 provides an additional set of coprocessor instructions.

CLZ   Count leading zeros

```
1.  CLZ<cond>  Rd, Rm                                ARMv5
```

Rd is set to the maximum left shift that can be applied to *Rm* without unsigned overflow. Equivalently, this is the number of zeros above the highest one in the binary representation of *Rm*. If *Rm* = 0, then *Rd* is set to 32. The following example normalizes the value in *r0* so that bit 31 is set. *Rd* and *Rm* must not be *pc*.

```
CLZ r1, r0             ; find normalization shift
MOV r0, r0, LSL r1     ; normalize so bit 31 is set (if r0!=0)
```

CMN   Compare negative

```
1. CMN<cond> Rn, #<rotated_immed>                    ARMv1
```

2. `CMN<cond> Rn, Rm {, <shift>}`   ARMv1

3. `CMN     Ln, Lm`   THUMBv1

Action

1. `cpsr flags set on the result of (Rn + <rotated_immed>)`

2. `cpsr flags set on the result of (Rn + <shifted_Rm>)`

3. `cpsr flags set on the result of (Ln + Lm)`

Notes

- In the *cpsr:* $N = $ *<Negative>*, $Z = $ *<Zero>*, $C = $ *<Unsigned-Overflow>*, $V = $ *<SignedOverflow>*. These are the same flags as generated by CMP with the second operand negated.
- If *Rn* or *Rm* is *pc*, then the value used is the address of the instruction plus eight bytes.

Example

```
CMN     r0, #3      ; compare r0 with -3
BLT     label       ; if (r0 <- 3) goto label
```

CMP   Compare two 32-bit integers

1. `CMP<cond> Rn, #<rotated_immed>`   ARMv1

2. `CMP<cond> Rn, Rm {, <shift>}`   ARMv1

3. `CMP     Ln, #<immed8>`   THUMBv1

4. `CMP     Rn, Rm`   THUMBv1

Action

1. `cpsr flags set on the result of (Rn - <rotated_immed>)`

2. `cpsr flags set on the result of (Rn - <shifted_Rm>)`

3. `cpsr flags set on the result of (Ln - <immed8>)`

4. `cpsr flags set on the result of (Rn - Rm)`

Notes

- In the *cpsr:* $N = $ *<Negative>*, $Z = $ *<Zero>*, $C = $ *<NoUnsigned-Overflow>*, $V = $ *<SignedOverflow>*. The carry flag is set this way because the subtract $x - y$ is implemented as the add $x + \sim y + 1$. The carry flag is one if $x + \sim y + 1$ overflows. This happens when $x \geq y$ (equivalently when $x - y$ doesn't overflow).

■ If *Rn* or *Rm* is *pc*, then the value used is the address of the instruction plus eight bytes for ARM instructions, or plus four bytes for Thumb instructions.

Example

```
CMP     r0, r1, LSR#2 ; compare r0 with (r1/4)
BHS     label         ; if (r0 >= (r1/4)) goto label;
```

CPS   Change processor state; modifies selected bits in the *cpsr*

1. CPS #<mode>	ARMv6
2. CPSID <flags> {, #<mode>}	ARMv6
3. CPSIE <flags> {, #<mode>}	ARMv6
4. CPSID <flags>	THUMBv3
5. CPSIE <flags>	THUMBv3

Action

1. cpsr[4:0] = <mode>

2. cpsr = cpsr | mask; { cpsr[4:0]=<mode> }

3. cpsr = cpsr & ~mask; { cpsr[4:0]=<mode> }

4. cpsr = cpsr | mask

5. cpsr = cpsr & ~mask

Bits are set in mask according to letters in the <flags> value as in Table A.4. The ID (interrupt disable) variants mask interrupts by setting cpsr bits. The IE (interrupt enable) variants unmask interrupts by clearing *cpsr* bits. CPS has no effect in User mode.

Table A.4   CPS flags characters.

Character	*cpsr* bit affected	Bit set in mask
a	imprecise data Abort mask bit	0x100 = 1 << 8
i	IRQ mask bit	0x080 = 1 << 7
f	FIQ mask bit	0x040 = 1 << 6

CPY	Copy one ARM register to another without affecting the *cpsr*.	
	1. CPY<cond> Rd, Rm	ARMv6
	2. CPY Rd, Rm	THUMBv3

This assembles to MOV<cond> *Rd, Rm* except in the case of Thumb where *Rd* and *Rm* are low registers in the range *r0* to *r7*. Then it is a new operation that sets *Rd=Rm* without affecting the *cpsr*.

EOR	Logical exclusive OR of two 32-bit values	
	1. EOR<cond>{S} Rd, Rn, #<rotated_immed>	ARMv1
	2. EOR<cond>{S} Rd, Rn, Rm {, <shift>}	ARMv1
	3. EOR Ld, Lm	THUMBv1

Action	Effect on the *cpsr*
1. Rd = Rn ^ <rotated_immed>	Updated if S suffix specified
2. Rd = Rn ^ <shifted_Rm>	Updated if S suffix specified
3. Ld = Ld ^ Lm	Updated (see Notes below)

Notes

- If the operation updates the *cpsr* and *Rd* is not *pc*, then N = <Negative>, Z = <Zero>, C = <shifter_C> (see Table A.3), V is preserved.
- If *Rd* is *pc*, then the instruction effects a jump to the calculated address. If the operation updates the *cpsr*, then the processor mode must have an *spsr*; in this case, the *cpsr* is set to the value of the *spsr*.
- If *Rn* or *Rm* is *pc*, then the value used is the address of the instruction plus eight bytes.

Example

```
     EOR    r0, r0, #1<<16      ; toggle bit 16
```

LDC	Load to coprocessor single or multiple 32-bit values	
	1. LDC<cond>{L} <copro>, Cd, [Rn {, #{-}<immed8>*4}]{!}	ARMv2
	2. LDC<cond>{L} <copro>, Cd, [Rn], #{-}<immed8>*4	ARMv2
	3. LDC<cond>{L} <copro>, Cd, [Rn], <option>	ARMv2

Table A.5   LDC addressing modes.

Addressing format	Address accessed	Value written back to *Rn*
`[Rn {,# {-}<immed>}]`	`Rn + {{-}<immed>}`	`Rn preserved`
`[Rn {,# {-}<immed>}]!`	`Rn + {{-}<immed>}`	`Rn + {{-}<immed>}`
`[Rn], # {-}<immed>`	`Rn`	`Rn + {-}<immed>`
`[Rn], <option>`	`Rn`	`Rn preserved`

4.	`LDC2{L}`	`<copro>, Cd, [Rn {, #{-}<immed8>*4}]{!}`	ARMv5
5.	`LDC2{L}`	`<copro>, Cd, [Rn], #{-}<immed8>*4`	ARMv5
6.	`LDC2{L}`	`<copro>, Cd, [Rn], <option>`	ARMv5

These instructions initiate a memory read, transferring data to the given coprocessor. `<copro>` is the number of the coprocessor in the range *p0* to *p15*. The core takes an undefined instruction trap if the coprocessor is not present. The memory read consists of a sequence of words from sequentially increasing addresses. The initial address is specified by the addressing mode in Table A.5. The coprocessor controls the number of words transferred, up to a maximum limit of 16 words. The fields *{L}* and *Cd* are interpreted by the coprocessor and ignored by the ARM. Typically *Cd* specifies the destination coprocessor register for the transfer. The `<option>` field is an eight-bit integer enclosed in {}. Its interpretation is coprocessor dependent.

If the address is not a multiple of four, then the access is *unaligned.* The restrictions on unaligned accesses are the same as for LDM.

LDM   Load multiple 32-bit words from memory to ARM registers

1.	`LDM<cond><amode>`	`Rn{!}, <register_list>{^}`	ARMv1
2.	`LDMIA`	`Rn!, <register_list>`	THUMBv1

These instructions load multiple words from sequential memory addresses. The `<register_list>` specifies a list of registers to load, enclosed in curly brackets {}. Although the assembler allows you to specify the registers in the list in any order, the order is not stored in the instruction, so it is good practice to write the list in increasing order of register number because this is the usual order of the memory transfer.

The following pseudocode shows the normal action of LDM. We use `<register_list>[i]` to denote the register appearing at position *i* in the list, starting at 0 for the first register. This assumes that the list is in order of increasing register number.

Table A.6   LDM addressing modes.

Addressing mode	Lowest address accessed	Highest address accessed	Value written back to Rn if ! specified
{IA|FD}	Rn	Rn + N*4 - 4	Rn + N*4
{IB|ED}	Rn + 4	Rn + N*4	Rn + N*4
{DA|FA}	Rn - N*4 + 4	Rn	Rn - N*4
{DB|EA}	Rn - N*4	Rn - 4	Rn - N*4

```
N = the number of registers in <register_list>
start = the lowest address accessed given in Table A.6
for (i=0; i<N; i++)
  <register_list>[i] = memory(start+i*4, 4);
if (! specified) then update Rn according to Table A.6
```

Note that memory(a, 4) returns the four bytes at address a packed according to the current processor data endianness. If a is not a multiple of four, then the load is unaligned. Because the behavior of an unaligned load depends on the architecture revision, memory system, and system coprocessor (CP15) configuration, it's best to avoid unaligned loads if possible. Assuming that the external memory system does not abort unaligned loads, then the following rules usually apply:

■   If the core has a system coprocessor and bit 1 (A-bit) or bit 22 (U-bit) of CP15:c1:c0:0 is set, then unaligned load multiples cause an alignment fault data abort exception.

■   Otherwise the access ignores the bottom two address bits.

Table A.6 lists the possible addressing modes specified by <amode>. If you specify the !, then the base address register is updated according to Table A.6; otherwise it is preserved. Note that the lowest register number is always read from the lowest address.

The first half of the addressing mode mnemonics stands for Increment After, Increment Before, Decrement After, and Decrement Before, respectively. Increment modes load the registers sequentially forward, starting from address Rn (increment after) or $Rn + 4$ (increment before). Decrement modes have the same effect as if you loaded the register list backwards from sequentially descending memory addresses, starting from address Rn (decrement after) or $Rn - 4$ (decrement before).

The second half of the addressing mode mnemonics stands for the stack type you can implement with that address mode: Full Descending, Empty Descending, Full Ascending, and Empty Ascending, With a full stack, Rn points to the last stacked value; with an empty stack, Rn points to the first unused stack location. ARM stacks are usually full descending.

You should use full descending or empty ascending stacks by preference, since LDC also supports these addressing modes.

Notes

- For Thumb (format 2), *Rn* and the register list registers must be in the range *r0* to *r7*.
- The number of registers *N* in the list must be nonzero.
- *Rn* must not be *pc*.
- *Rn* must not appear in the register list if ! (writeback) is specified.
- If *pc* appears in the register list, then on ARMv5 and above the processor performs a BX to the loaded address. For ARMv4 and below, the processor branches to the loaded address.
- If ^ is specified, then the operation is modified. The processor must not be in *user* or *system* mode. If *pc* is not in the register list, then the registers appearing in the register list refer to the *user* mode versions of the registers and writeback must not be specified. If *pc* is in the register list, then the *spsr* is copied to the *cpsr* in addition to the standard operation.
- The time order of the memory accesses may depend on the implementation. Be careful when using a load multiple to access I/O locations where the access order matters. If the order matters, then check that the memory locations are marked as I/O in the page tables, do not cross page boundaries, and do not use *pc* in the register list.

Examples

```
LDMIA    r4!, {r0, r1}   ; r0=*r4, r1=*(r4+4), r4+=8
LDMDB    r4!, {r0, r1}   ; r1=*(r4-4), r0=*(r4-8), r4-=8
LDMEQFD  sp!, {r0, pc}   ; if (result zero) then unstack r0, pc
LDMFD    sp, {sp}^       ; load sp_usr from sp_current
LDMFD    sp!, {r0-pc}^   ; return from exception, restore cpsr
```

LDR   Load a single value from a virtual address in memory

1.	LDR<cond>{|B}	Rd, [Rn {, #{-}<immed12>}]{!}	ARMv1
2.	LDR<cond>{|B}	Rd, [Rn, {-}Rm {,<imm_shift>}]{!}	ARMv1
3.	LDR<cond>{|B}{T}	Rd, [Rn], #{-}<immed12>	ARMv1
4.	LDR<cond>{|B}{T}	Rd, [Rn], {-}Rm {,<imm_shift>}	ARMv1
5.	LDR<cond>{H|SB|SH}	Rd, [Rn {, #{-}<immed8>}]{!}	ARMv4
6.	LDR<cond>{H|SB|SH}	Rd, [Rn, {-}Rm]{!}	ARMv4
7.	LDR<cond>{H|SB|SH}	Rd, [Rn], #{-}<immed8>	ARMv4

8.	LDR<cond>{H|SB|SH}	Rd, [Rn], {-}Rm	ARMv4
9.	LDR<cond>D	Rd, [Rn {, #{-}<immed8>}]{!}	ARMv5E
10.	LDR<cond>D	Rd, [Rn, {-}Rm]{!}	ARMv5E
11.	LDR<cond>D	Rd, [Rn], #{-}<immed8>	ARMv5E
12.	LDR<cond>D	Rd, [Rn], {-}Rm	ARMv5E
13.	LDREX<cond>	Rd, [Rn]	ARMv6
14.	LDR{|B|H}	Ld, [Ln, #<immed5>*<size>]	THUMBv1
15.	LDR{|B|H|SB|SH}	Ld, [Ln, Lm]	THUMBv1
16.	LDR	Ld, [pc, #<immed8>*4]	THUMBv1
17.	LDR	Ld, [sp, #<immed8>*4]	THUMBv1
18.	LDR<cond><type>	Rd, <label>	MACRO
19.	LDR<cond>	Rd, =<32-bit-value>	MACRO

Formats 1 to 17 load a single data item of the type specified by the opcode suffix, using a preindexed or postindexed addressing mode. Tables A.7 and A.8 show the different addressing modes and data types.

In Table A.8 memory(a, n) reads n sequential bytes from address a. The bytes are packed according to the configured processor data endianness. The function memoryT(a, n) performs the same access but with *user* mode privileges, regardless of the current processor mode. The function memoryEx(a, n) used by LDREX performs the access and marks the access as exclusive. If address a has the *shared* TLB attribute, then this marks address a as exclusive to the current processor and clears any other exclusive addresses for this processor.

Table A.7   LDR Addressing Modes.

Addressing format	Address a accessed	Value written back to *Rn*
[Rn {,#{-}<immed>}]	Rn + {{-}<immed>}	Rn preserved
[Rn {,#{-}<immed>}]!	Rn + {{-}<immed>}	Rn + {{-}<immed>}
[Rn, {-}Rm {,<shift>}]	Rn + {-}<shifted_Rm>	Rn preserved
[Rn, {-}Rm {,<shift>}]!	Rn + {-}<shifted_Rm>	Rn + {-}<shifted_Rm>
[Rn], #{-}<immed>	Rn	Rn + {-}<immed>
[Rn], {-}Rm {,<shift>}	Rn	Rn + {-}<shifted_Rm>

Table A.8   LDR datatypes.

Load	Datatype	<size> (bytes)	Action
LDR	word	4	Rd = memory(a, 4)
LDRB	unsigned Byte	1	Rd = (zero-extend)memory(a, 1)
LDRBT	Byte Translated	1	Rd = (zero-extend)memoryT(a, 1)
LDRD	Double word	8	Rd = memory(a, 4)
			R(d+1) = memory(a+4, 4)
LDREX	word EXclusive	4	Rd = memoryEx(a, 4)
LDRH	unsigned Halfword	2	Rd = (zero-extend)memory(a, 2)
LDRSB	Signed Byte	1	Rd = (sign-extend)memory(a, 1)
LDRSH	Signed Halfword	2	Rd = (sign-extend)memory(a, 2)
LDRT	word Translated	4	Rd = memoryT(a, 4)

Otherwise the processor remembers that there is an outstanding exclusive access. Exclusivity only affects the action of the STREX instruction.

If address a is not a multiple of <size>, then the load is *unaligned*. Because the behavior of an unaligned load depends on the architecture revision, memory system, and system coprocessor (CP15) configuration, it's best to avoid unaligned loads if possible. Assuming that the external memory system does not abort unaligned loads, then the following rules usually apply. In the rules, A is bit 1 of system coprocessor register CP15:c1:c0:0, and U is bit 22 of CP15:c1:c0:0, introduced in ARMv6. If there is no system coprocessor, then $A = U = 0$.

- If $A = 1$, then unaligned loads cause an alignment fault data abort exception except that word-aligned double-word loads are supported if $U = 1$.

- If $A = 0$ and $U = 1$, then unaligned loads are supported for LDR{|T|H|SH}. Word-aligned loads are supported for LDRD. A non-word-aligned LDRD generates an alignment fault data abort.

- If $A = 0$ and $U = 0$, then LDR and LDRT return the value memory(a & ~3, 4) ROR ((a&3)*8). All other unaligned operations are unpredictable but do not generate an alignment fault.

Format 18 generates a *pc*-relative load accessing the address specified by <label>. In other words, it assembles to LDR<cond><type> Rd, [pc, #<offset>] whenever this instruction is supported and <offset>=<label>-pc is in range.

Format 19 generates an instruction to move the given 32-bit value to the register *Rd*. Usually the instruction is LDR<cond> Rd, [pc, #<offset>], where the 32-bit value is stored in a literal pool at address pc+<offset>.

Notes

- For double-word loads (formats 9 to 12), *Rd* must be even and in the range *r0* to *r12*.
- If the addressing mode updates *Rn*, then *Rd* and *Rn* must be distinct.
- If *Rd* is *pc*, then *<size>* must be 4. Up to ARMv4, the core branches to the loaded address. For ARMv5 and above, the core performs a BX to the loaded address.
- If *Rn* is *pc*, then the addressing mode must not update *Rn*. The value used for *Rn* is the address of the instruction plus eight bytes for ARM or four bytes for Thumb.
- *Rm* must not be *pc*.
- For ARMv6 use LDREX and STREX to implement semaphores rather than SWP.

Examples

```
LDR     r0, [r0]              ; r0 = *(int*)r0;
LDRSH   r0, [r1], #4          ; r0 = *(short*)r1; r1 += 4;
LDRB    r0, [r1, #-8]!        ; r1 -= 8; r0 = *(char*)r1;
LDRD    r2, [r1]              ; r2 =* (int*)r1; r3 =* (int*)(r1+4);
LDRSB   r0, [r2, #55]         ; r0 = *(signed char*)(r2+55);
LDRCC   pc, [pc, r0, LSL #2]  ; if (C==0) goto *(pc+4*r0);
LDRB    r0, [r1], -r2, LSL #8 ; r0 = *(char*)r1; r1 -= 256*r2;
LDR     r0, =0x12345678       ; r0 = 0x12345678;
```

LSL Logical shift left for Thumb (see MOV for the ARM equivalent)

1.	LSL Ld, Lm, #<immed5>	THUMBv1
2.	LSL Ld, Ls	THUMBv1

Action		Effect on the *cpsr*
1.	Ld = Lm LSL #<immed5>	Updated (see Note below)
2.	Ld = Ld LSL Ls[7:0]	Updated

Note

- The *cpsr* is updated: N = *<Negative>*, Z = *<Zero>*, C = *<shifter_C>* (see Table A.3).

LSR Logical shift right for Thumb (see MOV for the ARM equivalent)

1.	LSR Ld, Lm, #<1-32>	THUMBv1
2.	LSR Ld, Ls	THUMBv1

Action	Effect on the *cpsr*
1. Ld = Lm LSR #<1-32>	Updated (see Note below)
2. Ld = Ld LSR Ls[7:0]	Updated

Note

- The *cpsr* is updated: $N = <Negative>$, $Z = <Zero>$, $C = <shifter\_C>$ (see Table A.3).

MCR
MCRR

Move to coprocessor from an ARM register

1.	MCR<cond>	<copro>, <op1>, Rd, Cn, Cm {, <op2>}	ARMv2
2.	MCR2	<copro>, <op1>, Rd, Cn, Cm {, <op2>}	ARMv5
3.	MCRR<cond>	<copro>, <op1>, Rd, Rn, Cm	ARMv5E
4.	MCRR2	<copro>, <op1>, Rd, Rn, Cm	ARMv6

These instructions transfer the value of ARM register *Rd* to the indicated coprocessor. Formats 3 and 4 also transfer a second register *Rn*. <copro> is the number of the coprocessor in the range *p0* to *p15*. The core takes an undefined instruction trap if the coprocessor is not present. The coprocessor operation specifiers <op1> and <op2>, and the coprocessor register numbers *Cn, Cm*, are interpreted by the coprocessor, and ignored by the ARM. *Rd* and *Rn* must not be *pc*. Coprocessor *p15* controls memory management options. See Chapters 13 and 14 for descriptions of the MPU and MMU memory management units. For example, the following code sequence enables alignment fault checking:

```
MRC    p15, 0, r0, c1, c0, 0   ; read the MMU register, c1
ORR    r0, r0, #2              ; set the A bit
MCR    p15, 0, r0, c1, c0, 0   ; write the MMU register, c1
```

MLA

Multiply with accumulate

1.	MLA<cond>{S} Rd, Rm, Rs, Rn	ARMv2

Action	Effect on the *cpsr*
1. Rd = Rn + Rm*Rs	Updated if S suffix supplied

Notes

- *Rd* is set to the lower 32 bits of the result.
- *Rd, Rm, Rs, Rn* must not be *pc*.

- *Rd* and *Rm* must be different registers prior to ARMv6.

- Implementations may terminate early on the value of the *Rs* operand. For this reason use small or constant values for *Rs* where possible. See Appendix D.

- If the *cpsr* is updated, then $N = $ <*Negative*>, $Z = $ <*Zero*>, *C* is unpredictable, and *V* is preserved. Avoid using the instruction MLAS because implementations often impose penalty cycles for this operation. Instead use MLA followed by a compare, and schedule the compare to avoid multiply result use interlocks.

MOV   Move a 32-bit value into a register

1.	MOV<cond>{S}	Rd, #<rotated_immed>	ARMv1
2.	MOV<cond>{S}	Rd, Rm {, <shift>}	ARMv1
3.	MOV	Ld, #<immed8>	THUMBv1
4.	MOV	Ld, Ln	THUMBv1
5.	MOV	Hd, Lm	THUMBv1
6.	MOV	Ld, Hm	THUMBv1
7.	MOV	Hd, Hm	THUMBv1

Action	Effect on the *cpsr*
1. Rd = <rotated_immed>	Updated if S suffix specified
2. Rd = <shifted_Rm>	Updated if S suffix specified
3. Ld = <immed8>	Updated (see Notes below)
4. Ld = Ln	Updated (see Notes below)
5. Hd = Lm	Preserved
6. Ld = Hm	Preserved
7. Hd = Hm	Preserved

Notes

- If the operation updates the *cpsr* and *Rd* is not *pc*, then $N = $ <*Negative*>, $Z = $ <*Zero*>, $C= $ <*shifter_C*> (see Table A.3), and *V* is preserved, for formats 1 to 3. For format 4, $N = $ <*Negative*>, $Z = $ <*Zero*>, $C = 0$, $V = 0$.

- If *Rd* or *Hd* is *pc*, then the instruction effects a jump to the calculated address. If the operation updates the *cpsr*, then the processor mode must have an *spsr*; in this case, the *cpsr* is set to the value of the *spsr*.

- If *Rm* is *pc*, then the value used is the address of the instruction plus eight bytes.
- If *Hm* is *pc*, then the value used is the address of the instruction plus four bytes.

Examples

```
MOV     r0, #0x00ff0000 ; r0 = 0x00ff0000
MOV     r0, r1, LSL#2   ; r0 = 4*r1
MOV     pc, lr       ; return from subroutine (pc=lr)
MOVS    pc, lr       ; return from exception (pc=lr, cpsr=spsr)
```

MRC MRRC	Move to ARM register from a coprocessor	
	1. MRC<cond> <copro>, <op1>, Rd, Cn, Cm , <op2>	ARMv2
	2. MRC2 <copro>, <op1>, Rd, Cn, Cm , <op2>	ARMv5
	3. MRRC<cond> <copro>, <op1>, Rd, Rn, Cm	ARMv5E
	4. MRRC2 <copro>, <op1>, Rd, Rn, Cm	ARMv6

These instructions transfer a 32-bit value from the indicated coprocessor to the ARM register *Rd*. Formats 3 and 4 also transfer a second 32-bit value to *Rn*. <copro> is the number of the coprocessor in the range *p0* to *p15*. The core takes an undefined instruction trap if the coprocessor is not present. The coprocessor operation specifiers <op1> and <op2>, and the coprocessor register numbers *Cn*, *Cm*, are interpreted by the coprocessor and ignored by the ARM. For formats 1 and 2, if *Rd* is *pc*, then the top four bits of the *cpsr* (the *NZCV* condition code flags) are set from the top four bits of the 32-bit value transferred; *pc* is not affected. For other formats, *Rd* and *Rn* must be distinct and not *pc*.

Coprocessor *p15* controls memory management options (see Chapters 12 and 13). For example, the following instruction reads the main ID register from *p15*:

```
MRC     p15, 0, r0, c0, c0      ; read the MMU ID register, c0
```

MRS	Move to ARM register from status register (*cpsr* or *spsr*)	
	1. MRS<cond> Rd, cpsr	ARMv3
	2. MRS<cond> Rd, spsr	ARMv3

These instructions set *Rd* = *cpsr* and *Rd* = *spsr*, respectively. *Rd* must not be *pc*. There is no *spsr* in User and System modes.

MSR	Move to status register (*cpsr* or *spsr*) from an ARM register	
	1. MSR<cond> cpsr_<fields>, #<rotated_immed>	ARMv3

Table A.9   Format of the `<fields>` specifier.

`<fields>` letter	Meaning	Bits set in `<mask>`
c	Control byte	0x000000ff
x	eXtension byte	0x0000ff00
s	Status byte	0x00ff0000
f	Flags byte	0xff000000

2. `MSR<cond> cpsr_<fields>, Rm`   ARMv3

3. `MSR<cond> spsr_<fields>, #<rotated_immed>`   ARMv3

4. `MSR<cond> spsr_<fields>, Rm`   ARMv3

Action

1. `cpsr = (cpsr & ~<mask>) | (<rotated_immed> & <mask>)`

2. `cpsr = (cpsr & ~<mask>) | (Rm & <mask>)`

3. `spsr = (spsr & ~<mask>) | (<rotated_immed> & <mask>)`

4. `spsr = (spsr & ~<mask>) | (Rm & <mask>)`

These instructions alter selected bytes of the *cpsr* or *spsr* according to the value of `<mask>`. The `<fields>` specifier is a sequence of one or more letters, determining which bytes of `<mask>` are set. See Table A.9. Bits [23:0] of the *cpsr* are unaffected in User mode. There is no *spsr* in User and System modes.

Some old ARM toolkits allowed *cpsr* or *cpsr_all* in place of *cpsr_fsxc*. They also used *cpsr_flg* and *cpsr_ctl* in place of *cpsr_f* and *cpsr_c*, respectively. These formats, and the *spsr* equivalents, are obsolete, so you should not use them. The following example changes to *system* mode and enables IRQ, which is useful in a reentrant interrupt handler:

```
MRS     r0, cpsr         ; read cpsr state
BIC     r0, r0, #0x9f     ; clear IRQ disable and mode bits
ORR     r0, r0, #0x1f     ; set system mode
MSR     cpsr_c, r0        ; update control byte of the cpsr
```

MUL   Multiply

1. `MUL<cond>{S} Rd, Rm, Rs`   ARMv2

2. `MUL        Ld, Lm`   THUMBv1

Action	Effect on the *cpsr*
1. Rd = Rm*Rs	Updated if S suffix supplied
2. Ld = Lm*Ld	Updated

Notes

- *Rd* or *Ld* is set to the lower 32 bits of the result.
- *Rd*, *Rm*, *Rs* must not be *pc*.
- *Rd* and *Rm* must be different registers. Similarly *Ld* and *Lm* must be different.
- Implementations may terminate early on the value of the *Rs* or *Ld* operand. For this reason use small or constant values for *Rs* or *Ld* where possible.
- If the *cpsr* is updated, then N = *<Negative>*, Z = *<Zero>*, C is unpredictable, and V is preserved. Avoid using the instruction MULS because implementations often impose penalty cycles for this operation. Instead use MUL followed by a compare, and schedule the compare, to avoid multiply result use interlocks.

MVN	Move the logical not of a 32-bit value into a register	
	1. MVN<cond>{S} Rd, #<rotated_immed>	ARMv1
	2. MVN<cond>{S} Rd, Rm {, <shift>}	ARMv1
	3. MVN Ld, Lm	THUMBv1

Action	Effect on the *cpsr*
1. Rd = ~<rotated_immed>	Updated if S suffix specified
2. Rd = ~<shifted_Rm>	Updated if S suffix specified
3. Ld = ~Lm	Updated (see Notes below)

Notes

- If the operation updates the *cpsr* and *Rd* is not *pc*, then N = *<Negative>*, Z = *<Zero>*, C = *<shifter_C>* (see Table A.3), and V is preserved.
- If *Rd* is *pc*, then the instruction effects a jump to the calculated address. If the operation updates the *cpsr*, then the processor mode must have an *spsr*; in this case, the *cpsr* is set to the value of the *spsr*.
- If *Rm* is *pc*, then the value used is the address of the instruction plus eight bytes.

Examples

```
MVN    r0, #0xff      ; r0 = 0xffffff00
MVN    r0, #0         ; r0 = -1
```

NEG   Negate value in Thumb (use RSB to negate in ARM state)

1. NEG Ld, Lm   THUMBv1

Action   Effect on the *cpsr*

1. Ld = -Lm   Updated (see Notes below)

Notes

- The *cpsr* is updated: N = *<Negative>*, Z = *<Zero>*, C = *<NoUnsignedOverflow>*, V = *<SignedOverflow>*. Note that $Z = C$ and $V = (Ld==0x80000000)$.
- This is the same as the operation RSBS Ld, Lm, #0 in ARM state.

NOP   No operation

1. NOP   MACRO

This is not an ARM instruction. It is an assembly macro that produces an instruction having no effect other than advancing the *pc* as normal. In ARM state it assembles to MOV r0,r0. In Thumb state it assembles to MOV r8,r8. The operation is not guaranteed to take one processor cycle. In particular, if you use NOP after a load of *r0*, then the operation may cause pipeline interlocks.

ORR   Logical bitwise OR of two 32-bit values

1. ORR<cond>{S} Rd, Rn, #<rotated_immed>   ARMv1

2. ORR<cond>{S} Rd, Rn, Rm {, <shift>}   ARMv1

3. ORR   Ld, Lm   THUMBv1

Action   Effect on the *cpsr*

1. Rd = Rn | <rotated_immed>   Updated if S suffix specified

2. Rd = Rn | <shifted_Rm>   Updated if S suffix specified

3. Ld = Ld | Lm   Updated (see Notes below)

Notes

- If the operation updates the *cpsr* and *Rd* is not *pc*, then *N* = *<Negative>*, *Z* = *<Zero>*, *C* = *<shifter_C>* (see Table A.3), and *V* is preserved.
- If *Rd* is *pc*, then the instruction effects a jump to the calculated address. If the operation updates the *cpsr*, then the processor mode must have an *spsr*, in this case, the *cpsr* is set to the value of the *spsr*.
- If *Rn* or *Rm* is *pc*, then the value used is the address of the instruction plus eight bytes.

Example

```
ORR     r0, r0,#1 << 13        ; set bit 13 of r0
```

PKH

Pack 16-bit halfwords into a 32-bit word

1.   PKHBT<cond> Rd, Rn, Rm {, LSL #<0-31>}   ARMv6
2.   PKHTB<cond> Rd, Rn, Rm {, ASR #<1-32>}   ARMv6

Action

1.   Rd[15:00] = Rn[15:00]; Rd[31:16]=<shifted_Rm>[31:16]
2.   Rd[31:16] = Rn[31:16]; Rd[15:00]=<shifted_Rm>[15:00]

Note

- *Rd, Rn, Rm* must not be *pc*. *cpsr* is not affected.

Examples

```
PKHBT   r0, r1, r2, LSL#16  ; r0 = (r2[15:00] << 16) | r1[15:00]
PKHTB   r0, r2, r1, ASR#16  ; r0 = (r2[31:15] << 16) | r1[31:15]
```

PLD

Preload hint instruction

1.   PLD [Rn {, #{-}<immed12>}]   ARMv5E
2.   PLD [Rn, {-}Rm {,<imm_shift>}]   ARMv5E

Action

1.   Preloads from address (Rn + {{-}<immed12>})
2.   Preloads from address (Rn + {-}<shifted_Rm>)

This instruction does not affect the processor registers (other than advancing *pc*). It merely hints that the programmer is likely to read from the given address in future. A cached processor may take this as a hint to load the cache line containing the address into the cache. The instruction should not generate a data abort or any other memory system error. If *Rn* is *pc*, then the value used for *Rn* is the address of the instruction plus eight. *Rm* must not be *pc*.

Examples

```
PLD     [r0, #7]          ; Preload from r0+7
PLD     [r0, r1, LSL#2]   ; Preload from r0+4*r1
```

| POP | Pops multiple registers from the stack in Thumb state (for ARM state use LDM) |

1. POP <regster_list>   THUMBv1

Action

1. equivalent to the ARM instruction LDMFD sp!, <register_list>

The <register_list> can contain registers in the range *r0* to *r7* and *pc*. The following example restores the low-numbered ARM registers and returns from a subroutine:

```
POP {r0-r7,pc}
```

| PUSH | Pushes multiple registers to the stack in Thumb state (for ARM state use STM) |

1. PUSH <regster_list>   THUMBv1

Action

1. equivalent to the ARM instruction STMFD sp!, <register_list>

The <register_list> can contain registers in the range *r0* to *r7* and *lr*. The following example saves the low-numbered ARM registers and link register.

```
PUSH {r0-r7,lr}
```

| QADD
QDADD
QDSUB
QSUB | Saturated signed and unsigned arithmetic |

1. QADD<cond>   Rd, Rm, Rn   ARMv5E

2. QDADD<cond>   Rd, Rm, Rn   ARMv5E

3.	QSUB<cond>	Rd, Rm, Rn	ARMv5E
4.	QDSUB<cond>	Rd, Rm, Rn	ARMv5E
5.	{U}QADD16<cond>	Rd, Rn, Rm	ARMv6
6.	{U}QADDSUBX<cond>	Rd, Rn, Rm	ARMv6
7.	{U}QSUBADDX<cond>	Rd, Rn, Rm	ARMv6
8.	{U}QSUB16<cond>	Rd, Rn, Rm	ARMv6
9.	{U}QADD8<cond>	Rd, Rn, Rm	ARMv6
10.	{U}QSUB8<cond>	Rd, Rn, Rm	ARMv6

Action

1. Rd = sat32(Rm+Rn)

2. Rd = sat32(Rm+sat32(2*Rn))

3. Rd = sat32(Rm-Rn)

4. Rd = sat32(Rm-sat32(2*Rn))

5. Rd[31:16] = sat16(Rn[31:16] + Rm[31:16]);
   Rd[15:00] = sat16(Rn[15:00] + Rm[15:00])

6. Rd[31:16] = sat16(Rn[31:16] + Rm[15:00]);
   Rd[15:00] = sat16(Rn[15:00] - Rm[31:16])

7. Rd[31:16] = sat16(Rn[31:16] - Rm[15:00]);
   Rd[15:00] = sat16(Rn[15:00] + Rm[31:16])

8. Rd[31:16] = sat16(Rn[31:16] - Rm[31:16]);
   Rd[15:00] = sat16(Rn[15:00] - Rm[15:00])

9. Rd[31:24] = sat8(Rn[31:24] + Rm[31:24]);
   Rd[23:16] = sat8(Rn[23:16] + Rm[23:16]);
   Rd[15:08] = sat8(Rn[15:08] + Rm[15:08]);
   Rd[07:00] = sat8(Rn[07:00] + Rm[07:00])

10. Rd[31:24] = sat8(Rn[31:24] - Rm[31:24]);
    Rd[23:16] = sat8(Rn[23:16] - Rm[23:16]);

```
Rd[15:08] = sat8(Rn[15:08] - Rm[15:08]);
Rd[07:00] = sat8(Rn[07:00] - Rm[07:00])
```

Notes

- The operations are signed unless the U prefix is present. For signed operations, $\mathrm{satN}(x)$ saturates x to the range $-2^{N-1} \leq x < 2^{N-1}$. For unsigned operations, $\mathrm{satN}(x)$ saturates x to the range $0 \leq x < 2^{N}$.

- For formats 1 to 4 the *cpsr* Q-flag is set if saturation occurred; otherwise it is preserved.

- *Rd*, *Rn*, *Rm* must not be *pc*.

- The X operations are useful for packed complex numbers. The following examples assume bits [15:00] hold the real part and [31:16] the imaginary part.

Examples

```
QDADD     r0, r0, r2  ; add Q30 value r2 to Q31 accumulator r0
QADD16    r0, r1, r2  ; SIMD saturating add
QADDSUBX  r0, r1, r2  ; r0=r1+i*r2 in packed complex arithmetic
QSUBADDX  r0, r1, r2  ; r0=r1-i*r2 in packed complex arithmetic
```

REV Reverse bytes within a word or halfword.

1. REV<cond>   Rd, Rm   ARMv6/THUMBv3

2. REV16<cond> Rd, Rm   ARMv6/THUMBv3

3. REVSH<cond> Rd, Rm   ARMv6/THUMBv3

Action

1. `Rd[31:24] = Rm[07:00]; Rd[23:16] = Rm[15:08];`

   `Rd[15:08] = Rm[23:16]; Rd[07:00] = Rm[31:24]`

2. `Rd[31:24] = Rm[23:16]; Rd[23:16] = Rm[31:24];`

   `Rd[15:08] = Rm[07:00]; Rd[07:00] = Rm[15:08]`

3. `Rd[31:08] = sign-extend(Rm[07:00]); Rd[07:00] = Rm[15:08]`

Notes

- *Rd* and *Rm* must not be *pc*.
- For Thumb, *Rd*, *Rm* must be in the range *r0* to *r7* and <cond> cannot be specified.

- These instructions are useful to convert big-endian data to little-endian and vice versa.

Examples

```
REV     r0, r0    ; switch endianness of a word
REV16   r0, r0    ; switch endianness of two packed halfwords
REVSH   r0, r0    ; switch endianness of a signed halfword
```

RFE

Return from exception

1.   RFE<amode> Rn!   ARMv6

This performs the operation that LDM<amode> Rn{!}, {pc, cpsr} would perform if LDM allowed a register list of {pc, cpsr}. See the entry for LDM.

ROR

Rotate right for Thumb (see MOV for the ARM equivalent)

1.   ROR Ld, Ls   THUMBv1

Action	Effect on the *cpsr*
1. Ld = Ld ROR Ls[7:0]	Updated

Notes

- The *cpsr* is updated: N = *<Negative>*, Z = *<Zero>*, C = *<shifter_C>* (see Table A.3).

RSB

Reverse subtract of two 32-bit integers

1.   RSB<cond>{S} Rd, Rn, #<rotated_immed>   ARMv1

2.   RSB<cond>{S} Rd, Rn, Rm {, <shift>}   ARMv1

Action	Effect on the *cpsr*
1. Rd = <rotated_immed> - Rn	Updated if S suffix present
2. Rd = <shifted_Rm> - Rn	Updated if S suffix present

Notes

- If the operation updates the *cpsr* and *Rd* is not *pc*, then N = *<Negative>*, Z = *<Zero>*, C = *<NoUnsignedOverflow>*, and V = *<SignedOverflow>*. The carry flag is set this way because the subtract $x - y$ is implemented as the add $x + {\sim}y + 1$. The carry flag is one if $x + {\sim}y + 1$ overflows. This happens when $x \geq y$, when $x - y$ doesn't overflow.

- If *Rd* is *pc*, then the instruction effects a jump to the calculated address. If the operation updates the *cpsr*, then the processor mode must have an *spsr* in this case, the *cpsr* is set to the value of the *spsr*.

- If *Rn* or *Rm* is *pc*, then the value used is the address of the instruction plus eight bytes.

Examples

```
RSB     r0, r0, #0          ; r0 = -r0
RSB     r0, r1, r1, LSL#3   ; r0 = 7*r1
```

RSC

Reverse subtract with carry of two 32-bit integers

1. `RSC<cond>{S} Rd, Rn, #<rotated_immed>`   ARMv1

2. `RSC<cond>{S} Rd, Rn, Rm {, <shift>}`   ARMv1

Action	Effect on the *cpsr*
1. Rd = <rotated_immed> - Rn - (~C)	Updated if S suffix present
2. Rd = <shifted_Rm> - Rn - (~C)	Updated if S suffix present

Notes

- If the operation updates the *cpsr* and *Rd* is not *pc*, then N = *<Negative>*, Z = *<Zero>*, C = *<NoUnsignedOverflow>*, V = *<SignedOverflow>*. The carry flag is set this way because the subtract $x - y - {\sim}C$ is implemented as the add $x + {\sim}y + C$. The carry flag is one if $x + {\sim}y + C$ overflows. This happens when $x - y - {\sim}C$ doesn't overflow.

- If *Rd* is *pc*, then the instruction effects a jump to the calculated address. If the operation updates the *cpsr*, then the processor mode must have an *spsr*; in this case the *cpsr* is set to the value of the *spsr*.

- If *Rn* or *Rm* is *pc*, then the value used is the address of the instruction plus eight bytes.

The following example negates a 64-bit integer where *r0* is the low 32 bits and *r1* the high 32 bits.

```
RSBS    r0, r0, #0          ; r0 = -r0  C=NOT(borrow)
RSC     r1, r1, #0          ; r1 = -r1-borrow
```

SADD

Parallel modulo add and subtract operations

1. `{S|U}ADD16<cond>    Rd, Rn, Rm`   ARMv6

2.	`{S|U}ADDSUBX<cond>    Rd, Rn, Rm`	ARMv6
3.	`{S|U}SUBADDX<cond>    Rd, Rn, Rm`	ARMv6
4.	`{S|U}SUB16<cond>      Rd, Rn, Rm`	ARMv6
5.	`{S|U}ADD8<cond>       Rd, Rn, Rm`	ARMv6
6.	`{S|U}SUB8<cond>       Rd, Rn, Rm`	ARMv6

Action   Effect on the *cpsr*

1. `Rd[31:16]=Rn[31:16]+Rm[31:16];`   `GE3=GE2=cmn(Rn[31:16],Rm[31:16])`

   `Rd[15:00]=Rn[15:00]+Rm[15:00]`   `GE1=GE0=cmn(Rn[15:00],Rm[15:00])`

2. `Rd[31:16]=Rn[31:16]+Rm[15:00];`   `GE3=GE2=cmn(Rn[31:16],Rm[15:00])`

   `Rd[15:00]=Rn[15:00]-Rm[31:16]`   `GE1=GE0=(Rn[15:00] >= Rm[31:16])`

3. `Rd[31:16]=Rn[31:16]-Rm[15:00];`   `GE3=GE2=(Rn[31:16] >= Rm[15:00])`

   `Rd[15:00]=Rn[15:00]+Rm[31:16]`   `GE1=GE0=cmn(Rn[15:00],Rm[31:16])`

4. `Rd[31:16]=Rn[31:16]-Rm[31:16];`   `GE3=GE2=(Rn[31:16] >= Rm[31:16])`

   `Rd[15:00]=Rn[15:00]-Rm[15:00]`   `GE1=GE0=(Rn[15:00] >= Rm[15:00])`

5. `Rd[31:24]=Rn[31:24]+Rm[31:24];`   `GE3 = cmn(Rn[31:24],Rm[31:24])`

   `Rd[23:16]=Rn[23:16]+Rm[23:16];`   `GE2 = cmn(Rn[23:16],Rm[23:16])`

   `Rd[15:08]=Rn[15:08]+Rm[15:08];`   `GE1 = cmn(Rn[15:08],Rm[15:08])`

   `Rd[07:00]=Rn[07:00]+Rm[07:00]`   `GE0 = cmn(Rn[07:00],Rm[07:00])`

6. `Rd[31:24]=Rn[31:24]-Rm[31:24];`   `GE3 = (Rn[31:24] >= Rm[31:24])`

   `Rd[23:16]=Rn[23:16]-Rm[23:16];`   `GE2 = (Rn[23:16] >= Rm[23:16])`

   `Rd[15:08]=Rn[15:08]-Rm[15:08];`   `GE1 = (Rn[15:08] >= Rm[15:08])`

   `Rd[07:00]=Rn[07:00]-Rm[07:00]`   `GE0 = (Rn[07:00] >= Rm[07:00])`

Notes

- If you specify the S prefix, then all comparisons are signed. The *cmn(x,y)* function returns $x \geq -y$ or equivalently $x + y \geq 0$.

- If you specify the U prefix, then all comparisons are unsigned. The *cmn(x,y)* function returns $x \geq (unsigned)(-y)$ or equivalently if the $x + y$ operation produces a carry.

- *Rd*, *Rn*, and *Rm* must not be *pc*.

- The X operations are useful for packed complex numbers. The following examples assume bits [15:00] hold the real part and [31:16] the imaginary part.

Examples

```
SADD16    r0, r1, r2  ; Signed 16-bit SIMD add
SADDSUBX  r0, r1, r2  ; r0=r1+i*r2 in packed complex arithmetic
SSUBADDX  r0, r1, r2  ; r0=r1-i*r2 in packed complex arithmetic
```

SBC   Subtract with carry

1. SBC<cond>{S} Rd, Rn, #<rotated_immed>	ARMv1
2. SBC<cond>{S} Rd, Rn, Rm {, <shift>}	ARMv1
3. SBC Ld, Lm	THUMBv1

Action	Effect on the *cpsr*
1. Rd = Rn - <rotated_immed> - (~C)	Updated if S suffix specified
2. Rd = Rn - <shifted_Rm> - (~C)	Updated if S suffix specified
3. Ld = Ld - Lm - (~C)	Updated (see Notes below)

Notes

- If the operation updates the *cpsr* and *Rd* is not *pc*, then $N = <Negative>$, $Z = <Zero>$, $C = <NoUnsignedOverflow>$, $V = <SignedOverflow>$. The carry flag is set this way because the subtract $x - y - \sim C$ is implemented as the add $x + \sim y + C$. The carry flag is one if $x + \sim y + C$ overflows. This happens when $x - y - \sim C$ doesn't overflow.
- If *Rd* is *pc*, then the instruction effects a jump to the calculated address. If the operation updates the *cpsr*, then the processor mode must have an *spsr*. In this case the *cpsr* is set to the value of the *spsr*.
- If *Rn* or *Rm* is *pc*, then the value used is the address of the instruction plus eight bytes.

The following example implements a 64-bit subtract:

```
SUBS   r0, r0, r2    ; subtract low words, C=NOT(borrow)
SBC    r1, r1, r3    ; subtract high words and borrow
```

SEL   Select between two source operands based on the *GE* flags

1. SEL<cond> Rd, Rn, Rm	ARMv6

Action

1. Rd[31:24] = GE3 ? Rn[31:24] : Rm[31:24];
   Rd[23:16] = GE2 ? Rn[23:16] : Rm[23:16];
   Rd[15:08] = GE1 ? Rn[15:08] : Rm[15:08];
   Rd[07:00] = GE0 ? Rn[07:00] : Rm[07:00]

Notes

- *Rd, Rn, Rm* must not be *pc*.
- See SADD for instructions that set the *GE* flags in the *cpsr*.

SETEND	Set the endianness for data accesses	

1. SETEND BE	ARMv6/THUMBv3
2. SETEND LE	ARMv6/THUMBv3

Action

1. In the cpsr E=1 so data accesses will be big-endian
2. In the cpsr E=0 so data accesses will be little-endian

Note

- ARMv6 uses a byte-invariant endianness model. This means that byte loads and stores are not affected by the configured endianess. For little-endian data access the byte at the lowest address appears in the least significant byte of the loaded word. For big-endian data accesses the byte at the lowest address appears in the most significant byte of the loaded word.

SHADD	Parallel halving add and subtract operations

1. {S|U}HADD16<cond> Rd, Rn, Rm	ARMv6
2. {S|U}HADDSUBX<cond> Rd, Rn, Rm	ARMv6
3. {S|U}HSUBADDX<cond> Rd, Rn, Rm	ARMv6
4. {S|U}HSUB16<cond> Rd, Rn, Rm	ARMv6
5. {S|U}HADD8<cond> Rd, Rn, Rm	ARMv6
6. {S|U}HSUB8<cond> Rd, Rn, Rm	ARMv6

Action

1. Rd[31:16] = (Rn[31:16] + Rm[31:16]) >> 1;

    Rd[15:00] = (Rn[15:00] + Rm[15:00]) >> 1

2. Rd[31:16] = (Rn[31:16] + Rm[15:00]) >> 1;

    Rd[15:00] = (Rn[15:00] - Rm[31:16]) >> 1

3. Rd[31:16] = (Rn[31:16] - Rm[15:00]) >> 1;

    Rd[15:00] = (Rn[15:00] + Rm[31:16]) >> 1

4. Rd[31:16] = (Rn[31:16] - Rm[31:16]) >> 1;

    Rd[15:00] = (Rn[15:00] - Rm[15:00]) >> 1

5. Rd[31:24] = (Rn[31:24] + Rm[31:24]) >> 1;

    Rd[23:16] = (Rn[23:16] + Rm[23:16]) >> 1;

    Rd[15:08] = (Rn[15:08] + Rm[15:08]) >> 1;

    Rd[07:00] = (Rn[07:00] + Rm[07:00]) >> 1

6. Rd[31:24] = (Rn[31:24] - Rm[31:24]) >> 1;

    Rd[23:16] = (Rn[23:16] - Rm[23:16]) >> 1;

    Rd[15:08] = (Rn[15:08] - Rm[15:08]) >> 1;

    Rd[07:00] = (Rn[07:00] - Rm[07:00]) >> 1

Notes

- If you use the S prefix, then all operations are signed and values are sign-extended before the addition.
- If you use the U prefix, then all operations are unsigned and values are zero-extended before the addition.
- *Rd*, *Rn*, and *Rm* must not be *pc*.
- These operations provide parallel arithmetic that cannot overflow, which is useful for DSP processing of normalized signals.

SMLA SMLS	Signed multiply accumulate instructions		
	1. SMLA\<x>\<y>\<cond>	Rd, Rm, Rs, Rn	ARMv5E
	2. SMLAW\<y>\<cond>	Rd, Rm, Rs, Rn	ARMv5E
	3. SMLAD{X}\<cond>	Rd, Rm, Rs, Rn	ARMv6

4.	`SMLSD{X}<cond>        Rd, Rm, Rs, Rn`	ARMv6
5.	`{U|S}MLAL<cond>{S} RdLo, RdHi, Rm, Rs`	ARMv3M
6.	`SMLAL<x><y><cond>  RdLo, RdHi, Rm, Rs`	ARMv5E
7.	`SMLALD{X}<cond>    RdLo, RdHi, Rm, Rs`	ARMv6
8.	`SMLSLD{X}<cond>    RdLo, RdHi, Rm, Rs`	ARMv6

Action

1.	`Rd`	`= Rn + (Rm.<x> * Rs.<y>)`
2.	`Rd`	`= Rn + (((signed)Rm * Rs.<y>) >> 16)`
3.	`Rd`	`= Rn + Rm.B*<rotated_Rs>.B + Rm.T*<rotated_Rs>.T`
4.	`Rd`	`= Rn + Rm.B*<rotated_Rs>.B - Rm.T*<rotated_Rs>.T`
5.	`RdHi:RdLo`	`= RdHi:RdLo + (Rm * Rs)`
6.	`RdHi:RdLo`	`= RdHi:RdLo + (Rm.<x> * Rm.<y>)`
7.	`RdHi:RdLo`	`= RdHi:RdLo + Rm.B*<rotated_Rs>.B + Rm.T*<rotated_Rs>.T`
8.	`RdHi:RdLo`	`= RdHi:RdLo + Rm.B*<rotated_Rs>.B - Rm.T*<rotated_Rs>.T`

Notes

- `<x>` and `<y>` can be B or T.
- *Rm.B* is shorthand for *(sign-extend)Rm*[15:00], the bottom 16 bits of *Rm*.
- *Rm.T* is shorthand for *(sign-extend)Rm*[31:16], the top 16 bits of *Rm*.
- *<rotated_Rs>* is *Rs* if you do not specify the X suffix or Rs ROR 16 if you do specify the X suffix.
- *RdHi* and *RdLo* must be different registers. For format 5 prior to ARMv6, *Rm* must be a different register from *RdHi* and *RdLo*.
- Formats 1 to 4 update the *cpsr* Q-flag: $Q = Q| <SignedOverflow>$.
- Format 5 implements an unsigned multiply with the U prefix or a signed multiply with the S prefix.
- Format 5 updates the *cpsr* if the S suffix is present: $N = RdHi[31]$, $Z = (RdHi==0$ && $RdLo==0)$; the *C* and *V* flags are unpredictable. Avoid using `{U|S}MLALS` because implementations often impose penalty cycles for this operation.

- Implementations may terminate early on the value of *Rs*. For this reason use small or constant values for *Rs* where possible.
- The X suffix and multiply subtract versions are useful for packed complex numbers. The following examples assume bits [15:00] hold the real part and [31:16] the imaginary part.

Examples

```
SMLABB   r0, r1, r2, r0  ; r0 += (short)r1 * (short)r2
SMLABT   r0, r1, r2, r0  ; r0 += (short)r1 * ((signed)r2 >> 16)
SMLAWB   r0, r1, r2, r0  ; r0 += (r1*(short)r2) >> 16
SMLAL    r0, r1, r2, r3  ; acc += r2*r3, acc is 64 bits [r1:r0]
SMLALTB  r0, r1, r2, r3  ; acc += ((signed)r2 >> 16)*((short)r3)
SMLSD    r0, r1, r2, r0  ; r0 += real(r1*r2) in complex maths
SMLADX   r0, r1, r2, r0  ; r0 += imag(r1*r2) in complex maths
```

SMMUL
SMMLA
SMMLS

Signed most significant word multiply instructions

1. SMMUL{R}<cond> Rd, Rm, Rs   ARMv6

2. SMMLA{R}<cond> Rd, Rm, Rs, Rn   ARMv6

3. SMMLS{R}<cond> Rd, Rm, Rs, Rn   ARMv6

Action

1. Rd = ((signed)Rm*(signed)Rs + round) >> 32

2. Rd = ((Rn << 32) + (signed)Rm*(signed)Rs + round) >> 32

3. Rd = ((Rn << 32) - (signed)Rm*(signed)Rs + round) >> 32

Notes

- If you specify the R suffix then $round = 2^{31}$; otherwise, $round = 0$.
- *Rd*, *Rm*, *Rs*, and *Rn* must not be *pc*.
- Implementations may terminate early on the value of *Rs*.
- For 32-bit DSP algorithms these operations have several advantages over using the high result register from SMLAL: They often take fewer cycles than SMLAL. They also implement rounding, multiply subtract, and don't require a temporary scratch register for the low 32 bits of result.

Example

```
SMMULR   r0, r1, r2      ; r0=r1*r2/2 using Q31 arithmetic
```

SMUL SMUAD SMUSD	Signed multiply instructions		
	1. SMUL<x><y><cond> Rd, Rm, Rs		ARMv5E
	2. SMULW<y><cond> Rd, Rm, Rs		ARMv5E
	3. SMUAD{X}<cond> Rd, Rm, Rs		ARMv6
	4. SMUSD{X}<cond> Rd, Rm, Rs		ARMv6
	5. {U|S}MULL<cond>{S} RdLo, RdHi, Rm, Rs		ARMv3M

Action

1. Rd   = Rm.<x> * Rs.<y>

2. Rd   = (Rm * Rs.<y>) >> 16

3. Rd   = Rm.B*<rotated_Rs>.B + Rm.T*<rotated_Rs>.T

4. Rd   = Rm.B*<rotated_Rs>.B - Rm.T*<rotated_Rs>.T

5. RdHi:RdLo = Rm*Rs

Notes

- <x> and <y> can be B or T.
- *Rm.B* is shorthand for *(sign-extend)Rm*[15:00], the bottom 16 bits of *Rm*.
- *Rm.T* is shorthand for *(sign-extend)Rm*[31:16], the top 16 bits of *Rm*.
- *<rotated_Rs>* is *Rs* if you do not specify the X suffix or Rs ROR 16 if you do specify the X suffix.
- *RdHi* and *RdLo* must be different registers. For format 5, *Rm* must be a different register from *RdHi* and *RdLo*.
- Format 3 updates the *cpsr* Q-flag: $Q = Q \mid <SignedOverflow>$.
- Format 5 implements an unsigned multiply with the U prefix or a signed multiply with the S prefix.
- Format 5 updates the *cpsr* if the *S* suffix is present: $N = RdHi[31]$, $Z = (RdHi==0 \&\& RdLo==0)$; the *C* and *V* flags are unpredictable. Avoid using {S|U}MULLS because implementations often impose penalty cycles for this operation.
- Implementations may terminate early on the value of *Rs*. For this reason use small or constant values for *Rs* where possible.
- The X suffix and multiply subtract versions are useful for packed complex numbers. The following examples assume bits [15:00] hold the real part and [31:16] the imaginary part.

Examples

```
SMULBB  r0, r1, r2      ; r0 = (short)r1 * (short)r2
SMULBT  r0, r1, r2      ; r0 = (short)r1 * ((signed)r2 >> 16)
SMULWB  r0, r1, r2      ; r0 = (r1*(short)r2) >> 16
SMULL   r0, r1, r2, r3  ; acc = r2*r3, acc is 64 bits [r1:r0]
SMUADX  r0, r1, r2      ; r0 = imag(r1*r2) in complex maths
```

SRS	Save return state

1. SRS<amode> #<mode>{!}   ARMv6

This performs the operation that *STM<amode> sp_<mode>{!}, {lr, spsr}* would perform if STM allowed a register list of *{lr, spsr}* and allowed you to reference the stack pointer of a different mode. See the entry for STM.

SSAT	Saturate to *n* bits

1. {S|U}SAT<cond>   Rd, #<n>, Rm {, LSL#<0-31>}   ARMv6

2. {S|U}SAT<cond>   Rd, #<n>, Rm {, ASR#<1-32>}   ARMv6

3. {S|U}SAT16<cond> Rd, #<n>, Rm   ARMv6

Action	Effect on the *cpsr*
1. Rd = sat(<shifted_Rm>, n);	Q=Q | 1 if saturation occurred
2. Rd = sat(<shifted_Rm>, n);	Q=Q | 1 if saturation occurred
3. Rd[31:16] = sat(Rm[31:16], n);	Q=Q | 1 if saturation occurred
Rd[15:00] = sat(Rm[15:00], n)	

Notes

- If you specify the S prefix, then $sat(x, n)$ saturates the signed value x to a signed n-bit value in the range $-2^{n-1} \le x < 2^{n-1}$. n is encoded as 1 + <immed5> for SAT and 1 + <immed4> for SAT16.

- If you specify the U prefix, then $sat(x, n)$ saturates the signed value x to an unsigned n-bit value in the range $0 \le x < 2^n$. n is encoded as <immed5> for SAT and <immed4> for SAT16.

- *Rd* and *Rm* must not be *pc*.

SSUB	Signed parallel subtract (see SADD)

STC	Store to coprocessor single or multiple 32-bit values

1. `STC<cond>{L}` `<copro>, Cd, [Rn {, #{-}<immed8>*4}]{!}`   ARMv2

2. `STC<cond>{L}` `<copro>, Cd, [Rn], #{-}<immed8>*4`   ARMv2

3. `STC<cond>{L}` `<copro>, Cd, [Rn], <option>`   ARMv2

4. `STC2{L}`   `<copro>, Cd, [Rn {, #{-}<immed8>*4}]{!}`   ARMv5

5. `STC2{L}`   `<copro>, Cd, [Rn], #{-}<immed8>*4`   ARMv5

6. `STC2{L}`   `<copro>, Cd, [Rn], <option>`   ARMv5

These instructions initiate a memory write, transferring data to memory from the given coprocessor. *<copro>* is the number of the coprocessor in the range *p0* to *p15*. The core takes an undefined instruction trap if the coprocessor is not present. The memory write consists of a sequence of words to sequentially increasing addresses. The initial address is specified by the addressing mode in Table A.10. The coprocessor controls the number of words transferred, up to a maximum limit of 16 words. The fields *{L}* and *Cd* are interpreted by the coprocessor and ignored by the ARM. Typically *Cd* specifies the source coprocessor register for the transfer. The *<option>* field is an eight-bit integer enclosed in *{}*. Its interpretation is coprocessor dependent.

If the address is not a multiple of four, then the access is unaligned. The restrictions on an unaligned access are the same as for STM.

Table A.10   STC addressing modes.

Addressing format	Address accessed	Value written back to *Rn*
`[Rn {,#{-}<immed>}]`	`Rn + {{-}<immed>}`	`Rn preserved`
`[Rn {,#{-}<immed>}]!`	`Rn + {{-}<immed>}`	`Rn + {{-}<immed>}`
`[Rn], #{-}<immed>`	`Rn`	`Rn + {-}<immed>`
`[Rn], <option>`	`Rn`	`Rn preserved`

STM	Store multiple 32-bit registers to memory

1. `STM<cond><amode> Rn{!}, <register_list>{^}`   ARMv1

2. `STMIA`   `Rn!, <register_list>`   THUMBv1

These instructions store multiple words to sequential memory addresses. The *<register_list>* specifies a list of registers to store, enclosed in curly brackets *{}*. Although the

Table A.11   STM addressing modes.

Addressing mode	Lowest address accessed	Highest address accessed	Value written back to Rn if ! specified
{IA|EA}	Rn	Rn + N*4 - 4	Rn + N*4
{IB|FA}	Rn + 4	Rn + N*4	Rn + N*4
{DA|ED}	Rn - N*4 + 4	Rn	Rn - N*4
{DB|FD}	Rn - N*4	Rn - 4	Rn - N*4

assembler allows you to specify the registers in the list in any order, the order is not stored in the instruction, so it is good practice to write the list in increasing order of register number since this is the usual order of the memory transfer.

The following pseudocode shows the normal action of STM. We use `<register_list>[i]` to denote the register appearing at position i in the list starting at 0 for the first register. This assumes that the list is in order of increasing register number.

```
N = the number of registers in <register_list>
start = the lowest address accessed given in Table A.11
for (i=0; i<N; i++)
  memory(start+i*4, 4) = <register_list>[i];
if (! specified) then update Rn according to Table A.11
```

Note that `memory(a, 4)` refers to the four bytes at address a packed according to the current processor data endianness. If a is not a multiple of four, then the store is unaligned. Because the behavior of an unaligned store depends on the architecture revision, memory system, and system coprocessor (CP15) configuration, it is best to avoid unaligned stores if possible. Assuming that the external memory system does not abort unaligned stores, then the following rules usually apply:

- If the core has a system coprocessor and bit 1 (*A*-bit) or bit 22 (*U*-bit) of CP15:c1:c0:0 is set, then unaligned store-multiples cause an alignment fault data abort exception.

- Otherwise, the access ignores the bottom two address bits.

Table A.11 lists the possible addressing modes specified by `<amode>`. If you specify the !, then the base address register is updated according to Table A.11; otherwise, it is preserved. Note that the lowest register number is always written to the lowest address.

The first half of the addressing mode mnemonics stands for Increment After, Increment Before, Decrement After, and Decrement Before, respectively. Increment modes store the registers sequentially forward starting from address Rn (increment after) or $Rn + 4$ (increment before). Decrement modes have the same effect as if you stored the register list backwards to sequentially descending memory addresses starting from address *Rn* (decrement after) or *Rn* − 4 (decrement before).

The second half of the addressing mode mnemonics stands for the stack type you can implement with that address mode: Full Descending, Empty Descending, Full Ascending, and Empty Ascending. With a full stack, *Rn* points to the last stacked value. With an empty stack, *Rn* points to the first unused stack location. ARM stacks are usually full descending. You should use full descending or empty ascending stacks by preference, since STC also supports these addressing modes.

Notes

- For Thumb (format 2), *Rn* and the register list registers must be in the range *r0* to *r7*.
- The number of registers *N* in the list must be nonzero.
- *Rn* must not be *pc*.
- If *Rn* appears in the register list and ! (writeback) is specified, the behavior is as follows: If *Rn* is the lowest register number in the list, then the original value is stored; otherwise, the stored value is unpredictable.
- If *pc* appears in the register list, then the value stored is implementation defined.
- If ^ is specified, then the operation is modified. The processor must not be in *user* or *system* mode. The registers appearing in the register list refer to the *user* mode versions of the registers and writeback must not be specified.
- The time order of the memory accesses may depend on the implementation. Be careful when using a store multiple to access I/O locations where the access order matters. If the order matters, then check that the memory locations are marked as I/O in the page tables. Do not cross page boundaries, and do not use *pc* in the register list.

Examples

```
STMIA    r4!, {r0, r1}   ; *r4=r0, *(r4+4)=r1, r4+=8
STMDB    r4!, {r0, r1}   ; *(r4-4)=r1, *(r4-8)=r0, r4-=8
STMEQFD  sp!, {r0, lr}   ; if (result zero) then stack r0, lr
STMFD    sp, {sp}^       ; store sp_usr on stack sp_current
```

STR Store a single value to a virtual address in memory

1.	STR<cond>{|B}	Rd, [Rn {, #{-}<immed12>}]{!}	ARMv1
2.	STR<cond>{|B}	Rd, [Rn, {-}Rm {,<imm_shift>}]{!}	ARMv1
3.	STR<cond>{|B}{T}	Rd, [Rn], #{-}<immed12>	ARMv1
4.	STR<cond>{|B}{T}	Rd, [Rn], {-}Rm {,<imm_shift>}	ARMv1
5.	STR<cond>{H}	Rd, [Rn {, #{-}<immed8>}]{!}	ARMv4

6.	STR<cond>{H}	Rd, [Rn, {-}Rm]{!}	ARMv4
7.	STR<cond>{H}	Rd, [Rn], #{-}<immed8>	ARMv4
8.	STR<cond>{H}	Rd, [Rn], {-}Rm	ARMv4
9.	STR<cond>D	Rd, [Rn {, #{-}<immed8>}]{!}	ARMv5E
10.	STR<cond>D	Rd, [Rn, {-}Rm]{!}	ARMv5E
11.	STR<cond>D	Rd, [Rn], #{-}<immed8>	ARMv5E
12.	STR<cond>D	Rd, [Rn], {-}Rm	ARMv5E
13.	STREX<cond>	Rd, Rm, [Rn]	ARMv6
14.	STR{|B|H}	Ld, [Ln, #<immed5>*<size>]	THUMBv1
15.	STR{|B|H}	Ld, [Ln, Lm]	THUMBv1
16.	STR	Ld, [sp, #<immed8>*4]	THUMBv1
17.	STR<cond><type>	Rd, <label>	MACRO

Formats 1 to 16 store a single data item of the type specified by the opcode suffix, using a preindexed or postindexed addressing mode. Tables A.12 and A.13 show the different addressing modes and data types.

In Table A.13, memory(a, n) refers to n sequential bytes at address a. The bytes are packed according to the configured processor data endianness. memoryT(a, n) performs the access with *user* mode privileges, regardless of the current processor mode. The act of function IsExclusive(a) used by STREX depends on address a. If a has the shared TLB attribute, then IsExclusive(a) is true if address a is marked as exclusive for this processor. It then clears any exclusive accesses on this processor and any exclusive accesses to address a on other processors in the system. If a does not have the shared TLB attribute, then IsExclusive(a) is true if there is an outstanding exclusive access on this processor. It then clears any such outstanding access.

Table A.12   STR addressing modes.

Addressing format	Address *a* accessed	Value written back to *Rn*
[Rn {,#{-}<immed>}]	Rn + {{-}<immed>}	Rn preserved
[Rn {,#{-}<immed>}]!	Rn + {{-}<immed>}	Rn + {{-}<immed>}
[Rn, {-}Rm {,<shift>}]	Rn + {-}<shifted_Rm>	Rn preserved
[Rn, {-}Rm {,<shift>}]!	Rn + {-}<shifted_Rm>	Rn + {-}<shifted_Rm>
[Rn], #{-}<immed>	Rn	Rn + {-}<immed>
[Rn], {-}Rm {,<shift>}	Rn	Rn + {-}<shifted_Rm>

Table A.13   STR data types.

Store	Datatype	`<size>` (bytes)	Action
STR	word	4	`memory(a, 4) = Rd`
STRB	unsigned Byte	1	`memory(a, 1) = (char)Rd`
STRBT	Byte Translated	1	`memoryT(a, 1) = (char)Rd`
STRD	Double word	8	`memory(a, 4) = Rd` `memory(a+4, 4) = R(d+1)`

STREX	word EXclusive	4	`if (IsExclsuive(a)) {`
			`  memory(a, 4) = Rm;`
			`  Rd = 0;`
			`} else {`
			`  Rd = 1;`
			`}`

STRH	unsigned Halfword	2	`memory(a, 2) = (short) Rd`
STRT	word Translated	4	`memoryT(a, 4) = Rd`

If the address a is not a multiple of *<size>*, then the store is unaligned. Because the behavior of an unaligned store depends on the architecture revision, memory system, and system coprocessor (CP15) configuration, it is best to avoid unaligned stores if possible. Assuming that the external memory system does not abort unaligned stores, then the following rules usually apply. In the rules, A is bit 1 of system coprocessor register CP15:c1:c0:0, and U is bit 22 of CP15:c1:c0:0, introduced in ARMv6. If there is no system coprocessor, then $A = U = 0$.

- If $A = 1$, then unaligned stores cause an alignment fault data abort exception except that word-aligned double-word stores are supported if $U = 1$.

- If $A = 0$ and $U = 1$, then unaligned stores are supported for STR{|T|H|SH}. Word-aligned stores are supported for STRD. A non-word-aligned STRD generates an alignment fault data abort.

- If $A = 0$ and $U = 0$, then STR and STRT write to *memory*(a & ~3, 4). All other unaligned operations are unpredictable but do not cause an alignment fault.

Format 17 generates a *pc* -relative store accessing the address specified by *<label>*. In other words it assembles to *STR<cond><type> Rd, [pc, #<offset>]* whenever this instruction is supported and *<offset>=<label>-pc* is in range.

Notes

- For double-word stores (formats 9 to 12), *Rd* must be even and in the range *r0* to *r12*.
- If the addressing mode updates *Rn*, then *Rd* and *Rn* must be distinct.

- If *Rd* is *pc*, then *<size>* must be 4. The value stored is implementation defined.
- If *Rn* is *pc*, then the addressing mode must not update *Rn* . The value used for *Rn* is the address of the instruction plus eight bytes.
- *Rm* must not be *pc*.

Examples

```
STR     r0, [r0]        ; *(int*)r0 = r0;
STRH    r0, [r1], #4    ; *(short*)r1 = r0; r1+=4;
STRD    r2, [r1, #-8]! ; r1-=8; *(int*)r1=r2; *(int*)(r1+4)=r3
STRB    r0, [r2, #55]        ; *(char*)(r2+55) = r0;
STRB    r0, [r1], -r2, LSL #8 ; *(char*)r1 = r0; r1-=256*r2;
```

SUB   Subtract two 32-bit values

1.	SUB<cond>{S} Rd, Rn, #<rotated_immed>	ARMv1
2.	SUB<cond>{S} Rd, Rn, Rm {, <shift>}	ARMv1
3.	SUB Ld, Ln, #<immed3>	THUMBv1
4.	SUB Ld, #<immed8>	THUMBv1
5.	SUB Ld, Ln, Lm	THUMBv1
6.	SUB sp, #<immed7>*4	THUMBv1

Action   Effect on the *cpsr*

1. Rd = Rn - <rotated_immed>	Updated if S suffix specified
2. Rd = Rn - <shifted_Rm>	Updated if S suffix specified
3. Ld = Ln - <immed3>	Updated (see Notes below)
4. Ld = Ld - <immed8>	Updated (see Notes below)
5. Ld = Ln - Lm	Updated (see Notes below)
6. sp = sp - <immed7>*4	Preserved

Notes

- If the operation updates the *cpsr* and *Rd* is not *pc*, then N = *<Negative>*, Z = *<Zero>*, C = *<NoUnsignedOverflow>*, and V = *<SignedOverflow>*. The carry flag is set this way because the subtract $x - y$ is implemented as the add $x + \sim y + 1$. The carry flag is one if $x + \sim y + 1$ overflows. This happens when $x \geq y$, when $x - y$ doesn't overflow.

- If *Rd* is *pc*, then the instruction effects a jump to the calculated address. If the operation updates the *cpsr*, then the processor mode must have an *spsr*; in this case, the *cpsr* is set to the value of the *spsr*.

- If *Rn* or *Rm* is *pc*, then the value used is the address of the instruction plus eight bytes.

Examples

```
SUBS    r0, r0, #1           ; r0-=1, setting flags
SUB     r0, r1, r1, LSL #2   ; r0 = -3*r1
SUBS    pc, lr, #4           ; jump to lr-4, set cpsr=spsr
```

SWI	Software interrupt	
	1. SWI<cond> <immed24>	ARMv1
	2. SWI <immed8>	THUMBv1

The SWI instruction causes the ARM to enter *supervisor* mode and start executing from the SWI vector. The return address and *cpsr* are saved in *lr_svc* and *spsr_svc*, respectively. The processor switches to ARM state and IRQ interrupts are disabled. The SWI vector is at address 0x00000008, unless high vectors are configured; then it is at address 0xFFFF0008.

The immediate operand is ignored by the ARM. It is normally used by the SWI exception handler as an argument determining which function to perform.

Example

```
SWI     0x123456 ; Used by the ARM tools to implement Semi-Hosting
```

SWP	Swap a word in memory with a register, without interruption	
	1. SWP<cond> Rd, Rm, [Rn]	ARMv2a
	2. SWP<cond>B Rd, Rm, [Rn]	ARMv2a

Action

1. temp=memory(Rn,4); memory(Rn,4)=Rm; Rd=temp;

2. temp=(zero extend)memory(Rn,1); memory(Rn,1)=(char)Rm; Rd=temp;

Notes

- The operations are atomic. They cannot be interrupted partway through.
- *Rd, Rm, Rn* must not be *pc*.

- *Rn* and *Rm* must be different registers. *Rn* and *Rd* must be different registers.

- *Rn* should be aligned to the size of the memory transfer.

- If a data abort occurs on the load, then the store does not occur. If a data abort occurs on the store, then *Rd* is not written.

You can use the SWP instruction to implement 8-bit or 32-bit semaphores on ARMv5 and below. For ARMv6 use LDREX and STREX in preference. As an example, suppose a byte semaphore register pointed to by *r1* can have the value 0xFF (claimed) or 0x00 (free). The following example claims the lock. If the lock is already claimed, then the code loops, waiting for an interrupt or task switch that will free the lock.

```
          MOV    r0, #0xFF      ; value to claim the lock
loop      SWPB   r0, r0, [r1]   ; try and claim the lock
          CMP    r0, #0xFF      ; check to see if it was already claimed
          BEQ    loop           ; if so wait for it to become free
```

SXT SXTA	Byte or halfword extract or extract with accumulate		

	1. {S|U}XTB16<cond>	Rd, Rm {, ROR#8*<rot> }	ARMv6
	2. {S|U}XTB<cond>	Rd, Rm {, ROR#8*<rot> }	ARMv6
	3. {S|U}XTH<cond>	Rd, Rm {, ROR#8*<rot> }	ARMv6
	4. {S|U}XTAB16<cond>	Rd, Rn, Rm {, ROR#8*<rot> }	ARMv6
	5. {S|U}XTAB<cond>	Rd, Rn, Rm {, ROR#8*<rot> }	ARMv6
	6. {S|U}XTAH<cond>	Rd, Rn, Rm {, ROR#8*<rot> }	ARMv6
	7. {S|U}XTB	Ld, Lm	THUMBv3
	8. {S|U}XTH	Ld, Lm	THUMBv3

Action

1. Rd[31:16] = extend(<shifted_Rm>[23:16]);

   Rd[15:00] = extend(<shifted_Rm>[07:00])

2. Rd = extend(<shifted_Rm>[07:00])

3. Rd = extend(<shifted_Rm>[15:00])

4. Rd[31:16] = Rn[31:16] + extend(<shifted_Rm>[23:16]);

   Rd[15:00] = Rn[15:00] + extend(<shifted_Rm>[07:00])

5. Rd = Rn + extend(<shifted_Rm>[07:00])

6. `Rd = Rn + extend(<shifted_Rm>[15:00])`

7. `Ld = extend(Lm[07:00])`

8. `Ld = extend(Lm[15:00])`

Notes

- If you specify the S prefix, then extend(x) sign extends x.
- If you specify the U prefix, then extend(x) zero extends x.
- *Rd, Rn* and *Rm* must not be *pc*.
- <*rot*> is an immediate in the range 0 to 3.

TEQ	Test for equality of two 32-bit values

1. `TEQ<cond> Rn, #<rotated_immed>`   ARMv1

2. `TEQ<cond> Rn, Rm {, <shift>}`   ARMv1

Action

1. Set the cpsr on the result of (Rn ^ <rotated_immed>)

2. Set the cpsr on the result of (Rn ^ <shifted_Rm>)

Notes

- The *cpsr* is updated: N = <*Negative*>, Z = <*Zero*>, C = <*shifter_C*> (see Table A.3).
- If *Rn* or *Rm* is *pc*, then the value used is the address of the instruction plus eight bytes.
- Use this instruction instead of CMP when you want to check for equality and preserve the carry flag.

Example

```
        TEQ    r0, #1      ; test to see if r0==1
```

TST	Test bits of a 32-bit value

1. `TST<cond> Rn, #<rotated_immed>`   ARMv1

```
2.  TST<cond> Rn, Rm {, <shift>}                ARMv1

3.  TST      Ln, Lm                             THUMBv1
```

Action

```
1. Set the cpsr on the result of (Rn & <rotated_immed>)

2. Set the cpsr on the result of (Rn & <shifted_Rm>)

3. Set the cpsr on the result of (Ln & Lm)
```

Notes

- The *cpsr* is updated: $N = <Negative>$, $Z = <Zero>$, $C = <shifter\_C>$ (see Table A.3).
- If *Rn* or *Rm* is *pc*, then the value used is the address of the instruction plus eight bytes.
- Use this instruction to test whether a selected set of bits are all zero.

Example

```
TST    r0, #0xFF     ; test if the bottom 8 bits of r0 are 0
```

UADD	Unsigned parallel modulo add (see the entry for SADD)

UHADD UHSUB	Unsigned halving add and subtract (see the entry for SHADD)

UMAAL   Unsigned multiply accumulate accumulate long

```
1.  UMAAL<cond> RdLo, RdHi, Rm, Rs               ARMv6
```

Action

```
1. RdHi:RdLo = (unsigned)Rm*Rs + (unsigned)RdLo + (unsigned)RdHi
```

Notes

- *RdHi* and *RdLo* must be different registers.
- *RdHi, RdLo, Rm, Rs* must not be *pc*.
- This operation cannot overflow because $(2^{32} - 1)(2^{32} - 1) + (2^{32} - 1) + (2^{32} - 1) = (2^{64} - 1)$. You can use it to synthesize the multiword multiplications used by public key cryptosystems.

UMLAL UMULL	Unsigned long multiply and multiply accumulate (see the SMLAL and SMULL entries)

UQADD UQSUB	Unsigned saturated add and subtract (see the QADD entry)

USAD	Unsigned sum of absolute differences

1. USAD8<cond> Rd, Rm, Rs   ARMv6

2. USADA8<cond> Rd, Rm, Rs, Rn   ARMv6

Action

1. Rd =   abs(Rm[31:24]-Rs[31:24]) + abs(Rm[23:16]-Rs[23:16])

               + abs(Rm[15:08]-Rs[15:08]) + abs(Rm[07:00]-Rs[07:00])

2. Rd = Rn + abs(Rm[31:24]-Rs[31:24]) + abs(Rm[23:16]-Rs[23:16])

               + abs(Rm[15:08]-Rs[15:08]) + abs(Rm[07:00]-Rs[07:00])

Notes

- *abs*(*x*) returns the absolute value of *x*. *Rm* and *Rs* are treated as unsigned.
- *Rd, Rn, Rm,* and *Rs* must not be *pc*.
- The sum of absolute differences operation is common in video codecs where it provides a metric to measure how similar two images are.

USAT	Unsigned saturation instruction (see the SSAT entry)

USUB	Unsigned parallel modulo subtracts (see the SADD entry)

UXT UXTA	Unsigned extract, extract with accumulate (see the entry for SXT)

A.4 ARM ASSEMBLER QUICK REFERENCE

This section summarizes the more useful commands and expressions available with the ARM assembler, *armasm*. Each assembly line has one of the following formats:

```
{<label>}    {<instruction>}                              ; comment
{<symbol>}   <directive>                                  ; comment
{<arg_0>}    <macro> {<arg_1>} {,<arg_2>} .. {,<arg_n>}   ; comment
```

where

- *<instruction>* is any ARM or Thumb instruction supported by the processor you are assembling for. See Section A.3.
- *<label>* is the name of a symbol to store the address of the instruction.
- *<directive>* is an ARM assembler directive. See Section A.4.4.
- *<symbol>* is the name of a symbol used by the *<directive>*.
- *<macro>* is the name of a new directive defined using the MACRO directive.
- *<arg_k>* is the *k*th macro argument.

You must use an AREA directive to define an area before any ARM or Thumb instructions appear. All assembly files must finish with the END directive. The following example shows a simple assembly file defining a function add that returns the sum of the two input arguments:

```
        AREA    maths_routines, CODE, READONLY
        EXPORT  add             ; give the symbol add external linkage

add     ADD     r0, r0, r1      ; add input arguments
        MOV     pc, lr          ; return from sub-routine

        END
```

A.4.1 ARM ASSEMBLER VARIABLES

The ARM assembler supports three types of assemble time variables (see Table A.14). Variable names are case sensitive and must be declared before use with the directives GBLx or LCLx.

You can use variables in expressions (see Section A.4.2), or substitute their value at assembly time using the $ operator. Specifically, $name. expands to the value of the variable

Table A.14   ARM assembler variable types.

Variable type	Declare globally	Declare locally to a macro	Set value	Example values
Unsigned 32-bit integer	GBLA	LCLA	SETA	15, 0xab
ASCII string	GBLS	LCLS	SETS	"", "ADD"
Logical	GBLL	LCLL	SETL	{TRUE}, {FALSE}

name before the line is assembled. You can omit the final period if name is not followed by an alphanumeric or underscore. Use $$ to produce a single $. Arithmetic variables expand to an eight-digit hexadecimal string on substitution. Logical variables expand to *T* or *F*.

The following example code shows how to declare and substitute variables of each type:

```
        ; arithmetic variables
        GBLA    count          ; declare an integer variable count
count   SETA    1              ; set count = 1
        WHILE   count<15
        BL      test$count     ; call test00000001, test00000002 ...
count   SETA    count+1        ;  .... test0000000E
        WEND

        ; string variables
        GBLS    cc             ; declare a string variable called cc
cc      SETS    "NE"           ; set cc="NE"
        ADD$cc   r0, r0, r0    ; assembles as ADDNE  r0,r0,r0
        STR$cc.B r0, [r1]      ; assembles as STRNEB r0,[r1]

        ; logical variable
        GBLL    debug          ; declare a logical variable called debug
debug   SETL    {TRUE}         ; set debug={TRUE}
        IF debug               ; if debug is TRUE then
        BL      print_debug    ; print out some debug information
        ENDIF
```

A.4.2   ARM ASSEMBLER LABELS

A label definition must begin on the first character of a line. The assembler treats indented text as an instruction, directive, or macro. It treats labels of the form <N><name> as a local label, where <N> is an integer in the range 0 to 99 and <name> is an optional textual name. Local labels are limited in scope by the ROUT directive. To reference a local label, you refer to it as %{|F|B}{|A|T}<N>{<name>}. The extra prefix letters tell the assembler how to search for the label:

- If you specify F, the assembler searches forward; if B, then the assembler searches backwards. Otherwise the assembler searches backwards and then forwards.

- If you specify T, the assembler searches the current macro only; if A, then the assembler searches all macro levels. Otherwise the assembler searches the current and higher macro nesting levels.

A.4.3 ARM ASSEMBLER EXPRESSIONS

The ARM assembler can evaluate a number of numeric, string, and logical expressions at assembly time. Table A.15 shows some of the unary and binary operators you can use within expressions. Brackets can be used to change the order of evaluation in the usual way.

Table A.15   ARM assembler unary and binary operators.

Expression	Result	Example
A+B, A-B	A plus or minus B	1-2 = 0xffffffff
A*B, A/B	A multiplied by or divided by B	2*3 = 6, 7/3 = 2
A:MOD:B	A modulo B	7:MOD:3 = 1
:CHR:A	string with ASCII code A	:CHR:32 = " "
'X'	the ASCII value of X	'a' = 0x61
:STR:A,	A or L converted to a string	:STR:32 = "00000020"
:STR:L		:STR:{TRUE} - "T"
A << B,	A shifted left by B bits	1<<3 = 8
A:SHL:B		
A >> B,	A shifted right by B bits (logical	0x80000000 >> 4 =
A:SHR:B	shift)	0x08000000
A:ROR:B,	A rotated right/left by B bits	1:ROR:1 = 0x80000000
A:ROL:B		0x80000000:ROL:1 = 1
A=B, A>B,	comparison of arithmetic or string	(1=2) = {FALSE},
A>=B, A<B,	variables (/= and <> both mean	(1<2) = {TRUE},
A<=B, A/=B,	not equal)	("a"="c") = {FALSE},
A<>B		("a"<"c") = {TRUE}
A:AND:B,	Bitwise AND, OR, exclusive OR of	1:AND:3 = 1
A:OR:B,	A and B; bitwise NOT of A.	1:OR:3 = 3
A:EOR:B,		:NOT:0 = 0xFFFFFFFF
:NOT:A		
:LEN:S	length of the string S	:LEN:"ABC" = 3
S:LEFT:B,	leftmost or rightmost B characters	"ABC":LEFT:2 = "AB",
S:RIGHT:B	of S	"ABC":RIGHT:2 = "BC"
S:CC:T	the concatenation of S, T	"AB":CC:"C" = "ABC"
L:LAND:M,	logical AND, OR, exclusive OR of	{TRUE}:LAND:{FALSE} =
L:LOR:M,	L and M	{FALSE}
L:LEOR:M		
:DEF:X	returns TRUE if a variable called X is defined	
:BASE:A	see the MAP directive	
:INDEX:A		

Table A.16   Predefined expressions.

Variable	Value
{ARCHITECURE}	The ARM architecture of the CPU ("4T" for ARMv4T)
{ARMASM_VERSION}	The assembler version number
{CONFIG} or	The bit width of the instructions being assembled (32 for
{CODESIZE}	ARM state, 16 for Thumb state)
{CPU}	The name of the CPU being assembled for
{ENDIAN}	The configured endianness, "big" or "little"
{INTER}	{TRUE} if ARM/Thumb interworking is on
{PC} (alias .)	The address of the current instruction being assembled
{ROPI}, {RWPI}	{TRUE} if read-only/read-write position independent
{VAR} (alias @)	The MAP counter (see the MAP directive)

In Table A.15, A and B represent arbitrary integers; S and T, strings; and L and M, logical values. You can use labels and other symbols in place of integers in many expressions.

A.4.3.1   Predefined Variables

Table A.16 shows a number of special variables that can appear in expressions. These are predefined by the assembler, and you cannot override them.

A.4.4   ARM ASSEMBLER DIRECTIVES

Here is an alphabetical list of the more common *armasm* directives.

ALIGN

        ALIGN   {<expression>, {<offset>}}

Aligns the address of the next instruction to the form q*<expression>+<offset>. The alignment is relative to the start of the ELF section so this must be aligned appropriately (see the AREA directive). <expression> must be a power of two; the default is 4. <offset> is zero if not specified.

AREA

        AREA   <section> {,<attr_1>} {,<attr_2>} ... {,<attr_k>}

Starts a new code or data section of name <section>. Table A.17 lists the possible attributes.

Table A.17   AREA attributes.

Attribute	Meaning
ALIGN=<expression>	Align the ELF section to a $2^{expression}$ byte boundary.
ASSOC=<sectionname>	If this section is linked, also link <sectionname>.
CODE	The section contains instructions and is read only.
DATA	The section contains data and is read write.
NOINIT	The data section does not require initialization.
READONLY	The section is read only.
READWRITE	The section is read write.

ASSERT

```
ASSERT   <logical-expression>
```

Assemble time assert. If the logical expression is false, then assembly terminates with an error.

CN

```
<name>   CN      <numeric-expression>
```

Set <name> to be an alias for coprocessor register <numeric-expression>.

CODE16, CODE32

CODE16 tells the assembler to assemble the following instructions as 16-bit Thumb instructions. CODE32 indicates 32-bit ARM instructions (the default for *armasm*).

CP

```
<name>   CP      <numeric-expression>
```

Set <name> to be an alias for coprocessor number <numeric-expression>.

DATA

```
<label> DATA
```

The DATA directive indicates that the label points to data rather than code. In Thumb state this prevents the linker from setting the bottom bit of the label. Bit 0 of a function pointer or code label is 0 for ARM code and 1 for Thumb code (see the BX instruction).

Table A.18   Memory initialization directives.

Directive	Alias	Data size (bytes)	Initialization value
DCB	=	1	byte or string
DCW		2	16-bit integer (aligned to 2 bytes)
DCD	&	4	32-bit integer (aligned to 4 bytes)
DCQ		8	64-bit integer (aligned to 4 bytes)
DCI		2 or 4	integer defining an ARM or Thumb instruction

DCB, DCD{U}, DCI, DCQ{U}, DCW{U}

These directives allocate one or more bytes of initialized memory according to Table A.18. Follow each directive with a comma-separated list of initialization values. If you specify the optional U suffix, then the assembler does not insert any alignment padding.

Examples

```
hello   DCB "hello", 0
powers  DCD 1, 2, 4, 8, 10, 0x20, 0x40, 0x80
        DCI 0xEA000000
```

ELSE (alias |)

See IF.

END

This directive must appear at the end of a source file. Assembler source after an END directive is ignored.

ENDFUNC (alias ENDP), ENDIF (alias])

See FUNCTION and IF, respectively.

ENTRY

This directive specifies the program entry point for the linker. The entry point is usually contained in the ARM C library.

EQU (alias *)

```
<name>  EQU <numeric-expression>
```

This directive is similar to #define in C. It defines a symbol <name> with value defined by the expression. This value cannot be redefined. See Section A.4.1 for the use of redefinable variables.

EXPORT (alias GLOBAL)

```
EXPORT  <symbol>{[WEAK]}
```

Assembler symbols are local to the object file unless exported using this command. You can link exported symbols with other object and library files. The optional [WEAK] suffix indicates that the linker should try and resolve references with other instances of this symbol before using this instance.

EXTERN, IMPORT

```
EXTERN  <symbol>{[WEAK]}
IMPORT  <symbol>{[WEAK]}
```

Both of these directives declare the name of an external symbol, defined in another object file or library. If you use this symbol, then the linker will resolve it at link time. For IMPORT, the symbol will be resolved even if you don't use it. For EXTERN, only used symbols are resolved. If you declare the symbol as [WEAK], then no error is generated if the linker cannot resolve the symbol; instead the symbol takes the value 0.

FIELD (alias #)

See MAP.

FUNCTION (alias PROC) and ENDFUNC (alias ENDP)

The FUNCTION and ENDFUNC directives mark the start and end of an ATPCS-compliant function. Their main use is to improve the debug view and allow backtracking of function calls during debugging. They also allow the profiler to more accurately profile assembly functions. You must precede the function directive with the ATPCS function name. For example:

```
sub     FUNCTION
        SUB     r0, r0, r1
        MOV     pc, lr
        ENDFUNC
```

GBLA, GBLL, GBLS

Directives defining global arithmetic, logic, and string variables, respectively. See Section A.4.1.

GET

See INCLUDE.

GLOBAL

See EXPORT.

IF (alias [), ELSE (alias |), ENDIF (alias])

These directives provide for conditional assembly. They are similar to #if, #else, #endif, available in C. The IF directive is followed by a logical expression. The ELSE directive may be omitted. For example:

```
IF {ARCHITECTURE}="5TE"
  SMULBB r0, r1, r1
ELSE
  MUL    r0, r1, r1
ENDIF
```

IMPORT

See EXTERN.

INCBIN

```
        INCBIN   <filename>
```

This directive includes the raw data contained in the binary file <filename> at the current point in the assembly. For example, INCBIN table.dat.

INCLUDE (alias GET)

```
        INCLUDE <filename>
```

Use this directive to include another assembly file. It is similar to the *#include* command in C. For example, INCLUDE header.h.

INFO (alias !)

```
        INFO    <numeric_expression>, <string_expression>
```

If <*numeric_expresssion*> is nonzero, then assembly terminates with error <*string_expresssion*>. Otherwise the assembler prints <*string_expression*> as an information message.

KEEP

```
KEEP    {<symbol>}
```

By default the assembler does not include local symbols in the object file, only exported symbols (see EXPORT). Use KEEP to include all local symbols or a specified local symbol. This aids the debug view.

LCLA, LCLL, LCLS

These directives declare macro-local arithmetic, logical, and string variables, respectively. See Section A.4.1.

LTORG

Use LTORG to insert a literal pool. The assembler uses literal pools to store the constants appearing in the *LDR Rd,=<value>* instruction. See LDR format 19. Usually the assembler inserts literal pools automatically, at the end of each area. However, if an area is too large, then the LDR instruction cannot reach this literal pool using *pc*-relative addressing. Then you need to insert a literal pool manually, near the LDR instruction.

MACRO, MEXIT, MEND

Use these directives to declare a new assembler macro or pseudoinstruction. The syntax is

```
           MACRO
{$<arg_0>}  <macro_name> {$<arg_1>} {,$<arg_2>} ... {,$<arg_k>}
           <macro_code>
           MEND
```

The macro parameters are stored in the dummy variables $<arg_i>. This argument is set to the empty string if you don't supply a parameter when calling the macro. The MEXIT directive terminates the macro early and is usually used inside IF statements. For example, the following macro defines a new pseudoinstruction SMUL, which evaluates to a SMULBB on an ARMv5TE processor, and an MUL otherwise.

```
        MACRO
$label  SMUL    $a, $b, $c
        IF {ARCHITECTURE}="5TE"
$label    SMULBB $a, $b, $c
          MEXIT
        ENDIF
$label  MUL     $a, $b, $c
        MEND
```

MAP (alias ^), FIELD (alias #)

These directives define objects similar to C structures. MAP sets the base address or offset of a structure, and FIELD defines structure elements. The syntax is

```
        MAP     <base> {, <base_register>}
<name>  FIELD   <field_size_in_bytes>
```

The MAP directive sets the value of the special assembler variable {VAR} to the base address of the structure. This is either the value <base> or the register relative value <base_register>+<base>. Each FIELD directive sets <name> to the value VAR and increments VAR by the specified number of bytes. For register relative values, the expressions :INDEX:<name> and :BASE:<name> return the element offset from base register, and base register number, respectively.

In practice the base register form is not that useful. Instead you can use the plain form and mention the base register explicitly in the instruction. This allows you to point to a structure of the same type with different base registers. The following example sets up a structure on the stack of two int variables:

```
        MAP     0               ; structure elements offset from 0
count   FIELD   4               ; define an int called count
type    FIELD   4               ; define an int called type
size    FIELD   0               ; record the struct size

        SUB     sp, sp, #size   ; make room on the stack
        MOV     r0, #0
        STR     r0, [sp, #count] ; clear the count element
        STR     r0, [sp, #type]  ; clear the type element
```

NOFP

This directive bans the use of floating-point instructions in the assembly file. We don't cover floating-point instructions and directives in this appendix.

OPT

The OPT directive controls the formatting of the *armasm -list* option. This is seldom used now that source-level debugging is available. See the *armasm* documentation.

PROC

See FUNCTION.

RLIST, RN

```
<name>  RN <numeric expression>
<name>  RLIST <list of ARM register enclosed in {}>
```

These directives name a list of ARM registers or a single ARM register. For example, the following code names *r0* as arg and the ATPCS preserved registers as saved.

```
arg     RN 0
saved   RLIST {r4-r11}
```

ROUT

The ROUT directive defines a new local label area. See Section A.4.2.

SETA, SETL, SETS

These directives set the values of arithmetic, logical, and string variables, respectively. See Section A.4.1.

SPACE (alias %)

```
{<label>} SPACE <numeric_expression>
```

This directive reserves <numeric_expression> bytes of space. The bytes are zero initialized.

WHILE, WEND

These directives supply an assemble-time looping structure. WHILE is followed by a logical expression. While this expression is true, the assembler repeats the code between WHILE and WEND. The following example shows how to create an array of powers of two from 1 to 65,536.

```
        GBLA    count
count   SETA    1
        WHILE   count<=65536
        DCD     count
count   SETA    2*count
        WEND
```

A.5 GNU ASSEMBLER QUICK REFERENCE

This section summarizes the more useful commands and expressions available with the GNU assembler, *gas*, when you target this assembler for ARM. Each assembly line has the format

```
{<label>:} {<instruction or directive>}        @ comment
```

Unlike the ARM assembler, you needn't indent instructions and directives. Labels are recognized by the following colon rather than their position at the start of the line. The following example shows a simple assembly file defining a function *add* that returns the sum of the two input arguments:

```
.section .text, "x"

.global  add                    @ give the symbol add external linkage

add:
        ADD     r0, r0, r1      @ add input arguments
        MOV     pc, lr          @ return from subroutine
```

A.5.1   GNU ASSEMBLER DIRECTIVES

Here is an alphabetical list of the more common *gas* directives.

.ascii "<string>"

Inserts the string as data into the assembly, as for DCB in *armasm*.

.asciz "<string>"

As for .ascii but follows the string with a zero byte.

.balign <power_of_2> {,<fill_value> {,<max_padding>} }

Aligns the address to *<power_of_2>* bytes. The assembler aligns by adding bytes of value *<fill_value>* or a suitable default. The alignment will not occur if more than *<max_padding>* fill bytes are required. Similar to ALIGN in *armasm*.

.byte <byte1> {,<byte2>} ...

Inserts a list of byte values as data into the assembly, as for DCB in *armasm*.

.code <number_of_bits>

Sets the instruction width in bits. Use 16 for Thumb and 32 for ARM assembly. Similar to CODE16 and CODE32 in *armasm*.

.else

Use with .if and .endif. Similar to ELSE in *armasm*.

.end

Marks the end of the assembly file. This is usually omitted.

.endif

Ends a conditional compilation code block. See `.if`, `.ifdef`, `.ifndef`. Similar to ENDIF in *armasm*.

.endm

Ends a macro definition. See `.macro`. Similar to MEND in *armasm*.

.endr

Ends a repeat loop. See `.rept` and `.irp`. Similar to WEND in *armasm*.

.equ <symbol name>, <value>

This directive sets the value of a symbol. It is similar to EQU in *armasm*.

.err

Causes assembly to halt with an error.

.exitm

Exit a macro partway through. See `.macro`. Similar to MEXIT in *armasm*.

.global <symbol>

This directive gives the symbol external linkage. It is similar to EXPORT in *armasm*.

.hword <short1> {,<short2>} ...

Inserts a list of 16-bit values as data into the assembly, as for DCW in *armasm*.

.if <logical_expression>

Makes a block of code conditional. End the block using `.endif`. Similar to IF in *armasm*. See also `.else`.

.ifdef <symbol>

Include a block of code if `<symbol>` is defined. End the block with `.endif`.

```
.ifndef <symbol>
```

Include a block of code if `<symbol>` is not defined. End the block with `.endif`.

```
.include "<filename>"
```

Includes the indicated source file. Similar to `INCLUDE` in *armasm* or `#include` in C.

```
.irp <param> {,<val_1>} {,<val_2>} ...
```

Repeats a block of code, once for each value in the value list. Mark the end of the block using a `.endr` directive. In the repeated code block, use `\<param>` to substitute the associated value in the value list.

```
.macro <name> {<arg_1>} {,<arg_1>} ... {,<arg_k>}
```

Defines an assembler macro called *<name>* with *k* parameters. The macro definition must end with `.endm`. To escape from the macro at an earlier point, use `.exitm`. These directives are similar to `MACRO`, `MEND`, and `MEXIT` in *armasm*. You must precede the dummy macro parameters by `\`. For example:

```
.macro SHIFTLEFT a, b
        .if \b < 0
          MOV   \a, \a, ASR #-\b
          .exitm
        .endif
        MOV \a, \a, LSL #\b
.endm
```

```
.rept <number_of_times>
```

Repeats a block of code the given number of times. End the block with `.endr`.

```
<register_name> .req <register_name>
```

This directive names a register. It is similar to the RN directive in *armasm* except that you must supply a name rather than a number on the right. For example, *acc .req r0*.

```
.section <section_name> {,"<flags>"}
```

Starts a new code or data section. Usually you should call a code section `.text`, an initialized data section `.data`, and an uninitialized data section `.bss` . These have default flags, and the linker understands these default names. The directive is similar to the *armasm*

Table A.19   `.section` flags for ELF format files.

Flag	Meaning
a	allocatable section
w	writable section
x	executable section

directive AREA. Table A.19 lists possible characters to appear in the `<flags>` string for ELF format files.

`.set <variable_name>, <variable_value>`

This directive sets the value of a variable. It is similar to SETA in *armasm*.

`.space <number_of_bytes> {,<fill_byte>}`

Reserves the given number of bytes. The bytes are filled with zero or `<fill_byte>` if specified. It is similar to SPACE in *armasm*.

`.word <word1> {,<word2>} ...`

Inserts a list of 32-bit word values as data into the assembly, as for DCD in *armasm*.

ARM AND THUMB INSTRUCTION ENCODINGS

This appendix gives tables for the instruction set encodings of the 32-bit ARM and 16-bit Thumb instruction sets. We also describe the fields of the processor status registers *cpsr* and *spsr*.

B.1 ARM INSTRUCTION SET ENCODINGS

Table B.1 summarizes the bit encodings for the 32-bit ARM instruction set architecture ARMv6. This table is useful if you need to decode an ARM instruction by hand. We've expanded the table to aid quick manual decode. Any bitmaps not listed are either unpredictable or undefined for ARMv6.

To use Table B.1 efficiently, follow this decoding procedure:

- Look at the leading hex digit of the instruction, bits 28 to 31. If this has a value 0xF, then jump to the end of Table B.1. Otherwise, the top hex digit represents a condition *cond*. Decode *cond* using Table B.2.
- Index through Table B.1 using the second hex digit, bits 24 to 27 (shaded).
- Index using bit 4, then bit 7 or bit 23 of the instruction where these bits are shaded.
- Once you have located the correct table entry, look at the bits named *op*. Concatenate these to form a binary number that indexes the I separated instruction list on the left.

For example if there are two *op* bits value 1 and 0, then the binary value 10 indicates instruction number 2 in the list (the third instruction).

- The instruction operands have the same name as in the instruction description of Appendix A.

The table uses the following abbreviations:

- *L* is 1 if the L suffix applies for LDC and STC operations.
- *M* is 1 if CPS changes processor mode. *mode* is defined in Table B.3.
- *op1* and *op2* are the opcode extension fields in coprocessor instructions.
- *post* indicates a postindexed addressing mode such as [Rn], Rm or [Rn], #immed.
- *pre* indicates a preindexed addressing mode such as [Rn, Rm] or [Rn, #immed].
- *register_list* is a bit field with bit *k* set if register *Rk* appears in the register list.
- *rot* is a byte rotate. The second operand is Rm ROR (8*rot).
- *rotate* is a bit rotate. The second operand is #immed ROR (2*rotate).
- *shift* and *sh* encode a shift type and direction. See Table B.4.
- *U* is the up/down select for addressing modes. If $U = 1$, then we add the offset to the base address, as in [Rn], #4 or [Rn, Rm]. If $U = 0$, then we subtract the offset from the base address, as in [Rn, #-4] or [Rn], -Rm.
- *unindexed* indicates an addressing mode of the form [Rn], {option}.
- *R* is 1 if the R (round) instruction suffix is present.
- *T* is 1 if the T suffix is present on load and store instructions.
- *W* is 1 if ! (writeback) is specified in the instruction mnemonic.
- *X* is 1 if the X (exchange) instruction suffix is present.
- *x* and *y* are 0 for the B suffix, 1 for the T suffix.
- ^ is 1 if the ^ suffix is applied in LDM or STM instructions.

B.2 THUMB INSTRUCTION SET ENCODINGS

Table B.5 summarizes the bit encodings for the 16-bit Thumb instruction set. This table is useful if you need to decode a Thumb instruction by hand. We've expanded the table to aid quick manual decode. The table contains instruction definitions up to architecture THUMBv3. Any bitmaps not listed are either unpredictable or undefined for THUMBv3.

Table B.1 ARM instruction decode table.

Instruction classes (indexed by *op*)	31–28	27–25	24–20	19–16	15–12	11–8	7	6–5	4	3–0
AND | EOR | SUB | RSB | ADD | ADC | SBC | RSC	cond	0 0 0	op S	Rn	Rd	shift_size		shift	0	Rm
AND | EOR | SUB | RSB | ADD | ADC | SBC | RSC	cond	0 0 0	op S	Rn	Rd	Rs	0	shift	1	Rm
MUL	cond	0 0 0	0 0 0 0 S	Rd	0 0 0 0	Rs	1	0 0	1	Rm
MLA	cond	0 0 0	0 0 0 1 S	Rd	Rn	Rs	1	0 0	1	Rm
UMAAL	cond	0 0 0	0 0 1 0 0	RdHi	RdLo	Rs	1	0 0	1	Rm
UMULL | UMLAL | SMULL | SMLAL	cond	0 0 0	0 1 op S	RdHi	RdLo	Rs	1	0 0	1	Rm
STRH | LDRH *post*	cond	0 0 0	0 U 0 0 op	Rn	Rd	0 0 0 0	1	0 1	1	Rm
STRH | LDRH *post*	cond	0 0 0	0 U 1 0 op	Rn	Rd	immed[7:4]	1	0 1	1	immed[3:0]
LDRD | STRD | LDRSB | LDRSH *post*	cond	0 0 0	0 U 0 0 op	Rn	Rd	0 0 0 0	1	1 op	1	Rm
LDRD | STRD | LDRSB | LDRSH *post*	cond	0 0 0	0 U 1 0 op	Rn	Rd	immed[7:4]	1	1 op	1	immed[3:0]
MRS Rd, cpsr | MRS Rd, spsr	cond	0 0 0	1 0 op 0 0	1 1 1 1	Rd	0 0 0 0	0	0 0	0	0 0 0 0
MSR cpsr, Rm | MSR spsr, Rm	cond	0 0 0	1 0 op 1 0	f s x c	1 1 1 1	0 0 0 0	0	0 0	0	Rm
BXJ	cond	0 0 0	1 0 0 1 0	1 1 1 1	1 1 1 1	1 1 1 1	0	0 1	0	Rm
SMLAxy	cond	0 0 0	1 0 0 0 0	Rd	Rn	Rs	1	y x	0	Rm
SMLAWy	cond	0 0 0	1 0 0 1 0	Rd	Rn	Rs	1	y 0	0	Rm
SMULWy	cond	0 0 0	1 0 0 1 0	Rd	0 0 0 0	Rs	1	y 1	0	Rm
SMLALxy	cond	0 0 0	1 0 1 0 0	RdHi	RdLo	Rs	1	y x	0	Rm
SMULxy	cond	0 0 0	1 0 1 1 0	Rd	0 0 0 0	Rs	1	y x	0	Rm
TST | TEQ | CMP | CMN	cond	0 0 0	1 0 op 1	Rn	0 0 0 0	shift_size		shift	0	Rm
ORR | BIC	cond	0 0 0	1 1 op 0 S	Rn	Rd	shift_size		shift	0	Rm
MOV | MVN	cond	0 0 0	1 1 op 1 S	0 0 0 0	Rd	shift_size		shift	0	Rm
BX | BLX	cond	0 0 0	1 0 0 1 0	1 1 1 1	1 1 1 1	1 1 1 1	0	0 op	1	Rm
CLZ	cond	0 0 0	1 0 1 1 0	1 1 1 1	Rd	1 1 1 1	0	0 0	1	Rm
QADD | QSUB | QDADD | QDSUB	cond	0 0 0	1 0 op 0	Rn	Rd	0 0 0 0	0	1 0	1	Rm
BKPT	1 1 1 0	0 0 0	1 0 0 1 0	immed[15:4]			0	1 1	1	immed[3:0]
TST | TEQ | CMP | CMN	cond	0 0 0	1 0 op 1	Rn	0 0 0 0	Rs	0	shift	1	Rm
ORR | BIC	cond	0 0 0	1 1 op 0 S	Rn	Rd	Rs	0	shift	1	Rm
MOV | MVN	cond	0 0 0	1 1 op 1 S	0 0 0 0	Rd	Rs	0	shift	1	Rm
SWP | SWPB	cond	0 0 0	1 0 op 0 0	Rn	Rd	0 0 0 0	1	0 0	1	Rm
STREX	cond	0 0 0	1 1 0 0 0	Rn	Rd	1 1 1 1	1	0 0	1	Rm
LDREX	cond	0 0 0	1 1 0 0 1	Rn	Rd	1 1 1 1	1	0 0	1	1 1 1 1

Table B.1   ARM instruction decode table. (*Continued.*)

Instruction classes (indexed by *op*)	31–28	27	26	25	24	23	22	21	20	19–16	15–12	11	10	9	8	7	6	5	4	3–0
STRH | LDRH *pre*	cond	0	0	0	1	U	0	W	op	Rn	Rd	0	0	0	0	1	0	1	1	Rm
STRH | LDRH *pre*	cond	0	0	0	1	U	1	W	op	Rn	Rd	immed [7:4]				1	0	1	1	immed [3:0]
LDRD | STRD | LDRSB | LCRSH *pre*	cond	0	0	0	1	U	0	W	op	Rn	Rd	0	0	0	0	1	1	op	1	Rm
LDRD | STRD | LDRSB | LCRSH *pre*	cond	0	0	0	1	U	1	W	op	Rn	Rd	immed [7:4]				1	1	op	1	immed [3:0]
AND | EOR | SUB | RSB | ADD | ADC | SBC | RSC	cond	0	0	1	0	op			S	Rn	Rd	rotate				immed				
MSR cpsr, #imm | MSR spsr, #imm	cond	0	0	1	1	0	op	1	0	f s x c	1 1 1 1	rotate				immed				
TST | TEQ | CMP | CMN	cond	0	0	1	1	0	op		1	Rn	0 0 0 0	rotate				immed				
ORR | BIC	cond	0	0	1	1	1	op	0	S	Rn	Rd	rotate				immed				
MOV | MVN	cond	0	0	1	1	1	op	1	S	0 0 0 0	Rd	rotate				immed				
STR | LDR | STRB | LDRB *post*	cond	0	1	0	0	U	op	T	op	Rn	Rd	immed12								
STR | LDR | STRB | LDRB *pre*	cond	0	1	0	1	U	op	W	op	Rn	Rd	immed12								
STR | LDR | STRB | LDRB *post*	cond	0	1	1	0	U	op	T	op	Rn	Rd	shift_size					shift		0	Rm
{S|Q|SH|U|UQ|UH}ADD16	cond	0	1	1	0	0	op			Rn	Rd	1	1	1	1	0	0	0	1	Rm
{S|Q|SH|U|UQ|UH}ADDSUBX	cond	0	1	1	0	0	op			Rn	Rd	1	1	1	1	0	0	1	1	Rm
{S|Q|SH|U|UQ|UH}SUBADDX	cond	0	1	1	0	0	op			Rn	Rd	1	1	1	1	0	1	0	1	Rm
{S|Q|SH|U|UQ|UH}SUB16	cond	0	1	1	0	0	op			Rn	Rd	1	1	1	1	0	1	1	1	Rm
{S|Q|SH|U|UQ|UH}ADD8	cond	0	1	1	0	0	op			Rn	Rd	1	1	1	1	1	0	0	1	Rm
{S|Q|SH|U|UQ|UH}SUB8	cond	0	1	1	0	0	op			Rn	Rd	1	1	1	1	1	1	1	1	Rm
PKHBT | PKHTB	cond	0	1	1	0	1	0	0	0	Rn	Rd	shift_size					op	0	1	Rm
{S|U}SAT	cond	0	1	1	0	1	op	1	immed5		Rd	shift_size					sh	0	1	Rm
{S|U}SAT16	cond	0	1	1	0	1	op	1	0	immed4	Rd	1	1	1	1	0	0	1	1	Rm
SEL	cond	0	1	1	0	1	0	0	0	Rn	Rd	1	1	1	1	1	0	1	1	Rm
REV | REV16 | REVSH	cond	0	1	1	0	1	op	1	1	1 1 1 1	Rd	1	1	1	1	op	0	1	1	Rm
{S|U}XTAB16	cond	0	1	1	0	1	op	0	0	Rn!=1111	Rd	rot		0	0	0	1	1	1	Rm
{S|U}XTB16	cond	0	1	1	0	1	op	0	0	1 1 1 1	Rd	rot		0	0	0	1	1	1	Rm
{S|U}XTAB	cond	0	1	1	0	1	op	1	0	Rn!=1111	Rd	rot		0	0	0	1	1	1	Rm
{S|U}XTB	cond	0	1	1	0	1	op	1	0	1 1 1 1	Rd	rot		0	0	0	1	1	1	Rm
{S|U}XTAH	cond	0	1	1	0	1	op	1	1	Rn!=1111	Rd	rot		0	0	0	1	1	1	Rm
{S|U}XTH	cond	0	1	1	0	1	op	1	1	1 1 1 1	Rd	rot		0	0	0	1	1	1	Rm
STR | LDR | STRB | LDRB *pre*	cond	0	1	1	1	U	op	W	op	Rn	Rd	shift_size					shift		0	Rm
SMLAD | SMLSD	cond	0	1	1	1	0	0	0	0	Rd	Rn!=1111	Rs				0	op	X	1	Rm
SMUAD | SMUSD	cond	0	1	1	1	0	0	0	0	Rd	1 1 1 1	Rs				0	op	X	1	Rm
SMLALD | SMLSLD	cond	0	1	1	1	0	1	0	0	RdHi	RdLo	Rs				0	op	X	1	Rm

Table B.1   ARM instruction decode table. (Continued.)

Instruction classes (indexed by *op*)	31 30 29 28	27 26 25	24 23 22 21 20	19 18 17 16	15 14 13 12	11 10 9 8	7 6 5 4	3 2 1 0
SMMLA | | | SMMLS	cond	0 1 1	1 0 1 0 1	Rd	Rn!=1111	Rs	op R 1	Rm
SMMUL	cond	0 1 1	1 0 1 0 1	Rd	1 1 1 1	Rs	0 0 R 1	Rm
USADA8	cond	0 1 1	1 1 0 0 0	Rd	Rn!=1111	Rs	0 0 0 1	Rm
USAD8	cond	0 1 1	1 1 0 0 0	Rd	1 1 1 1	Rs	0 0 0 1	Rm
Undefined and expected to stay so	cond	0 1 1	1 1 1 x x	x			1 1 1 1	x
STMDA | STMIA | LDMDA | LDMIA	cond	1 0 0	op 0 0 W op	Rn	register_list			
STMDB | STMIB | LDMDB | LDMIB	cond	1 0 0	op 0 1 W op	Rn	register_list			
B to instruction_address+8+4*offset	cond	1 0 1	0	signed 24-bit branch offset				
BL to instruction_address+8+4*offset	cond	1 0 1	1	signed 24-bit branch offset				
MCRR | MRRC	cond	1 1 0	0 0 1 0 op	Rn	Rd	copro	op1	Cm
STC{L} | LDC{L} *unindexed*	cond	1 1 0	0 1 L 0 op	Rn	Cd	copro	option	
STC{L} | LDC{L} *post*	cond	1 1 0	0 U L 1 op	Rn	Cd	copro	immed8	
STC{L} | LDC{L} *pre*	cond	1 1 0	1 U L 1 op	Rn	Cd	copro	immed8	
CDP	cond	1 1 1	0 op1	Cn	Cd	copro	op2 0	Cm
MCR | MRC	cond	1 1 1	0 op1 op	Cn	Rd	copro	op2 1	Cm
SWI	cond	1 1 1	1	immed24				
CPS | | CPSIE | CPSID	1 1 1 1	0 0 0	1 0 0 0 0	op M 0	0 0 0 0	0 a i f 0		mode
SETEND LE | SETEND BE	1 1 1 1	0 0 0	1 0 0 0 0	0 0 0 1	0 0 op 0	0 0 0 0	0 0 0 0	
PLD *pre*	1 1 1 1	0 1 0	1 U 1 0 1	Rn	1 1 1 1	immed12		
PLD *pre*	1 1 1 1	0 1 1	1 U 1 0 1	Rn	1 1 1 1	shift_size	shift 0	Rm
RFEDA | RFEIA | RFEDB | RFEIB	1 1 1 1	1 0 0	op op 0 W 1	Rn	0 0 0 0	1 0 1 0	0 0 0 0	0 0 0 0
SRSDA | SRSIA | SRSDB | SRSIB	1 1 1 1	1 0 0	op op 1 W 0	1 1 0 1	0 0 0 0	1 0 1 0	0 0 0	mode
BLX instruction+8+4*offset+2*a	1 1 1 1	1 0 1	a	signed 24-bit branch offset				
MCRR2 | MRRC2	1 1 1 1	1 1 0	0 0 1 0 op	Rn	Rd	copro	op1	Cm
STC2{L} | LDC2{L} *unindexed*	1 1 1 1	1 1 0	0 1 L 0 op	Rn	Cd	copro	option	
STC2{L} | LDC2{L} *post*	1 1 1 1	1 1 0	0 U L 1 op	Rn	Cd	copro	immed8	
STC2{L} | LDC2{L} *pre*	1 1 1 1	1 1 0	1 U L 1 op	Rn	Cd	copro	immed8	
CDP2	1 1 1 1	1 1 1	0 op1	Cn	Cd	copro	op2 0	Cm
MCR2 | MRC2	1 1 1 1	1 1 1	0 op1 op	Cn	Cd	copro	op2 1	Cm

Table B.2   Decoding table for *cond*.

Binary	Hex	*cond*	Binary	Hex	*cond*
0000	0	EQ	1000	8	HI
0001	1	NE	1001	9	LS
0010	2	CS/HS	1010	A	GE
0011	3	CC/LO	1011	B	LT
0100	4	MI	1100	C	GT
0101	5	PL	1101	D	LE
0110	6	VS	1110	E	{AL}
0111	7	VC			

Table B.3   Decoding table for *mode*.

Binary	Hex	*mode*
10000	0x10	*user* mode (_usr)
10001	0x11	*FIQ* mode (_fiq)
10010	0x12	*IRQ* mode (_irq)
10011	0x13	*supervisor* mode (_svc)
10111	0x17	*abort* mode (_abt)
11011	0x1B	*undefined* mode (_und)
11111	0x1F	*system* mode

Table B.4   Decoding table for *shift*, *shift_size*, and *Rs*.

shift	*shift_size*	*Rs*	Shift action
00	0 to 31	N/A	LSL #shift_size
00	N/A	*Rs*	LSL Rs
01	0	N/A	LSR #32
01	1 to 31	N/A	LSR #shift_size
01	N/A	*Rs*	LSR Rs
10	0	N/A	ASR #32
10	1 to 31	N/A	ASR #shift_size
10	N/A	*Rs*	ASR Rs
11	0	N/A	RRX
11	1 to 31	N/A	ROR #shift_size
11	N/A	*Rs*	ROR Rs
N/A	0 to 31	N/A	The *shift* value is implicit: For PKHBT it is 00. For PKHTB it is 10. For SAT it is 2*sh.

To use the table efficiently, follow this decoding procedure:

- Index through the table using the first hex digit of the instruction, bits 12 to 15 (shaded).
- Index on any shaded bits from bits 0 to 11.
- Once you have located the correct table entry, look at the bits named *op*. Concatenate these to form a binary number that indexes the | separated instruction list on the left. For example, if there are two *op* bits value 1 and 0, then the binary value 10 indicates instruction number 2 in the list (the third instruction).
- The instruction operands have the same name as in the instruction description of Appendix A.

The table uses the following abbreviations:

- *register_list* is a bit field with bit *k* set if register *Rk* appears in the register list.
- *R* is 1 if *lr* is in the register list of PUSH or *pc* is in the register list of POP.

Table B.5   Thumb instruction decode table.

Instruction classes (indexed by *op*)	15	14	13	12	11	10	9	8	7	6	5	4	3	2	1	0
LSL | LSR	0	0	0	0	op	shift_size					Lm			Ld		
ASR	0	0	0	1	0	shift_size					Lm			Ld		
ADD | SUB	0	0	0	1	1	0	op	Lm			Ln			Ld		
ADD | SUB	0	0	0	1	1	1	op	immed3			Ln			Ld		
MOV | CMP	0	0	1	0	op	Ld/Ln			immed8							
ADD | SUB	0	0	1	1	op	Ld			immed8							
AND | EOR | LSL | LSR	0	1	0	0	0	0	0	0	op		Lm/Ls			Ld		
ASR | ADC | SBC | ROR	0	1	0	0	0	0	0	1	op		Lm/Ls			Ld		
TST | NEG | CMP | CMN	0	1	0	0	0	0	1	0	op		Lm			Ld/Ln		
ORR | MUL | BIC | MVN	0	1	0	0	0	0	1	1	op		Lm			Ld		
CPY Ld, Lm	0	1	0	0	0	1	1	0	0	0	Lm			Ld		
ADD | MOV Ld, Hm	0	1	0	0	0	1	op	0	0	1	Hm & 7			Ld		
ADD | MOV Hd, Lm	0	1	0	0	0	1	op	0	1	0	Lm			Hd & 7		
ADD | MOV Hd, Hm	0	1	0	0	0	1	op	0	1	1	Hm & 7			Hd & 7		
CMP	0	1	0	0	0	1	0	1	0	1	Hm & 7			Ln		
CMP	0	1	0	0	0	1	0	1	1	0	Lm			Hn & 7		
CMP	0	1	0	0	0	1	0	1	1	1	Hm & 7			Hn & 7		
BX | BLX	0	1	0	0	0	1	1	1	op		Rm			0	0	0
LDR Ld, [pc, #immed*4]	0	1	0	0	1	Ld			immed8							
STR | STRH | STRB | LDRSB *pre*	0	1	0	1	0	op		Lm			Ln			Ld		
LDR | LDRH | LDRB | LDRSH *pre*	0	1	0	1	1	op		Lm			Ln			Ld		
STR | LDR Ld, [Ln, #immed*4]	0	1	1	0	op	immed5					Ln			Ld		
STRB | LDRB Ld, [Ln, #immed]	0	1	1	1	op	immed5					Ln			Ld		
STRH | LDRH Ld, [Ln, #immed*2]	1	0	0	0	op	immed5					Ln			Ld		

Table B.5 Thumb instruction decode table. (*Continued.*)

Instruction classes (indexed by *op*)	15	14	13	12	11	10	9	8	7	6	5	4	3	2	1	0
STR | LDR Ld, [sp, #immed*4]	1	0	0	1	*op*		*Ld*					*immed8*				
ADD Ld, pc, #immed*4 | ADD Ld, sp, #immed*4	1	0	1	0	*op*		*Ld*					*immed8*				
ADD sp, #immed*4 | SUB sp, #immed*4	1	0	1	1	0	0	0	0	*op*				*immed7*			
SXTH | SXTB | UXTH | UXTB	1	0	1	1	0	0	1	0	*op*			*Lm*			*Ld*	
REV | REV16 | | REVSH	1	0	1	1	1	0	1	0	*op*			*Lm*			*Ld*	
PUSH | POP	1	0	1	1	*op*	1	0	*R*				*register_list*				
SETEND LE | SETEND BE	1	0	1	1	0	1	1	0	0	1	0	1	*op*	0	0	0
CPSIE | CPSID	1	0	1	1	0	1	1	0	0	1	1	*op*	0	*a*	*i*	*f*
BKPT immed8	1	0	1	1	1	1	1	0				*immed8*				
STMIA | LDMIA Ln!, {register-list}	1	1	0	0	*op*		*Ln*					*register_list*				
B<cond> instruction_address+ 4+offset*2	1	1	0	1	*cond* < 1110				signed 8-bit offset							
Undefined and expected to remain so	1	1	0	1	1	1	1	0				*x*				
SWI immed8	1	1	0	1	1	1	1	1				*immed8*				
B instruction_address+4+offset*2	1	1	1	0	0				signed 11-bit *offset*							
BLX ((instruction+4+ (poff<<12)+offset*4) &~ 3) This must be preceded by a branch prefix instruction.	1	1	1	0	1				unsigned 10-bit *offset*							0
This is the branch prefix instruction. It must be followed by a relative BL or BLX instruction.	1	1	1	1	0				signed 11-bit prefix offset *poff*							
BL instruction+4+ (poff<<12)+ offset*2 This must be preceded by a branch prefix instruction.	1	1	1	1	1				unsigned 11-bit *offset*							

B.3 Program Status Registers

Table B.6 shows how to decode the 32-bit program status registers for ARMv6.

Table B.6   *cpsr* and *spsr* decode table.

31	30	29	28	27	26 25	24	23 22 21 20	19 18 17 16	15 14 13 12 11 10 9	8	7	6	5	4 3 2 1 0
N	Z	C	V	Q	Res	J	Res	GE[3:0]	Res	E	A	I	F T	mode

Field	Use
N	Negative flag, records bit 31 of the result of flag-setting operations.
Z	Zero flag, records if the result of a flag-setting operation is zero.
C	Carry flag, records unsigned overflow for addition, not-borrow for subtraction, and is also used by the shifting circuit. See Table A.3.
V	Overflow flag, records signed overflows for flag-setting operations.
Q	Saturation flag. Certain operations set this flag on saturation. See for example QADD in Appendix A (ARMv5E and above).
J	$J = 1$ indicates Java execution (must have $T = 0$). Use the BXJ instruction to change this bit (ARMv5J and above).
Res	These bits are reserved for future expansion. Software should preserve the values in these bits.
GE[3:0]	The SIMD greater-or-equal flags. See SADD in Appendix A (ARMv6).
E	Controls the data endianness. See SETEND in Appendix A (ARMv6).
A	$A = 1$ disables imprecise data aborts (ARMv6).
I	$I = 1$ disables IRQ interrupts.
F	$F = 1$ disables FIQ interrupts.
T	$T = 1$ indicates Thumb state. $T = 0$ indicates ARM state. Use the BX or BLX instructions to change this bit (ARMv4T and above).
mode	The current processor mode. See Table B.4.

A P P E N D I X C

PROCESSORS AND ARCHITECTURE

This appendix lists ARM processor names together with their core name and Instruction Set Architecture (ISA). We have omitted processors designed prior to the ARM7TDMI.

For example, Table C.3 shows that the ARM966E-S processor has a ARM9E core and implements ARM architecture version 5TE. Any ARMv5TE binaries will execute on an ARM966E-S processor.

C.1 ARM NAMING CONVENTION

All ARM processors share a common naming convention that has evolved over time. ARM cores have the name ARM{x}{*labels*}, where x is the number of the core and *labels* are letters representing extra features, described in Table C.1. ARM processors have the name ARM{x}{y}{z}{*labels*}, where y and z are numbers defining the processor cache size and memory management model. Table C.2 lists the rules for ARM processor numbering.

The labels, or attributes, are often subsumed into the architecture version over time. For example, the T label indicates the inclusion of Thumb in ARMv4 processors. However, Thumb is included in ARMv5 and later processors, so it is not necessary to specify the T after this point.

C.2 CORE AND ARCHITECTURES

Table C.3 shows each ARM processor together with the core and architecture versions that the processor uses.

Table C.1   Label attributes.

Attribute	Description
D	The ARM core supports debug via the JTAG interface. The *D* is automatic for ARMv5 and above.
E	The ARM core supports the Enhanced DSP instruction additions to ARMv5. The *E* is automatic for ARMv6 and above.
F	The ARM core supports hardware floating point via the Vector Floating Point (VFP) architecture.
I	The ARM core supports hardware breakpoints and watchpoints via the EmbeddedICE cell. The *I* is automatic for ARMv5 and above.
J	The ARM core supports the Jazelle Java acceleration architecture.
M	The ARM core supports the long multiply instructions for ARMv3. The *M* is automatic for ARMv4 and above.
-S	The ARM processor uses a synthesizable hardware design.
T	The ARM core supports the Thumb instruction set for ARMv4 and above. The *T* is automatic for ARMv6 and above.

Table C.2   ARM processor numbering: ARM$\{x\}\{y\}\{z\}$.

x	y	z	Description	Example
7	*	*	ARM7 processor core	ARM7TDMI
9	*	*	ARM9 processor core	ARM926EJ-S
10	*	*	ARM10 processor core	ARM1026EJ-S
11	*	*	ARM11 processor core	ARM1136J S
*	2	*	cache and MMU	ARM920T
*	3	*	cache and MMU with physical address tagging	ARM1136J-S
*	4	*	cache and an MPU	ARM946E-S
*	6	*	write buffer but no cache(s)	ARM966E-S
*	*	0	standard cache size	ARM920T
*	*	2	reduced cache size	ARM922T
*	*	6	includes tightly coupled SRAM memory (TCM)	ARM946E-S

Table C.3   Processors, cores, and architecture versions.

Processor product	Processor core	ARM ISA	Thumb ISA	VFP ISA
ARM7TDMI	ARM7TDMI	v4T	v1	
ARM7TDMI-S	ARM7TDMI-S	v4T	v1	
ARM7EJ-S	ARM7EJ	v5TEJ	v2	
ARM740T	ARM7TDMI	v4T	v1	
ARM720T	ARM7TDMI	v4T	v1	
ARM920T	ARM9TDMI	v4T	v1	
ARM922T	ARM9TDMI	v4T	v1	
ARM940T	ARM9TDMI	v4T	v1	
Intel SA-110	StrongARM1	v4		
ARM926EJ-S	ARM9EJ	v5TEJ	v2	
ARM946E-S	ARM9E	v5TE	v2	
ARM966E-S	ARM9E	v5TE	v2	
ARM1020E	ARM10E	v5TE	v2	
ARM1022E	ARM10E	v5TE	v2	
ARM1026EJ-S	ARM10EJ	v5TEJ	v2	
Intel XScale™	XScale	v5TE	v2	
ARM1136J-S	ARM11	v6J	v3	
ARM1136JF-S	ARM11	v6J	v3	v2

APPENDIX D

INSTRUCTION CYCLE TIMINGS

This appendix lists the instruction cycle timings for some common ARM implementions. Timings can vary between different revisions of an implementation and are also affected by external events such as interrupts, memory speed, and cache misses. You should treat these numbers as a guide only and verify performance measurements on real hardware. Refer to the manufacturer's data sheets for the latest timing information.

ARM cores use pipelined implementations. The number of cycles that an instruction takes may depend on the previous and following instructions. When you optimize code, you need to be aware of these interactions, described in the "Notes" column of the timing tables.

D.1 USING THE INSTRUCTION CYCLE TIMING TABLES

Use the following steps to calculate the number of cycles taken by an instruction:

- Use Table C.3 in Appendix C to find which ARM core you are using. For example, ARM7xx parts usually contain an ARM7TDMI core; ARM9xx parts, an ARM9TDMI core; and ARM9xxE, parts an ARM9E core.

- Find the table in this appendix for the ARM core you are using.

- Find the relevant instruction class in the left-hand column of the table. The class "ALU" is shorthand for all of the arithmetic and logical instructions: ADD, ADC, SUB, RSB, SBC, RSC, AND, ORR, BIC, EOR, CMP, CMN, TEQ, TST, MOV, MVN, CLZ.

651

Table D.1   Standard cycle abbreviations.

Abbreviation	Meaning
B	The number of busy-wait cycles issued by a coprocessor. This depends on the coprocessor design.
M	The number of multiplier iteration cycles. This depends on the value in register *Rs*. Each implementation section contains a table showing how to calculate *M* from *Rs* for that implementation.
N	The number of words to transfer in a load or store multiple. This includes *pc* if it is in the register list. *N* must be at least one.

- Read the value in the "Cycles" column. This is the number of cycles the instruction usually takes, assuming the instruction passes its condition codes and there are no interactions with other instructions. The cycle count may depend on one of the abbreviations in Table D.1.

- If the "Notes" column contains any notes of the form +*k* *if condition*, then add on to your cycle count all the additions that apply.

- Look for interlock conditions that will cause the processor to stall. These are occasions where an instruction attempts to use the result of a previous instruction before it is ready. Unless otherwise stated, input registers are required on the first cycle of the instruction and output results are available at the end of the last cycle of the instruction. However, implementations with multiple execute stage pipelines can require input operands early and produce output operands later. Table D.2 defines the statements we use in the "Notes" sections to describe this.

- If your instruction fails its condition codes, then it is not executed. Usually this costs one cycle. However, on some implementations, instructions may cost multiple cycles even if they are not executed. Look for a note of the form "[*k* cycles if not executed]."

Table D.2   Pipeline behavior statements.

Statement	Meaning
Rd is not available for *k* cycles.	The result register *Rd* of the instruction is not available as the input to another instruction for *k* cycles after the end of the instruction. If you attempt to use *Rd* earlier, then the core will stall until the *k* cycles have elapsed.
Rn is required *k* cycles early.	The input register *Rn* of the instruction must be available *k* cycles before the start of the instruction. If it was the result of a later operation, then the core will stall until this condition is met.
Rn is not required until the *k*th cycle.	The input register *Rn* is not read on the first cycle of the instruction. Instead it is read on the *k*th cycle of the instruction. Therefore the core will not stall if *Rn* is available by this point.
You cannot start a type *X* instruction for *k* cycles.	The instruction uses a resource also used by type X instructions. Moreover the instruction continues to use this resource for *k* cycles after the last cycle of the instruction. If you attempt to execute a type *X* instruction before *k* cycles have elapsed, then the core will stall until *k* cycles have elapsed.

D.2 ARM7TDMI INSTRUCTION CYCLE TIMINGS

The ARM7TDMI core is based on a three-stage pipeline with a single execute stage. The number of cycles an instruction takes does not usually depend on preceding or following instructions. The multiplier circuit uses a 32-bit by 8-bit multiplier array with early termination. The number of multiply iteration cycles M depends on the value of register Rs according to Table D.3. Table D.4 gives the ARM7TDMI instruction cycle timings.

Table D.3   ARM7TDMI multiplier early termination.

M	Rs range (use the first applicable range)	Rs bitmap s = sign bit x = wildcard-bit
1	$-2^8 \leq x < 2^8$	SSSSSSSS SSSSSSSS SSSSSSSS XXXXXXXX
2	$-2^{16} \leq x < 2^{16}$	SSSSSSSS SSSSSSSS XXXXXXXX XXXXXXXX
3	$-2^{24} \leq x < 2^{24}$	SSSSSSSS XXXXXXXX XXXXXXXX XXXXXXXX
4	remaining x	XXXXXXXX XXXXXXXX XXXXXXXX XXXXXXXX

Table D.4   ARM7TDMI (ARMv4T) instruction cycle timings.

Instruction class	Cycles	Notes
ALU	1	+1 if you use a register-specified shift *Rs*. +2 if *Rd* is *pc*.
B, BL, BX	3	
CDP	$1 + B$	
LDC	$1 + B + N$	
LDR/B/H/SB/SH	3	+2 if *Rd* is *pc*.
LDM	$2 + N$	+2 if *pc* is in the register list.
MCR	$2 + B$	
MLA	$2 + M$	
xMLAL	$3 + M$	
MRC	$3 + B$	
MRS, MSR	1	
MUL	$1 + M$	
xMULL	$2 + M$	
STC	$1 + B + N$	
STR/B/H	2	
STM	$1 + N$	
SWI	3	
SWP/B	4	

D.3   ARM9TDMI INSTRUCTION CYCLE TIMINGS

The ARM9TDMI core is based on a five-stage pipeline with a single execute stage and two memory fetch stages. There is usually a one- or two-cycle delay following a load instruction before you can use the data. Using data immediately after a load will add interlock cycles. The multiplier circuit uses a 32-bit by 8-bit multiplier array with early termination. The number of multiply iteration cycles M depends on the value of register *Rs* according to Table D.5. Table D.6 gives the ARM9TDMI instruction cycle timings.

Table D.5   ARM9TDMI multiplier early termination.

M	*Rs* range (use the first applicable range)	Rs bitmap s = sign bit x = wildcard-bit			
1	$-2^8 \le x < 2^8$	ssssssss	ssssssss	ssssssss	xxxxxxxx
2	$-2^{16} \le x < 2^{16}$	ssssssss	ssssssss	xxxxxxxx	xxxxxxxx
3	$-2^{24} \le x < 2^{24}$	ssssssss	xxxxxxxx	xxxxxxxx	xxxxxxxx
4	remaining x	xxxxxxxx	xxxxxxxx	xxxxxxxx	xxxxxxxx

Table D.6   ARM9TDMI (ARMv4T) instruction cycle timings.

Instruction class	Cycles	Notes
ALU	1	+1 if a register-specified shift Rs is used. +2 if Rd is pc.
B, BL, BX	3	
CDP	$1 + B$	
LDC	$B + N$	
LDRB/H/SB/SH	1	Rd is not available for two cycles.
LDR Rd not pc	1	Rd is not available for one cycle.
LDR Rd is pc	5	
LDM not loading pc	N	+1 if $N = 1$ or the last loaded register used in the next cycle.
LDM loading pc	$N + 4$	
MCR	$1 + B$	
MRC Rd not pc	$1 + B$	Rd is not available for one cycle.
MRC Rd is pc	$3 + B$	
MRS	1	
MSR	1	+2 if any of the csx fields are updated.
MUL, MLA	$2 + M$	
xMULL, xMLAL	$3 + M$	
STC	$B + N$	
STR/B/H	1	
STM	N	+1 if $N = 1$.
SWI	3	
SWP/B	2	Rd is not available for one cycle.

D.4 STRONGARM1 INSTRUCTION CYCLE TIMINGS

The StrongARM1 core is based on a five-stage pipeline. There is usually a one-cycle delay following a load or multiply instruction before you can use the data. Additionally, there is often a one-cycle delay if you start a new multiply instruction immediately following a previous multiply instruction. The multiplier circuit uses a 32-bit by 12-bit multiplier array with early termination. The number of multiply iteration cycles M depends on the value of register Rs according to Table D.7. Table D.8 gives the StrongARM1 instruction cycle timings.

Table D.7   StrongARM1 multiplier early termination.

M	Rs range (use the first applicable range)	Rs bitmap s = sign bit x = wildcard bit
1	$-2^{11} \leq x < 2^{11}$	SSSSSSSS SSSSSSSS SSSSSXXX XXXXXXXX
2	$-2^{23} \leq x < 2^{23}$	SSSSSSSS SXXXXXXX XXXXXXXX XXXXXXXX
3	remaining x	XXXXXXXX XXXXXXXX XXXXXXXX XXXXXXXX

Table D.8   StrongARM1 (ARMv4) instruction cycle timings.

Instruction class	Cycles	Notes
ALU	1	+1 if a register-specified shift is used [even if the instruction is not executed]. +2 if *Rd* is *pc* [only if executed].
B, BL	2	
LDR/B/H *Rd* not *pc*	1	*Rd* is not available for one cycle.
LDRSB/SH *Rd* not *pc*	2	*Rd* is not available for one cycle.
LDR *Rd* is *pc*	4	
LDM $N = 1$, not *pc*	2	[2 cycles if not executed.]
LDM $N > 1$, not *pc*	N	The last loaded value is not available for one cycle. [N cycles if not executed.]
LDM loading *pc*	$N+3$	[max(N,2) if not executed.]
MRS	1	*Rd* is not available for one cycle.
MSR to *cpsr*	3	+1 if any of the *csx* fields are updated.
MSR to *spsr*	1	
MUL, MLA	M	*Rd* is not available for one cycle. You cannot start another multiply on the next cycle.
MULS, MLAS	4	
xMULL, xMLAL	$1 + M$	*RdHi* is not available for one cycle. You cannot start a multiply on the next cycle. [2 if instruction not executed.]
xMULLS, xMLALS	5	[2 if instruction not executed.]
STR/B/H	1	
STM	N	+1 if $N = 1$. [Same number of cycles if not executed.]
SWP/B	2	[2 if instruction not executed.]

D.5   ARM9E INSTRUCTION CYCLE TIMINGS

The ARM9E core is based on a five-stage pipeline. There is usually a one- or two-cycle delay following a load or multiply instruction before you can use the data. The multiplier circuit uses a 32-bit by 16-bit multiplier array. The multiplier does not terminate early. Table D.9 gives the ARM9E instruction cycle timings.

Table D.9   ARM9Erev2 (ARMv5TE) instruction cycle timings.

Instruction Class	Cycles	Notes
ALU Rd not pc	1	+1 if a register-specified shift is used.
ALU Rd is pc	3	+1 if the operation is logical or any shift is used.
B, BL, BX, BLX	3	
CDP	$1 + B$	
LDC	$B + N$	
LDRB/H/SB/SH	1	Rd is not available for two cycles. +1 if the load offset is shifted.
LDR Rd not pc	1	Rd is not available for one cycle. +1 if the load offset is shifted.
LDR Rd is pc	5	+1 if the load offset is shifted.
LDRD	2	$R(d+1)$ is not available for one cycle.
LDM not loading pc	N	+1 if $N = 1$ or the last loaded register used in the next cycle.
LDM loading pc	$N + 4$	
MCR	$1 + B$	
MCRR	$2 + B$	
MRC Rd not pc	$1 + B$	Rd is not available for one cycle.
MRC Rd is pc	$4 + B$	
MRRC	$2 + B$	Rn is not available for one cycle.
MRS	2	
MSR	1	+2 if any of the csx fields are updated.
MUL, MLA	2	Rd is not available for one cycle, except as an accumulator input for a multiply accumulate.
MULS, MLAS	4	
xMULL, xMLAL	3	$RdHi$ is not available for one cycle, except as an accumulator input for a multiply accumulate.
xMULLS, xMLALS	5	
PLD	1	
QxADD, QxSUB	1	Rd is not available for one cycle.
SMULxy, SMLAxy, SMULWx, SMLAWx	1	Rd is not available for one cycle, except as an accumulator input for a multiply accumulate.
SMLALxy	2	$RdHi$ is not available for one cycle, except as an accumulator input for a multiply accumulate.
STC	$B + N$	
STR/B/H	1	+1 if a shifted offset is used.
STRD	2	
STM	N	+1 if $N = 1$.
SWI	3	
SWP/B	2	Rd is not available for one cycle.

D.6 ARM10E INSTRUCTION CYCLE TIMINGS

The ARM10E core is based on a five-stage pipeline with branch prediction. There is usually a one-cycle delay following a load or multiply instruction before you can use the data. The ARM10E uses a 64-bit-wide data bus, so load and store instructions can transfer 64 bits per cycle. The multiplier does not use early termination. Table D.10 gives the ARM10E instruction cycle timings.

Table D.10   ARM10E (ARMv5TE) instruction cycle timings.

Instruction class	Cycles	Notes
ALU	1	+1 if a register-specified shift, or RRX, is used.
		+4 if *Rd* is *pc*.
		An exception is MOV *pc, Rn*. This takes 4 cycles.
B, BX	0-2	+4 if the branch is mispredicted.
BL, BLX	1-2	+4 if the branch is mispredicted.
CDP	1	
LDC	1	Data availability depends on the coprocessor.
LDR/B/H/SB/SH	1	*Rd* is not available for one cycle.
Rd not *pc*		+1 if the addressing mode is register preindexed with the option of a (constant) shift.
LDR *Rd* is *pc*	6	+1 if the offset (pre- or postindex) is a shifted register.
		[2 cycles if not executed].
LDRD	1	*Rd* and $R(d + 1)$ are not available for one cycle.
LDM not loading *pc*	1	The first data item is not available for one cycle. Once the address is 8-byte aligned, data items are loaded in pairs, at two per cycle. Therefore the *k*th data item will be available after $(k + a + 1)/2$ cycles, where *a* is bit 2 of the base address. You cannot start another load or store until this one has finished.
LDM loading *pc*	$L + 6$	$L = (N + a)/2$, and *a* is bit 2 of the base address.
MCR, MCCR	1	
MR{R}C *Rd* not *pc*	1	*Rd* is not available for one cycle.
MRC *Rd* is *pc*	2	
MRS	1	
MSR to *cpsr*	1	+3 if any of the *csx* fields are updated.
MSR to *spsr*	3	[2 if the instruction is not executed.]
MUL, MLA	2	*Rd* is not available for one cycle.
MULS, MLAS	4	
xMULL, xMLAL	3	*RdHi* is not available for one cycle.
xMULLS, xMLALS	5	

Table D.10   ARM10E (ARMv5TE) instruction cycle timings. (*continued*)

Instruction class	Cycles	Notes
PLD	1	+1 if a shifted register offset is used.
QxADD, QxSUB	1	*Rd* is not available for one cycle.
SMULxy, SMULWx	1	*Rd* is not available for one cycle.
SMLAxy, SMLAWx	2	
SMLALxy	2	*RdHi* is not available for one cycle.
STC	1	
STR/B/H	1	+1 if a preindexed shifted register offset is used.
STRD	1	
STM	1	Registers are stored two per cycle once the address is 8-byte aligned. You cannot write a register in the register list until its value has been stored. You cannot start another load or store until this one is complete.
SWP/B	2	

D.7 INTEL XSCALE INSTRUCTION CYCLE TIMINGS

The Intel XScale is based on a seven-stage pipeline. There is usually a two-cycle delay following a load instruction before you can use the data. Multiply instructions usually issue in a fixed number of cycles, but then the result is not available for a variable number of cycles, depending on the value of *Rs*. Table D.11 shows how the number of multiply iteration cycles *M* depends on the value of *Rs*. Table D.12 gives the Intel XScale instruction cycle timings.

Table D.11   Intel XScale multiplier early termination.

M	*Rs* range (use the first applicable range)	Rs bitmap s = sign bit x = wildcard bit
1	$-2^{15} \leq x < 2^{15}$	SSSSSSSS SSSSSSSS SXXXXXXX XXXXXXXX
2	$-2^{27} \leq x < 2^{27}$	SSSSSXXX XXXXXXXX XXXXXXXX XXXXXXXX
3	remaining *x*	XXXXXXXX XXXXXXXX XXXXXXXX XXXXXXXX

Table D.12   Intel XScale (ARMv5TE) instruction cycle timings.

Instruction class	Cycles	Notes
ALU	1	+1 if a register-specified shift, or RRX, is used. +4 if *Rd* is *pc*.
B, BL	1	+4 if the branch is mispredicted.
BX, BLX	5	[1 cycle if not executed.]
LDR/B/H/SB/SH *Rd* not *pc*	1	*Rd* is not available for two cycles.
LDR *Rd* is *pc*	8	[2 cycles if not executed.]
LDRD	1	*Rd* is not available for two cycles. $R(d + 1)$ is not available for three cycles. +1 if *Rd* is *r12*.
LDM not loading *pc*	$2 + N$	The last value loaded is not available for two cycles. The value previous to that is not available for one cycle.
LDM loading *pc*	$7 + N$	Increase to 10 cycles if $N < 3$. $[3 + N$ cycles if not executed.]
MCR to copro 15	2	
MRC from copro 15	4	
MRS	1	*Rd* is not available for one cycle.
MSR	2	+4 if any of the *csx* fields are updated.
MUL, MLA	1	*Rd* is not available for *M* cycles. You cannot start another multiply in the next $M - 1$ cycles.
MULS, MLAS	$1 + M$	
xMULL	1	*RdHi* is not available for $M + 1$ cycles. *RdLo* is not available for *M* cycles. You cannot start another multiply in the next *M* cycles.
xMLAL	2	*RdHi* is not available for *M* cycles. *RdLo* is not available for $M - 1$ cycles. You cannot start another multiply in the next $M - 1$ cycles.
xMULLS, xMLALS	$2 + M$	
PLD	1	
QxADD, QxSUB	1	*Rd* is not available for one cycle.
SMULxy, SMLAxy	1	*Rd* is not available for one cycle.
SMULWx, SMLAWx	1	*Rd* is not available for two cycles. You cannot start another multiply for one cycle.
SMLALxy	2	*RdHi* is not available for one cycle.
STR/B/H	1	
STRD	2	
STM	$2 + N$	
SWI	6	
SWP/B	5	

D.8 ARM11 CYCLE TIMINGS

The ARM11 core uses an eight-stage pipeline with three execute stages. There is usually a two-cycle delay following a load instruction before you can use the data. Some operations such as shift, multiply, and address calculations require their input registers a cycle early.

For example, the following code sequence will stall the core for three cycles because the result of the load is not available for two cycles, and the input to the shift is required one cycle early:

```
LDR     r0, [r1]         ; r0 not available for 2 cycles
MOV     r2, r0, ASR#3    ; r0 required one cycle early
```

The ARM11 core has a separate address generation unit that can calculate simple addresses in one cycle. More complicated addresses take two cycles. Table D.13 defines the number of address calculation cycles A for each addressing mode.

Table D.13   ARM11 address calculation cycles.

A	Addressing modes
1	[Rn, #<signed-offset>]{!}
	[Rn], #<signed-offset>
	[Rn, Rm {, LSL #2}]{!}
	[Rn], Rm {, LSL #2}
2	[Rn, -Rm] {!}
	[Rn], -Rm
	[Rn, {-}<shifted_Rm>]{!} where shift is not LSL #0 or LSL #2
	[Rn], {-}<shifted_Rm> where shift is not LSL #0 or LSL #2

The ARM11 core uses prediction to minimize the number of cycles caused by a change in program flow. To enable prediction, set bit 11 of CP15 register c1. There are three branch predictors.

A *static predictor* predicts relative branches that are not recorded in the branch prediction cache. This is the case the first time the processor sees a given branch. The static predictor predicts forward conditional branches as not taken and backward conditional branches as taken.

A *dynamic predictor* predicts relative branches that are recorded in the branch prediction cache. The branch prediction cache has 128 entries based on the branch instruction address. Each cache entry predicts the branch destination and if the branch is taken. A cache entry has four states: strongly not taken, weakly not taken, weakly taken, strongly taken. Each time the branch is taken, the state moves one to the right in this list (if it can), and each time the branch is not taken, the state moves one to the left in this list (if it can).

A *return stack* predicts unconditional subroutine return instructions. The stack has three entries storing the return address from the three deepest BL, BLX subroutine calls.

Table D.14 gives the ARM11 instruction cycle timings.

Table D.14   ARM11 (ARMv6) instruction cycle timings.

Instruction class	Cycles	Notes
ALU operations except a MOV to *pc* (for MOV to *pc*, see BX)	1	*Rm* is required one cycle early if shifted by a constant shift. +1 if a register-specified shift is used. In this case *Rs* is required one cycle early and *Rn* is not required until the second cycle. +6 if *Rd* is *pc*.
B <*immed*> BL <*immed*> BLX <*immed*>	1	Assumes successful dynamic prediction. Some dynamically predicted branches may be folded, to be zero cycles. +3 for successful static prediction. +4 for unsuccessful static or dynamic prediction. In this case the flags are required two cycles early.
BX *lr* MOV *pc*, *lr*	4	+1 if unconditional and return stack is empty. +3 if unconditional and return stack mispredicts. +1 if conditional. In this case the flags are required two cycles early.
BX *Rm* (not *lr*) BLX *Rm* MOV *pc*, *Rm* (not *lr*)	5	If no shift on MOV and conditional, the flags are required two cycles early. +1 if a constant shift is used for MOV. In this case *Rm* is required one cycle early. If conditional, then the flags are required one cycle early. +2 if a register-specified shift is used for MOV. In this case *Rs* is required one cycle early, and *Rn* is not used until the second cycle.
CPS	1	+1 if a mode change occurs.
LDR/B/H/SB/SH/D *Rd* not *pc*	*A*	*Rd* is not available for two cycles. $R(d+1)$ is not available for two cycles for LDRD. If the load is potentially unaligned (base or offset unaligned), then you cannot start another memory access on the next cycle. If the load is unaligned, then *Rd* is not available for three cycles for LDR/H/SH. For LDRD *Rd* is not available for two cycles and $R(d+1)$ for three cycles.

Table D.14   ARM11 (ARMv6) instruction cycle timings. (*Continued.*)

Instruction class	Cycles	Notes
LDR *pc*, [*sp*, #*off*] {!} LDR *pc*, [*sp*], #*off*	4	+4 if unconditional and return stack is empty. +5 if unconditional and return stack mispredicts +4 if conditional.
LDR *pc* not using a constant stack offset	$A+7$	
LDM not loading *pc*	1	You cannot start another memory access for the next $(N + a - 1)/2$ cycles, where *a* is bit 2 of the address. The *k*th register in the list not available for $(k + a + 3)/2$ cycles.
LDM *sp*{!} loading *pc*	4	+5 if conditional or return stack empty or return stack mispredicts. You cannot start another memory access for $(N + a)/2$ cycles. The *k*th register in the list not available for $(k + a + 5)/2$ cycles.
LDM loading *pc* not from the stack	8	You cannot start another memory access for $(N + a)/2$ cycles. The *k*th register in the list not available for $(k + a + 5)/2$ cycles.
MCR/MCRR	1	This counts as a memory access.
MRC/MRRC	1	This counts as a memory access. The result registers are not available for two cycles.
MRS	1	
MSR to *cpsr*	1	+3 if any of the *csx* fields are updated.
MSR to *spsr*	5	
MUL, MLA	2	*Rd* is not available for two cycles, except as an accumulator input for another multiply accumulate when it is not available for one cycle. *Rm* and *Rs* are required one cycle early. *Rn* is not required until the second cycle for MLA.
MULS, MLAS	5	*Rm* and *Rs* are required one cycle early. *Rn* is not required until the second cycle for MLAS.
xMULL, xMLAL	3	*RdLo* is not available for one cycle. *RdHi* is not available for two cycles. Reduce these latencies by one if these registers are used as accumulator inputs for another multiply accumulate. *Rm* and *Rs* are required one cycle early. *RdLo* is not required until the second cycle for MLAL.
xMULLS, xMLALS	6	*Rm* and *Rs* are required one cycle early. *RdLo* is not required until the second cycle for MLAL.
PKHBT, PKHTB	1	*Rm* is required one cycle early.

Table D.14   ARM11 (ARMv6) instruction cycle timings. (*Continued.*)

Instruction class	Cycles	Notes
PLD	*A*	
QxADD, QxSUB	1	*Rd* is not available for one cycle. *Rn* is required one cycle early for QDADD and QDSUB.
REV, REV16, REVSH	1	*Rm* is required one cycle early.
{S,SH,Q,U,UH,UQ} ADD16, ADDSUBX, SUBADDX, SUB16, ADD8, SUB8	1	*Rd* is not available for one cycle for saturating or halving operations (SH, Q, UH, UQ prefix). *Rm* is required one cycle early for ADDSUBX and SUBADDX operations.
SEL	1	
SETEND	1	
SMULxy, SMLAxy, SMULWy, SMLAWy SMUAD, SMLAD, SMUSD, SMLSD	1	*Rd* is not available for two cycles, except as an accumulator input for another multiply accumulate when it is not available for one cycle. *Rm* and *Rs* are required one cycle early.
SMLALxy, SMLALD{X}, SMLSLD{X}	2	*RdLo* is not available for one cycle. *RdHi* is not available for two cycles. Reduce these latencies by one if these registers are used as accumulator inputs for another multiply accumulate. *Rm* and *Rs* are required one cycle early. *RdHi* is not required until the second cycle.
SMMUL{R}, SMMLA{R}, SMMLS{R}	2	*Rd* is not available for two cycles, except as an accumulator input for another multiply accumulate when it is not available for one cycle. *Rm* and *Rs* are required one cycle early. *Rn* is not required until the second cycle.
SSAT, USAT, SSAT16, USAT16	1	*Rd* is not available for one cycle. *Rm* is required one cycle early for SSAT and USAT.
STR/B/H/D	*A*	If the store is potentially unaligned (base or offset unaligned), then you cannot start a memory access on the next cycle. For STRD you cannot start another instruction that writes to $R(d + 1)$ for one cycle.
STM	1	You cannot start another memory access for the next $(N + a - 1)/2$ cycles, where *a* is bit 2 of the address. You cannot start an instruction that writes to the *k*th register in the list for *k*/2 cycles.
SWI	8	
SWP/B	2	*Rd* is not available for one cycle.
SXT, UXT	1	*Rm* is required one cycle early.

Table D.14   ARM11 (ARMv6) instruction cycle timings. (*Continued.*)

Instruction class	Cycles	Notes
UMAAL	3	*RdLo* is not available for one cycle. *RdHi* is not available for two cycles. These latencies are reduced by one for another accumulate. *Rm* and *Rs* are required one cycle early. *RdLo* is not required until the second cycle.
USAD8, USADA8	1	*Rd* is not available for two cycles, with the exception that the result of USAD8 is available as the accumulator for USADA8 after one cycle. *Rm* and *Rs* are required one cycle early.

APPENDIX E

SUGGESTED READING

E.1 ARM REFERENCES

- *ARM Architecture Reference Manual*, Second Edition, Published 2001, edited by David Seal. Addison-Wesley. The definitive reference for the ARM architecture definition.

- *ARM System-on-Chip Architecture*, Second Edition, Published 2000, by Steve Furber. Addison-Wesley. Covers the hardware aspects of ARM processors and SOC design.

E.2 ALGORITHM REFERENCES

- *Digital Signal Processing: Principles, Algorithms, and Applications*, by John G. Proakis and Dimitris G. Manolakis. Published 1996. PrenticeHall. This is a solid book on DSP algorithms.

- *The Art of Computer Programming: Seminumerical Algorithms*, by Donald E. Knuth. Third Edition, Published 1998. Addison-Wesley. A highly respected work covering random number generation, algorithms used for extended-precision arithmetic, as well as many other fundamental algorithms.

E.3 MEMORY MANAGEMENT AND CACHE ARCHITECTURE (HARDWARE OVERVIEW AND REFERENCE)

- *The Cache Memory Book*, by Jim Handy. Second edition (1998). Academic Press. Provides a detailed discussion of cache design.

- *Computer Architecture: A Quantitative Approach*, by John L. Hennessy et al. Morgan Kaufmann. 2nd edition (1996). A classic text on computer hardware design.

- *Computer Organization and Design: The Hardware/Software Interface*, by David A. Patterson et al. 1997. Morgan Kaufmann. A solid textbook showing the relationship between hardware and software in modern computer systems.

E.4 OPERATING SYSTEM REFERENCES

- *Design of the UNIX Operating System*, by Maurice J. Bach (1986). Prentice-Hall. Describes the internal algorithms and structures of the UNIX System V kernel.

- *Operating Systems*, 2nd edition (1990) by Harvey M. Deitel. Addison-Wesley. A very good introductory text on operating systems.

- *Modern Operating Systems*, 2nd edition (2001) by Andrew Tanenbaum. Prentice-Hall. A thorough overview of operating system design.

INDEX

Page numbers followed by "f" denote figures and "t" denote tables

669